About Pearson

Pearson is the world's learning company, with presence across 70 countries worldwide. Our unique insights and world-class expertise comes from a long history of working closely with renowned teachers, authors and thought leaders, as a result of which, we have emerged as the preferred choice for millions of teachers and learners across the world.

We believe learning opens up opportunities, creates fulfilling careers and hence better lives. We hence collaborate with the best of minds to deliver you class-leading products, spread across the Higher Education and K12 spectrum.

Superior learning experience and improved outcomes are at the heart of everything we do. This product is the result of one such effort.

Your feedback plays a critical role in the evolution of our products and you can contact us - reachus@pearson.com. We look forward to it.

Twelfth Edition

MODERN DATABASE MANAGEMENT

Twelfth Edition

MODERN DATABASE MANAGEMENT

Jeffrey A. Hoffer
University of Dayton

V. Ramesh
Indiana University

Heikki Topi
Bentley University

 Pearson

Credits and acknowledgments borrowed from other sources and reproduced, with permission, in this textbook appear on the appropriate page within text.

Microsoft and/or its respective suppliers make no representations about the suitability of the information contained in the documents and related graphics published as part of the services for any purpose. All such documents and related graphics are provided "as is" without warranty of any kind. Microsoft and/or its respective suppliers hereby disclaim all warranties and conditions with regard to this information, including all warranties and conditions of merchantability, whether express, implied or statutory, fitness for a particular purpose, title and non-infringement. In no event shall Microsoft and/or its respective suppliers be liable for any special, indirect or consequential damages or any damages whatsoever resulting from loss of use, data or profits, whether in an action of contract, negligence or other tortious action, arising out of or in connection with the use or performance of information available from the services.

The documents and related graphics contained herein could include technical inaccuracies or typographical errors. Changes are periodically added to the information herein. Microsoft and/or its respective suppliers may make improvements and/or changes in the product(s) and/or the program(s) described herein at any time. Partial screen shots may be viewed in full within the software version specified.

Trademarks
Microsoft® windows®, and Microsoft office® are registered trademarks of the Microsoft corporation in the U.S.A. and other countries. This book is not sponsored or endorsed by or affiliated with the Microsoft Corporation.

Acknowledgements of third party content appear on the appropriate page within the text, which constitutes an extension of this copyright page.

Unless otherwise indicated herein, any third-party trademarks that may appear in this work are the property of their respective owners and any references to third-party trademarks, logos or other trade dress are for demonstrative or descriptive purposes only. Such references are not intended to imply any sponsorship, endorsement, authorization, or promotion of Pearson's products by the owners of such marks, or any relationship between the owner and Pearson Education, Inc. or its affiliates, authors, licensees or distributors.

Authorized adaptation from the United States edition, entitled *Modern Database Management, 12th Edition,* ISBN 9780133544619, by Hoffer, Jeffrey A., Ramesh, V. and Topi, Heikki, published by Pearson Education, Inc, Copyright © 2016.

Indian Subcontinent Adaptation
Copyright © 2018 Pearson India Education Services Pvt. Ltd

This book is sold subject to the condition that it shall not, by way of trade or otherwise, be lent, resold, hired out, or otherwise circulated without the publisher's prior written consent in any form of binding or cover other than that in which it is published and without a similar condition including this condition being imposed on the subsequent purchaser and without limiting the rights under copyright reserved above, no part of this publication may be reproduced, stored in or introduced into a retrieval system, or transmitted in any form or by any means (electronic, mechanical, photocopying, recording or otherwise), without the prior written permission of both the copyright owner and the publisher of this book.

ISBN 978-93-868-7326-2

First Impression 2018

Third Impression

This edition is manufactured in India and is authorized for sale only in India, Bangladesh, Bhutan, Pakistan, Nepal, Sri Lanka and the Maldives. Circulation of this edition outside of these territories is UNAUTHORIZED.

Published by Pearson India Education Services Pvt Ltd, CIN: U72200TN2005PTC057128
Head Office: 15th Floor, Tower-B, World Trade Tower, Plot No. 1, Block-C, Sector 16, Noida 201 301, Uttar Pradesh, India
Registered Office: 4th Floor, Software Block, Elnet Software City, TS-140,Block 2 and 9, Rajiv Gandhi Salai, Taramani, Chennai 600 113, Tamil Nadu, India.Fax: 080-30461003,Phone: 080-30461060, www.in.pearson.com, Email: companysecretary.india@pearson.com

Printed in India by HT Media Ltd, Gr. Noida

To Patty, for her sacrifices, encouragement, and support for more than 30 years of being a textbook author widow. To my students and colleagues, for being receptive and critical and for challenging me to be a better teacher.

—J.A.H.

To Gayathri, for her sacrifices and patience these past 25 years. To my parents, for letting me make the journey abroad, and to my cat, Raju, who was a part of our family for more than 20 years.

—V.R.

To Anne-Louise, for her loving support, encouragement, and patience. To Leila and Saara, whose laughter and joy of life continue to teach me about what is truly important. To my teachers, colleagues, and students, from whom I continue to learn every day.

—H.T.

BRIEF CONTENTS

CONTENTS

 – Learning Objectives   PINE VALLEY FURNITURE – Company   – Case

ONLINE CHAPTERS

PINE VALLEY FURNITURE

PREFACE

This text is designed to be used with an introductory course in database management. Such a course is usually required as part of an information systems curriculum in business schools, computer technology programs, and applied computer science departments. The Association for Information Systems (AIS), the Association for Computing Machinery (ACM), and the International Federation of Information Processing Societies (IFIPS) curriculum guidelines (e.g., IS 2010) all outline this type of database management course. Previous editions of this text have been used successfully for more than 33 years at both the undergraduate and graduate levels, as well as in management and professional development programs.

WHAT'S NEW IN THIS EDITION?

This 12th edition of *Modern Database Management* updates and expands materials in areas undergoing rapid change as a result of improved managerial practices, database design tools and methodologies, and database technology. Later, we detail changes to each chapter. The themes of this 12th edition reflect the major trends in the information systems field and the skills required of modern information systems graduates:

- Given the explosion in interest in the topics of big data and analytics, we have added an entire new chapter (Chapter 11) dedicated to this area. The chapter provides in-depth coverage of big data technologies such as NoSQL, Hadoop, MapReduce, Pig, and Hive and provides an introduction to the different types of analytics (descriptive, predictive, and prescriptive) and their use in business.
- We have also introduced this topic in relevant places throughout the textbook, e.g., in the revised introduction section in Chapter 1 as well as in a new section titled "The Future of Data Warehousing: Integration with Big Data and Analytics" in the data warehousing chapter (Chapter 9).
- Topics such as in-memory databases, in-database analytics, data warehousing in the cloud, and massively parallel processing are covered in sections of Chapter 9 and Chapter 11.
- The Mountain View Community Hospital (MVCH) case study (a staple of many past editions) has been replaced with a simpler mini-case titled "Forondo Artist Management Excellence Inc." (FAME). The case focuses on the development of a system to support the needs of a small artist management company. The case is presented in the form of stakeholder e-mails describing the current challenges faced by the organization as well as the features they would like to see in a new system. Each chapter presents a set of project exercises that serve as guidelines for deliverables for students.
- We have updated the section on routines in Chapter 7 to provide clarity on the nature of routines and how to use them.
- New material added to Chapter 2 on why data modeling is important provides several compelling reasons for why data modeling is still crucial.

In addition to the new topics covered, specific improvements to the textbook have been made in the following areas:

- Every chapter went through significant edits to streamline coverage to ensure relevance with current technologies and eliminate redundancies.
- End-of-chapter material (review questions, problems and exercises, and/or field exercises) in every chapter has been revised with new questions and exercises.
- The figures in several chapters were updated to reflect the changing landscape of technologies that are being used in modern organizations.
- The Web Resources section in each chapter was updated to ensure that the student has information on the latest database trends and expanded background details on important topics covered in the text.

- We have continued to focus on reducing the length of the printed book, an effort that began with the eighth edition. The reduced length is more consistent with what our reviewers say can be covered in a database course today, given the need for depth of coverage in the most important topics. The reduced length should encourage more students to purchase and read the text, without any loss of coverage and learning. The book continues to be available through CourseSmart, an innovative e-book delivery system, and as an electronic book in the Kindle format.

    Also, we continue to provide on the student Companion Web site several custom-developed short videos that address key concepts and skills from different sections of the book. These videos, produced by the textbook authors, help students learn difficult material by using both the printed text and a mini lecture or tutorial. Videos have been developed to support Chapters 1 (introduction to database), 2 and 3 (conceptual data modeling), 4 (normalization), and 6 and 7 (SQL). More will be produced with future editions. Look for special icons on the opening page of these chapters to call attention to these videos, and go to **www.pearsonhighered.com/hoffer** to find these videos.

FOR THOSE NEW TO *MODERN DATABASE MANAGEMENT*

Modern Database Management has been a leading text since its first edition in 1983. In spite of this market leadership position, some instructors have used other good database management texts. Why might you want to switch at this time? There are several good reasons:

- One of our goals, in every edition, has been to lead other books in coverage of the latest principles, concepts, and technologies. See what we have added for the 12th edition in "What's New in This Edition?" In the past, we have led in coverage of object-oriented data modeling and UML, Internet databases, data warehousing, and the use of CASE tools in support of data modeling. For the 12th edition, we continue this tradition by providing significant coverage on the important topic of big data and analytics, focusing on what every database student needs to understand about these topics.
- While remaining current, this text focuses on what leading practitioners say is most important for database developers. We work with many practitioners, including the professionals of the Data Management Association (DAMA) and The Data Warehousing Institute (TDWI), leading consultants, technology leaders, and authors of articles in the most widely read professional publications. We draw on these experts to ensure that what the book includes is important and covers not only important entry-level knowledge and skills, but also those fundamentals and mind-sets that lead to long-term career success.
- In the 12th edition of this highly successful book, material is presented in a way that has been viewed as very accessible to students. Our methods have been refined through continuous market feedback for more than 30 years, as well as through our own teaching. Overall, the pedagogy of the book is sound. We use many illustrations that help make important concepts and techniques clear. We use the most modern notations. The organization of the book is flexible, so you can use chapters in whatever sequence makes sense for your students. We supplement the book with data sets to facilitate hands-on, practical learning, and with new media resources to make some of the more challenging topics more engaging.
- Our text can accommodate structural flexibility. For example, you may have particular interest in introducing SQL early in your course. Our text makes this possible. First, we cover SQL in depth, devoting two full chapters to this core technology of the database field. Second, we include many SQL examples in early chapters. Third, many instructors have successfully used the two SQL chapters early in their course. Although logically appearing in the life cycle of systems development as Chapters 6 and 7, part of the implementation section of the text, many instructors have used these chapters immediately after Chapter 1 or in parallel with other early chapters. Finally, we use SQL throughout the book, for example, to illustrate Web application connections to relational databases in Chapter 8 and online analytical processing in Chapter 11.

- We have the latest in supplements and Web site support for the text. See the supplement package for details on all the resources available to you and your students.
- This text is written to be part of a modern information systems curriculum with a strong business systems development focus. Topics are included and addressed so as to reinforce principles from other typical courses, such as systems analysis and design, networking, Web site design and development, MIS principles, and computer programming. Emphasis is on the development of the database component of modern information systems and on the management of the data resource. Thus, the text is practical, supports projects and other hands-on class activities, and encourages linking database concepts to concepts being learned throughout the curriculum the student is taking.

SUMMARY OF ENHANCEMENTS TO EACH CHAPTER

The following sections present a chapter-by-chapter description of the major changes in this edition. Each chapter description presents a statement of the purpose of that chapter, followed by a description of the changes and revisions that have been made for the 12th edition. Each paragraph concludes with a description of the strengths that have been retained from prior editions.

PART I: THE CONTEXT OF DATABASE MANAGEMENT

Chapter 1: The Database Environment and Development Process

This chapter discusses the role of databases in organizations and previews the major topics in the remainder of the text. The primary change in this chapter has been in how we use current examples around the explosion in the amount of data being generated and the benefits that can be gained by harnessing the power data (through analytics) to help set the stage for the entire book. A few new exercises have also been added, and the new Forondo Artist Management Excellence (FAME) case is introduced. After presenting a brief introduction to the basic terminology associated with storing and retrieving data, the chapter presents a well-organized comparison of traditional file processing systems and modern database technology. The chapter then introduces the core components of a database environment. It then goes on to explain the process of database development in the context of structured life cycle, prototyping, and agile methodologies. The presentation remains consistent with the companion textbook, *Modern Systems Analysis and Design* by Hoffer, George, and Valacich. The chapter also discusses important issues in database development, including management of the diverse group of people involved in database development and frameworks for understanding database architectures and technologies (e.g., the three-schema architecture). Reviewers frequently note the compatibility of this chapter with what students learn in systems analysis and design classes. A brief history of the evolution of database technology, from pre-database files to modern object-relational technologies, is presented. The chapter also provides an overview of the range of database applications that are currently in use within organizations—personal, two-tier, multitier, and enterprise applications. The explanation of enterprise databases includes databases that are part of enterprise resource planning systems and data warehouses. The chapter concludes with a description of the process of developing a database in a fictitious company, Pine Valley Furniture. This description closely mirrors the steps in database development described earlier in the chapter.

PART II: DATABASE ANALYSIS

Chapter 2: Modeling Data in the Organization

This chapter presents a thorough introduction to conceptual data modeling with the entity-relationship (E-R) model. The chapter title emphasizes the reason for the entity-relationship model: to unambiguously document the rules of the business that influence database design. New material on why data modeling is important helps set the stage for the rest of the discussion that follows. Specific subsections explain in detail how to name and define elements of a data model, which are essential in developing an unambiguous E-R diagram. The chapter continues to proceed from simple to more complex examples, and it concludes with a comprehensive E-R diagram for the Pine Valley Furniture Company. In the 12th edition, we have provided three new problems and exercises, and the second part of the new FAME case is introduced. Appendix A provides information on different data modeling tools and notations.

Chapter 3: The Enhanced E-R Model

This chapter presents a discussion of several advanced E-R data model constructs, primarily supertype/subtype relationships. As in Chapter 2, problems and exercises have been revised. The third part of the new FAME case is presented in this chapter. The chapter continues to present thorough coverage of supertype/subtype relationships and includes a comprehensive example of an extended E-R data model for the Pine Valley Furniture Company.

PART III: DATABASE DESIGN

Chapter 4: Logical Database Design and the Relational Model

This chapter describes the process of converting a conceptual data model to the relational data model, as well as how to merge new relations into an existing normalized database. It provides a conceptually sound and practically relevant introduction to normalization, emphasizing the importance of the use of functional dependencies and determinants as the basis for normalization. Concepts of normalization and normal forms are extended in Appendix B. The chapter features a discussion of the characteristics of foreign keys and introduces the important concept of a nonintelligent enterprise key. Enterprise keys (also called surrogate keys for data warehouses) are emphasized as some concepts of object orientation have migrated into the relational technology world. Eight new review questions and problems and exercises are included, and the revision has further clarified the coverage of some of the key concepts and the visual quality of the presentation. The chapter continues to emphasize the basic concepts of the relational data model and the role of the database designer in the logical design process. The new FAME case continues in this chapter.

Chapter 5: Physical Database Design and Performance

This chapter describes the steps that are essential in achieving an efficient database design, with a strong focus on those aspects of database design and implementation that are typically within the control of a database professional in a modern database environment. Five new review questions and problems and exercises are included. In addition, the language of the chapter was streamlined to improve readability. References to Oracle (including the visual coverage of database terminology) were updated to cover the latest version (at the time of this writing), 12c. New coverage of heap file organization was added to the chapter. The chapter contains an emphasis on ways to improve database performance, with references to specific techniques available in Oracle and other DBMSs to improve database processing performance. The discussion of indexes includes descriptions of the types of indexes (primary and secondary indexes, join index, hash index table) that are widely available in database technologies as techniques to improve query processing speed. Appendix C provides excellent background on fundamental data structures for programs of study that need coverage of this topic. The chapter continues to emphasize the physical design process and the goals of that process. The new FAME case continues with questions related to the material covered in this chapter.

PART IV: IMPLEMENTATION

Chapter 6: Introduction to SQL

This chapter presents a thorough introduction to the SQL used by most DBMSs (SQL:1999) and introduces the changes that are included in the latest standard (SQL:2011). This edition adds coverage of the new features of SQL:2011. The coverage of SQL is extensive and divided into this and the next chapter. This chapter includes examples of SQL code, using mostly SQL:1999 and SQL:2011 syntax, as well as some Oracle 12c and Microsoft SQL Server syntax. Some unique features of MySQL are mentioned. Both dynamic and materialized views are also covered. This revision links Chapter 6 explicitly with the material covered in the new Chapter 11 on big data and analytics. Chapter 6 explains the SQL commands needed to create and maintain a database and to program single-table queries. The revised version of the chapter provides the reader with improved guidance regarding alternate sequences for learning the material. Coverage of dual-table, IS NULL/IS NOT NULL, more built-in functions, derived tables, and rules for aggregate functions and the GROUP BY clause is included or improved. Three review questions and eight problems and exercises have been added to the chapter. The chapter continues to use the Pine Valley Furniture Company case to illustrate a wide variety of practical queries and query results. Questions related to the new FAME case also are available in the context of this chapter.

Chapter 7: Advanced SQL

This chapter continues the description of SQL, with a careful explanation of multiple-table queries, transaction integrity, data dictionaries, triggers and stored procedures (the differences between them are now more clearly explained), and embedded SQL in other programming language programs. All forms of the OUTER JOIN command are covered. Standard SQL (with an updated focus on SQL:2011) is also used. The revised version of the chapter includes a new section on the temporal features introduced in SQL:2011. This chapter illustrates how to store the results of a query in a derived table, the CAST command to convert data between different data types, and the CASE command for doing conditional processing in SQL. Emphasis continues on the set-processing style of SQL compared with the record processing of programming languages with which the student may be familiar. The section on routines has been revised to provide clarified, expanded, and more current coverage of this topic. New and updated problems and exercises have been added to the chapter. The chapter continues to contain a clear explanation of subqueries and correlated subqueries, two of the most complex and powerful constructs in SQL. This chapter also includes relevant FAME case questions.

Chapter 8: Database Application Development

This chapter provides a modern discussion of the concepts of client/server architecture and applications, middleware, and database access in contemporary database environments. The section has been revised to ensure that the applicability of the concepts presented in the chapter is clear in the era of modern devices such as smartphones, tablets, etc. Review questions and problems and exercises have been updated. The chapter focuses on technologies that are commonly used to create two- and three-tier applications. Many figures are included to show the options in multitiered networks, including application and database servers, database processing distribution alternatives among network tiers, and browser (thin) clients. The chapter also presents sample application programs that demonstrate how to access databases from popular programming languages such as Java, VB.NET, ASP.NET, JSP, and PHP. This chapter lays the technology groundwork for the Internet topics presented in the remainder of the text and highlights some of the key considerations in creating three-tier Internet-based applications. The chapter also provides coverage of the role of Extensible Markup Language (XML) and related technologies in data storage and retrieval. Topics covered include basics of XML schemas, XQuery, and XSLT. The chapter concludes with an overview of Web services; associated standards and technologies; and their role in seamless, secure movement of data in Web-based applications. A brief introduction to service-oriented architecture (SOA) is also presented. Security topics, including Web security, are covered in Chapter 12. This chapter includes the final questions related to the new FAME case.

Chapter 9: Data Warehousing

This chapter describes the basic concepts of data warehousing, the reasons data warehousing is regarded as critical to competitive advantage in many organizations, and the database design activities and structures unique to data warehousing. A new section on the future of data warehousing provides a preview of the topics that will be covered in the new chapter (Chapter 11) on big data and analytics and serves as the link between these two chapters. Some of the material that previously belonged to this chapter is now covered in an expanded fashion in Chapter 11. Topics covered in this chapter include alternative data warehouse architectures and the dimensional data model (or star schema) for data warehouses. Coverage of architectures has been streamlined consistent with trends in data warehousing, and a deep explanation of how to handle slowly changing dimensional data is provided. Operational data store and independent, dependent, and logical data marts are defined.

PART V: ADVANCED DATABASE TOPICS

Chapter 10: Data Quality and Integration

In this chapter, the principles of data governance, which are at the core of enterprise data management (EDM) activities, are introduced. This is followed by coverage of data quality. This chapter describes the need for an active program to manage data quality in organizations and outlines the steps that are considered today to be best practices for data quality management. Quality data are defined, and reasons for poor-quality data are identified. Methods for data quality improvement, such as data auditing, improving data capturing (a key part of database design), data stewardship and governance, TQM principles, modern data management technologies, and high-quality data models are all discussed. The topic of master data management, one approach to integrating key business data, is introduced and explained. Different approaches to data integration are overviewed, and the reasons for each are outlined. The extract, transform, load (ETL) process for data warehousing is discussed in detail.

Chapter 11: Big Data and Analytics

Chapter 11 on big data and analytics is new in this edition, and it extends the coverage of the text in three important ways: First, this chapter provides a systematic introduction to the technologies that are currently discussed under the label *big data* and the impact of these technologies on the overall enterprise data management architecture. Specifically, the chapter focuses on the Hadoop infrastructure and four categories of so-called NoSQL (Not only SQL) database management systems. Second, the chapter offers integrated coverage of analytics, including descriptive, predictive, and prescriptive analytics. The discussion on analytics is linked not only to the coverage of big data but also the material on data warehousing in Chapter 9 and the general discussion on data management in Chapter 1. The chapter also briefly covers approaches and technologies used by analytics professionals, such as OLAP, data visualization, business performance management and dashboards, data mining, and text mining. Third, the chapter integrates the coverage of big data and analytics technologies to the individual, organizational, and societal implications of these capabilities.

Chapter 12: Data and Database Administration

This chapter presents a thorough discussion of the importance and roles of data and database administration and describes a number of the key issues that arise when these functions are performed. This chapter emphasizes the changing roles and approaches of data and database administration, with emphasis on data quality and high performance. We also briefly touch upon the impact of cloud computing on the data/database administration. The chapter contains a thorough discussion of database backup procedures, as well as extensively expanded and consolidated coverage of data security threats and responses and data availability. The data security topics include database security policies, procedures, and technologies (including encryption and smart cards). The role of databases in Sarbanes-Oxley compliance is also examined. We also discuss open source DBMS, the benefits and hazards of this technology, and how to choose an open source DBMS. In addition, the topic of heartbeat queries is included in the coverage of database performance improvements. The chapter continues to emphasize the critical importance of data and database management in managing data as a corporate asset.

Chapter 13: Distributed Databases

This chapter reviews the role, technologies, and unique database design opportunities of distributed databases. The objectives and trade-offs for distributed databases, data replication alternatives, factors in selecting a data distribution strategy, and distributed database vendors and products are covered. This chapter provides thorough coverage of database concurrency access controls. The chapter introduces several technical updates that are related to the significant advancements in both data management and networking technologies, which form the context for a distributed database. The full version of this chapter is available on the textbook's Web site. Many reviewers indicated that they are seldom able to cover this chapter in an introductory course, but having the material available is critical for advanced students or special topics.

Chapter 14: Object-Oriented Data Modeling

This chapter presents an introduction to object-oriented modeling using Object Management Group's Unified Modeling Language (UML). This chapter has been carefully reviewed to ensure consistency with the latest UML notation and best industry practices. UML provides an industry-standard notation for representing classes and objects. The chapter continues to emphasize basic object-oriented concepts, such as inheritance, encapsulation, composition, and polymorphism. The revised version of the chapter also includes brand-new review questions and modeling exercises. As with Chapter 13, Chapter 14 is available on the textbook's Web site.

APPENDICES

In the 12th edition three appendices are available on the Web and are intended for those who wish to explore certain topics in greater depth.

Appendix A: Data Modeling Tools and Notation

This appendix addresses a need raised by many readers—how to translate the E-R notation in the text into the form used by the CASE tool or the DBMS used in class. Specifically, this appendix compares the notations of CA ERwin Data Modeler r9.5, Oracle SQL Data Modeler 4.0, SAP Sybase PowerDesigner 16.5, and Microsoft Visio Professional 2013. Tables and illustrations show the notations used for the same constructs in each of these popular software packages.

Appendix B: Advanced Normal Forms

This appendix presents a description (with examples) of Boyce-Codd and fourth normal forms, including an example of BCNF to show how to handle overlapping candidate keys. Other normal forms are briefly introduced. The Web Resources section includes a reference for information on many advanced normal form topics.

Appendix C: Data Structures

This appendix describes several data structures that often underlie database implementations. Topics include the use of pointers, stacks, queues, sorted lists, inverted lists, and trees.

PEDAGOGY

A number of additions and improvements have been made to end-of-chapter materials to provide a wider and richer range of choices for the user. The most important of these improvements are the following:

1. *Review Questions* Questions have been updated to support new and enhanced chapter material.
2. *Problems and Exercises* This section has been reviewed in every chapter, and many chapters contain new problems and exercises to support updated chapter material.

Of special interest are questions in many chapters that give students opportunities to use the data sets provided for the text. Also, Problems and Exercises have been re-sequenced into roughly increasing order of difficulty, which should help instructors and students find exercises appropriate for what they want to accomplish.

3. *Field Exercises* This section provides a set of "hands-on" mini cases that can be assigned to individual students or to small teams of students. Field exercises range from directed field trips to Internet searches and other types of research exercises.

4. *Case* The 12th edition of this book has a brand new mini case: Forondo Artist Management Excellence Inc. (FAME). In the first three chapters, the case begins with a description provided in the "voice" of one or more stakeholders, revealing a new dimension of requirements to the reader. Each chapter has project assignments intended to provide guidance on the types of deliverables instructors could expect from students, some of which tie together issues and activities across chapters. These project assignments can be completed by individual students or by small project teams. This case provides an excellent means for students to gain hands-on experience with the concepts and tools they have studied.

5. *Web Resources* Each chapter contains a list of updated and validated URLs for Web sites that contain information that supplements the chapter. These Web sites cover online publication archives, vendors, electronic publications, industry standards organizations, and many other sources. These sites allow students and instructors to find updated product information, innovations that have appeared since the printing of the book, background information to explore topics in greater depth, and resources for writing research papers.

We continue to provide several pedagogical features that help make the 12th edition widely accessible to instructors and students. These features include the following:

1. *Learning objectives* appear at the beginning of each chapter, as a preview of the major concepts and skills students will learn from that chapter. The learning objectives also provide a great study review aid for students as they prepare for assignments and examinations.

2. *Chapter introductions and summaries* both encapsulate the main concepts of each chapter and link material to related chapters, providing students with a comprehensive conceptual framework for the course.

3. *The chapter review* includes the Review Questions, Problems and Exercises, and Field Exercises discussed earlier and also contains a Key Terms list to test the student's grasp of important concepts, basic facts, and significant issues.

4. *A running glossary* defines key terms in the page margins as they are discussed in the text. These terms are also defined at the end of the text, in the Glossary of Terms. Also included is the end-of-book Glossary of Acronyms for abbreviations commonly used in database management.

ORGANIZATION

We encourage instructors to customize their use of this book to meet the needs of both their curriculum and student career paths. The modular nature of the text, its broad coverage, extensive illustrations, and its inclusion of advanced topics and emerging issues make customization easy. The many references to current publications and Web sites can help instructors develop supplemental reading lists or expand classroom discussion beyond material presented in the text. The use of appendices for several advanced topics allows instructors to easily include or omit these topics.

The modular nature of the text allows the instructor to omit certain chapters or to cover chapters in a different sequence. For example, an instructor who wishes to emphasize data modeling may cover Chapter 14 (available on the book's Web site) on object-oriented data modeling along with or instead of Chapters 2 and 3. An instructor who wishes to cover only basic entity-relationship concepts (but not the enhanced E-R model) may skip Chapter 3 or cover it after Chapter 4 on the relational model.

We have contacted many adopters of *Modern Database Management* and asked them to share with us their syllabi. Most adopters cover the chapters in sequence, but several alternative sequences have also been successful. These alternatives include the following:

- Some instructors cover Chapter 12 on data and database administration immediately after Chapter 5 on physical database design and the relational model.
- To cover SQL as early as possible, instructors have effectively covered Chapters 6 and 7 immediately after Chapter 4; some have even covered Chapter 6 immediately after Chapter 1.
- Many instructors have students read appendices along with chapters, such as reading Appendix on data modeling notations with Chapter 2 or Chapter 3 on E-R modeling, Appendix B on advanced normal forms with Chapter 4 on the relational model, and Appendix C on data structures with Chapter 5.

THE SUPPLEMENT PACKAGE:

All Instructor and student resources will be available at www.pearsoned.co.in/hoffer12e

ACKNOWLEDGMENTS

We are grateful to numerous individuals who contributed to the preparation of *Modern Database Management*, 12th edition. First, we wish to thank our reviewers for their detailed suggestions and insights, characteristic of their thoughtful teaching style. As always, analysis of topics and depth of coverage provided by the reviewers were crucial. Our reviewers and others who gave us many useful comments to improve the text include Tamara Babaian, Bentley University; Gary Baram, Temple University; Bijoy Bordoloi, Southern Illinois University, Edwardsville; Timothy Bridges, University of Central Oklahoma; Traci Carte, University of Oklahoma; Wingyan Chung, Santa Clara University; Jagdish Gangolly, State University of New York at Albany; Jon Gant, Syracuse University; Jinzhu Gao, University of the Pacific; Monica Garfield, Bentley University; Rick Gibson, American University; Chengqi Guo, James Madison University; William H. Hochstettler III, Franklin University; Weiling Ke, Clarkson University; Dongwon Lee, Pennsylvania State University; Ingyu Lee, Troy University; Chang-Yang Lin, Eastern Kentucky University; Brian Mennecke, Iowa State University; Dat-Dao Nguyen, California State University, Northridge; Fred Niederman, Saint Louis University; Lara Preiser-Houy, California State Polytechnic University, Pomona; John Russo, Wentworth Institute of Technology; Ioulia Rytikova, George Mason University; Richard Segall, Arkansas State University; Chelley Vician, University of St. Thomas; and Daniel S. Weaver, Messiah College.

We received excellent input from people in industry, including Todd Walter, Carrie Ballinger, Rob Armstrong, and David Schoeff (all of Teradata Corp); Chad Gronbach and Philip DesAutels (Microsoft Corp.); Peter Gauvin (Ball Aerospace); Paul Longhurst (Overstock.com); Derek Strauss (Gavroshe International); Richard Hackathorn (Bolder Technology); and Michael Alexander (Open Access Technology, International).

We have special admiration for and gratitude to Heikki Topi, Bentley University, author of the *Instructor's Resource Manual*. In addition to his duties as author, Heikki took on this additional task and has been extremely careful in preparing the *Instructor's Resource Manual*; in the process he has helped us clarify and fix various parts of the text. We also want to recognize the important role played by Chelley Vician of the University of St. Thomas, the author of several previous editions of the *Instructor's Resource Manual*; her work added great value to this book. We also thank Sven Aelterman, Troy University, for his many excellent suggestions for improvements and clarifications throughout the text.

We are also grateful to the staff and associates of Pearson for their support and guidance throughout this project. In particular, we wish to thank retired Executive Editor Bob Horan for his support through many editions of this text book, Project Manager Ilene Kahn, who kept us on track and made sure everything was complete; Acquisitions Editor Nicole Sam; Program Manager Denise Weiss; and Editorial Assistant Olivia

Vignone. We extend special thanks to George Jacob at Integra, whose supervision of the production process was excellent.

While finalizing this edition of *MDBM*, we learned that one of the co-authors of previous editions, Dr. Mary Prescott, passed away after many years of battling and beating, but ultimately losing one last round of cancer. Mary was a co-author for the 5th through 9th editions, and she was integrally involved as a reviewer and contributor of ideas and teaching methods for several prior editions. Dr. Prescott was a dedicated and inspiring member of the author team and co-author of many of the innovations in *MDBM*, including the first material on data warehousing and significant updates of the coverage of SQL and data administration. Mary was an outstanding educator and academic administrator at the University of South Florida and University of Tampa. She was also involved in leadership development for Florida Polytechnic University (USF Polytechnic). Mary's multiple talents, built on an academic background of BA and MA in Psychology, MBA with a concentration in Accounting, and PhD in MIS, as well as a crisp writing style, contributed greatly to her significant value to this text. Mary's contributions to *MDBM*, both content and spirit, will be directly and indirectly included in this book for many years to come.

Finally, we give immeasurable thanks to our spouses, who endured many evenings and weekends of solitude for the thrill of seeing a book cover hang on a den wall. In particular, we marvel at the commitment of Patty Hoffer, who has lived the lonely life of a textbook author's spouse through 12 editions over more than 30 years of late-night and weekend writing. We also want to sincerely thank Anne-Louise Klaus for being willing to continue her wholehearted support for Heikki's involvement in the project. Although the book project was no longer new for Gayathri Mani, her continued support and understanding are very much appreciated. Much of the value of this text is due to their patience, encouragement, and love, but we alone bear the responsibility for any errors or omissions between the covers.

Jeffrey A. Hoffer

V. Ramesh

Heikki Topi

ABOUT THE CONTRIBUTOR

Malathi Sriram is driven by technology and innovation in the Information Systems field. She is an Associate Professor in the area of Systems at Shri Dharmasthala Manajunatheshwara Institute for Management Development (SDMIMD) at Mysuru, India. It is the only B-School in India to be internationally accredited by both E-PAS (EFMD) and ACBSP.

She has conducted a number of corporate programs on OOAD, SSAD, RDBMS and Course Management System. She is currently in-charge of the Management Development Programs at SDMIMD.

She has written a number of research articles, book chapters and case studies. She has presented her papers in National and International Conferences in India and abroad. Her current area of research and interest is Massive Open Online Courses (MOOCs). She is currently pursuing her Ph.D. from the University of Mysore on MOOCs.

She teaches the core course – Management Information Systems for the PG students of Business Management. Also teaches specialization courses such as Social Media, Mobility, Analytics, Cloud (SMAC), Managing Software Projects, RDBMS and part of the interdisciplinary course – Customer Relationship Management (CRM).

She has served as Secretary and Executive council member for the Greater Mysore Management Association (GMMA) a subsidiary of All India Management Association (AIMA), New Delhi. She is currently a member of the IT Panel, CII, Mysuru.

PART I

The Context of Database Management

AN OVERVIEW OF PART ONE

In this chapter and opening part of the book, we set the context and provide basic database concepts and definitions used throughout the text. In this part, we portray database management as an exciting, challenging, and growing field that provides numerous career opportunities for information systems students. Databases continue to become a more common part of everyday living and a more central component of business operations. From the database that stores contact information in your smartphone or tablet to the very large databases that support enterprise-wide information systems, databases have become the central points of data storage that were envisioned decades ago. Customer relationship management and Internet shopping are examples of two database-dependent activities that have developed in recent years. The development of data warehouses and "big data" repositories that provide managers the opportunity for deeper and broader historical analysis of data also continues to take on more importance.

We begin by providing basic definitions of *data, database, metadata, database management system, data warehouse,* and other terms associated with this environment. We compare databases with the older file management systems they replaced and describe several important advantages that are enabled by the carefully planned use of databases.

The chapter also describes the general steps followed in the analysis, design, implementation, and administration of databases. Further, this chapter also illustrates how the database development process fits into the overall information systems development process. Database development for both structured life cycle and prototyping methodologies is explained. We introduce enterprise data modeling, which sets the range and general contents of organizational databases. This is often the first step in database development. We introduce the concept of schemas and the three-schema architecture, which is the dominant approach in modern database systems. We describe the major components of the database environment and the types of applications, as well as multitier and enterprise databases. Enterprise databases include those that are used to support enterprise resource planning systems and data warehouses. Finally, we describe the roles of the various people who are typically involved in a database development project. The Pine Valley Furniture Company case is introduced and used to illustrate many of the principles and concepts of database management. This case is used throughout the text as a continuing example of the use of database management systems.

Chapter 1

The Database Environment and Development Process

The Database Environment and Development Process

Visit www.pearsonhighered.com/hoffer to view the accompanying video for this chapter.

LEARNING OBJECTIVES

After studying this chapter, you should be able to:

- Concisely define each of the following key terms: **data, database, database management system, data model, information, metadata, enterprise data model, entity, relational database, enterprise resource planning (ERP) system, database application, data warehouse, data independence, repository, user view, enterprise data modeling, systems development life cycle (SDLC), prototyping, agile software development, data modeling and design tools, conceptual schema, logical schema,** and **physical schema.**
- Name several limitations of conventional file processing systems.
- Explain at least 10 advantages of the database approach, compared to traditional file processing.
- Identify several costs and risks of the database approach.
- List and briefly describe nine components of a typical database environment.
- Identify four categories of applications that use databases and their key characteristics.
- Describe the life cycle of a systems development project, with an emphasis on the purpose of database analysis, design, and implementation activities.
- Explain the prototyping and agile-development approaches to database and application development.
- Explain the roles of individuals who design, implement, use, and administer databases.
- Explain the differences among external, conceptual, and internal schemas and the reasons for the three-schema architecture for databases.

DATA MATTER!

The amount of data being generated, stored and processed is growing by leaps and bounds. According to a McKinsey Global Institute Report (Manikay et al. 2011), it is estimated 50 percent reduction in product development costs.

The availability of large amounts of data is also fueling innovation in companies and allowing them to think differently and creatively about various aspects of their business and also the use of data. Apart from the routine innovative ways of offering products and services companies also are now contemplating how to monetize their data. Putting it simply, can the companies sell their data without violating the legal and ethical framework of the national and business eco-system. Putting it simply - Can companies use their data as any other corporate resource to generate a revenue model for itself?

Below we provide some examples from a variety of domains where companies exploit the data generated, collected, stored and processed are used for innovation and/or monetization.

1. Equifax On the surface: Equifax is a company that sells data and enriched data in the form of credit scores and ratings to risk managers, marketing officers, compliance heads, demand managers, and the like. It is also an anomalous success; its stock price has risen by 50 percent over the past two years, more than double the growth of the S&P 500. What sets Equifax apart is its ability to develop business opportunities across the entire data and analytics spectrum. Like many financial companies, Equifax interacts with a large and diverse set of data assets: customer wealth, fraud and authentication, securities compliance, telephone and utility exchange, and income and employment data. The company's ability to develop products and services across the entire data and analytics spectrum is clearly driving growth. In fact, Equifax predicts multiyear growth of 7 to 10 percent (with acquisitions), including 2 to 3 percent growth fueled by new products and innovation in data and analytics. (http://www.strategyand.pwc.com/media/file/Strategyand_The-Data-Gold-Rush.pdf)

2. DIGILocker: Digital Locker is one of the key initiatives under the Digital India Programme. A beta version of the same has been already released by the Department of Electronics and Information Technology (DeitY), Govt. of India in Feb 2015. The Prime Minister, Mr. Narendra Modi launched the final version of the Digital Locker is on 1st July 2015. The Digital Locker is aimed at minimizing the usage of physical documents and enable sharing of e-documents across agencies.

   With the help of this Portal, the sharing of the e-documents will be done through registered repositories thereby ensuring the authenticity of the documents online. Residents can also upload their own electronic documents and digitally sign them using the e-sign facility. These digitally signed documents can be shared with Government organizations or other entities. It is a dedicated personal storage space for e-documents as well as Uniform Resource Identifier (URI) of e-documents issued by government departments. Individual locker will be linked to the resident's **Aadhaar** number, and enable sharing of e-documents across agencies whenever required. The sharing of these e-documents will be done through registered repositories thereby ensuring the authenticity of the documents online, and also minimize the loss and damage of important documents like birth certificate etc. (Source: http://india.gov.in/spotlight/digilocker-online-document-storage-facility)

INTRODUCTION

Over the past two decades, data has become a strategic asset for most organizations. Databases are used to store, manipulate, and retrieve data in nearly every type of organization, including business, health care, education, government, and libraries. Database technology is routinely used by individuals on personal computers and by employees using enterprise-wide distributed applications. Databases are also accessed by customers and other remote users through diverse technologies, such as automated teller machines, Web browsers, smartphones, and intelligent living and office environments. Most Web-based applications depend on a database foundation.

Following this period of rapid growth, will the demand for databases and database technology level off? Very likely not! In the highly competitive environment of today, there is every indication that database technology will assume even greater importance. Managers seek to use knowledge derived from databases for competitive advantage. For example, detailed sales databases can be mined to determine customer buying patterns as a basis for advertising and marketing campaigns. Organizations embed procedures called *alerts* in databases to warn of unusual conditions, such as impending stock shortages or opportunities to sell additional products, and to trigger appropriate actions.

Although the future of databases is assured, much work remains to be done. Many organizations have a proliferation of incompatible databases that were developed to meet immediate needs rather than based on a planned strategy or a well-managed evolution. Enormous amounts of data are trapped in older, "legacy" systems, and the data are often of poor quality. New skills are required to design and manage data warehouses and other repositories of data and to fully leverage all the data that is being captured in the organization. There is a shortage of skills in areas such as database analysis, database design, database application development, and business analytics. We address these and other important issues in this textbook to equip you for the jobs of the future.

A course in database management has emerged as one of the most important courses in the information systems curriculum today. Further, many schools have added an additional elective course in data warehousing and/or business analytics to provide in-depth coverage of these important topics. As information systems professionals, you must be prepared to analyze database requirements and design and implement databases within the context of information systems development. You also must be prepared to consult with end users and show them how they can use databases (or data warehouses) to build decision models and systems for competitive advantage. And, the widespread use of databases attached to Web sites that return dynamic information to users of these sites requires that you understand not only how to link databases to the Web-based applications but also how to secure those databases so that their contents can be viewed but not compromised by outside users.

In this chapter, we introduce the basic concepts of databases and database management systems (DBMSs). We describe traditional file management systems and some of their shortcomings that led to the database approach. Next, we consider the benefits, costs, and risks of using the database approach. We review the range of technologies used to build, use, and manage databases; describe the types of applications that use databases—personal, multitier, and enterprise; and describe how databases have evolved over the past five decades.

Because a database is one part of an information system, this chapter also examines how the database development process fits into the overall information systems development process. The chapter emphasizes the need to coordinate database development with all the other activities in the development of a complete information system. It includes highlights from a hypothetical database development process at Pine Valley Furniture Company. Using this example, the chapter introduces tools for developing databases on personal computers and the process of extracting data from enterprise databases for use in stand-alone applications.

There are several reasons for discussing database development at this point. First, although you may have used the basic capabilities of a database management system, such as Microsoft Access, you may not yet have developed an understanding of how these databases were developed. Using simple examples, this chapter briefly illustrates what you will be able to do after you complete a database course using this text. Thus, this chapter helps you develop a vision and context for each topic developed in detail in subsequent chapters.

Second, many students learn best from a text full of concrete examples. Although all of the chapters in this text contain numerous examples, illustrations, and actual database designs and code, each chapter concentrates on a specific aspect of database management. We have designed this chapter to help you understand, with minimal technical details, how all of these individual aspects of database management are related and how database development tasks and skills relate to what you are learning in other information systems courses.

Finally, many instructors want you to begin the initial steps of a database development group or individual project early in your database course. This chapter gives you an idea of how to structure a database development project sufficient to begin a course exercise. Obviously, because this is only the first chapter, many of the examples and notations we will use will be much simpler than those required for your project, for other course assignments, or in a real organization.

One note of caution: You will not learn how to design or develop databases just from this chapter. Sorry! We have purposely kept the content of this chapter introductory and simplified. Many of the notations used in this chapter are not exactly like the ones you will learn in subsequent chapters. Our purpose in this chapter is to give you a general understanding of the key steps and types of skills, not to teach you specific techniques. You will, however, learn fundamental concepts and definitions and develop an intuition and motivation for the skills and knowledge presented in later chapters.

BASIC CONCEPTS AND DEFINITIONS

We define a **database** as an organized collection of logically related data. Not many words in the definition, but have you looked at the size of this book? There is a lot to do to fulfill this definition.

Database
An organized collection of logically related data.

A database may be of any size and complexity. For example, a salesperson may maintain a small database of customer contacts—consisting of a few megabytes of data—on her laptop computer. A large corporation may build a large database consisting of several terabytes of data (a *terabyte* is a trillion bytes) on a large mainframe computer that is used for decision support applications (Winter, 1997). Very large data warehouses contain more than a petabyte of data. (A *petabyte* is a quadrillion bytes.) (We assume throughout the text that all databases are computer based.)

Data

Historically, the term *data* referred to facts concerning objects and events that could be recorded and stored on computer media. For example, in a salesperson's database, the data would include facts such as customer name, address, and telephone number. This type of data is called *structured* data. The most important structured data types are numeric, character, and dates. Structured data are stored in tabular form (in tables, relations, arrays, spreadsheets, etc.) and are most commonly found in traditional databases and data warehouses.

The traditional definition of data now needs to be expanded to reflect a new reality: Databases today are used to store objects such as documents, e-mails, tweets, Facebook posts, GPS information, maps, photographic images, sound, and video segments in addition to structured data. For example, the salesperson's database might include a photo image of the customer contact. It might also include a sound recording or video clip about the most recent product. This type of data is referred to as *unstructured* data, or as multimedia data. Today structured and unstructured data are often combined in the same database to create a true multimedia environment. For example, an automobile repair shop can combine structured data (describing customers and automobiles) with multimedia data (photo images of the damaged autos and scanned images of insurance claim forms).

An expanded definition of **data** that includes structured and unstructured types is "a stored representation of objects and events that have meaning and importance in the user's environment."

Data
Stored representations of objects and events that have meaning and importance in the user's environment.

Data Versus Information

The terms *data* and *information* are closely related and in fact are often used interchangeably. However, it is useful to distinguish between data and information. We define **information** as data that have been processed in such a way that the knowledge of the person who uses the data is increased. For example, consider the following list of facts:

Information
Data that have been processed in such a way as to increase the knowledge of the person who uses the data.

Bohra, Kiran D.	180991
Singh, Seema	179878
Arora, Ankit	231456
Chakraborty, Sunad	239807
Sharma, Arun	789342
Avdhani, Suresh	318529

FIGURE 1-1 Converting data to information
(a) Data in context

(b) Summarized data

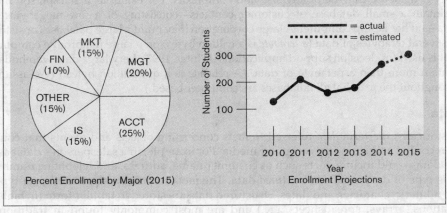

These facts satisfy our definition of data, but most people would agree that the data are useless in their present form. Even if we guess that this is a list of people's names paired with their Social Security numbers, the data remain useless because we have no idea what the entries mean. Notice what happens when we place the same data in a context, as shown in Figure 1-1a.

By adding a few additional data items and providing some structure, we recognize a class roster for a particular course. This is useful information to some users, such as the course instructor and the registrar's office. Of course, as general awareness of the importance of strong data security has increased, few organizations still use Social Security numbers as identifiers. Instead, most organizations use an internally generated number for identification purposes.

Another way to convert data into information is to summarize them or otherwise process and present them for human interpretation. For example, Figure 1-1b shows summarized student enrollment data presented as graphical information. This information could be used as a basis for deciding whether to add new courses or to hire new faculty members.

In practice, according to our definitions, databases today may contain either data or information (or both). For example, a database may contain an image of the class roster document shown in Figure 1-1a. Also, data are often preprocessed and stored in summarized form in databases that are used for decision support. Throughout this text we use the term *database* without distinguishing its contents as data or information.

Metadata

Metadata
Data that describe the properties or characteristics of end-user data and the context of those data.

As we have indicated, data become useful only when placed in some context. The primary mechanism for providing context for data is metadata. **Metadata** are data

TABLE 1-1   Example Metadata for Class Roster

Data Item			Metadata			
Name	**Type**	**Length**	**Min**	**Max**	**Description**	**Source**
Course	Alphanumeric	30			Course ID and name	Academic Unit
Section	Integer	1	1	9	Section number	Registrar
Semester	Alphanumeric	10			Semester and year	Registrar
Name	Alphanumeric	30			Student name	Student IS
ID	Integer	9			Student ID (SSN)	Student IS
Major	Alphanumeric	4			Student major	Student IS
GPA	Decimal	3	0.0	4.0	Student grade point average	Academic Unit

that describe the properties or characteristics of end-user data and the context of that data. Some of the properties that are typically described include data names, definitions, length (or size), and allowable values. Metadata describing data context include the source of the data, where the data are stored, ownership (or steward-ship), and usage. Although it may seem circular, many people think of metadata as "data about data."

Some sample metadata for the Class Roster (Figure 1-1a) are listed in Table 1-1. For each data item that appears in the Class Roster, the metadata show the data item name, the data type, length, minimum and maximum allowable values (where appropriate), a brief description of each data item, and the source of the data (sometimes called the *system of record*). Notice the distinction between data and metadata. Metadata are once removed from data. That is, metadata describe the properties of data but are separate from that data. Thus, the metadata shown in Table 1-1 do not include any sample data from the Class Roster of Figure 1-1a. Metadata enable database designers and users to understand what data exist, what the data mean, and how to distinguish between data items that at first glance look similar. Managing metadata is at least as crucial as managing the associated data because data without clear meaning can be confusing, misinterpreted, or erroneous. Typically, much of the metadata are stored as part of the database and may be retrieved using the same approaches that are used to retrieve data or information.

Data can be stored in files (think Excel sheets) or in databases. In the following sections, we examine the progression from file processing systems to databases and the advantages and disadvantages of each.

TRADITIONAL FILE PROCESSING SYSTEMS

When computer-based data processing was first available, there were no databases. To be useful for business applications, computers had to store, manipulate, and retrieve large files of data. Computer file processing systems were developed for this purpose. Although these systems have evolved over time, their basic structure and purpose have changed little over several decades.

As business applications became more complex, it became evident that traditional file processing systems had a number of shortcomings and limitations (described next). As a result, these systems have been replaced by database processing systems in most business applications today. Nevertheless, you should have at least some familiarity with file processing systems since understanding the problems and limitations inher-ent in file processing systems can help you avoid these same problems when design-ing database systems. It should be noted that Excel files, in general, fall into the same category as file systems and suffer from the same drawbacks listed below.

File Processing Systems at Pine Valley Furniture Company

Early computer applications at Pine Valley Furniture used the traditional file processing approach. This approach to information systems design met the data processing needs of individual departments rather than the overall information needs of the organization. The information systems group typically responded to users' requests for new systems by developing (or acquiring) new computer programs for individual applications such as inventory control, accounts receivable, or human resource management. No overall map, plan, or model guided application growth.

   Three of the computer applications based on the file processing approach are shown in Figure 1-2. The systems illustrated are Order Filling, Invoicing, and Payroll. The figure also shows the major data files associated with each application. A *file* is a collection of related records. For example, the Order Filling System has three files: Customer Master, Inventory Master, and Back Order. Notice that there is duplication of some of the files used by the three applications, which is typical of file processing systems.

Disadvantages of File Processing Systems

Several disadvantages associated with conventional file processing systems are listed in Table 1-2 and described briefly next. It is important to understand these issues because if we don't follow the database management practices described in this book, some of these disadvantages can also become issues for databases as well.

Database application

An application program (or set of related programs) that is used to perform a series of database activities (create, read, update, and delete) on behalf of database users.

PROGRAM-DATA DEPENDENCE File descriptions are stored within each **database application** program that accesses a given file. For example, in the Invoicing System in Figure 1-2, Program A accesses the Inventory Pricing File and the Customer Master File. Because the program contains a detailed file description for these files, any change to a file structure requires changes to the file descriptions for all programs that access the file.

   Notice in Figure 1-2 that the Customer Master File is used in the Order Filling System and the Invoicing System. Suppose it is decided to change the customer address field length in the records in this file from 30 to 40 characters. The file descriptions in each program that is affected (up to five programs) would have to be modified. It is often difficult even to locate all programs affected by such changes. Worse, errors are often introduced when making such changes.

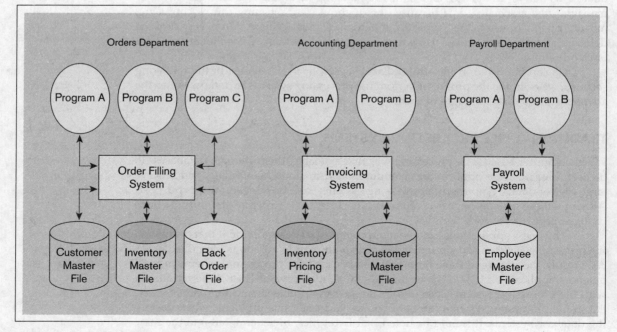

FIGURE 1-2   Old file processing systems at Pine Valley Furniture Company

DUPLICATION OF DATA   Because applications are often developed independently in file processing systems, unplanned duplicate data files are the rule rather than the exception. For example, in Figure 1-2, the Order Filling System contains an Inventory Master File, whereas the Invoicing System contains an Inventory Pricing File. These files contain data describing Pine Valley Furniture Company's products, such as product description, unit price, and quantity on hand. This duplication is wasteful because it requires additional storage space and increased effort to keep all files up to date. Data formats may be inconsistent or data values may not agree (or both). Reliable metadata are very difficult to establish in file processing systems. For example, the same data item may have different names in different files or, conversely, the same name may be used for different data items in different files.

LIMITED DATA SHARING   With the traditional file processing approach, each application has its own private files, and users have little opportunity to share data outside their own applications. Notice in Figure 1-2, for example, that users in the Accounting Department have access to the Invoicing System and its files, but they probably do not have access to the Order Filling System or to the Payroll System and their files. Managers often find that a requested report requires a major programming effort because data must be drawn from several incompatible files in separate systems. When different organizational units own these different files, additional management barriers must be overcome.

LENGTHY DEVELOPMENT TIMES   With traditional file processing systems, each new application requires that the developer essentially start from scratch by designing new file formats and descriptions and then writing the file access logic for each new program. The lengthy development times required are inconsistent with today's fast-paced business environment, in which time to market (or time to production for an information system) is a key business success factor.

EXCESSIVE PROGRAM MAINTENANCE   The preceding factors all combined to create a heavy program maintenance load in organizations that relied on traditional file processing systems. In fact, as much as 80 percent of the total information system's development budget might be devoted to program maintenance in such organizations. This in turn means that resources (time, people, and money) are not being spent on developing new applications.

It is important to note that many of the disadvantages of file processing we have mentioned can also be limitations of databases if an organization does not properly apply the database approach. For example, if an organization develops many separately managed databases (say, one for each division or business function) with little or no coordination of the metadata, then uncontrolled data duplication, limited data sharing, lengthy development time, and excessive program maintenance can occur. Thus, the database approach, which is explained in the next section, is as much a way to manage organizational data as it is a set of technologies for defining, creating, maintaining, and using these data.

THE DATABASE APPROACH

So, how do we overcome the flaws of file processing? No, we don't call Ghostbusters, but we do something better: We follow the database approach. We first begin by defining some core concepts that are fundamental in understanding the database approach to managing data. We then describe how the database approach can overcome the limitations of the file processing approach.

Data Models

Designing a database properly is fundamental to establishing a database that meets the needs of the users. **Data models** capture the nature of and relationships among data and are used at different levels of abstraction as a database is conceptualized and designed. The effectiveness and efficiency of a database is directly associated with the structure of the database. Various graphical systems exist that convey this structure and are used to

TABLE 1-2   Disadvantages of File Processing Systems

Program-data dependence

Duplication of data

Limited data sharing

Lengthy development times

Excessive program maintenance

Data model

Graphical systems used to capture the nature and relationships among data.

produce data models that can be understood by end users, systems analysts, and database designers. Chapters 2 and 3 are devoted to developing your understanding of data modeling, as is Chapter 14, on the book's Web site which addresses a different approach using object-oriented data modeling. A typical data model is made up of entities, attributes, and relationships and the most common data modeling representation is the entity-relationship model. A brief description is presented next. More details will be forthcoming in Chapters 2 and 3.

ENTITIES   Customers and orders are objects about which a business maintains information. They are referred to as "entities." An **entity** is like a noun in that it describes a person, a place, an object, an event, or a concept in the business environment for which information must be recorded and retained. CUSTOMER and ORDER are entities in Figure 1-3a. The data you are interested in capturing about the entity (e.g., Customer Name) is called an *attribute*. Data are recorded for many customers. Each customer's information is referred to as an *instance* of CUSTOMER.

Entity

A person, a place, an object, an event, or a concept in the user environment about which the organization wishes to maintain data.

FIGURE 1-3 Comparison of enterprise and project-level data models
(a) Segment of an enterprise data model

(b) Segment of a project data model

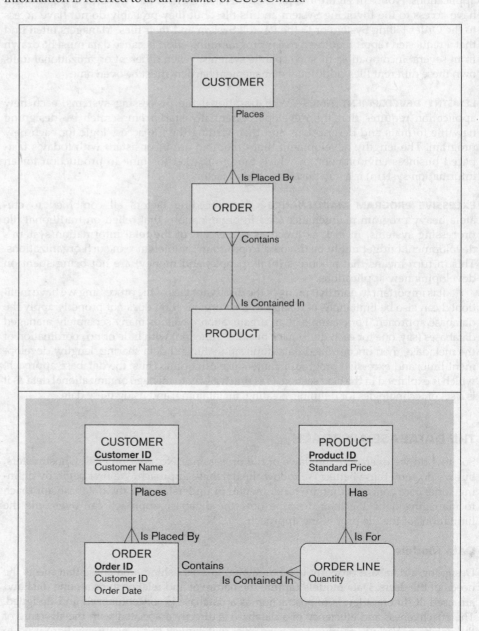

RELATIONSHIPS   A well-structured database establishes the *relationships* between entities that exist in organizational data so that desired information can be retrieved. Most relationships are one-to-many (*1:M*) or many-to-many (*M:N*). A customer can place (the Places relationship) more than one order with a company. However, each order is usually associated with (the Is Placed By relationship) a particular customer. Figure 1-3a shows the *1:M* relationship of customers who may place one or more orders; the *1:M* nature of the relationship is marked by the crow's foot attached to the rectangle (entity) labeled ORDER. This relationship appears to be the same in Figures 1-3a and 1-3b. However, the relationship between orders and products is *M:N*. An order may be for one or more products, and a product may be included on more than one order. It is worthwhile noting that Figure 1-3a is an enterprise-level model, where it is necessary to include only the higher-level relationships of customers, orders, and products. The project-level diagram shown in Figure 1-3b includes additional levels of details, such as the further details of an order.

Relational Databases

Relational databases establish the relationships between entities by means of common fields included in a file, called a relation. The relationship between a customer and the customer's order depicted in the data models in Figure 1-3 is established by including the customer number with the customer's order. Thus, a customer's identification number is included in the file (or relation) that holds customer information such as name, address, and so forth. Every time the customer places an order, the customer identification number is also included in the relation that holds order information. Relational databases use the identification number to establish the relationship between customer and order.

Relational database

A database that represents data as a collection of tables in which all data relationships are represented by common values in related tables.

Database Management Systems

A **database management system (DBMS)** is a software system that enables the use of a database approach. The primary purpose of a DBMS is to provide a systematic method of creating, updating, storing, and retrieving the data stored in a database. It enables end users and application programmers to share data, and it enables data to be shared among multiple applications rather than propagated and stored in new files for every new application (Mullins, 2002). A DBMS also provides facilities for controlling data access, enforcing data integrity, managing concurrency control, and restoring a database. We describe these DBMS features in detail in Chapter 12.

Database management system (DBMS)

A software system that is used to create, maintain, and provide controlled access to user databases.

Now that we understand the basic elements of a database approach, let us try to understand the differences between a database approach and file-based approach. Let us begin by comparing Figures 1-2 and 1-4. Figure 1-4 depicts a representation (entities) of how the data can be considered to be stored in the database. Notice that unlike Figure 1-2, in Figure 1-4, there is only one place where the CUSTOMER information is stored rather than the two Customer Master Files. Both the Order Filling System and the Invoicing System will access the data contained in the single CUSTOMER entity. Further, what CUSTOMER information is stored, how it is stored and how it is accessed is likely not closely tied to either of the two systems. All of this enables us to achieve the advantages listed in the next section. Of course, it is important to note that a real-life database will likely include thousands of entities and relationships among them.

Advantages of the Database Approach

The primary advantages of a database approach, enabled by DBMSs, are summarized in Table 1-3 and described next.

PROGRAM-DATA INDEPENDENCE   The separation of data descriptions (metadata) from the application programs that use the data is called **data independence**. With the database approach, data descriptions are stored in a central location called the *repository*. This property of database systems allows an organization's data to change and evolve (within limits) without changing the application programs that process the data.

Data independence

The separation of data descriptions from the application programs that use the data.

FIGURE 1-4 Enterprise model for Figure 1-3 segments

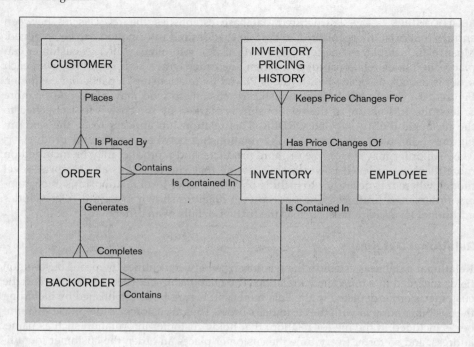

PLANNED DATA REDUNDANCY Good database design attempts to integrate previously separate (and redundant) data files into a single, logical structure. Ideally, each primary fact is recorded in only one place in the database. For example, facts about a product, such as the Pine Valley oak computer desk, its finish, price, and so forth, are recorded together in one place in the Product table, which contains data about each of Pine Valley's products. The database approach does not eliminate redundancy entirely, but it enables the designer to control the type and amount of redundancy. At other times, it may be desirable to include some limited redundancy to improve database performance, as we will see in later chapters.

IMPROVED DATA CONSISTENCY By eliminating or controlling data redundancy, we greatly reduce the opportunities for inconsistency. For example, if a customer's address is stored only once, we cannot disagree about the customer's address. When the customer's address changes, recording the new address is greatly simplified because the address is stored in a single place. Finally, we avoid the wasted storage space that results from redundant data storage.

IMPROVED DATA SHARING A database is designed as a shared corporate resource. Authorized internal and external users are granted permission to use the database, and

TABLE 1-3 Advantages of the Database Approach
Program-data independence
Planned data redundancy
Improved data consistency
Improved data sharing
Increased productivity of application development
Enforcement of standards
Improved data quality
Improved data accessibility and responsiveness
Reduced program maintenance
Improved decision support

each user (or group of users) is provided one or more user views into the database to facilitate this use. A **user view** is a logical description of some portion of the database that is required by a user to perform some task. A user view is often developed by identifying a form or report that the user needs on a regular basis. For example, an employee working in human resources will need access to confidential employee data; a customer needs access to the product catalog available on Pine Valley's Web site. The views for the human resources employee and the customer are drawn from completely different areas of one unified database.

User view

A logical description of some portion of the database that is required by a user to perform some task.

INCREASED PRODUCTIVITY OF APPLICATION DEVELOPMENT   A major advantage of the database approach is that it greatly reduces the cost and time for developing new business applications. There are three important reasons that database applications can often be developed much more rapidly than conventional file applications:

1. Assuming that the database and the related data capture and maintenance applications have already been designed and implemented, the application developer can concentrate on the specific functions required for the new application, without having to worry about file design or low-level implementation details.
2. The database management system provides a number of high-level productivity tools, such as forms and report generators, and high-level languages that automate some of the activities of database design and implementation. We describe many of these tools in subsequent chapters.
3. Significant improvement in application developer productivity, estimated to be as high as 60 percent (Long, 2005), is currently being realized through the use of Web services, based on the use of standard Internet protocols and a universally accepted data format (XML). Web services and XML are covered in Chapter 8.

ENFORCEMENT OF STANDARDS   When the database approach is implemented with full management support, the database administration function should be granted single-point authority and responsibility for establishing and enforcing data standards. These standards will include naming conventions, data quality standards, and uniform procedures for accessing, updating, and protecting data. The data repository provides database administrators with a powerful set of tools for developing and enforcing these standards. Unfortunately, the failure to implement a strong database administration function is perhaps the most common source of database failures in organizations. We describe the database administration (and related data administration) functions in Chapter 12.

IMPROVED DATA QUALITY   Concern with poor quality data is a common theme in strategic planning and database administration today. In 2011 alone, poor data quality is estimated to have cost the U.S. economy almost $3 trillion dollars, almost twice the size of the federal deficit (http://hollistibbetts.sys-con.com/node/1975126). The database approach provides a number of tools and processes to improve data quality. Two of the more important are the following:

1. Database designers can specify integrity constraints that are enforced by the DBMS. A **constraint** is a rule that cannot be violated by database users. We describe numerous types of constraints (also called "business rules") in Chapters 2 and 3. If a customer places an order, the constraint that ensures that the customer and the order remain associated is called a "relational integrity constraint," and it prevents an order from being entered without specifying who placed the order.

Constraint

A rule that cannot be violated by database users.

2. One of the objectives of a data warehouse environment is to clean up (or "scrub") operational data before they are placed in the data warehouse (Jordan, 1996). Do you ever receive multiple copies of a catalog? The company that sends you three copies of each of its mailings could recognize significant postage and printing savings if its data were scrubbed, and its understanding of its customers would also be enhanced if it could determine a more accurate count of existing customers. We describe data warehouses in Chapter 9 and the potential for improving data quality in Chapter 10.

IMPROVED DATA ACCESSIBILITY AND RESPONSIVENESS With a relational database, end users without programming experience can often retrieve and display data, even when they cross traditional departmental boundaries. For example, an employee can display information about computer desks at Pine Valley Furniture Company with the following query:

```
SELECT *
FROM Product_T
WHERE ProductDescription = "Computer Desk";
```

The language used in this query is called Structured Query Language, or SQL. (You will study this language in detail in Chapters 6 and 7.) Although the queries constructed can be *much* more complex, the basic structure of the query is easy for even novice, non-programmers to grasp. If they understand the structure and names of the data that fit within their view of the database, they soon gain the ability to retrieve answers to new questions without having to rely on a professional application developer. This can be dangerous; queries should be thoroughly tested to be sure they are returning accurate data before relying on their results, and novices may not understand that challenge.

REDUCED PROGRAM MAINTENANCE Stored data must be changed frequently for a variety of reasons: New data item types are added, data formats are changed, and so on. A celebrated example of this problem was the well-known "year 2000" problem, in which common two-digit year fields were extended to four digits to accommodate the rollover from the year 1999 to the year 2000.

In a file processing environment, the data descriptions and the logic for accessing data are built into individual application programs (this is the program-data dependence issue described earlier). As a result, changes to data formats and access methods inevitably result in the need to modify application programs. In a database environment, data are more independent of the application programs that use them. Within limits, we can change either the data or the application programs that use the data without necessitating a change in the other factor. As a result, program maintenance can be significantly reduced in a modern database environment.

IMPROVED DECISION SUPPORT Some databases are designed expressly for decision support applications. For example, some databases are designed to support customer relationship management, whereas others are designed to support financial analysis or supply chain management. You will study how databases are tailored for different decision support applications and analytical styles in Chapter 9.

Cautions About Database Benefits

The previous section identified 10 major potential benefits of the database approach. However, we must caution you that many organizations have been frustrated in attempting to realize some of these benefits. For example, the goal of data independence (and, therefore, reduced program maintenance) has proven elusive due to the limitations of older data models and database management software. Fortunately, the relational model and the newer object-oriented model provide a significantly better environment for achieving these benefits. Another reason for failure to achieve the intended benefits is poor organizational planning and database implementation; even the best data management software cannot overcome such deficiencies. For this reason, we stress database planning and design throughout this text.

Costs and Risks of the Database Approach

TABLE 1-4 Costs and Risks of the Database Approach

New, specialized personnel

Installation and management cost and complexity

Conversion costs

Need for explicit backup and recovery

Organizational conflict

A database is not a silver bullet, and it does not have the magic power of Harry Potter. As with any other business decision, the database approach entails some additional costs and risks that must be recognized and managed when it is implemented (see Table 1-4).

NEW, SPECIALIZED PERSONNEL   Frequently, organizations that adopt the database approach need to hire or train individuals to design and implement databases, provide database administration services, and manage a staff of new people. Further, because of the rapid changes in technology, these new people will have to be retrained or upgraded on a regular basis. This personnel increase may be more than offset by other productivity gains, but an organization should recognize the need for these specialized skills, which are required to obtain the most from the potential benefits. We discuss the staff requirements for database management in Chapter 12.

INSTALLATION AND MANAGEMENT COST AND COMPLEXITY   A multiuser database management system is a large and complex suite of software that has a high initial cost, requires a staff of trained personnel to install and operate, and has substantial annual maintenance and support costs. Installing such a system may also require upgrades to the hardware and data communications systems in the organization. Substantial training is normally required on an ongoing basis to keep up with new releases and upgrades. Additional or more sophisticated and costly database software may be needed to provide security and to ensure proper concurrent updating of shared data.

CONVERSION COSTS   The term *legacy system* is widely used to refer to older applications in an organization that are based on file processing and/or older database technology. The cost of converting these older systems to modern database technology—measured in terms of dollars, time, and organizational commitment—may often seem prohibitive to an organization. The use of data warehouses is one strategy for continuing to use older systems while at the same time exploiting modern database technology and techniques (Ritter, 1999).

NEED FOR EXPLICIT BACKUP AND RECOVERY   A shared corporate database must be accurate and available at all times. This requires that comprehensive procedures be developed and used for providing backup copies of data and for restoring a database when damage occurs. These considerations have acquired increased urgency in today's security-conscious environment. A modern database management system normally automates many more of the backup and recovery tasks than a file system. We describe procedures for security, backup, and recovery in Chapter 12.

ORGANIZATIONAL CONFLICT   A shared database requires a consensus on data definitions and ownership, as well as responsibilities for accurate data maintenance. Experience has shown that conflicts on data definitions, data formats and coding, rights to update shared data, and associated issues are frequent and often difficult to resolve. Handling these issues requires organizational commitment to the database approach, organizationally astute database administrators, and a sound evolutionary approach to database development.

   If strong top management support of and commitment to the database approach are lacking, end-user development of stand-alone databases is likely to proliferate. These databases do not follow the general database approach that we have described, and they are unlikely to provide the benefits described earlier. In the extreme, they may lead to a pattern of inferior decision making that threatens the well-being or existence of an organization.

COMPONENTS OF THE DATABASE ENVIRONMENT

Now that you have seen the advantages and risks of using the database approach to managing data, let us examine the major components of a typical database environment and their relationships (see Figure 1-5). You have already been introduced to some (but not all) of these components in previous sections. Following is a brief description of the nine components shown in Figure 1-5:

1. *Data modeling and design tools*   **Data modeling and design tools** are automated tools used to design databases and application programs. These tools help with creation of data models and in some cases can also help automatically generate

Data modeling and design tools
Software tools that provide automated support for creating data models.

FIGURE 1-5 Components of the database environment

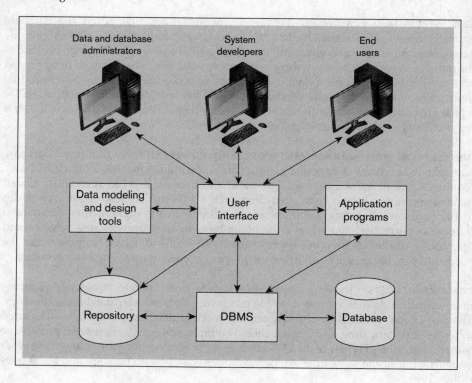

Repository

A centralized knowledge base of all data definitions, data relationships, screen and report formats, and other system components.

the "code" needed to create the database. We reference the use of automated tools for database design and development throughout the text.

2. *Repository* A **repository** is a centralized knowledge base for all data definitions, data relationships, screen and report formats, and other system components. A repository contains an extended set of metadata important for managing databases as well as other components of an information system. We describe the repository in Chapter 12.

3. *DBMS* A DBMS is a software system that is used to create, maintain, and provide controlled access to user databases. We describe the functions of a DBMS in Chapter 12.

4. *Database* A database is an organized collection of logically related data, usually designed to meet the information needs of multiple users in an organization. It is important to distinguish between the database and the repository. The repository contains definitions of data, whereas the database contains occurrences of data. We describe the activities of database design in Chapters 4 and 5 and of implementation in Chapters 6 through 9.

5. *Application programs* Computer-based application programs are used to create and maintain the database and provide information to users. Key database-related application programming skills are described in Chapters 6 through 9.

6. *User interface* The user interface includes languages, menus, and other facilities by which users interact with various system components, such as data modeling and design tools, application programs, the DBMS, and the repository. User interfaces are illustrated throughout this text.

7. *Data and database administrators* Data administrators are persons who are responsible for the overall management of data resources in an organization. Database administrators are responsible for physical database design and for managing technical issues in the database environment. We describe these functions in detail in Chapter 12.

8. *System developers* System developers are persons such as systems analysts and programmers who design new application programs.

9. *End users*   End users are persons throughout the organization who add, delete, and modify data in the database and who request or receive information from it. All user interactions with the database must be routed through the DBMS.

In summary, the database operational environment shown in Figure 1-5 is an integrated system of hardware, software, and people, designed to facilitate the storage, retrieval, and control of the information resource and to improve the productivity of the organization.

THE DATABASE DEVELOPMENT PROCESS

How do organizations start developing a database? In many organizations, database development begins with **enterprise data modeling**, which establishes the range and general contents of organizational databases. Its purpose is to create an overall picture or explanation of organizational data, not the design for a particular database. A particular database provides the data for one or more information systems, whereas an enterprise data model, which may encompass many databases, describes the scope of data maintained by the organization. In enterprise data modeling, you review current systems, analyze the nature of the business areas to be supported, describe the data needed at a very high level of abstraction, and plan one or more database development projects.

Enterprise data modeling
The first step in database development, in which the scope and general contents of organizational databases are specified.

Figure 1-3a showed a segment of an enterprise data model for Pine Valley Furniture Company, using a simplified version of the notation you will learn in Chapters 2 and 3. Besides such a graphical depiction of the entity types, a thorough enterprise data model would also include business-oriented descriptions of each entity type and a compendium of various statements about how the business operates, called *business rules*, which govern the validity of data. Relationships between business objects (business functions, units, applications, etc.) and data are often captured using matrixes and complement the information captured in the enterprise data model. Figure 1-6 shows an example of such a matrix.

Enterprise data modeling as a component of a top-down approach to information systems planning and development represents one source of database projects. Such projects often develop new databases to meet strategic organizational goals, such as improved customer support, better production and inventory management, or more accurate sales forecasting. Many database projects arise, however, in a more bottom-up fashion. In this case, projects are requested by information systems users, who need certain information to do their jobs, or by other information systems professionals, who see a need to improve data management in the organization.

FIGURE 1-6   Example business function-to-data entity matrix

Business Functions \ Data Entity Types	Customer	Product	Raw Material	Order	Work Center	Work Order	Invoice	Equipment	Employee
Business Planning	X	X						X	X
Product Development		X	X		X			X	
Materials Management		X	X	X	X	X		X	
Order Fulfillment	X	X	X	X	X	X	X	X	X
Order Shipment	X	X		X	X		X		X
Sales Summarization	X	X		X			X		X
Production Operations		X	X	X	X	X		X	X
Finance and Accounting	X	X	X	X	X		X	X	X

X = data entity is used within business function

A typical bottom-up database development project usually focuses on the creation of one database. Some database projects concentrate only on defining, designing, and implementing a database as a foundation for subsequent information systems development. In most cases, however, a database and the associated information processing functions are developed together as part of a comprehensive information systems development project.

Systems Development Life Cycle

As you may know from other information systems courses you've taken, a traditional process for conducting an information systems development project is called the **systems development life cycle (SDLC)**. The SDLC is a complete set of steps that a team of information systems professionals, including database designers and programmers, follow in an organization to specify, develop, maintain, and replace information systems. Textbooks and organizations use many variations on the life cycle and may identify anywhere from 3 to 20 different phases.

The various steps in the SDLC and their associated purpose are depicted in Figure 1-7 (Hoffer et al., 2014). The process appears to be circular and is intended to convey the iterative nature of systems development projects. The steps may overlap in time, they may be conducted in parallel, and it is possible to backtrack to previous steps when prior decisions need to be reconsidered. Some believe that the most common path through the development process is to cycle through the steps depicted in Figure 1-7, but at more detailed levels on each pass, as the requirements of the system become more concrete.

Figure 1-7 also provides an outline of the database development activities typically included in each phase of the SDLC. Note that there is not always a one-to-one correspondence between SDLC phases and database development steps. For example, conceptual data modeling occurs in both the Planning and the Analysis phases. We will briefly illustrate each of these database development steps for Pine Valley Furniture Company later in this chapter.

PLANNING—ENTERPRISE MODELING The database development process begins with a review of the enterprise modeling components that were developed during the information systems planning process. During this step, analysts review current databases and information systems; analyze the nature of the business area that is the subject of the development project; and describe, in general terms, the data needed for each information system under consideration for development. They determine what data are already available in existing databases and what new data will need to be added to support the proposed new project. Only selected projects move into the next phase based on the projected value of each project to the organization.

PLANNING—CONCEPTUAL DATA MODELING For an information systems project that is initiated, the overall data requirements of the proposed information system must be analyzed. This is done in two stages. First, during the Planning phase, the analyst develops a diagram similar to Figure 1-3a, as well as other documentation, to outline the scope of data involved in this particular development project without consideration of what databases already exist. Only high-level categories of data (entities) and major relationships are included at this point. This step in the SDLC is critical for improving the chances of a successful development process. The better the definition of the specific needs of the organization, the closer the conceptual model should come to meeting the needs of the organization, and the less recycling back through the SDLC should be needed.

ANALYSIS—CONCEPTUAL DATA MODELING During the Analysis phase of the SDLC, the analyst produces a detailed data model that identifies all the organizational data that must be managed for this information system. Every data attribute is defined, all categories of data are listed, every business relationship between data entities is represented, and every rule that dictates the integrity of the data is specified. It is also during the Analysis phase that the conceptual data model is checked for consistency

Systems development life cycle (SDLC)

The traditional methodology used to develop, maintain, and replace information systems.

FIGURE 1-7   Database development activities during the systems development life cycle (SDLC)

Planning

Purpose: To develop a preliminary understanding of a business situation and how information systems might help solve a problem or make an opportunity possible

Enterprise modeling
• Analyze current data processing
• Analyze the general business functions and their database needs
• Justify need for new data and databases in support of business

Conceptual data modeling
• Identify scope of database requirements for proposed information system
• Analyze overall data requirements for business function(s) supported by database

Maintenance

Purpose: To monitor the operation and usefulness of the system, and to repair and enhance the system

Database maintenance
• Analyze database and database applications to ensure that evolving information requirements are met
• Tune database for improved performance
• Fix errors in database and database applications and recover database when it is contaminated

Analysis

Purpose: To analyze the business situation thoroughly to determine requirements, to structure those requirements, and to select among competing system features

Conceptual data modeling, cont'd.
• Develop preliminary conceptual data model, including entities and relationships
• Compare preliminary conceptual data model with enterprise data model
• Develop detailed conceptual data model, including all entities, relationships, attributes, and business rules
• Make conceptual data model consistent with other models of information system
• Populate repository with all conceptual database specifications

Implementation

Purpose: To write programs, build databases, test and install the new system, train users, and finalize documentation

Database implementation
• Code and test database processing programs
• Complete database documentation and training materials
• Install database and convert data from prior systems

Design

Purpose: To elicit and structure all information requirements; to develop all technology and organizational specifications

Logical database design
• Analyze in detail the transactions, forms, displays, and inquiries (database views) required by the business functions supported by the database
• Integrate database views into conceptual data model
• Identify data integrity and security requirements, and populate repository

Physical database design and definition
• Define database to DBMS (often generated from repository)
• Decide on physical organization of data
• Design database processing programs

with other types of models developed to explain other dimensions of the target information system, such as processing steps, rules for handling data, and the timing of events. However, even this detailed conceptual data model is preliminary, because subsequent SDLC activities may find missing elements or errors when designing specific transactions, reports, displays, and inquiries. With experience, the database developer gains mental models of common business functions, such as sales or financial record keeping, but must always remain alert for the exceptions to common practices followed by an organization. The output of the conceptual modeling phase is a **conceptual schema**.

DESIGN—LOGICAL DATABASE DESIGN   Logical database design approaches database development from two perspectives. First, the conceptual schema must be transformed into a logical schema, which describes the data in terms of the data management technology that will be used to implement the database. For example, if relational technology will be used, the conceptual data model is transformed and represented using

Conceptual schema

A detailed, technology-independent specification of the overall structure of organizational data.

elements of the relational model, which include tables, columns, rows, primary keys, foreign keys, and constraints. (You will learn how to conduct this important process in Chapter 4.) This representation is referred to as the **logical schema**.

Logical schema

The representation of a database for a particular data management technology.

Then, as each application in the information system is designed, including the program's input and output formats, the analyst performs a detailed review of the transactions, reports, displays, and inquiries supported by the database. During this so-called bottom-up analysis, the analyst verifies exactly what data are to be maintained in the database and the nature of those data as needed for each transaction, report, and so forth. It may be necessary to refine the conceptual data model as each report, business transaction, and other user view is analyzed. In this case, one must combine, or integrate, the original conceptual data model along with these individual user views into a comprehensive design during logical database design. It is also possible that additional information processing requirements will be identified during logical information systems design, in which case these new requirements must be integrated into the previously identified logical database design.

The final step in logical database design is to transform the combined and reconciled data specifications into basic, or atomic, elements following well-established rules for well-structured data specifications. For most databases today, these rules come from relational database theory and a process called *normalization*, which we will describe in detail in Chapter 4. The result is a complete picture of the database without any reference to a particular database management system for managing these data. With a final logical database design in place, the analyst begins to specify the logic of the particular computer programs and queries needed to maintain and report the database contents.

Physical schema

Specifications for how data from a logical schema are stored in a computer's secondary memory by a database management system.

DESIGN—PHYSICAL DATABASE DESIGN AND DEFINITION   A **physical schema** is a set of specifications that describe how data from a logical schema are stored in a computer's secondary memory by a specific database management system. There is one physical schema for each logical schema. Physical database design requires knowledge of the specific DBMS that will be used to implement the database. In physical database design and definition, an analyst decides on the organization of physical records, the choice of file organizations, the use of indexes, and so on. To do this, a database designer needs to outline the programs to process transactions and to generate anticipated management information and decision-support reports. The goal is to design a database that will efficiently and securely handle all data processing against it. Thus, physical database design is done in close coordination with the design of all other aspects of the physical information system: programs, computer hardware, operating systems, and data communications networks.

IMPLEMENTATION—DATABASE IMPLEMENTATION   In database implementation, a designer writes, tests, and installs the programs/scripts that access, create, or modify the database. The designer might do this using standard programming languages (e.g., Java, C#, or Visual Basic.NET) or in special database processing languages (e.g., SQL) or use special-purpose nonprocedural languages to produce stylized reports and displays, possibly including graphs. Also, during implementation, the designer will finalize all database documentation, train users, and put procedures into place for the ongoing support of the information system (and database) users. The last step is to load data from existing information sources (files and databases from legacy applications plus new data now needed). Loading is often done by first unloading data from existing files and databases into a neutral format (such as binary or text files) and then loading these data into the new database. Finally, the database and its associated applications are put into production for data maintenance and retrieval by the actual users. During production, the database should be periodically backed up and recovered in case of contamination or destruction.

MAINTENANCE—DATABASE MAINTENANCE   The database evolves during database maintenance. In this step, the designer adds, deletes, or changes characteristics of the structure of a database in order to meet changing business conditions, to correct errors in database design, or to improve the processing speed of database applications. The designer might also need to rebuild a database if it becomes contaminated or destroyed due to a program or computer system malfunction. This is typically the longest step of database development, because it lasts throughout the life of the database and its associated applications. Each time the database evolves, view it as an abbreviated database development process in which conceptual data modeling, logical and physical database design, and database implementation occur to deal with proposed changes.

Alternative Information Systems (IS) Development Approaches

The systems development life cycle or slight variations on it are often used to guide the development of information systems and databases. The SDLC is a methodical, highly structured approach, which includes many checks and balances to ensure that each step produces accurate results and the new or replacement information system is consistent with existing systems with which it must communicate or for which there needs to be consistent data definitions. Whew! That's a lot of work! Consequently, the SDLC is often criticized for the length of time needed until a working system is produced, which occurs only at the end of the process. Instead, organizations increasingly use rapid application development (RAD) methods, which follow an iterative process of rapidly repeating analysis, design, and implementation steps until they converge on the system the user wants. These RAD methods work best when most of the necessary database structures already exist, and hence for systems that primarily retrieve data, rather than for those that populate and revise databases.

One of the most popular RAD methods is **prototyping**, which is an iterative process of systems development in which requirements are converted to a working system that is continually revised through close work between analysts and users. Figure 1-8 shows the prototyping process. This figure includes annotations to indicate roughly which database development activities occur in each prototyping phase. Typically, you make only a very cursory attempt at conceptual data modeling when the information system problem is identified. During the development of the initial prototype, you simultaneously design the displays and reports the user wants while

Prototyping

An iterative process of systems development in which requirements are converted to a working system that is continually revised through close work between analysts and users.

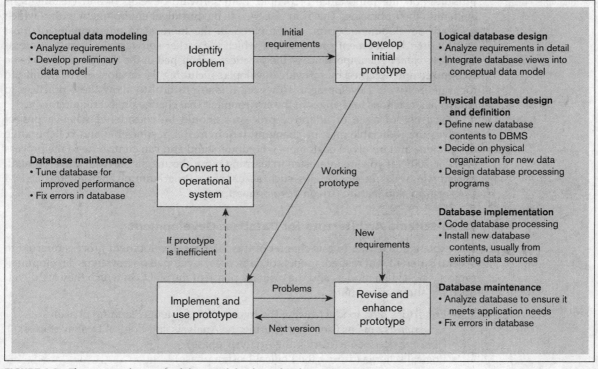

FIGURE 1-8 The prototyping methodology and database development process

understanding any new database requirements and defining a database to be used by the prototype. This is typically a new database, which is a copy of portions of existing databases, possibly with new content. If new content is required, it will usually come from external data sources, such as market research data, general economic indicators, or industry standards.

Database implementation and maintenance activities are repeated as new versions of the prototype are produced. Often security and integrity controls are minimal because the emphasis is on getting working prototype versions ready as quickly as possible. Also, documentation tends to be delayed until the end of the project, and user training occurs from hands-on use. Finally, after an accepted prototype is created, the developer and the user decide whether the final prototype, and its database, can be put into production as is. If the system, including the database, is too inefficient, the system and database might need to be reprogrammed and reorganized to meet performance expectations. Inefficiencies, however, have to be weighed against violating the core principles behind sound database design.

With the increasing popularity of visual programming tools (such as Visual Basic, Java, or C#) that make it easy to modify the interface between user and system, prototyping is becoming the systems development methodology of choice to develop new applications internally. With prototyping, it is relatively easy to change the content and layout of user reports and displays.

The benefits from iterative approaches to systems development demonstrated by RAD and prototyping approaches have resulted in further efforts to create ever more responsive development approaches. In February 2001, a group of 17 individuals interested in supporting these approaches created "The Manifesto for Agile Software Development." For them, **agile software development** practices include valuing **(www. agilemanifesto.org)**:

Individuals and interactions over processes and tools

Working software over comprehensive documentation

Customer collaboration over contract negotiation, and

Responding to change over following a plan

Agile software development
An approach to database and software development that emphasizes "**individuals and interactions** over processes and tools, **working software** over comprehensive documentation, **customer collaboration** over contract negotiation, and **response to change** over following a plan."

Emphasis on the importance of people, both software developers and customers, is evident in their phrasing. This is in response to the turbulent environment within which software development occurs, as compared to the more staid environment of most engineering development projects from which the earlier software development methodologies came. The importance of the practices established in the SDLC continues to be recognized and accepted by software developers including the creators of The Manifesto for Agile Software Development. However, it is impractical to allow these practices to stifle quick reactions to changes in the environment that change project requirements.

The use of agile or adaptive processes should be considered when a project involves unpredictable and/or changing requirements, responsible and collaborative developers, and involved customers who understand and can contribute to the process (Fowler, 2005). If you are interested in learning more about agile software development, investigate agile methodologies such as eXtreme Programming, Scrum, the DSDM Consortium, and feature-driven development.

Three-Schema Architecture for Database Development

The explanation earlier in this chapter of the database development process referred to several different, but related, models of databases developed on a systems development project. These data models and the primary phase of the SDLC in which they are developed are summarized here:

- Enterprise data model (during the Information Systems Planning phase)
- External schema or user view (during the Analysis and Logical Design phases)
- Conceptual schema (during the Analysis phase)
- Logical schema (during the Logical Design phase)
- Physical schema (during the Physical Design phase)

FIGURE 1-9 **Three-schema architecture**

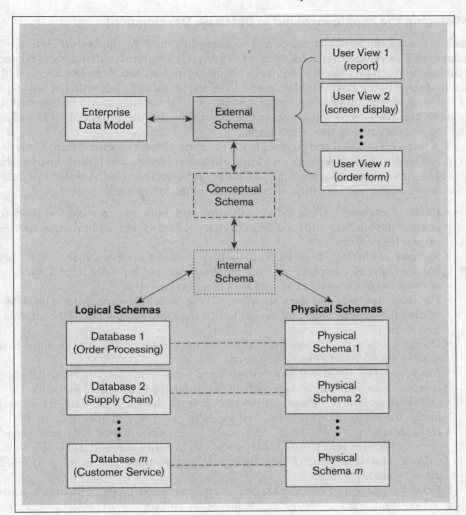

In 1978, an industry committee commonly known as ANSI/SPARC published an important document that described three-schema architecture—external, conceptual, and internal schemas—for describing the structure of data. Figure 1-9 shows the relationship between the various schemas developed during the SDLC and the ANSI three-schema architecture. It is important to keep in mind that all these schemas are just different ways of visualizing the structure of the same database by different stakeholders.

The three schemas as defined by ANSI (depicted down the center of Figure 1-9) are as follows:

1. *External schema* This is the view (or views) of managers and other employees who are the database users. As shown in Figure 1-9, the external schema can be represented as a combination of the enterprise data model (a top-down view) and a collection of detailed (or bottom-up) user views.

2. *Conceptual schema* This schema combines the different external views into a single, coherent, and comprehensive definition of the enterprise's data. The conceptual schema represents the view of the data architect or data administrator.

3. *Internal schema* As shown in Figure 1-9, an internal schema today really consists of two separate schemas: a logical schema and a physical schema. The logical schema is the representation of data for a type of data management technology (e.g., relational). The physical schema describes how data are to be represented and stored in secondary storage using a particular DBMS (e.g., Oracle).

Managing the People Involved in Database Development

Project

A planned undertaking of related activities to reach an objective that has a beginning and an end.

Isn't it always ultimately about people working together? As implied in Figure 1-7, a database is developed as part of a project. A **project** is a planned undertaking of related activities to reach an objective that has a beginning and an end. A project begins with the first steps of the Project Initiation and Planning phase and ends with the last steps of the Implementation phase. A senior systems or database analyst will be assigned to be project leader. This person is responsible for creating detailed project plans as well as staffing and supervising the project team.

A project is initiated and planned in the Planning phase; executed during Analysis, Logical Design, Physical Design, and Implementation phases; and closed down at the end of implementation. During initiation, the project team is formed. A systems or database development team can include one or more of the following:

- *Business analysts*   These individuals work with both management and users to analyze the business situation and develop detailed system and program specifications for projects.
- *Systems analysts*   These individuals may perform business analyst activities but also specify computer systems requirements and typically have a stronger systems development background than business analysts.
- *Database analysts and data modelers*   These individuals concentrate on determining the requirements and design for the database component of the information system.
- *Users*   Users provide assessments of their information needs and monitor that the developed system meets their needs.
- *Programmers*   These individuals design and write computer programs that have commands to maintain and access data in the database embedded in them.
- *Database architects*   These individuals establish standards for data in business units, striving to attain optimum data location, currency, and quality.
- *Data administrators*   These individuals have responsibility for existing and future databases and ensure consistency and integrity across databases, and as experts on database technology, they provide consulting and training to other project team members.
- *Project managers*   Project managers oversee assigned projects, including team composition, analysis, design, implementation, and support of projects.
- *Other technical experts*   Other individuals are needed in areas such as networking, operating systems, testing, data warehousing, and documentation.

It is the responsibility of the project leader to select and manage all of these people as an effective team. See Hoffer et al. (2014) for details on how to manage a systems development project team. See Henderson et al. (2005) for a more detailed description of career paths and roles in data management. The emphasis on people rather than roles when agile development processes are adopted means that team members will be less likely to be constrained to a particular role. They will be expected to contribute and collaborate across these roles, thus using their particular skills, interests, and capabilities more completely.

EVOLUTION OF DATABASE SYSTEMS

Database management systems were first introduced during the 1960s and have continued to evolve during subsequent decades. Figure 1-10a sketches this evolution by highlighting the database technology (or technologies) that were dominant during each decade. In most cases, the period of introduction was quite long, and the technology was first introduced during the decade preceding the one shown in the figure. For example, the relational model was first defined by E. F. Codd, an IBM research fellow, in a paper published in 1970 (Codd, 1970). However, the relational model did not realize widespread commercial success until the 1980s. For example, the challenge of the 1970s when programmers needed to write complex programs to access data was addressed by the introduction of the Structured Query Language (SQL) in the 1980s.

FIGURE 1-10 The range of database technologies: past and present

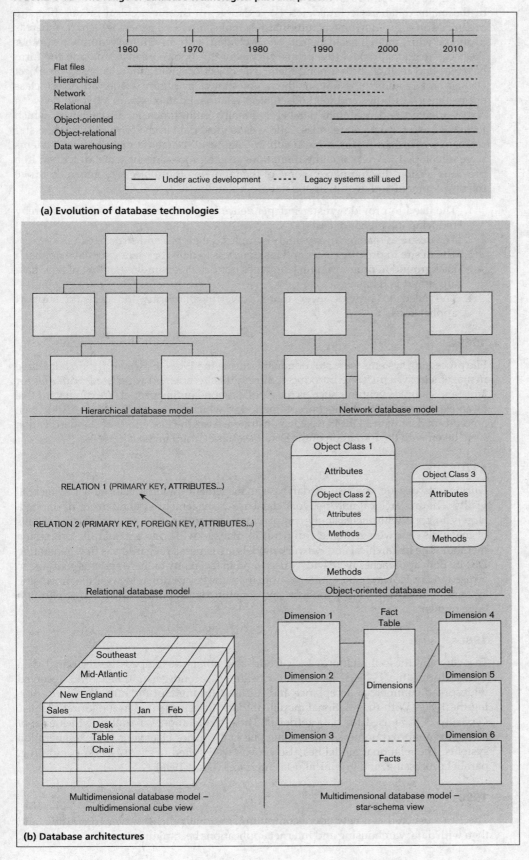

(a) Evolution of database technologies

(b) Database architectures

Figure 1-10b shows a visual depiction of the organizing principle underlying each of the major database technologies. For example, in the hierarchical model, files are organized in a top-down structure that resembles a tree or genealogy chart, whereas in the network model, each file can be associated with an arbitrary number of other files. The relational model (the primary focus of this book) organizes data in the form of tables and relationships among them. The object-oriented model is based on object classes and relationships among them. As shown in Figure 1-10b, an object class encapsulates attributes and methods. Object-relational databases are a hybrid between object-oriented and relational databases. Finally, multidimensional databases, which form the basis for data warehouses, allow us to view data in the form of cubes or a star schema; we discuss this in more detail in Chapter 9. Database management systems were developed to overcome the limitations of file processing systems, described in a previous section. To summarize, some of the following four objectives generally drove the development and evolution of database technology:

1. The need to provide greater independence between programs and data, thereby reducing maintenance costs
2. The desire to manage increasingly complex data types and structures
3. The desire to provide easier and faster access to data for users who have neither a background in programming languages nor a detailed understanding of how data are stored in databases
4. The need to provide ever more powerful platforms for decision support applications

1960s

File processing systems were still dominant during the 1960s. However, the first database management systems were introduced during this decade and were used primarily for large and complex ventures such as the Apollo moon-landing project. We can regard this as an experimental "proof-of-concept" period in which the feasibility of managing vast amounts of data with a DBMS was demonstrated. Also, the first efforts at standardization were taken with the formation of the Data Base Task Group in the late 1960s.

1970s

During this decade, the use of database management systems became a commercial reality. The hierarchical and network database management systems were developed, largely to cope with increasingly complex data structures such as manufacturing bills of materials that were extremely difficult to manage with conventional file processing methods. The hierarchical and network models are generally regarded as first-generation DBMS. Both approaches were widely used, and in fact many of these systems continue to be used today. However, they suffered from the same key disadvantages as file processing systems: limited data independence and lengthy development times for application development.

1980s

To overcome these limitations, E. F. Codd and others developed the relational data model during the 1970s. This model, considered second-generation DBMS, received widespread commercial acceptance and diffused throughout the business world during the 1980s. With the relational model, all data are represented in the form of tables. Typically, SQL is used for data retrieval. Thus, the relational model provides ease of access for nonprogrammers, overcoming one of the major objections to first-generation systems. The relational model has also proven well suited to client/server computing, parallel processing, and graphical user interfaces (Gray, 1996).

1990s

The 1990s ushered in a new era of computing, first with client/server computing, and then with data warehousing and Internet applications becoming increasingly important.

Whereas the data managed by a DBMS during the 1980s were largely structured (such as accounting data), multimedia data (including graphics, sound, images, and video) became increasingly common during the 1990s. To cope with these increasingly complex data, object-oriented databases (considered third generation) were introduced during the late 1980s (Grimes, 1998).

Because organizations must manage a vast amount of structured and unstructured data, both relational and object-oriented databases are still of great importance today. In fact, some vendors are developing combined object-relational DBMSs that can manage both types of data.

2000 and Beyond

Currently, the major type of database that is still most widely used is the relational database. However, a recent trend is the emergence of NoSQL (Not Only SQL) databases. NoSQL is an umbrella term that refers to a set of database technologies that is specifically designed to address large (structured and unstructured) data that are potentially stored across various locations. Popular examples of NoSQL databases are Apache Cassandra **(http://cassandra.apache.org/)** and MongoDB. Hadoop is an example of a non-relational technology that is designed to handle the processing of large amounts of data. This search for non-relational database technologies is fueled by the needs of Web 2.0 applications such as blogs, wikis, and social networking sites (Facebook, Twitter, LinkedIn, etc.) and partially by how easy it has become to generate unstructured data such as pictures and images from devices such as smartphones, tablets, etc. Developing effective database practices to deal with these diverse types of data is going to continue to be of prime importance as we move into the next decade. As larger computer memory chips become less expensive, new database technologies to manage in-memory databases are emerging. This trend opens up new possibilities for even faster database processing. We cover some of these new trends in Chapter 11.

Recent regulations such as Sarbanes-Oxley, Health Insurance Portability and Accountability Act (HIPAA), and the Basel Convention have highlighted the importance of good data management practices, and the ability to reconstruct historical positions has gained prominence. This has led to developments in computer forensics with increased emphasis and expectations around discovery of electronic evidence. The importance of good database administration capabilities also continues to rise because effective disaster recovery and adequate security are mandated by these regulations.

An emerging trend that is making it more convenient to use database technologies (and to tackle some of the regulatory challenges identified here) is that of cloud computing. One popular technology available in the cloud is databases. Databases, relational and non-relational, can now be created, deployed, and managed through the use of technologies provided by a service provider. We examine issues surrounding cloud databases in Chapters 8 and 12.

THE RANGE OF DATABASE APPLICATIONS

What can databases help us do? Recall that Figure 1-5 showed that there are several methods for people to interact with the data in the database. First, users can interact directly with the database using the user interface provided by the DBMS. In this manner, users can issue commands (called *queries*) against the database and examine the results or potentially even store them inside a Microsoft Excel spreadsheet or Word document. This method of interaction with the database is referred to as ad hoc querying and requires a level of understanding the query language on the part of the user.

Because most business users do not possess this level of knowledge, the second and more common mechanism for accessing the database is using application programs. An application program consists of two key components. A graphical user interface accepts the users' request (e.g., to input, delete, or modify data) and/or provides a mechanism for displaying the data retrieved from the database. The business logic contains the programming logic necessary to act on the users' commands. The machine that runs the user interface (and sometimes the business logic) is referred to as the *client*. The machine that runs the DBMS and contains the database is referred to as the *database server*.

It is important to understand that the applications and the database need not reside on the same computer (and, in most cases, they don't). In order to better understand the range of database applications, we divide them into three categories based on the location of the client (application) and the database software itself: personal and multitier databases. We introduce each category with a typical example, followed by some issues that generally arise within that category of use.

Personal Databases

Personal databases are designed to support one user. Personal databases have long resided on personal computers (PCs), including laptops, and now increasingly reside on smartphones, tablets, phablets, etc. The purpose of these databases is to provide the user with the ability to manage (store, update, delete, and retrieve) small amounts of data in an efficient manner. Simple database applications that store customer information and the details of contacts with each customer can be used from a PC and easily transferred from one device to the other for backup and work purposes. For example, consider a company that has a number of salespersons who call on actual or prospective customers. A database of customers and a pricing application can enable the salesperson to determine the best combination of quantity and type of items for the customer to order.

Personal databases are widely used because they can often improve personal productivity. However, they entail a risk: The data cannot easily be shared with other users. For example, suppose the sales manager wants a consolidated view of customer contacts. This cannot be quickly or easily provided from an individual salesperson's databases. This illustrates a common problem: If data are of interest to one person, they probably are or will soon become of interest to others as well. For this reason, personal databases should be limited to those rather special situations (e.g., in a very small organization) where the need to share the data among users of the personal database is unlikely to arise.

Multitier Client/Server Databases

As noted earlier, the utility of a personal (single-user) database is quite limited. Often, what starts off as a single-user database evolves into something that needs to be shared among several users.

To overcome these limitations, most modern applications that need to support a large number of users are built using the concept of multitiered architecture. In most organizations, these applications are intended to support a department (such as marketing or accounting) or a division (such as a line of business), which is generally larger than a workgroup (typically between 25 and 100 persons).

An example of a company that has several multitier applications is shown in Figure 1-11. In a multitiered architecture, the user interface is accessible on the individual users' computers. This user interface may be either Web browser based or written using programming languages such as Visual Basic.NET, Visual C#, or Java. The application layer/Web server layer contains the business logic required to accomplish the business transactions requested by the users. This layer in turn talks to the database server. The most significant implication for database development from the use of multitier client/server architectures is the ease of separating the development of the database and the modules that maintain the data from the information systems modules that focus on business logic and/or presentation logic. In addition, this architecture allows us to improve performance and maintainability of the application and database. We will consider both two and multitier client/server architectures in more detail in Chapter 8.

FIGURE 1-11   Multitiered client/server database architecture

Enterprise Applications

An enterprise (that's small "e," not capital "E," as in *Starship*) application/database is one whose scope is the entire organization or enterprise (or, at least, many different departments). Such databases are intended to support organization-wide operations and decision making. Note that an organization may have several enterprise databases, so such a database is not inclusive of all organizational data. A single operational enterprise database is impractical for many medium to large organizations due to difficulties in performance for very large databases, diverse needs of different users, and the complexity of achieving a single definition of data (metadata) for all database users. An enterprise database does, however, support information needs from many departments and divisions. The evolution of enterprise databases has resulted in two major developments:

1. Enterprise resource planning (ERP) systems
2. Data warehousing implementations

Enterprise applications are the backbone for virtually every modern organization because they form the foundation for the processes that control and execute basic business tasks. They are the systems that keep an organization running, whether it is a neighborhood grocery store with a few employees or a multinational corporation with dozens of divisions around the world and tens of thousands of employees. The focus of these applications is on capturing the data surrounding the "*transactions*," that is, the hundreds or millions (depending on the size of the organization and the nature of the business) of events that take place in an organization every day and define how a business is conducted. For example, when you registered for your database course, you engaged in a transaction that captured data about your registration. Similarly, when you go to a store to buy a candy bar, a transaction takes place between you and the store, and data are captured about your purchase. When Wal-Mart pays its hundreds of thousands of hourly employees, data regarding these transactions are captured in Wal-Mart's systems.

Enterprise resource planning (ERP)

A business management system that integrates all functions of the enterprise, such as manufacturing, sales, finance, marketing, inventory, accounting, and human resources. ERP systems are software applications that provide the data necessary for the enterprise to examine and manage its activities.

Data warehouse

An integrated decision support database whose content is derived from the various operational databases.

It is very typical these days that organizations use packaged systems offered by outside vendors for their transaction processing needs. Examples of these types of systems include **enterprise resource planning (ERP)**, customer relationship management (CRM), supply chain management (SCM), human resource management, and payroll. All these systems are heavily dependent on databases for storing the data.

Whereas ERP systems work with the current operational data of the enterprise, **data warehouses** collect content from the various operational databases, including personal, workgroup, department, and ERP databases. Data warehouses provide users with the opportunity to work with historical data to identify patterns and trends and answers to strategic business questions. Figure 1-12 presents an example of what an output from a data warehouse might look like. We describe data warehouses in detail in Chapter 9.

Finally, one change that has dramatically affected the database environment is the ubiquity of the Internet, and the subsequent development of applications that are used by the masses. Acceptance of the Internet by businesses has resulted in important changes in long-established business models. Even extremely successful companies have been shaken by competition from new businesses that have employed the Internet to provide improved customer information and service, to eliminate traditional marketing and distribution channels, and to implement employee relationship management. For example, customers configure and order their personal computers directly from the computer manufacturers. Bids are accepted for airline tickets and collectables within seconds of submission, sometimes resulting in substantial savings for the end consumer. Information about open positions and company

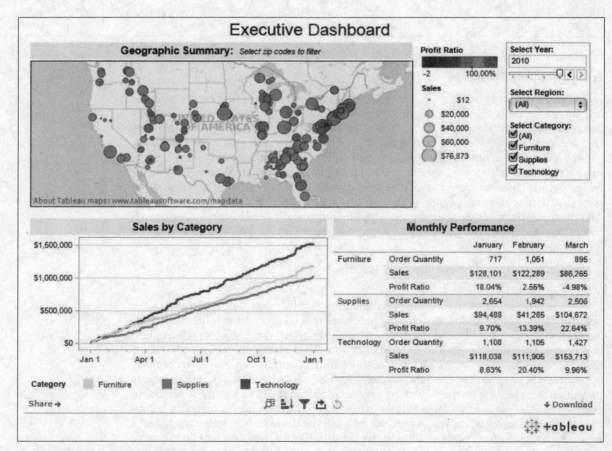

FIGURE 1-12   An example of an executive dashboard
(http://public.tableausoftware.com/profile/mirandali#!/vizhome/Executive-Dashboard_7/ExecutiveDashboard)
Courtesy Tableau Software

TABLE 1-5 Summary of Database Applications

Type of Database / Application	Typical Number of Users	Typical Size of Database
Personal	1	Megabytes
Multitier Client/Server	100–1000	Gigabytes
Enterprise resource planning	>100	Gigabytes–terabytes
Data warehousing	>100	Terabytes–petabytes

activities is readily available within many companies. Each of these Web-based applications use databases extensively.

In the previous examples, the Internet is used to facilitate interaction between the business and the customer (B2C) because the customers are necessarily external to the business. However, for other types of applications, the customers of the businesses are other businesses. Those interactions are commonly referred to as B2B relationships and are enabled by extranets. An *extranet* uses Internet technology, but access to the extranet is not universal, as is the case with an Internet application. Rather, access is restricted to business suppliers and customers with whom an agreement has been reached about legitimate access and use of one another's data and information. Finally, an *intranet* is used by employees of the firm to access applications and databases within the company.

Allowing such access to a business's database raises data security and integrity issues that are new to the management of information systems, whereby data have traditionally been closely guarded and secured within each company. These issues become even more complex as companies take advantage of the cloud. Now data are stored on servers that are not within the control of the company that is generating the data. We cover these issues in more detail in Chapter 12.

Table 1-5 presents a brief summary of the types of databases outlined in this section.

DEVELOPING A DATABASE APPLICATION FOR PINE VALLEY FURNITURE COMPANY

Pine Valley Furniture Company was introduced earlier in this chapter. By the late 1990s, competition in furniture manufacturing had intensified, and competitors seemed to respond more rapidly than Pine Valley Furniture to new business opportunities. While there were many reasons for this trend, managers believed that the computer information systems they had been using (based on traditional file processing) had become outdated. After attending an executive development session led by Heikki Topi and Jeff Hoffer (we wish!), the company started a development effort that eventually led to adopting a database approach for the company. Data previously stored in separate files have been integrated into a single database structure. Also, the metadata that describe these data reside in the same structure. The DBMS provides the interface between the various database applications for organizational users and the database (or databases). The DBMS allows users to share the data and to query, access, and update the stored data.

To facilitate the sharing of data and information, Pine Valley Furniture Company uses a local area network (LAN) that links employee workstations in the various departments to a database server, as shown in Figure 1-13. During the early 2000s, the company mounted a two-phase effort to introduce Internet technology. First, to improve intracompany communication and decision making, an intranet was installed that allows employees fast Web-based access to company information, including phone directories, furniture design specifications, e-mail, and so forth. In addition, Pine Valley Furniture Company also added a Web interface to some of its business applications, such as order entry, so that more internal business activities that require access to data in the database server could also be conducted by employees through

FIGURE 1-13   Computer
System for Pine Valley
Furniture Company

its intranet. However, most applications that use the database server still do not have a Web interface and require that the application itself be stored on employees' workstations.

Database Evolution at Pine Valley Furniture Company

A trait of a good database is that it does and can evolve! Helen Jarvis, product manager for home office furniture at Pine Valley Furniture Company, knows that competition has become fierce in this growing product line. Thus, it is increasingly important to Pine Valley Furniture that Helen be able to analyze sales of her products more thoroughly. Often these analyses are ad hoc, driven by rapidly changing and unanticipated business conditions, comments from furniture store managers, trade industry gossip, or personal experience. Helen has requested that she be given direct access to sales data with an easy-to-use interface so that she can search for answers to the various marketing questions she will generate.

Chris Martin is a systems analyst in Pine Valley Furniture's information systems development area. Chris has worked at Pine Valley Furniture for five years and has experience with information systems from several business areas within Pine Valley. With this experience, his information systems education at Western Florida University, and the extensive training Pine Valley has given him, he has become one of Pine Valley's best systems developers. Chris is skilled in data modeling and is familiar with several relational database management systems used within the firm. Because of his experience, expertise, and availability, the head of information systems has assigned Chris to work with Helen on her request for a marketing support system.

Because Pine Valley Furniture has been careful in the development of its systems, especially since adopting the database approach, the company already has databases that support its operational business functions. Thus, it is likely that Chris will be able to extract the data Helen needs from existing databases. Pine Valley's information systems architecture calls for systems such as the one Helen is requesting to be built as stand-alone databases so that the unstructured and unpredictable use of data will not interfere with the access to the operational databases needed to support efficient transaction processing systems.

Further, because Helen's needs are for data analysis, not creation and mainte-nance, and are personal, not institutional, Chris decides to follow a combination of prototyping and life-cycle approaches in developing the system Helen has requested. This means that Chris will follow all the life-cycle steps but focus his energy on the steps that are integral to prototyping. Thus, he will quickly address project planning and then use an iterative cycle of analysis, design, and implementation to work closely with Helen to develop a working prototype of the system she needs. Because the sys-tem will be personal and likely will require a database with limited scope, Chris hopes the prototype will end up being the actual system Helen will use. Chris has chosen to develop the system using Microsoft Access, Pine Valley's preferred technology for personal databases.

Project Planning

Chris begins the project by interviewing Helen. Chris asks Helen about her business area, taking notes about business area objectives, business functions, data entity types, and other business objects with which she deals. At this point, Chris listens more than he talks so that he can concentrate on understanding Helen's business area; he interjects questions and makes sure that Helen does not try to jump ahead to talk about what she thinks she needs with regards to computer screens and reports from the informa-tion system. Chris asks general questions, using business and marketing terminology as much as possible. For example, Chris asks Helen what issues she faces managing the home office products; what people, places, and things are of interest to her in her job; how far back in time she needs data to go to do her analyses; and what events occur in the business that are of interest to her. Chris pays particular attention to Helen's objectives as well as the data entities that she is interested in.

Chris does two quick analyses before talking with Helen again. First, he iden-tifies all of the databases that contain data associated with the data entities Helen mentioned. From these databases, Chris makes a list of all of the data attributes from these data entities that he thinks might be of interest to Helen in her analy-ses of the home office furniture market. Chris's previous involvement in projects that developed Pine Valley's standard sales tracking and forecasting system and cost accounting system helps him speculate on the kinds of data Helen might want. For example, the objective to exceed sales goals for each product finish category of office furniture suggests that Helen wants product annual sales goals in her system; also, the objective of achieving at least an 8 percent annual sales growth means that the prior year's orders for each product need to be included. He also concludes that Helen's database must include all products, not just those in the office furniture line, because she wants to compare her line to others. However, he is able to eliminate many of the data attributes kept on each data entity. For example, Helen does not appear to need various customer data such as address, phone number, contact per-son, store size, and salesperson. Chris does, though, include a few additional attri-butes, customer type and zip code, which he believes might be important in a sales forecasting system.

Second, from this list, Chris draws a conceptual data model (Figure 1-14) that represents the data entities with the associated data attributes, as well as the major rela-tionships among these data entities. The data model is represented using a notation called the Entity-Relationship (E-R) model. You will learn more about this notation in

FIGURE 1-14   Preliminary data
model for Home Office product
line marketing support system

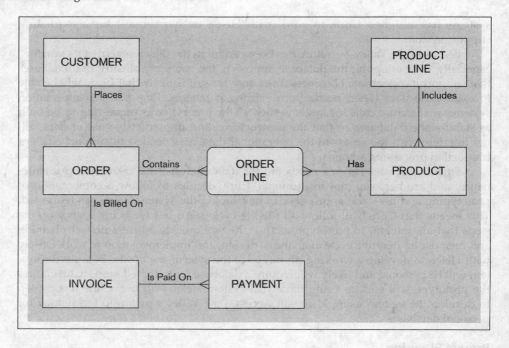

Chapters 2 and 3. The data attributes of each entity Chris thinks Helen wants for the system are listed in Table 1-6. Chris lists in Table 1-6 only basic data attributes from existing databases, because Helen will likely want to combine these data in various ways for the analyses she will want to do.

Analyzing Database Requirements

Prior to their next meeting, Chris sends Helen a rough project schedule outlining the steps he plans to follow and the estimated length of time each step will take. Because prototyping is a user-driven process, in which the user says when to stop iterating on the new prototype versions, Chris can provide only rough estimates of the duration of certain project steps.

Chris does more of the talking at this second meeting, but he pays close attention to Helen's reactions to his initial ideas for the database application. He methodically walks through each data entity in Figure 1-14, explaining what it means and what business policies and procedures are represented by each line between entities.

A few of the rules he summarizes are listed here:

1. Each CUSTOMER *Places* any number of ORDERs. Conversely, each ORDER *Is Placed By* exactly one CUSTOMER.
2. Each ORDER *Contains* any number of ORDER LINEs. Conversely, each ORDER LINE *Is Contained In* exactly one ORDER.
3. Each PRODUCT *Has* any number of ORDER LINEs. Conversely, each ORDER LINE *Is For* exactly one PRODUCT.
4. Each ORDER *Is Billed On* one INVOICE and each INVOICE *Is a Bill for* exactly one ORDER.

Places, *Contains*, and *Has* are called one-to-many relationships because, for example, one customer places potentially many orders and one order is placed by exactly one customer.

In addition to the relationships, Chris also presents Helen with some detail on the data attributes captured in Table 1-6. For example, Order Number uniquely identifies each order. Other data about an order Chris thinks Helen might want to know include

TABLE 1-6 Data Attributes for Entities in the Preliminary Data Model (Pine Valley Furniture Company)

Entity Type	Attribute
Customer	Customer Identifier
	Customer Name
	Customer Type
	Customer Zip Code
Product	Product Identifier
	Product Description
	Product Finish
	Product Price
	Product Cost
	Product Annual Sales Goal
	Product Line Name
Product Line	Product Line Name
	Product Line Annual Sales Goal
Order	Order Number
	Order Placement Date
	Order Fulfillment Date
	Customer Identifier
Ordered Product	Order Number
	Product Identifier
	Order Quantity
Invoice	Invoice Number
	Order Number
	Invoice Date
Payment	Invoice Number
	Payment Date
	Payment Amount

the date when the order was placed and the date when the order was filled. (This would be the latest shipment date for the products on the order.) Chris also explains that the Payment Date attribute represents the most recent date when the customer made any payments, in full or partial, for the order.

Maybe because Chris was so well prepared or so enthusiastic, Helen is excited about the possibilities, and this excitement leads her to tell Chris about some additional data she wants (the number of years a customer has purchased products from Pine Valley Furniture Company and the number of shipments necessary to fill each order). Helen also notes that Chris has only one year of sales goals indicated for a product line. She reminds him that she wants these data for both the past and current years. As she reacts to the data model, Chris asks her how she intends to use the data she wants. Chris does not try to be thorough at this point because he knows that Helen has not worked with an information set like the one being developed; thus, she may not yet be positive about what data she wants or what she wants to do with it. Rather, Chris's objective is to understand a few ways in which Helen intends to use the data so he can develop an initial prototype, including the database and several computer displays or reports. The final list of attributes that Helen agrees she needs appears in Table 1-7.

TABLE 1-7   Data Attributes for Entities in Final Data Model (Pine Valley Furniture Company)

Entity Type	Attribute
Customer	Customer Identifier
	Customer Name
	Customer Type
	Customer Zip Code
	Customer Years
Product	Product Identifier
	Product Description
	Product Finish
	Product Price
	Product Cost
	Product Prior Year Sales Goal
	Product Current Year Sales Goal
	Product Line Name
Product Line	Product Line Name
	Product Line Prior Year Sales Goal
	Product Line Current Year Sales Goal
Order	Order Number
	Order Placement Date
	Order Fulfillment Date
	Order Number of Shipments
	Customer Identifier
Ordered Product	Order Number
	Product Identifier
	Order Quantity
Invoice	Invoice Number
	Order Number
	Invoice Date
Payment	Invoice Number
	Payment Date
	Payment Amount

*Changes from preliminary list of attributes appear in italics.

Designing the Database

Because Chris is following a prototyping methodology and the first two sessions with Helen quickly identified the data Helen might need, Chris is now ready to build a prototype. His first step is to create a project data model like the one shown in Figure 1-15. Notice the following characteristics of the project data model:

1. It is a model of the organization that provides valuable information about how the organization functions, as well as important constraints.
2. The project data model focuses on entities, relationships, and business rules. It also includes attribute labels for each piece of data that will be stored in each entity.

Second, Chris translates the data model into a set of tables for which the columns are data attributes and the rows are different sets of values for those attributes.

FIGURE 1-15   Project data model for Home Office product line marketing support system

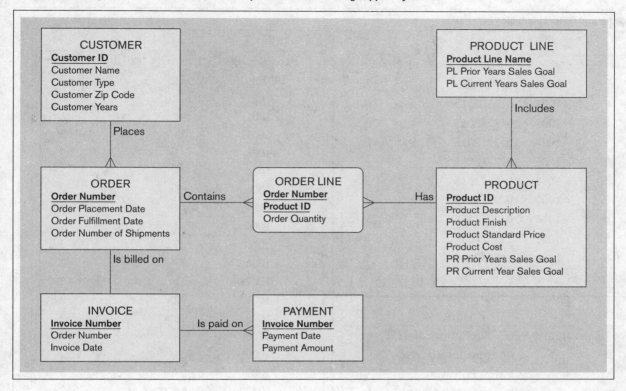

Tables are the basic building blocks of a relational database (we will learn about this in Chapter 4), which is the database style for Microsoft Access. Figure 1-16 shows four tables with sample data: Customer, Product, Order, and OrderLine. Notice that these tables represent the four entities shown in the project data model (Figure 1-15). Each column of a table represents an attribute (or characteristic) of an entity. For example, the attributes shown for Customer are CustomerID and CustomerName. Each row of a table represents an instance (or occurrence) of the entity. The design of the database also required Chris to specify the format, or properties, for each attribute (MS Access calls attributes *fields*). These design decisions were easy in this case because most of the attributes were already specified in the corporate data dictionary.

The tables shown in Figure 1-14 were created using SQL (you will learn about this in Chapters 6 and 7). Figures 1-17 and 1-18 show the SQL statements that Chris would have likely used to create the structure of the ProductLine and Product tables. It is customary to add the suffix _T to a table name. Also note that because Access does not allow for spaces between names, the individual words in the attributes from the data model have now been concatenated. Hence, Product Description in the data model has become ProductDescription in the table. Chris did this translation so that each table had an attribute, called the table's "primary key," which will be distinct for each row in the table. The other major properties of each table are that there is only one value for each attribute in each row; if we know the value of the identifier, there can be only one value for each of the other attributes. For example, for any product line, there can be only one value for the current year's sales goal.

A final key characteristic of the relational model is that it represents relationships between entities by values stored in the columns of the corresponding tables. For example, notice that CustomerID is an attribute of both the Customer table and the Order table. As a result, we can easily link an order to its associated customer. For example, we can determine that OrderID 1003 is associated with CustomerID 1. Can you determine which ProductIDs are associated with OrderID 1004?

FIGURE 1-16   Four relations (Pine Valley Furniture Company)

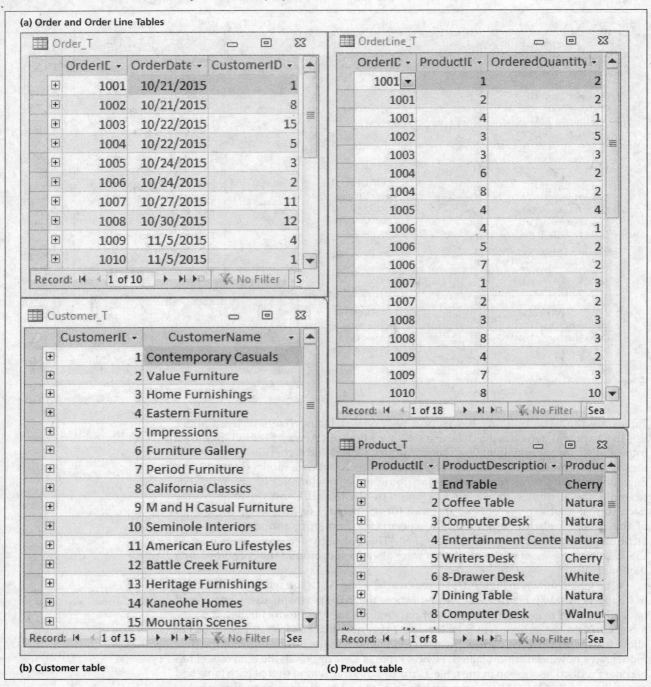

(a) Order and Order Line Tables

(b) Customer table

(c) Product table

In Chapters 6 and 7, you will also learn how to retrieve data from these tables by using SQL, which exploits these linkages. The other major decision Chris has to make about database design is how to physically organize the database to respond as fast as possible to the queries Helen will write. Because the database will be used for decision support, neither Chris nor Helen can anticipate all of the queries that will arise; thus, Chris must make the physical design choices from experience rather than precise knowledge of the way the database will be used. The key physical

FIGURE 1-17 SQL definition of ProductLine table

```
CREATE TABLE ProductLine_T

(ProductLineID        VARCHAR (40) NOT NULL PRIMARY KEY,

PlPriorYearGoal       DECIMAL,

PlCurrentYearGoal   DECIMAL);
```

FIGURE 1-18 SQL definition of Product table

```
CREATE TABLE Product_T

(ProductID                    NUMBER(11,0) NOT NULL PRIMARY KEY

ProductDescription          VARCHAR (50),

ProductFinish               VARCHAR (20),

ProductStandardPrice        DECIMAL(6,2),

ProductCost                 DECIMAL,

ProductPriorYearGoal        DECIMAL,

ProductCurrentYearGoal      DECIMAL,

ProductLineID               VARCHAR (40),

FOREIGN KEY                 (ProductLineID)  REFERENCES ProductLine_T (ProductLineID));
```

database design decision that SQL allows a database designer to make is on which attributes to create indexes. All primary key attributes (such as OrderNumber for the Order_T table)—those with unique values across the rows of the table—are indexed. In addition to this, Chris uses a general rule of thumb: Create an index for any attribute that has more than 10 different values and that Helen might use to segment the database. For example, Helen indicated that one of the ways she wants to use the database is to look at sales by product finish. Thus, it might make sense to create an index on the Product_T table using the Product Finish attribute.

However, Pine Valley uses only six product finishes, or types of wood, so this is not a useful index candidate. On the other hand, OrderPlacementDate (called a secondary key because there may be more than one row in the Order_T table with the same value of this attribute), which Helen also wants to use to analyze sales in different time periods, is a good index candidate.

Using the Database

Helen will use the database Chris has built mainly for ad hoc questions, so Chris will train her so that she can access the database and build queries to answer her ad hoc questions. Helen has indicated a few standard questions she expects to ask periodically. Chris will develop several types of prewritten routines (forms, reports, and queries) that can make it easier for Helen to answer these standard questions (so she does not have to program these questions from scratch).

During the prototyping development process, Chris may develop many examples of each of these routines as Helen communicates more clearly what she wants the system to be able to do. At this early stage of development, however, Chris wants to develop one routine to create the first prototype. One of the standard sets of information Helen says she wants is a list of each of the products in the Home Office product line showing each product's total sales to date compared with its current year sales goal. Helen may want

FIGURE 1-19 SQL query for
Home Office sales-to-goal
comparison

SELECT Product.ProductID, Product.ProductDescription, Product.PRCurrentYearSalesGoal,

    (OrderQuantity * ProductPrice) AS SalesToDate

FROM Order.OrderLine, Product.ProductLine

WHERE Order.OrderNumber = OrderLine.OrderNumber

AND Product.ProductID = OrderedProduct.ProductID

AND Product.ProductID = ProductLine.ProductID

AND Product.ProductLineName = "Home Office";

FIGURE 1-20 Home Office
product line sales comparison

Home Office Sales to Date : Select Query

Product ID	Product Description	PR Current Year Sales Goal	Sales to Date
3	Computer Desk	$23,500.00	5625
10	96" Bookcase	$22,500.00	4400
5	Writer's Desk	$26,500.00	650
3	Computer Desk	$23,500.00	3750
7	48" Bookcase	$17,000.00	2250
5	Writer's Desk	$26,500.00	3900

the results of this query to be displayed in a more stylized fashion—an opportunity to use a report—but for now Chris will present this feature to Helen only as a query.

The query to produce this list of products appears in Figure 1-19, with sample output in Figure 1-20. The query in Figure 1-19 uses SQL. You can see three of the six standard SQL clauses in this query: SELECT, FROM, and WHERE. SELECT indicates which attributes will be shown in the result. One calculation is also included and given the label "Sales to Date." FROM indicates which tables must be accessed to retrieve data. WHERE defines the links between the tables and indicates that results from only the Home Office product line are to be included. Only limited data are included for this example, so the Total Sales results in Figure 1-20 are fairly small, but the format is the result of the query in Figure 1-19.

Chris is now ready to meet with Helen again to see if the prototype is beginning to meet her needs. Chris shows Helen the system. As Helen makes suggestions, Chris is able to make a few changes online, but many of Helen's observations will have to wait for more careful work at his desk.

Space does not permit us to review the whole project to develop the Home Office marketing support system. Chris and Helen ended up meeting about a dozen times before Helen was satisfied that all the attributes she needed were in the database; that the standard queries, forms, and reports Chris wrote were of use to her; and that she knew how to write queries for unanticipated questions. Chris will be available to Helen at any time to provide consulting support when she has trouble with the system, including writing more complex queries, forms, or reports. One final decision that Chris and Helen made was that the performance of the final prototype was efficient enough that the prototype did not have to be rewritten or redesigned. Helen was now ready to use the system.

Administering the Database

The administration of the Home Office marketing support system is fairly simple. Helen decided that she could live with weekly downloads of new data from Pine Valley's operational databases into her MS Access database. Chris wrote a C# program with SQL commands embedded in it to perform the necessary extracts from the corporate databases and wrote an MS Access program in Visual Basic to rebuild the Access tables from these extracts; he scheduled these jobs to run every Sunday evening. Chris also updated the corporate information systems architecture model to include the Home Office marketing support system. This step was important so that when changes occurred to formats for data included in Helen's system, the corporate data modeling and design tools could alert Chris that changes might also have to be made in her system.

Future of Databases at Pine Valley

Although the databases currently in existence at Pine Valley adequately support the daily operations of the company, requests such as the one made by Helen have highlighted that the current databases are often inadequate for decision support applications. For example, following are some types of questions that cannot be easily answered:

1. What is the pattern of furniture sales this year, compared with the same period last year?
2. Who are our 10 largest customers, and what are their buying patterns?
3. Why can't we easily obtain a consolidated view of any customer who orders through different sales channels, rather than viewing each contact as representing a separate customer?

To answer these and other questions, an organization often needs to build a separate database that contains historical and summarized information. Such a database is usually called a *data warehouse* or, in some cases, a *data mart*. Also, analysts need specialized decision support tools to query and analyze the database. One class of tools used for this purpose is called online analytical processing (OLAP) tools. We describe data warehouses, data marts, and related decision support tools in Chapter 11. There you will learn of the interest in building a data warehouse that is now growing within Pine Valley Furniture Company.

Summary

Over the past two decades, there has been enormous growth in the number and importance of database applications. Databases are used to store, manipulate, and retrieve data in every type of organization. In the highly competitive environment of today, there is every indication that database technology will assume even greater importance. A course in modern database management is one of the most important courses in the information systems curriculum.

A database is an organized collection of logically related data. We define *data* as stored representations of objects and events that have meaning and importance in the user's environment. Information is data that have been processed in such a way that the knowledge of the person who uses the data increases. Both data and information may be stored in a database.

Metadata are data that describe the properties or characteristics of end-user data and the context of that data. A database management system (DBMS) is a software system that is used to create, maintain, and provide controlled access to user databases. A DBMS stores metadata in a repository, which is a central storehouse for all data definitions, data relationships, screen and report formats, and other system components.

Computer file processing systems were developed early in the computer era so that computers could store, manipulate, and retrieve large files of data. These systems (still in use today) have a number of important limitations such as dependence between programs and data, data duplication, limited data sharing, and lengthy development times. The database approach was developed to overcome these limitations. This approach emphasizes the integration and sharing of data across the organization. Advantages of this approach include program-data independence, improved data sharing, minimal data redundancy, and improved productivity of application development.

Database development begins with enterprise data modeling, during which the range and general contents of organizational databases are established. In addition to the relationships among the data entities themselves, their relationship to other organizational planning objects, such as organizational units, locations, business functions, and information systems, also need to be established.

Relationships between data entities and the other organizational planning objects can be represented at a high level by planning matrixes, which can be manipulated to understand patterns of relationships. Once the need for a database is identified, either from a planning exercise or from a specific request (such as the one from Helen Jarvis for a Home Office products marketing support system), a project team is formed to develop all elements. The project team follows a systems development process, such as the systems development life cycle or prototyping. The systems development life cycle can be represented by five methodical steps: (1) planning, (2) analysis, (3) design, (4) implementation, and (5) maintenance. Database development activities occur in each of these overlapping phases, and feedback may occur that causes a project to return to a prior phase. In prototyping, a database and its applications are iteratively refined through a close interaction of systems developers and users. Prototyping works best when the database application is small and stand-alone, and a small number of users exist.

Those working on a database development project deal with three views, or schemas, for a database: (1) a conceptual schema, which provides a complete, technology-independent picture of the database; (2) an internal schema, which specifies the complete database as it will be stored in computer secondary memory in terms of a logical schema and a physical schema; and (3) an external schema or user view, which describes the database relevant to a specific set of users in terms of a set of user views combined with the enterprise data model.

Database applications can be arranged into the following categories: personal databases, multitier databases, and enterprise databases. Enterprise databases include data warehouses and integrated decision support databases whose content is derived from the various operational databases. Enterprise resource planning (ERP) systems rely heavily on enterprise databases. A modern database and the applications that use it may be located on multiple computers. Although any number of tiers may exist (from one to many), three tiers of computers relate to the client/server architecture for database processing: (1) the client tier, where database contents are presented to the user; (2) the application/Web server tier, where analyses on database contents are made and user sessions are managed; and (3) the enterprise server tier, where the data from across the organization are merged into an organizational asset.

We closed the chapter with the review of a hypothetical database development project at Pine Valley Furniture Company. This system to support marketing a Home Office furniture product line illustrated the use of a personal database management system and SQL coding for developing a retrieval-only database. The database in this application contained data extracted from the enterprise databases and then stored in a separate database on the client tier. Prototyping was used to develop this database application because the user, Helen Jarvis, had rather unstructured needs that could best be discovered through an iterative process of developing and refining the system. Also, her interest and ability to work closely with Chris was limited.

Chapter Review

Key Terms

Agile software development 22
Conceptual schema 19
Constraint 13
Data 5
Data independence 11
Data model 9
Data modeling and design tools 15
Data warehouse 30
Database 5
Database application 8
Database management system (DBMS) 11
Enterprise data modeling 17
Enterprise resource planning (ERP) 30
Entity 10
Information 5
Logical schema 20
Metadata 6
Physical schema 20
Project 24
Prototyping 21
Relational database 11
Repository 16
Systems development life cycle (SDLC) 18
User view 13

Review Questions

1-1. Define each of the following terms:
   a. data
   b. information
   c. metadata
   d. enterprise resource planning
   e. data warehouse
   f. constraint
   g. database
   h. entity

   i. database management system
   j. client/server architecture
   k. systems development life cycle (SDLC)
   l. prototyping
   m. enterprise data model
   n. conceptual data model
   o. logical data model
   p. physical data model

1-2. Match the following terms and definitions:

___ data	a. data placed in context or summarized
___ database application	b. application program(s)
	c. facts, text, graphics, images, etc.
___ constraint	d. a graphical model that shows the high-level entities for the organization and the relationships among those entities
___ repository	
___ metadata	e. organized collection of related data
___ data warehouse	f. includes data definitions and constraints
___ information	g. centralized storehouse for all data definitions
___ user view	h. separation of data description from programs
___ database management system	i. a business management system that integrates all functions of the enterprise
___ data independence	j. logical description of portion of database
___ database	k. a software application that is used to create, maintain, and provide controlled access to user databases
___ enterprise resource planning (ERP)	l. a rule that cannot be violated by database users
___ systems development life cycle (SDLC)	m. integrated decision support database
	n. consist of the enterprise data model and multiple user views
___ prototyping	o. a rapid approach to systems development
___ enterprise data model	p. consists of two data models: a logical model and a physical model
___ conceptual schema	q. a comprehensive description of business data
___ internal schema	r. a structured, step-by-step approach to systems development
___ external schema	

1-3. Contrast the following terms:
 a. data dependence; data independence
 b. structured data; unstructured data
 c. data; information
 d. repository; database
 e. entity; enterprise data model
 f. data warehouse; ERP system
 g. personal databases; multitier databases
 h. systems development life cycle; prototyping
 i. enterprise data model; conceptual data model
 j. prototyping; agile software development

1-4. List five disadvantages of file processing systems.

1-5. List the nine major components in a database system environment.

1-6. How are relationships between tables expressed in a relational database?

1-7. What does the term *data independence* mean, and why is it an important goal?

1-8. List 10 potential benefits of the database approach over conventional file systems.

1-9. List five costs or risks associated with the database approach.

1-10. List nine key components that comprise a typical database environment.

1-11. In the multitiered database architecture, is it possible for there to be no database on a particular tier? If not, why? If yes, give an example.

1-12. Name the five phases of the traditional systems development life cycle, and explain the purpose and deliverables of each phase.

1-13. In which of the five phases of the SDLC do database development activities occur?

1-14. Are there procedures and processes that are common to the use of SDLC, prototyping, and agile methodologies? Explain any that you can identify and then indicate why the methodologies are considered to be different even though fundamental procedures and processes are still included.

1-15. Explain the differences between user views, a conceptual schema, and an internal schema as different perspectives of the same database.

1-16. In the three-schema architecture:
 a. The view of a manager or other type of user is called the ___ schema.
 b. The view of the data architect or data administrator is called the ___ schema.
 c. The view of the database administrator is called the ___ schema.

1-17. Revisit the section titled "Developing a Database Application for Pine Valley Furniture Company." What phase(s) of the database development process (Figure 1-8) do the activities that Chris performs in the following sub-sections correspond to:
 a. Project planning
 b. Analyzing database requirements
 c. Designing the database
 d. Using the database
 e. Administering the database

1-18. Why might Pine Valley Furniture Company need a data warehouse?

1-19. As the ability to handle large amounts of data improves, describe three business areas where these very large databases are being used effectively.

1-20. How does data and information vary from each other? Is metadata an improvement over data and how is it useful?

1-21. What do you understand by the term data models, entities, and relationships?

1-22. How do file processing systems differ from database approach—Give an assessment of the pros and cons of these two systems?

1-23. What are the different types of databases and what key parameters affect their implementation?

1-24. Can a well designed DBMS help an organization control and utilize its resources properly to achieve improvements in its productivity? If so, how?

1-25. Why is the traditional file-processing system disadvantageous?

1-26. Why are Data Models very important for designing a Database?

1-27. Name and explain at least five different roles that people need to don for the development of the Database Systems.

Problems and Exercises

1-28. For each of the following pairs of related entities, indicate whether (under typical circumstances) there is a one-to-many or a many-to-many relationship. Then, using the shorthand notation introduced in the text, draw a diagram for each of the relationships.
  a. STUDENT and COURSE (students register for courses)
  b. BOOK and BOOK COPY (books have copies)
  c. COURSE and SECTION (courses have sections)
  d. SECTION and ROOM (sections are scheduled in rooms)
  e. INSTRUCTOR and COURSE

1-29. Reread the definitions for *data* and *database* in this chapter. Database management systems only recently began to include the capability to store and retrieve more than numeric and textual data. What special data storage, retrieval, and maintenance capabilities do images, sound, video, and other advanced data types require that are not required or are simpler with numeric and textual data?

1-30. Table 1-1 shows example metadata for a set of data items. Identify three other columns for these data (i.e., three other metadata characteristics for the listed attributes) and complete the entries of the table in Table 1-1 for these three additional columns.

1-31. In the section "Disadvantages of File Processing Systems," the statement is made that the disadvantages of file processing systems can also be limitations of databases, depending on how an organization manages its databases. First, why do organizations create multiple databases, not just one all-inclusive database supporting all data processing needs? Second, what organizational and personal factors are at work that might lead an organization to have multiple, independently managed databases (and, hence, not completely follow the database approach)?

1-32. Consider the data needs of the student-run newspaper in your university or high school. What are the data entities of this enterprise? List and define each entity. Then, develop an enterprise data model (such as Figure 1-3a) showing these entities and important relationships between them.

1-33. A driver's license bureau maintains a database of licensed drivers. State whether each of the following represents data or metadata. If it represents data, state whether it is structured or unstructured data. If it represents metadata, state whether it is a fact describing a property of data or a fact describing the context of data.
  a. Driver's name, address, and birth date
  b. The fact that the driver's name is a 30-character field
  c. A photo image of the driver
  d. An image of the driver's fingerprint
  e. The make and serial number of the scanning device that was used to scan the fingerprint
  f. The resolution (in megapixels) of the camera that was used to photograph the driver
  g. The fact that the driver's birth date must precede today's date by at least 16 years

1-34. Great Lakes Insurance would like to implement a relational database for both its in-house and outside agents. The outside agents will use both tablets and notebook computers to keep track of customers and policy information. Based on what you have learned in this chapter, what type (or types) of database(s) would you recommend for this application?

1-35. Figure 1-21 shows an enterprise data model for a music store.

FIGURE 1-21   Data model for Problem and Exercise 1-35

  a. What is the relationship between Album and Store (one-to-one, many-to-many, or one-to-many)?
  b. What is the relationship between Artist and Album?
  c. Do you think there should be a relationship between Artist and Store?

1-36. Consider Figure 1-11, which depicts a hypothetical multitiered database architecture. Identify potential duplications of data across all the databases listed on this figure. What problems might arise because of this duplication? Does this duplication violate the principles of the database approach outlined in this chapter? Why or why not?

1-37. What is your reaction to the representation of the systems development life cycle included in this chapter? Explain any problems you have with it.

1-38. List three additional entities that might appear in an enterprise data model for Pine Valley Furniture Company (Figure 1-3a).

1-39. Consider your business school or other academic unit as a business enterprise.
  a. Define several major data entity types and draw a preliminary enterprise data model (similar in notation to Figure 1-3a).
  b. Would your business school or academic unit benefit from a multitiered architecture for data? Why or why not?

1-40. Contrast the top-down nature of database development during conceptual data modeling with the bottom-up nature of database development during logical database design. What major differences exist in the type of information considered in each of these two database development steps?

1-41. The objective of the prototyping systems development methodology is to rapidly build and rebuild an information system as the user and systems analyst learn from use of the prototype what features should be included in the evolving information system. Because the final prototype does not have to become the working system, where do you think would be an ideal location to develop a prototype: on a personal computer, department server, or enterprise server? Does your answer depend on any assumptions?

1-42. Explain the differences between an enterprise data model and a conceptual data model. How many databases does each represent? What scope of the organization does each address? What are other salient differences?

1-43. Is it possible that during the physical database design and creation step of database development you might want to return to the logical database design activity? Why or why not? If it is possible, give an example of what might arise during physical database design and creation that would cause you to want to reconsider the conceptual and external database designs from prior steps.

1-44. Consider an organization with which you frequently interact, such as a bank, credit card company, university, or insurance company, from which you receive several computer-generated messages, such as monthly statements, transaction slips, and so forth. Depict the data included in each message you receive from the organization as its own user view; use the notation of Figure 1-3a to represent these views. Now, combine all of these user views together into one conceptual data model, also using the notation of Figure 1-3a. What did you observe about the process of combining the different user views? Were there inconsistencies across the user views? Once you have created the conceptual data model, would you like to change anything about any of the user views?

1-45. Consider Figure 1-14. Explain the meaning of the line that connects CUSTOMER to ORDER and the line that connects ORDER to INVOICE. What does this say about how Pine Valley Furniture Company does business with its customers?

1-46. Consider the project data model shown in Figure 1-15.
 a. Create a textual description of the diagrammatic representation shown in the figure. Ensure that the description captures the rules/constraints conveyed by the model.
 b. In arriving at the requirements document, what aspect of the diagram did you find was the most difficult to describe? Which parts of the requirements do you still consider to be a little ambiguous? In your opinion, what is the underlying reason for this ambiguity?

1-47. Answer the following questions concerning Figures 1-17 and 1-18:
 a. What will be the field size for the ProductLineName field in the Product table? Why?

 b. In Figure 1-18, how is the ProductID field in the Product table specified to be required? Why is it a required attribute?
 c. In Figure 1-18, explain the function of the FOREIGN KEY definition.

1-48. Consider the SQL query in Figure 1-19.
 a. How is Sales to Date calculated?
 b. How would the query have to change if Helen Jarvis wanted to see the results for all of the product lines, not just the Home Office product line?

1-49. Helen Jarvis wants to determine the most important customers for Home Office products. She requests a listing of total dollar sales year-to-date for each customer who bought these products, as revealed by invoiced payments. The list is to be sorted in descending order, so that the largest customer heads the list.
 a. Look at Figure 1-15 and determine what entities are required to produce this list.
 b. Which entities will be involved in the SQL query that will give Helen the information she needs?

1-50. In this chapter, we described four important data models and their properties: enterprise, conceptual, logical, and physical. In the following table, summarize the important properties of these data models by entering a Y (for Yes) or an N (for No) in each cell of the table.

1-51. Refer to the figure 1-1b. Explain how from the data stored in a database the visual/graphical representation can be produced? Discuss how this type of data representation helps data analysis.

1-52. Astra-Pharma, a pharmaceutical company in the US has worldwide operations? The company has its direct agents/employee who sells samples and offer free samples to hospitals and doctors worldwide. Having learnt about databases, suggest from the range of database applications that is the most suitable one for Astra-Pharma.

Table for Problem and Exercise 1-47

	All Entities?	All Attributes?	Technology Independent?	DBMS Independent?	Record Layouts?
Enterprise					
Conceptual					
Logical					
Physical					

1-53. A FMCG Marketing Company wants to release its new Product to the Market; a Market survey needs to be done. It wants to employ an outside agency for carrying out the survey. What data needs to be collected internal in the organization and what data is needed from the outside of the organization? Based on this information, what type of databases would you recommend for this survey?

1-54. A automobile accessories dealer has been in the business for around 8-10 years. But the sales have been stagnating over a couple years. While company has been using IT for its Accounting related business processes, it has not implemented IT for its Sales. Sales personnel are taking a long time to complete the sales

transactions manually. The sales data was found wanting and incomplete to take any decisions. The CEO feels that having a proper database of the transacted sales and projected sales would help. What would be your recommendation to the CEO to go about analyzing the Database Requirements for the Sales related database?

1-55. A multiplex screening movies has hosted its ticketing system online. At the end of the day, the Theatre Manager wants to analyse the counter collections with respect to the movies screenings. There are many ad-hoc queries that the Theatre manager wants to use apart from the standard ones. As a database analyst and designer how would you go about helping the Theatre Manager using the database?

Field Exercises

For Questions 1 through 8, choose an organization with a fairly extensive information systems department and set of information system applications. You should choose one with which you are familiar, possibly your employer, your university, or an organization where a friend works. Use the same organization for each question.

1-56. Investigate whether the organization follows more of a traditional file processing approach or the database approach to organizing data. How many different databases does the organization have? Try to draw a figure, similar to Figure 1-2, to depict some or all of the files and databases in this organization.

1-57. Talk with a database administrator or designer from the organization. What type of metadata does this organization maintain about its databases? Why did the organization choose to keep track of these and not other metadata? What tools are used to maintain these metadata?

1-58. Determine the company's use of intranet, extranet, or other Web-enabled business processes. For each type of process, determine its purpose and the database management system that is being used in conjunction with the networks. Ask what the company's plans are for the next year with regard to using intranets, extranets, or the Web in its business activities. Ask what new skills the company is looking for in order to implement these plans.

1-59. Consider a major database in this organization, such as one supporting customer interactions, accounting, or manufacturing. What is the architecture for this database? Is the organization using some form of client/server architecture? Interview information systems managers in this organization to find out why they chose the architecture for this database.

1-60. Interview systems and database analysts at this organization. Ask them to describe their systems development process. Which does it resemble more: the systems development life cycle or prototyping? Do they use methodologies similar to both? When do they use their different methodologies? Explore the methodology used for developing applications to be used through the Web. How have they adapted their methodology to fit this new systems development process?

1-61. Interview a systems analyst or database analyst and ask questions about the typical composition of an information systems development team. Specifically, what role does a database analyst play in project teams? Is a database analyst used throughout the systems development process or is the database analyst used only at selected points?

1-62. Interview a systems analyst or database analyst and ask questions about how that organization uses data modeling and design tools in the systems development process. Concentrate your questions on how data modeling and design tools are used to support data modeling and database design and how the data modeling and design tool's repository maintains the information collected about data, data characteristics, and data usage. If multiple data modeling and design tools are used on one or many projects, ask how the organization attempts to integrate data models and data definitions. Finally, inquire how satisfied the systems and database analysts are with data modeling and design tool support for data modeling and database design.

1-63. Interview one person from a key business function, such as finance, human resources, or marketing. Concentrate your questions on the following items: How does he or she retrieve data needed to make business decisions? From what kind of system (personal database, enterprise system, or data warehouse) are the data retrieved? How often are these data accessed? Is this person satisfied with the data available for decision making? If not, what are the main challenges in getting access to the right data?

1-64. You may want to keep a personal journal of ideas and observations about database management while you are studying this book. Use this journal to record comments you hear, summaries of news stories or professional articles you read, original ideas or hypotheses you create, uniform resource locators (URLs) for and comments about Web sites related to databases, and questions that require further analysis. Keep your eyes and ears open for anything related to database management. Your instructor may ask you to turn in a copy of your journal from time to time in order to provide feedback and reactions. The journal is an unstructured set of personal notes that will supplement your class notes and can stimulate you to think beyond the topics covered within the time limitations of most courses.

References

Anderson-Lehman, R., H. J. Watson, B. Wixom, and J. A. Hoffer. 2004. "Continental Airlines Flies High with Real-Time Business Intelligence." *MIS Quarterly Executive* 3,4 (December).

Codd, E. F. 1970. "A Relational Model of Data for Large Shared Data Banks." *Communications of the ACM* 13,6 (June): 377–87.

Fowler, M. 2005. "The New Methodology" available at **www.martinfowler.com/articles/newMethodology.html** (access verified November 27, 2011).

Gray, J. 1996. "Data Management: Past, Present, and Future." *IEEE Computer* 29,10: 38–46.

Grimes, S. 1998. "Object/Relational Reality Check." *Database Programming & Design* 11,7 (July): 26–33.

Henderson, D., B. Champlin, D. Coleman, P. Cupoli, J. Hoffer, L. Howarth et al. 2005. "Model Curriculum Framework for Post Secondary Education Programs in Data Resource Management." The Data Management Association International Foundation Committee on the Advancement of Data Management in Post Secondary Institutions Sub Committee on Curriculum Framework Development. DAMA International Foundation.

Hoffer, J. A., J. F. George, and J. S. Valacich. 2014. *Modern Systems Analysis and Design*, 6th ed. Upper Saddle River, NJ: Prentice Hall.

IBM. 2011. "The Essential CIO: Insights from the 2011 IBM Global CIO Study."

Jordan, A. 1996. "Data Warehouse Integrity: How Long and Bumpy the Road?" *Data Management Review* 6,3 (March): 35–37.

Laskowski, Nicole (2014). "Ten Big Data Case Studies in a Nutshell" available at **http://searchcio.techtarget.com/opinion/Ten-big-data-case-studies-in-a-nutshell** (access verified October 25, 2014).

Long, D. 2005. Presentation. ".Net Overview," Tampa Bay Technology Leadership Association, May 19, 2005.

Mullins, C. S. 2002. *Database Administration: The Complete Guide to Practices and Procedures*. New York: Addison-Wesley.

Manyika, J., M. Chui, B. Brown, J. Bughin, R. Dobbs, C. Roxburgh, and A. H. Byers. 2011. "Big Data: The Next Frontier for Innovation, Competition and Productivity." *McKinsey Global Institute* (May).

Ritter, D. 1999. "Don't Neglect Your Legacy." *Intelligent Enterprise* 2,5 (March 30): 70–72.

Winter, R. 1997. "What, After All, Is a Very Large Database?" *Database Programming & Design* 10,1 (January): 23–26.

Further Reading

Ballou, D. P., and G. K. Tayi. 1999. "Enhancing Data Quality in Data Warehouse Environments." *Communications of the ACM* 42,1 (January): 73–78.

Date, C. J. 1998. "The Birth of the Relational Model, Part 3." *Intelligent Enterprise* 1,4 (December 10): 45–48.

Kimball, R., and M. Ross. 2002. The *Data Warehouse Toolkit: The Complete Guide to Dimensional Data Modeling*, 2d ed. New York: Wiley.

Ritter, D. 1999. "The Long View." *Intelligent Enterprise* 2,12 (August 24): 58–67.

Silverston, L. 2001a. *The Data Model Resource Book, Vol. 1: A Library of Universal Data Models for all Enterprises*. New York: Wiley.

Silverston, L. 2001b. *The Data Model Resource Book, Vol 2: A Library of Data Models for Specific Industries*. New York: Wiley.

Winter, R. 1997. "What, After All, Is a Very Large Database?" *Database Programming & Design* 10,1 (January): 23–26.

Web Resources

www.webopedia.com An online dictionary and search engine for computer terms and Internet technology.

www.techrepublic.com A portal site for information technology professionals that users can customize to their own particular interests.

www.zdnet.com A portal site where users can review recent articles on information technology subjects.

www.information-management.com *DM Review* magazine Web site, with the tagline "Covering Business Intelligence, Integration and Analytics." Provides a comprehensive list of links to relevant resource portals in addition to providing many of the magazine articles online.

www.dbta.com *Data Base Trends and Applications* magazine Web site. Addresses enterprise-level information issues.

http://databases.about.com A comprehensive site with many feature articles, links, interactive forum, chat rooms, and so forth.

http://groups.google.com/group/comp.software-eng? lnk=gsch&hl=en The software engineering archives for a Google group that focuses on software engineering and related topics. This site contains many links that you may want to explore.

www.acinet.org/acinet America's Career InfoNet, which provides information about careers, outlook, requirements, and so forth.

www.collegegrad.com/salaries/index.shtml A site for finding recent salary information for a wide range of careers, including database-related careers.

www.essentialstrategies.com/publications/methodology/ zachman.htm David Hay's Web site, which has considerable information on universal data models as well as how database development fits into the Zachman information systems architecture.

www.inmondatasystems.com Web site for one of the pioneers of data warehousing.

www.agilemanifesto.org Web site that explains the viewpoints of those who created The Manifesto for Agile Software Development.

CASE

Forondo Artist Management Excellence Inc.

Case Description

FAME (Forondo Artist Management Excellence) Inc. is an artist management company that represents classical music artists (only soloists) both nationally and internationally. FAME has more than 500 artists under its management, and wants to replace its spreadsheet-based system with a new state-of-the-art computerized information system.

Their core business idea is simple: FAME finds paid performance opportunities for the artists whom it represents and receives a 10–30 percent royalty for all the fees the artists earn (the royalties vary by artist and are based on a contract between FAME and each artist). To accomplish this objective, FAME needs technology support for several tasks. For example, it needs to keep track of prospective artists. FAME receives information regarding possible new artists both from promising young artists themselves and as recommendations from current artists and a network of music critics. FAME employees collect information regarding promising prospects and maintain that information in the system. When FAME management decides to propose a contract to a prospect, it first sends the artist a tentative contract, and if the response is positive, a final contract is mailed to the prospect. New contracts are issued annually to all artists.

FAME markets its artists to opera houses and concert halls (customers); in this process, a customer normally requests a specific artist for a specific date. FAME maintains the artists' calendars and responds back based on the requested artist's availability. After the performance, FAME sends an invoice to the customer, who sends a payment to FAME (please note that FAME requires a security deposit, but you do not need to capture that aspect in your system). Finally, FAME pays the artist after deducting its own fee.

Currently, FAME has no IT staff. Its technology infrastructure consists of a variety of desktops, printers, laptops, tablets, and smartphones all connected with a simple wired and wireless network. A local company manages this infrastructure and provides the required support.

E-mail from Martin Forondo, Owner

Martin Forondo, the owner of FAME, has commissioned your team to design and develop a database application. In his e-mail soliciting your help he provides the following information:

"My name is Martin Forondo, and I am the owner and founder of FAME. I have built this business over the past thirty years together with my wonderful staff and I am very proud of my company. We are in the business of creating bridges between the finest classical musicians and the best concert venues and opera houses of the world and finding the best possible opportunities for the musicians we represent. It is very important for us to provide the best possible service to the artists we represent.

It used to be possible to run our business without any technology, particularly when the number of the artists we represented was much smaller than it currently is. The situation is, however, changing, and we seem to have a need to get some

technical help for us. At this moment we have about 500 different artists and every one of them is very special for us. We have about 20 artist managers who are responsible for different numbers of artists; some of them have only 10, but some manage as many as 30 artists. The artist managers really keep this business going, and each of them has the ultimate responsibility for the artists for whom they work. Every manager has an administrative assistant to help him or her with daily routine work—the managers are focusing on relationship building and finding new talent for our company. The managers report to me but they are very independent in their work, and I am very pleased that I only very seldom have to deal with operational issues related to the managers' work. By the way, I also have my own artists (only a few but, of course, the very best within the company, if I may say so).

As I said, we find performance opportunities for the artists and, in practice, we organize their entire professional lives—of course, in agreement with them. Our main source of revenue consists of the royalties we get when we are successful in finding a performance opportunity for an artist: We get up to 30 percent of the fee paid to an artist (this is agreed separately with every artist and is a central part of our contract with the artist). Of course, we get the money only after the artist has successfully completed the performance; thus, if an artist has to cancel the performance, for example, because of illness, we will not get anything. Within the company the policy is very clear: A manager gets 50 percent of the royalties we earn based on the work of the artists he or she manages, and the remaining 50 percent will be used to cover administrative costs (including the administrative assistants' salaries), rent, electricity, computer systems, accounting services, and, of course, my modest profits. Each manager pays their own travel expenses from their 50 percent. Keeping track of the revenues by manager and by artist is one of the most important issues in running this business. Right now, we take care of it manually, which occasionally leads to unfortunate mistakes and a lot of extra work trying to figure out what the problem is. It is amazing how difficult simple things can sometimes become.

When thinking about the relationship between us and an artist whom we represent, it is important to remember that the artists are ultimately responsible for a lot of the direct expenses we pay when working for them, such as flyers, photos, prints of photos, advertisements, and publicity mailings. We don't, however, charge for phone calls made on behalf of a certain artist, but rather this is part of the general overhead. We would like to settle the accounts with each of the artists once per month so that either we pay them what we owe after our expenses are deducted from their portion of the fee or they pay us, if the expenses are higher than a particular month's fees. The artists take care of their own travel expenses, meals, etc.

From my perspective, the most important benefit of a new system would be an improved ability to know real-time how my managers are serving their artists. Are they finding opportunities for them and how good are the opportunities, what are the fees that their artists have earned and what are they projected to be, etc. Furthermore, the better the system could predict the future revenues of the company, the better for me. Whatever we could do with the system to better cultivate new relationships between promising young artists, it would be great. I am not very computer savvy; thus, it is essential that the system will be easy to use.

Project Questions

1-59. Create a memo describing your initial analysis of the situation at FAME as it relates to the design of the database application. Write this as though you are writing a memo to Martin Forondo. Ensure that your memo addresses the following points:

  a. Your approach to addressing the problem at hand (for example, specify the systems development life cycle or whatever approach you plan on taking).

  b. What will the new system accomplish? What functions will it perform? Which organizational goals will it support?

  c. What will be the benefits of using the new system? Use concrete examples to illustrate this. Outline general categories of costs and resources needed for the project and implementation of the ultimate system.

  d. A timeline/roadmap for the project.

  e. Questions, if any, you have for Mr. Forondo for which you need answers before you would be willing to begin the project.

1-60. Create an enterprise data model that captures the data needs of FAME. Use a notation similar to the one shown in Figure 1-4.

PART II

Database Analysis

AN OVERVIEW OF PART TWO

The first step in database development is database analysis, in which we determine user requirements for data and develop data models to represent those requirements. The two chapters in Part II describe in depth the de facto standard for conceptual data modeling—entity-relationship diagramming. A conceptual data model represents data from the viewpoint of the organization, independent of any technology that will be used to implement the model.

Chapter 2 ("Modeling Data in the Organization") begins by describing business rules, which are the policies and rules about the operation of a business that a data model represents. Characteristics of good business rules are described, and the process of gathering business rules is discussed. General guidelines for naming and defining elements of a data model are presented within the context of business rules.

Chapter 2 introduces the notations and main constructs of this modeling technique, including entities, relationships, and attributes; for each construct, we provide specific guidelines for naming and defining these elements of a data model. We distinguish between strong and weak entity types and the use of identifying relationships. We describe different types of attributes, including required versus optional attributes, simple versus composite attributes, single-valued versus multivalued attributes, derived attributes, and identifiers. We contrast relationship types and instances and introduce associative entities. We describe and illustrate relationships of various degrees, including unary, binary, and ternary relationships. We also describe the various relationship cardinalities that arise in modeling situations. We discuss the common problem of how to model time-dependent data. Finally, we describe the situation in which multiple relationships are defined between a given set of entities. The E-R modeling concepts are illustrated with an extended example for Pine Valley Furniture Company. This final example, as well as a few other examples throughout the chapter, is presented using Microsoft Visio, which shows how many data modeling tools represent data models.

Chapter 3 ("The Enhanced E-R Model") presents advanced concepts in E-R modeling; these additional modeling features are often required to cope with the increasingly complex business environment encountered in organizations today.

The most important modeling construct incorporated in the enhanced entity-relationship (EER) diagram is supertype/subtype relationships. This facility allows us to model a general entity type (called a supertype) and then subdivide it into several specialized entity types called subtypes. For example, sports cars and sedans are subtypes of automobiles. We introduce a simple notation for representing supertype/subtype relationships and several refinements. We also introduce generalization and specialization as two contrasting techniques for identifying supertype/subtype relationships. Supertype/subtype notation is necessary for the increasingly popular universal data model, which is motivated and explained in Chapter 3. The comprehensiveness of a well-documented relationship can be overwhelming, so we introduce a technique called entity clustering for simplifying the presentation of an E-R diagram to meet the needs of a given audience.

The concept of patterns has become a central element of many information systems development methodologies. The notion is that there are reusable component designs that can be combined and tailored to meet new information system requests. In the database world, these patterns are called universal data models, prepackaged data models, or logical data models. These patterns can be purchased or may be inherent in a commercial off-the-shelf package, such as an ERP or CRM application. Increasingly, it is from these patterns that new databases are designed. In Chapter 3, we describe the usefulness of such patterns and outline a modification of the database development process when such patterns are the starting point. Universal industry or business function data models extensively use the extended entity-relationship diagramming notations introduced in this chapter.

There is another, alternative notation for data modeling: the Unified Modeling Language class diagrams for systems developed using object-oriented technologies. This technique is presented in a supplement found on this book's Web site. It is possible to read this supplement immediately after Chapter 3 if you want to compare these alternative, but conceptually similar, approaches.

The conceptual data modeling concepts presented in the two chapters in Part II provide the foundation for your career in database analysis and design. As a database analyst, you will be expected to apply the E-R notation in modeling user requirements for data and information.

CHAPTER 2

Modeling Data in the Organization

LEARNING OBJECTIVES

After studying this chapter, you should be able to:

- Concisely define each of the following key terms: **business rule, term, fact, entity-relationship model (E-R model), entity-relationship diagram (E-R diagram), entity, entity type, entity instance, strong entity type, weak entity type, identifying owner, identifying relationship, attribute, required attribute, optional attribute, composite attribute, simple attribute, multivalued attribute, derived attribute, identifier, composite identifier, relationship type, relationship instance, associative entity, degree, unary relationship, binary relationship, ternary relationship, cardinality constraint, minimum cardinality, maximum cardinality,** and **time stamp**.

Visit www.pearsonhighered.com/ hoffer to view the accompanying video for this chapter.

- State reasons why many system developers and business leaders believe that data modeling is the most important part of the systems development process with a high return on investment.

- Write good names and definitions for entities, relationships, and attributes.

- Distinguish unary, binary, and ternary relationships and give a common example of each.

- Model each of the following constructs in an E-R diagram: composite attribute, multivalued attribute, derived attribute, associative entity, identifying relationship, and minimum and maximum cardinality constraints.

- Draw an E-R diagram to represent common business situations.

- Convert a many-to-many relationship to an associative entity type.

- Model simple time-dependent data using time stamps and relationships in an E-R diagram.

INTRODUCTION

You have already been introduced to modeling data and the entity-relationship (E-R) data model through simplified examples in Chapter 1. (You may want to review, for example, the E-R models in Figures 1-3 and 1-4.) In this chapter, we formalize data modeling based on the powerful concept of business rules and describe the E-R data model in detail. This chapter begins your journey of learning how to design and use databases. It is exciting to create information systems that run organizations and help people do their jobs well.

Our excitement can, of course, lead to mistakes if we are not careful to follow best practices. When we fail to follow best practices of database design, Embarcadero

Technologies, a leader in database design tools and processes, has identified "seven deadly sins" that are the culprits (Embarcadero Technologies, 2014):

1. Poor or missing documentation for database(s) in production (this will be addressed in Chapters 2 and 3 via the topics of business rules and data modeling with entity relationship diagramming)
2. Little or no normalization (this will be a central topic of Chapter 4 on the relational data model)
3. Not treating the data model like a living, breathing organism (we encourage you through exercises and projects to develop database designs in phases and to realize that requirements evolve and emerge over time; in other words, design for change)
4. Improper storage of reference data (we will address this briefly in subsequent chapters in Parts II and III of this text)
5. Not using foreign keys or check constraints (this will be a significant topic in Chapters 4 and 5)
6. Not using domains and naming standards (we emphasize naming standards in Chapter 2 and provide guidelines on good standards to adopt in your practice)
7. Not choosing primary keys (we emphasize entity identifiers in Chapter 2 and address considerations in choosing primary keys in Chapters 4 and 5)

A specific quote from the referenced Embarcadero report that we believe sets the tone for the importance of what we present in this and subsequent chapters is "In the data management arena, you may constantly hear from data professionals that if you don't get the data right, nothing else matters. However, the business focus on applications often overshadows the priority for a well-organized database design. The database just comes along for the ride as the application grows in scope and functionality." That is, often in practice there is an emphasis on functionality over architecture and engineering. If the architecture and engineering are bad, you can never achieve the functionality the organization requires. So, let's begin at the beginning for the architecture and engineering of a database with business rules.

Business rules, the foundation of data models, are derived from policies, procedures, events, functions, and other business objects, and they state constraints on the organization. Business rules represent the language and fundamental structure of an organization (Hay, 2003). Business rules formalize the understanding of the organization by organization owners, managers, and leaders with that of information systems architects.

Business rules are important in data modeling because they govern how data are handled and stored. Examples of basic business rules are data names and definitions. This chapter explains guidelines for the clear naming and definition of data objects in a business. In terms of conceptual data modeling, names and definitions must be provided for the main data objects: entity types (e.g., Customer), attributes (Customer Name), and relationships (Customer Places Orders). Other business rules may state constraints on these data objects. These constraints can be captured in a data model, such as an entity-relationship diagram, and associated documentation. Additional business rules govern the people, places, events, processes, networks, and objectives of the organization, which are all linked to the data requirements through other system documentation.

After decades of use, the E-R model remains the mainstream approach for conceptual data modeling. Its popularity stems from factors such as relative ease of use, widespread computer-aided software engineering (CASE) tool support, and the belief that entities and relationships are natural modeling concepts in the real world.

The E-R model is most used as a tool for communications between database designers and end users during the analysis phase of database development (described in Chapter 1). The E-R model is used to construct a conceptual data model, which is a representation of the structure and constraints of a database that is independent of software (such as a database management system).

Some authors introduce terms and concepts peculiar to the relational data model when discussing E-R modeling; the relational data model is the basis for most database management systems in use today. In particular, they recommend that the E-R model be completely normalized, with full resolution of primary and foreign keys. However, we believe that this forces a premature commitment to the relational data model. In today's database environment, the database may be implemented with object-oriented technology or with a mixture of object-oriented and relational technology. Therefore, we defer discussion of normalization concepts to Chapter 4.

The E-R model was introduced in a key article by Chen (1976), in which he described the main constructs of the E-R model—entities and relationships—and their associated attributes. The model has subsequently been extended to include additional constructs by Chen and others; for example, see Teorey et al. (1986) and Storey (1991). The E-R model continues to evolve, but unfortunately there is not yet a standard notation for E-R modeling. Song et al. (1995) present a side-by-side comparison of 10 different E-R modeling notations, explaining the major advantages and disadvantages of each approach. Because data modeling software tools are now commonly used by professional data modelers, we adopt for use in this text a variation of the notation used in professional modeling tools. Appendix A, found on this book's Web site, will help you translate between our notation and other popular E-R diagramming notations.

As said in a popular travel service TV commercial, "we are doing important stuff here." Many systems developers believe that data modeling is the most important part of the systems development process for the following reasons (Hoffer et al., 2014):

1. The characteristics of data captured during data modeling are crucial in the design of databases, programs, and other system components. The facts and rules captured during the process of data modeling are essential in assuring data integrity in an information system.
2. Data rather than processes are the most complex aspect of many modern information systems and hence require a central role in structuring system requirements. Often the goal is to provide a rich data resource that might support any type of information inquiry, analysis, and summary.
3. Data tend to be more stable than the business processes that use that data. Thus, an information system design that is based on a data orientation should have a longer useful life than one based on a process orientation.

Of course, we are all eager to build something new, so data modeling may still seem like a costly and unnecessary activity that simply delays getting to "the real work." If the above reasons for why data modeling is important are not enough to convince you, the following reasons are derived from what one industry leader demonstrates with examples are the benefits from and return on investment for data modeling (Haughey, 2010):

- Data modeling facilitates interaction/communication between designer, application programmer, and end user, thus reducing misunderstandings and improving the thoroughness of resultant systems; this is accomplished, in part, by providing a simplified (visual) understanding of data (data model) with agreed upon supporting documentation (metadata).
- Data modeling can foster understanding of the organization (rules) for which the data model is being developed; consistency and completeness of rules can be verified; otherwise, it is possible to create systems that are incorrect or inconsistent and unable to accommodate changes in user requirements (such as processing certain transactions or producing specific reports).
- The value of data modeling can be demonstrated as an overall savings in maintenance or development costs by determining the right requirements before the more costly steps of software development and hardware acquisition; further, data models can be reused in whole or in part on multiple projects, which can result in significant savings to any organization by reducing the costs for building redundant systems or complex interfaces between systems.

- Data modeling results in improved data quality because of consistent business data definitions (metadata), and hence greater accuracy of reporting and consistency across systems, and less organizational confusion; data modeling across the organization results in everyone having the same understanding of the same data.
- Data modeling reduces the significant costs of moving and translating data from one system to another; decisions can be made about the efficacy of sharing or having redundant data because data modeling creates a consistent enterprise-wide understanding of data; and when data must be transferred to achieve efficiencies, they do not have to be collected (possibly with inconsistencies) in multiple systems or from multiple sources.

To state it as simply as possible, the value of data modeling can be summarized by the phrase "measure twice, cut once."

In an actual work environment, you may not have to develop a data model from scratch. Because of the increased acceptance of packaged software (for example, enterprise resource planning with a predefined data model) and purchased business area or industry data models (which we discuss in Chapter 3), your job of data modeling has a jump start. This is good because such components and patterns give you a starting point based on generally accepted practices. However, your job is not done for several reasons:

1. There are still many times when a new, custom-built application is being developed along with the associated database. The business rules for the business area supported by this application need to be modeled.
2. Purchased applications and data models need to be customized for your particular setting. Predefined data models tend to be very extensive and complex; hence, they require significant data modeling skill to tailor the models to be effective and efficient in a given organization. Although this effort can be much faster, thorough, and accurate than starting from scratch, the ability to understand a particular organization to match the data model to its business rules is an essential task.

In this chapter, we present the main features of E-R modeling, using common notation and conventions. We begin with a sample E-R diagram, including the basic constructs of the E-R model—entities, attributes, and relationships—and then we introduce the concept of business rules, which is the foundation for all the data modeling constructs. We define three types of entities that are common in E-R modeling: strong entities, weak entities, and associative; a few more entity types are defined in Chapter 3. We also define several important types of attributes, including required and optional attributes, single- and multivalued attributes, derived attributes, and composite attributes. We then introduce three important concepts associated with relationships: the degree of a relationship, the cardinality of a relationship, and participation constraints in a relationship. We conclude with an extended example of an E-R diagram for Pine Valley Furniture Company.

THE E-R MODEL: AN OVERVIEW

Entity-relationship model (E-R model)

A logical representation of the data for an organization or for a business area, using entities for categories of data and relationships for associations between entities.

Entity-relationship diagram (E-R diagram, or ERD)

A graphical representation of an entity-relationship model.

An **entity-relationship model (E-R model)** is a detailed, logical representation of the data for an organization or for a business area. The E-R model is expressed in terms of entities in the business environment, the relationships (or associations) among those entities, and the attributes (or properties) of both the entities and their relationships. An E-R model is normally expressed as an **entity-relationship diagram (E-R diagram, or ERD),** which is a graphical representation of an E-R model.

Sample E-R Diagram

To jump-start your understanding of E-R diagrams, Figure 2-1 presents a simplified E-R diagram for a small furniture manufacturing company, Pine Valley Furniture Company. (This figure, which does not include attributes, is often called an *enterprise*

FIGURE 2-1   Sample E-R diagram

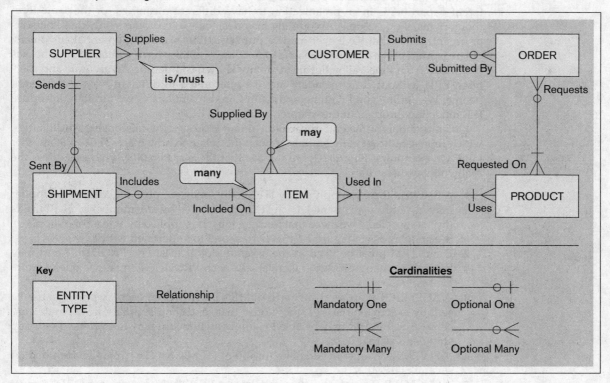

data model, which we introduced in Chapter 1.) A number of suppliers supply and ship different items to Pine Valley Furniture. The items are assembled into products that are sold to customers who order the products. Each customer order may include one or more lines corresponding to the products appearing on that order.

The diagram in Figure 2-1 shows the entities and relationships for this company. (Attributes are omitted to simplify the diagram for now.) Entities (the objects of the organization) are represented by the rectangle symbol, whereas relationships between entities are represented by lines connecting the related entities. The entities in Figure 2-1 include the following:

CUSTOMER	A person or an organization that has ordered or might order products. *Example*: L. L. Fish Furniture.
PRODUCT	A type of furniture made by Pine Valley Furniture that may be ordered by customers. Note that a product is not a specific bookcase, because individual bookcases do not need to be tracked. *Example*: A 6-foot, 5-shelf, oak bookcase called O600.
ORDER	The transaction associated with the sale of one or more products to a customer and identified by a transaction number from sales or accounting. *Example*: The event of L. L. Fish buying one product O600 and four products O623 on September 10, 2015.
ITEM	A type of component that goes into making one or more products and can be supplied by one or more suppliers. *Example*: A 4-inch ball-bearing caster called I-27–4375.
SUPPLIER	Another company that may provide items to Pine Valley Furniture. *Example*: Sure Fasteners, Inc.
SHIPMENT	The transaction associated with items received in the same package by Pine Valley Furniture from a supplier. All items in a shipment appear on one bill-of-lading document. *Example*: The receipt of 300 I-27-4375 and 200 I-27-4380 items from Sure Fasteners, Inc., on September 9, 2015.

Note that it is important to clearly define, as metadata, each entity. For example, it is important to know that the CUSTOMER entity includes persons or organizations that have not yet purchased products from Pine Valley Furniture. It is common for different departments in an organization to have different meanings for the same term (homonyms). For example, Accounting may designate as customers only those persons or organizations that have ever made a purchase, thus excluding potential customers, whereas Marketing designates as customers anyone they have contacted or who has purchased from Pine Valley Furniture or any known competitor. An accurate and thorough ERD without clear metadata may be interpreted in different ways by different people. We outline good naming and definition conventions as we formally introduce E-R modeling throughout this chapter.

The symbols at the end of each line on an ERD specify relationship cardinalities, which represent how many entities of one kind relate to how many entities of another kind. On examining Figure 2-1, we can see that these cardinality symbols express the following business rules:

1. A SUPPLIER <u>may</u> supply <u>many</u> ITEMs (by "may supply," we mean the supplier may not supply any items). Each ITEM <u>is</u> supplied by any number of SUPPLIERs (by "is supplied," we mean that the item <u>must</u> be supplied by at least one supplier). See annotations in Figure 2-1 that correspond to underlined words.
2. Each ITEM must be used in the assembly of at least one PRODUCT and may be used in many products. Conversely, each PRODUCT must use one or more ITEMs.
3. A SUPPLIER may send many SHIPMENTs. However, each shipment must be sent by exactly one SUPPLIER. Notice that sends and supplies are separate concepts. A SUPPLIER may be able to supply an item but may not yet have sent any shipments of that item.
4. A SHIPMENT must include one (or more) ITEMs. An ITEM may be included on several SHIPMENTs.
5. A CUSTOMER may submit any number of ORDERs. However, each ORDER must be submitted by exactly one CUSTOMER. Given that a CUSTOMER may not have submitted any ORDERs, some CUSTOMERs must be potential, inactive, or some other customer possibly without any related ORDERs.
6. An ORDER must request one (or more) PRODUCTs. A given PRODUCT may not be requested on any ORDER or may be requested on one or more orders.

There are actually two business rules for each relationship, one for each direction from one entity to the other. Note that each of these business rules roughly follows a certain grammar:

<entity> <minimum cardinality> <relationship> <maximum cardinality> <entity>

For example, rule 5 is

<CUSTOMER> <may> <Submit> <any number> <ORDER>

This grammar gives you a standard way to put each relationship into a natural English business rule statement.

E-R Model Notation

The notation we use for E-R diagrams is shown in Figure 2-2. As indicated in the previous section, there is no industry-standard notation (in fact, you saw a slightly simpler notation in Chapter 1). The notation in Figure 2-2 combines most of the desirable features of the different notations that are commonly used in E-R drawing tools today and also allows us to model accurately most situations that are encountered in practice. We introduce additional notation for enhanced entity-relationship models (including class-subclass relationships) in Chapter 3.

FIGURE 2-2   Basic E-R notation

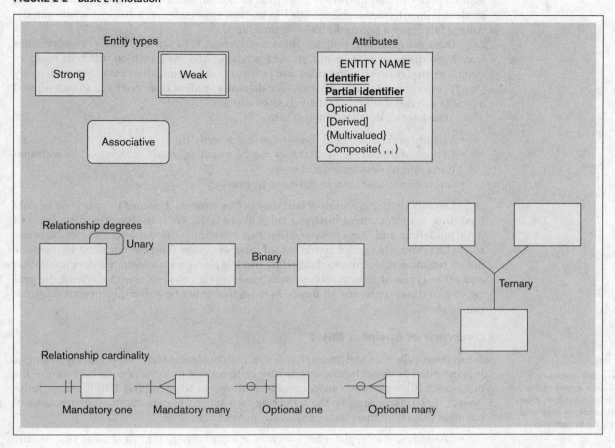

In many situations, however, a simpler E-R notation is sufficient. Most drawing tools, either stand-alone ones such as Microsoft Visio or SmartDraw (which we use in the video associated with this chapter) or those in CASE tools such as Oracle Designer, CA ERwin, or PowerDesigner, do not show all the entity and attribute types we use. It is important to note that any notation requires special annotations, not always present in a diagramming tool, to show all the business rules of the organizational situation you are modeling. We will use the Visio notation for a few examples throughout the chapter and at the end of the chapter so that you can see the differences. Appendix A, found on this book's Web site, llustrates the E-R notation from several commonly used guidelines and diagramming tools. This appendix may help you translate between the notations in the text and the notations you use in classes.

MODELING THE RULES OF THE ORGANIZATION

Now that you have an example of a data model in mind, let's step back and consider more generally what a data model is representing. We will see in this and the next chapter how to use data models, in particular the entity-relationship notation, to document rules and policies of an organization. *In fact, documenting rules and policies of an organization that govern data is exactly what data modeling is all about.* Business rules and policies govern creating, updating, and removing data in an information processing and storage system; thus, they must be described along with the data to which they are related. For example, the policy "every student in the university must have a faculty adviser" forces data (in a database) about each student to be associated with data about some student adviser. Also, the statement "a student is any person who has applied for admission or taken a course or training program from any credit or noncredit unit of the university" not only defines the concept of "student" for a particular university but also states a policy of that university (e.g., implicitly, alumni are students, and a high school student who attended a college fair but has not applied is not a student, assuming the college fair is not a noncredit training program).

Business rules and policies are not universal; for example, different universities may have different policies for student advising and may include different types of people as students. Also, the rules and policies of an organization may change (usually slowly) over time; a university may decide that a student does not have to be assigned a faculty adviser until the student chooses a major.

Your job as a database analyst is to

- Identify and understand those rules *that govern data*
- Represent those rules so that they can be unambiguously understood by information systems developers and users
- Implement those rules in database technology

Data modeling is an important tool in this process. Because the purpose of data modeling is to document business rules about data, we introduce the discussion of data modeling and the entity-relationship notation with an overview of business rules. Data models cannot represent all business rules (and do not need to, because not all business rules govern data); data models along with associated documentation and other types of information system models (e.g., models that document the processing of data) represent all business rules that must be enforced through information systems.

Overview of Business Rules

Business rule

A statement that defines or constrains some aspect of the business. It is intended to assert business structure or to control or influence the behavior of the business.

A **business rule** is "a statement that defines or constrains some aspect of the business. It is intended to assert business structure or to control or influence the behavior of the business...rules prevent, cause, or suggest things to happen" (GUIDE Business Rules Project, 1997). For example, the following two statements are common expressions of business rules that affect data processing and storage:

- "A student may register for a section of a course only if he or she has successfully completed the prerequisites for that course."
- "A preferred customer qualifies for a 10 percent discount, unless he has an overdue account balance."

Most organizations (and their employees) today are guided by thousands of combinations of such rules. In the aggregate, these rules influence behavior and determine how the organization responds to its environment (Gottesdiener, 1997; von Halle, 1997). Capturing and documenting business rules is an important, complex task. Thoroughly capturing and structuring business rules, then enforcing them through database technologies, helps ensure that information systems work right and that users of the information understand what they enter and see.

THE BUSINESS RULES PARADIGM The concept of business rules has been used in information systems for some time. There are many software products that help organizations manage their business rules (for example, JRules from ILOG, an IBM company). In the database world, it has been more common to use the related term *integrity constraint* when referring to such rules. The intent of this term is somewhat more limited in scope, usually referring to maintaining valid data values and relationships in the database.

A business rules approach is based on the following premises:

- Business rules are a core concept in an enterprise because they are an expression of business policy and guide individual and aggregate behavior. Well-structured business rules can be stated in natural language for end users and in a data model for systems developers.
- Business rules can be expressed in terms that are familiar to end users. Thus, users can define and then maintain their own rules.
- Business rules are highly maintainable. They are stored in a central repository, and each rule is expressed only once, then shared throughout the organization. Each

rule is discovered and documented only once, to be applied in all systems development projects.
- Enforcement of business rules can be automated through the use of software that can interpret the rules and enforce them using the integrity mechanisms of the database management system (Moriarty, 2000).

Although much progress has been made, the industry has not realized all of these objectives to date (Owen, 2004). Possibly the premise with greatest potential benefit is "Business rules are highly maintainable." The ability to specify and maintain the requirements for information systems as a set of rules has considerable power when coupled with an ability to generate automatically information systems from a repository of rules. Automatic generation and maintenance of systems will not only simplify the systems development process but also will improve the quality of systems.

Scope of Business Rules

In this chapter and the next, we are concerned with business rules that impact only an organization's databases. Most organizations have a host of rules and/or policies that fall outside this definition. For example, the rule "Friday is business casual dress day" may be an important policy statement, but it has no immediate impact on databases. In contrast, the rule "A student may register for a section of a course only if he or she has successfully completed the prerequisites for that course" is within our scope because it constrains the transactions that may be processed against the database. In particular, it causes any transaction that attempts to register a student who does not have the necessary prerequisites to be rejected. Some business rules cannot be represented in common data modeling notation; those rules that cannot be represented in a variation of an entity-relationship diagram are stated in natural language, and some can be represented in the relational data model, which we describe in Chapter 4.

GOOD BUSINESS RULES   Whether stated in natural language, a structured data model, or other information systems documentation, a business rule will have certain characteristics if it is to be consistent with the premises outlined previously. These characteristics are summarized in Table 2-1. These characteristics will have a better chance of being satisfied if a business rule is defined, approved, and owned by business, not technical, people. Businesspeople become stewards of the business rules. You, as the database analyst, facilitate the surfacing of the rules and the transformation of ill-stated rules into ones that satisfy the desired characteristics.

TABLE 2-1   Characteristics of a Good Business Rule

Characteristic	Explanation
Declarative	A business rule is a statement of policy, not how policy is enforced or conducted; the rule does not describe a process or implementation, but rather describes what a process validates.
Precise	With the related organization, the rule must have only one interpretation among all interested people, and its meaning must be clear.
Atomic	A business rule marks one statement, not several; no part of the rule can stand on its own as a rule (that is, the rule is indivisible, yet sufficient).
Consistent	A business rule must be internally consistent (that is, not contain conflicting statements) and must be consistent with (and not contradict) other rules.
Expressible	A business rule must be able to be stated in natural language, but it will be stated in a structured natural language so that there is no misinterpretation.
Distinct	Business rules are not redundant, but a business rule may refer to other rules (especially to definitions).
Business-oriented	A business rule is stated in terms businesspeople can understand, and because it is a statement of business policy, only businesspeople can modify or invalidate a rule; thus, a business rule is owned by the business.

Source: Based on Gottesdiener (1999) and Plotkin (1999).

GATHERING BUSINESS RULES   Business rules appear (possibly implicitly) in descriptions of business functions, events, policies, units, stakeholders, and other objects. These descriptions can be found in interview notes from individual and group information systems requirements collection sessions, organizational documents (e.g., personnel manuals, policies, contracts, marketing brochures, and technical instructions), and other sources. Rules are identified by asking questions about the who, what, when, where, why, and how of the organization. Usually, a data analyst has to be persistent in clarifying initial statements of rules because initial statements may be vague or imprecise (what some people have called "business ramblings"). Thus, precise rules are formulated from an iterative inquiry process. You should be prepared to ask such questions as "Is this always true?" "Are there special circumstances when an alternative occurs?" "Are there distinct kinds of that person?" "Is there only one of those or are there many?" and "Is there a need to keep a history of those, or is the current data all that is useful?" Such questions can be useful for surfacing rules for each type of data modeling construct we introduce in this chapter and the next.

Data Names and Definitions

Fundamental to understanding and modeling data are naming and defining data objects. Data objects must be named and defined before they can be used unambiguously in a model of organizational data. In the entity-relationship notation you will learn in this chapter, you have to give entities, relationships, and attributes clear and distinct names and definitions.

DATA NAMES   We will provide specific guidelines for naming entities, relationships, and attributes as we develop the entity-relationship data model, but there are some general guidelines about naming any data object. Data names should (Salin, 1990; ISO/IEC, 2005)

- *Relate to business, not technical (hardware or software), characteristics;* so, Customer is a good name, but File10, Bit7, and Payroll Report Sort Key are not good names.
- *Be meaningful,* almost to the point of being self-documenting (i.e., the definition will refine and explain the name without having to state the essence of the object's meaning); you should avoid using generic words such as *has, is, person,* or *it*.
- *Be unique* from the name used for every other distinct data object; words should be included in a data name if they distinguish the data object from other similar data objects (e.g., Home Address versus Campus Address).
- *Be readable,* so that the name is structured as the concept would most naturally be said (e.g., Grade Point Average is a good name, whereas Average Grade Relative To A, although possibly accurate, is an awkward name).
- *Be composed of words taken from an approved list;* each organization often chooses a vocabulary from which significant words in data names must be chosen (e.g., maximum is preferred, never upper limit, ceiling, or highest); alternative, or alias names, also can be used as can approved abbreviations (e.g., CUST for CUSTOMER), and you may be encouraged to use the abbreviations so that data names are short enough to meet maximum length limits of database technology.
- *Be repeatable,* meaning that different people or the same person at different times should develop exactly or almost the same name; this often means that there is a standard hierarchy or pattern for names (e.g., the birth date of a student would be Student Birth Date and the birth date of an employee would be Employee Birth Date).
- *Follow a standard syntax,* meaning that the parts of the name should follow a standard arrangement adopted by the organization.

Salin (1990) suggests that you develop data names by

1. Preparing a definition of the data. (We talk about definitions next.)
2. Removing insignificant or illegal words (words not on the approved list for names); note that the presence of AND and OR in the definition may imply that

two or more data objects are combined, and you may want to separate the objects and assign different names.

3. Arranging the words in a meaningful, repeatable way.
4. Assigning a standard abbreviation for each word.
5. Determining whether the name already exists, and if so, adding other qualifiers that make the name unique.

We will see examples of good data names as we develop a data modeling notation in this chapter.

DATA DEFINITIONS   A definition (sometimes called a *structural assertion*) is considered a type of business rule (GUIDE Business Rules Project, 1997). A definition is an explanation of a term or a fact. A **term** is a word or phrase that has a specific meaning for the business. Examples of terms are *course*, *section*, *rental car*, *flight*, *reservation*, and *passenger*. Terms are often the key words used to form data names. Terms must be defined carefully and concisely. However, there is no need to define common terms such as *day*, *month*, *person*, or *television*, because these terms are understood without ambiguity by most persons.

A **fact** is an association between two or more terms. A fact is documented as a simple declarative statement that relates terms. Examples of facts that are definitions are the following (the defined terms are underlined):

- "A <u>course</u> is a module of instruction in a particular subject area." This definition associates two terms: *module of instruction* and *subject area*. We assume that these are common terms that do not need to be further defined.
- "A <u>customer</u> may request a <u>model of car</u> from a <u>rental branch</u> on a particular <u>date</u>." This fact, which is a definition of *model rental request*, associates the four underlined terms (GUIDE Business Rules Project, 1997). Three of these terms are business-specific terms that would need to be defined individually (date is a common term).

A fact statement places no constraints on instances of the fact. For example, it is inappropriate in the second fact statement to add that a customer may not request two different car models on the same date. Such constraints are separate business rules.

GOOD DATA DEFINITIONS   We will illustrate good definitions for entities, relationships, and attributes as we develop the entity-relationship notation in this and the next chapters.There are, however, some general guidelines to follow (Aranow, 1989; ISO/IEC, 2004):

- Definitions (and all other types of business rules) are gathered from the same sources as all requirements for information systems. Thus, systems and data analysts should be looking for data objects and their definitions as these sources of information systems requirements are studied.
- Definitions will usually be accompanied by diagrams, such as entity-relationship diagrams. The definition does not need to repeat what is shown on the diagram but rather supplement the diagram.
- Definitions will be stated in the singular and explain what the data element is, not what it is not. A definition will use commonly understood terms and abbreviations and stand alone in its meaning and not embed other definitions within it. It should be concise and concentrate on the essential meaning of the data, but it may also state such characteristics of a data object as
  - Subtleties
  - Special or exceptional conditions
  - Examples
  - Where, when, and how the data are created or calculated in the organization
  - Whether the data are static or change over time
  - Whether the data are singular or plural in their atomic form
  - Who determines the value for the data
  - Who owns the data (i.e., who controls the definition and usage)

Term

A word or phrase that has a specific meaning for the business.

Fact

An association between two or more terms.

- Whether the data are optional or whether empty (what we will call null) values are allowed
- Whether the data can be broken down into more atomic parts or are often combined with other data into some more composite or aggregate form

If not included in a data definition, these characteristics need to be documented elsewhere, where other metadata are stored.

- A data object should not be added to a data model, such as an entity-relationship diagram, until after it has been carefully defined (and named) and there is agreement on this definition. But expect the definition of the data to change once you place the object on the diagram because the process of developing a data model tests your understanding of the meaning of data. (In other words, *modeling data is an iterative process*.)

There is an unattributed phrase in data modeling that highlights the importance of good data definitions: "The person who controls the meaning of data controls the data." It might seem that obtaining concurrence in an organization on the definitions to be used for the various terms and facts should be relatively easy. However, this is usually far from the case. In fact, it is likely to be one of the most difficult challenges you will face in data modeling or, for that matter, in any other endeavor. It is not unusual for an organization to have multiple definitions (perhaps a dozen or more) for common terms such as *customer* or *order*.

To illustrate the problems inherent in developing definitions, consider a data object of Student found in a typical university. A sample definition for Student is "a person who has been admitted to the school and who has registered for at least one course during the past year." This definition is certain to be challenged, because it is probably too narrow. A person who is a student typically proceeds through several stages in relationship with the school, such as the following:

1. Prospect—some formal contact, indicating an interest in the school
2. Applicant—applies for admission
3. Admitted applicant—admitted to the school and perhaps to a degree program
4. Matriculated student—registers for at least one course
5. Continuing student—registers for courses on an ongoing basis (no substantial gaps)
6. Former student—fails to register for courses during some stipulated period (now may reapply)
7. Graduate—satisfactorily completes some degree program (now may apply for another program)

Imagine the difficulty of obtaining consensus on a single definition in this situation! It would seem you might consider three alternatives:

1. *Use multiple definitions to cover the various situations.* This is likely to be highly confusing if there is only one entity type, so this approach is not recommended (multiple definitions are not good definitions). It might be possible to create multiple entity types, one for each student situation. However, because there is likely considerable similarity across the entity types, the fine distinctions between the entity types may be confusing, and the data model will show many constructs.
2. *Use a very general definition that will cover most situations.* This approach may necessitate adding additional data about students to record a given student's actual status. For example, data for a student's status, with values of prospect, applicant, and so forth, might be sufficient. On the other hand, if the same student could hold multiple statuses (e.g., prospect for one degree and matriculated for another degree), this might not work.
3. *Consider using multiple, related data objects for Student.* For example, we could create a general entity type for Student and then other specific entity types for kinds of students with unique characteristics. We describe the conditions that suggest this approach in Chapter 3.

MODELING ENTITIES AND ATTRIBUTES

The basic constructs of the E-R model are entities, relationships, and attributes. As shown in Figure 2-2, the model allows numerous variations for each of these constructs. The richness of the E-R model allows designers to model real-world situations accurately and expressively, which helps account for the popularity of the model.

Entities

An **entity** is a person, a place, an object, an event, or a concept in the user environment about which the organization wishes to maintain data. Thus, an entity has a noun name. Some examples of each of these *kinds* of entities follow:

Person:	EMPLOYEE, STUDENT, PATIENT
Place:	STORE, WAREHOUSE, STATE
Object:	MACHINE, BUILDING, AUTOMOBILE
Event:	SALE, REGISTRATION, RENEWAL
Concept:	ACCOUNT, COURSE, WORK CENTER

Entity

A person, a place, an object, an event, or a concept in the user environment about which the organization wishes to maintain data.

ENTITY TYPE VERSUS ENTITY INSTANCE There is an important distinction between entity types and entity instances. An **entity type** is a collection of entities that share common properties or characteristics. Each entity type in an E-R model is given a name. Because the name represents a collection (or set) of items, it is always singular. We use capital letters for names of entity type(s). In an E-R diagram, the entity name is placed inside the box representing the entity type (see Figure 2-1).

Entity type

A collection of entities that share common properties or characteristics.

An **entity instance** is a single occurrence of an entity type. Figure 2-3 illustrates the distinction between an entity type and two of its instances. An entity type is described just once (using metadata) in a database, whereas many instances of that entity type may be represented by data stored in the database. For example, there is one EMPLOYEE entity type in most organizations, but there may be hundreds (or even thousands) of instances of this entity type stored in the database. We often use the single term *entity* rather than *entity instance* when the meaning is clear from the context of our discussion.

Entity instance

A single occurrence of an entity type.

ENTITY TYPE VERSUS SYSTEM INPUT, OUTPUT, OR USER A common mistake people make when they are learning to draw E-R diagrams, especially if they are already familiar with data process modeling (such as data flow diagramming), is to confuse data entities with other elements of an overall information systems model. A simple rule to avoid such confusion is that *a true data entity will have many possible instances, each with a distinguishing characteristic, as well as one or more other descriptive pieces of data.*

Entity type: EMPLOYEE

Attributes	Attribute Data Type	Example Instance	Example Instance
Employee Number	CHAR (10)	642-17-8360	534-10-1971
Name	CHAR (25)	Michelle Brady	David Johnson
Address	CHAR (30)	100 Pacific Avenue	450 Redwood Drive
City	CHAR (20)	San Francisco	Redwood City
State	CHAR (2)	CA	CA
Zip Code	CHAR (9)	98173	97142
Date Hired	DATE	03-21-1992	08-16-1994
Birth Date	DATE	06-19-1968	09-04-1975

FIGURE 2-3   Entity type EMPLOYEE with two instances

FIGURE 2-4 Example of inappropriate entities (a) System user (Treasurer) and output (Expense Report) shown as entities

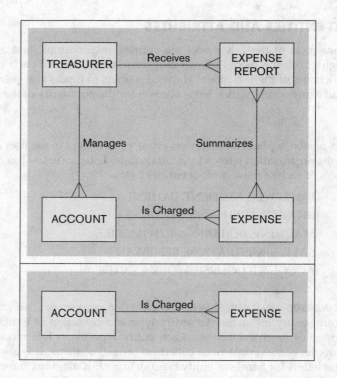

(b) E-R diagram with only the necessary entities

Consider Figure 2-4a, which might be drawn to represent a database needed for a college sorority's expense system. (For simplicity in this and some other figures, we show only one name for a relationship.) In this situation, the sorority treasurer manages accounts, receives expense reports, and records expense transactions against each account. However, do we need to keep track of data about the Treasurer (the TREASURER entity type) and her supervision of accounts (the Manages relationship) and receipt of reports (the Receives relationship)? The Treasurer is the person entering data about accounts and expenses and receiving expense reports. That is, she is a user of the database. Because there is only one Treasurer, TREASURER data do not need to be kept. Further, is the EXPENSE REPORT entity necessary? Because an expense report is computed from expense transactions and account balances, it is the result of extracting data from the database and received by the Treasurer. Even though there will be multiple instances of expense reports given to the Treasurer over time, data needed to compute the report contents each time are already represented by the ACCOUNT and EXPENSE entity types.

Another key to understanding why the ERD in Figure 2-4a might be in error is the nature of the *relationship names*, Receives and Summarizes. These relationship names refer to business activities that transfer or translate data, not to simply the association of one kind of data with another kind of data. The simple E-R diagram in Figure 2-4b shows entities and a relationship that would be sufficient to handle the sorority expense system as described here. See Problem and Exercise 2-43 for a variation on this situation.

STRONG VERSUS WEAK ENTITY TYPES   Most of the basic entity types to identify in an organization are classified as strong entity types. A **strong entity type** is one that exists independently of other entity types. (Some data modeling software, in fact, use the term *independent entity*.) Examples include STUDENT, EMPLOYEE, AUTOMOBILE, and COURSE. Instances of a strong entity type always have a unique characteristic (called an *identifier*)—that is, an attribute or a combination of attributes that uniquely distinguish each occurrence of that entity.

In contrast, a **weak entity type** is an entity type whose existence depends on some other entity type. (Some data modeling software, in fact, use the term *dependent entity*.) A weak entity type has no business meaning in an E-R diagram without the

Strong entity type

An entity that exists independently of other entity types.

Weak entity type

An entity type whose existence depends on some other entity type.

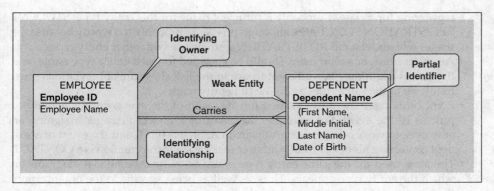

FIGURE 2-5 **Example of a weak entity and its identifying relationship**

entity on which it depends. The entity type on which the weak entity type depends is called the **identifying owner** (or simply *owner* for short). A weak entity type does not typically have its own identifier. Generally, on an E-R diagram, a weak entity type has an attribute that serves as a *partial* identifier. During a later design stage (described in Chapter 4), a full identifier will be formed for the weak entity by combining the partial identifier with the identifier of its owner or by creating a surrogate identifier attribute.

An example of a weak entity type with an identifying relationship is shown in Figure 2-5. EMPLOYEE is a strong entity type with identifier Employee ID (we note the identifier attribute by underlining it). DEPENDENT is a weak entity type, as indicated by the double-lined rectangle. The relationship between a weak entity type and its owner is called an **identifying relationship**. In Figure 2-5, Carries is the identifying relationship (indicated by the double line). The attribute Dependent Name serves as a *partial* identifier. (Dependent Name is a composite attribute that can be broken into component parts, as we describe later.) We use a double underline to indicate a partial identifier. During a later design stage, Dependent Name will be combined with Employee ID (the identifier of the owner) to form a full identifier for DEPENDENT. Some additional examples of strong and weak entity pairs are: BOOK–BOOK COPY, PRODUCT–SERIAL PRODUCT, and COURSE–COURSE OFFERING.

Identifying owner
The entity type on which the weak entity type depends.

Identifying relationship
The relationship between a weak entity type and its owner.

NAMING AND DEFINING ENTITY TYPES   In addition to the general guidelines for naming and defining data objects, there are a few special guidelines for *naming* entity types, which follow:

- An entity type name is a *singular noun* (such as CUSTOMER, STUDENT, or AUTOMOBILE); an entity is a person, a place, an object, an event, or a concept, and the name is for the entity type, which represents a set of entity instances (i.e., STUDENT represents students Hank Finley, Jean Krebs, and so forth). It is common to also specify the plural form (possibly in a CASE tool repository accompanying the E-R diagram), because sometimes the E-R diagram is read best by using plurals. For example, in Figure 2-1, we would say that a SUPPLIER may supply ITEMs. Because plurals are not always formed by adding an *s* to the singular noun, it is best to document the exact plural form.
- An entity type name should be *specific to the organization*. Thus, one organization may use the entity type name CUSTOMER, and another organization may use the entity type name CLIENT (this is one task, for example, done to customize a purchased data model). The name should be descriptive for everyone in the organization and distinct from all other entity type names within that organization. For example, a PURCHASE ORDER for orders placed with suppliers is distinct from a CUSTOMER ORDER for orders placed with a company by its customers. Both of these entity types cannot be named ORDER.
- An entity type name should be *concise*, using as few words as possible. For example, in a university database, an entity type REGISTRATION for the event of a student

registering for a class is probably a sufficient name for this entity type; STUDENT REGISTRATION FOR CLASS, although precise, is probably too wordy because the reader will understand REGISTRATION from its use with other entity types.

- An *abbreviation*, or a *short name*, should be specified for each entity type name, and the abbreviation may be sufficient to use in the E-R diagram; abbreviations must follow all of the same rules as do the full entity names.
- *Event entity types* should be named for the result of the event, not the activity or process of the event. For example, the event of a project manager assigning an employee to work on a project results in an ASSIGNMENT, and the event of a student contacting his or her faculty adviser seeking some information is a CONTACT.
- The *name* used for the same entity type *should be the same* on all E-R diagrams on which the entity type appears. Thus, as well as being specific to the organization, the name used for an entity type should be a standard, adopted by the organization for all references to the same kind of data. However, some entity types will have aliases, or alternative names, which are synonyms used in different parts of the organization. For example, the entity type ITEM may have aliases of MATERIAL (for production) and DRAWING (for engineering). Aliases are specified in documentation about the database, such as the repository of a CASE tool.

There are also some specific guidelines for *defining* entity types, which follow:

- *An entity type definition usually starts with* "An X is…." This is the most direct and clear way to state the meaning of an entity type.
- An entity type definition should *include a statement of what the unique characteristic is for each instance of the entity type*. In many cases, stating the identifier for an entity type helps convey the meaning of the entity. An example for Figure 2-4b is "An expense is a payment for the purchase of some good or service. An expense is identified by a journal entry number."
- An entity type definition should make it clear what *entity instances are included and not included* in the entity type; often, it is necessary to list the kinds of entities that are excluded. For example, "A customer is a person or organization that has placed an order for a product from us or one that we have contacted to advertise or promote our products. A customer does not include persons or organizations that buy our products only through our customers, distributors, or agents."
- An entity type definition often includes a description of *when an instance of the entity type is created and deleted*. For example, in the previous bullet point, a customer instance is implicitly created when the person or organization places its first order; because this definition does not specify otherwise, implicitly a customer instance is never deleted, or it is deleted based on general rules that are specified about the purging of data from the database. A statement about when to delete an entity instance is sometimes referred to as the retention of the entity type. A possible deletion statement for a customer entity type definition might be "A customer ceases to be a customer if it has not placed an order for more than three years."
- For some entity types, the definition must specify *when an instance might change into an instance of another entity type*. For example, consider the situation of a construction company for which bids accepted by potential customers become contracts. In this case, a bid might be defined by "A bid is a legal offer by our organization to do work for a customer. A bid is created when an officer of our company signs the bid document; a bid becomes an instance of contract when we receive a copy of the bid signed by an officer of the customer." This definition is also a good example to note how one definition can use other entity type names (in this case, the definition of bid uses the entity type name CUSTOMER).
- For some entity types, the definition must specify *what history is to be kept about instances of the entity type*. For example, the characteristics of an ITEM in Figure 2-1 may change over time, and we may need to keep a complete history of the individual values and when they were in effect. As we will see in some examples later, such statements about keeping history may have ramifications about how we represent the entity type on an E-R diagram and eventually how we store data for the entity instances.

Attributes

Each entity type has a set of attributes associated with it. An **attribute** is a property or characteristic of an entity type that is of interest to the organization. (Later, we will see that some types of relationships may also have attributes.) Thus, an attribute has a noun name. Following are some typical entity types and their associated attributes:

Attribute
A property or characteristic of an entity or relationship type that is of interest to the organization.

STUDENT	Student ID, Student Name, Home Address, Phone Number, Major
AUTOMOBILE	Vehicle ID, Color, Weight, Horsepower
EMPLOYEE	Employee ID, Employee Name, Payroll Address, Skill

In naming attributes, we use an initial capital letter followed by lowercase letters. If an attribute name consists of more than one word, we use a space between the words and we start each word with a capital letter, for example, Employee Name or Student Home Address. In E-R diagrams, we represent an attribute by placing its name in the entity it describes. Attributes may also be associated with relationships, as described later. Note that an attribute is associated with exactly one entity or relationship.

Notice in Figure 2-5 that all of the attributes of DEPENDENT are characteristics only of an employee's dependent, not characteristics of an employee. In traditional E-R notation, an entity type (not just weak entities but any entity) does not include attributes of entities to which it is related (what might be called foreign attributes). For example, DEPENDENT does not include any attribute that indicates to which employee this dependent is associated. This nonredundant feature of the E-R data model is consistent with the shared data property of databases. Because of relationships, which we discuss shortly, someone accessing data from a database will be able to associate attributes from related entities (e.g., show on a display screen a Dependent Name and the associated Employee Name).

REQUIRED VERSUS OPTIONAL ATTRIBUTES Each entity (or instance of an entity type) potentially has a value associated with each of the attributes of that entity type. An attribute that must be present for each entity instance is called a **required attribute**, whereas an attribute that may not have a value is called an **optional attribute**. For example, Figure 2-6 shows two STUDENT entities (instances) with their respective attribute values. The only optional attribute for STUDENT is Major. (Some students, specifically Melissa Kraft in this example, have not chosen a major yet; MIS would, of course, be a great career choice!) However, every student must, by the rules of the organization, have values for all the other attributes; *that is, we cannot store any data about a student in a STUDENT entity instance unless there are values for all the required attributes.* In various E-R diagramming notations, a symbol might appear in front of each attribute to indicate whether it is required (e.g., *) or optional (e.g., o), or required attributes will be

Required attribute
An attribute that must have a value for every entity (or relationship) instance with which it is associated.

Optional attribute
An attribute that may not have a value for every entity (or relationship) instance with which it is associated.

FIGURE 2-6 Entity type STUDENT with required and optional attributes

Entity type: STUDENT				
Attributes	**Attribute Data Type**	**Required or Optional**	**Example Instance**	**Example Instance**
Student ID	CHAR (10)	Required	876-24-8217	822-24-4456
Student Name	CHAR (40)	Required	Michael Grant	Melissa Kraft
Home Address	CHAR (30)	Required	314 Baker St.	1422 Heft Ave
Home City	CHAR (20)	Required	Centerville	Miami
Home State	CHAR (2)	Required	OH	FL
Home Zip Code	CHAR (9)	Required	45459	33321
Major	CHAR (3)	Optional	MIS	

in **boldface**, whereas optional attributes will be in normal font (the format we use in this text); in many cases, required or optional is indicated within supplemental documentation. In Chapter 3, when we consider entity supertypes and subtypes, we will see how sometimes optional attributes imply that there are different types of entities. (For example, we may want to consider students who have not declared a major as a subtype of the student entity type.) An attribute without a value is said to be null. Thus, each entity has an identifying attribute, which we discuss in a subsequent section, plus one or more other attributes. If you try to create an entity that has only an identifier, that entity is likely not legitimate. Such a data structure may simply hold a list of legal values for some attribute, which is better kept outside the database.

SIMPLE VERSUS COMPOSITE ATTRIBUTES   Some attributes can be broken down into meaningful component parts (detailed attributes). A common example is Name, which we saw in Figure 2-5; another is Address, which can usually be broken down into the following component attributes: Street Address, City, State, and Postal Code. A **composite attribute** is an attribute, such as Address, that has meaningful component parts, which are more detailed attributes. Figure 2-7 shows the notation that we use for composite attributes applied to this example. Most drawing tools do not have a notation for composite attributes, so you simply list all the component parts.

Composite attribute

An attribute that has meaningful component parts (attributes).

Composite attributes provide considerable flexibility to users, who can either refer to the composite attribute as a single unit or else refer to individual components of that attribute. Thus, for example, a user can either refer to Address or refer to one of its components, such as Street Address. The decision about whether to subdivide an attribute into its component parts depends on whether users will need to refer to those individual components, and hence, they have organizational meaning. Of course, the designer must always attempt to anticipate possible future usage patterns for the database.

A **simple (or atomic) attribute** is an attribute that cannot be broken down into smaller components that are meaningful for the organization. For example, all the attributes associated with AUTOMOBILE are simple: Vehicle ID, Color, Weight, and Horsepower.

Simple (or atomic) attribute

An attribute that cannot be broken down into smaller components that are meaningful to the organization.

SINGLE-VALUED VERSUS MULTIVALUED ATTRIBUTES   Figure 2-6 shows two entity instances with their respective attribute values. For each entity instance, each of the attributes in the figure has one value. It frequently happens that there is an attribute that may have more than one value for a given instance. For example, the EMPLOYEE entity type in Figure 2-8 has an attribute named Skill, whose values record the skill (or skills) for that employee. Of course, some employees may have more than one skill, such as PHP Programmer and C++ Programmer. A **multivalued attribute** is an attribute that may take on more than one value for a given entity (or relationship) instance. In this text, we indicate a multivalued attribute with curly brackets around the attribute name, as shown for the Skill attribute in the EMPLOYEE example in Figure 2-8. In Microsoft Visio, once an attribute is placed in an entity, you can edit that attribute (column), select the Collection tab, and choose one of the options. (Typically, MultiSet will be your choice, but one of the other options may be more appropriate for a given situation.) Other E-R diagramming tools may use an asterisk (*) after the attribute name, or you may have to use supplemental documentation to specify a multivalued attribute.

Multivalued attribute

An attribute that may take on more than one value for a given entity (or relationship) instance.

FIGURE 2-7   A composite attribute

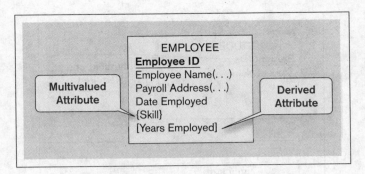

FIGURE 2-8 Entity with multivalued attribute (Skill) and derived attribute (Years Employed)

Multivalued and composite are different concepts, although beginner data modelers often confuse these terms. Skill, a multivalued attribute, may occur multiple times for each employee; Employee Name and Payroll Address are both likely composite attributes, each of which occurs once for each employee, but which have component, more atomic attributes, which are not shown in Figure 2-8 for simplicity. See Problem and Exercise 2-38 to review the concepts of composite and multivalued attributes.

STORED VERSUS DERIVED ATTRIBUTES Some attribute values that are of interest to users can be calculated or derived from other related attribute values that are stored in the database. For example, suppose that for an organization, the EMPLOYEE entity type has a Date Employed attribute. If users need to know how many years a person has been employed, that value can be calculated using Date Employed and today's date. A **derived attribute** is an attribute whose values can be calculated from related attribute values (plus possibly data not in the database, such as today's date, the current time, or a security code provided by a system user). We indicate a derived attribute in an E-R diagram by using square brackets around the attribute name, as shown in Figure 2-8 for the Years Employed attribute. Some E-R diagramming tools use a notation of a forward slash (/) in front of the attribute name to indicate that it is derived. (This notation is borrowed from UML for a virtual attribute.)

> **Derived attribute**
> An attribute whose values can be calculated from related attribute values.

In some situations, the value of an attribute can be derived from attributes in related entities. For example, consider an invoice created for each customer at Pine Valley Furniture Company. Order Total would be an attribute of the INVOICE entity, which indicates the total dollar amount that is billed to the customer. The value of Order Total can be computed by summing the Extended Price values (unit price times quantity sold) for the various line items that are billed on the invoice. Formulas for computing values such as this are one type of business rule.

IDENTIFIER ATTRIBUTE An **identifier** is an attribute (or combination of attributes) whose value distinguishes individual instances of an entity type. That is, no two instances of the entity type may have the same value for the identifier attribute. The identifier for the STUDENT entity type introduced earlier is Student ID, whereas the identifier for AUTOMOBILE is Vehicle ID. Notice that an attribute such as Student Name is not a candidate identifier, because many students may potentially have the same name, and students, like all people, can change their names. To be a candidate identifier, each entity instance must have a single value for the attribute and the attribute must be associated with the entity. We underline identifier names on the E-R diagram, as shown in the STUDENT entity type example in Figure 2-9a. To be an identifier, the attribute is also required (so the distinguishing value must exist), so an identifier is also in bold. Some E-R drawing software will place a symbol, called a stereotype, in front of the identifier (e.g., <<ID>> or <<PK>>).

> **Identifier**
> An attribute (or combination of attributes) whose value distinguishes instances of an entity type.

For some entity types, there is no single (or atomic) attribute that can serve as the identifier (i.e., that will ensure uniqueness). However, two (or more) attributes used in combination may serve as the identifier. A **composite identifier** is an identifier that consists of a composite attribute. Figure 2-9b shows the entity FLIGHT with the composite identifier Flight ID. Flight ID in turn has component attributes Flight Number and Date. This combination is required to identify uniquely individual occurrences of FLIGHT.

> **Composite identifier**
> An identifier that consists of a composite attribute.

FIGURE 2-9 Simple and composite identifier attributes
(a) Simple identifier attribute

(b) Composite identifier attribute

We use the convention that the composite attribute (Flight ID) is underlined to indicate it is the identifier, whereas the component attributes are not underlined. Some data modelers think of a composite identifier as "breaking a tie" created by a simple identifier. Even with Flight ID, a data modeler would ask a question, such as "Can two flights with the same number occur on the same date?" If so, yet another attribute is needed to form the composite identifier and to break the tie.

Some entities may have more than one candidate identifier. If there is more than one candidate identifier, the designer must choose one of them as the identifier. Bruce (1992) suggests the following criteria for selecting identifiers:

1. Choose an identifier that will not change its value over the life of each instance of the entity type. For example, the combination of Employee Name and Payroll Address (even if unique) would be a poor choice as an identifier for EMPLOYEE because the values of Employee Name and Payroll Address could easily change during an employee's term of employment.
2. Choose an identifier such that for each instance of the entity, the attribute is guaranteed to have valid values and not be null (or unknown). If the identifier is a composite attribute, such as Flight ID in Figure 2-9b, make sure that all parts of the identifier will have valid values.
3. Avoid the use of so-called intelligent identifiers (or keys), whose structure indicates classifications, locations, and so on. For example, the first two digits of an identifier value may indicate the warehouse location. Such codes are often changed as conditions change, which renders the identifier values invalid.
4. Consider substituting single-attribute surrogate identifiers for large composite identifiers. For example, an attribute called Game Number could be used for the entity type GAME instead of the combination of Home Team and Visiting Team.

NAMING AND DEFINING ATTRIBUTES   In addition to the general guidelines for naming data objects, there are a few special guidelines for naming attributes, which follow:

- An attribute name is a *singular noun or noun phrase* (such as Customer ID, Age, Product Minimum Price, or Major). Attributes, which materialize as data values, are concepts or physical characteristics of entities. Concepts and physical characteristics are described by nouns.
- An attribute name should be *unique*. No two attributes of the same entity type may have the same name, and it is desirable, for clarity purposes, that no two attributes across all entity types have the same name.
- To make an attribute name unique and for clarity purposes, *each attribute name should follow a standard format*. For example, your university may establish Student

GPA, as opposed to GPA of Student, as an example of the standard format for attribute naming. The format to be used will be established by each organization. A common format is [Entity type name { [Qualifier] }] Class, where [...] is an optional clause, and {...} indicates that the clause may repeat. *Entity type name* is the name of the entity with which the attribute is associated. The entity type name may be used to make the attribute name explicit. It is almost always used for the identifier attribute (e.g., Customer ID) of each entity type. *Class* is a phrase from a list of phrases defined by the organization that are the permissible characteristics or properties of entities (or abbreviations of these characteristics). For example, permissible values (and associated approved abbreviations) for Class might be Name (Nm), Identifier (ID), Date (Dt), or Amount (Amt). Class is, obviously, required. *Qualifier* is a phrase from a list of phrases defined by the organization that are used to place constraints on classes. One or more qualifiers may be needed to make each attribute of an entity type unique. For example, a qualifier might be Maximum (Max), Hourly (Hrly), or State (St). A qualifier may not be necessary: Employee Age and Student Major are both fully explicit attribute names. Sometimes a qualifier is necessary. For example, Employee Birth Date and Employee Hire Date are two attributes of Employee that require one qualifier. More than one qualifier may be necessary. For example, Employee Residence City Name (or Emp Res Cty Nm) is the name of an employee's city of residence, and Employee Tax City Name (or Emp Tax Cty Nm) is the name of the city in which an employee pays city taxes.

• *Similar attributes* of different entity types *should use the same qualifiers and classes*, as long as those are the names used in the organization. For example, the city of residence for faculty and students should be, respectively, Faculty Residence City Name and Student Residence City Name. Using similar names makes it easier for users to understand that values for these attributes come from the same possible set of values, what we will call *domains*. Users may want to take advantage of common domains in queries (e.g., find students who live in the same city as their adviser), and it will be easier for users to recognize that such a matching may be possible if the same qualifier and class phrases are used.

There are also some specific guidelines for defining attributes, which follow:

• An attribute definition states *what the attribute is and possibly why it is important*. The definition will often parallel the attribute's name; for example, Student Residence City Name could be defined as "The name of the city in which a student maintains his or her permanent residence."

• An attribute definition should make it clear *what is included and not included* in the attribute's value; for example, "Employee Monthly Salary Amount is the amount of money paid each month in the currency of the country of residence of the employee exclusive of any benefits, bonuses, reimbursements, or special payments."

• Any *aliases*, or alternative names, for the attribute can be specified in the definition or may be included elsewhere in documentation about the attribute, possibly stored in the repository of a CASE tool used to maintain data definitions.

• It may also be desirable to state in the definition *the source of values for the attribute*. Stating the source may make the meaning of the data clearer. For example, "Customer Standard Industrial Code is an indication of the type of business for the customer. Values for this code come from a standard set of values provided by the Federal Trade Commission and are found on a CD we purchase named SIC provided annually by the FTC."

• An attribute definition (or other specification in a CASE tool repository) also should indicate *if a value for the attribute is required or optional*. This business rule about an attribute is important for maintaining data integrity. The identifier attribute of an entity type is, by definition, required. If an attribute value is required, then to create an instance of the entity type, a value of this attribute must be provided. Required means that an entity instance must always have a value for this attribute, not just when an instance is created. Optional means that a value may not exist for an instance of an entity instance to be stored. Optional can be further qualified by stating whether once a value is entered, a value must always exist. For example, "Employee Department ID is the identifier of the department to which the employee is assigned. An employee may not be assigned to a department when hired (so this attribute is initially optional), but once an employee is assigned to a department, the employee must always be assigned to some department."

• An attribute definition (or other specification in a CASE tool repository) may also indicate *whether a value for the attribute may change* once a value is provided and before the entity instance is deleted. This business rule also controls data integrity. Nonintelligent identifiers may not change values over time. To assign a new nonintelligent identifier to an entity instance, that instance must first be deleted and then re-created.

• For a multivalued attribute, the attribute definition should indicate *the maximum and minimum number of occurrences of an attribute value for an entity instance*. For example, "Employee Skill Name is the name of a skill an employee possesses. Each employee must possess at least one skill, and an employee can choose to list at most 10 skills." The reason for a multivalued attribute may be that a history of the attribute needs to be kept. For example, "Employee Yearly Absent Days Number is the number of days in a calendar year the employee has been absent from work. An employee is considered absent if he or she works less than 50 percent of the scheduled hours in the day. A value for this attribute should be kept for each year in which the employee works for our company."

• An attribute definition may also indicate *any relationships that attribute has with other attributes*. For example, "Employee Vacation Days Number is the number of days of paid vacation for the employee. If the employee has a value of 'Exempt' for Employee Type, then the maximum value for Employee Vacation Days Number is determined by a formula involving the number of years of service for the employee."

MODELING RELATIONSHIPS

Relationships are the glue that holds together the various components of an E-R model. Intuitively, a *relationship* is an association representing an interaction among the instances of one or more entity types that is of interest to the organization. Thus, a relationship has a verb phrase name. Relationships and their characteristics (degree and cardinality) represent business rules, and usually relationships represent the most complex business rules shown in an ERD. In other words, this is where data modeling gets really interesting and fun, as well as crucial for controlling the integrity of a database. Relationships are essential for almost every meaningful use of a database; for example, relationships allow iTunes to find the music you've purchased, your cell phone company to find all the text messages in one of your SMS threads, or the campus nurse to see how different students have reacted to different treatments to the latest influenza on campus. So, fun and essential—modeling relationships will be a rewarding skill for you.

To understand relationships more clearly, we must distinguish between relationship types and relationship instances. To illustrate, consider the entity types EMPLOYEE and COURSE, where COURSE represents training courses that may be taken by employees. To track courses that have been completed by particular employees, we define a relationship called Completes between the two entity types (see Figure 2-10a). This is a many-to-many relationship, because each employee may complete any number of courses (zero, one, or many courses), whereas a given course may be completed by any number of employees (nobody, one employee, many employees). For example, in Figure 2-10b, the employee Milan Shah has completed three courses (.NET, SQL, and Perl). The SQL course has been completed by two employees (Chirag and Ganesh), and the Visual Basic course has not been completed by anyone.

In this example, there are two entity types (EMPLOYEE and COURSE) that participate in the relationship named Completes. In general, any number of entity types (from one to many) may participate in a relationship.

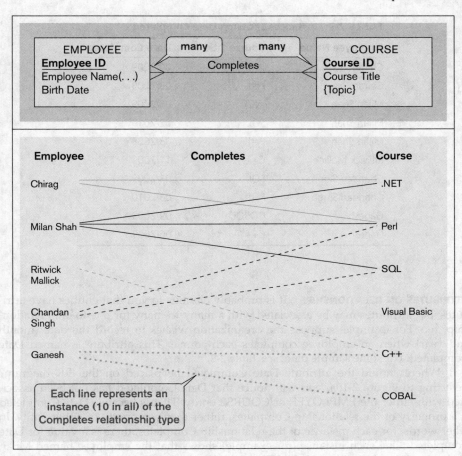

FIGURE 2-10   Relationship type
and instances
(a) Relationship type (Complete)

(b) Relationship instances

We frequently use in this and subsequent chapters the convention of a single verb phrase label to represent a relationship. Because relationships often occur due to an organizational event, entity instances are related because an action was taken; thus, a verb phrase is appropriate for the label. This verb phrase should be in the present tense and descriptive. There are, however, many ways to represent a relationship. Some data modelers prefer the format with two relationship names, one to name the relationship in each direction. One or two verb phrases have the same structural meaning, so you may use either format as long as the meaning of the relationship in each direction is clear.

Basic Concepts and Definitions in Relationships

A **relationship type** is a meaningful association between (or among) entity types. The phrase *meaningful association* implies that the relationship allows us to answer questions that could not be answered given only the entity types. A relationship type is denoted by a line labeled with the name of the relationship, as in the example shown in Figure 2-10a, or with two names, as in Figure 2-1. We suggest you use a short, descriptive verb phrase that is meaningful to the user in naming the relationship. (We say more about naming and defining relationships later in this section.)

A **relationship instance** is an association between (or among) entity instances, where each relationship instance associates exactly one entity instance from each participating entity type (Elmasri and Navathe, 1994). For example, in Figure 2-10b, each of the 10 lines in the figure represents a relationship instance between one employee and one course, indicating that the employee has completed that course. For example, the line between Employee Ritchie and Course Perl is one relationship instance.

Relationship type

A meaningful association between (or among) entity types.

Relationship instance

An association between (or among) entity instances where each relationship instance associates exactly one entity instance from each participating entity type.

TABLE 2-2   Instances Showing Date Completed

Employee Name	Course Title	Date Completed
Chirag	.NET	06/2009
Chirag	Perl	09/2009
Milan Shah	.NET	06/2009
Milan Shah	SQL	02/2010
Milan Shah	Perl	03/2009
Ritwick Mallick	C++	11/2009
Chandan Singh	SQL	03/2009
Chandan Singh	Perl	03/2010
Ganesh	COBOL	09/2009
Ganesh	C++	06/2009

ATTRIBUTES ON RELATIONSHIPS   It is probably obvious to you that entities have attributes, but attributes may be associated with a many-to-many (or one-to-one) relationship, too. For example, suppose the organization wishes to record the date (month and year) when an employee completes each course. This attribute is named Date Completed. For some sample data, see Table 2-2.

Where should the attribute Date Completed be placed on the E-R diagram? Referring to Figure 2-10a, you will notice that Date Completed has not been associated with either the EMPLOYEE or COURSE entity. That is because Date Completed is a property of the relationship Completes, rather than a property of either entity. In other words, for each instance of the relationship Completes, there is a value for Date Completed. One such instance (for example) shows that the employee named Milan Shah completed the course titled .NET in 06/2014.

A revised version of the ERD for this example is shown in Figure 2-11a. In this diagram, the attribute Date Completed is in a rectangle connected to the Completes relationship line. Other attributes might be added to this relationship if appropriate, such as Course Grade, Instructor, and Room Location.

It is interesting to note that an attribute cannot be associated with a one-to-many relationship, such as Carries in Figure 2-5. For example, consider Dependent Date, similar to Date Completed above, for when the DEPENDENT begins to be carried by the EMPLOYEE. Because each DEPENDENT is associated with only one EMPLOYEE, such a date is unambiguously a characteristic of the DEPENDENT (i.e., for a given DEPENDENT, Dependent Date cannot vary by EMPLOYEE). So, if you ever have the urge to associate an attribute with a one-to-many relationship, "step away from the relationship!"

ASSOCIATIVE ENTITIES   The presence of one or more attributes on a relationship suggests to the designer that the relationship should perhaps instead be represented as an entity type. To emphasize this point, most E-R drawing tools require that such attributes be placed in an entity type. An **associative entity** is an entity type that associates the instances of one or more entity types and contains attributes that are peculiar to the relationship between those entity instances. The associative entity CERTIFICATE is represented with the rectangle with rounded corners, as shown in Figure 2-11b. Most E-R drawing tools do not have a special symbol for an associative entity. Associative entities are sometimes referred to as gerunds, because the relationship name (a verb) is usually converted to an entity name that is a noun. Note in Figure 2-11b that there are no relationship names on the lines between an associative entity and a strong entity. This is because the associative entity represents the relationship. Figure 2-11c shows how associative entities are drawn using Microsoft Visio, which is representative of how you

Associative entity

An entity type that associates the instances of one or more entity types and contains attributes that are peculiar to the relationship between those entity instances.

FIGURE 2-11   An associative entity

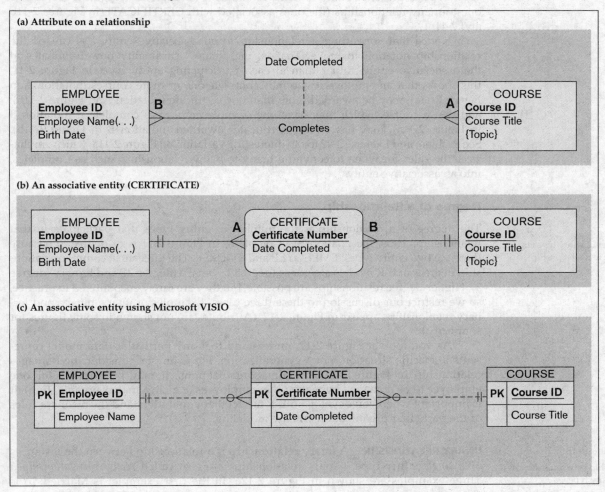

(a) Attribute on a relationship

EMPLOYEE
Employee ID
Employee Name(. . .)
Birth Date

B

Date Completed

Completes

A

COURSE
Course ID
Course Title
{Topic}

(b) An associative entity (CERTIFICATE)

EMPLOYEE
Employee ID
Employee Name(. . .)
Birth Date

A

CERTIFICATE
Certificate Number
Date Completed

B

COURSE
Course ID
Course Title
{Topic}

(c) An associative entity using Microsoft VISIO

EMPLOYEE	
PK	**Employee ID**
	Employee Name

CERTIFICATE	
PK	**Certificate Number**
	Date Completed

COURSE	
PK	**Course ID**
	Course Title

would draw an associative entity with most E-R diagramming tools. In Visio, the relationship lines are dashed because CERTIFICATE does not include the identifiers of the related entities in its identifier. (Certificate Number is sufficient.)

How do you know whether to convert a relationship to an associative entity type? Following are four conditions that should exist:

1. All the relationships for the participating entity types are "many" relationships.
2. The resulting associative entity type has independent meaning to end users and, preferably, can be identified with a single-attribute identifier.
3. The associative entity has one or more attributes in addition to the identifier.
4. The associative entity participates in one or more relationships independent of the entities related in the associated relationship.

Figure 2-11b shows the relationship Completes converted to an associative entity type. In this case, the training department for the company has decided to award a certificate to each employee who completes a course. Thus, the entity is named CERTIFICATE, which certainly has independent meaning to end users. Also, each certificate has a number (Certificate Number) that serves as the identifier.

The attribute Date Completed is also included. Note also in Figure 2-11b and the Visio version of Figure 2-11c that both EMPLOYEE and COURSE are mandatory participants in the two relationships with CERTIFICATE. This is exactly what occurs when you have to represent a many-to-many relationship (Completes in Figure 2-11a) as two one-to-many relationships (the ones associated with CERTIFICATE in Figures 2-11b and 2-11c).

Notice that converting a relationship to an associative entity has caused the relationship notation to move. That is, the "many" cardinality now terminates at the associative entity, rather than at each participating entity type. In Figure 2-11, this shows that an employee, who may complete one or more courses (notation A in Figure 2-11a), may be awarded more than one certificate (notation A in Figure 2-11b); and that a course, which may have one or more employees complete it (notation B in Figure 2-11a), may have many certificates awarded (notation B in Figure 2-11b). See Problem and Exercise 2-42 for an interesting variation on Figure 2-11a, which empha-sizes the rules for when to convert a many-to-many relationship, such as Completes, into an associative entity.

Degree of a Relationship

Degree

The number of entity types that participate in a relationship.

The **degree** of a relationship is the number of entity types that participate in that relationship. Thus, the relationship Completes in Figure 2-11 is of degree 2, because there are two entity types: EMPLOYEE and COURSE. The three most common relation-ship degrees in E-R models are unary (degree 1), binary (degree 2), and ternary (degree 3). Higher-degree relationships are possible, but they are rarely encountered in practice, so we restrict our discussion to these three cases. Examples of unary, binary, and ter-nary relationships appear in Figure 2-12. (Attributes are not shown in some figures for simplicity.)

As you look at Figure 2-12, understand that any particular data model repre-sents a specific situation, not a generalization. For example, consider the Manages relationship in Figure 2-12a. In some organizations, it may be possible for one employee to be managed by many other employees (e.g., in a matrix organization). It is important when you develop an E-R model that you understand the business rules of the particular organization you are modeling.

Unary relationship

A relationship between instances of a single entity type.

UNARY RELATIONSHIP   A **unary relationship** is a relationship between the instances of a *single* entity type. (Unary relationships are also called *recursive relationships*.) Three examples are shown in Figure 2-12a. In the first example, Is Married To is shown as a one-to-one relationship between instances of the PERSON entity type. Because this is a one-to-one relationship, this notation indicates that only the current marriage, if one exists, needs to be kept about a person. What would change if we needed to retain the history of marriages for each person? See Review Question 2-20 and Problem and Exercise 2-34 for other business rules and their effect on the Is Married To relationship representation. In the second example, Manages is shown as a one-to-many relationship between instances of the EMPLOYEE entity type. Using this relationship, we could identify, for example, the employees who report to a particular manager. The third example is one case of using a unary relation-ship to represent a sequence, cycle, or priority list. In this example, sports teams are related by their standing in their league (the Stands After relationship). (Note: In these examples, we ignore whether these are mandatory- or optional-cardinality relationships or whether the same entity instance can repeat in the same relationship instance; we will introduce mandatory and optional cardinality in a later section of this chapter.)

Figure 2-13 shows an example of another unary relationship, called a *bill-of-materials structure*. Many manufactured products are made of assemblies, which in turn are composed of subassemblies and parts, and so on. As shown in Figure 2-13a, we can represent this structure as a many-to-many unary relationship. In this figure, the entity type ITEM is used to represent all types of components, and we use Has Components for the name of the relationship type that associates lower-level items with higher-level items.

Two occurrences of this bill-of-materials structure are shown in Figure 2-13b. Each of these diagrams shows the immediate components of each item as well as the

FIGURE 2-12   Examples of relationships of different degrees

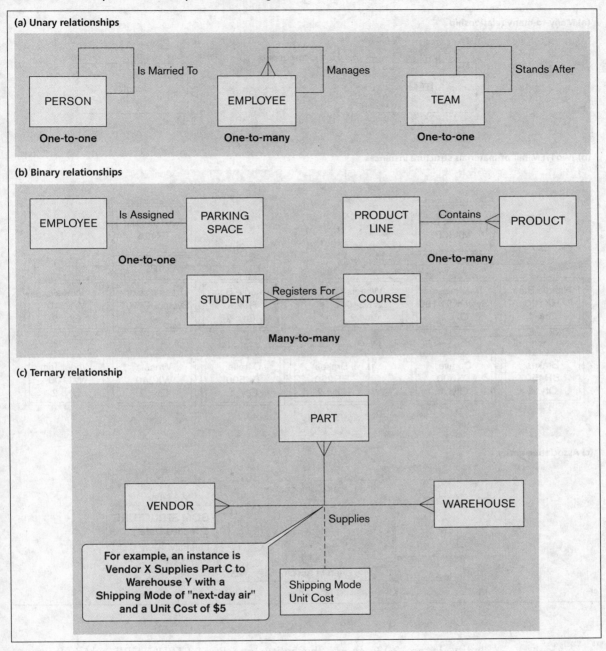

quantities of that component. For example, item TX100 consists of item BR450 (quantity 2) and item DX500 (quantity 1). You can easily verify that the associations are in fact many-to-many. Several of the items have more than one component type (e.g., item MX300 has three immediate component types: HX100, TX100, and WX240). Also, some of the components are used in several higher-level assemblies. For example, item WX240 is used in both item MX300 and item WX340, even at different levels of the bill-of-materials. The many-to-many relationship guarantees that, for example, the same subassembly structure of WX240 (not shown) is used each time item WX240 goes into making some other item.

The presence of the attribute Quantity on the relationship suggests that the analyst consider converting the relationship Has Components to an associative

FIGURE 2-13   Representing a bill-of-materials structure

(a) Many-to-many relationship

ITEM — Has Components — Quantity

(b) Two ITEM bill-of-materials structure instances

Mountain Bike MX300

- Handle Bars HX100 Qty: 1
- Transmission System TX100 Qty: 1
  - Brakes BR450 Qty: 2
  - Derailer DX500 Qty: 1
- Wheels WX240 Qty: 2

Tandem Bike TR425

- Handle Bars HT200 Qty: 2
- Transmission System TX101
  - Brakes BR250 Qty: 2
  - Derailer DX500 Qty: 1
- Wheels WX340 Qty: 2
  - Wheels WX240 Qty: 2
  - Wheel Trim WT100 Qty: 2

(c) Associative entity

ITEM — Has Components — BOM STRUCTURE **Effective Date** Quantity — Used In Assemblies

entity. Figure 2-13c shows the entity type BOM STRUCTURE, which forms an association between instances of the ITEM entity type. A second attribute (named Effective Date) has been added to BOM STRUCTURE to record the date when this component was first used in the related assembly. Effective dates are often needed when a history of values is required. Other data model structures can be used for unary relationships involving such hierarchies; we show some of these other structures in Chapter 9.

Binary relationship

A relationship between the instances of two entity types.

BINARY RELATIONSHIP   A **binary relationship** is a relationship between the instances of two entity types and is the most common type of relationship encountered in data modeling. Figure 2-12b shows three examples. The first (one-to-one) indicates that an employee is assigned one parking place, and that each parking place is assigned to one employee. The second (one-to-many) indicates that a product line may contain several products, and that each product belongs to only one product line. The third (many-to-many) shows that a student may register for more than one course, and that each course may have many student registrants.

TERNARY RELATIONSHIP   A **ternary relationship** is a *simultaneous* relationship among the instances of three entity types. A typical business situation that leads to a ternary relationship is shown in Figure 2-12c. In this example, vendors can supply various parts to warehouses. The relationship Supplies is used to record the specific parts that are supplied by a given vendor to a particular warehouse. Thus, there are three entity types: VENDOR, PART, and WAREHOUSE. There are two attributes on the relationship Supplies: Shipping Mode and Unit Cost. For example, one instance of Supplies might record the fact that vendor X can ship part C to warehouse Y, that the shipping mode is next-day air, and that the cost is $5 per unit.

> Don't be confused: A ternary relationship is not the same as three binary relationships. For example, Unit Cost is an attribute of the Supplies relationship in Figure 2-12c. Unit Cost cannot be properly associated with any one of the three possible binary relationships among the three entity types, such as that between PART and WAREHOUSE. Thus, for example, if we were told that vendor X can ship part C for a unit cost of $8, those data would be incomplete because they would not indicate to which warehouse the parts would be shipped.

> As usual, the presence of an attribute on the relationship Supplies in Figure 2-12c suggests converting the relationship to an associative entity type. Figure 2-14 shows an alternative (and preferable) representation of the ternary relationship shown in Figure 2-12c. In Figure 2-14, the (associative) entity type SUPPLY SCHEDULE is used to replace the Supplies relationship from Figure 2-12c. Clearly, the entity type SUPPLY SCHEDULE is of independent interest to users. However, notice that an identifier has not yet been assigned to SUPPLY SCHEDULE. This is acceptable. If no identifier is assigned to an associative entity during E-R modeling, an identifier (or key) will be assigned during logical modeling (discussed in Chapter 4). This will be a composite identifier whose components will consist of the identifier for each of the participating entity types (in this example, PART, VENDOR, and WAREHOUSE). Can you think of other attributes that might be associated with SUPPLY SCHEDULE?

> As noted earlier, we do not label the lines from SUPPLY SCHEDULE to the three entities. This is because these lines do not represent binary relationships. To keep the same meaning as the ternary relationship of Figure 2-12c, we cannot break the Supplies relationship into three binary relationships, as we have already mentioned.

> So, here is a guideline to follow: Convert all ternary (or higher) relationships to associative entities, as in this example. Song et al. (1995) show that participation constraints (described in a following section on cardinality constraints) cannot be accurately represented for a ternary relationship, given the notation with attributes on the relationship line. However, by converting to an associative entity, the constraints can be

Ternary relationship
A simultaneous relationship among the instances of three entity types.

FIGURE 2-14   Ternary relationship as an associative entity

accurately represented. Also, many E-R diagram drawing tools, including most CASE tools, cannot represent ternary relationships. So, although not semantically accurate, you must use these tools to represent the ternary or higher order relationship with an associative entity and three binary relationships, which have a mandatory association with each of the three related entity types.

Attributes or Entity?

Sometimes you will wonder if you should represent data as an attribute or an entity; this is a common dilemma. Figure 2-15 includes three examples of situations when an attribute could be represented via an entity type. We use this text's E-R notation in the left column and the notation from Microsoft Visio in the right column; it is important that you learn how to read ERDs in several notations because you will encounter various styles in different publications and organizations. In Figure 2-15a, the potentially multiple prerequisites of a course (shown as a multivalued attribute in the Attribute cell) are also courses (and a course may be a prerequisite for many other courses). Thus, prerequisite could be viewed as a bill-of-materials structure (shown in the Relationship & Entity cell) between courses, not a multivalued attribute of COURSE. Representing prerequisites via a bill-of-materials structure also means that finding the prerequisites of a course and finding the courses for which a course is prerequisite both deal with relationships between entity types. When a prerequisite is a multivalued attribute of COURSE, finding the courses for which a course is a prerequisite means looking for a specific value for a prerequisite across all COURSE instances. As was shown in Figure 2-13a, such a situation could also be modeled as a unary relationship among instances of the COURSE entity type. In Visio, this specific situation requires creating the equivalent of an associative entity (see the Relationship & Entity cell in Figure 2-15a; Visio does not use the rectangle with rounded corners symbol). By creating the associative entity, it is now easy to add characteristics to the relationship, such as a minimum grade required. Also note that Visio shows the identifier (in this case compound) with a PK stereotype symbol and boldface on the component attribute names, signifying these are required attributes.

In Figure 2-15b, employees potentially have multiple skills (shown in the Attribute cell), but skill could be viewed instead as an entity type (shown in the Relationship & Entity cell as the equivalent of an associative entity) about which the organization wants to maintain data (the unique code to identify each skill, a descriptive title, and the type of skill, for example, technical or managerial). An employee has skills, which are not viewed as attributes, but rather as instances of a related entity type. In the cases of Figures 2-15a and 2-15b, representing the data as a multivalued attribute rather than via a relationship with another entity type may, in the view of some people, simplify the diagram. On the other hand, the right-hand drawings in these figures are closer to the way the database would be represented in a standard relational database management system, the most popular type of DBMS in use today. Although we are not concerned with implementation during conceptual data modeling, there is some logic for keeping the conceptual and logical data models similar. Further, as we will see in the next example, there are times when an attribute, whether simple, composite, or multivalued, should be in a separate entity.

So, when *should* an attribute be linked to an entity type via a relationship? The answer is when the attribute is the identifier or some other characteristic of an entity type in the data model and multiple entity instances need to share these same attributes. Figure 2-15c represents an example of this rule. In this example, EMPLOYEE has a composite attribute of Department. Because Department is a concept of the business, and multiple employees will share the same department data, department data could be represented (nonredundantly) in a DEPARTMENT entity type, with attributes for the data about departments that all other related entity instances need to know. With this approach, not only can different employees share the storage of the same department data, but projects (which are assigned to a department) and organizational units (which are composed of departments) also can share the storage of this same department data.

FIGURE 2-15 Using relationships and entities to link related attributes

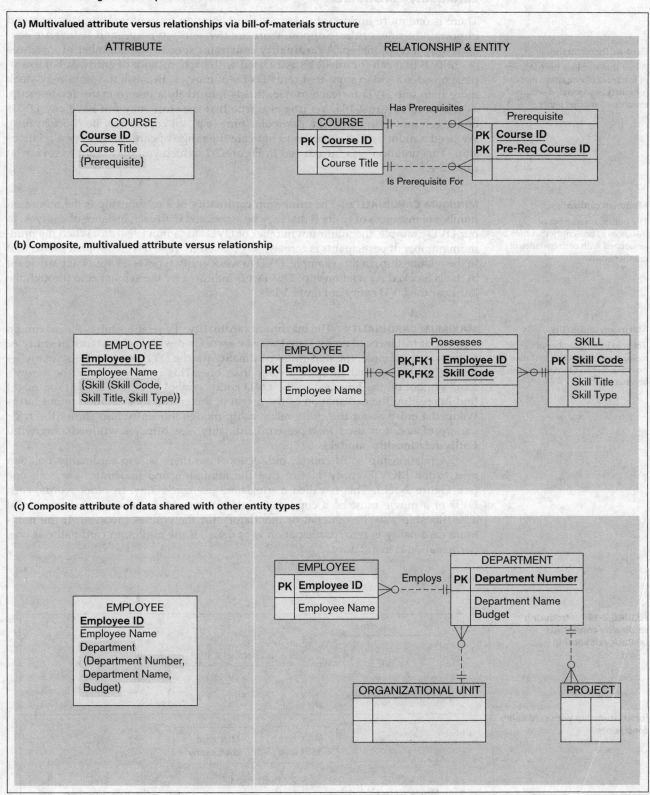

(a) Multivalued attribute versus relationships via bill-of-materials structure

ATTRIBUTE

RELATIONSHIP & ENTITY

(b) Composite, multivalued attribute versus relationship

(c) Composite attribute of data shared with other entity types

Cardinality Constraints

There is one more important data modeling notation for representing common and important business rules. Suppose there are two entity types, A and B, that are connected by a relationship. A **cardinality constraint** specifies the number of instances of entity B that can (or must) be associated with each instance of entity A. For example, consider a video store that rents DVDs of movies. Because the store may stock more than one DVD for each movie, this is intuitively a one-to-many relationship, as shown in Figure 2-16a. Yet it is also true that the store may not have any DVDs of a given movie in stock at a particular time (e.g., all copies may be checked out). We need a more precise notation to indicate the range of cardinalities for a relationship. This notation was introduced in Figure 2-2, which you may want to review at this time.

Cardinality constraint

A rule that specifies the number of instances of one entity that can (or must) be associated with each instance of another entity.

MINIMUM CARDINALITY   The **minimum cardinality** of a relationship is the minimum number of instances of entity B that may be associated with each instance of entity A. In our DVD example, the minimum number of DVDs for a movie is zero. When the minimum number of participants is zero, we say that entity type B is an optional participant in the relationship. In this example, DVD (a weak entity type) is an optional participant in the Is Stocked As relationship. This fact is indicated by the symbol zero through the line near the DVD entity in Figure 2-16b.

Minimum cardinality

The minimum number of instances of one entity that may be associated with each instance of another entity.

MAXIMUM CARDINALITY   The **maximum cardinality** of a relationship is the maximum number of instances of entity B that may be associated with each instance of entity A. In the video example, the maximum cardinality for the DVD entity type is "many"— that is, an unspecified number greater than one. This is indicated by the "crow's foot" symbol on the line next to the DVD entity symbol in Figure 2-16b. (You might find interesting the explanation of the origin of the crow's foot notation found in the Wikipedia entry about the entity-relationship model; this entry also shows the wide variety of notation used to represent cardinality; see **http://en.wikipedia.org/wiki/Entity-relationship_model.**)

Maximum cardinality

The maximum number of instances of one entity that may be associated with each instance of another entity.

A relationship is, of course, bidirectional, so there is also cardinality notation next to the MOVIE entity. Notice that the minimum and maximum are both one (see Figure 2-16b). This is called a *mandatory one* cardinality. In other words, each DVD of a movie must be a copy of exactly one movie. In general, participation in a relationship may be optional or mandatory for the entities involved. If the minimum cardinality is zero, participation is optional; if the minimum cardinality is one, participation is mandatory.

FIGURE 2-16 Introducing cardinality constraints
(a) Basic relationship

(b) Relationship with cardinality constraints

In Figure 2-16b, some attributes have been added to each of the entity types. Notice that DVD is represented as a weak entity. This is because a DVD cannot exist unless the owner movie also exists. The identifier of MOVIE is Movie Name. DVD does not have a unique identifier. However, Copy Number is a *partial* identifier, which together with Movie Name would uniquely identify an instance of DVD.

Some Examples of Relationships and Their Cardinalities

Examples of three relationships that show all possible combinations of minimum and maximum cardinalities appear in Figure 2-17. Each example states the business rule for each cardinality constraint and shows the associated E-R notation. Each example also shows some relationship instances to clarify the nature of the relationship. You should study each of these examples carefully. Following are the business rules for each of the examples in Figure 2-17:

1. *PATIENT Has Recorded PATIENT HISTORY (Figure 2-17a)* Each patient has one or more patient histories. (The initial patient visit is always recorded as an instance of PATIENT HISTORY.) Each instance of PATIENT HISTORY "belongs to" exactly one PATIENT.
2. *EMPLOYEE Is Assigned To PROJECT (Figure 2-17b)* Each PROJECT has at least one EMPLOYEE assigned to it. (Some projects have more than one.) Each EMPLOYEE may or (optionally) may not be assigned to any existing PROJECT (e.g., employee Pete) or may be assigned to one or more PROJECTs.
3. *PERSON Is Married To PERSON (Figure 2-17c)* This is an optional zero or one cardinality in both directions, because a person may or may not be married at a given point in time.

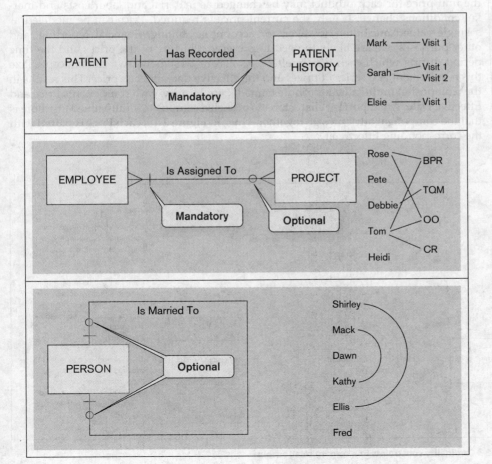

FIGURE 2-17 Examples of cardinality constraints
(a) Mandatory cardinalities

(b) One optional, one mandatory cardinality

(c) Optional cardinalities

It is possible for the maximum cardinality to be a fixed number, not an arbitrary "many" value. For example, suppose corporate policy states that an employee may work on at most five projects at the same time. We could show this business rule by placing a 5 above or below the crow's foot next to the PROJECT entity in Figure 2-17b.

A TERNARY RELATIONSHIP   We showed the ternary relationship with the associative entity type SUPPLY SCHEDULE in Figure 2-14. Now let's add cardinality constraints to this diagram, based on the business rules for this situation. The E-R diagram, with the relevant business rules, is shown in Figure 2-18. Notice that PART and WAREHOUSE must relate to some SUPPLY SCHEDULE instance, and a VENDOR optionally may not participate. The cardinality at each of the participating entities is a mandatory one, because each SUPPLY SCHEDULE instance must be related to exactly one instance of each of these participating entity types. (Remember, SUPPLY SCHEDULE is an associative entity.)

As noted earlier, a ternary relationship is not equivalent to three binary relationships. Unfortunately, you are not able to draw ternary relationships with many CASE tools; instead, you are forced to represent ternary relationships as three binaries (i.e., an associative entity with three binary relationships). If you are forced to draw three binary relationships, then do not draw the binary relationships with names, and be sure that the cardinality next to the three strong entities is a mandatory one.

Modeling Time-Dependent Data

Database contents vary over time. With renewed interest today in traceability and reconstruction of a historical picture of the organization for various regulatory requirements, such as HIPAA and Sarbanes-Oxley, the need to include a time series of data has become essential. For example, in a database that contains product information, the unit price for each product may be changed as material and labor costs and market conditions change. If only the current price is required, Price can be modeled as a single-valued attribute. However, for accounting, billing, financial reporting, and other purposes, we are likely to need to preserve a history of the prices and the time period during which each was in effect. As Figure 2-19 shows, we can conceptualize this requirement as a series of prices and the effective date for each price. This results in the (composite) multivalued attribute named Price History, with components Price and Effective Date. An important characteristic of such a composite, multivalued attribute is that the component attributes go together. Thus, in Figure 2-19, each Price is paired with the corresponding Effective Date.

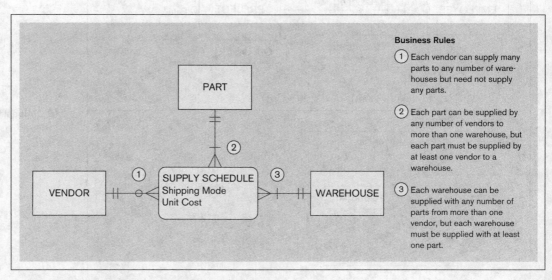

FIGURE 2-18   Cardinality constraints in a ternary relationship

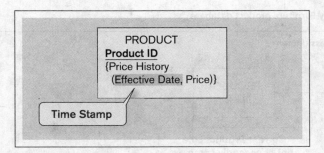

FIGURE 2-19   **Simple example of time stamping**

In Figure 2-19, each value of the attribute Price is time stamped with its effective date. A **time stamp** is simply a time value, such as date and time, that is associated with a data value. A time stamp may be associated with any data value that changes over time when we need to maintain a history of those data values. Time stamps may be recorded to indicate the time the value was entered (transaction time); the time the value becomes valid or stops being valid; or the time when critical actions were performed, such as updates, corrections, or audits. This situation is similar to the employee skill diagrams in Figure 2-15b; thus, an alternative, not shown in Figure 2-19, is to make Price History a separate entity type, as was done with Skill using Microsoft Visio.

The use of simple time stamping (as in the preceding example) is often adequate for modeling time-dependent data. However, time can introduce subtler complexities to data modeling. For example, consider again Figure 2-17c. This figure is drawn for a given point in time, not to show history. If, on the other hand, we needed to record the full history of marriages for individuals, the Is Married To relationship would be an optional many-to-many relationship. Further, we might want to know the beginning and ending date (optional) of each marriage; these dates would be, similar to the bill-of-materials structure in Figure 2-13c, attributes of the relationship or associative entity.

Financial and other compliance regulations, such as Sarbanes-Oxley and Basel II, require that a database maintain history rather than just current status of critical data. In addition, some data modelers will argue that a data model should always be able to represent history, even if today's users say they need only current values. These factors suggest that all relationships should be modeled as many-to-many (which is often done in purchased data model). Thus, for most databases, this will necessitate forming an associative entity along every relationship. There are two obvious negatives to this approach. First, many additional (associative) entities are created, thus cluttering ERDs. Second, a many-to-many ($M{:}N$) relationship is less restrictive than a one-to-many ($1{:}M$). So, if initially you want to enforce only one associated entity instance for some entity (i.e., the "one" side of the relationships), this cannot be enforced by the data model with an $M{:}N$ relationship. It would seem likely that some relationships would never be $M{:}N$; for example, would a $1{:}M$ relationship between customer and order ever become $M{:}N$ (but, of course, maybe someday our organization would sell items that would allow and often have joint purchasing, like vehicles or houses)? The conclusion is that if history or a time series of values might ever be desired or required by regulation, you should consider using an $M{:}N$ relationship.

An even more subtle situation of the effect of time on data modeling is illustrated in Figure 2-20a, which represents a portion of an ERD for Pine Valley Furniture Company. Each product is assigned (i.e., current assignment) to a product line (or related group of products). Customer orders are processed throughout the year, and monthly summaries are reported by product line and by product within product line.

Suppose that in the middle of the year, due to a reorganization of the sales function, some products are reassigned to different product lines. The model shown in Figure 2-20a is not designed to track the reassignment of a product to a new product line. Thus, all sales reports will show cumulative sales for a product based on its current

Time stamp

A time value that is associated with a data value, often indicating when some event occurred that affected the data value.

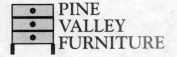

FIGURE 2-20   Example of time in Pine Valley Furniture product database

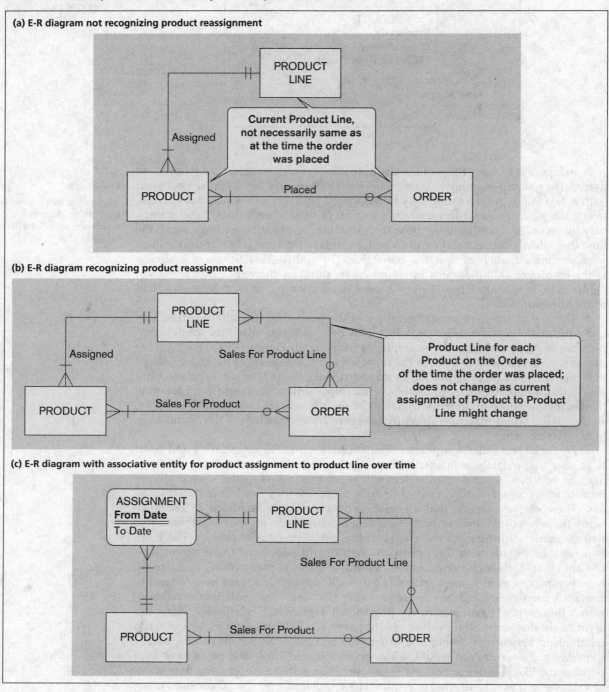

(a) E-R diagram not recognizing product reassignment

PRODUCT LINE

Assigned

Current Product Line, not necessarily same as at the time the order was placed

PRODUCT

Placed

ORDER

(b) E-R diagram recognizing product reassignment

PRODUCT LINE

Assigned

Sales For Product Line

Product Line for each Product on the Order as of the time the order was placed; does not change as current assignment of Product to Product Line might change

PRODUCT

Sales For Product

ORDER

(c) E-R diagram with associative entity for product assignment to product line over time

ASSIGNMENT
From Date
To Date

PRODUCT LINE

Sales For Product Line

PRODUCT

Sales For Product

ORDER

product line rather than the one at the time of the sale. For example, a product may have total year-to-date sales of $50,000 and be associated with product line B, yet $40,000 of those sales may have occurred while the product was assigned to product line A. This fact will be lost using the model in Figure 2-20a. The simple design change shown in Figure 2-20b will correctly recognize product reassignments. A new relationship, called Sales For Product Line, has been added between ORDER and PRODUCT LINE. As customer orders are processed, they are credited to both the correct product (via Sales For Product) and the correct product line (via Sales For Product Line) as of the time of the sale. The approach of Figure 2-20b is similar to what is done in a data warehouse to retain historical records of the precise situation at any point in time. (We will return to dealing with the time dimension in Chapter 9.)

Another aspect of modeling time is recognizing that although the requirements of the organization today may be to record only the current situation, the design of the database may need to change if the organization ever decides to keep history. In Figure 2-20b, we know the current product line for a product and the product line for the product each time it is ordered. But what if the product were ever reassigned to a product line during a period of zero sales for the product? Based on this data model in Figure 2-20b, we would not know of these other product line assignments. A common solution to this need for greater flexibility in the data model is to consider whether a one-to-many relationship, such as Assigned, should become a many-to-many relationship. Further, to allow for attributes on this new relationship, this relationship should actually be an associative entity. Figure 2-20c shows this alternative data model with the ASSIGNMENT associative entity for the Assigned relationship. The advantage of the alternative is that we now will not miss recording any product line assignment, and we can record information about the assignment (such as the from and to effective dates of the assignment); the disadvantage is that the data model no longer has the restriction that a product may be assigned to only one product line at a time.

We have discussed the problem of time-dependent data with managers in several organizations who are considered leaders in the use of data modeling and database management. Before the recent wave of financial reporting disclosure regulations, these discussions revealed that data models for operational databases were generally inadequate for handing time-dependent data, and that organizations often ignored this problem and hoped that the resulting inaccuracies balanced out. However, with these new regulations, you need to be alert to the complexities posed by time-dependent data as you develop data models in your organization. For a thorough explanation of time as a dimension of data modeling, see a series of articles by T. Johnson and R. Weis beginning in May 2007 in *DM Review* (now *Information Management*; see References at the end of this chapter).

Modeling Multiple Relationships Between Entity Types

There may be more than one relationship between the same entity types in a given organization. Two examples are shown in Figure 2-21. Figure 2-21a shows two relationships between the entity types EMPLOYEE and DEPARTMENT. In this figure, we use the notation with names for the relationship in each direction; this notation makes explicit what the cardinality is for each direction of the relationship (which becomes important for clarifying the meaning of the unary relationship on EMPLOYEE). One relationship associates employees with the department in which they work. This relationship is one-to-many in the Has Workers direction and is mandatory in both directions. That is, a department must have at least one employee who works there (perhaps the department manager), and each employee must be assigned to exactly one department. (Note: These are specific business rules we assume for this illustration. It is crucial when you develop an E-R diagram for a particular situation that you understand the business rules that apply for that setting. For example, if EMPLOYEE were to include retirees, then each employee may not be currently assigned to exactly one department; further, the E-R model in Figure 2-21a assumes that the organization needs to remember in which DEPARTMENT each EMPLOYEE currently works, rather than remembering the history of department assignments. Again, the structure of the data model reflects the information the organization needs to remember.)

The second relationship between EMPLOYEE and DEPARTMENT associates each department with the employee who manages that department. The relationship from DEPARTMENT to EMPLOYEE (called Is Managed By in that direction) is a mandatory one, indicating that a department must have exactly one manager. From EMPLOYEE to DEPARTMENT, the relationship (Manages) is optional because a given employee either is or is not a department manager.

Figure 2-21a also shows the unary relationship that associates each employee with his or her supervisor, and vice versa. This relationship records the business rule that

FIGURE 2-21   Examples of
multiple relationships
(a) Employees and departments

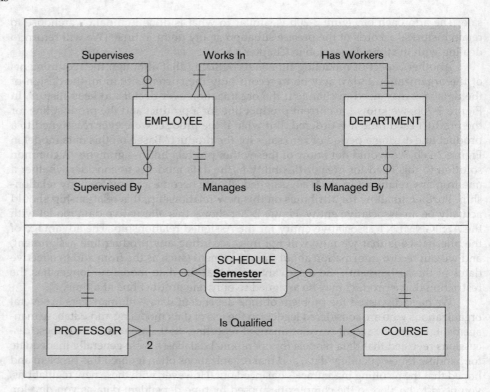

(b) Professors and courses (fixed
lower limit constraint)

each employee may have exactly one supervisor (Supervised By). Conversely, each employee may supervise any number of employees or may not be a supervisor.

The example in Figure 2-21b shows two relationships between the entity types PROFESSOR and COURSE. The relationship Is Qualified associates professors with the courses they are qualified to teach. A given course must have at a minimum two qualified instructors (an example of how to use a fixed value for a minimum or maximum cardinality). This might happen, for example, so that a course is never the "property" of one instructor. Conversely, each instructor must be qualified to teach at least one course (a reasonable expectation).

The second relationship in this figure associates professors with the courses they are actually scheduled to teach during a given semester. Because Semester is a characteristic of the relationship, we place an associative entity, SCHEDULE, between PROFESSOR and COURSE.

One final point about Figure 2-21b: Have you figured out what the identifier is for the SCHEDULE associative entity? Notice that Semester is a partial identifier; thus, the full identifier will be the identifier of PROFESSOR along with the identifier of COURSE as well as Semester. Because such full identifiers for associative entities can become long and complex, it is often recommended that surrogate identifiers be created for each associative entity; so, Schedule ID would be created as the identifier of SCHEDULE, and Semester would be an attribute. What is lost in this case is the explicit business rule that the combination of the PROFESSOR identifier, COURSE identifier, and Semester must be unique for each SCHEDULE instance (because this combination is the identifier of SCHEDULE). Of course, this can be added as another business rule.

Naming and Defining Relationships

In addition to the general guidelines for naming data objects, there are a few special guidelines for naming relationships, which follow:

- A relationship name is a *verb phrase* (such as Assigned To, Supplies, or Teaches). Relationships represent actions being taken, usually in the present tense, so transitive verbs (an action on something) are the most appropriate. A relationship name states the action taken, not the result of the action (e.g., use Assigned To, not Assignment). The name states the essence of the interaction between the participating entity types, not the process involved (e.g., use an Employee is *Assigned To* a project, not an Employee is *Assigning* a project).

- You should *avoid vague names*, such as Has or Is Related To. Use descriptive, powerful verb phrases, often taken from the action verbs found in the definition of the relationship.

There are also some specific guidelines for defining relationships, which follow:

- A relationship definition *explains what action is being taken and possibly why it is important*. It may be important to state who or what does the action, but it is not important to explain how the action is taken. Stating the business objects involved in the relationship is natural, but because the E-R diagram shows what entity types are involved in the relationship and other definitions explain the entity types, you do not have to describe the business objects.

- It may also be important to *give examples to clarify the action*. For example, for a relationship of Registered For between student and course, it may be useful to explain that this covers both on-site and online registration and includes registrations made during the drop/add period.

- The definition should explain any *optional participation*. You should explain what conditions lead to zero associated instances, whether this can happen only when an entity instance is first created, or whether this can happen at any time. For example, "Registered For links a course with the students who have signed up to take the course, and the courses a student has signed up to take. A course will have no students registered for it before the registration period begins and may never have any registered students. A student will not be registered for any courses before the registration period begins and may not register for any classes (or may register for classes and then drop any or all classes)."

- A relationship definition should also *explain the reason for any explicit maximum cardinality* other than many. For example, "Assigned To links an employee with the projects to which that employee is assigned and the employees assigned to a project. Due to our labor union agreement, an employee may not be assigned to more than four projects at a given time." This example, typical of many upper-bound business rules, suggests that maximum cardinalities tend not to be permanent. In this example, the next labor union agreement could increase or decrease this limit. Thus, the implementation of maximum cardinalities must be done to allow changes.

- A relationship definition should *explain any mutually exclusive relationships*. Mutually exclusive relationships are ones for which an entity instance can participate in only one of several alternative relationships. We will show examples of this situation in Chapter 3. For now, consider the following example: "Plays On links an intercollegiate sports team with its student players and indicates on which teams a student plays. Students who play on intercollegiate sports teams cannot also work in a campus job (i.e., a student cannot be linked to both an intercollegiate sports team via Plays On and a campus job via the Works On relationship)." Another example of a mutually exclusive restriction is when an employee cannot both be Supervised By and be Married To the same employee.

- A relationship definition should *explain any restrictions on participation in the relationship*. Mutual exclusivity is one restriction, but there can be others. For example, "Supervised By links an employee with the other employees he or she supervises and links an employee with the other employee who supervises him or her. An employee cannot supervise him- or herself, and an employee cannot supervise other employees if his or her job classification level is below 4."

- A relationship definition should *explain the extent of history that is kept in the relationship*. For example, "Assigned To links a hospital bed with a patient. Only the current bed assignment is stored. When a patient is not admitted, that patient is not assigned to a bed, and a bed may be vacant at any given point in time." Another example of describing history for a relationship is "Places links a customer with the orders he or she has placed with our company and links an order with the associated customer. Only two years of orders are maintained in the database, so not all orders can participate in this relationship."

- A relationship definition should *explain whether an entity instance involved in a relationship instance can transfer participation to another relationship instance.* For example, "Places links a customer with the orders he or she has placed with our company and links an order with the associated customer. An order is not transferable to another customer." Another example is "Categorized As links a product line with the products sold under that heading and links a product to its associated product line. Due to changes in organization structure and product design features, products may be recategorized to a different product line. Categorized As keeps track of only the current product line to which a product is linked."

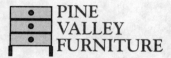

E-R MODELING EXAMPLE: PINE VALLEY FURNITURE COMPANY

Developing an E-R diagram can proceed from one (or both) of two perspectives. With a top-down perspective, the designer proceeds from basic descriptions of the business, including its policies, processes, and environment. This approach is most appropriate for developing a high-level E-R diagram with only the major entities and relationships and with a limited set of attributes (such as just the entity identifiers). With a bottom-up approach, the designer proceeds from detailed discussions with users, and from a detailed study of documents, screens, and other data sources. This approach is necessary for developing a detailed, "fully attributed" E-R diagram.

In this section, we develop a high-level ERD for Pine Valley Furniture Company, based largely on the first of these approaches (see Figure 2-22 for a Microsoft Visio version). For simplicity, we do not show any composite or multivalued attributes (e.g., skill is shown as a separate entity type associated with EMPLOYEE via an associative entity, which allows an employee to have many skills and a skill to be held by many employees).

Figure 2-22 provides many examples of common E-R modeling notations, and hence, it can be used as an excellent review of what you have learned in this chapter. In a moment, we will explain the business rules that are represented in this figure. However, before you read that explanation, one way to use Figure 2-22 is to search for typical E-R model constructs in it, such as one-to-many, binary, or unary relationships. Then, ask yourself why the business data was modeled this way. For example, ask yourself

- Where is a unary relationship, what does it mean, and for what reasons might the cardinalities on it be different in other organizations?
- Why is Includes a one-to many relationship, and why might this ever be different in some other organization?
- Does Includes allow for a product to be represented in the database before it is assigned to a product line (e.g., while the product is in research and development)?
- If there were a different customer contact person for each sales territory in which a customer did business, where in the data model would we place this person's name?
- What is the meaning of the Does Business In associative entity, and why does each Does Business In instance have to be associated with exactly one SALES TERRITORY and one CUSTOMER?
- In what way might Pine Valley change the way it does business that would cause the Supplies associative entity to be eliminated and the relationships around it to change?

Each of these questions is included in Problem and Exercise 2-25 at the end of the chapter, but we suggest you use these now as a way to review your understanding of E-R diagramming.

FIGURE 2-22   Data model for Pine Valley Furniture Company in Microsoft Visio notation

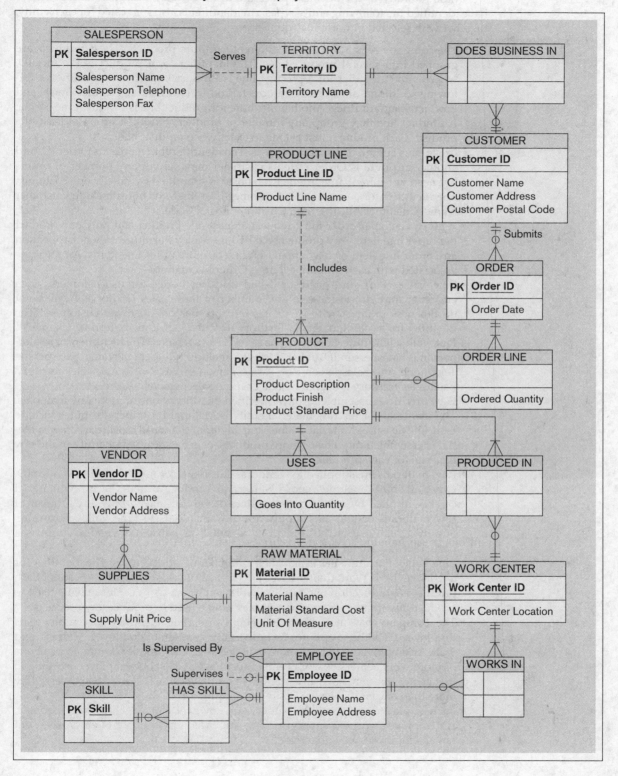

From a study of the business processes at Pine Valley Furniture Company, we have identified the following entity types. An identifier is also suggested for each entity, together with selected important attributes:

- The company sells a number of different furniture products. These products are grouped into several product lines. The identifier for a product is Product ID, whereas the identifier for a product line is Product Line ID. We identify the following additional attributes for product: Product Description, Product Finish, and Product Standard Price. Another attribute for product line is Product Line Name. A product line may group any number of products but must group at least one product. Each product must belong to exactly one product line.

- Customers submit orders for products. The identifier for an order is Order ID, and another attribute is Order Date. A customer may submit any number of orders but need not submit any orders. Each order is submitted by exactly one customer. The identifier for a customer is Customer ID. Other attributes include Customer Name, Customer Address, and Customer Postal Code.

- A given customer order must request at least one product and only one product per order line item. Any product sold by Pine Valley Furniture may not appear on any order line item or may appear on one or more order line items. An attribute associated with each order line item is Ordered Quantity.

- Pine Valley Furniture has established sales territories for its customers. Each customer may do business in any number of these sales territories or may not do business in any territory. A sales territory has one to many customers. The identifier for a sales territory is Territory ID and an attribute is Territory Name.

- Pine Valley Furniture Company has several salespersons. The identifier for a salesperson is Salesperson ID. Other attributes include Salesperson Name, Salesperson Telephone, and Salesperson Fax. A salesperson serves exactly one sales territory. Each sales territory is served by one or more salespersons.

- Each product is assembled from a specified quantity of one or more raw materials. The identifier for the raw material entity is Material ID. Other attributes include Unit Of Measure, Material Name, and Material Standard Cost. Each raw material is assembled into one or more products, using a specified quantity of the raw material for each product.

- Raw materials are supplied by vendors. The identifier for a vendor is Vendor ID. Other attributes include Vendor Name and Vendor Address. Each raw material can be supplied by one or more vendors. A vendor may supply any number of raw materials or may not supply any raw materials to Pine Valley Furniture. Supply Unit Price is the unit price at which a particular vendor supplies a particular raw material.

- Pine Valley Furniture has established a number of work centers. The identifier for a work center is Work Center ID. Another attribute is Work Center Location. Each product is produced in one or more work centers. A work center may be used to produce any number of products or may not be used to produce any products.

- The company has more than 100 employees. The identifier for employee is Employee ID. Other attributes include Employee Name, Employee Address, and Skill. An employee may have more than one skill. Each employee may work in one or more work centers. A work center must have at least one employee working in that center but may have any number of employees. A skill may be possessed by more than one employee or possibly no employees.

- Each employee has exactly one supervisor; however, a manager has no supervisor. An employee who is a supervisor may supervise any number of employees, but not all employees are supervisors.

DATABASE PROCESSING AT PINE VALLEY FURNITURE

The purpose of the data model diagram in Figure 2-22 is to provide a conceptual design for the Pine Valley Furniture Company database. It is important to check the quality of such a design through frequent interaction with the persons who will use the database after it is implemented. An important and often performed type of quality check is to determine whether the E-R model can easily satisfy user requests for data and/or information. Employees at Pine Valley Furniture have many data retrieval and reporting requirements. In this section, we show how a few of these information requirements can be satisfied by database processing against the database shown in Figure 2-22.

We use the SQL database processing language (explained in Chapters 6 and 7) to state these queries. To fully understand these queries, you will need to understand concepts introduced in Chapter 4. However, a few simple queries in this chapter should help you understand the capabilities of a database to answer important organizational questions and give you a jump-start toward understanding SQL queries in Chapter 6 as well as in later chapters.

Showing Product Information

Many different users have a need to see data about the products Pine Valley Furniture produces (e.g., salespersons, inventory managers, and product managers). One specific need is for a salesperson who wants to respond to a request from a customer for a list of products of a certain type. An example of this query is

> List all details for the various computer desks that are stocked by the company.

The data for this query are maintained in the PRODUCT entity (see Figure 2-22). The query scans this entity and displays all the attributes for products that contain the description Computer Desk.

The SQL code for this query is

```
SELECT *
FROM Product
WHERE ProductDescription LIKE "Computer Desk%";
```

Typical output for this query is

PRODUCTID	PRODUCTDESCRIPTION	PRODUCTFINISH	PRODUCTSTANDARDPRICE
3	Computer Desk 48"	Oak	375.00
8	Computer Desk 64"	Pine	450.00

SELECT * FROM Product says display all attributes of PRODUCT entities. The WHERE clause says to limit the display to only products whose description begins with the phrase Computer Desk.

Showing Product Line Information

Another common information need is to show data about Pine Valley Furniture product lines. One specific type of person who needs this information is a product manager. The following is a typical query from a territory sales manager:

> List the details of products in product line 4.

The data for this query are maintained in the PRODUCT entity. As we explain in Chapter 4, the attribute Product Line ID will be added to the PRODUCT entity when a data model in Figure 2-22 is translated into a database that can be accessed via SQL. The query scans the PRODUCT entity and displays all attributes for products that are in the selected product line.

The SQL code for this query is

```
SELECT *
FROM Product
WHERE ProductLineID = 4;
```

Typical output for this query is

PRODUCTID	PRODUCTDESCRIPTION	PRODUCTFINISH	PRODUCTSTANDARDPRICE	PRODUCTONHAND	PRODUCTLINEID
18	Grandfather Clock	Oak	890.0000	0	4
19	Grandfather Clock	Oak	1100.0000	0	4

The explanation of this SQL query is similar to the explanation of the previous one.

Showing Customer Order Status

The previous two queries are relatively simple, involving data from only one table in each case. Often, data from multiple tables are needed in one information request. Although the previous query is simple, we did have to look through the whole database to find the entity and attributes needed to satisfy the request.

To simplify query writing and for other reasons, many database management systems support creating restricted views of a database suitable for the information needs of a particular user. For queries related to customer order status, Pine Valley utilizes such a user view called "Orders for customers," which is created from the segment of an E-R diagram for PVFC shown in Figure 2-23a. This user view allows users to see only CUSTOMER and ORDER entities in the database, and only the attributes of these entities shown in the figure. For the user, there is only one (virtual) table, ORDERS FOR CUSTOMERS, with the listed attributes. As we explain in Chapter 4, the attribute Customer ID will be added to the ORDER entity (as shown in Figure 2-23a). A typical order status query is

How many orders have we received from Value Furniture?

Assuming that all the data we need are pulled together into this one user view, or virtual entity, called OrdersForCustomers, we can simply write the query as follows:

```
SELECT COUNT(Order ID)
FROM OrdersForCustomers
WHERE CustomerName = "Value Furniture";
```

FIGURE 2-23 Two user views for Pine Valley Furniture **(a)** User View 1: Orders for customers

(b) User View 2: Orders for products

Without the user view, we can write the SQL code for this query in several ways. The way we have chosen is to compose a query within a query, called a *subquery*. (We will explain subqueries in Chapter 7, with some diagramming techniques to assist you in composing the query.) The query is performed in two steps. First, the subquery (or inner query) scans the CUSTOMER entity to determine the Customer ID for the customer named Value Furniture. (The ID for this customer is 5, as shown in the output for the previous query.) Then the query (or outer query) scans the ORDER entity and counts the order instances for this customer.

The SQL code for this query without the "Orders for customer" user view is as follows:

```
SELECT COUNT (OrderID)
FROM Order
WHERE CustomerID =
  (SELECT CustomerID
  FROM Customer
  WHERE CustomerName = "Value Furniture");
```

For this example query, using a subquery rather than a view did not make writing the query much more complex.

Typical output for this query using either of the query approaches above is

```
COUNT(ORDERID)
      4
```

Showing Product Sales

Salespersons, territory managers, product managers, production managers, and others have a need to know the status of product sales. One kind of sales question is what products are having an exceptionally strong sales month. Typical of this question is the following query:

> What products have had total sales exceeding $25,000 during the past month (June, 2014)?

This query can be written using the user view "Orders for products," which is created from the segment of an E-R diagram for PVFC shown in Figure 2-23b. Data to respond to the query are obtained from the following sources:

- Order Date from the ORDER entity (to find only orders in the desired month)
- Ordered Quantity for each product on each order from the associative entity ORDER LINE for an ORDER entity in the desired month
- Standard Price for the product ordered from the PRODUCT entity associated with the ORDER LINE entity

For each item ordered during the month of June 2014, the query needs to multiply Ordered Quantity by Product Standard Price to get the dollar value of a sale. For the user, there is only one (virtual) table, ORDERS FOR PRODUCTS, with the listed attributes. The total amount is then obtained for that item by summing all orders. Data are displayed only if the total exceeds $25,000.

The SQL code for this query is beyond the scope of this chapter, because it requires techniques introduced in Chapter 7. We introduce this query now only to suggest the power that a database such as the one shown in Figure 2-22 has to find information for management from detailed data. In many organizations today, users can use a Web browser to obtain the information described here. The programming code associated with a Web page then invokes the required SQL commands to obtain the requested information.

Summary

This chapter has described the fundamentals of modeling data in the organization. Business rules, derived from policies, procedures, events, functions, and other business objects, state constraints that govern the organization and, hence, how data are handled and stored. Using business rules is a powerful way to describe the requirements for an information system, especially a database. The power of business rules results from business rules being core concepts of the business; being able to be expressed in terms familiar to end users; being highly maintainable; and being able to be enforced through automated means, mainly through a database. Good business rules are ones that are declarative, precise, atomic, consistent, expressible, distinct, and business oriented.

Examples of basic business rules are data names and definitions. This chapter explained guidelines for the clear naming and definition of data objects in a business. In terms of conceptual data modeling, names and definitions must be provided for entity types, attributes, and relationships. Other business rules may state constraints on these data objects. These constraints can be captured in a data model and associated documentation.

The data modeling notation most frequently used today is the entity-relationship data model. An E-R model is a detailed, logical representation of the data for an organization. An E-R model is usually expressed in the form of an E-R diagram, which is a graphical representation of an E-R model. The E-R model was introduced by Chen in 1976. However, at the present time, there is no standard notation for E-R modeling. Notations such as those found in Microsoft Visio are used in many CASE tools.

The basic constructs of an E-R model are entity types, relationships, and related attributes. An entity is a person, a place, an object, an event, or a concept in the user environment about which the organization wishes to maintain data. An entity type is a collection of entities that share common properties, whereas an entity instance is a single occurrence of an entity type. A strong entity type is an entity that has its own identifier and can exist without other entities. A weak entity type is an entity whose existence depends on the existence of a strong entity type. Weak entities do not have their own identifier, although they normally have a partial identifier. Weak entities are identified through an identifying relationship with their owner entity type.

An attribute is a property or characteristic of an entity or relationship that is of interest to the organization. There are several types of attributes. A required attribute must have a value for an entity instance, whereas an optional attribute value may be null. A simple attribute is one that has no component parts. A composite attribute is an attribute that can be broken down into component parts. For example, Person Name can be broken down into the parts First Name, Middle Initial, and Last Name.

A multivalued attribute is one that can have multiple values for a single instance of an entity. For example, the attribute College Degree might have multiple values for an individual. A derived attribute is one whose values can be calculated from other attribute values. For example, Average Salary can be calculated from values of Salary for all employees.

An identifier is an attribute that uniquely identifies individual instances of an entity type. Identifiers should be chosen carefully to ensure stability and ease of use. Identifiers may be simple attributes, or they may be composite attributes with component parts.

A relationship type is a meaningful association between (or among) entity types. A relationship instance is an association between (or among) entity instances. The degree of a relationship is the number of entity types that participate in the relationship. The most common relationship types are unary (degree 1), binary (degree 2), and ternary (degree 3).

In developing E-R diagrams, we sometimes encounter many-to-many (and one-to-one) relationships that have one or more attributes associated with the relationship, rather than with one of the participating entity types. In such cases, we might consider converting the relationship to an associative entity. This type of entity associates the instances of one or more entity types and contains attributes that are peculiar to the relationship. Associative entity types may have their own simple identifier, or they may be assigned a composite identifier during logical design.

A cardinality constraint is a constraint that specifies the number of instances of entity B that may (or must) be associated with each instance of entity A. Cardinality constraints normally specify the minimum and maximum number of instances. The possible constraints are mandatory one, mandatory many, optional one, optional many, and a specific number. The minimum cardinality constraint is also referred to as the participation constraint. A minimum cardinality of zero specifies optional participation, whereas a minimum cardinality of one specifies mandatory participation.

Because many databases need to store the value of data over time, modeling time-dependent data is an important part of data modeling. Data that repeat over time may be modeled as multivalued attributes or as separate entity instances; in each case, a time stamp is necessary to identify the relevant date and time for the data value. Sometimes separate relationships need to be included in the data model to represent associations at different points in time. The recent wave of financial reporting disclosure regulations have made it more important to include time-sensitive and historical data in databases.

Chapter Review

Key Terms

Associative entity 76	Entity 65	Identifying owner 67	Simple (or atomic)
Attribute 69	Entity instance 65	Identifying relationship 67	attribute 70
Binary relationship 80	Entity-relationship diagram	Maximum cardinality 84	Strong entity type 66
Business rule 60	(E-R diagram) 56	Minimum cardinality 84	Term 63
Cardinality constraint 84	Entity-relationship model	Multivalued attribute 70	Ternary relationship 81
Composite attribute 70	(E-R model) 56	Optional attribute 69	Time stamp 87
Composite identifier 71	Entity type 65	Relationship instance 75	Unary relationship 78
Degree 78	Fact 63	Relationship type 75	Weak entity type 66
Derived attribute 71	Identifier 71	Required attribute 69	

Review Questions

2-1. Define each of the following terms:
   a. entity type
   b. entity-relationship model
   c. entity instance
   d. attribute
   e. relationship type
   f. strong entity type
   g. multivalued attribute
   h. associative entity
   i. cardinality constraint
   j. weak entity
   k. identifying relationship
   l. derived attribute
   m. business rule

2-2. Match the following terms and definitions.

____composite attribute	a. uniquely identifies entity instances
____associative entity	b. relates instances of a single
____unary relationship	entity type
____weak entity	c. specifies maximum and minimum
____attribute	number of instances
____entity	d. relationship modeled as an entity type
____relationship type	e. association between entity types
____cardinality	f. collection of similar entities
constraint	g. number of participating entity types
____degree	in relationship
____identifier	h. property of an entity
____entity type	i. can be broken into component parts
____ternary	j. depends on the existence of another
____bill-of-materials	entity type
	k. relationship of degree 3
	l. many-to-many unary relationship
	m. person, place, object, concept, event

2-3. Contrast the following terms:
   a. stored attribute; derived attribute
   b. simple attribute; composite attribute
   c. entity type; relationship type
   d. strong entity type; weak entity type
   e. degree; cardinality
   f. required attribute; optional attribute
   g. composite attribute; multivalued attribute
   h. ternary relationship; three binary relationships

2-4. Give four reasons why many system designers believe that data modeling is important and arguably the most important part of the systems development process.

2-5. Give four reasons why a business rules approach is advocated as a new paradigm for specifying information systems requirements.

2-6. Explain where you can find business rules in an organization.

2-7. State six general guidelines for naming data objects in a data model.

2-8. State four criteria for selecting identifiers for entities.

2-9. Why must some identifiers be composite rather than simple?

2-10. State three conditions that suggest the designer should model a relationship as an associative entity type.

2-11. List the four types of cardinality constraints, and draw an example of each.

2-12. Give an example, other than those described in this chapter, of a weak entity type. Why is it necessary to indicate an identifying relationship?

2-13. What is the degree of a relationship? List the three types of relationship degrees described in the chapter and give an example of each.

2-14. Give an example (other than those described in this chapter) for each of the following, and justify your answer:
   a. derived attribute
   b. multivalued attribute
   c. atomic attribute
   d. composite attribute
   e. composite identifier attribute
   f. optional attribute

2-15. Give an example of each of the following, other than those described in this chapter, and clearly explain why your example is this type of relationship and not of some other degree.
   a. ternary relationship
   b. unary relationship

2-16. Give an example of the use of effective (or effectivity) dates as attributes of an entity.

2-17. State a rule that says when to extract an attribute from one entity type and place it in a linked entity type.

2-18. What are the special guidelines for naming relationships?

2-19. In addition to explaining what action is being taken, what else should a relationship definition explain?

2-20. For the Manages relationship in Figure 2-12a, describe one or more situations that would result in different cardinalities on the two ends of this unary relationship. Based on your description for this example, do you think it is always clear simply from an E-R diagram what the business rule is that results in certain cardinalities? Justify your answer.

2-21. Explain the distinction between entity type and entity instance.

2-22. Why is it recommended that every ternary relationship be converted into an associative entity?

2-23. Why does it become important to have a time-series of data in today context of business? Illustrate the same with an example.

2-24. With an example explain how would you identify and differentiate between and entity and an attribute.

2-25. Compare and contrast with examples—Ternary and Binary Relationships.

2-26. What are the key components of Information System Architecture and how important is ISA in the creation of a database?

2-27. What are the important steps to be undertaken in a proper information system planning?

2-28. a. What is system Development Life cycle?
b. What are its core components?

2-29. Compare SDLC with RAD and Agile Software Development and discuss the radical differences in the approaches to IS development.

2-30. How do packaged data models affect the implementation and design of a database?

2-31. What is the three-schema architecture for database development and what is its significance?

Problems and Exercises

2-32. A cellular operator needs a database to keep track of its customers, their subscription plans, and the handsets (mobile phones) that they are using. The E-R diagram in Figure 2-24 illustrates the key entities of interest to the operator and the relationships between them. Based on the figure, answer the following questions and explain the rationale for your response. For each question, identify the element(s) in the E-R diagram that you used to determine your answer.

a. Can a customer have an unlimited number of plans?

b. Can a customer exist without a plan?

c. Is it possible to create a plan without knowing who the customer is?

d. Does the operator want to limit the types of handsets that can be linked to a specific plan type?

e. Is it possible to maintain data regarding a handset without connecting it to a plan?

f. Can a handset be associated with multiple plans?

g. Assume a handset type exists that can utilize multiple operating systems. Could this situation be accommodated within the model included in Figure 2-24?

h. Is the company able to track a manufacturer without maintaining information about its handsets?

i. Can the same operating system be used on multiple handset types?

j. There are two relationships between Customer and Plan. Explain how they differ.

k. Characterize the degree and the cardinalities of the relationship that connects Customer to itself. Explain its meaning.

l. Is it possible to link a handset to a specific customer in a plan with multiple customers?

m. Can the company track a handset without identifying its operating system?

2-33. For each of the descriptions below, perform the following tasks:

i. Identify the degree and cardinalities of the relationship.

ii. Express the relationships in each description graphically with an E-R diagram.

a. A book is identified by its ISBN number, and it has a title, a price, and a date of publication. It is published by a publisher, which has its own ID number and a name.

FIGURE 2-24   Diagram for Problem and Exercise 2-32

Each book has exactly one publisher, but one publisher typically publishes multiple books over time.

b. A book (see 2a) is written by one or multiple authors. Each author is identified by an author number and has a name and date of birth. Each author has either one or multiple books; in addition, occasionally data are needed regarding prospective authors who have not yet published any books.

c. In the context specified in 2a and 2b, better information is needed regarding the relationship between a book and its authors. Specifically, it is important to record the percentage of the royalties that belongs to a specific author, whether or not a specific author is a lead author of the book, and each author's position in the sequence of the book's authors.

d. A book (see 2a) can be part of a series, which is also identified as a book and has its own ISBN number. One book can belong to several sets, and a set consists of at least one but potentially many books.

e. A piano manufacturer wants to keep track of all the pianos it makes individually. Each piano has an identifying serial number and a manufacturing completion date. Each instrument represents exactly one piano model, all of which have an identification number and a name. In addition, the company wants to maintain information about the designer of the model. Over time, the company often manufactures thousands of pianos of a certain model, and the model design is specified before any single piano exists.

f. A piano manufacturer (see 2e) employs piano technicians who are responsible for inspecting the instruments before they are shipped to the customers. Each piano is inspected by at least two technicians (identified by their employee number). For each separate inspection, the company needs to record its date and a quality evaluation grade.

g. The piano technicians (see 2f) have a hierarchy of reporting relationships: Some of them have supervisory responsibilities in addition to their inspection role and have multiple other technicians report to them. The supervisors themselves report to the chief technician of the company.

h. A vendor builds multiple types of tablet computers. Each has a type identification number and a name. The key specifications for each type include amount of storage space and display type. The company uses multiple processor types, exactly one of which is used for a specific tablet computer type; obviously, the same processor can be used in multiple types of tablets. Each processor has a manufacturer and a manufacturer's unique code that identifies it.

i. Each individual tablet computer manufactured by the vendor (see 2h) is identified by the type identification number and a serial number that is unique within the type identification. The vendor wants to maintain information about when each tablet is shipped to a customer.

j. Each of the tablet computer types (see 2h) has a specific operating system. Each technician the company employs is certified to assemble a specific tablet type–operating system combination. The validity of a certification starts on the day the employee passes a certification examination for the combination, and the certification is valid for a specific period of time that varies depending on tablet type–operating system combination.

2-34. Answer the following questions concerning Figure 2-22:
a. Where is a unary relationship, what does it mean, and for what reasons might the cardinalities on it be different in other organizations?
b. Why is Includes a one-to many relationship, and why might this ever be different in some other organization?
c. Does Includes allow for a product to be represented in the database before it is assigned to a product line (e.g., while the product is in research and development)?
d. If there is a rating of the competency for each skill an employee possesses, where in the data model would we place this rating?

e. What is the meaning of the DOES BUSINESS IN associative entity, and why does each DOES BUSINESS IN instance have to be associated with exactly one TERRITORY and one CUSTOMER?
f. In what way might Pine Valley change the way it does business that would cause the Supplies associative entity to be eliminated and the relationships around it to change?

2-35. There is a bulleted list associated with Figure 2-22 that describes the entities and their relationships in Pine Valley Furniture. For each of the 10 points in the list, identify the subset of Figure 2-22 described by that point.

2-36. You may have been assigned a CASE or a drawing tool to develop conceptual data models. Using this tool, attempt to redraw all the E-R diagrams in this chapter. What difficulties did you encounter? What E-R notations did not translate well to your tool? How did you incorporate the E-R notation that did not directly translate into the tool's notation?

2-37. Consider the two E-R diagrams in Figure 2-25, which represent a database of community service agencies and volunteers in two different cities (A and B). For each of the following three questions, place a check mark under City A, City B, or Can't Tell for the choice that is the best answer.

	City A	City B	Can't Tell
a. Which city maintains data about only those volunteers who currently assist agencies?			
b. In which city would it be possible for a volunteer to assist more than one agency?			
c. In which city would it be possible for a volunteer to change which agency or agencies he or she assists?			

2-38. The entity type STUDENT has the following attributes: Student Name, Address, Phone, Age, Activity, and No of Years. Activity represents some campus-based student activity, and No of Years represents the number of years the student has engaged in this activity. A given student may engage in more than one activity. Draw an ERD for this situation. What attribute or attributes did you designate as the identifier for the STUDENT entity? Why?

2-39. Are associative entities also weak entities? Why or why not? If yes, is there anything special about their "weakness"?

2-40. Because Visio does not explicitly show associative entities, it is not clear in Figure 2-22 which entity types are associative. List the associative entities in this figure. Why are there so many associative entities in Figure 2-22?

2-41. Figure 2-26 shows a grade report that is mailed to students at the end of each semester. Prepare an ERD reflecting the data contained in the grade report. Assume that

FIGURE 2-25 Diagram for Problem and Exercise 2-37

FIGURE 2-26 Grade report

```
                    MILLENNIUM COLLEGE
                    GRADE REPORT
                    FALL SEMESTER 2015

    NAME:              Emily Williams         ID: 268300458
    CAMPUS ADDRESS:    208 Brooks Hall
    MAJOR:             Information Systems
```

COURSE ID	TITLE	INSTRUCTOR NAME	INSTRUCTOR LOCATION	GRADE
IS 350	Database Mgt.	Codd	B104	A
IS 465	System Analysis	Parsons	B317	B

each course is taught by one instructor. Also, draw this data model using the tool you have been told to use in the course. Explain what you chose for the identifier of each entity type on your ERD.

2-42. Add minimum and maximum cardinality notation to each of the following figures, as appropriate:
   a. Figure 2-5
   b. Figure 2-10a
   c. Figure 2-11b
   d. Figure 2-12 (all parts)
   e. Figure 2-13c
   f. Figure 2-14

2-43. The Is Married To relationship in Figure 2-12a would seem to have an obvious answer in Problem and Exercise 2-42d—that is, until time plays a role in modeling data. Draw a data model for the PERSON entity type and the Is Married To relationship for each of the following variations by showing the appropriate cardinalities and including, if necessary, any attributes:
   a. All we need to know is who a person is currently married to, if anyone. (This is likely what you represented in your answer to Problem and Exercise 2-42d.)
   b. We need to know who a person has ever been married to, if anyone.
   c. We need to know who a person has ever been married to, if anyone, as well as the date of their marriage and the date, if any, of the dissolution of their marriage.
   d. The same situation as in c, but now assume (which you likely did not do in c) that the same two people can remarry each other after a dissolution of a prior marriage to each other.
   e. In history, and even in some cultures today, there may be no legal restriction on the number of people to whom one can be currently married. Does your answer to part c of this Problem and Exercise handle this situation or must you make some changes (if so, draw a new ERD).

2-44. Figure 2-27 represents a situation of students who attend and work in schools and who also belong to certain clubs that are located in different schools. Study this diagram carefully to try to discern what business rules are represented.
   a. You will notice that cardinalities are not included on the Works For relationship. State a business rule for

FIGURE 2-27 E-R diagram for Problem and Exercise 2-44

this relationship, and then represent this rule with the cardinalities that match your rule.
   b. State a business rule that would make the Located In relationship redundant (i.e., where the school in which a club is located can be surmised or derived in some way from other relationships).
   c. Suppose a student could work for only a school the student attends but might not work. Would the Works For relationship still be necessary, or could you represent whether a student works for the school she attends in some other way (if so, how)?
   d. Based on the rules of the ERD in Figure 2-27, is it possible for a student to belong to a club located in a school that the student does not attend? Explain.

2-45. Figure 2-28 shows two diagrams (A and B), both of which are legitimate ways to represent that a stock has a history of many prices. Which of the two diagrams do you consider a better way to model this situation and why?

2-46. Modify Figure 2-11a to model the following additional information requirements: The training director decides for each employee who completes each class who (what employees) should be notified of the course completion. The training director needs to keep track of which employees are notified about each course completion by a student. The date of notification is the only attribute recorded about this notification.

2-47. Review Figure 2-8 and Figure 2-22.
   a. Identify any attributes in Figure 2-22 that might be composite attributes but are not shown that way. Justify your suggestions. Redraw the ERD to reflect any changes you suggest.

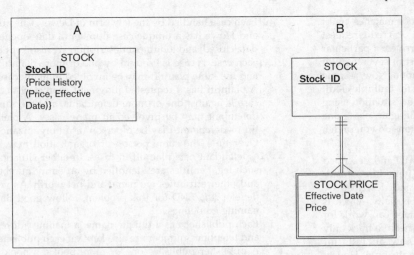

FIGURE 2-28 E-R diagram for
Problem and Exercise 2-45

b. Identify any attributes in Figure 2-22 that might be multivalued attributes but are not shown that way. Justify your suggestions. Redraw the ERD to reflect any changes you suggest.

c. Is it possible for the same attribute to be both composite and multivalued? If no, justify your answer; if yes, give an example. (Hint: Consider the CUSTOMER attributes in Figure 2-22.)

2-48. Draw an ERD for each of the following situations. (If you believe that you need to make additional assumptions, clearly state them for each situation.) Draw the same situation using the tool you have been told to use in the course.

a. A company has a number of employees. The attributes of EMPLOYEE include Employee ID (identifier), Name, Address, and Birthdate. The company also has several projects. Attributes of PROJECT include Project ID (identifier), Project Name, and Start Date. Each employee may be assigned to one or more projects or may not be assigned to a project. A project must have at least one employee assigned and may have any number of employees assigned. An employee's billing rate may vary by project, and the company wishes to record the applicable billing rate (Billing Rate) for each employee when assigned to a particular project. Do the attribute names in this description follow the guidelines for naming attributes? If not, suggest better names. Do you have any associative entities on your ERD? If so, what are the identifiers for those associative entities? Does your ERD allow a project to be created before it has any employees assigned to it? Explain. How would you change your ERD if the Billing Rate could change in the middle of a project?

b. A laboratory has several chemists who work on one or more projects. Chemists also may use certain kinds of equipment on each project. Attributes of CHEMIST include Employee ID (identifier), Name, and Phone No. Attributes of PROJECT include Project ID (identifier) and Start Date. Attributes of EQUIPMENT include Serial No and Cost. The organization wishes to record Assign Date—that is, the date when a given equipment item was assigned to a particular chemist working on a specified project. A chemist must be assigned to at least one project and one equipment item. A given

equipment item need not be assigned, and a given project need not be assigned either a chemist or an equipment item. Provide good definitions for all of the relationships in this situation.

c. A college course may have one or more scheduled sections or may not have a scheduled section. Attributes of COURSE include Course ID, Course Name, and Units. Attributes of SECTION include Section Number and Semester ID. Semester ID is composed of two parts: Semester and Year. Section Number is an integer (such as 1 or 2) that distinguishes one section from another for the same course but does not uniquely identify a section. How did you model SECTION? Why did you choose this way versus alternative ways to model SECTION?

d. A hospital has a large number of registered physicians. Attributes of PHYSICIAN include Physician ID (the identifier) and Specialty. Patients are admitted to the hospital by physicians. Attributes of PATIENT include Patient ID (the identifier) and Patient Name. Any patient who is admitted must have exactly one admitting physician. A physician may optionally admit any number of patients. Once admitted, a given patient must be treated by at least one physician. A particular physician may treat any number of patients, or may not treat any patients. Whenever a patient is treated by a physician, the hospital wishes to record the details of the treatment (Treatment Detail). Components of Treatment Detail include Date, Time, and Results. Did you draw more than one relationship between physician and patient? Why or why not? Did you include hospital as an entity type? Why or why not? Does your ERD allow for the same patient to be admitted by different physicians over time? How would you include on the ERD the need to represent the date on which a patient is admitted for each time he or she is admitted?

e. The loan office in a bank receives from various parties requests to investigate the credit status of a customer. Each credit request is identified by a Request ID and is described by a Request Date and Requesting Party Name. The loan office also received results of credit checks. A credit check is identified by a Credit Check ID and is described by the Credit Check Date and the Credit Rating. The loan office matches credit requests with credit check results. A credit request may be recorded before its result arrives; a particular credit result may be used in support of several credit requests. Draw an ERD for this situation. Now, assume that credit results may not be reused for multiple credit requests. Redraw the ERD for this new situation using two entity types, and then redraw it again using one entity type. Which of these two versions do you prefer, and why?

f. Companies, identified by Company ID and described by Company Name and Industry Type, hire consultants, identified by Consultant ID and described by Consultant Name and Consultant Specialty, which is multivalued. Assume that a consultant can work for only one company at a time, and we need to track only current consulting engagements. Draw an ERD for this situation. Now, consider a new attribute, Hourly Rate, which is the rate a consultant charges a company for each hour of his or her services. Redraw the ERD to include this new attribute. Now, consider that each time a consultant works for a company, a contract is written describing the terms for this consulting engagement. Contract is identified by a composite identifier of Company ID, Consultant ID, and Contract Date. Assuming that a consultant can still work for only one company at a time, redraw the ERD for this new situation. Did you move any attributes to different entity types in this latest situation? As a final situation, now consider that although a consultant can work for only one company at a time, we now need to keep the complete history of all consulting engagements for each consultant and company. Draw an ERD for this final situation. Explain why these different changes to the situation led to different data models, if they did.

g. An art museum owns a large volume of works of art. Each work of art is described by an item code (identifier), title, type, and size; size is further composed of height, width, and weight. A work of art is developed by an artist, but the artist for some works is unknown. An artist is described by an artist ID (identifier), name, date of birth, and date of death (which is null for still living artists). Only data about artists for works currently owned by the museum are kept in the database. At any point in time, a work of art is either on display at the museum, held in storage, away from the museum as part of a traveling show, or on loan to another gallery. If on display at the museum, a work of art is also described by its location within the museum. A traveling show is described by a show ID (identifier), the city in which the show is currently appearing, and the start and end dates of the show. Many of the museum works may be part of a given show, and only active shows with at least one museum work of art need be represented in the database. Finally, another gallery is described by a gallery ID (identifier), name, and city. The museum wants to retain a complete history of loaning a work of art to other galleries, and each time a work is loaned, the museum wants to know the date the work was loaned and the date it was returned. As you develop the ERD for this problem, follow good data naming guidelines.

h. Each case handled by the law firm of Dewey, Cheetim, and Howe has a unique case number; a date opened, date closed, and judgment description are also kept on each case. A case is brought by one or more plaintiffs, and the same plaintiff may be involved in many cases. A plaintiff has a requested judgment characteristic. A case is against one or more defendants, and the same defendant may be involved in many cases. A plaintiff or defendant may be a person or an organization. Over time, the same person or organization may be a defendant or a plaintiff in cases. In either situation, such legal entities are identified by an entity number, and other attributes are name and net worth. As you develop the ERD for this problem, follow good data naming guidelines.

i. Each publisher has a unique name; a mailing address and telephone number are also kept on each publisher. A publisher publishes one or more books; a book is published by exactly one publisher. A book is identified by its ISBN, and other attributes are title, price, and number of pages. Each book is written by one or more authors; an author writes one or more books, potentially for different publishers. Each author is uniquely described by an author ID, and we know each author's name and address. Each author is paid a certain royalty rate on each book he or she authors, which potentially varies for each book and for each author. An author receives a separate royalty check for each book he or she writes. Each check is identified by its check number, and we also keep track of the date and amount of each check. As you develop the ERD for this problem, follow good data naming guidelines.

2-49. Assume that at Pine Valley Furniture, each product (described by product number, description, and cost) is composed of three components (described by component number, description, and unit of measure), and components are used to make one or many products. In addition, assume that components are used to make other components, and that raw materials are also considered to be components. In both cases of components, we need to keep track of how many components go into making something else. Draw an ERD for this situation, and place minimum and maximum cardinalities on the diagram. Also, draw a data model for this situation using the tool you have been told to use in your course.

2-50. Emerging Electric wishes to create a database with the following entities and attributes:
- Customer, with attributes Customer ID, Name, Address (Street, City, State, Zip Code), and Telephone
- Location, with attributes Location ID, Address (Street, City, State, Zip Code), and Type (values of Business or Residential)
- Rate, with attributes Rate Class and RatePerKWH

After interviews with the owners, you have come up with the following business rules:
- Customers can have one or more locations.
- Each location can have one or more rates, depending on the time of day.

Draw an ERD for this situation and place minimum and maximum cardinalities on the diagram. Also, draw a data model for this situation using the tool you have been told to use in your course. State any assumptions that you have made.

2-51. Each semester, each student must be assigned an adviser who counsels students about degree requirements and helps students register for classes. Each student must register for classes with the help of an adviser, but if the student's assigned adviser is not available, the student may register with any adviser. We must keep track of students, the assigned adviser for each, and the name of the adviser with whom the student registered for the current term. Represent this situation of students and advisers with an E-R diagram. Also, draw a data model for this situation using the tool you have been told to use in your course.

2-52. In the chapter, when describing Figure 2-4a, it was argued that the Received and Summarizes relationships and TREASURER entity were not necessary. Within the context of this explanation, this is true. Now, consider a slightly different situation. Suppose it is necessary, for compliance purposes (e.g., Sarbanes-Oxley compliance), to know when each expense report was produced and which officers (not just the treasurer) received each expense report and when each signed off on that report. Redraw Figure 2-4a, now including any attributes and relationships required for this revised situation.

2-53. Virtual Campus (VC) is a social media firm that specializes in creating virtual meeting places for students, faculty, staff, and others associated with different college campuses. VC was started as a student project in a database class at Cyber University, an online polytechnic college, with headquarters in a research park in Dayton, Ohio. The following parts of this exercise relate to different phases in the development of the database VC now provides to client institutions to support a threaded discussion application. Your assignment is to draw an ERD to represent each phase of the development of the VC database and to answer questions that clients raised about the capabilities (business rules) of the database in each phase. The description of each phase will state specific requirements as seen by clients, but other requirements may be implied or possibly should be implemented in the design slightly differently than the clients might see them, so be careful to not limit yourself to only the specifics provided.

    a. The first phase was fairly simplistic. Draw an ERD to represent this initial phase, described by the following:
- A client may maintain several social media sites (e.g., for intercollegiate sports, academics, local food and beverage outlets, or a specific student organization). Each site has attributes of Site Identifier, Site Name, Site Purpose, Site Administrator, and Site Creation Date.
- Any person may become a participant in any public site. Persons need to register with the client's social media presence to participate in any site, and when they do the person is assigned a Person Identifier; the person provides his or her Nickname and Status (e.g., student, faculty, staff, or friend, or possibly several such values); the Date Joined the site is automatically generated. A person may also include other information, which is available to other persons on the site; this information includes Name, Twitter Handle, Facebook Page link, and SMS Contact Number. Anyone may register (no official association with the client is necessary).
- An account is created each time a person registers to use a particular site. An account is described by an Account ID, User Name, Password, Date Created, Date Terminated, and Date/Time the person most recently used that account.
- Using an account, a person creates a posting, or message, for others to read. A posting has a Posting Date/Time and Content. The person posting the message may also add a Date when the posting should be made invisible to other users.
- A person is permitted to have multiple accounts, each of which is for only one site.
- A person, over time, may create multiple postings from an account.

    b. After the first phase, a representative from one of the initial clients asked if it were possible for a person to have multiple accounts on the same site. Answer this question based on your ERD from part a of this exercise. If your answer is yes, could you enforce via the ERD a business rule of only one account per site per person, or would other than a data modeling requirement be necessary? If your answer is no, justify how your ERD enforces this rule.

    c. The database for the first phase certainly provided only the basics. VC quickly determined that two additional features needed to be added to the database design, as follows (draw a revised ERD to represent the expanded second phase database):
- From their accounts, persons might respond to postings with an additional posting. Thus, postings may form threads, or networks of response postings, which then may have other response postings, and so forth.
- It also became important to track not only postings but also when persons from their accounts read a posting. This requirement is needed to produce site usage reports concerning when postings are made, when they are read and by whom, frequency of reading, etc.

    d. Clients liked the improvements to the social media application supported by the database from the second phase. How useful the social media application is depends, in part, on questions administrators at a client organization might be able to answer from inquiries against the database using reports or online queries. For each of the example client inquiries that follow, justify for your answer to part c whether your database could provide answers to that inquiry (if you already know SQL, you could provide justification by showing the appropriate SQL query; otherwise, explain the entities, attributes, and relationships from your ERD in part c that would be necessary to produce the desired result):
- How many postings has each person created for each site?
- Which postings appear under multiple sites?
- Has any person created a posting and then responded to his or her own posting before any other person has read the original posting?
- Which sites, if any, have no associated postings?

    e. The third phase of database development by VC dealt with one of the hazards of social media sites— irresponsible, objectionable, or harmful postings (e.g., bullying or inappropriate language). So for phase three, draw a revised ERD to the ERD you drew for the second phase to represent the following:

- Any person from one of their accounts may file a complaint about any posting. Most postings, of course, are legitimate and not offensive, but some postings generate lots of complaints. Each complaint has a Complaint ID, Date/Time the complaint is posted, the Content of the complaint, and a Resolution Code. Complaints and the status of resolution are visible to only the person making the complaint and to the site administrator.
- The administrator for the site about which a complaint has been submitted (not necessarily a person in the database, and each site may have a different administrator) reviews complaints. If a complaint is worthy, the associated offensive posting is marked as removed from the site; however, the posting stays in the database so that special reports can be produced to summarize complaints in various ways, such as by person, so that persons who make repeated objectionable postings can be dealt with. In any case, the site administrator after his or her review fills in the date of resolution and the Resolution Code value for the complaint. As stated, only the site administrator and the complaining person, not other persons with accounts on the site, see complaints for postings on the associated site. Postings marked as removed as well as responses to these postings are then no longer seen by the other persons.

f. You may see various additional capabilities for the VC database. However, in the final phase you will consider in this exercise, you are to create an expansion of the ERD you drew for phase three to handle the following:
- Not all sites are public; that is, open for anyone to create an account. A person may create one or more sites as well as groups, and then invite other persons in a group to be part of a site he or she has created. A group has a Group ID, Group Name, Date Created, Date Terminated, Purpose, and Number of Members.
- The person creating a "private" site is then, by default, the site administrator for that site.
- Only the members of a group associated with a private site may then create accounts for that site, post to that site, and perform any other activities for that site.

2-54. After completing a course in database management, you are asked to develop a preliminary ERD for a symphony orchestra. You discover the entity types that should be included as shown in Table 2-3.

During further discussions you discover the following:
- A concert season schedules one or more concerts. A particular concert is scheduled for only one concert season.
- A concert includes the performance of one or more compositions. A composition may be performed at one or more concerts or may not be performed.
- For each concert there is one conductor. A conductor may conduct any number of concerts or may not conduct any concerts.
- Each composition may require one or more soloists or may not require a soloist. A soloist may perform one or more compositions at a given concert or may not perform any composition. The symphony orchestra wishes to record the date when a soloist last performed a given composition (Date Last Performed).

Draw an ERD to represent what you have discovered. Identify a business rule in this description and explain how this business rule is modeled on the E-R diagram. Also draw a data model for this situation using the tool you have been told to use in your course.

2-55. Obtain several common user views such as a credit card receipt, credit card statement, and annual summary or some other common document from one organization with which you interact.
a. Prepare an ERD for one of these documents. Also prepare a data model for this document, using the tool you have been told to use in your course.
b. Prepare an ERD for another of these documents. Also prepare a data model for this document, using the tool you have been told to use in your course.
c. Do you find the same entities, attributes, and relationships in the two ERDs you developed for parts a and b? What differences do you find in modeling the same data entities, attributes, and relationships between the two ERDs? Can you combine the two ERDs into one ERD for which the original two are subsets? Do you encounter any issues in trying to combine the ERDs? Suggest some issues that might arise if two different data modelers had independently developed the two data models.
d. How might you use data naming and definition standards to overcome the issues you identified in part c?

TABLE 2-3	Entity Types for Problem and Exercise 2-54
CONCERT SEASON	The season during which a series of concerts will be performed. Identifier is Opening Date, which includes Month, Day, and Year.
CONCERT	A given performance of one or more compositions. Identifier is Concert Number. Another important attribute is Concert Date, which consists of the following: Month, Day, Year, and Time. Each concert typically has more than one concert date.
COMPOSITION	Compositions to be performed at each concert. Identifier is Composition ID, which consists of the following: Composer Name and Composition Name. Another attribute is Movement ID, which consists of two parts: Movement Number and Movement Name. Many, but not all, compositions have multiple movements.
CONDUCTOR	Person who will conduct the concert. Identifier is Conductor ID. Another attribute is Conductor Name.
SOLOIST	Solo artist who performs a given composition on a particular concert. Identifier is Soloist ID. Another attribute is Soloist Name.

2-56. Draw an ERD for the following situation (Batra et al., 1988). Also, develop the list of words for qualifiers and classes that you use to form attribute names. Explain why you chose the words on your list. Also, draw a data model for this situation using the tool you have been told to use in your course.

Projects, Inc., is an engineering firm with approximately 500 employees. A database is required to keep track of all employees, their skills, projects assigned, and departments worked in. Every employee has a unique number assigned by the firm and is required to store his or her name and date of birth. If an employee is currently married to another employee of Projects, Inc., the date of marriage and who is married to whom must be stored; however, no record of marriage is required if an employee's spouse is not also an employee. Each employee is given a job title (e.g., engineer, secretary, and so on). An employee does only one type of job at any given time, and we only need to retain information for an employee's current job.

There are 11 different departments, each with a unique name. An employee can report to only 1 department. Each department has a phone number.

To procure various kinds of equipment, each department deals with many vendors. A vendor typically supplies equipment to many departments. We are required to store the name and address of each vendor and the date of the last meeting between a department and a vendor.

Many employees can work on a project. An employee can work on many projects (e.g., Southwest Refinery, California Petrochemicals, and so on) but can only be assigned to at most one project in a given city. For each city, we are interested in its state and population. An employee can have many skills (preparing material requisitions, checking drawings, and so on), but she or he may use only a given set of skills on a particular project. (For example, an employee MURPHY may prepare requisitions for the Southwest Refinery project and prepare requisitions as well as check drawings for California Petrochemicals.) Employees use each skill that they possess in at least one project. Each skill is assigned a number, and we must store a short description of each skill. Projects are distinguished by project numbers, and we must store the estimated cost of each project.

2-57. Draw an ERD for the following situation. (State any assumptions you believe you have to make in order to develop a complete diagram.) Also, draw a data model for this situation using the tool you have been told to use in your course: Stillwater Antiques buys and sells one-of-a-kind antiques of all kinds (e.g., furniture, jewelry, china, and clothing). Each item is uniquely identified by an item number and is also characterized by a description, asking price, condition, and open-ended comments. Stillwater works with many different individuals, called clients, who sell items to and buy items from the store. Some clients only sell items to Stillwater, some only buy items, and some others both sell and buy. A client is identified by a client number and is also described by a client name and client address. When Stillwater sells an item in stock to a client, the owners want to record the commission paid, the actual selling price, sales tax (tax of zero indicates a tax exempt sale), and date sold. When Stillwater buys an item from a client, the owners want to record the purchase cost, date purchased, and condition at time of purchase.

2-58. Draw an ERD for the following situation. (State any assumptions you believe you have to make in order to develop a complete diagram.) Also, draw a data model for this situation using the tool you have been told to use in your course: The A. M. Honka School of Business operates international business programs in 10 locations throughout Europe. The school had its first class of 9,000 graduates in 1965. The school keeps track of each graduate's student number, name when a student, country of birth, current country of citizenship, current name, and current address, as well as the name of each major the student completed. (Each student has one or two majors.) To maintain strong ties to its alumni, the school holds various events around the world. Events have a title, date, location, and type (e.g., reception, dinner, or seminar). The school needs to keep track of which graduates have attended which events. For an attendance by a graduate at an event, a comment is recorded about information school officials learned from that graduate at that event. The school also keeps in contact with graduates by mail, e-mail, telephone, and fax interactions. As with events, the school records information learned from the graduate from each of these contacts. When a school official knows that he or she will be meeting or talking to a graduate, a report is produced showing the latest information about that graduate and the information learned during the past two years from that graduate from all contacts and events the graduate attended.

2-59. Wally Los Gatos, owner of Wally's Wonderful World of Wallcoverings, Etc., has hired you as a consultant to design a database management system for his new online marketplace for wallpaper, draperies, and home decorating accessories. He would like to track sales, prospective sales, and customers. Ultimately, he'd like to become the leading online retailer for all things related to home decorating. During an initial meeting with Wally, you and Wally developed a list of business requirements to begin the design of an E-R model for the database to support his business needs.

a. Wally was called away unexpectedly after only a short discussion with you, due to a sticky situation with the pre-pasted line of wallcoverings he sells. He gave you only a brief description of his needs and asked that you fill in details for what you expect he might need for these requirements. Wally expected to be away for only a short time, so he asked that you go ahead with some first suggestions for the database; but he said "keep it basic for now, we'll do the faux finishes later." Before Wally left, he requested the following features for his system:

- At a basic level, Wally needs to track his customers (both those who have bought and those Wally has identified as prospective buyers based on his prior brick-and-mortar business outlets), the products he sells, and the products they have bought.

- Wally wants a variety of demographic data about his customers so he can better understand who is buying his products. He'd like a few suggestions from you on appropriate demographic data, but he definitely wants to know customer interests, hobbies, and activities that might help him proactively suggest products customers might like.

b. True to his word, Wally soon returned, but said he could only step into the room for a short time because the new Tesla he had ordered had been delivered, and he wanted to take it for a test drive. But before he and his friend Elon left, he had a few questions that he wanted the database to allow him to answer, including the following (you can answer Wally with an SQL query that would produce the result, because Wally is proficient in SQL, or by explaining the entities, attributes, and relationships that would allow the questions to be answered):
   • Would the database be able to tell him which other customers had bought the same product a given customer or prospective customer had bought or was considering buying?
   • Would the database be able to tell him even something deeper, that is, what other products other customers bought who also bought the product the customer just bought (that is, an opportunity for cross-selling)?
   • Would he be able to find other customers with at least three interests that overlap with those of a given customer so that he can suggest to these other customers other products they might want to purchase?

Prepare queries or explanations to demonstrate for Wally why your database design in part a of this exercise can support these needs, or draw a revised design to support these specific questions.

c. Wally is thrilled with his new Tesla and returns from the test drive eager to expand his business to now pay for this new car. The test drive was so invigorating that it helped him to generate more ideas for the new online shopping site, including the following requirements:
   • Wally wants to be able to suggest products for customers to buy. Wally knows that most of the products he sells have similar alternatives that a customer might want to consider. Similarity is fairly subtle, so he or his staff would have to specify for each product what other products, if any, are similar.
   • Wally also thinks that he can improve sales by reminding customers about products they have previously considered or viewed when on his online marketplace.

Unfortunately, Wally's administrative assistant, Helen, in her hunt for Wally, knocked on the door and told Wally that his first-born child, Julia, had just come in asking to see her father so that she could show him her new tattoo, introduce him to her new "goth" boyfriend, and let him know about her new life plans. This declaration, obviously, got Wally's attention. Wally left abruptly, but asked that you fill in the blanks for these new database requirements.

d. Fortunately, Wally's assistant was just kidding, and the staff had actually thrown a surprise birthday party for Wally. They needed Wally in the staff dining room quickly before the ice cream melted and the festive draperies adorning the table of presents had to be returned to the warehouse for shipment to Rio for display at the summer Olympics. Now overjoyed by the warm reception from his trusted associates, Wally

was even more enthusiastic about making his company successful. Wally came in with two additional requirements for this database:
   • Wally had learned the hard way that in today's world, some of his customers have multiple homes or properties for which they order his products. Thus, different orders for the same customer may go to different addresses, but several orders for the same customer often go to the same address.
   • Customers also like to see what other people think about products they are considering to buy. So, the database needs to be able to allow customers to rate and review products they buy, and for other customers considering purchasing a product to see the reviews and ratings from those who have already purchased the product being considered. Wally also wants to know what reviews customers have viewed, so he can tell which reviews might be influencing purchases.

Yet again, Wally has to leave the meeting, this time because it is time for his weekly pickle ball game, and he doesn't want to brush off his partner in the ladder tournament, which he and partner now lead. He asks that you go ahead and work on adding these requirements to the database, and he'll be back after he and his partner hang their new trophy in Wally's den.

e. Although still a little sweaty and not in his normal dapper business attire, Wally triumphantly hobbled back to the meeting room. Wally's thigh was wrapped in what seemed to be a whole reel of painter's tape (because he didn't have any sports tape), nursing his agony of victory. Before limping off to his doctor, Wally, ever engaged in his business, wanted to make sure your database design could handle the following needs:
   • One of the affinities people have for buying is what other people in their same geographical area are buying (a kind of "keep up with the Jones" phenomenon). Justify to Wally why your database design can support this requirement, or suggest how the design can be changed to meet this need.
   • Customers want to search for possible products based on categories and characteristics, such as paint brushes, lamps, bronze color, etc.
   • Customers want to have choices for the sequence in which products are shown to them, such as by rating, popularity, and price.

Justify to Wally why your database design can support these needs, or redesign your database to support these additional requirements.

2-60. Doctors Information Technology (DocIT) is an IT services company supporting medical practices with a variety of computer technologies to make medical offices more efficient and less costly to run. Medical offices are rapidly becoming automated with electronic medical records, automated insurance claims processing and prescription submissions, patient billing, and other typical aspects of medical practices. In this assignment you will address only insurance claims processing; however, what you develop must be able to be generalized and expanded to these other areas of a medical practice. Your assignment is to draw an ERD to represent each phase of the development of an insurance claims processing database and to answer questions that clients might raise about the capabilities of the application the database supports in each phase.

a. The first phase deals with a few core elements. Draw an ERD to represent this initial phase, described by the following:

- A patient is assigned a patient ID and you need to keep track of a patient's gender, date of birth, name, current address, and list of allergies.
- A staff member (doctor, nurse, physician's assistant, etc.) has a staff ID, job title, gender, name, address, and list of degrees or qualifications.
- A patient may be included in the database even if no staff member has ever seen the patient (e.g., family member of another patient or a transfer from another medical practice). Similarly, some staff members never have a patient contact that requires a claim to be processed (e.g., a receptionist greeting a patient does not generate a claim).
- A patient sees a staff member via an appointment. An appointment has an appointment ID, a date and time of when the appointment is scheduled or when it occurred as well as a date and time when the appointment was made, and a list of reasons for the appointment.

b. As was noted in part a of this exercise the first phase, information about multiple members of the same family may need to be stored in the database because they are all patients. Actually, there is a broader need. A medical practice may need to recognize various people related to a particular patient (e.g., spouse, child, caregiver, power of attorney, an administrator at a nursing home, etc.) who can see patient information and make emergency medical decisions on behalf of the patient. Augment your answer to part a of this exercise, to represent the relationships between people in the database and the nature of any relationships.

c. In the next phase, you will extend the database design to begin to handle insurance claims. Draw a revised ERD to your answer to part b of this exercise, to represent the expanded second phase database:

- Each appointment may generate several insurance claims (some patients are self-pay, with no insurance coverage). Each claim is for a specific action taken in the medical practice, such as seeing a staff member, performing a test, administering a specific treatment, etc. Each claim has an ID, a claim code (taken from a list of standard codes that all insurance companies recognize), date the action was done, date the claim was filed, amount claimed, amount paid on the claim, optionally a reason code for not paying full amount, and the date the claim was (partially) paid.
- Each patient may be insured under policies with many insurance companies. Each patient policy has a policy number; possibly a group code; a designation of whether the policy is primary, secondary, tertiary, or whatever in the sequence of processing claims for a given patient; and the type of coverage (e.g., medicines, office visit, outpatient procedure).
- A medical practice deals with many insurance companies because of the policies for their patients. Each company has an ID, name, mailing address, IP address, and company contact person.
- Each claim is filed under exactly one policy with one insurance company. If for some reason a particular action with a patient necessitates more than one insurance company to be involved, then a separate claim is filed with each insurance company (e.g., a patient might reach some reimbursement limit under her primary policy, so a second claim must be filed for the same action with the company associated with the secondary policy).

d. How useful and sufficient a database is depends, in part, on questions it can be used to answer using reports or online queries. For each of the example inquiries that follow, justify for your answer to part c of this exercise whether your database could provide answers to that inquiry (if you already know SQL, you could provide justification by showing the appropriate SQL query; otherwise, explain the entities, attributes, and relationships from your ERD in part c that would be necessary to produce the desired result):

- How many claims are currently fully unreimbursed?
- Which insurance company has the most fully or partially unreimbursed claims?
- What is the total claims amount per staff member?
- Is there a potential conflict of interest in which a staff member is related to a patient for which that staff member has generated a claim?

e. As was stated in previous parts of this exercise, some claims may be only partially paid or even denied by the insurance company. When this occurs, the medical practice may take follow-up steps to resolve the disputed claim, and this can cycle through various negotiation stages. Draw a revised ERD to replace the ERD you drew for part c to represent the following:

- Each disputed claim may be processed through several stages. In each stage, the medical practice needs to know the date processed, the dispute code causing the processing step, the staff person handling the dispute in this stage, the date when this stage ends, and a description of the dispute status at the end of the stage.
- There is no limit to the number of stages a dispute may go through.
- One possible result of a disputed claim processing stage is the submission of a new claim, but usually it is the same original claim that is processed in subsequent stages.

2-61. Review your answer to Problem and Exercise 2-59; if necessary, change the names of the entities, attributes, and relationships to conform to the naming guidelines presented in this chapter. Then, using the definition guidelines, write a definition for each entity, attribute, and relationship. If necessary, state assumptions so that each definition is as complete as possible.

2-62.

FIGURE 2-29   E-R diagram for Problem and Exercise 2-62

Identify (as bullet points) the Business Rules applicable to the entities involved in the relationships given above.

2-63. Mysore One is a single point entry/access application to various local governing revenue payments. Mysore One operates as a kiosk in Mysore city at numerous locations to facilitate the citizens of Mysore to make a one stop payment of the electricity bill, property tax, road tax, water bill etc. Discuss how you would draw up an enterprise data model for such a scenario.

2-64. A business school offering post graduate diploma in Management admits students to the PGDM program. You are required to design a DBMS for the admission office. You have developed a list of business rules.

   • Students apply to the college by getting the application form from the local branches of a nationalized bank
   • Students who have taken the Common Admission Test only are eligible
   • Applicant's Details: Application No., Applicant's Name, Applicant's Address, Applicant's DOB , Applicant's Qualification and CAT No. and CAT Score are stored by the Admission Office.
   • An applicant, if eligible may get admission to any of the campuses of the B – School.
   • Eligibility of the student is based on a number of parameters:
      o Applicant's GPA in graduation degree
      o Applicant 's performance in High School
      o Applicant's score in CAT
      o Applicant's meeting the criteria for the above components are called for a personal interview and Group Discussion.

   • The Applicants finally admitted to the college will be evaluated on the following parameters with revised weightages.
      o Applicant's GPA in graduation
      o Applicant's performance in 10th Standard
      o Applicant's score in CAT
      o Applicant's performance in Group Discussion
      o Applicant's performance in personal interview
      o Each Applicant will get admitted into only one of the campuses
   • A final list of admitted students is sent along with their photographs to the PGP Office for further process.

Draw a E-R model for the above business rules and constraints.

2-65.

FIGURE 2-30   Diagram for Problem and Exercise 2-65

For the above ERD fill in the Minimum and Maximum Cardinality as appropriate.

2-66. For the **(example given in 16)** develop a business function—data entity matrix. Explain any assumption you make for developing the matrix.

Field Exercises

2-67. Interview a database analyst or systems analyst and document how he or she decides on names for data objects in data models. Does the organization in which this person works have naming guidelines? If so, describe the pattern used. If there are no guidelines, ask whether your contact has ever had any problems because guidelines did not exist. Does the organization use any tool to help manage metadata, including data names?

2-68. Visit two local small businesses, one in the service sector (e.g., dry cleaner, auto repair shop, veterinarian, or bookstore) and one that manufactures tangible goods. Interview employees from these organizations to elicit from them the entities, attributes, and relationships that are commonly encountered in these organizations. Use this information to construct E-R diagrams. What differences and similarities are there between the diagrams for the service- and the product-oriented companies? Does the E-R diagramming technique handle both situations equally well? Why or why not?

2-69. Ask a database or systems analyst to give you examples of unary, binary, and ternary relationships that the analyst has dealt with personally at his or her company. Ask which is most common and why.

2-70. Ask a database or systems analyst in a local company to show you an E-R diagram for one of the organization's primary databases. Ask questions to be sure you understand what each entity, attribute, and relationship means. Does this organization use the same E-R notation used in this text? If not, what other or alternative symbols are used and what do these symbols mean? Does this organization model associative entities on the E-R diagram? If not, how are associative entities modeled? What metadata are kept about the objects on the E-R diagram?

2-71. For the same E-R diagram used in Field Exercise 2-70 or for a different database in the same or a different organization, identify any uses of time stamping or other means to model time-dependent data. Why are time-dependent data necessary for those who use this database? Would the E-R diagram be much simpler if it were not necessary to represent the history of attribute values?

2-72. Research various graphics and drawing packages (e.g., Microsoft Office, SmartDraw) and compare the E-R diagramming capabilities of each. Is each package capable of using the notation found in this text? Is it possible to draw a ternary or higher-order relationship with each package?

References

Aranow, E. B. 1989. "Developing Good Data Definitions." *Database Programming & Design* 2,8 (August): 36–39.

Batra, D., J. A. Hoffer, and R. B. Bostrom. 1988. "A Comparison of User Performance Between the Relational and Extended Entity Relationship Model in the Discovery Phase of Database Design." *Proceedings of the Ninth International Conference on Information Systems.* Minneapolis, November 30–December 3: 295–306.

Bruce, T. A. 1992. *Designing Quality Databases with IDEF1X Information Models.* New York: Dorset House.

Chen, P. P.-S. 1976. "The Entity-Relationship Model—Toward a Unified View of Data." *ACM Transactions on Database Systems* 1,1 (March): 9–36.

Elmasri, R., and S. B. Navathe. 1994. *Fundamentals of Database Systems.* 2d ed. Menlo Park, CA: Benjamin/Cummings.

Embarcadero Technologies. 2014. "Seven Deadly Sins of Database Design: How to Avoid the Worst Problems in Database Design." April. Available at **www.embarcadero.com**.

Gottesdiener, E. 1997. "Business Rules Show Power, Promise." *Application Development Trends* 4,3 (March): 36–54.

Gottesdiener, E. 1999. "Turning Rules into Requirements." *Application Development Trends* 6,7 (July): 37–50.

Hay, D. C. 2003. "What Exactly IS a Data Model?" Parts 1, 2, and 3. *DM Review* 13,2 (February: 24–26), 3 (March: 48–50), and 4 (April: 20–22, 46).

GUIDE. 1997 (October)."GUIDE Business Rules Project." Final Report, revision 1.2.

Haughey, T. 2010 (March) "The Return on Investment (ROI) of Data Modeling." White paper published by Computer Associates–Erwin Division.

Hoffer, J. A., J. F. George, and J. S. Valacich. 2014. *Modern Systems Analysis and Design.* 7th ed. Upper Saddle River, NJ: Prentice Hall.

ISO/IEC. 2004. "Information Technology—Metadata Registries (MDR)—Part 4: Formulation of Data Definitions." July. Switzerland. Available at **http://metadata-standards.org/11179**.

ISO/IEC. 2005. "Information Technology—Metadata Registries (MDR)—Part 5: Naming and Identification Principles." September. Switzerland. Available at **http://metadata-standards.org/11179**.

Johnson, T. and R. Weis. 2007. "Time and Time Again: Managing Time in Relational Databases, Part 1." May. *DM Review.* This and other related articles by Johnson and Weis on "Time and Time Again" can be found by doing a search on Weis at **www.information-management.com**.

Moriarty, T. 2000. "The Right Tool for the Job." *Intelligent Enterprise* 3,9 (June 5): 68, 70–71.

Owen, J. 2004. "Putting Rules Engines to Work." *InfoWorld* (June 28): 35–41.

Plotkin, D. 1999. "Business Rules Everywhere." *Intelligent Enterprise* 2,4 (March 30): 37–44.

Salin, T. 1990. "What's in a Name?" *Database Programming & Design* 3,3 (March): 55–58.

Song, I.-Y., M. Evans, and E. K. Park. 1995. "A Comparative Analysis of Entity-Relationship Diagrams." *Journal of Computer & Software Engineering* 3,4: 427–59.

Storey, V. C. 1991. "Relational Database Design Based on the Entity-Relationship Model." *Data and Knowledge Engineering* 7: 47–83.

Teorey, T. J., D. Yang, and J. P. Fry. 1986. "A Logical Design Methodology for Relational Databases Using the Extended Entity-Relationship Model." *Computing Surveys* 18, 2 (June): 197–221.

von Halle, B. 1997. "Digging for Business Rules." *Database Programming & Design* 8,11: 11–13.

Further Reading

Batini, C., S. Ceri, and S. B. Navathe. 1992. *Conceptual Database Design: An Entity-Relationship Approach.* Menlo Park, CA: Benjamin/Cummings.

Bodart, F., A. Patel, M. Sim, and R. Weber. 2001. "Should Optional Properties Be Used in Conceptual Modelling? A Theory and Three Empirical Tests." *Information Systems Research* 12,4 (December): 384–405.

Carlis, J., and J. Maguire. 2001. *Mastering Data Modeling: A User-Driven Approach.* Upper Saddle River, NJ: Prentice Hall.

Keuffel, W. 1996. "Battle of the Modeling Techniques." *DBMS* 9,8 (August): 83, 84, 86, 97.

Moody, D. 1996. "The Seven Habits of Highly Effective Data Modelers." *Database Programming & Design* 9,10 (October): 57, 58, 60–62, 64.

Teorey, T. 1999. *Database Modeling & Design.* 3d ed. San Francisco, CA: Morgan Kaufman.

Tillman, G. 1994. "Should You Model Derived Data?" *DBMS* 7,11 (November): 88, 90.

Tillman, G. 1995. "Data Modeling Rules of Thumb." *DBMS* 8,8 (August): 70, 72, 74, 76, 80–82, 87.

Web Resources

http://dwr.ais.columbia.edu/info/Data%20Naming%20Standards.html Web site that provides guidelines for naming entities, attributes, and relationships similar to those suggested in this chapter.

www.adtmag.com Web site of *Application Development Trends*, a leading publication on the practice of information systems development.

www.axisboulder.com Web site for one vendor of business rules software.

www.businessrulesgroup.org Web site of the Business Rules Group, formerly part of GUIDE International, which formulates and supports standards about business rules.

http://en.wikipedia.org/wiki/Entity-relationship_model The Wikipedia entry for entity-relationship model, with an explanation of the origins of the crow's foot notation, which is used in this book.

http://ss64.com/ora/syntax-naming.html Web site that suggests naming conventions for entities, attributes, and relationships within an Oracle database environment.

www.tdan.com Web site of *The Data Administration Newsletter*, an online journal that includes articles on a wide variety of data management topics. This Web site is considered a "must follow" Web site for data management professionals.

CASE

Forondo Artist Management Excellence Inc.

Case Description

Martin was very impressed with your project plan and has given you the go ahead for the project. He also indicates to you that he has e-mails from several key staff members that should help with the design of the system. The first is from Alex Martin (administrative assistant to Pat Smith, an artist manager). Pat is on vacation and Martin has promised that Pat's perspective will be provided at a later date. The other two are from Dale Dylan, an artist that Pat manages, and Sandy Wallis, an event organizer. The text of these e-mails is provided below.

E-mail from Alex Martin, Administrative Assistant

My name is Alex Martin, and I am the administrative assistant to Pat Smith. While Pat's role is to create and maintain relationships with our clients and the event organizers, I am responsible for running the show at the operational level. I take care of Pat's phone calls while Pat is on the road, respond to inquiries and relay the urgent ones to Pat, write letters to organizers and artists, collect information on prospective artists, send bills to the event organizers and make sure that they pay their bills, take care of the artist accounts, and arrange Pat's travel (and keep track of travel costs). Most of my work I manage with Word and simple Excel spreadsheets, but it would be very useful to be able to have a system that would help me to keep track of the event fees that have been agreed upon, the events that have been successfully completed, cancellations (in the current system, I sometimes don't get information about a cancellation and I end up sending an invoice for a cancelled concert—pretty embarrassing), payments that need to be made to the artists, etc. Pat and other managers seem to think that it would be a good idea if they could better track their travel costs and the impact these costs have on their income.

We don't have a very good system for managing our artist accounts because we have separate spreadsheets for keeping track of a particular artist's fees earned and the expenses incurred, and then at the end of each month we manually create a simple statement for each of the artists. This is a lot of work, and it would make much more sense to have a computer system that would allow us to be able to keep the books constantly up to date.

A big thing for me is to keep track of the artists whom Pat manages. We need to keep in our databases plenty of information on them—their name, gender, address (including country, as they live all over the world), phone number(s), instrument(s), e-mail, etc. We also try to keep track of how they are doing in terms of the reviews they get, and thus we are subscribing to a clipping service that provides us articles on the artists whom we manage. For some of the artists, the amount of material we get is huge, and we would like to reduce it somehow. At any rate, we would at least like to be able to have a better idea of what we have in our archives on a particular artist, and thus we should probably start to maintain some kind of a list of the news items we have for a particular artist. I don't know if this is worth it but it would be very useful if we could get it done.

Scheduling is, of course, a major headache for me. Although Pat and the artists negotiate the final schedules, I do, in practice, at this point maintain a big schedule book for each artist whom we manage. You know, somebody has to have the central copy. This means that Pat, the artists, and the event organizers are calling me all the time to verify the current situation and make changes to the schedule. Sometimes things get mixed up and we don't get the latest changes to the central calendar (for example, an artist schedules a vacation and forgets to tell us—as you can understand, this can lead to a pretty difficult situation). It would be so wonderful to get a centralized calendar which both Pat and the artists could access; it is probably, however, better if Pat (and the other managers for the other artists, of course) was the only person in addition to me who had the right to change the calendar. Hmmm...I guess it would be good if the artists could block time out if they decide that they need if for personal purposes (they are not, however, allowed to book any performances without discussing it first with us).

One more thing: I would need to have something that would remind me of the upcoming changes in artist contracts. Every artist's contract has to be renewed annually, and sometimes I forget to remind Pat to do this with the artist. Normally this is not a big deal, but occasionally we have had a situation where the lack of a valid contract led to unfortunate and unnecessary problems. It seems that we would need to maintain some type of list of the contracts with their start dates, end dates, royalty percentages, and simple notes related to each of the contracts.

This is a pretty hectic job, and I have not had time to get as good computer training as I would have wanted. I think I am still doing pretty well. It is very important that whatever you develop for us, it has to be easy to use because we are in such a hurry all the time and we cannot spend much time learning complex commands.

E-mail from Dale Dylan, Established Artist

Hi! I am Dale Dylan, a pianist from Austin, TX. I have achieved reasonable success during my career and I am very thankful that I have been able to work with Pat Smith and Mr. Forondo during the past five years. They have been very good at finding suitable performance opportunities for me, particularly after I won an international piano competition in Amsterdam a few years ago. Compared to some other people with whom I have worked, Pat is very conscientious and works hard for me.

During the recent months, FAME and its managers' client base has grown quite a lot, and unfortunately I have seen this in the service they have been able to provide to me. I know that Pat and Alex don't mean any harm but it seems that they simply have too much to do, particularly in scheduling and getting my fees to me. Sometimes things seem to get lost pretty easily these days, and occasionally I have been waiting for my money for 2–3 months. This was never the case earlier but it has been pretty typical during the last year or so. Please don't say anything to Pat or Alex about this; I don't want to hurt their feelings, but it just simply seems that they have too much to do. Do you think your new system could help them?

What I would like to see in a new system—if you will develop one for them—are just simple facilities that would help them do even better what they have always done pretty well (except very recently): collecting money from the concert organizers and getting it to me fast (they are, after all, taking 20 percent of my money—at least they should get the rest of it to me quickly) and maintaining my schedule. I have either a laptop or at least my smartphone/iPad with me all the time while I am on the road, thus I certainly should be able to check my schedule on the Web. Now I always need to call Alex to get any last-minute changes. It seems pretty silly that Pat has to be in touch with Alex before any changes can be made to the calendar; I feel that I should be allowed to make my own changes. Naturally, I would always notify Pat about anything that changes (or maybe the system could do that for me). The calendar system should be able to give me at least a simple list of the coming events in the chronological order for any time period I want. Furthermore, I would like to be able to search for events using specific criteria (location, type, etc.).

In addition, we do, of course, get annual summaries from FAME regarding the fees we have earned, but it would be nice to have this information a bit more often. I don't need it on paper but if I could access that information on the Web, it would be very, very good. It seems to me that Alex is doing a lot of work with these reports by hand; if you could help her with any of the routine work she is doing, I am sure she would be quite happy. Maybe then she and Pat would have more time for getting everything done as they always did earlier.

E-mail from Sandy Wallis, Event Organizer

I am Sandy Wallis, the executive director of the Greater Tri-State Area Concert Halls, and it has been a pleasure to have a good working relationship with Pat Smith at FAME for many years. Pat has provided me and my annual concert series several excellent artists per year, and I believe that our cooperation has a potential to continue into the foreseeable future. This does, however, require that Pat is able to continue to give me the best service in the industry during the years to come.

Our business is largely based on personal trust, and the most important aspect of our cooperation is that I can know that I can rely on the artists managed by Pat. I am not interested in the technology Pat is using, but it is important for us that practical matters such as billing and scheduling work smoothly and that technology does not prevent us from

making decisions fast, if necessary. We don't want to be billed for events that were cancelled and never rescheduled, and we are quite unhappy if we need to spend our time on these types of technicalities.

At times, we need a replacement artist to substitute for a musician who becomes ill or cancels for some other reason, and the faster we can get information about the availability of world-class performers in these situations, the better it is for us. Yes, we work in these situations directly with Pat, but we have seen that occasionally all the information required for fast decision making is not readily available, and this is something that is difficult for us to understand. We would like to be able to assume that Pat's able assistant Alex should be able to give us information regarding the availability of a certain artist on a certain date on the phone without any problems. Couldn't this information be available on the Web, too? Of course, we don't want anybody to know in advance whom we have booked before we announce our annual program; therefore, security is very important for us.

I hope you understand that we run multiple venues but we definitely still want to be treated as one customer. With some agencies we have seen silly problems that have forced them to send us invoices with several different names and customer numbers, which does not make any sense from our perspective and causes practical problems with our systems.

Project Questions

2-74. Redo the enterprise data model you created in Chapter 1 to accommodate the information gleaned from Alex Martin, Dale Dylan, and Sandy Wallis' e-mails.

2-75. Create an E-R diagram for FAME based on the enterprise data model you developed in 1-67. Clearly state any assumptions you made in developing the diagram.

2-76. Use the narratives in Chapter 1 and above to identify the typical outputs (reports and displays) the various stakeholders might want to retrieve from your database. Now, revisit the E-R diagram you created in 2-75 to ensure that your model has captured the information necessary to generate the outputs desired. Update your E-R diagram as necessary.

2-77. Prepare a list of questions that you have as a result of your E-R modeling efforts, and that need to be answered to clarify your understanding of FAME's business rules and data requirements.

CHAPTER 3

The Enhanced E-R Model

Visit www.pearsonhighered.com/ hoffer to view the accompanying video for this chapter.

LEARNING OBJECTIVES

After studying this chapter, you should be able to:

- Concisely define each of the following key terms: **enhanced entity-relationship (EER) model, subtype, supertype, attribute inheritance, generalization, specialization, completeness constraint, total specialization rule, partial specialization rule, disjointness constraint, disjoint rule, overlap rule, subtype discriminator, supertype/ subtype hierarchy, entity cluster,** and **universal data model.**
- Recognize when to use supertype/subtype relationships in data modeling.
- Use both specialization and generalization as techniques for defining supertype/ subtype relationships.
- Specify both completeness constraints and disjointness constraints in modeling supertype/subtype relationships.
- Develop a supertype/subtype hierarchy for a realistic business situation.
- Develop an entity cluster to simplify presentation of an E-R diagram.
- Explain the major features and data modeling structures of a universal (packaged) data model.
- Describe the special features of a data modeling project when using a packaged data model.

INTRODUCTION

The basic E-R model described in Chapter 2 was first introduced during the mid-1970s. It has been suitable for modeling most common business problems and has enjoyed widespread use. However, the business environment has changed dramatically since that time. Business relationships are more complex, and as a result, business data are much more complex as well. For example, organizations must be prepared to segment their markets and to customize their products, which places much greater demands on organizational databases.

To cope better with these changes, researchers and consultants have continued to enhance the E-R model so that it can more accurately represent the complex data encountered in today's business environment. The term **enhanced entity-relationship (EER) model** is used to identify the model that has resulted from extending the original E-R model with these new modeling constructs. These extensions make the EER model semantically similar to object-oriented data modeling; visit www.pearsonhighered. com/hoffer for a supplement on the object-oriented data model.

The most important modeling construct incorporated in the EER model is supertype/subtype relationships. This facility enables us to model a general entity type (called the *supertype*) and then subdivide it into several specialized entity

Enhanced entity-relationship (EER) model

A model that has resulted from extending the original E-R model with new modeling constructs.

types (called *subtypes*). Thus, for example, the entity type CAR can be modeled as a supertype, with subtypes SEDAN, SPORTS CAR, COUPE, and so on. Each subtype inherits attributes from its supertype and in addition may have special attributes and be involved in relationships of its own. Adding new notation for modeling supertype/subtype relationships has greatly improved the flexibility of the basic E-R model.

E-R, and especially EER, diagrams can become large and complex, requiring multiple pages (or very small font) for display. Some commercial databases include hundreds of entities. Many users and managers specifying requirements for or using a database do not need to see all the entities, relationships, and attributes to understand the part of the database with which they are most interested. Entity clustering is a way to turn a part of an entity-relationship data model into a more macro-level view of the same data. Entity clustering is a hierarchical decomposition technique (a nesting process of breaking a system into further and further subparts), which can make E-R diagrams easier to read and databases easier to design. By grouping entities and relationships, you can lay out an E-R diagram in such a way that you give attention to the details of the model that matter most in a given data modeling task.

As introduced in Chapter 2, universal and industry-specific generalizable data models, which extensively utilized EER capabilities, have become very important for contemporary data modelers. These packaged data models and data model patterns have made data modelers more efficient and produce data models of higher quality. The EER features of supertypes/subtypes are essential to create generalizable data models; additional generalizing constructs, such as typing entities and relationships, are also employed. It has become very important for data modelers to know how to customize a data model pattern or data model for a major software package (e.g., enterprise resource planning or customer relationship management), just as it has become commonplace for information system builders to customize off-the-shelf software packages and software components.

REPRESENTING SUPERTYPES AND SUBTYPES

Recall from Chapter 2 that an entity type is a collection of entities that share common properties or characteristics. Although the entity instances that comprise an entity type are similar, we do not expect them to have exactly the same attributes. For example, recall required and optional attributes from Chapter 2. One of the major challenges in data modeling is to recognize and clearly represent entities that are almost the same, that is, entity types that share common properties but also have one or more distinct properties that are of interest to the organization.

For this reason, the E-R model has been extended to include supertype/subtype relationships. A **subtype** is a subgrouping of the entities in an entity type that is meaningful to the organization. For example, STUDENT is an entity type in a university. Two subtypes of STUDENT are GRADUATE STUDENT and UNDERGRADUATE STUDENT. In this example, we refer to STUDENT as the supertype. A **supertype** is a generic entity type that has a relationship with one or more subtypes.

In the E-R diagramming we have done so far, supertypes and subtypes have been hidden. For example, consider again Figure 2-22, which is the E-R diagram (in Microsoft Visio) for Pine Valley Furniture Company. Notice that it is possible for a customer to not do business in any territory (i.e., no associated instances of the DOES BUSINESS IN associative entity). Why is this? One possible reason is that there are two types of customers—national account customers and regular customers—and only regular customers are assigned to a sales territory. Thus, in that figure the reason for the optional cardinality next to the DOES BUSINESS IN associative entity coming from CUSTOMER is obscured. Explicitly drawing a customer entity supertype and several entity subtypes will help us make the E-R diagram more meaningful. Later in this chapter, we show a revised E-R diagram for Pine Valley Furniture, which demonstrates several EER notations to make vague aspects of Figure 2-22 more explicit.

Subtype
A subgrouping of the entities in an entity type that is meaningful to the organization and that shares common attributes or relationships distinct from other subgroupings.

Supertype
A generic entity type that has a relationship with one or more subtypes.

Basic Concepts and Notation

The notation that is used for supertype/subtype relationships in this text is shown in Figure 3-1a. The supertype is connected with a line to a circle, which in turn is connected with a line to each subtype that has been defined. The U-shaped symbol on each line connecting a subtype to the circle emphasizes that the subtype is a subset of the supertype. It also indicates the direction of the subtype/supertype relationship. (This U is optional because the meaning and direction of the supertype/subtype relationship is usually obvious; in most examples, we will not include this symbol.) Figure 3-1b shows the type of EER notation used by Microsoft Visio (which is very similar to that used in this text), and Figure 3-1c shows the type of EER notation used by some CASE tools (e.g., Oracle Designer); the notation in Figure 3-1c is also the form often used for universal and industry-specific data models. These different formats have identical basic features, and you should easily become comfortable using any of these forms. We primarily use the text notation for examples in this chapter because advanced EER features are more standard with this format.

Attributes that are shared by all entities (including the identifier) are associated with the supertype. Attributes that are unique to a particular subtype are associated with that subtype. The same is true for relationships. Other components will be added to this notation to provide additional meaning in supertype/subtype relationships as we proceed through the remainder of this chapter.

FIGURE 3-1 Basic notation for supertype/subtype relationships
(a) EER notation

(b) Microsoft Visio notation

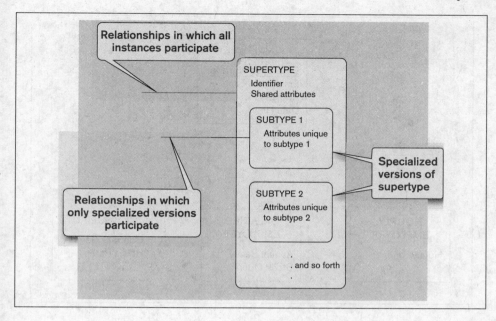

FIGURE 3-1   (*continued*)
(c) Subtypes inside supertypes notation

AN EXAMPLE OF A SUPERTYPE/SUBTYPE RELATIONSHIP   Let us illustrate supertype/subtype relationships with a simple yet common example. Suppose that an organization has three basic types of employees: hourly employees, salaried employees, and contract consultants. The following are some of the important attributes for each of these types of employees:

- *Hourly employees* Employee Number, Employee Name, Address, Date Hired, Hourly Rate
- *Salaried employees* Employee Number, Employee Name, Address, Date Hired, Annual Salary, Stock Option
- *Contract consultants* Employee Number, Employee Name, Address, Date Hired, Contract Number, Billing Rate

Notice that all of the employee types have several attributes in common: Employee Number, Employee Name, Address, and Date Hired. In addition, each type has one or more attributes distinct from the attributes of other types (e.g., Hourly Rate is unique to hourly employees). If you were developing a conceptual data model in this situation, you might consider three choices:

1. Define a single entity type called EMPLOYEE. Although conceptually simple, this approach has the disadvantage that EMPLOYEE would have to contain all of the attributes for the three types of employees. For an instance of an hourly employee (for example), attributes such as Annual Salary and Contract Number would not apply (optional attributes) and would be null or not used. When taken to a development environment, programs that use this entity type would necessarily need to be quite complex to deal with the many variations.
2. Define a separate entity type for each of the three entities. This approach would fail to exploit the common properties of employees, and users would have to be careful to select the correct entity type when using the system.
3. Define a supertype called EMPLOYEE with subtypes HOURLY EMPLOYEE, SALARIED EMPLOYEE, and CONSULTANT. This approach exploits the common properties of all employees, yet it recognizes the distinct properties of each type.

Figure 3-2 shows a representation of the EMPLOYEE supertype with its three subtypes, using enhanced E-R notation. Attributes shared by all employees are associated with the EMPLOYEE entity type. Attributes that are peculiar to each subtype are included with that subtype only.

FIGURE 3-2 Employee
supertype with three
subtypes

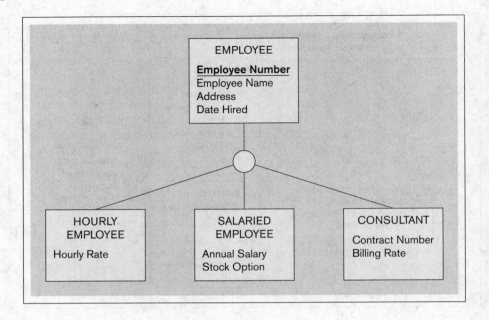

ATTRIBUTE INHERITANCE   A subtype is an entity type in its own right. An entity instance of a subtype represents the same entity instance of the supertype. For example, if "Therese Jones" is an occurrence of the CONSULTANT subtype, then this same person is necessarily an occurrence of the EMPLOYEE supertype. As a consequence, an entity in a subtype must possess not only values for its own attributes, but also values for its attributes as a member of the supertype, including the identifier.

Attribute inheritance

A property by which subtype
entities inherit values of all
attributes and instances of all
relationships of their supertype.

    Attribute inheritance is the property by which subtype entities inherit values of all attributes and instance of all relationships of the supertype. This important property makes it unnecessary to include supertype attributes or relationships redundantly with the subtypes (remember, when it comes to data modeling, redundancy = bad, simplicity = good). For example, Employee Name is an attribute of EMPLOYEE (Figure 3-2) but not of the subtypes of EMPLOYEE. Thus, the fact that the employee's name is "Therese Jones" is inherited from the EMPLOYEE supertype. However, the Billing Rate for this same employee is an attribute of the subtype CONSULTANT.

    We have established that a member of a subtype must be a member of the supertype. Is the converse also true—that is, is a member of the supertype also a member of one (or more) of the subtypes? This may or may not be true, depending on the business situation. (Sure, "it depends" is the classic academic answer, but it's true in this case.) We discuss the various possibilities later in this chapter.

WHEN TO USE SUPERTYPE/SUBTYPE RELATIONSHIPS   So, how do you know when to use a supertype/subtype relationship? You should consider using subtypes when either (or both) of the following conditions are present:

1. There are attributes that apply to some (but not all) instances of an entity type. For example, see the EMPLOYEE entity type in Figure 3-2.
2. The instances of a subtype participate in a relationship unique to that subtype.

    Figure 3-3 is an example of the use of subtype relationships that illustrates both of these situations. The hospital entity type PATIENT has two subtypes: OUTPATIENT and RESIDENT PATIENT. (The identifier is Patient ID.) All patients have an Admit Date attribute, as well as a Patient Name. Also, every patient is cared for by a RESPONSIBLE PHYSICIAN who develops a treatment plan for the patient.

    Each subtype has an attribute that is unique to that subtype. Outpatients have Checkback Date, whereas resident patients have Date Discharged. Also, resident patients have a unique relationship that assigns each patient to a bed. (Notice that this is a

FIGURE 3-3 Supertype/subtype
relationships in a hospital

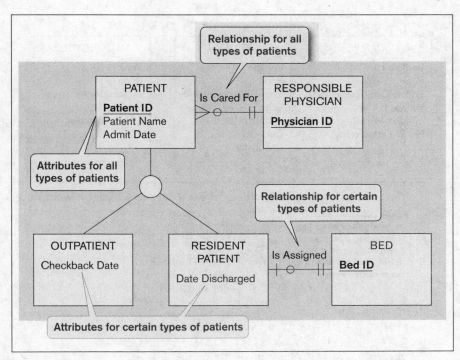

mandatory relationship; it would be optional if it were attached to PATIENT.) Each bed
may or may not be assigned to a patient.

Earlier we discussed the property of attribute inheritance. Thus, each outpatient
and each resident patient inherits the attributes of the parent supertype PATIENT:
Patient ID, Patient Name, and Admit Date. Figure 3-3 also illustrates the principle of
relationship inheritance. OUTPATIENT and RESIDENT PATIENT are also instances of
PATIENT; therefore, each Is Cared For by a RESPONSIBLE PHYSICIAN.

Representing Specialization and Generalization

We have described and illustrated the basic principles of supertype/subtype relationships, including the characteristics of "good" subtypes. But in developing real-world
data models, how can you recognize opportunities to exploit these relationships? There
are two processes—generalization and specialization—that serve as mental models in
developing supertype/subtype relationships.

GENERALIZATION   A unique aspect of human intelligence is the ability and propensity
to classify objects and experiences and to generalize their properties. In data modeling,
generalization is the process of defining a more general entity type from a set of more
specialized entity types. Thus generalization is a bottom-up process.

An example of generalization is shown in Figure 3-4. In Figure 3-4a, three entity
types have been defined: CAR, TRUCK, and MOTORCYCLE. At this stage, the data
modeler intends to represent these separately on an E-R diagram. However, on closer
examination, we see that the three entity types have a number of attributes in common:
Vehicle ID (identifier), Vehicle Name (with components Make and Model), Price, and
Engine Displacement. This fact (reinforced by the presence of a common identifier) suggests that each of the three entity types is really a version of a more general entity type.

This more general entity type (named VEHICLE) together with the resulting
supertype/subtype relationships is shown in Figure 3-4b. The entity CAR has the specific
attribute No Of Passengers, whereas TRUCK has two specific attributes: Capacity and
Cab Type. Thus, generalization has allowed us to group entity types along with their
common attributes and at the same time preserve specific attributes that are peculiar to
each subtype.

Generalization

The process of defining a more
general entity type from a set of
more specialized entity types.

FIGURE 3-4 Example of generalization
(a) Three entity types: CAR, TRUCK, and MOTORCYCLE

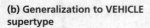

(b) Generalization to VEHICLE supertype

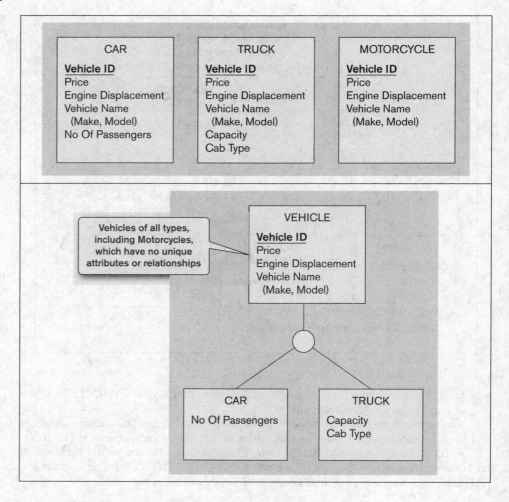

Notice that the entity type MOTORCYCLE is not included in the relationship. Is this simply an omission? No. Instead, it is deliberately not included because it does not satisfy the conditions for a subtype discussed earlier. Comparing Figure 3-4 parts a and b, you will notice that the only attributes of MOTORCYCLE are those that are common to all vehicles; there are no attributes specific to motorcycles. Furthermore, MOTORCYCLE does not have a relationship to another entity type. Thus, there is no need to create a MOTORCYCLE subtype.

The fact that there is no MOTORCYCLE subtype suggests that it must be possible to have an instance of VEHICLE that is not a member of any of its subtypes. We discuss this type of constraint in the section on specifying constraints.

Specialization

The process of defining one or more subtypes of the supertype and forming supertype/subtype relationships.

SPECIALIZATION   As we have seen, generalization is a bottom-up process. **Specialization** is a top-down process, the direct reverse of generalization. Suppose that we have defined an entity type with its attributes. Specialization is the process of defining one or more subtypes of the supertype and forming supertype/subtype relationships. Each subtype is formed based on some distinguishing characteristic, such as attributes or relationships specific to the subtype.

An example of specialization is shown in Figure 3-5. Figure 3-5a shows an entity type named PART, together with several of its attributes. The identifier is Part No, and other attributes are Description, Unit Price, Location, Qty On Hand, Routing Number, and Supplier. (The last attribute is multivalued and composite because there may be more than one supplier with an associated unit price for a part.)

In discussions with users, we discover that there are two possible sources for parts: Some are manufactured internally, whereas others are purchased from outside

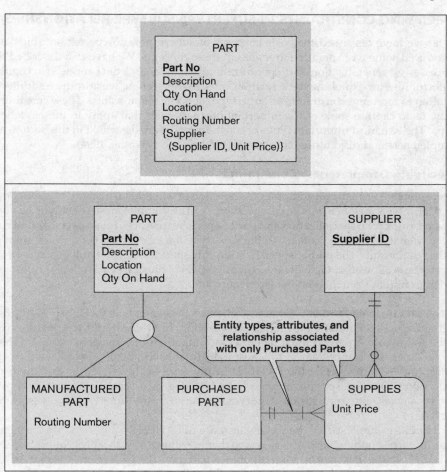

FIGURE 3-5 Example of specialization
(a) Entity type PART

suppliers. Further, we discover that some parts are obtained from both sources. In this case, the choice depends on factors such as manufacturing capacity, unit price of the parts, and so on.

Some of the attributes in Figure 3-5a apply to all parts, regardless of source. However, others depend on the source. Thus, Routing Number applies only to manufactured parts, whereas Supplier ID and Unit Price apply only to purchased parts. These factors suggest that PART should be specialized by defining the subtypes MANUFACTURED PART and PURCHASED PART (Figure 3-5b).

In Figure 3-5b, Routing Number is associated with MANUFACTURED PART. The data modeler initially planned to associate Supplier ID and Unit Price with PURCHASED PART. However, in further discussions with users, the data modeler suggested instead that they create a SUPPLIER entity type and an associative entity linking PURCHASED PART with SUPPLIER. This associative entity (named SUPPLIES in Figure 3-5b) allows users to more easily associate purchased parts with their suppliers. Notice that the attribute Unit Price is now associated with the associative entity so that the unit price for a part may vary from one supplier to another. In this example, specialization has permitted a preferred representation of the problem domain.

COMBINING SPECIALIZATION AND GENERALIZATION Specialization and generalization are both valuable techniques for developing supertype/subtype relationships. The technique you use at a particular time depends on several factors, such as the nature of the problem domain, previous modeling efforts, and personal preference. You should be prepared to use both approaches and to alternate back and forth as dictated by the preceding factors.

SPECIFYING CONSTRAINTS IN SUPERTYPE/SUBTYPE RELATIONSHIPS

So far we have discussed the basic concepts of supertype/subtype relationships and introduced some basic notation to represent these concepts. We have also described the processes of generalization and specialization, which help a data modeler recognize opportunities for exploiting these relationships. In this section, we introduce additional notation to represent constraints on supertype/subtype relationships. These constraints allow us to capture some of the important business rules that apply to these relationships. The two most important types of constraints that are described in this section are completeness and disjointness constraints (Elmasri and Navathe, 1994).

Specifying Completeness Constraints

Completeness constraint

A type of constraint that addresses whether an instance of a supertype must also be a member of at least one subtype.

Total specialization rule

A rule that specifies that each entity instance of a supertype must be a member of some subtype in the relationship.

Partial specialization rule

A rule that specifies that an entity instance of a supertype is allowed not to belong to any subtype.

A **completeness constraint** addresses the question of whether an instance of a supertype must also be a member of at least one subtype. The completeness constraint has two possible rules: total specialization and partial specialization. The **total specialization rule** specifies that each entity instance of the supertype must be a member of some subtype in the relationship. The **partial specialization rule** specifies that an entity instance of the supertype is allowed not to belong to any subtype. We illustrate each of these rules with earlier examples from this chapter (see Figure 3-6).

TOTAL SPECIALIZATION RULE   Figure 3-6a repeats the example of PATIENT (Figure 3-3) and introduces the notation for total specialization. In this example, the business rule is the following: A patient must be either an outpatient or a resident patient. (There are no other types of patient in this hospital.) Total specialization is indicated by the *double* line extending from the PATIENT entity type to the circle. (In the Microsoft Visio notation, total specialization is called "Category is complete" and is shown also by a *double* line under the category circle between the supertype and associated subtypes.)

In this example, every time a new instance of PATIENT is inserted into the supertype, a corresponding instance is inserted into either OUTPATIENT or RESIDENT PATIENT. If the instance is inserted into RESIDENT PATIENT, an instance of the relationship Is Assigned is created to assign the patient to a hospital bed.

PARTIAL SPECIALIZATION RULE   Figure 3-6b repeats the example of VEHICLE and its subtypes CAR and TRUCK from Figure 3-4. Recall that in this example, motorcycle is a type of vehicle, but it is not represented as a subtype in the data model. Thus, if

FIGURE 3-6 Examples of completeness constraints (a) Total specialization rule

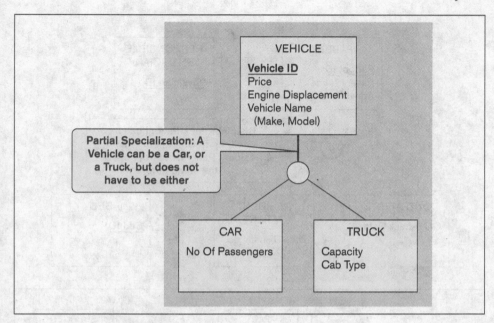

FIGURE 3-6 *(continued)*
(b) Partial specialization rule

a vehicle is a car, it must appear as an instance of CAR, and if it is a truck, it must appear as an instance of TRUCK. However, if the vehicle is a motorcycle, it cannot appear as an instance of any subtype. This is an example of partial specialization, and it is specified by the single line from the VEHICLE supertype to the circle.

Specifying Disjointness Constraints

A **disjointness constraint** addresses whether an instance of a supertype may simultaneously be a member of two (or more) subtypes. The disjointness constraint has two possible rules: the disjoint rule and the overlap rule. The disjoint rule specifies that if an entity instance (of the supertype) is a member of one subtype, it cannot simultaneously be a member of any other subtype. The overlap rule specifies that an entity instance can simultaneously be a member of two (or more) subtypes. An example of each of these rules is shown in Figure 3-7.

Disjointness constraint

A constraint that addresses whether an instance of a supertype may simultaneously be a member of two (or more) subtypes.

DISJOINT RULE Figure 3-7a shows the PATIENT example from Figure 3-6a. The business rule in this case is the following: *At any given time,* a patient must be either an outpatient or a resident patient, but cannot be both. This is the **disjoint rule,** as specified by the letter *d* in the circle joining the supertype and its subtypes. Note in this figure, the subclass of a PATIENT may change over time, but at a given time, a PATIENT is of only one type. (The Microsoft Visio notation does not have a way to designate disjointness or overlap; however, you can place a *d* or an *o* inside the category circle using the Text tool.)

Disjoint rule

A rule that specifies that an instance of a supertype may not simultaneously be a member of two (or more) subtypes.

OVERLAP RULE Figure 3-7b shows the entity type PART with its two subtypes, MANUFACTURED PART and PURCHASED PART (from Figure 3-5b). Recall from our discussion of this example that some parts are both manufactured and purchased. Some clarification of this statement is required. In this example, an instance of PART is a particular part number (i.e., a *type of part*), not an individual part (indicated by the identifier, which is Part No). For example, consider part number 4000. At a given time, the quantity on hand for this part might be 250, of which 100 are manufactured and the remaining 150 are purchased parts. In this case, it is not important to keep track of individual parts. When tracking individual parts is important, each part is assigned a serial number identifier, and the quantity on hand is one or zero, depending on whether that individual part exists or not.

FIGURE 3-7 Examples of disjointness constraints
(a) Disjoint rule

(b) Overlap rule

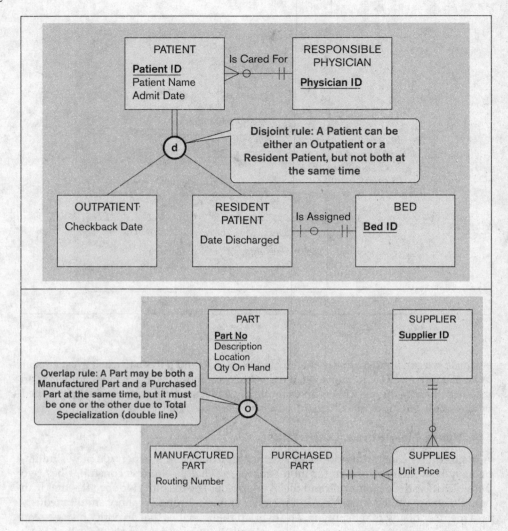

Overlap rule

A rule that specifies that an instance of a supertype may simultaneously be a member of two (or more) subtypes.

The **overlap rule** is specified by placing the letter *o* in the circle, as shown in Figure 3-7b. Notice in this figure that the total specialization rule is also specified, as indicated by the double line. Thus, any part must be either a purchased part or a manufactured part, or it may simultaneously be both of these.

Defining Subtype Discriminators

Given a supertype/subtype relationship, consider the problem of inserting a new instance of a supertype. Into which of the subtypes (if any) should this instance be inserted? We have already discussed the various possible rules that apply to this situation. We need a simple mechanism to implement these rules, if one is available. Often this can be accomplished by using a subtype discriminator. A **subtype discriminator** is an attribute of a supertype whose values determine the target subtype or subtypes.

Subtype discriminator

An attribute of a supertype whose values determine the target subtype or subtypes.

DISJOINT SUBTYPES An example of the use of a subtype discriminator is shown in Figure 3-8. This example is for the EMPLOYEE supertype and its subtypes, introduced in Figure 3-2. Notice that the following constraints have been added to this figure: total specialization and disjoint subtypes. Thus, each employee must be either hourly, salaried, or a consultant.

A new attribute (Employee Type) has been added to the supertype to serve as a subtype discriminator. When a new employee is added to the supertype, this attribute

FIGURE 3-8 Introducing
a subtype discriminator
(disjoint rule)

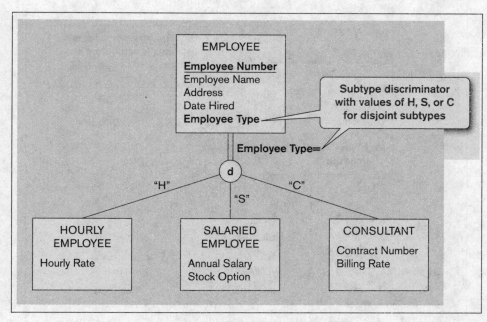

is coded with one of three values, as follows: "H" (for Hourly), "S" (for Salaried), or "C" (for Consultant). Depending on this code, the instance is then assigned to the appropriate subtype. (An attribute of the supertype may be selected in the Microsoft Visio notation as a discriminator, which is shown similarly next to the category symbol.)

The notation we use to specify the subtype discriminator is also shown in Figure 3-8. The expression Employee Type= (which is the left side of a condition statement) is placed next to the line leading from the supertype to the circle. The value of the attribute that selects the appropriate subtype (in this example, either "H," "S," or "C") is placed adjacent to the line leading to that subtype. Thus, for example, the condition Employee Type="S" causes an entity instance to be inserted into the SALARIED EMPLOYEE subtype.

OVERLAPPING SUBTYPES When subtypes overlap, a slightly modified approach must be applied for the subtype discriminator. The reason is that a given instance of the supertype may require that we create an instance in more than one subtype.

An example of this situation is shown in Figure 3-9 for PART and its overlapping subtypes. A new attribute named Part Type has been added to PART. Part Type is a composite attribute with components Manufactured? and Purchased? Each of these attributes is a Boolean variable (i.e., it takes on only the values yes, "Y," and no, "N"). When a new instance is added to PART, these components are coded as follows:

Type of Part	Manufactured?	Purchased?
Manufactured only	"Y"	"N"
Purchased only	"N"	"Y"
Purchased and manufactured	"Y"	"Y"

The method for specifying the subtype discriminator for this example is shown in Figure 3-9. Notice that this approach can be used for any number of overlapping subtypes.

Defining Supertype/Subtype Hierarchies

We have considered a number of examples of supertype/subtype relationships in this chapter. It is possible for any of the subtypes in these examples to have other subtypes defined on it (in which case, the subtype becomes a supertype for the newly

FIGURE 3-9 Subtype
discriminator
(overlap rule)

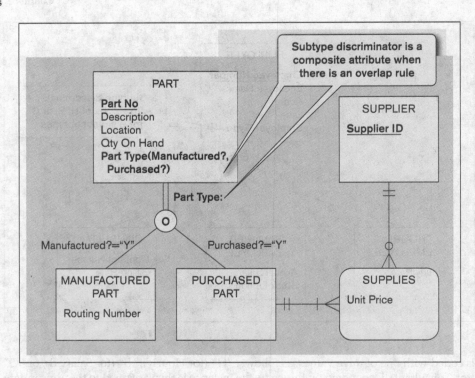

Supertype/subtype hierarchy

A hierarchical arrangement of
supertypes and subtypes in
which each subtype has only one
supertype.

defined subtypes). A **supertype/subtype hierarchy** is a hierarchical arrangement of
supertypes and subtypes, where each subtype has only one supertype (Elmasri and
Navathe, 1994).

We present an example of a supertype/subtype hierarchy in this section in
Figure 3-10. (For simplicity, we do not show subtype discriminators in this and most
subsequent examples. See Problems and Exercises 3-19 and 3-20.) This example
includes most of the concepts and notation we have used in this chapter to this point.
It also presents a methodology (based on specialization) that you can use in many data
modeling situations.

AN EXAMPLE OF A SUPERTYPE/SUBTYPE HIERARCHY Suppose that you are asked to
model the human resources in a university. Using specialization (a top-down approach),
you might proceed as follows: Starting at the top of a hierarchy, model the most general
entity type first. In this case, the most general entity type is PERSON. List and associate all attributes of PERSON. The attributes shown in Figure 3-10 are SSN (identifier),
Name, Address, Gender, and Date Of Birth. The entity type at the top of a hierarchy is
sometimes called the *root*.

Next, define all major subtypes of the root. In this example, there are three
subtypes of PERSON: EMPLOYEE (persons who work for the university), STUDENT
(persons who attend classes), and ALUMNUS (persons who have graduated).
Assuming that there are no other types of persons of interest to the university, the
total specialization rule applies, as shown in the figure. A person might belong to
more than one subtype (e.g., ALUMNUS and EMPLOYEE), so the overlap rule is used.
Note that overlap allows for any overlap. (A PERSON may be simultaneously in any
pair or in all three subtypes.) If certain combinations are not allowed, a more refined
supertype/subtype hierarchy would have to be developed to eliminate the prohibited
combinations.

Attributes that apply specifically to each of these subtypes are shown in the figure.
Thus, each instance of EMPLOYEE has a value for Date Hired and Salary. Major Dept is
an attribute of STUDENT, and Degree (with components Year, Designation, and Date)
is a multivalued, composite attribute of ALUMNUS.

FIGURE 3-10   Example of supertype/subtype hierarchy

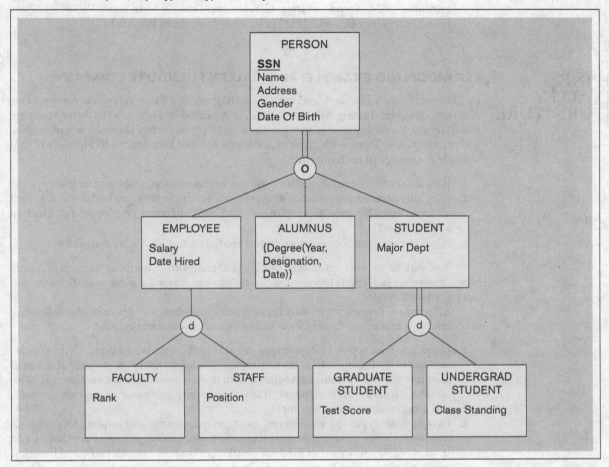

The next step is to evaluate whether any of the subtypes already defined qualify for further specialization. In this example, EMPLOYEE is partitioned into two subtypes: FACULTY and STAFF. FACULTY has the specific attribute Rank, whereas STAFF has the specific attribute Position. Notice that in this example the subtype EMPLOYEE becomes a supertype to FACULTY and STAFF. Because there may be types of employees other than faculty and staff (such as student assistants), the partial specialization rule is indicated. However, an employee cannot be both faculty and staff at the same time. Therefore, the disjoint rule is indicated in the circle.

Two subtypes are also defined for STUDENT: GRADUATE STUDENT and UNDERGRAD STUDENT. UNDERGRAD STUDENT has the attribute Class Standing, whereas GRADUATE STUDENT has the attribute Test Score. Notice that total specialization and the disjoint rule are specified; you should be able to state the business rules for these constraints.

SUMMARY OF SUPERTYPE/SUBTYPE HIERARCHIES   We note two features concerning the attributes contained in the hierarchy shown in Figure 3-10:

1. Attributes are assigned at the highest logical level that is possible in the hierarchy. For example, because SSN (i.e., Social Security Number) applies to all persons, it is assigned to the root. In contrast, Date Hired applies only to employees, so it is assigned to EMPLOYEE. This approach ensures that attributes can be shared by as many subtypes as possible.
2. Subtypes that are lower in the hierarchy inherit attributes not only from their immediate supertype, but from all supertypes higher in the hierarchy, up to the

root. Thus, for example, an instance of faculty has values for all of the following attributes: SSN, Name, Address, Gender, and Date Of Birth (from PERSON); Date Hired and Salary (from EMPLOYEE); and Rank (from FACULTY).

EER MODELING EXAMPLE: PINE VALLEY FURNITURE COMPANY

In Chapter 2, we presented a sample E-R diagram for Pine Valley Furniture. (This diagram, developed using Microsoft Visio, is repeated in Figure 3-11.) After studying this diagram, you might use some questions to help you clarify the meaning of entities and relationships. Three such areas of questions are (see annotations in Figure 3-11 that indicate the source of each question):

1. Why do some customers not do business in one or more sales territories?
2. Why do some employees not supervise other employees, and why are they not all supervised by another employee? And, why do some employees not work in a work center?
3. Why do some vendors not supply raw materials to Pine Valley Furniture?

You may have other questions, but we will concentrate on these three to illustrate how supertype/subtype relationships can be used to convey a more specific (semantically rich) data model.

After some investigation into these three questions, we discover the following business rules that apply to how Pine Valley Furniture does business:

1. There are two types of customers: regular and national account. Only regular customers do business in sales territories. A sales territory exists only if it has at least one regular customer associated with it. A national account customer is associated with an account manager. It is possible for a customer to be both a regular and a national account customer.
2. Two special types of employees exist: management and union. Only union employees work in work centers, and a management employee supervises union employees. There are other kinds of employees besides management and union. A union employee may be promoted into management, at which time that employee stops being a union employee.
3. Pine Valley Furniture keeps track of many different vendors, not all of which have ever supplied raw materials to the company. A vendor is associated with a contract number once that vendor becomes an official supplier of raw materials.

These business rules have been used to modify the E-R diagram in Figure 3-11 into the EER diagram in Figure 3-12. (We have left most attributes off this diagram except for those that are essential to see the changes that have occurred.) Rule 1 means that there is a total, overlapping specialization of CUSTOMER into REGULAR CUSTOMER and NATIONAL ACCOUNT CUSTOMER. A composite attribute of CUSTOMER, Customer Type (with components National and Regular), is used to designate whether a customer instance is a regular customer, a national account, or both. Because only regular customers do business in sales territories, only regular customers are involved in the Does Business In relationship (associative entity).

Rule 2 means that there is a partial, disjoint specialization of EMPLOYEE into MANAGEMENT EMPLOYEE and UNION EMPLOYEE. An attribute of EMPLOYEE, Employee Type, discriminates between the two special types of employees. Specialization is partial because there are other kinds of employees besides these two types. Only union employees are involved in the Works In relationship, but all union employees work in some work center, so the minimum cardinality next to Works In from UNION EMPLOYEE is now mandatory. Because an employee cannot be both management and union at the same time (although he or she can change status over time), the specialization is disjoint.

FIGURE 3-11   E-R diagram for Pine Valley Furniture Company

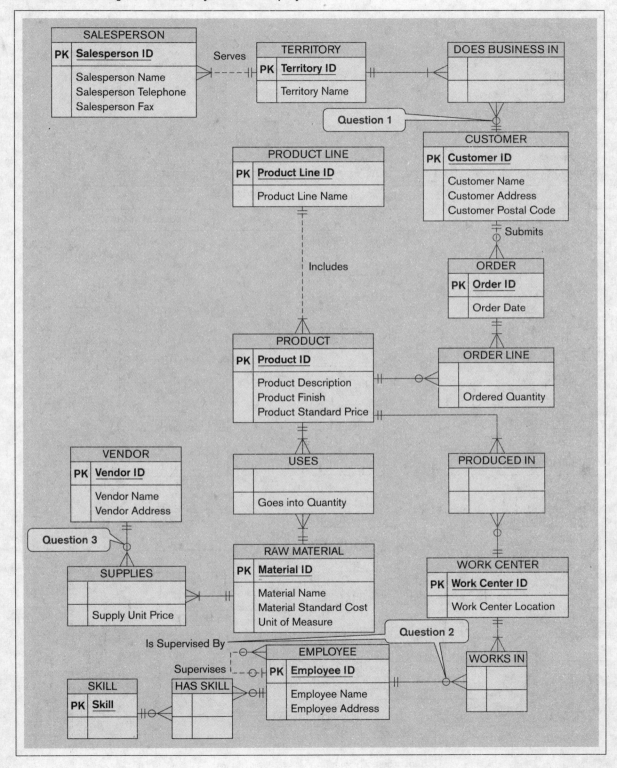

FIGURE 3-12 EER diagram for Pine Valley Furniture Company using Microsoft Visio

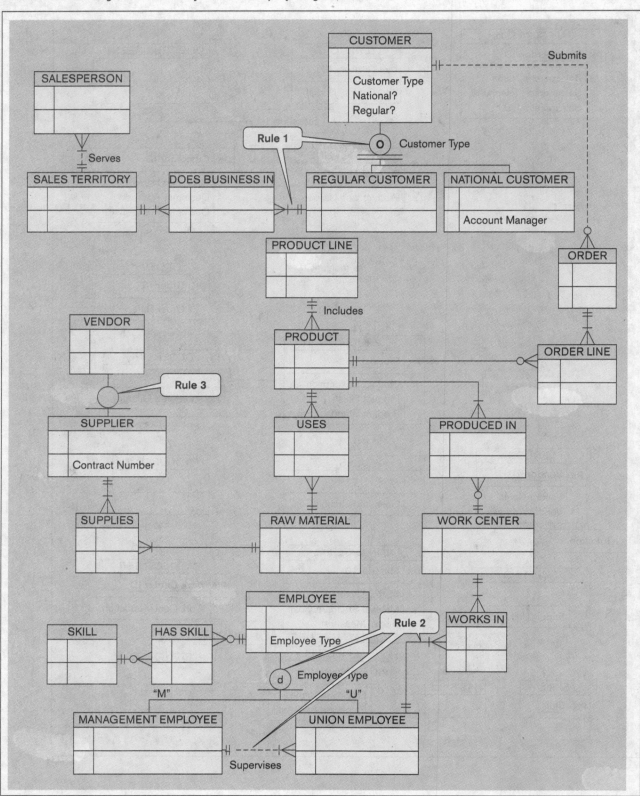

Rule 3 means that there is a partial specialization of VENDOR into SUPPLIER because only some vendors become suppliers. A supplier, not a vendor, has a contract number. Because there is only one subtype of VENDOR, there is no reason to specify a disjoint or overlap rule. Because all suppliers supply some raw material, the minimum cardinality next to RAW MATERIAL in the Supplies relationship (associative entity in Visio) now is one.

This example shows how an E-R diagram can be transformed into an EER diagram once generalization/specialization of entities is understood. Not only are supertype and subtype entities now in the data model, but additional attributes, including discriminating attributes, also are added, minimum cardinalities change (from optional to mandatory), and relationships move from the supertype to a subtype.

This is a good time to emphasize a point made earlier about data modeling. A data model is a conceptual picture of the data required by an organization. A data model does not map one-for-one to elements of an implemented database. For example, a database designer may choose to put all customer instances into one database table, not separate ones for each type of customer. Such details are not important now. The purpose now is to explain all the rules that govern data, not how data will be stored and accessed to achieve efficient, required information processing. We will address technology and efficiency issues in subsequent chapters when we cover database design and implementation.

Although the EER diagram in Figure 3-12 clarifies some questions and makes the data model in Figure 3-11 more explicit, it still can be difficult for some people to comprehend. Some people will not be interested in all types of data, and some may not need to see all the details in the EER diagram to understand what the database will cover. The next section addresses how we can simplify a complete and explicit data model for presentation to specific user groups and management.

ENTITY CLUSTERING

Some enterprise-wide information systems have more than 1,000 entity types and relationships. How do we present such an unwieldy picture of organizational data to developers and users? With a *really big* piece of paper? On the wrap-around walls of a large conference room? (Don't laugh about that one; we've seen it done!) Well, the answer is that we don't have to. In fact, there would be very few people who need to see the whole ERD in detail. If you are familiar with the principles of systems analysis and design (see, e.g., Hoffer et al., 2014), you know about the concept of functional decomposition. Briefly, functional decomposition is an iterative approach to breaking a system down into related components so that each component can be redesigned by itself without destroying the connections with other components. Functional decomposition is powerful because it makes redesign easier and allows people to focus attention on the part of the system in which they are interested. In data modeling, a similar approach is to create multiple, linked E-R diagrams, each showing the details of different (possibly overlapping) segments or subsets of the data model (e.g., different segments that apply to different departments, information system applications, business processes, or corporate divisions).

Entity clustering (Teorey, 1999) is a useful way to present a data model for a large and complex organization. An **entity cluster** is a set of one or more entity types and associated relationships grouped into a single abstract entity type. Because an entity cluster behaves like an entity type, entity clusters and entity types can be further grouped to form a higher-level entity cluster. Entity clustering is a hierarchical decomposition of a macro-level view of the data model into finer and finer views, eventually resulting in the full, detailed data model.

Entity cluster
A set of one or more entity types and associated relationships grouped into a single abstract entity type.

Figure 3-13 illustrates one possible result of entity clustering for the Pine Valley Furniture Company data model of Figure 3-12. Figure 3-13a shows the complete data model with shaded areas around possible entity clusters; Figure 3-13b shows the final result of transforming the detailed EER diagram into an EER diagram of only entity clusters and relationships. (An EER diagram may include both entity

FIGURE 3-13 Entity clustering for Pine Valley Furniture Company
(a) Possible entity clusters (using Microsoft Visio)

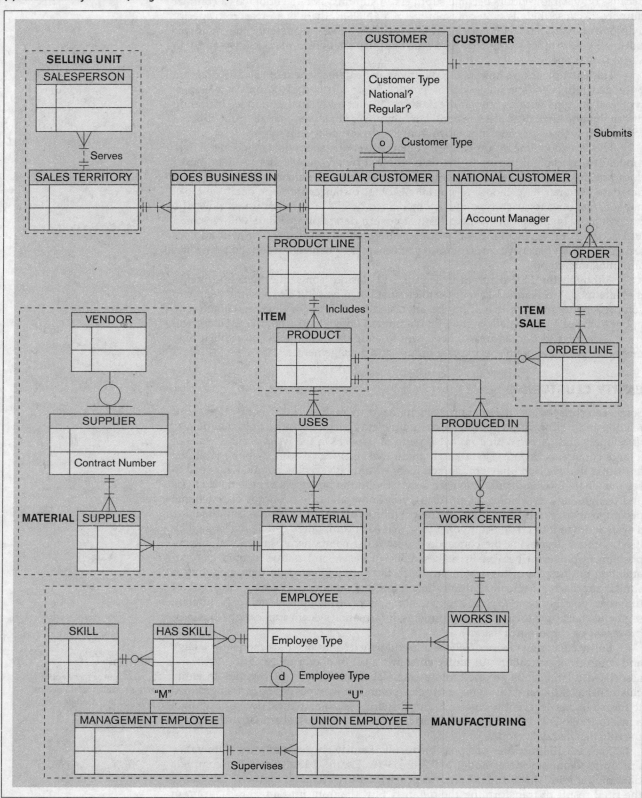

FIGURE 3-13 *(continued)*
(b) EER diagram for entity clusters (using Microsoft Visio)

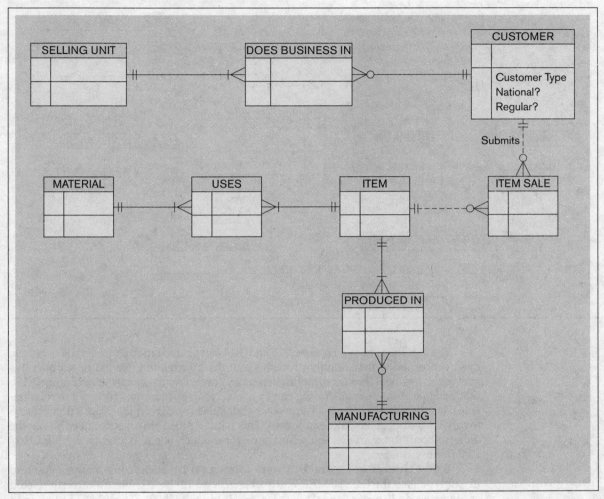

clusters and entity types, but this diagram includes only entity clusters.) In this figure, the entity cluster

- SELLING UNIT represents the SALESPERSON and SALES TERRITORY entity types and the Serves relationship
- CUSTOMER represents the CUSTOMER entity supertype, its subtypes, and the relationship between supertype and subtypes
- ITEM SALE represents the ORDER entity type and ORDER LINE associative entity as well as the relationship between them
- ITEM represents the PRODUCT LINE and PRODUCT entity types and the Includes relationship
- MANUFACTURING represents the WORK CENTER and EMPLOYEE supertype entity and its subtypes as well as the Works In associative entity and Supervises relationships and the relationship between the supertype and its subtypes. (Figure 3-14 shows an explosion of the MANUFACTURING entity cluster into its components.)
- MATERIAL represents the RAW MATERIAL and VENDOR entity types, the SUPPLIER subtype, the Supplies associative entity, and the supertype/subtype relationship between VENDOR and SUPPLIER.

FIGURE 3-14 MANUFACTURING entity cluster

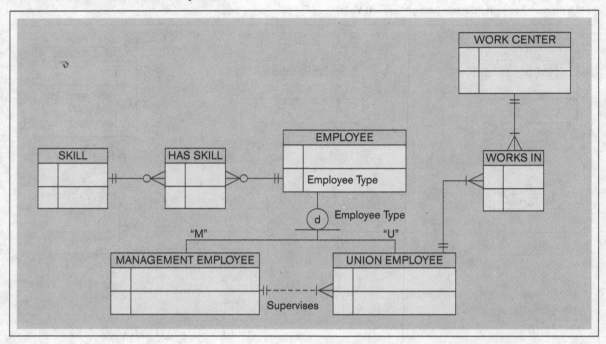

The E-R diagrams in Figures 3-13 and 3-14 can be used to explain details to people most concerned with assembly processes and the information needed to support this part of the business. For example, an inventory control manager can see in Figure 3-13b that the data about manufacturing can be related to item data (the Produced In relationship). Furthermore, Figure 3-14 shows what detail is kept about the production process involving work centers and employees. This person probably does not need to see the details about, for example, the selling structure, which is embedded in the SELLING UNIT entity cluster.

Entity clusters in Figure 3-13 were formed (1) by abstracting a supertype and its subtype (see the CUSTOMER entity cluster) and (2) by combining directly related entity types and their relationships (see the SELLING UNIT, ITEM, MATERIAL, and MANUFACTURING entity clusters). An entity cluster can also be formed by combining a strong entity and its associated weak entity types (not illustrated here). Because entity clustering is hierarchical, if it were desirable, we could draw another EER diagram in which we combine the SELLING UNIT and CUSTOMER entity clusters with the DOES BUSINESS IN associative entity one entity cluster, because these are directly related entity clusters.

An entity cluster should focus on an area of interest to some community of users, developers, or managers. Which entity types and relationships are grouped to form an entity cluster depends on your purpose. For example, the ORDER entity type could be grouped in with the CUSTOMER entity cluster and the ORDER LINE entity type could be grouped in with the ITEM entity cluster in the example of entity clustering for the Pine Valley Furniture data model. This regrouping would eliminate the ITEM SALE cluster, which might not be of interest to any group of people. Also, you can do several different entity clusterings of the full data model, each with a different focus.

PACKAGED DATA MODELS

According to Len Silverston (1998), "The age of the data modeler as artisan is passing. Organizations can no longer afford the labor or time required for handcrafting data models from scratch. In response to these constraints, the age of the data modeler as engineer is dawning." As one executive explained to us, "the acquisition of a [packaged data model] was one of the key strategic things his organization did to gain quick results and long-term success" for the business. Packaged data models are a game-changer for data modeling.

As introduced in Chapter 2, an increasingly popular approach to beginning a data modeling project is to acquire a packaged or predefined data model, either a so-called universal model or an industry-specific model (some providers call these logical data models [LDMs], but these are really EER diagrams as explained in this chapter; the data model may also be part of a purchased software package, such as an enterprise resource planning or customer relationship management system). These packaged data models are not fixed; rather, the data modeler customizes the predefined model to fit the business rules of his or her organization based on a best-practices data model for the industry (e.g., transportation or communications) or chosen functional area (e.g., finance or manufacturing). The key assumption of this data modeling approach is that underlying structures or patterns of enterprises in the same industry or functional area are similar. Packaged data models are available from various consultants and database technology vendors. Although packaged data models are not inexpensive, many believe the total cost is lower and the quality of data modeling is better by using such resources. Some generic data models can be found in publications (e.g., see articles and books by Hay and by Silverston listed at the end of this chapter).

A **universal data model** is a generic or template data model that can be reused as a starting point for a data modeling project. Some people call these data model patterns, similar to the notion of patterns of reusable code for programming. A universal data model is not the "right" data model, but it is a successful starting point for developing an excellent data model for an organization.

Universal data model
A generic or template data model that can be reused as a starting point for a data modeling project.

Why has this approach of beginning from a universal data model for conducting a data modeling project become so popular? The following are some of the most compelling reasons professional data modelers are adopting this approach (we have developed this reasoning from Hoberman, 2006, and from an in-depth study we have conducted at the leading online retailer Overstock.com, which has adopted several packaged data models from Teradata Corporation):

- Data models can be developed using proven components evolved from cumulative experiences (as stated by the data administrator in the company we studied, "why reinvent when you can adapt?"). These data models are kept up-to-date by the provider as new kinds of data are recognized in an industry (e.g., RFID).
- Projects take less time and cost because the essential components and structures are already defined and only need to be quickly customized to the particular situation. The company we studied stated that the purchased data model was about 80 percent right before customization and that the cost of the package was about equal to the cost of one database modeler for one year.
- Data models are less likely to miss important components or make modeling errors due to not recognizing common possibilities. For example, the company we studied reported that its packaged data models helped it avoid the temptation of simply mirroring existing databases, with all the historical "warts" of poor naming conventions, data structures customized for some historical purpose, and the inertia of succumbing to the pressure to simply duplicate the inadequate past practices. As another example, one vendor of packaged data models, Teradata, claims that one of its data models was scoped using more than 1,000 business questions and key performance indicators.
- Because of a holistic, enterprise view and development from best practices of data modeling experts found in a universal data model, the resulting data model for a particular enterprise tends to be easier to evolve as additional data requirements are identified for the given situation. A purchased model results in reduced rework in the future because the package gets it correct right out of the box and anticipates the future needs.
- The generic model provides a starting point for asking requirements questions so that most likely all areas of the model are addressed during requirements

determination. In fact, the company we studied said that their staff was "intrigued by all the possibilities" to meet even unspoken requirements from the capabilities of the prepackaged data models.

- Data models of an existing database are easier to read by data modelers and other data management professionals the first time because they are based on common components seen in similar situations.
- Extensive use of supertype/subtype hierarchies and other structures in universal data models promotes reusing data and taking a holistic, rather than narrow, view of data in an organization.
- Extensive use of many-to-many relationships and associative entities even where a data modeler might place a one-to-many relationship gives the data model greater flexibility to fit any situation, and naturally handles time stamping and retention of important history of relationships, which can be important to comply with regulations and financial record-keeping rules.
- Adaptation of a data model from your DBMS vendor usually means that your data model will easily work with other applications from this same vendor or its software partners.
- If multiple companies in the same industry use the same universal data model as the basis for their organizational databases, it may be easier to share data for interorganizational systems (e.g., reservation systems between rental car and airline firms).

A Revised Data Modeling Process with Packaged Data Models

Data modeling from a packaged data model requires no less skill than data modeling from scratch. Packaged data models are not going to put data modelers out of work (or keep you from getting that job as an entry-level data analyst you want now that you've started studying database management!). In fact, working with a package requires advanced skills, like those you are learning in this chapter and Chapter 2. As we will see, the packaged data models are rather complex because they are thorough and developed to cover all possible circumstances. A data modeler has to be very knowledgeable of the organization as well as the package to customize the package to fit the specific rules of that organization.

What do you get when you purchase a data model? What you are buying is metadata. You receive, usually on a CD, a fully populated description of the data model, usually specified in a structured data modeling tool, such as ERwin from Computer Associates or Oracle Designer from Oracle Corporation. The supplier of the data model has drawn the EER diagram; named and defined all the elements of the data model; and given all the attributes characteristics of data type (character, numeric, image), length, format, and so forth. You can print the data model and various reports about its contents to support the customization process. Once you customize the model, you can then use the data modeling tool to automatically generate the SQL commands to define the database to a variety of database management systems.

How is the data modeling process different when starting with a purchased solution? The following are the key differences (our understanding of these differences is enhanced by the interviews we conducted at Overstock.com):

- Because a purchased data model is extensive, you begin by identifying the parts of the data model that apply to your data modeling situation. Concentrate on these parts first and in the most detail. Start, as with most data modeling activities, first with entities, then attributes, and finally relationships. Consider how your organization will operate in the future, not just today.
- You then rename the identified data elements to terms local to the organization rather than the generic names used in the package.
- In many cases, the packaged data model will be used in new information systems that replace existing databases as well as to extend into new areas. So the next step is to map the data to be used from the package to data in current databases.

One way this mapping will be used is to design migration plans to convert existing databases to the new structures. The following are some key points about this mapping process:

- There will be data elements from the package that are not in current systems, and there will be some data elements in current databases not in the package. Thus, some elements won't map between the new and former environments. This is to be expected because the package anticipates information needs you have not, yet, satisfied by your current databases and because you do some special things in your organization that you want to retain but that are not standard practices. However, be sure that each non-mapped data element is really unique and needed. For example, it is possible that a data element in a current database may actually be derived from other more atomic data in the purchased data model. Also, you need to decide if data elements unique to the purchased data model are needed now or can be added on when you are ready to take advantage of these capabilities in the future.
- In general, the business rules embedded in the purchased data model cover all possible circumstances (e.g., the maximum number of customers associated with a customer order). The purchased data model allows for great flexibility, but a general-purpose business rule may be too weak for your situation (e.g., you are sure you will never allow more than one customer per customer order). As you will see in the next section, the flexibility and generalizability of a purchased data model results in complex relationships and many entity types. Although the purchased model alerts you to what is possible, you need to decide if you really need this flexibility and if the complexity is worthwhile.
- Because you are starting with a prototypical data model, it is possible to engage users and managers to be supported by the new database early and often in the data modeling project. Interviews, JAD sessions, and other requirements gathering activities are based on concrete ERDs rather than wish lists. The purchased data model essentially suggests specific questions to be asked or issues to discuss (e.g., "Would we ever have a customer order with more than one customer associated with it?" or "Might an employee also be a customer?"). The purchased model in a sense provides a visual checklist of items to discuss (e.g., Do we need these data? Is this business rule right for us?); further, it is comprehensive, so it is less likely that an important requirement will be missed.
- Because the purchased data model is comprehensive, there is no way you will be able to build and populate the full database or even customize the whole data model in one project. However, you don't want to miss the opportunity to visualize future requirements shown in the full data model. Thus, you will get to a point where you have to make a decision on what will be built first and possible future phases to build out as much of the purchased data model as will make sense. One approach to explaining the build-out schedule is to use entity clustering to show segments of the full data model that will be built in different phases. Future mini-projects will address detailed customization for new business needs and other segments of the data model not developed in the initial project.

You will learn in subsequent chapters of this book important database modeling and design concepts and skills that are important in any database development effort, including those based on purchased data models. There are, however, some important things to note about projects involving purchased data models. Some of these involve using existing databases to guide how to customize a purchased data model, including the following:

- Over time the same attribute may have been used for different purposes—what people call overloaded columns in current systems. This means that the data values in existing databases may not have uniform meaning for the migration to the new database. Often these multiple uses are not documented and are not known until the migration begins. Some data may no longer be needed (maybe used for a special business project), or there may be hidden requirements that were not formally incorporated into the database design. More on how to deal with this in a moment.

- Similarly, some attributes may be empty (i.e., have no values), at least for some periods of time. For example, some employee home addresses could be missing, or product engineering attributes for a given product line might be absent for products developed a few years ago. This could have occurred because of application software errors, human data entry mistakes, or other reasons. As we have studied, missing data may suggest optional data, and the need for entity subtypes. So missing data need to be studied to understand why the data are sparse.

- A good method for understanding hidden meaning and identifying inconsistencies in existing data models, and hence data and business rules that need to be included in the customized purchased data model, is data profiling. Profiling is a way to statistically analyze data to uncover hidden patterns and flaws. Profiling can find outliers, identify shifts in data distribution over time, and identify other phenomena. Each perturbation of the distribution of data may tell a story, such as showing when major application system changes occurred, or when business rules changed. Often these patterns suggest poorly designed databases (e.g., data for separate entities were combined to improve processing speed for a special set of queries but the better structure was never restored). Data profiling can also be used to assess how accurate current data are and anticipate the clean-up effort that will be needed to populate the purchased data model with high-quality data.

- Arguably the most important challenge of customizing a purchased data model is determining the business rules that will be established through the data model. A purchased data model will anticipate the vast majority of the needed rules, but each rule must be verified for your organization. Fortunately, you don't have to guess which ones to address; each is laid out by the entities, attributes, and relationships with their metadata (names, definitions, data types, formats, lengths, etc.) in the purchased model. It simply takes time to go through each of these data elements with the right subject matter experts to make sure you have the relationship cardinalities and all other aspects of the data model right.

Packaged Data Model Examples

What, then, do packaged or universal data models look like? Central to the universal data model approach are supertype/subtype hierarchies. For example, a core structure of any universal data model is the entity type PARTY, which generalizes persons or organizations as actors for the enterprise, and an associated entity type PARTY ROLE, which generalizes various roles parties can play at different times. A PARTY ROLE instance is a situation in which a PARTY acts in a particular ROLE TYPE. These notions of PARTY, PARTY ROLE, and ROLE TYPE supertypes and their relationship are shown in Figure 3-15a. We use the supertype/subtype notation from Figure 3-1c because this is the notation most frequently used in publically available universal data models. (Most packaged data models are proprietary intellectual property of the vendor, and, hence, we cannot show them in this text.) This is a very generic data model (albeit simple to begin our discussion). This type of structure allows a specific party to serve in different roles during different time periods (specified by From Date and Thru Date). It allows attribute values of a party to be "overridden" (if necessary in the organization) by values pertinent to the role being played during the given time period (e.g., although a PERSON of the PARTY supertype has a Current Last Name as of now, when in the party role of BILL TO CUSTOMER a different Current Last Name could apply during the particular time period [From Date to Thru Date] of that role). Note that even for this simple situation, the data model is trying to capture the most general circumstances. For example, an instance of the EMPLOYEE subtype of the PERSON ROLE subtype of PARTY ROLE would be associated with an instance of the ROLE TYPE that describes the employee-person role-party role. Thus, one description of a role type explains all the instances of the associated party roles of that role type.

An interesting aspect of Figure 3-15a is that PARTY ROLE actually simplifies what could be a more extensive set of subtypes of PARTY. Figure 3-15b shows one PARTY

FIGURE 3-15 PARTY, PARTY ROLE, and ROLE TYPE in a universal data model

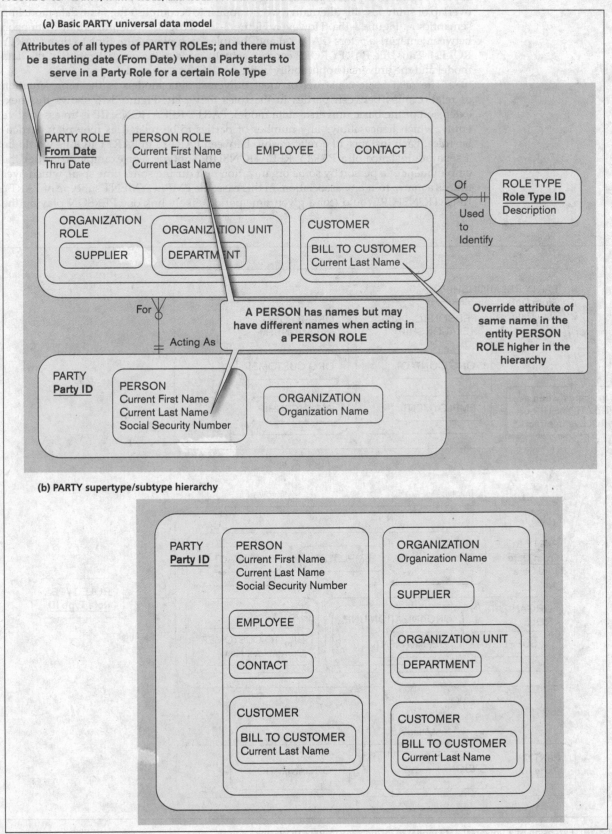

supertype with many subtypes covering many party roles. With partial specialization and overlap of subtypes, this alternative would appear to accomplish the same data modeling semantics as Figure 3-15a. However, Figure 3-15a recognizes the important distinction between enterprise actors (PARTYs) and the roles each plays from time to time (PARTY ROLEs). Thus, the PARTY ROLE concept actually adds to the generalization of the data model and the universal applicability of the predefined data model.

The next basic construct of most universal data models is the representation of relationships between parties in the roles they play. Figure 3-16 shows this next extension of the basic universal data model. PARTY RELATIONSHIP is an associative entity, which hence allows any number of parties to be related as they play particular roles. Each instance of a relationship between PARTYs in PARTY ROLEs would be a separate instance of a PARTY RELATIONSHIP subtype. For example, consider the employment of a person by some organization unit during some time span, which over time is a many-to-many association. In this case, the EMPLOYMENT subtype of PARTY RELATIONSHIP would (for a given time period) likely link one PERSON playing the

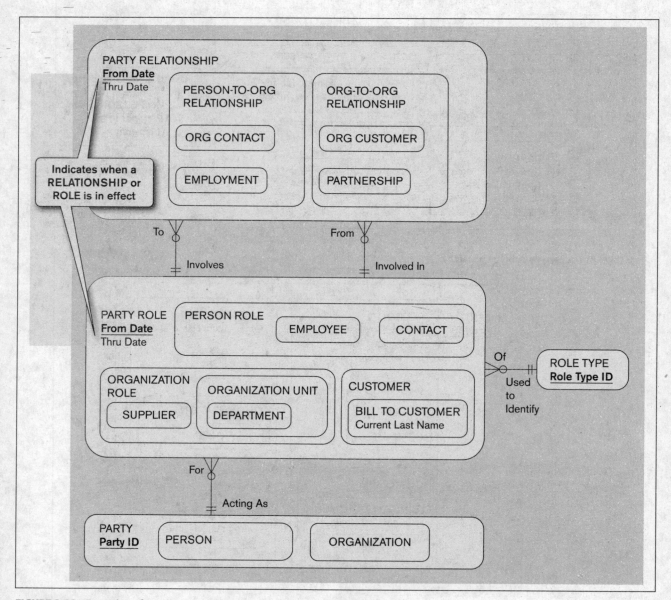

FIGURE 3-16 Extension of a universal data model to include PARTY RELATIONSHIPs

role of an EMPLOYEE subtype of PARTY ROLE with one ORGANIZATION ROLE playing some pertinent party role, such as ORGANIZATION UNIT. (That is, a person is employed in an organization unit during a period of From Date to Thru Date in PARTY RELATIONSHIP.)

PARTY RELATIONSHIP is represented very generally, so it really is an associative entity for a unary relationship among PARTY ROLE instances. This makes for a very general, flexible pattern of relationships. What might be obscured, however, are which subtypes might be involved in a particular PARTY RELATIONSHIP, and stricter relationships that are not many-to-many, probably because we don't need to keep track of the relationship over time. For example, because the Involves and Involved In relationships link the PARTY ROLE and PARTY RELATIONSHIP supertypes, this does not restrict EMPLOYMENT to an EMPLOYEE with an ORGANIZATION UNIT. Also, if the enterprise needs to track only current employment associations, the data model in Figure 3-16 will not enforce that a PERSON PARTY in an EMPLOYEE PARTY ROLE can be associated with only one ORGANIZATION UNIT at a time. We will see in the next section how we can include additional business rule notation on an EER diagram to make this specific. Alternatively, we could draw specific relationships from just the EMPLOYEE PARTY ROLE and the ORGANIZATION UNIT PARTY ROLE to the EMPLOYMENT PARTY RELATIONSHIP to represent this particular one-to-many association. As you can imagine, to handle very many special cases like this would create a diagram with a large number of relationships between PARTY ROLE and PARTY RELATIONSHIP, and, hence, a very busy diagram. Thus, more restrictive cardinality rules (at least most of them) would likely be implemented outside the data model (e.g., in database stored procedures or application programs) when using a packaged data model.

We could continue introducing various common, reusable building blocks of universal data models. However, Silverston in a two-volume set (2001a, 2001b) and Hay (1996) provide extensive coverage. To bring our discussion of packaged, universal data models to a conclusion, we show in Figure 3-17, a universal data model for a relationship development organization. In this figure, we use the original notation of Silverston (see several references at the end of the chapter), which is pertinent to Oracle data modeling tools. Now that you have studied EER concepts and notations and have been introduced to universal data models, you can understand more about the power of this data model.

To help you better understand the EER diagram in Figure 3-17, consider the definitions of the highest-level entity type in each supertype/subtype hierarchy:

PARTY	Persons and organizations independent of the roles they play
PARTY ROLE	Information about a party for an associated role, thus allowing a party to act in multiple roles
PARTY RELATIONSHIP	Information about two parties (those in the "to" and "from" roles) within the context of a relationship
EVENT	Activities that may occur within the context of relationships (e.g., a CORRESPONDENCE can occur within the context of a PERSON-CUSTOMER relationship in which the "to" party is a CUSTOMER role for an ORGANIZATION and the from party is an EMPLOYEE role for a PERSON)
PRIORITY TYPE	Information about a priority that may set the priority for a given PARTY RELATIONSHIP
STATUS TYPE	Information about the status (e.g., active, inactive, pending) of events or party relationships
EVENT ROLE	Information about all of the PARTYs involved in an EVENT
ROLE TYPE	Information about the various PARTY ROLEs and EVENT ROLEs

In Figure 3-17, supertype/subtype hierarchies are used extensively. For example, in the PARTY ROLE entity type, the hierarchy is as many as four levels deep (e.g., PARTY ROLE to PERSON ROLE to CONTACT to CUSTOMER CONTACT). Attributes can be located with any entity type in the hierarchy (e.g., PARTY has

FIGURE 3-17 A universal data model for relationship development

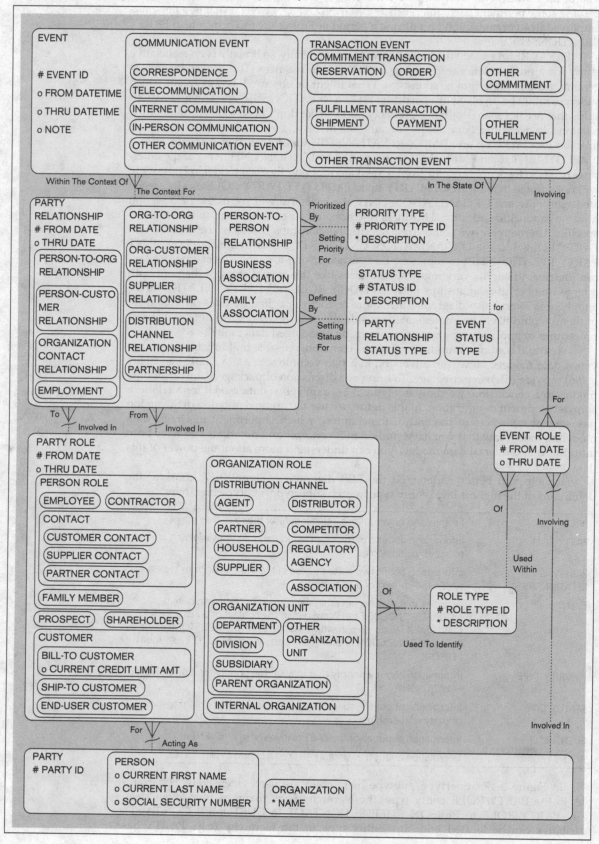

the identifier PARTY ID [# means identifier], PERSON has three optional attributes [o means optional], and ORGANIZATION has a required attribute [* means required]). Relationships can be between entity types anywhere in the hierarchy. For example, any EVENT is "in the state of" an EVENT STATUS TYPE, a subtype, whereas any EVENT is "within the context of" a PARTY RELATIONSHIP, a supertype.

As stated previously, packaged data models are not meant to be exactly right straight out of the box for a given organization; they are meant to be customized. To be the most generalized, such models have certain properties before they are customized for a given situation:

1. Relationships are connected to the highest-level entity type in a hierarchy that makes sense. Relationships can be renamed, eliminated, added, and moved as needed for the organization.
2. Strong entities almost always have *M:N* relationships between them (e.g., EVENT and PARTY), so at least one, and sometimes many, associative entities are used. Consequently, all relationships are 1:*M*, and there is an entity type in which to store intersection data. Intersection data are often dates, showing over what span of time the relationship was valid. Thus, the packaged data model is designed to allow tracking of relationships over time. (Recall that this is a common issue that was discussed with Figure 2-20.) 1:*M* relationships are optional, at least on the many side (e.g., the dotted line next to EVENT for the "involving" relationship signifies that an EVENT may involve an EVENT ROLE, as is done with Oracle Designer).
3. Although not clear on this diagram, all supertype/subtype relationships follow the total specialization and overlap rules, which makes the diagram as thorough and flexible as possible.
4. Most entities on the many side of a relationship are weak, thus inheriting the identifier of the entity on the one side (e.g., the ~ on the "acting as" relationship from PARTY to PARTY ROLE signifies that PARTY ROLE implicitly includes PARTY ID).

Summary

This chapter has described how the basic E-R model has been extended to include supertype/subtype relationships. A *supertype* is a generic entity type that has a relationship with one or more subtypes. A *subtype* is a grouping of the entities in an entity type that is meaningful to the organization. For example, the entity type PERSON is frequently modeled as a supertype. Subtypes of PERSON may include EMPLOYEE, VOLUNTEER, and CLIENT. Subtypes inherit the attributes and relationships associated with their supertype.

Supertype/subtype relationships should normally be considered in data modeling with either (or both) of the following conditions present: First, there are attributes that apply to some (but not all) of the instances of an entity type. Second, the instances of a subtype participate in a relationship unique to that subtype.

The techniques of generalization and specialization are important guides in developing supertype/subtype relationships. Generalization is the bottom-up process of defining a generalized entity type from a set of more specialized entity types. Specialization is the top-down process of defining one or more subtypes of a supertype that has already been defined.

The EER notation allows us to capture the important business rules that apply to supertype/subtype

relationships. The completeness constraint allows us to specify whether an instance of a supertype must also be a member of at least one subtype. There are two cases: With total specialization, an instance of the supertype must be a member of at least one subtype. With partial specialization, an instance of a supertype may or may not be a member of any subtype. The disjointness constraint allows us to specify whether an instance of a supertype may simultaneously be a member of two or more subtypes. Again, there are two cases. With the disjoint rule, an instance can be a member of only one subtype at a given time. With the overlap rule, an entity instance can simultaneously be a member of two (or more) subtypes.

A subtype discriminator is an attribute of a supertype whose values determine to which subtype (or subtypes) a supertype instance belongs. A supertype/subtype hierarchy is a hierarchical arrangement of supertypes and subtypes, where each subtype has only one supertype.

There are extensions to the E-R notation other than supertype/subtype relationships. One of the other useful extensions is aggregation, which represents how some entities are part of other entities (e.g., a PC is composed of a disk drive, RAM, a motherboard). Due to space limitations, we have not discussed these extensions here.

Most of these extensions, like aggregation, are also a part of object-oriented data modeling, which is explained in Chapter 14, on the book Web site.

E-R diagrams can become large and complex, including hundreds of entities. Many users and managers do not need to see all the entities, relationships, and attributes to understand the part of the database with which they are most interested. Entity clustering is a way to turn a part of an entity-relationship data model into a more macro-level view of the same data. An entity cluster is a set of one or more entity types and associated relationships grouped into a single abstract entity type. Several entity clusters and associated relationships can be further grouped into even a higher entity cluster, so entity clustering is a hierarchical decomposition technique. By grouping entities and relationships, you can lay out an E-R diagram to allow you to give attention to the details of the model that matter most in a given data modeling task.

Packaged data models, so called universal and industry-specific data models, extensively utilize EER features. These generalizable data models often use multiple level supertype/subtype hierarchies and associative entities. Subjects and the roles subjects play are separated, creating many entity types; this complexity can be simplified when customized for a given organization, and entity clusters can be used to present simpler views of the data model to different audiences.

The use of packaged data models can save considerable time and cost in data modeling. The skills required for a data modeling project with a packaged data model are quite advanced and are built on the data modeling principles covered in this text. You have to consider not only current needs but also future requirements to customize the general-purpose package. Data elements must be renamed to local terms, and current data need to be mapped to the target database design. This mapping can be challenging due to various forms of mismatches between the data in current databases with those found in the best-practices purchased database model. Fortunately, having actual data models "right out of the box" helps structure the customization process for completeness and ease of communication with subject matter experts. Overloaded columns, poor metadata, and abuses of the structure of current databases can make the customization and migration processes challenging. Data profiling can be used to understand the current data and uncover hidden meanings and business rules in data for your organization.

Chapter Review

Key Terms

Attribute inheritance *118*
Completeness
  constraint *122*
Disjoint rule *123*
Disjointness
  constraint *123*

Enhanced entity-
  relationship (EER)
  model *114*
Entity cluster *131*
Generalization *119*
Overlap rule *124*

Partial specialization
  rule *122*
Specialization *120*
Subtype *115*
Subtype discriminator *124*
Supertype *115*

Supertype/subtype
  hierarchy *126*
Total specialization
  rule *122*
Universal data model *135*

Review Questions

3-1. Define each of the following terms:
  a. supertype
  b. subtype
  c. specialization
  d. entity cluster
  e. completeness constraint
  f. enhanced entity-relationship (EER) model
  g. subtype discriminator
  h. total specialization rule
  i. generalization
  j. disjoint rule
  k. overlap rule
  l. partial specialization rule
  m. universal data model

3-2. Match the following terms and definitions:
  _____ supertype
  _____ entity cluster
  _____ subtype
  _____ specialization
  _____ subtype
      discriminator
  _____ attribute
      inheritance
  _____ overlap rule

  a. subset of supertype
  b. entity belongs to two subtypes
  c. subtype gets supertype attributes
  d. generalized entity type
  e. creating subtypes for an entity type
  f. a group of associated entity types and relationships
  g. locates target subtype for an entity

3-3. Contrast the following terms:
  a. supertype; subtype
  b. generalization; specialization
  c. disjoint rule; overlap rule

d. total specialization rule; partial specialization rule

e. PARTY; PARTY ROLE

f. entity; entity cluster

3-4. State two conditions that indicate when a database designer should consider using supertype/subtype relationships.

3-5. State the reason for entity clustering.

3-6. Give an example (other than those discussed in the chapter) of a supertype/subtype relationship.

3-7. What is attribute inheritance? Why is it important?

3-8. Give an example of each of the following:

a. a supertype/subtype relationship where the disjoint rule applies

b. a supertype/subtype relationship where the overlap rule applies

3-9. What types of business rules are normally captured in an EER diagram?

3-10. What is the purpose of a subtype discriminator?

3-11. When would a packaged data model be useful?

3-12. In what ways is starting a data modeling project with a packaged data model different from starting a data modeling project with a clean sheet of paper?

3-13. How can data profiling be used during a data modeling project, especially one using a packaged data model?

3-14. Does a data modeling project using a packaged data model require less or greater skill than a project not using a packaged data model? Why or why not?

3-15. What do you purchase when you acquire a packaged data model?

3-16. When might a supertype/subtype hierarchy be useful?

3-17. When is a member of a supertype always a member of at least one subtype?

3-18. How are attributes associated with entities? Explain the different types of attributes with examples? What are the naming and defining conventions for attributes?

3-19. What are relationships? Compare and contrast the different degrees of relationships.

3-20. How do cardinality constraints come into play in relationships? Explain the various facets of such constraints.

Problems and Exercises

3-21. Examine the hierarchy for the university EER diagram (Figure 3-10). As a student, you are an instance of one of the subtypes: either UNDERGRAD STUDENT or GRADUATE STUDENT. List the names of all the attributes that apply to you. For each attribute, record the data value that applies to you.

3-22. Add a subtype discriminator for each of the supertypes shown in Figure 3-10. Show the discriminator values that assign instances to each subtype. Use the following subtype discriminator names and values:

a. PERSON: Person Type (Employee? Alumnus? Student?)

b. EMPLOYEE: Employee Type (Faculty, Staff)

c. STUDENT: Student Type (Grad, Undergrad)

3-23. For simplicity, subtype discriminators were left off many figures in this chapter. Add subtype discriminator notation in each figure listed below. If necessary, create a new attribute for the discriminator.

a. Figure 3-2

b. Figure 3-3

c. Figure 3-4b

d. Figure 3-7a

e. Figure 3-7b

3-24. Refer to the employee EER diagram in Figure 3-2. Make any assumptions that you believe are necessary. Develop a sample definition for each entity type, attribute, and relationship in the diagram.

3-25. Refer to the EER diagram for patients in Figure 3-3. Make any assumptions you believe are necessary. Develop sample definitions for each entity type, attribute, and relationship in the diagram.

3-26. Figure 3-13 shows the development of entity clusters for the Pine Valley Furniture E-R diagram. In Figure 3-13b, explain the following:

a. Why is the minimum cardinality next to the DOES BUSINESS IN associative entity coming from CUSTOMER zero?

b. What would be the attributes of ITEM (refer to Figure 2-22)?

c. What would be the attributes of MATERIAL (refer to Figure 2-22)?

3-27. Refer to Problem and Exercise 2-53 in Chapter 2, Part f. Redraw the ERD for your answer to this exercise using appropriate supertypes and subtypes.

3-28. For a library, the entity type HOLDING has four subtypes: BOOK, AUDIO BOOK, DVD, and SOFTWARE. Draw a separate EER diagram segment for each of the following situations:

a. At a given time, a holding must be exactly one of these subtypes.

b. A holding may or may not be one of these subtypes. However, a holding that is one of these subtypes cannot at the same time be one of the other subtypes.

c. A holding may or may not be one of these subtypes. On the other hand, a holding may be any two (or even four) of these subtypes at the same time.

d. At a given time, a holding must be at least one of these subtypes.

3-29. A bank has three types of accounts: checking, savings, and loan. Following are the attributes for each type of account:

CHECKING: Acct No, Date Opened, Balance, Service Charge

SAVINGS: Acct No, Date Opened, Balance, Interest Rate

LOAN: Acct No, Date Opened, Balance, Interest Rate, Payment

Assume that each bank account must be a member of exactly one of these subtypes. Using generalization, develop an EER model segment to represent this situation using the traditional EER notation, the Visio notation, or the subtypes inside supertypes notation, as specified by your instructor. Remember to include a subtype discriminator.

3-30. Refer to your answer to Problem and Exercise 2-53 in Chapter 2. Develop entity clusters for this E-R diagram and redraw the diagram using the entity clusters. Explain why you chose the entity clusters you used.

3-31. Refer to your answer to Problem and Exercise 3-27. Develop entity clusters for this E-R diagram and redraw the diagram using the entity clusters. Explain why you chose the entity clusters you used.

3-32. Draw an EER diagram for the following problem using this text's EER notation, the Visio notation, or the subtypes inside supertypes notation, as specified by your instructor.

A nonprofit organization depends on a number of different types of persons for its successful operation. The organization is interested in the following attributes for all of these persons: SSN, Name, Address, City/State/Zip, and Telephone. Three types of persons are of greatest interest: employees, volunteers, and donors. Employees have only a Date Hired attribute, and volunteers have only a Skill attribute. Donors have only a relationship (named Donates) with an Item entity type. A donor must have donated one or more items, and an item may have no donors, or one or more donors.

There are persons other than employees, volunteers, and donors who are of interest to the organization so that a person need not belong to any of these three groups. On the other hand, at a given time a person may belong to two or more of these groups (e.g., employee and donor).

3-33. Add a subtype discriminator (named Person Type) to the diagram you created in Problem and Exercise 2-38.

3-34. Develop an EER model for the following situation, using the traditional EER notation, the Visio notation, or the subtypes inside supertypes notation, as specified by your instructor:

A technology company provides offerings to its customers. Offerings are of two separate types: products and services. Offerings are identified by an offering ID and an attribute of description. In addition, products are described by product name, standard price, and date of first release; services are described by name of the company's unit responsible for the service and conditions of service. There are repair, maintenance, and other types of services. A repair service has a cost and is the repair of some product; a maintenance service has an hourly rate. Fortunately, some products never require repair. However, there are many potential repair services for a product. A customer may purchase an offering, and the company needs to keep track of when the offering was purchased and the contact person for that offering with the customer. Unfortunately, not all offerings are purchased. Customers are identified by customer ID and have descriptive data of name, address, and phone number. When a service is performed, that service is billed to some customer. Because some customers purchase offerings for their clients, a customer may be billed for services he or she did not purchase, as well as for ones that were purchased. When a customer is billed for a service (although some may never require a service of any type), the company needs to keep track of the date the service was performed, the date the bill is due, and the amount due.

3-35. Draw an EER diagram for the following description of a law firm:

Each case handled by the firm has a unique case number; a date opened, date closed, and judgment description are also kept on each case. A case is brought by one or more plaintiffs, and the same plaintiff may be involved in many cases. A plaintiff has a requested judgment characteristic. A case is against one or more defendants, and the same defendant may be involved in many cases. A plaintiff or defendant may be a person or an organization. Over time, the same person or organization may be a defendant or a plaintiff in cases. In either situation, such legal entities are identified by an entity number, and other attributes are name and net worth.

3-36. Develop an EER model for the following situation using the traditional EER notation, the Visio notation, or the subtypes inside supertypes notation, as specified by your instructor:

An international school of technology has hired you to create a database management system to assist in scheduling classes. After several interviews with the president, you have come up with the following list of entities, attributes, and initial business rules:

- Room is identified by Building ID and Room No and also has a Capacity. A room can be either a lab or a classroom. If it is a classroom, it has an additional attribute called Board Type.
- Media is identified by MType ID and has attributes of Media Type and Type Description. Note: Here we are tracking type of media (such as a VCR, projector, etc.), not the individual piece of equipment. Tracking of equipment is outside the scope of this project.
- Computer is identified by CType ID and has attributes Computer Type, Type Description, Disk Capacity, and Processor Speed. Please note: As with Media Type, we are tracking only the type of computer, not an individual computer. You can think of this as a class of computers (e.g., PIII 900MHZ).
- Instructor has identifier Emp ID and has attributes Name, Rank, and Office Phone.
- Timeslot has identifier TSIS and has attributes Day Of Week, Start Time, and End Time.
- Course has identifier Course ID and has attributes Course Description and Credits. Courses can have one, none, or many prerequisites. Courses also have one or more sections.
- Section has identifier Section ID and attribute Enrollment Limit.

After some further discussions, you have come up with some additional business rules to help you create the initial design:

- An instructor teaches one, none, or many sections of a course in a given semester.
- An instructor specifies preferred time slots.
- Scheduling data are kept for each semester, uniquely identified by semester and year.
- A room can be scheduled for one section or no section during one time slot in a given semester of a given year. However, one room can participate in many schedules, one schedule, or no schedules; one time slot can participate in many schedules, one schedule, or no schedules; one section can participate in many schedules, one schedule, or no schedules. Hint: Can you associate this to anything that you have seen before?
- A room can have one type of media, several types of media, or no media.
- Instructors are trained to use one, none, or many types of media.

- A lab has one or more computer types. However, a classroom does not have any computers.
- A room cannot be both a classroom and a lab. There also are no other room types to be incorporated into the system.

3-37. Develop an EER model for the following situation using the traditional EER notation, the Visio notation, or the subtypes inside supertypes notation, as specified by your instructor:

Wally Los Gatos and his partner Henry Chordate have formed a new limited partnership, Fin and Finicky Security Consultants. Fin and Finicky consults with corporations to determine their security needs. You have been hired by Wally and Henry to design a database management system to help them manage their business.

Due to a recent increase in business, Fin and Finicky has decided to automate its client tracking system. You and your team have done a preliminary analysis and come up with the following set of entities, attributes, and business rules:

Consultant

There are two types of consultants: business consultants and technical consultants. Business consultants are contacted by a business in order to first determine security needs and provide an estimate for the actual services to be performed. Technical consultants perform services according to the specifications developed by the business consultants.

Attributes of business consultant are the following: Employee ID (identifier), Name, Address (which is composed of Street, City, State, and Zip Code), Telephone, Date Of Birth, Age, Business Experience (which is composed of Number of Years, Type of Business [or businesses], and Degrees Received).

Attributes of technical consultant are the following: Employee ID (identifier), Name, Address (which is composed of Street, City, State, and Zip Code), Telephone, Date Of Birth, Age, Technical Skills, and Degrees Received.

Customer

Customers are businesses that have asked for consulting services. Attributes of customer are Customer ID (identifier), Company Name, Address (which is composed of Street, City, State, and Zip Code), Contact Name, Contact Title, Contact Telephone, Business Type, and Number Of Employees.

Location

Customers can have multiple locations. Attributes of location are Customer ID (identifier), Location ID (which is unique only for each Customer ID), Address (which is composed of Street, City, State, and Zip Code), Telephone, and Building Size.

Service

A security service is performed for a customer at one or more locations. Before services are performed, an estimate is prepared. Attributes of service are Service ID (identifier), Description, Cost, Coverage, and Clearance Required.

Additional Business Rules

In addition to the entities outlined previously, the following information will need to be stored to tables and should be shown in the model. These may be entities, but they also reflect a relationship between more than one entity:

- Estimates, which have characteristics of Date, Amount, Business Consultant, Services, and Customer
- Services Performed, which have characteristics of Date, Amount, Technical Consultant, Services, and Customer

In order to construct the EER diagram, you may assume the following:

A customer can have many consultants providing many services. You wish to track both actual services performed as well as services offered. Therefore, there should be two relationships between customer, service, and consultant, one to show services performed and one to show services offered as part of the estimate.

3-38. Based on the EER diagram constructed for Problem and Exercise 3-37, develop a sample definition for each entity type, attribute, and relationship in the diagram.

3-39. Refer to your answer to Problem and Exercise 2-60 in Chapter 2. The description for DocIT explained that there were to be data in the database about people who are not patients but are related to patients. Also, it is possible for some staff members to be patients or to be related to patients. And, some staff members have no reason to see patients in appointments, but these staff members provide functions related to only claims processing. Develop supertypes and subtypes to more clearly represent these distinctions, and draw a new EER diagram to show your revised data model.

3-40. Draw an EER diagram for the following situation:

TomKat Entertainment is a chain of theaters owned by former husband and wife actors/entertainers who, for some reason, can't get a job performing anymore. The owners want a database to track what is playing or has played on each screen in each theater of their chain at different times of the day. A theater (identified by a Theater ID and described by a theater name and location) contains one or more screens for viewing various movies. Within each theater each screen is identified by its number and is described by the seating capacity for viewing the screen. Movies are scheduled for showing in time slots each day. Each screen can have different time slots on different days (i.e., not all screens in the same theater have movies starting at the same time, and even on different days the same movie may play at different times on the same screen). For each time slot, the owners also want to know the end time of the time slot (assume all slots end on the same day the slot begins), attendance during that time slot, and the price charged for attendance in that time slot. Each movie (which can be either a trailer, feature, or commercial) is identified by a Movie ID and further described by its title, duration, and type (i.e., trailer, feature, or commercial). In each time slot, one or more movies are shown. The owners want to also keep track of in what sequence the movies are shown (e.g., in a time slot there might be two trailers, followed by two commercials, followed by a feature film, and closed with another commercial).

3-41. Add the following to Figure 3-16: An EMPLOYMENT party relationship is further explained by the positions and assignments to positions during the time a person is employed. A position is defined by an organization unit, and a unit may define many positions over time. Over time, positions are assigned to various employment relationships (i.e., somebody employed by some organization unit is assigned a particular position). For example, a position of Business Analyst is defined by the Systems Development organization unit. Carl Gerber, while employed by the Data Warehousing organization unit, is assigned the position of Systems Analyst. In the spirit of universal data modeling, enhance Figure 3-16 for the most general case consistent with this description.

3-42. A business school offering post graduate diploma in Management admits students to the PGDM program. You are required to design a DBMS for the admission office. You have developed a list of business rules.

a. Students apply to the college by getting the application form from the local branches of a nationalized bank

b. Students who have taken the Common Admission Test only are eligible

c. Applicant's Details: Application No., Applicant's Name, Applicant's Address, Applicant's DOB, Applicant's Qualification and CAT No. and CAT Score are stored by the Admission Office.

d. An applicant, if eligible may get admission to any of the campuses of the B-School.

e. Eligibility of the student is based on a number of parameters:
- Applicant's GPA in graduation degree
- Applicant's performance in High School
- Applicant's score in CAT
- Applicant's meeting the criteria for the above components are called for a personal interview and Group Discussion.

f. The Applicants finally admitted to the college will be evaluated on the following parameters with revised weightages.
- Applicant's GPA in graduation
- Applicant's performance in 10th Standard
- Applicant's score in CAT
- Applicant's performance in Group Discussion
- Applicant's performance in personal interview
- Each Applicant will get admitted into only one of the campuses

g. A final list of admitted students is sent along with their photographs to the PGP Office for further process.

Draw a E-R model for the above business rules and constraints.

Field Exercises

3-43. Interview a friend or family member to elicit common examples of supertype/subtype relationships he or she may come into contact with at work. You will have to explain the meaning of this term to the person you are interviewing and provide a common example, such as PROPERTY: RESIDENTIAL, COMMERCIAL, or BONDS: CORPORATE, MUNICIPAL. Use the information the person provides to construct an EER diagram segment and present it to the person. Revise, if necessary, until it seems appropriate to you and your friend or family member.

3-44. Visit two local small businesses, one in the service sector and one in manufacturing. Interview employees from these organizations to obtain examples of both supertype/subtype relationships and business rules (such as "A customer can return merchandise only with a valid sales slip"). In which of these environments is it easier to find examples of these constructs? Why?

3-45. Ask a database administrator or database or system analyst in a local company to show you an EER (or E-R) diagram for one of the organization's primary databases.

Does this organization model have supertype/subtype relationships? If so, what notation is used, and does the CASE tool the company uses support these relationships? Also, what types of business rules are included during the EER modeling phase? How are business rules represented, and how and where are they stored?

3-46. Read the summary of business rules published by the GUIDE Business Rules Project (1997) and the article by Gottesdiener (1997). Search the Web for additional information on business rules. Then write a three-page executive summary of current directions in business rules and their potential impact on systems development and maintenance.

3-47. Research universal data models. Find articles on universal (or packaged, industry, or functional area) data models, or find information on some commercial offerings. Identify common features across these models as well as different ways to model the same concepts. Discuss what you think are the advantages and disadvantages of the different ways used to model the same concepts.

References

Elmasri, R., and S. B. Navathe. 1994. *Fundamentals of Database Systems*. Menlo Park, CA: Benjamin/Cummings.

Gottesdiener, E. 1997. "Business Rules Show Power, Promise." *Application Development Trends* 4,3 (March): 36–54.

GUIDE. 1997 (October). "GUIDE Business Rules Project." Final Report, revision 1.2.

Hay, D. C. 1996. *Data Model Patterns: Conventions of Thought*. New York: Dorset House Publishing.

Hoberman, S. 2006. "Industry Logical Data Models." *Teradata Magazine*. Available at **www.teradata.com**.

Hoffer, J. A., J. F. George, and J. S. Valacich. 2014. *Modern Systems Analysis and Design*. 7th ed. Upper Saddle River, NJ: Prentice Hall.

Silverston, L. 1998. "Is Your Organization Too Unique to Use Universal Data Models?" *DM Review* 8,8 (September), accessed at **www.information-management.com/issues/19980901/425-1.html**.

Silverston, L. 2001a. *The Data Model Resource Book, Volume 1*, Rev. ed. New York: Wiley.

Silverston, L. 2001b. *The Data Model Resource Book, Volume 2*, Rev. ed. New York: Wiley.

Silverston, L. 2002. "A Universal Data Model for Relationship Development." *DM Review* 12,3 (March): 44–47, 65.

Teorey, T. 1999. *Database Modeling & Design*. San Francisco: Morgan Kaufman Publishers.

Further Reading

Frye, C. 2002. "Business Rules Are Back." *Application Development Trends* 9, 7 (July): 29–35.

Moriarty, T. "Using Scenarios in Information Modeling: Bringing Business Rules to Life." *Database Programming & Design* 6, 8 (August): 65–67.

Ross, R. G. 1997. *The Business Rule Book*. Version 4. Boston: Business Rule Solutions, Inc.

Ross, R. G. 1998. *Business Rule Concepts: The New Mechanics of Business Information Systems.* Boston: Business Rule Solutions, Inc.

Ross, R. G. 2003. *Principles of the Business Rule Approach*. Boston: Addison-Wesley.

Schmidt, B. 1997. "A Taxonomy of Domains." *Database Programming & Design* 10, 9 (September): 95, 96, 98, 99.

Silverston, L. 2002. Silverston has a series of articles in *DM Review* that discuss universal data models in different settings. See in particular Vol. 12 issues 1 (January) on clickstream analysis, 5 (May) on health care, 7 (July) on financial services, and 12 (December) on manufacturing.

von Halle, B. 1996. "Object-Oriented Lessons." *Database Programming & Design* 9,1 (January): 13–16.

von Halle, B. 2001. von Halle has a series of articles in *DM Review* on building a business rules system. These articles are in Vol. 11, issues 1–5 (January–May).

von Halle, B., and R. Kaplan. 1997. "Is IT Falling Short?" *Database Programming & Design* 10, 6 (June): 15–17.

Web Resources

www.adtmag.com Web site of *Application Development Trends,* a leading publication on the practice of information systems development.

www.brsolutions.com Web site of Business Rule Solutions, the consulting company of Ronald Ross, a leader in the development of a business rule methodology. Or you can check out **www.BRCommunity.com**, which is a virtual community site for people interested in business rules (sponsored by Business Rule Solutions).

www.businessrulesgroup.org Web site of the Business Rules Group, formerly part of GUIDE International, which formulates and supports standards about business rules.

www.databaseanswers.org/data_models A fascinating site that shows more than 100 sample E-R diagrams for a wide variety of applications and organizations. A variety of notations are used, so this a good site to also learn about variations in E-R diagramming.

http://researchlibrary.theserverside.net/detail/RES/1214505974_136.html Link to the white paper "Modeling Unstructured Data" by Steve Hoberman. Unstructured data (e.g., e-mails, images, sounds) is an emerging area for databases, and there are some special issues in data modeling for unstructured data.

www.tdan.com Web site of *The Data Administration Newsletter*, which regularly publishes new articles, special reports, and news on a variety of data modeling and administration topics.

www.teradatauniversitynetwork.com Web site for Teradata University Network, a free resource for a wide variety of information about database management and related topics. Go to this site and search on "entity relationship" to see many articles and assignments related to EER data modeling.

CASE

Forondo Artist Management Excellence Inc.

Case Description

Martin is encouraged by the progress you have made so far. As promised, he forwards you an e-mail from one of the key members of his staff, Pat Smith (an artist manager). He also provides you with an e-mail from Shannon Howard, a prospective artist who might use FAME's services.

E-mail from Pat Smith, Artist Manager

I am Pat Smith, and I am one of the 20 artist managers working for Mr. Forondo. I have worked for him for 15 years, and I am one of the most senior managers within the company. I enjoy working here because Mr. Forondo trusts me and knows that I will do my job. One area we have been lacking in during the last 10–15 years is the use of computers to support our jobs, and it is great to hear and notice that something is happening in this area.

There are two areas that I find particularly important for me. First, I would like to have a system that would help me track prospective artists. There are so many talented musicians around the world that it is almost impossible to know who is doing what and where without keeping very good records and it seems that this would be an area where computers really could help. There are a lot of sources from which I get hints about young artists whose career I should start to follow. Sometimes my friends who are music critics call me and recommend a particular young artist they have heard; sometimes I myself hear a promising artist perform; sometimes we find a jewel among the unsolicited recordings that are sent or referred to us; and we also follow a large number of newspapers, magazines, and websites that review performances. Over the years we have learned to value the opinions of certain critics who write reviews, thus it is very important to know the source of a recommendation or an opinion. Sometimes I deal with dozens or even hundreds of recommendations per day and thus the lists that I maintain in a Word file on my laptop just are not very easy to use and organize.

The system for managing prospective artists should keep track of the artists (including their name, gender, year of birth, instrument(s), university degrees, address, phone number, e-mail, honors, etc.) and all the situations in which we have heard of them (including the source, a brief summary, a brief quality evaluation, and space for storing the original story or a reference to it if it was a review either in a newspaper or on the Web). It is essential that I can get this data reported quickly and in an easy-to-read format. It would be fantastic if I could query the database from my personal tablet and smartphone; I definitely need access to my laptop while on the road. This info would be maintained by any of the managers in the company or their administrative assistants (the assistants take care of most of the work with the reviews). I don't know if Mr. Forondo told you but he makes the final decisions regarding who becomes the artist manager for a new artist if there is any question about the contributions in recruiting the artist.

The second system I would find very helpful would be an application that reports the revenues my artists have earned in the past (we should be able to choose the period freely) and are predicted to earn in the future based on the contracts we have signed for them with our clients. This way, I would know how much I am earning and going to earn in the future. Somehow, it would be great if the system could also tell how much money I have spent on travel; as you might have learned, we managers pay our own travel costs from the 60 percent of royalties we receive. I am really happy we don't need to pay the assistant's salaries, too.

E-mail from Shannon Howard, Prospective Artist

I am Shannon Howard, a soprano from Bloomington, Indiana, and I have had some initial discussions with Pat Smith at FAME regarding the possibility that they might take me under management. I feel that having a good manager would be very important for my career, and I believe that FAME would provide excellent service for me.

One area where FAME is not yet very strong is marketing their artists on the Internet, and maybe your project could have some impact in this area. I think it would be an excellent idea if prospective concert organizers could see an artist's information on the Web and also hear samples of his/her music. In addition, information about an artist's availability should be available on the Internet. By the way, has anybody remembered to tell you that an artist may be prevented from performing somewhere not only because of an earlier commitment to perform but also because of rehearsals or time needed for travel? Sometimes large productions need long practice times and transcontinental travel also can take several days away from an artist's schedule. For me it is very important that I can personally negotiate with my manager what I will perform and what I won't, and I think it would be great if my manager would know what repertoire I have already prepared and what I am not willing or able to perform at this time. Also, it would be great if I could block time away from my calendar in different priority groups so that I could say that certain days I am definitely not available, certain days are not very good but I can perform if Pat can find an excellent opportunity for me, and on certain days I can take any work. I don't know if this is realistic technologically and whether or not Pat would accept the idea, but it sure would be nice from my perspective.

The smoother all types of practical issues go, the better I can focus on my actual work, i.e., singing. Therefore, I feel that it is very important that FAME has a good computer system to help them in their work for me (assuming I can sign up with them—wish me luck!). I would find it very helpful if they could tell me at the end of the year how much money I have made and from whom I received it—it won't be a long list in the beginning but hopefully it will become much more extensive over time.

I don't know if you have thought about it but just in case I have gigs around the world it would be very nice if the system could also tell how much (if anything) each of the governments withheld from my pay at the source before it was forwarded to FAME and if the payments could be sorted and subtotaled by country. If you wonder what this could mean in practice, let me give you an example. Let's say I am performing in Finland

and Finland has an at-the-source tax for artists of 15 percent. If my fee there is $2,000, my employer in Finland has to withdraw 15 percent of my fee and pay it to the Finnish government; therefore, FAME will receive only $1,700, and if their royalty is 30 percent, I will receive only $1,190. At the end of the year, FAME should give me a report including four columns: my original fee (i.e., $2,000 in this case), tax-at-source ($300), FAME's share ($510), and finally my share ($1,190). The math is simple but it is essential that this is done correctly so that I won't be in trouble with the tax authorities either in foreign countries or here in the United States.

Project Questions

3-48. Create an EER diagram for FAME that extends the E-R diagram you developed in Chapter 2, 2-75, but accommodates the information gleaned from the e-mails from Pat Smith and Shannon Howard.

3-49. Document your thought process around what changes you made to the model developed in Chapter 2, 2-75, to accommodate the new information. Pay particular attention to what changes you had to make to the original model to accommodate the need for supertype/subtype relationships that emerged from the new information.

3-50. Use the narratives in Chapters 1, 2, and above to identify the typical outputs (reports and displays) the various stakeholders might want to retrieve from your database. Now, revisit the EER diagram you created in 3-49 to ensure that your model has captured the information necessary to generate the outputs desired. Update your EER diagram as necessary.

3-51. Create a plan for reviewing your deliverables with the appropriate stakeholders. Which stakeholders should you meet with? Would you conduct the reviews separately or together? Who do you think should sign off on your EER model before you move to the next phase of the project?

PART III

Database Design

AN OVERVIEW OF PART THREE

By the end of the database analysis phase of database development, systems and database analysts have a fairly clear understanding of data storage and access requirements. However, the data model developed during analysis explicitly avoids any ties to database technologies. Before we can implement a database, the conceptual data model must be mapped into a data model that is compatible with the database management system to be used.

The activities of database design transform the requirements for data storage developed during database analysis into specifications to guide database implementation. There are two forms of specifications:

1. Logical specifications, which map the conceptual requirements into the data model associated with a specific database management system.
2. Physical specifications, which indicate all the parameters for data storage that are then used as input for database implementation. During this phase, a database is actually defined using a data definition language.

In Chapter 4 ("Logical Database Design and the Relational Model"), we describe logical database design, with special emphasis on the relational data model. Logical database design is the process of transforming the conceptual data model (described in Chapters 2 and 3) into a logical data model. Most database management systems in use today are based on the relational data model, so this data model is the basis for our discussion of logical database design.

In Chapter 4, we first define the important terms and concepts for this model, including *relation*, *primary key* and *surrogate primary key*, *foreign key*, *anomaly*, *normal form*, *normalization*, *functional dependency*, *partial functional dependency*, and *transitive dependency*. We next describe and illustrate the process of transforming an E-R model to the relational model. Many modeling tools support this transformation; however, it is important that you understand the underlying principles and procedures. We then describe and illustrate in detail the important concepts of normalization (the process of designing well-structured relations). Appendix B, on the book's Web site, includes further discussion of normalization. Finally, we describe how to merge relations from separate logical design activities (e.g., different groups within a large project team) while avoiding common pitfalls that may occur in this process. We end this discussion with a presentation of enterprise keys, which make relational keys distinct across relations.

The purpose of physical database design, the topic of Chapter 5 ("Physical Database Design and Performance"), is to translate the logical description of data into the technical specifications for storing and retrieving data. The goal is to create a design for storing data that will provide adequate performance and ensure

Chapter 4

Logical Database Design and the Relational Model

Chapter 5

Physical Database Design and Performance

database integrity, security, and recoverability. Physical database design produces the technical specifications that programmers and others involved in information systems construction will use during the implementation phase, which we discuss in Chapters 6 through 9.

In Chapter 5, you will learn key terms and concepts for physical database design, including *data type*, *page*, *pointer*, *denormalization*, *partitioning*, *indexed file organization*, and *hashed file organization*. You will study the basic steps in developing an efficient physical database design. You will learn about choices for storing attribute values and how to select among these choices. You will also learn why normalized tables do not always form the best physical data files and how you can, if necessary, denormalize the data to achieve data retrieval speed improvements. You will learn about different file organizations and different types of indexes, which are important in speeding the retrieval of data. Appendix C, on the book's Web site, addresses some additional constructs for physical data storage. In addition, you will learn how physical database design choices that improve data quality affect the process of validating the accuracy of financial reporting. These are essential issues today because of government regulations, such as Sarbanes-Oxley, and because of the growing realization that ensuring high data quality makes business sense.

You must carefully perform physical database design because decisions made during this stage have a major impact on data accessibility, response times, security, user friendliness, information quality, and similarly important information system design factors. Database administration (described in Chapter 12) plays a major role in physical database design, so we will return to some advanced design issues in that chapter, and Chapter 13, on the book's Web site, addresses distributed database design issues.

CHAPTER 4

Logical Database Design and the Relational Model

LEARNING OBJECTIVES

After studying this chapter, you should be able to:

- Concisely define each of the following key terms: **relation, primary key, composite key, foreign key, null, entity integrity rule, referential integrity constraint, well-structured relation, anomaly, surrogate primary key, recursive foreign key, normalization, normal form, functional dependency, determinant, candidate key, first normal form, second normal form, partial functional dependency, third normal form, transitive dependency, synonyms, alias, homonym,** and **enterprise key.**
- List five properties of relations.
- State two essential properties of a candidate key.
- Give a concise definition of each of the following: first normal form, second normal form, and third normal form.
- Briefly describe four problems that may arise when merging relations.
- Transform an E-R (or EER) diagram into a logically equivalent set of relations.
- Create relational tables that incorporate entity integrity and referential integrity constraints.
- Use normalization to decompose a relation with anomalies into well-structured relations.

Visit www.pearsonhighered.com/ hoffer to view the accompanying video for this chapter.

INTRODUCTION

In this chapter, we describe logical database design, with special emphasis on the relational data model. Logical database design is the process of transforming the conceptual data model (described in Chapters 2 and 3) into a logical data model—one that is consistent and compatible with a specific type of database technology. An experienced database designer often will do logical database design in parallel with conceptual data modeling if he or she knows the type of database technology that will be used. It is, however, important to treat these as separate steps so that you concentrate on each important part of database development. Conceptual data modeling is about understanding the organization—getting the requirements right. Logical database design is about creating stable database structures—correctly expressing the requirements in a technical language. Both are important steps that must be performed carefully.

Although there are other logical data models, we have two reasons for emphasizing the relational data model in this chapter. First, the relational data model is by far the one most commonly used in contemporary database applications. Second, some of the principles of logical database design for the relational model apply to the other logical models as well.

We have introduced the relational data model informally through simple examples in earlier chapters. It is important, however, to note that the relational data model is a form of logical data model, and as such it is different from the conceptual data models. Thus, an E-R data model is not a relational data model, and an E-R model may not obey the rules for a well-structured relational data model, called *normalization*, which we explain in this chapter. That is okay, because the E-R model was developed for other purposes—understanding data requirements and business rules about the data—not structuring the data for sound database processing, which is the goal of logical database design.

In this chapter, we first define the important terms and concepts for the relational data model. (We often use the abbreviated term *relational model* when referring to the relational data model.) We next describe and illustrate the process of transforming an EER model into the relational model. Many CASE tools support this transformation today at the technical level. It is, however, important that you understand the underlying principles and procedures. We then describe the concepts of normalization in detail. Normalization, which is the process of designing well-structured relations, is an important component of logical design for the relational model. Finally, we describe how to merge relations while avoiding common pitfalls that may occur in this process.

The objective of logical database design is to translate the conceptual design (which represents an organization's requirements for data) into a logical database design that can be implemented via a chosen database management system. The resulting databases must meet user needs for data sharing, flexibility, and ease of access. The concepts presented in this chapter are essential to your understanding of the database development process.

THE RELATIONAL DATA MODEL

The relational data model was first introduced in 1970 by E. F. Codd, then of IBM (Codd, 1970). Two early research projects were launched to prove the feasibility of the relational model and to develop prototype systems. The first of these, at IBM's San Jose Research Laboratory, led to the development of System R (a prototype relational DBMS [RDBMS]) during the late 1970s. The second, at the University of California at Berkeley, led to the development of Ingres, an academically oriented RDBMS. Commercial RDBMS products from numerous vendors started to appear about 1980. (See the Web site for this text for links to DBMS vendors.) Today, RDBMSs have become the dominant technology for database management, and there are literally hundreds of RDBMS products for computers ranging from smartphones and personal computers to mainframes. In Chapter 11 we will discuss a new set of DBMS technologies under the umbrella of NoSQL (Not Only SQL); although increasing in popularity, the use of these technologies is still not anywhere close to that of RDBMSs.

Basic Definitions

The relational data model represents data in the form of tables. The relational model is based on mathematical theory and therefore has a solid theoretical foundation. However, we need only a few simple concepts to describe the relational model. Therefore, it can be easily understood and used even by those unfamiliar with the underlying theory. The relational data model consists of the following three components (Fleming and von Halle, 1989):

1. *Data structure* Data are organized in the form of tables, with rows and columns.
2. *Data manipulation* Powerful operations (typically implemented using the SQL language) are used to manipulate data stored in the relations.
3. *Data integrity* The model includes mechanisms to specify business rules that maintain the integrity of data when they are manipulated.

EMPLOYEE1

EmpID	Name	DeptName	Salary
100	Malini Srivastav	Marketing	48,000
140	Akash Bahety	Accounting	52,000
110	Chandan Shetty	Info Systems	43,000
190	Lakshmi Dave	Finance	55,000
150	Sushma Murthy	Marketing	42,000

FIGURE 4-1 EMPLOYEE1 relation with sample data

We discuss data structure and data integrity in this section. Data manipulation is discussed primarily in Chapters 6 and 7, and presented in an application context in Chapter 8.

RELATIONAL DATA STRUCTURE   A **relation** is a named, two-dimensional table of data. Each relation (or table) consists of a set of named columns and an arbitrary number of unnamed rows. An attribute, consistent with its definition in Chapter 2, is a named column of a relation. Each row of a relation corresponds to a record that contains data (attribute) values for a single entity. Figure 4-1 shows an example of a relation named EMPLOYEE1. This relation contains the following attributes describing employees: EmpID, Name, DeptName, and Salary. The five rows of the table correspond to five employees. It is important to understand that the sample data in Figure 4-1 are intended to illustrate the structure of the EMPLOYEE1 relation; they are not part of the relation itself. Even if we add another row of data to the figure or change any of the data in the existing rows, it is still the same EMPLOYEE1 relation. Nor does deleting a row change the relation. In fact, we could delete all of the rows shown in Figure 4-1, and the EMPLOYEE1 relation would still exist. In other words, Figure 4-1 is an instance of the EMPLOYEE1 relation.

Relation
A named two-dimensional table of data.

We can express the structure of a relation by using a shorthand notation in which the name of the relation is followed (in parentheses) by the names of the attributes in that relation. For EMPLOYEE1 we would have

EMPLOYEE1(EmpID, Name, DeptName, Salary)

RELATIONAL KEYS   We must be able to store and retrieve a row of data in a relation, based on the data values stored in that row. To achieve this goal, every relation must have a primary key. A **primary key** is an attribute or a combination of attributes that uniquely identifies each row in a relation. We designate a primary key by underlining the attribute name(s). For example, the primary key for the relation EMPLOYEE1 is EmpID. Notice that this attribute is underlined in Figure 4-1. In shorthand notation, we express this relation as follows:

Primary key
An attribute or a combination of attributes that uniquely identifies each row in a relation.

EMPLOYEE1(EmpID, Name, DeptName, Salary)

The concept of a primary key is related to the term *identifier* defined in Chapter 2. The attribute or a collection of attributes indicated as an entity's identifier in an E-R diagram may be the same attributes that comprise the primary key for the relation representing that entity. There are exceptions: For example, associative entities do not have to have an identifier, and the (partial) identifier of a weak entity forms only part of a corresponding relation's primary key. In addition, there may be several attributes of an entity that may serve as the associated relation's primary key. All of these situations will be illustrated later in this chapter.

A **composite key** is a primary key that consists of more than one attribute. For example, the primary key for a relation DEPENDENT would likely consist of the

Composite key
A primary key that consists of more than one attribute.

combination EmpID and DependentName. We show several examples of composite keys later in this chapter.

Often we must represent the relationship between two tables or relations. This is accomplished through the use of foreign keys. A **foreign key** is an attribute (possibly composite) in a relation that serves as the primary key of another relation. For example, consider the relations EMPLOYEE1 and DEPARTMENT:

Foreign key

An attribute in a relation that serves as the primary key of another relation in the same database.

EMPLOYEE1(EmpID, Name, DeptName, Salary)
DEPARTMENT(DeptName, Location, Fax)

The attribute DeptName is a foreign key in EMPLOYEE1. It allows a user to associate any employee with the department to which he or she is assigned. Some authors emphasize the fact that an attribute is a foreign key by using a dashed underline, like this:

EMPLOYEE1(EmpID, Name, DeptName, Salary)

We provide numerous examples of foreign keys in the remainder of this chapter and discuss the properties of foreign keys under the heading "Referential Integrity."

PROPERTIES OF RELATIONS We have defined relations as two-dimensional tables of data. However, not all tables are relations. Relations have several properties that distinguish them from non-relational tables. We summarize these properties next:

1. Each relation (or table) in a database has a unique name.
2. An entry at the intersection of each row and column is atomic (or single valued). There can be only one value associated with each attribute on a specific row of a table; no multivalued attributes are allowed in a relation.
3. Each row is unique; no two rows in a relation can be identical.
4. Each attribute (or column) within a table has a unique name.
5. The sequence of columns (left to right) is insignificant. The order of the columns in a relation can be changed without changing the meaning or use of the relation.
6. The sequence of rows (top to bottom) is insignificant. As with columns, the order of the rows of a relation may be changed or stored in any sequence.

REMOVING MULTIVALUED ATTRIBUTES FROM TABLES The second property of relations listed in the preceding section states that no multivalued attributes are allowed in a relation. Thus, a table that contains one or more multivalued attributes is not a relation. For example, Figure 4-2a shows the employee data from the EMPLOYEE1 relation extended to include courses that have been taken by those employees. Because a given employee may have taken more than one course, CourseTitle and DateCompleted are multivalued attributes. For example, the employee with EmpID 100 has taken two courses, therefore, there are two values of both CourseTitle (SPSS and Surveys) and DateCompleted (6/9/2015 and 10/7/2015) associated with one value of EmpID (100). If an employee has not taken any courses, the CourseTitle and DateCompleted attribute values are null. (See the employee with EmpID 190 for an example.)

We show how to eliminate the multivalued attributes in Figure 4-2b by filling the relevant data values into the previously vacant cells of Figure 4-2a. As a result, the table in Figure 4-2b has only single-valued attributes and now satisfies the atomic property of relations. The name EMPLOYEE2 is given to this relation to distinguish it from EMPLOYEE1. However, as you will see, this new relation does have some undesirable properties. We will discuss some of them later in the chapter, but one of them is that the primary key column EmpID no longer uniquely identifies each of the rows.

Sample Database

A relational database may consist of any number of relations. The structure of the database is described through the use of a schema (defined in Chapter 1), which is

FIGURE 4-2 Eliminating multivalued attributes

(a) Table with repeating groups

EmpID	Name	DeptName	Salary	CourseTitle	DateCompleted
100	Malini Srivastav	Marketing	48,000	SPSS	6/19/201X
				Surveys	10/7/201X
140	Akash Bahety	Accounting	52,000	Tax Acc	12/8/201X
110	Chandan Shetty	Info Systems	43,000	Visual Basic	1/12/201X
				C++	4/22/201X
190	Lakshmi Dave	Finance	55,000		
150	Sushma Murthy	Marketing	42,000	SPSS	6/16/201X
				Java	8/12/201X

(b) EMPLOYEE2 relation

EMPLOYEE2

EmpID	Name	DeptName	Salary	CourseTitle	DateCompleted
100	Malini Srivastav	Marketing	48,000	SPSS	6/19/201X
100	Malini Srivastav	Marketing	48,000	Surveys	10/7/201X
140	Akash Bahety	Accounting	52,000	Tax Acc	12/8/201X
110	Chandan Shetty	Info Systems	43,000	Visual Basic	1/12/201X
110	Chandan Shetty	Info Systems	43,000	C++	4/22/201X
190	Lakshmi Dave	Finance	55,000		
150	Sushma Murthy	Marketing	42,000	SPSS	6/19/201X
150	Sushma Murthy	Marketing	42,000	Java	8/12/201X

a description of the overall logical structure of the database. There are two common methods for expressing a schema:

1. Short text statements, in which each relation is named and the names of its attributes follow in parentheses. (See the EMPLOYEE1 and DEPARTMENT relations defined earlier in this chapter.)
2. A graphical representation, in which each relation is represented by a rectangle containing the attributes for the relation.

Text statements have the advantage of simplicity. However, a graphical representation provides a better means of expressing referential integrity constraints (as you will see shortly). In this section, we use both techniques for expressing a schema so that you can compare them.

A schema for four relations at Pine Valley Furniture Company is shown in Figure 4-3. The four relations shown in this figure are CUSTOMER, ORDER, ORDER LINE, and PRODUCT. The key attributes for these relations are underlined, and other important attributes are included in each relation. We show how to design these relations using the techniques of normalization later in this chapter.

Following is a text description of these relations:

CUSTOMER(CustomerID, CustomerName, CustomerAddress,
    CustomerCity, CustomerState, CustomerPostalCode)
ORDER(OrderID, OrderDate, CustomerID)
ORDER LINE(OrderID, ProductID, OrderedQuantity)
PRODUCT(ProductID, ProductDescription, ProductFinish,
    ProductStandardPrice, ProductLineID)

Notice that the primary key for ORDER LINE is a composite key consisting of the attributes OrderID and ProductID. Also, CustomerID is a foreign key in the ORDER relation; this allows the user to associate an order with the customer who submitted the order. ORDER LINE has two foreign keys: OrderID and ProductID. These keys allow

FIGURE 4-3 Schema for four
relations (Pine Valley Furniture
Company)

CUSTOMER

CustomerID	CustomerName	CustomerAddress	CustomerCity*	CustomerState*	CustomerPostalCode

ORDER

OrderID	OrderDate	CustomerID

ORDER LINE

OrderID	ProductID	OrderedQuantity

PRODUCT

ProductID	ProductDescription	ProductFinish	ProductStandardPrice	ProductLineID

* Not in Figure 2-22 for simplicity.

the user to associate each line on an order with the relevant order and product. In cases when a foreign key is also part of a composite key (such as this), frequently only the primary key role of the attribute is marked with a solid underline.

An instance of this database is shown in Figure 4-4. This figure shows four tables with sample data. Notice how the foreign keys allow us to associate the various tables. It is a good idea to create an instance of your relational schema with sample data for four reasons:

1. The sample data allow you to test your assumptions regarding the design.
2. The sample data provide a convenient way to check the accuracy of your design.
3. The sample data help improve communications with users in discussing your design.
4. The sample data can be used to develop prototype applications and to test queries.

INTEGRITY CONSTRAINTS

The relational data model includes several types of constraints, or rules limiting acceptable values and actions, whose purpose is to facilitate maintaining the accuracy and integrity of data in the database. The major types of integrity constraints are domain constraints, entity integrity, and referential integrity.

Domain Constraints

All of the values that appear in a column of a relation must be from the same domain. A domain is the set of values that may be assigned to an attribute. A domain definition usually consists of the following components: domain name, meaning, data type, size (or length), and allowable values or allowable range (if applicable). Table 4-1 (page 162) shows domain definitions for the domains associated with the attributes in Figures 4-3 and 4-4.

Entity Integrity

The entity integrity rule is designed to ensure that every relation has a primary key and that the data values for that primary key are all valid. In particular, it guarantees that every primary key attribute is non-null.

In some cases, a particular attribute cannot be assigned a data value. There are two situations in which this is likely to occur: Either there is no applicable data value or the applicable data value is not known when values are assigned. Suppose, for example, that you fill out an employment form that has a space reserved for a fax number. If you have no fax number, you leave this space empty because it does not apply to you. Or suppose that you are asked to fill in the telephone number of your previous employer.

FIGURE 4-4   **Instance of a relational schema (Pine Valley Furniture Company)**

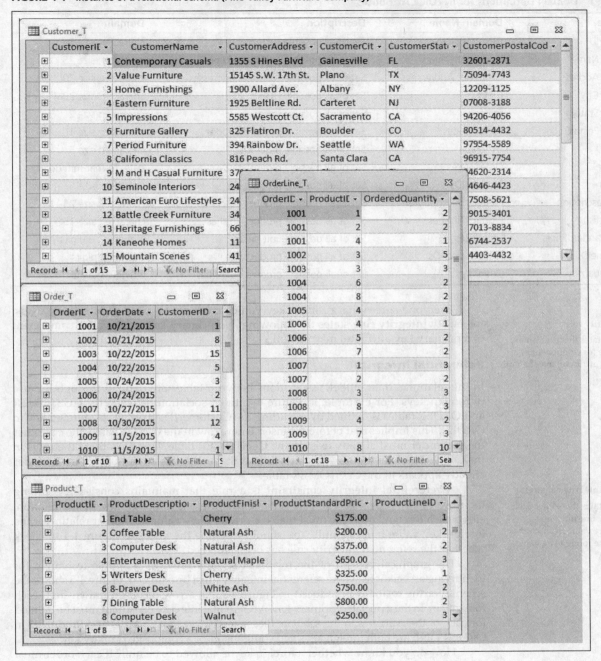

If you do not recall this number, you may leave it empty because that information is not known. You might also want to leave it empty because you do not want your current employer to know that you are seeking for another position.

The relational data model allows us to assign a null value to an attribute in the just described situations. A **null** is a value that may be assigned to an attribute when no other value applies or when the applicable value is unknown. In reality, a null is not a value, but rather it indicates the absence of a value. For example, it is not the same as a numeric zero or a string of blanks. The inclusion of nulls in the relational model is somewhat controversial, because it sometimes leads to anomalous results (Date, 2003). However, Codd, the inventor of the relational model, advocates the use of nulls for missing values (Codd, 1990).

Null

A value that may be assigned to an attribute when no other value applies or when the applicable value is unknown.

TABLE 4-1 Domain Definitions for INVOICE Attributes

Attribute	Domain Name	Description	Domain
CustomerID	Customer IDs	Set of all possible customer IDs	character: size 5
CustomerName	Customer Names	Set of all possible customer names	character: size 25
CustomerAddress	Customer Addresses	Set of all possible customer addresses	character: size 30
CustomerCity	Cities	Set of all possible cities	character: size 20
CustomerState	States	Set of all possible states	character: size 2
CustomerPostalCode	Postal Codes	Set of all possible postal zip codes	character: size 10
OrderID	Order IDs	Set of all possible order IDs	character: size 5
OrderDate	Order Dates	Set of all possible order dates	date: format mm/dd/yy
ProductID	Product IDs	Set of all possible product IDs	character: size 5
ProductDescription	Product Descriptions	Set of all possible product descriptions	character: size 25
ProductFinish	Product Finishes	Set of all possible product finishes	character: size 15
ProductStandardPrice	Unit Prices	Set of all possible unit prices	monetary: 6 digits
ProductLineID	Product Line IDs	Set of all possible product line IDs	integer: 3 digits
OrderedQuantity	Quantities	Set of all possible ordered quantities	integer: 3 digits

Entity integrity rule

A rule that states that no primary key attribute (or component of a primary key attribute) may be null.

Everyone agrees that primary key values must not be allowed to be null. Thus, the **entity integrity rule** states the following: No primary key attribute (or component of a primary key attribute) may be null.

Referential Integrity

In the relational data model, associations between tables are defined through the use of foreign keys. For example, in Figure 4-4, the association between the CUSTOMER and ORDER tables is defined by including the CustomerID attribute as a foreign key in ORDER. This implies that before we insert a new row in the ORDER table, the customer for that order must already exist in the CUSTOMER table. If you examine the rows in the ORDER table in Figure 4-4, you will find that every customer number for an order already appears in the CUSTOMER table.

Referential integrity constraint

A rule that states that either each foreign key value must match a primary key value in another relation or the foreign key value must be null.

A **referential integrity constraint** is a rule that maintains consistency among the rows of two relations. The rule states that if there is a foreign key in one relation, either each foreign key value must match a primary key value in another relation or the foreign key value must be null. You should examine the tables in Figure 4-4 to check whether the referential integrity rule has been enforced.

The graphical version of the relational schema provides a simple technique for identifying associations where referential integrity must be enforced. Figure 4-5 shows the schema for the relations introduced in Figure 4-3. An arrow has been drawn from each foreign key to the associated primary key. A referential integrity constraint must be defined for each of these arrows in the schema. Please remember that OrderID and ProductID in ORDER LINE are both foreign keys and components of a composite primary key.

How do you know whether a foreign key is allowed to be null? If each order must have a customer (a mandatory relationship), then the foreign key CustomerID cannot be null in the ORDER relation. If the relationship is optional, then the foreign key could be null. Whether a foreign key can be null must be specified as a property of the foreign key attribute when the database is defined.

Actually, whether a foreign key can be null is more complex to model on an E-R diagram and to determine than we have shown so far. For example, what happens to order data if we choose to delete a customer who has submitted orders? We may want to see sales even if we do not care about the customer any more. Three choices are possible:

1. Delete the associated orders (called a cascading delete), in which case we lose not only the customer but also all the sales history.
2. Prohibit deletion of the customer until all associated orders are first deleted (a safety check).

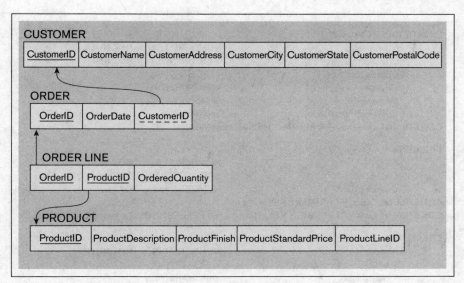

FIGURE 4-5 Referential integrity constraints (Pine Valley Furniture Company)

3. Place a null value in the foreign key (an exception stating that although an order must have a CustomerID value when the order is created, CustomerID can become null later if the associated customer is deleted).

We will see how each of these choices is implemented when we describe the SQL database query language in Chapter 6. Please note that in practice, organizational rules and various regulations regarding data retention often determine what data can be deleted and when, and they therefore govern the choice between various deletion options.

Creating Relational Tables

In this section, we create table definitions for the four tables shown in Figure 4-5. These definitions are created using the **CREATE TABLE** statements of the SQL data definition language. In practice, these table definitions are actually created during the implementation phase later in the database development process. However, we show these sample tables in this chapter for continuity and especially to illustrate the way the integrity constraints described previously are implemented in SQL.

The SQL table definitions are shown in Figure 4-6. One table is created for each of the four relations shown in the relational schema (Figure 4-5). Each attribute for a table is then defined. Notice that the data type and length for each attribute are taken from the domain definitions (Table 4-1). For example, the attribute CustomerName in the Customer_T table is defined as VARCHAR (variable character) data type with length 25. By specifying NOT NULL, each attribute can be constrained from being assigned a null value.

The primary key is specified for each table using the **PRIMARY KEY** clause at the end of each table definition. The OrderLine_T table illustrates how to specify a primary key when that key is a composite attribute. In this example, the primary key of OrderLine_T is the combination of OrderID and ProductID. Each primary key attribute in the four tables is constrained with **NOT NULL**. This enforces the entity integrity constraint described in the previous section. Notice that the **NOT NULL** constraint can also be used with non-primary-key attributes.

Referential integrity constraints are easily defined, based on the graphical schema shown in Figure 4-5. An arrow originates from each foreign key and points to the related primary key in the associated relation. In the SQL table definition, a **FOREIGN KEY REFERENCES** statement corresponds to each of these arrows. Thus, for the table Order_T, the foreign key CustomerID references the primary key of Customer_T, which is also called CustomerID. Although in this case the foreign key and primary key have the same name, this is not required. For example, the foreign key attribute could be named CustNo instead of CustomerID. However, the foreign and primary keys must be from the same domain (i.e., they must have the same data type).

FIGURE 4-6 SQL table definitions

```
CREATE TABLE Customer_T
        (CustomerID                    NUMBER(11,0)      NOT NULL,
        CustomerName                   VARCHAR2(25)      NOT NULL,
        CustomerAddress                VARCHAR2(30),
        CustomerCity                   VARCHAR2(20),
        CustomerState                  CHAR(2),
        CustomerPostalCode             VARCHAR2(9),
CONSTRAINT Customer_PK PRIMARY KEY (CustomerID));

CREATE TABLE Order_T
        (OrderID                       NUMBER(11,0)      NOT NULL,
        OrderDate                      DATE DEFAULT SYSDATE,
        CustomerID                     NUMBER(11,0),
CONSTRAINT Order_PK PRIMARY KEY (OrderID),
CONSTRAINT Order_FK FOREIGN KEY (CustomerID) REFERENCES Customer_T (CustomerID));

CREATE TABLE Product_T
        (ProductID                     NUMBER(11,0)      NOT NULL,
        ProductDescription             VARCHAR2(50),
        ProductFinish                  VARCHAR2(20),
        ProductStandardPrice           DECIMAL(6,2),
        ProductLineID                  NUMBER(11,0),
CONSTRAINT Product_PK PRIMARY KEY (ProductID));

CREATE TABLE OrderLine_T
        (OrderID                       NUMBER(11,0)      NOT NULL,
        ProductID                      NUMBER(11,0)      NOT NULL,
        OrderedQuantity                NUMBER(11,0),
CONSTRAINT OrderLine_PK PRIMARY KEY (OrderID, ProductID),
CONSTRAINT OrderLine_FK1 FOREIGN KEY (OrderID) REFERENCES Order_T (OrderID),
CONSTRAINT OrderLine_FK2 FOREIGN KEY (ProductID) REFERENCES Product_T (ProductID));
```

The OrderLine_T table provides an example of a table that has two foreign keys. Foreign keys in this table reference the Order_T and Product_T tables, respectively. Please note that these two foreign keys are also the components of the primary key of OrderLine_T. This type of structure is very common as an implementation of a many-to-many relationship.

Well-Structured Relations

Well-structured relation
A relation that contains minimal redundancy and allows users to insert, modify, and delete the rows in a table without errors or inconsistencies.

To prepare for our discussion of normalization, we need to address the following question: What constitutes a well-structured relation? Intuitively, a **well-structured relation** contains minimal redundancy and allows users to insert, modify, and delete the rows in a table without errors or inconsistencies. EMPLOYEE1 (Figure 4-1) is such a relation. Each row of the table contains data describing one employee, and any modification to an employee's data (such as a change in salary) is confined to one row of the table. In contrast, EMPLOYEE2 (Figure 4-2b) is not a well-structured relation. If you examine the sample data in the table, you will notice considerable redundancy. For example, values for EmpID, Name, DeptName, and Salary appear in two separate rows for employees 100, 110, and 150. Consequently, if the salary for employee 100 changes, we must record this fact in two rows.

Anomaly
An error or inconsistency that may result when a user attempts to update a table that contains redundant data. The three types of anomalies are insertion, deletion, and modification anomalies.

Redundancies in a table may result in errors or inconsistencies (called **anomalies**) when a user attempts to update the data in the table. We are typically concerned about three types of anomalies:

1. *Insertion anomaly* Suppose that we need to add a new employee to EMPLOYEE2. The primary key for this relation is the combination of EmpID and CourseTitle (as noted earlier). Therefore, to insert a new row, the user must supply values for both EmpID and CourseTitle (because primary key values cannot be null or nonexistent). This is an anomaly because the user should be able to enter employee data without supplying course data.

FIGURE 4-7 EMP COURSE

EmpID	CourseTitle	DateCompleted
100	SPSS	6/19/2015
100	Surveys	10/7/2015
140	Tax Acc	12/8/2015
110	Visual Basic	1/12/2015
110	C++	4/22/2015
150	SPSS	6/19/2015
150	Java	8/12/2015

2. *Deletion anomaly* Suppose that the data for employee number 140 are deleted from the table. This will result in losing the information that this employee completed a course (Tax Acc) on 12/8/2015. In fact, it results in losing the information that this course had an offering that completed on that date.

3. *Modification anomaly* Suppose that employee number 100 gets a salary increase. We must record the increase in each of the rows for that employee (two occurrences in Figure 4-2); otherwise, the data will be inconsistent.

These anomalies indicate that EMPLOYEE2 is not a well-structured relation. The problem with this relation is that it contains data about two entities: EMPLOYEE and COURSE. We will use normalization theory (described later in this chapter) to divide EMPLOYEE2 into two relations. One of the resulting relations is EMPLOYEE1 (Figure 4-1). The other we will call EMP COURSE, which appears with sample data in Figure 4-7. The primary key of this relation is the combination of EmpID and CourseTitle, and we underline these attribute names in Figure 4-7 to highlight this fact. Examine Figure 4-7 to verify that EMP COURSE is free of the types of anomalies described previously and is therefore well structured.

TRANSFORMING EER DIAGRAMS INTO RELATIONS

During logical design, you transform the E-R (and EER) diagrams that were developed during conceptual design into relational database schemas. The inputs to this process are the entity-relationship (and enhanced E-R) diagrams that you studied in Chapters 2 and 3. The outputs are the relational schemas described in the first two sections of this chapter.

Transforming (or mapping) EER diagrams into relations is a relatively straightforward process with a well-defined set of rules. In fact, many CASE tools can automatically perform many of the conversion steps. However, it is important that you understand the steps in this process for four reasons:

1. CASE tools often cannot model more complex data relationships such as ternary relationships and supertype/subtype relationships. In these situations, you may have to perform the steps manually.

2. There are sometimes legitimate alternatives for which you will need to choose a particular solution.

3. You must be prepared to perform a quality check on the results obtained with a CASE tool.

4. Understanding the transformation process helps you understand why conceptual data modeling (modeling the real-world domain) is different from logical data modeling (i.e., representing the data items within the domain in a way that can be implemented with a DBMS).

In the following discussion, we illustrate the steps in the transformation with examples taken from Chapters 2 and 3. It will help for you to recall that we discussed three types of entities in those chapters:

1. *Regular entities* are entities that have an independent existence and generally represent real-world objects, such as persons and products. Regular entity types are represented by rectangles with a single line.

FIGURE 4-8 Example of
mapping a regular entity
(a) CUSTOMER entity type

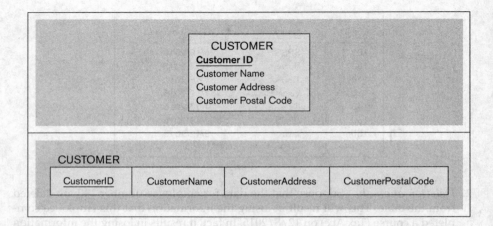

(b) CUSTOMER relation

2. *Weak entities* are entities that cannot exist except with an identifying relationship with an owner (regular) entity type. Weak entities are identified by a rectangle with a double line.
3. *Associative entities* (also called gerunds) are formed from many-to-many relationships between other entity types. Associative entities are represented by a rectangle with rounded corners.

Step 1: Map Regular Entities

Each regular entity type in an E-R diagram is transformed into a relation. The name given to the relation is generally the same as the entity type. Each simple attribute of the entity type becomes an attribute of the relation. The identifier of the entity type becomes the primary key of the corresponding relation. You should check to make sure that this primary key satisfies the desirable properties of identifiers outlined in Chapter 2.

Figure 4-8a shows a representation of the CUSTOMER entity type for Pine Valley Furniture Company from Chapter 2 (see Figure 2-22). The corresponding CUSTOMER relation is shown in graphical form in Figure 4-8b. In this figure and those that follow in this section, we show only a few key attributes for each relation to simplify the figures.

COMPOSITE ATTRIBUTES When a regular entity type has a composite attribute, only the simple components of the composite attribute are included in the new relation as its attributes. Figure 4-9 shows a variant of the example in Figure 4-8, where Customer Address is represented as a composite attribute with components Street, City, and State (see Figure 4-9a). This entity is mapped to the CUSTOMER relation, which contains the simple address attributes, as shown in Figure 4-9b. Although Customer Name is modeled as a simple attribute in Figure 4-9a, it could have been (and, in practice, would have been) modeled as a composite attribute with components Last Name, First Name, and Middle

FIGURE 4-9 Example of
mapping a composite attribute
**(a) CUSTOMER entity type with
composite attribute**

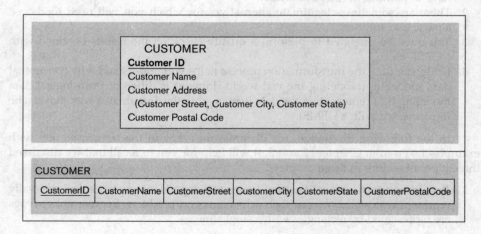

**(b) CUSTOMER relation with
address detail**

FIGURE 4-10 Example of
mapping an entity with a
multivalued attribute
(a) EMPLOYEE entity type with
multivalued attribute

**(b) EMPLOYEE and EMPLOYEE
SKILL relations**

Initial. In designing the CUSTOMER relation (Figure 4-9b), you may choose to use these simple attributes instead of CustomerName. Compared to composite attributes, simple attributes improve data accessibility and facilitate maintaining data quality. For example, for data reporting and other output purposes it is much easier if CustomerName is represented with its components (last name, first name, and middle initial separately). This way, any process reporting the data can easily create any format it needs to.

MULTIVALUED ATTRIBUTES   When the regular entity type contains a multivalued attribute, two new relations (rather than one) are created. The first relation contains all of the attributes of the entity type except the multivalued attribute. The second relation contains two attributes that form the primary key of the second relation. The first of these attributes is the primary key from the first relation, which becomes a foreign key in the second relation. The second is the multivalued attribute. The name of the second relation should capture the meaning of the multivalued attribute.

An example of this procedure is shown in Figure 4-10. This is the EMPLOYEE entity type for Pine Valley Furniture Company. As shown in Figure 4-10a, EMPLOYEE has Skill as a multivalued attribute. Figure 4-10b shows the two relations that are created. The first (called EMPLOYEE) has the primary key EmployeeID. The second relation (called EMPLOYEE SKILL) has the two attributes, EmployeeID and Skill, which form the primary key. The relationship between foreign and primary keys is indicated by the arrow in the figure.

The relation EMPLOYEE SKILL contains no nonkey attributes (also called *descriptors*). Each row simply records the fact that a particular employee possesses a particular skill. This provides an opportunity for you to suggest to users that new attributes can be added to this relation. For example, the attributes YearsExperience and/or CertificationDate might be appropriate new values to add to this relation. (See Figure 2-15b for another variation on employee skills.) If SKILL itself needs additional attributes, you can create a separate SKILL relation. In this case, EMPLOYEE SKILL becomes an associative entity between EMPLOYEE and SKILL.

If an entity type contains multiple multivalued attributes, each of them will be converted to a separate relation.

Step 2: Map Weak Entities

Recall that a weak entity type does not have an independent existence but exists only through an identifying relationship with another entity type called the *owner*. A weak entity type does not have a complete identifier but must have an attribute called a

FIGURE 4-11 Example of mapping a weak entity
(a) Weak entity DEPENDENT

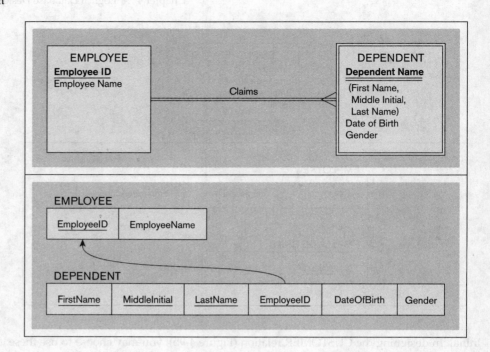

(b) Relations resulting from weak entity

partial identifier that permits distinguishing the various occurrences of the weak entity for each owner entity instance.

The following procedure assumes that you have already created a relation corresponding to the identifying entity type during Step 1. If you have not, you should create that relation now, using the process described in Step 1.

For each weak entity type, create a new relation and include all of the simple attributes (or simple components of composite attributes) as attributes of this relation. Then include the primary key of the *identifying* relation as a foreign key attribute in this new relation. The primary key of the new relation is the combination of this primary key of the identifying relation and the partial identifier of the weak entity type.

An example of this process is shown in Figure 4-11. Figure 4-11a shows the weak entity type DEPENDENT and its identifying entity type EMPLOYEE, linked by the identifying relationship Claims (see Figure 2-5). Notice that the attribute Dependent Name, which is the partial identifier for this relation, is a composite attribute with components First Name, Middle Initial, and Last Name. Thus, we assume that, *for a given employee*, these items will uniquely identify a dependent (a notable exception being the case of prizefighter George Foreman, who has named all his sons after himself).

Figure 4-11b shows the two relations that result from mapping this E-R segment. The primary key of DEPENDENT consists of four attributes: EmployeeID, FirstName, MiddleInitial, and LastName. DateOfBirth and Gender are the nonkey attributes. The foreign key relationship with its primary key is indicated by the arrow in the figure.

In practice, an alternative approach is often used to simplify the primary key of the DEPENDENT relation: Create a new attribute (called DependentID), which will be used as a **surrogate primary key** in Figure 4-11b. With this approach, the relation DEPENDENT has the following attributes:

Surrogate primary key

A serial number or other system-assigned primary key for a relation.

DEPENDENT(DependentID, EmployeeID, FirstName, MiddleInitial, LastName, DateOfBirth, Gender)

DependentID is simply a serial number that is assigned to each dependent of an employee. Notice that this solution will ensure unique identification for each dependent (even for those of George Foreman!).

WHEN TO CREATE A SURROGATE KEY   A surrogate key is usually created to simplify the key structures. According to Hoberman (2006), a surrogate key should be created when any of the following conditions hold:

- There is a composite primary key, as in the case of the DEPENDENT relation shown previously with the four-component primary key.
- The natural primary key (i.e., the key used in the organization and recognized in conceptual data modeling as the identifier) is inefficient. For example, it may be very long and hence costly for database software to handle if it is used as a foreign key that references other tables.
- The natural primary key is recycled (i.e., the key is reused or repeated periodically, so it may not actually be unique over time); a more general statement of this condition is when the natural primary key cannot, in fact, be guaranteed to be unique over time (e.g., there could be duplicates, such as with names or titles).

Whenever a surrogate key is created, the natural key is always kept as nonkey data in the same relation because the natural key has organizational meaning that has to be captured in the database. In fact, surrogate keys mean nothing to users, so they are usually never shown to the user. Instead, the natural keys are used as identifiers in searches.

Step 3: Map Binary Relationships

The procedure for representing relationships depends on both the degree of the relationships (unary, binary, or ternary) and the cardinalities of the relationships. We describe and illustrate the important cases in the following discussion.

MAP BINARY ONE-TO-MANY RELATIONSHIPS   For each binary 1:*M* relationship, first create a relation for each of the two entity types participating in the relationship, using the procedure described in Step 1. Next, include the primary key attribute (or attributes) of the entity on the one-side of the relationship as a foreign key in the relation that is on the many-side of the relationship. (A mnemonic you can use to remember this rule is this: The primary key migrates to the many side.)

To illustrate this simple process, we use the Submits relationship between customers and orders for Pine Valley Furniture Company (see Figure 2-22). This 1:*M* relationship is illustrated in Figure 4-12a. (Again, we show only a few attributes for simplicity.) Figure 4-12b shows the result of applying this rule to map the entity types with the 1:*M* relationship. The primary key CustomerID of CUSTOMER (the one side) is included as a foreign key in ORDER (the many side). The foreign key relationship

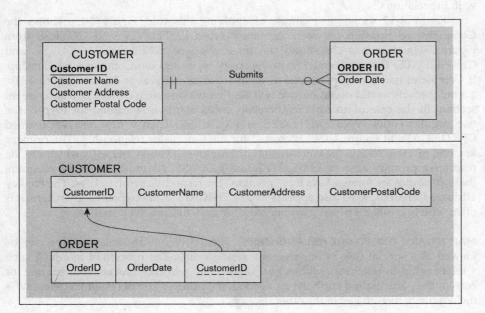

FIGURE 4-12   Example of mapping a 1:*M* relationship (a) Relationship between CUSTOMER and ORDER entities

(b) CUSTOMER and ORDER relations with a foreign key in ORDER

FIGURE 4-13   Example of mapping a *M:N* relationship
(a) Completes relationship (*M:N*)

(b) Three resulting relations

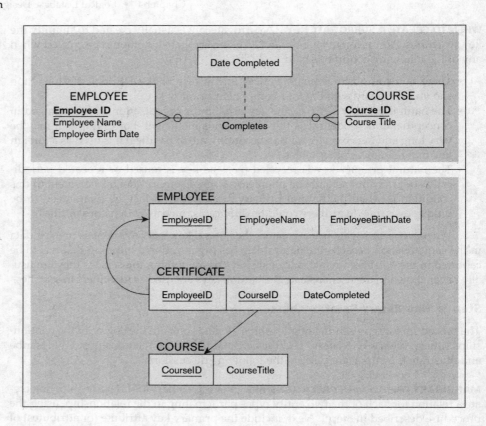

FIGURE 4-13   Example of mapping a *M:N* relationship
(a) Completes relationship (*M:N*)

(b) Three resulting relations

is indicated with an arrow. Please note that it is not necessary to name the foreign key attribute CustomerID. It is, however, essential that it has the same domain as the primary key it references.

MAP BINARY MANY-TO-MANY RELATIONSHIPS   Suppose that there is a binary many-to-many (*M:N*) relationship between two entity types, A and B. For such a relationship, create a new relation, C. Include as foreign key attributes in C the primary key for each of the two participating entity types. These attributes together become the primary key of C. Any nonkey attributes that are associated with the *M:N* relationship are included with the relation C.

Figure 4-13 shows an example of applying this rule. Figure 4-13a shows the Completes relationship between the entity types EMPLOYEE and COURSE from Figure 2-11a. Figure 4-13b shows the three relations (EMPLOYEE, COURSE, and CERTIFICATE) that are formed from the entity types and the Completes relationship. If Completes had been represented as an associative entity, as is done in Figure 2-11b, a similar result would occur, but we will deal with associative entities in a subsequent section. In the case of an *M:N* relationship, a relation is first created for each of the two regular entity types EMPLOYEE and COURSE. Then a new relation (named CERTIFICATE in Figure 4-13b) is created for the Completes relationship. The primary key of CERTIFICATE is the combination of EmployeeID and CourseID, which are the respective primary keys of EMPLOYEE and COURSE. As indicated in the diagram, these attributes are foreign keys that "point to" the respective primary keys. The nonkey attribute DateCompleted also appears in CERTIFICATE. Although not shown here, it is often wise to create a surrogate primary key for the CERTIFICATE relation.

MAP BINARY ONE-TO-ONE RELATIONSHIPS   Binary one-to-one relationships can be viewed as a special case of one-to-many relationships. The process of mapping such a relationship to relations requires two steps. First, two relations are created, one for each of the participating entity types. Second, the primary key of one of the relations is included as a foreign key in the other relation.

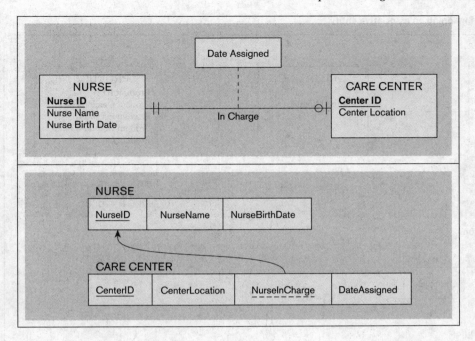

(b) Resulting relations

In a 1:1 relationship, the association in one direction is nearly always an optional one, whereas the association in the other direction is a mandatory one. (You can review the notation for these terms in Figure 2-1.) You should include in the relation on the optional side of the relationship a foreign key referencing the primary key of the entity type that has the mandatory participation in the 1:1 relationship. This approach will prevent the need to store null values in the foreign key attribute. Any attributes associated with the relationship itself are also included in the same relation as the foreign key.

An example of applying this procedure is shown in Figure 4-14. Figure 4-14a shows a binary 1:1 relationship between the entity types NURSE and CARE CENTER. Each care center must have a nurse who is in charge of that center. Thus, the association from CARE CENTER to NURSE is a mandatory one, whereas the association from NURSE to CARE CENTER is an optional one (since any nurse may or may not be in charge of a care center). The attribute Date Assigned is attached to the In Charge relationship.

The result of mapping this relationship to a set of relations is shown in Figure 4-14b. The two relations NURSE and CARE CENTER are created from the two entity types. Because CARE CENTER is the optional participant, the foreign key is placed in this relation. In this case, the foreign key is NurseInCharge. It has the same domain as NurseID, and the relationship with the primary key is shown in the figure. The attribute DateAssigned is also located in CARE CENTER and would not be allowed to be null.

Step 4: Map Associative Entities

As explained in Chapter 2, when a data modeler encounters a many-to-many relationship, he or she may choose to model that relationship as an associative entity in the E-R diagram. This approach is most appropriate when the end user can best visualize the relationship as an entity type rather than as an *M:N* relationship. Mapping the associative entity involves essentially the same steps as mapping an *M:N* relationship, as described in Step 3.

The first step is to create three relations: one for each of the two participating entity types and a third for the associative entity. We refer to the relation formed from the associative entity as the *associative relation*. The second step then depends on whether on the E-R diagram an identifier was assigned to the associative entity.

FIGURE 4-15   Example of mapping an associative entity

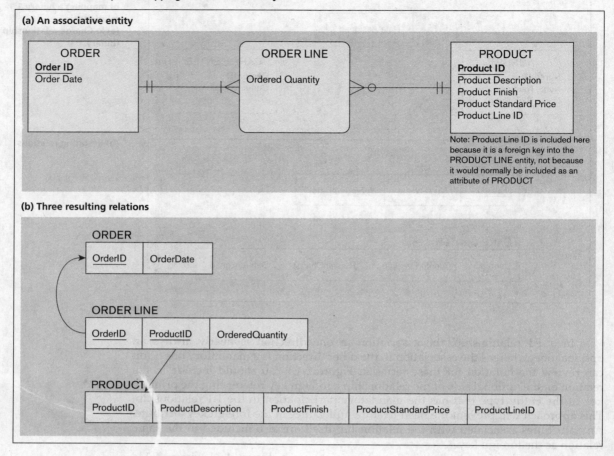

(a) An associative entity

ORDER
Order ID
Order Date

ORDER LINE
Ordered Quantity

PRODUCT
Product ID
Product Description
Product Finish
Product Standard Price
Product Line ID

Note: Product Line ID is included here because it is a foreign key into the PRODUCT LINE entity, not because it would normally be included as an attribute of PRODUCT

(b) Three resulting relations

ORDER

OrderID	OrderDate

ORDER LINE

OrderID	ProductID	OrderedQuantity

PRODUCT

ProductID	ProductDescription	ProductFinish	ProductStandardPrice	ProductLineID

IDENTIFIER NOT ASSIGNED   If an identifier was not assigned, the default primary key for the associative relation is a composite key that consists of the two primary key attributes from the other two relations. These attributes are then foreign keys that reference the other two relations.

An example of this case is shown in Figure 4-15. Figure 4-15a shows the associative entity ORDER LINE that links the ORDER and PRODUCT entity types at Pine Valley Furniture Company (see Figure 2-22). Figure 4-15b shows the three relations that result from this mapping. Note the similarity of this example to that of an *M:N* relationship shown in Figure 4-13.

PINE
VALLEY
FURNITURE

IDENTIFIER ASSIGNED   Sometimes a data modeler will assign a single-attribute identifier to the associative entity type on the E-R diagram. Two reasons may have motivated the data modeler to assign a single-attribute key during conceptual data modeling:

1. The associative entity type has a natural single-attribute identifier that is familiar to end users.
2. The default identifier (consisting of the identifiers for each of the participating entity types) may not uniquely identify instances of the associative entity.

These motivations are in addition to the reasons mentioned earlier in this chapter to create a surrogate primary key.

The process for mapping the associative entity in this case is now modified as follows. As before, a new (associative) relation is created to represent the associative entity. However, the primary key for this relation is the identifier assigned on the E-R diagram (rather than the default key). The primary keys for the two participating entity types are then included as foreign keys in the associative relation.

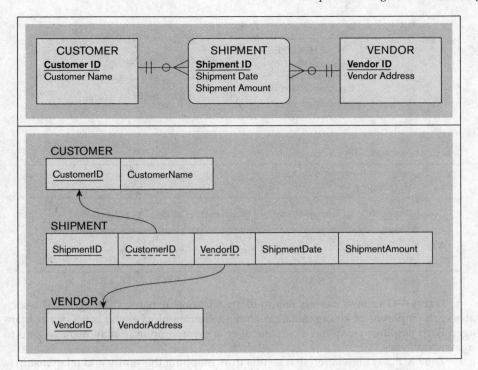

An example of this process is shown in Figure 4-16. Figure 4-16a shows the associative entity type SHIPMENT that links the CUSTOMER and VENDOR entity types. Shipment ID has been chosen as the identifier for SHIPMENT for two reasons:

1. Shipment ID is a natural identifier for this entity that is very familiar to end users.
2. The default identifier consisting of the combination of Customer ID and Vendor ID does not uniquely identify the instances of SHIPMENT. In fact, a given vendor typically makes many shipments to a given customer. Even including the attribute Date does not guarantee uniqueness, since there may be more than one shipment by a particular vendor on a given date. The surrogate key ShipmentID will, however, uniquely identify each shipment.

Two nonkey attributes associated with the SHIPMENT associative entity are Shipment Date and Shipment Amount.

The result of mapping this entity to a set of relations is shown in Figure 4-16b. The new associative relation is named SHIPMENT. The primary key is ShipmentID. CustomerID and VendorID are included as foreign keys in this relation, and ShipmentDate and ShipmentAmount are nonkey attributes. It is also possible that the designer decides as part of the logical modeling process to add a surrogate key into a relation that did not have it earlier. In these cases, it is highly recommended to update the conceptual model to keep it consistent.

Step 5: Map Unary Relationships

In Chapter 2, we defined a unary relationship as a relationship between the instances of a single entity type. Unary relationships are also called *recursive relationships*. The two most important cases of unary relationships are one-to-many and many-to-many relationships. We discuss these two cases separately because the approach to mapping is somewhat different for the two types.

UNARY ONE-TO-MANY RELATIONSHIPS The entity type in the unary relationship is mapped to a relation using the procedure described in Step 1. Next, a foreign key attribute is added to the same relation; this attribute references the primary key values in the same relation. (This foreign key must have the same domain as the primary key.) This type of a foreign key is called a **recursive foreign key.**

Recursive foreign key

A foreign key in a relation that references the primary key values of the same relation.

FIGURE 4-17 Example
of mapping a unary 1:*M*
relationship
(a) EMPLOYEE entity with unary
relationship

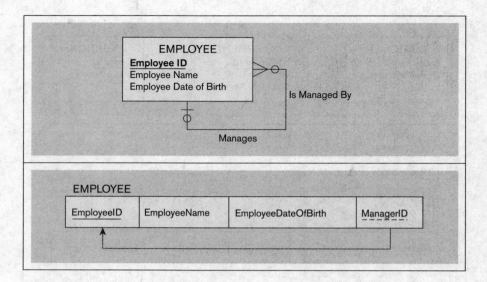

**(b) EMPLOYEE relation with
recursive foreign key**

Figure 4-17a shows a unary one-to-many relationship named Manages that associates each employee of an organization with another employee who is his or her manager. Each employee may have one manager; a given employee may manage zero to many employees.

The EMPLOYEE relation that results from mapping this entity and relationship is shown in Figure 4-17b. The (recursive) foreign key in the relation is named ManagerID. This attribute has the same domain as the primary key EmployeeID. Each row of this relation stores the following data for a given employee: EmployeeID, EmployeeName, EmployeeDateOfBirth, and ManagerID (i.e., EmployeeID for this employee's manager). Notice that because it is a foreign key, ManagerID references EmployeeID.

UNARY MANY-TO-MANY RELATIONSHIPS With this type of relationship, two relations are created: one to represent the entity type in the relationship and an associative relation to represent the *M:N* relationship itself. The primary key of the associative relation consists of two attributes. These attributes (which need not have the same name) both take their values from the primary key of the other relation. Any nonkey attribute of the relationship is included in the associative relation.

An example of mapping a unary *M:N* relationship is shown in Figure 4-18. Figure 4-18a shows a bill-of-materials relationship among items that are assembled from other items or components. (This structure was described in Chapter 2, and an example appears in Figure 2-13.) The relationship (called Contains) is *M:N* because a given item can contain numerous component items, and, conversely, an item can be used as a component in numerous other items.

The relations that result from mapping this entity and its relationship are shown in Figure 4-18b. The ITEM relation is mapped directly from the same entity type. COMPONENT is an associative relation whose primary key consists of two attributes that are arbitrarily named ItemNo and ComponentNo. The attribute Quantity is a nonkey attribute of this relation that, for a given item, records the quantity of a particular component item used in that item. Notice that both ItemNo and ComponentNo reference the primary key (ItemNo) of the ITEM relation. It is not unusual to give this relation a surrogate key to avoid any practical complexities related to the composite key.

We can easily query these relations to determine, for example, the components of a given item. The following SQL query will list the immediate components (and their quantity) for item number 100:

```
SELECT ComponentNo, Quantity
FROM Component_T
WHERE ItemNo = 100;
```

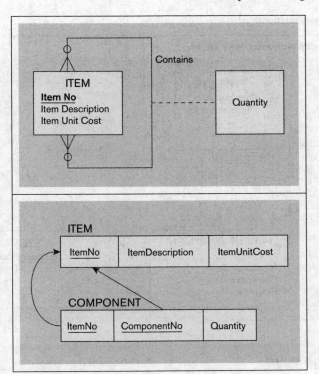

FIGURE 4-18   **Example
of mapping a unary *M:N*
relationship
(a) Bill-of-materials relationship
Contains (*M:N*)**

**(b) ITEM and COMPONENT
relations**

Step 6: Map Ternary (and *n*-ary) Relationships

Recall from Chapter 2 that a ternary relationship is a relationship among three entity
types. In that chapter, we recommended that you convert a ternary relationship to an
associative entity to represent participation constraints more accurately.

To map an associative entity type that links three regular entity types, we create
a new associative relation. The default primary key of this relation consists of the three
primary key attributes for the participating entity types. (In some cases, additional attributes are required to form a unique primary key.) These attributes then act in the role of
foreign keys that reference the individual primary keys of the participating entity types.
Any attributes of the associative entity type become attributes of the new relation.

An example of mapping a ternary relationship (represented as an associative entity type) is shown in Figure 4-19. Figure 4-19a is an E-R segment (or view)
that represents a *patient* receiving a *treatment* from a *physician*. The associative entity
type PATIENT TREATMENT has the attributes PTreatment Date, PTreatment Time,
and PTreatment Results; values are recorded for these attributes for each instance of
PATIENT TREATMENT.

The result of mapping this view is shown in Figure 4-19b. The primary key attributes PatientID, PhysicianID, and TreatmentCode become foreign keys in PATIENT
TREATMENT. The foreign key into TREATMENT is called PTreatmentCode in PATIENT
TREATMENT. We are using this column name to illustrate that the foreign key name
does not have to be the same as the name of the primary key to which it refers, as long
as the values come from the same domain. These three attributes are components of
the primary key of PATIENT TREATMENT. However, they do not uniquely identify
a given treatment, because a patient may receive the same treatment from the same
physician on more than one occasion. Does including the attribute Date as part of the
primary key (along with the other three attributes) result in a primary key? This would
be so if a given patient receives only one treatment from a particular physician on a
given date. However, this is not likely to be the case. For example, a patient may receive
a treatment in the morning, then the same treatment again in the afternoon. To resolve
this issue, we include PTreatmentDate and PTreatmentTime as part of the primary key.
Therefore, the primary key of PATIENT TREATMENT consists of the five attributes

FIGURE 4-19   Example of mapping a ternary relationship

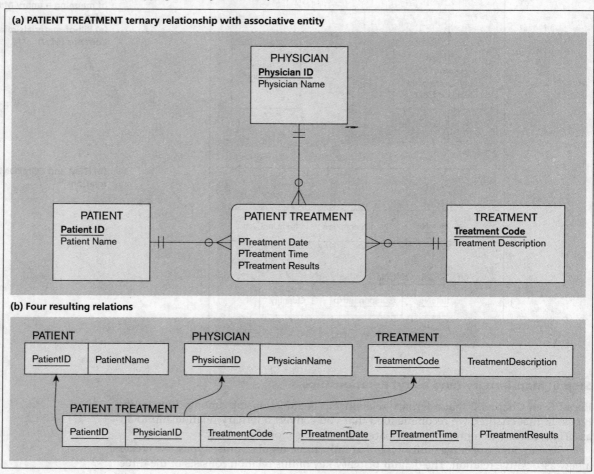

shown in Figure 4-19b: PatientID, PhysicianID, TreatmentCode, PTreatmentDate, and PTreatmentTime. The only nonkey attribute in the relation is PTreatmentResults.

Although this primary key is technically correct, it is complex and therefore difficult to manage and prone to errors. A better approach is to introduce a surrogate key, such as PTreatmentID, that is, a serial number that uniquely identifies each treatment. In this case, each of the former primary key attributes except for PTreatmentDate and PTreatmentTime becomes a foreign key in the PATIENT TREATMENT relation. Another similar approach is to use an enterprise key, as described at the end of this chapter.

Step 7: Map Supertype/Subtype Relationships

The relational data model does not yet directly support supertype/subtype relationships. Fortunately, there are various strategies that database designers can use to represent these relationships with the relational data model (Chouinard, 1989). For our purposes, we use the following strategy, which is the one most commonly employed:

1. Create a separate relation for the supertype and for each of its subtypes.
2. Assign to the relation created for the supertype the attributes that are common to all members of the supertype, including the primary key.
3. Assign to the relation for each subtype the primary key of the supertype and only those attributes that are unique to that subtype.
4. Assign one (or more) attributes of the supertype to function as the subtype discriminator. (The role of the subtype discriminator was discussed in Chapter 3.)

FIGURE 4-20 Supertype/subtype relationships

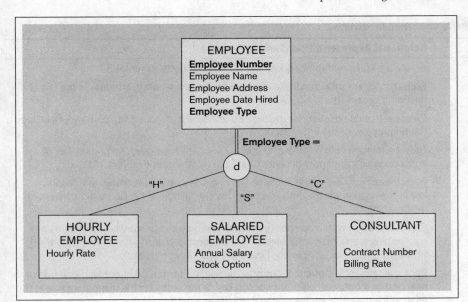

An example of applying this procedure is shown in Figures 4-20 and 4-21. Figure 4-20 shows the supertype EMPLOYEE with subtypes HOURLY EMPLOYEE, SALARIED EMPLOYEE, and CONSULTANT. (This example is described in Chapter 3, and Figure 4-20 is a repeat of Figure 3-8.) The primary key of EMPLOYEE is Employee Number, and the attribute Employee Type is the subtype discriminator.

The result of mapping this diagram to relations using these rules is shown in Figure 4-21. There is one relation for the supertype (EMPLOYEE) and one for each of the three subtypes. The primary key for each of the four relations is EmployeeNumber. A prefix is used to distinguish the name of the primary key for each subtype. For example, SEmployeeNumber is the name for the primary key of the relation SALARIED EMPLOYEE. Each of these attributes is a foreign key that references the supertype primary key, as indicated by the arrows in the diagram. Each subtype relation contains only those attributes unique to the subtype.

For each subtype, a relation can be produced that contains all of the attributes of that subtype (both specific and inherited) by using an SQL command that joins the

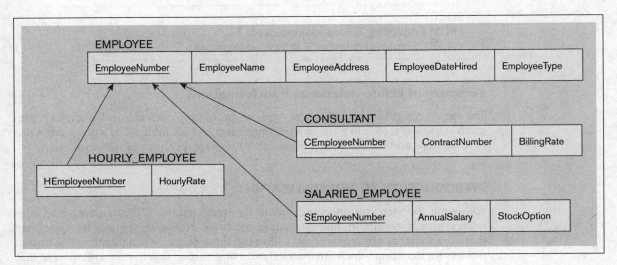

FIGURE 4-21 Mapping supertype/subtype relationships to relations

TABLE 4-2 Summary of EER-to-Relational Transformations

EER Structure	Relational Representation (Sample Figure)
Regular entity	Create a relation with primary key and nonkey attributes (Figure 4-8)
Composite attribute	Each component of a composite attribute becomes a separate attribute in the target relation (Figure 4-9)
Multivalued attribute	Create a separate relation for multivalued attribute with composite primary key, including the primary key of the entity (Figure 4-10)
Weak entity	Create a relation with a composite primary key (which includes the primary key of the entity on which this entity depends) and nonkey attributes (Figure 4-11)
Binary or unary 1:*M* relationship	Place the primary key of the entity on the one side of the relationship as a foreign key in the relation for the entity on the many side (Figure 4-12; Figure 4-17 for unary relationship)
Binary or unary *M:N* relationship or associative entity without its own key	Create a relation with a composite primary key using the primary keys of the related entities plus any nonkey attributes of the relationship or associative entity (Figure 4-13, Figure 4-15 for associative entity, Figure 4-18 for unary relationship)
Binary or unary 1:1 relationship	Place the primary key of either entity in the relation for the other entity; if one side of the relationship is optional, place the foreign key of the entity on the mandatory side in the relation for the entity on the optional side (Figure 4-14)
Binary or unary *M:N* relationship or associative entity with its own key	Create a relation with the primary key associated with the associative entity plus any nonkey attributes of the associative entity and the primary keys of the related entities as foreign keys (Figure 4-16)
Ternary and *n*-ary relationships	Same as binary *M:N* relationships above; without its own key, include as part of primary key of relation for the relationship or associative entity the primary keys from all related entities; with its own surrogate key, the primary keys of the associated entities are included as foreign keys in the relation for the relationship or associative entity (Figure 4-19)
Supertype/subtype relationship	Create a relation for the superclass, which contains the primary and all nonkey attributes in common with all subclasses, plus create a separate relation for each subclass with the same primary key (with the same or local name) but with only the nonkey attributes related to that subclass (Figure 4-20 and 4-21)

subtype with its supertype. For example, suppose that we want to display a table that contains all of the attributes for SALARIED EMPLOYEE. The following command is used:

```
SELECT *
FROM Employee_T, SalariedEmployee_T
WHERE EmployeeNumber = SEmployeeNumber;
```

Summary of EER-to-Relational Transformations

The steps provide a comprehensive explanation of how each element of an EER diagram is transformed into parts of a relational data model. Table 4-2 is a quick reference to these steps and the associated figures that illustrate each type of transformation.

INTRODUCTION TO NORMALIZATION

Following the steps outlined previously for transforming EER diagrams into relations typically results in well-structured relations. However, there is no guarantee that all anomalies are removed by following these steps. Normalization is a formal process for deciding which attributes should be grouped together in a relation so that all anomalies are removed. For example, we used the principles of normalization to convert the EMPLOYEE2 table (with its redundancy) to EMPLOYEE1 (Figure 4-1) and EMP COURSE (Figure 4-7). There are two major occasions during the overall database development process when you can usually benefit from using normalization:

1. *During logical database design (described in this chapter)* You should use normalization concepts to verify the quality of the relations that are obtained from mapping E-R diagrams.
2. *When reverse-engineering older systems* Many of the tables and user views for older systems are redundant and subject to the anomalies we describe in this chapter.

So far we have presented an intuitive discussion of well-structured relations; however, we need formal definitions of such relations, together with a process for designing them. **Normalization** is the process of successively reducing relations with anomalies to produce smaller, well-structured relations. Following are some of the main goals of normalization:

Normalization
The process of decomposing relations with anomalies to produce smaller, well-structured relations.

1. Minimize data redundancy, thereby avoiding anomalies and conserving storage space.
2. Simplify the enforcement of referential integrity constraints.
3. Make it easier to maintain data (insert, update, and delete).
4. Provide a better design that is an improved representation of the real world and a stronger basis for future growth.

Normalization makes no assumptions about how data will be used in displays, queries, or reports. Normalization, based on what we will call *normal forms* and *functional dependencies*, defines rules of the business, not data usage. Further, remember that data are normalized by the end of logical database design. Thus, normalization, as we will see in Chapter 5, places no constraints on how data can or should be physically stored or, therefore, on processing performance. Normalization is a logical data-modeling technique used to ensure that data are well structured from an organization-wide view.

Steps in Normalization

Normalization can be accomplished and understood in stages, each of which corresponds to a normal form (see Figure 4-22). A **normal form** is a state of a relation that requires that certain rules regarding relationships between attributes (or functional dependencies) are satisfied. We describe these rules briefly in this section and illustrate them in detail in the following sections:

Normal form
A state of a relation that requires that certain rules regarding relationships between attributes (or functional dependencies) are satisfied.

1. *First normal form* Any multivalued attributes (also called *repeating groups*) have been removed, so there is a single value (possibly null) at the intersection of each row and column of the table (as in Figure 4-2b).
2. *Second normal form* Any partial functional dependencies have been removed (i.e., nonkey attributes are identified by the whole primary key).
3. *Third normal form* Any transitive dependencies have been removed (i.e., nonkey attributes are identified by only the primary key).
4. *Boyce-Codd normal form* Any remaining anomalies that result from functional dependencies have been removed (because there was more than one possible primary key for the same nonkeys).
5. *Fourth normal form* Any multivalued dependencies have been removed.
6. *Fifth normal form* Any remaining anomalies have been removed.

We describe and illustrate the first through the third normal forms in this chapter. The remaining normal forms are described in Appendix B, available on the book's Web site. These other normal forms are in an appendix only to save space in this chapter, not because they are less important. In fact, you can easily continue with Appendix B immediately after the section on the third normal form.

Functional Dependencies and Keys

Up to the Boyce-Codd normal form, normalization is based on the analysis of functional dependencies. A **functional dependency** is a constraint between two attributes or two

Functional dependency
A constraint between two attributes in which the value of one attribute is determined by the value of another attribute.

FIGURE 4-22 Steps in normalization

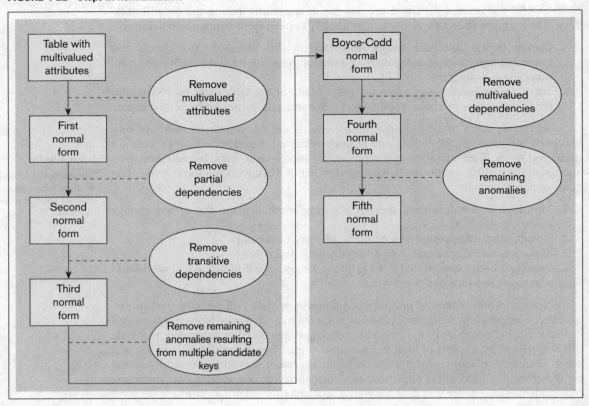

sets of attributes. For any relation R, attribute B is functionally dependent on attribute A if, for every valid instance of A, that value of A uniquely determines the value of B (Dutka and Hanson, 1989). The functional dependency of B on A is represented by an arrow, as follows: A → B. A functional dependency is not a mathematical dependency: B cannot be computed from A. Rather, if you know the value of A, there can be only one value for B. An attribute may be functionally dependent on a combination of two (or more) attributes rather than on a single attribute. For example, consider the relation EMP COURSE (EmpID, CourseTitle, DateCompleted) shown in Figure 4-7. We represent the functional dependency in this relation as follows:

EmpID, CourseTitle → DateCompleted

The comma between EmpID and CourseTitle stands for the logical AND operator, because DateCompleted is functionally dependent on EmpID and CourseTitle in combination.

The functional dependency in this statement implies that the date when a course is completed is determined by the identity of the employee and the title of the course. Typical examples of functional dependencies are the following:

1. *SSN → Name, Address, Birthdate*   A person's name, address, and birth date are functionally dependent on that person's Social Security number (in other words, there can be only one Name, one Address, and one Birthdate for each SSN).
2. *VIN → Make, Model, Color*   The make, model, and the original color of a vehicle are functionally dependent on the vehicle identification number (as above, there can be only one value of Make, Model, and Color associated with each VIN).
3. *ISBN → Title, FirstAuthorName, Publisher*   The title of a book, the name of the first author, and the publisher are functionally dependent on the book's international standard book number (ISBN).

DETERMINANTS   The attribute on the left side of the arrow in a functional dependency is called a **determinant**. SSN, VIN, and ISBN are determinants in the preceding three examples. In the EMP COURSE relation (Figure 4-7), the combination of EmpID and CourseTitle is a determinant.

CANDIDATE KEYS   A **candidate key** is an attribute, or combination of attributes, that uniquely identifies a row in a relation. A candidate key must satisfy the following properties (Dutka and Hanson, 1989), which are a subset of the six properties of a relation previously listed:

1. *Unique identification*   For every row, the value of the key must uniquely identify that row. This property implies that each nonkey attribute is functionally dependent on that key.
2. *Nonredundancy*   No attribute in the key can be deleted without destroying the property of unique identification.

Let's apply the preceding definition to identify candidate keys in two of the relations described in this chapter. The EMPLOYEE1 relation (Figure 4-1) has the following schema: EMPLOYEE1(EmpID, Name, DeptName, Salary). EmpID is the only determinant in this relation. All of the other attributes are functionally dependent on EmpID. Therefore, EmpID is a candidate key and (because there are no other candidate keys) also is the primary key.

We represent the functional dependencies for a relation using the notation shown in Figure 4-23. Figure 4-23a shows the representation for EMPLOYEE1. The horizontal line in the figure portrays the functional dependencies. A vertical line drops from the primary key (EmpID) and connects to this line. Vertical arrows then point to each of the nonkey attributes that are functionally dependent on the primary key.

For the relation EMPLOYEE2 (Figure 4-2b), notice that (unlike EMPLOYEE1) EmpID does not uniquely identify a row in the relation. For example, there are two rows in the table for EmpID number 100. There are two types of functional dependencies in this relation:

1. EmpID → Name, DeptName, Salary
2. EmpID, CourseTitle → DateCompleted

The functional dependencies indicate that the combination of EmpID and CourseTitle is the only candidate key (and therefore the primary key) for EMPLOYEE2. In other words, the primary key of EMPLOYEE2 is a composite key. Neither EmpID

Determinant

The attribute on the left side of the arrow in a functional dependency.

Candidate key

An attribute, or combination of attributes, that uniquely identifies a row in a relation.

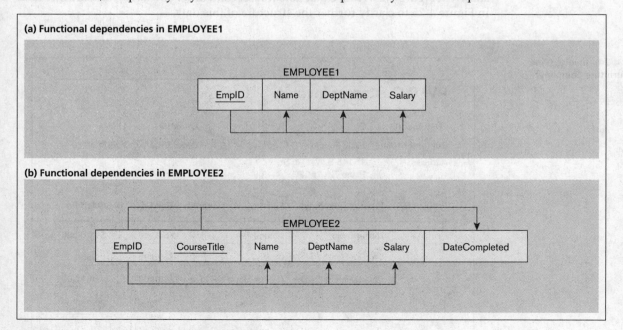

(a) Functional dependencies in EMPLOYEE1

(b) Functional dependencies in EMPLOYEE2

FIGURE 4-23   Representing functional dependencies

nor CourseTitle uniquely identifies a row in this relation and therefore (according to property 1) cannot by itself be a candidate key. Examine the data in Figure 4-2b to verify that the combination of EmpID and CourseTitle does uniquely identify each row of EMPLOYEE2. We represent the functional dependencies in this relation in Figure 4-23b. Notice that DateCompleted is the only attribute that is functionally dependent on the full primary key consisting of the attributes EmpID and CourseTitle.

We can summarize the relationship between determinants and candidate keys as follows: A candidate key is always a determinant, whereas a determinant may or may not be a candidate key. For example, in EMPLOYEE2, EmpID is a determinant but not a candidate key. A candidate key is a determinant that uniquely identifies the remaining (nonkey) attributes in a relation. A determinant may be a candidate key (such as EmpID in EMPLOYEE1), part of a composite candidate key (such as EmpID in EMPLOYEE2), or a nonkey attribute. We will describe examples of this shortly.

As a preview to the following illustration of what normalization accomplishes, normalized relations have as their primary key the determinant for each of the nonkeys, and within that relation there are no other functional dependencies.

NORMALIZATION EXAMPLE: PINE VALLEY FURNITURE COMPANY

Now that we have examined functional dependencies and keys, we are ready to describe and illustrate the steps of normalization. If an EER data model has been transformed into a comprehensive set of relations for the database, then each of these relations needs to be normalized. In other cases in which the logical data model is being derived from user interfaces, such as screens, forms, and reports, you will want to create relations for each user interface and normalize those relations.

For a simple illustration, we use a customer invoice from Pine Valley Furniture Company (see Figure 4-24.)

Step 0: Represent the View in Tabular Form

The first step (preliminary to normalization) is to represent the user view (in this case, an invoice) as a single table, or relation, with the attributes recorded as column headings. Sample data should be recorded in the rows of the table, including any repeating groups that are present in the data. The table representing the invoice is shown in Figure 4-25. Notice that data for a second order (OrderID 1007) are included in Figure 4-25 to clarify further the structure of this data.

FIGURE 4-24 Invoice (Pine Valley Furniture Company)

PVFC Customer Invoice

Customer ID	2		Order ID	1006
Customer Name	Value Furniture		Order Date	10/24/2015
Address	15145 S.W. 17th St. Plano TX 75022			

Product ID	Product Description	Finish	Quantity	Unit Price	Extended Price
7	Dining Table	Natural Ash	2	$800.00	$1,600.00
5	Writer's Desk	Cherry	2	$325.00	$650.00
4	Entertainment Center	Natural Maple	1	$650.00	$650.00
				Total	$2,900.00

FIGURE 4-25 INVOICE data (Pine Valley Furniture Company)

OrderID	Order Date	Customer ID	Customer Name	Customer Address	ProductID	Product Description	Product Finish	Product StandardPrice	Ordered Quantity
1006	10/24/2015	2	Value Furniture	Plano, TX	7	Dining Table	Natural Ash	800.00	2
					5	Writer's Desk	Cherry	325.00	2
					4	Entertainment Center	Natural Maple	650.00	1
1007	10/25/2015	6	Furniture Gallery	Boulder, CO	11	4–Dr Dresser	Oak	500.00	4
					4	Entertainment Center	Natural Maple	650.00	3

Step 1: Convert to First Normal Form

A relation is in **first normal form (1NF)** if the following two constraints both apply:

1. There are no repeating groups in the relation (thus, there is a single fact at the intersection of each row and column of the table).
2. A primary key has been defined, which uniquely identifies each row in the relation.

First normal form (1NF)

A relation that has a primary key and in which there are no repeating groups.

REMOVE REPEATING GROUPS As you can see, the invoice data in Figure 4-25 contain a repeating group for each product that appears on a particular order. Thus, OrderID 1006 contains three repeating groups, corresponding to the three products on that order.

In a previous section, we showed how to remove repeating groups from a table by filling relevant data values into previously vacant cells of the table (see Figures 4-2a and 4-2b). Applying this procedure to the invoice table yields the new relation (named INVOICE) shown in Figure 4-26.

SELECT THE PRIMARY KEY There are four determinants in INVOICE, and their functional dependencies are the following:

> OrderID → OrderDate, CustomerID, CustomerName, CustomerAddress
> CustomerID → CustomerName, CustomerAddress
> ProductID → ProductDescription, ProductFinish, ProductStandardPrice
> OrderID, ProductID → OrderedQuantity

Why do we know these are the functional dependencies? These business rules come from the organization. We know these from studying the nature of the Pine Valley Furniture Company business. We can also see that no data in Figure 4-26 violates any of these functional dependencies. But because we don't see all possible rows of this table, we cannot be sure that there wouldn't be some invoice that would violate one of these functional dependencies. Thus, we must depend on our understanding of the rules of the organization.

As you can see, the only candidate key for INVOICE is the composite key consisting of the attributes OrderID and ProductID (because there is only one row in the table for any combination of values for these attributes). Therefore, OrderID and ProductID are underlined in Figure 4-26, indicating that they compose the primary key.

When forming a primary key, you must be careful not to include redundant (and therefore unnecessary) attributes. Thus, although CustomerID is a determinant in INVOICE, it is not included as part of the primary key because all of the nonkey attributes are identified by the combination of OrderID and ProductID. We will see the role of CustomerID in the normalization process that follows.

FIGURE 4-26 INVOICE relation (1NF) (Pine Valley Furniture Company)

OrderID	Order Date	Customer ID	Customer Name	Customer Address	ProductID	Product Description	Product Finish	Product StandardPrice	Ordered Quantity
1006	10/24/2015	2	Value Furniture	Plano, TX	7	Dining Table	Natural Ash	800.00	2
1006	10/24/2015	2	Value Furniture	Plano, TX	5	Writer's Desk	Cherry	325.00	2
1006	10/24/2015	2	Value Furniture	Plano, TX	4	Entertainment Center	Natural Maple	650.00	1
1007	10/25/2015	6	Furniture Gallery	Boulder, CO	11	4–Dr Dresser	Oak	500.00	4
1007	10/25/2015	6	Furniture Gallery	Boulder, CO	4	Entertainment Center	Natural Maple	650.00	3

A diagram that shows these functional dependencies for the INVOICE relation is shown in Figure 4-27. This diagram is a horizontal list of all the attributes in INVOICE, with the primary key attributes (OrderID and ProductID) underlined. Notice that the only attribute that depends on the full key is OrderedQuantity. All of the other functional dependencies are either partial dependencies or transitive dependencies (both are defined next).

ANOMALIES IN 1NF Although repeating groups have been removed, the data in Figure 4-26 still contain considerable redundancy. For example, CustomerID, CustomerName, and CustomerAddress for Value Furniture are recorded in three rows (at least) in the table. As a result of these redundancies, manipulating the data in the table can lead to anomalies such as the following:

1. *Insertion anomaly* With this table structure, the company is not able to introduce a new product (say, Breakfast Table with ProductID 8) and add it to the database before it is ordered the first time: No entries can be added to the table without both ProductID *and* OrderID. As another example, if a customer calls and requests another product be added to his OrderID 1007, a new row must be inserted in which the order date and all of the customer information must be repeated. This leads to data replication and potential data entry errors (e.g., the customer name may be entered as "Valley Furniture").
2. *Deletion anomaly* If a customer calls and requests that the Dining Table be deleted from her OrderID 1006, this row must be deleted from the relation, and we lose the information concerning this item's finish (Natural Ash) and price ($800.00).
3. *Update anomaly* If Pine Valley Furniture (as part of a price adjustment) increases the price of the Entertainment Center (ProductID 4) to $750.00, this change must be recorded in all rows containing that item. (There are two such rows in Figure 4-26.)

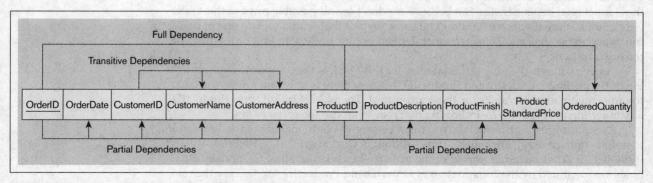

FIGURE 4-27 Functional dependency diagram for INVOICE

Step 2: Convert to Second Normal Form

We can remove many of the redundancies (and resulting anomalies) in the INVOICE relation by converting it to second normal form. A relation is in **second normal form (2NF)** if it is in first normal form and contains no partial functional dependencies. A **partial functional dependency** exists when a nonkey attribute is functionally dependent on part (but not all) of the primary key. As you can see, the following partial dependencies exist in Figure 4-27:

Second normal form (2NF)
A relation in first normal form in which every nonkey attribute is fully functionally dependent on the primary key.

Partial functional dependency
A functional dependency in which one or more nonkey attributes are functionally dependent on part (but not all) of the primary key.

OrderID → OrderDate, CustomerID, CustomerName, CustomerAddress
ProductID → ProductDescription, ProductFinish, ProductStandardPrice

The first of these partial dependencies (for example) states that the date on an order is uniquely determined by the order number and has nothing to do with the ProductID.

To convert a relation with partial dependencies to second normal form, the following steps are required:

1. Create a new relation for each primary key attribute (or combination of attributes) that is a determinant in a partial dependency. That attribute is the primary key in the new relation.
2. Move the nonkey attributes that are only dependent on this primary key attribute (or attributes) from the old relation to the new relation.

The results of performing these steps for the INVOICE relation are shown in Figure 4-28. Removal of the partial dependencies results in the formation of two new relations: PRODUCT and CUSTOMER ORDER. The INVOICE relation is now left with just the primary key attributes (OrderID and ProductID) and OrderedQuantity, which is functionally dependent on the whole key. We rename this relation ORDER LINE, because each row in this table represents one line item on an order.

As indicated in Figure 4-28, the relations ORDER LINE and PRODUCT are in third normal form. However, CUSTOMER ORDER contains transitive dependencies and therefore (although in second normal form) is not yet in third normal form.

A relation that is in first normal form will be in second normal form if any one of the following conditions applies:

1. The primary key consists of only one attribute (e.g., the attribute ProductID in the PRODUCT relation in Figure 4-28). By definition, there cannot be a partial dependency in such a relation.
2. No nonkey attributes exist in the relation (thus all of the attributes in the relation are components of the primary key). There are no functional dependencies in such a relation.

FIGURE 4-28 Removing partial dependencies

3. Every nonkey attribute is functionally dependent on the full set of primary key attributes (e.g., the attribute OrderedQuantity in the ORDER LINE relation in Figure 4-28).

Step 3: Convert to Third Normal Form

Third normal form (3NF)

A relation that is in second normal form and has no transitive dependencies.

Transitive dependency

A functional dependency between the primary key and one or more nonkey attributes that are dependent on the primary key via another nonkey attribute.

A relation is in **third normal form (3NF)** if it is in second normal form and no transitive dependencies exist. A **transitive dependency** in a relation is a functional dependency between the primary key and one or more nonkey attributes that are dependent on the primary key via another nonkey attribute. For example, there are two transitive dependencies in the CUSTOMER ORDER relation shown in Figure 4-28:

OrderID → CustomerID → CustomerName
OrderID → CustomerID → CustomerAddress

In other words, both customer name and address are uniquely identified by CustomerID, but CustomerID is not part of the primary key (as we noted earlier).

Transitive dependencies create unnecessary redundancy that may lead to the type of anomalies discussed earlier. For example, the transitive dependency in CUSTOMER ORDER (Figure 4-28) requires that a customer's name and address be reentered every time a customer submits a new order, regardless of how many times they have been entered previously. You have no doubt experienced this type of annoying requirement when ordering merchandise online, visiting a doctor's office, or any number of similar activities.

REMOVING TRANSITIVE DEPENDENCIES   You can easily remove transitive dependencies from a relation by means of a three-step procedure:

1. For each nonkey attribute (or set of attributes) that is a determinant in a relation, create a new relation. That attribute (or set of attributes) becomes the primary key of the new relation.
2. Move all of the attributes that are functionally dependent only on the primary key of the new relation from the old to the new relation.
3. Leave the attribute that serves as a primary key in the new relation in the old relation to serve as a foreign key that allows you to associate the two relations.

The results of applying these steps to the relation CUSTOMER ORDER are shown in Figure 4-29. A new relation named CUSTOMER has been created to receive the components of the transitive dependency. The determinant CustomerID becomes the primary key of this relation, and the attributes CustomerName and CustomerAddress are moved to the relation. CUSTOMER ORDER is renamed ORDER, and the attribute CustomerID remains as a foreign key in that relation. This allows us to associate an order with the customer who submitted the order. As indicated in Figure 4-29, these relations are now in third normal form.

Normalizing the data in the INVOICE view has resulted in the creation of four relations in third normal form: CUSTOMER, PRODUCT, ORDER, and ORDER LINE. A relational schema showing these four relations and their associations (developed

FIGURE 4-29 Removing transitive dependencies

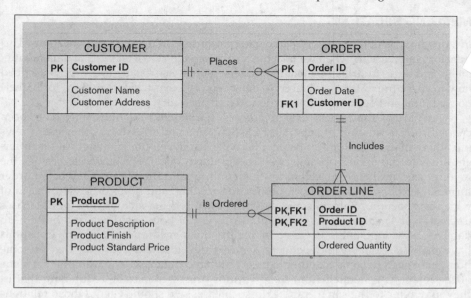

using Microsoft Visio) is shown in Figure 4-30. Note that CustomerID is a foreign key in ORDER, and OrderID and ProductID are foreign keys in ORDER LINE. (Foreign keys are shown in Visio for logical, but not conceptual, data models.) Also note that minimum cardinalities are shown on the relationships even though the normalized relations provide no evidence of what the minimum cardinalities should be. Sample data for the relations might include, for example, a customer with no orders, thus providing evidence of the optional cardinality for the relationship Places. However, even if there were an order for every customer in a sample data set, this would not prove mandatory cardinality. Minimum cardinalities must be determined from business rules, not illustrations of reports, screens, and transactions. The same statement is true for specific maximum cardinalities (e.g., a business rule that no order may contain more than 100 line items).

Determinants and Normalization

We demonstrated normalization through 3NF in steps. There is an easy shortcut, however. If you look back at the original set of four determinants and the associated functional dependencies for the invoice user view, each of these corresponds to one of the relations in Figure 4-30. Each determinant is the primary key of a relation, and the nonkeys of each relation are those attributes that are functionally dependent on each determinant. There is a subtle but important difference: Because OrderID determines CustomerID, CustomerName, and CustomerAddress and CustomerID determines its dependent attributes, CustomerID becomes a foreign key in the ORDER relation, which is where CustomerName and CustomerAddress are represented. If you can determine determinants that have no overlapping dependent attributes, then you have defined the relations. Thus, you can do normalization step by step as illustrated for the Pine Valley Furniture invoice, or you can create relations in 3NF straight from determinants' functional dependencies.

Step 4: Further Normalization

After completing Steps 0 through 3, all nonkeys will be dependent on the primary key, the whole primary key, and nothing but the primary key ("so help you Codd!"). Actually, normal forms are rules about functional dependencies and, hence, are the result of finding determinants and their associated nonkeys. The steps we outlined above are an aid in creating a relation for each determinant and its associated nonkeys.

You will recall from the beginning of our discussion of normalization that we identified additional normal forms beyond 3NF. The most commonly enforced of these additional normal forms are explained in Appendix B (available on the book's Web site), which you might want to read or scan now.

MERGING RELATIONS

In a previous section, we described how to transform EER diagrams into relations. This transformation occurs when we take the results of a top-down analysis of data requirements and begin to structure them for implementation in a database. We then described how to check the resulting relations to determine whether they are in third (or higher) normal form and perform normalization steps if necessary.

As part of the logical design process, normalized relations may have been created from a number of separate EER diagrams and (possibly) other user views (i.e., there may be bottom-up or parallel database development activities for different areas of the organization as well as top-down ones). For example, besides the invoice used in the prior section to illustrate normalization, there may be an order form, an account balance report, production routing, and other user views, each of which has been normalized separately. The three-schema architecture for databases (see Chapter 1) encourages the simultaneous use of both top-down and bottom-up database development processes. In reality, most medium-to-large organizations have many reasonably independent systems development activities that at some point may need to come together to create a shared database. The result is that some of the relations generated from these various processes may be redundant; that is, they may refer to the same entities. In such cases, we should merge those relations to remove the redundancy. This section describes merging relations (also called *view integration*). An understanding of how to merge relations is important for three reasons:

1. On large projects, the work of several subteams comes together during logical design, so there is often a need to merge relations.
2. Integrating existing databases with new information requirements often leads to the need to integrate different views.
3. New data requirements may arise during the life cycle, so there is a need to merge any new relations with what has already been developed.

An Example

Suppose that modeling a user view results in the following 3NF relation:

EMPLOYEE1(EmployeeID, Name, Address, Phone)

Modeling a second user view might result in the following relation:

EMPLOYEE2(EmployeeID, Name, Address, Jobcode, NoYears)

Because these two relations have the same primary key (EmployeeID), they likely describe the same entity and may be merged into one relation. The result of merging the relations is the following relation:

EMPLOYEE(EmployeeID, Name, Address, Phone, Jobcode, NoYears)

Notice that an attribute that appears in both relations (e.g., Name in this example) appears only once in the merged relation.

View Integration Problems

When integrating relations as in the preceding example, a database analyst must understand the meaning of the data and must be prepared to resolve any problems that may arise in that process. In this section, we describe and briefly illustrate four problems that arise in view integration: *synonyms*, *homonyms*, *transitive dependencies*, and *supertype/subtype relationships*.

SYNONYMS In some situations, two (or more) attributes may have different names but the same meaning (e.g., when they describe the same characteristic of an entity). Such attributes are called **synonyms.** For example, EmployeeID and EmployeeNo may be synonyms. When merging the relations that contain synonyms, you should obtain agreement (if possible) from users on a single, standardized name for the attribute and eliminate any other synonyms. (Another alternative is to choose a third name to replace the synonyms.) For example, consider the following relations:

Synonyms
Two (or more) attributes that have different names but the same meaning.

STUDENT1(<u>StudentID</u>, Name)
STUDENT2(<u>MatriculationNo</u>, Name, Address)

In this case, the analyst recognizes that both StudentID and MatriculationNo are synonyms for a person's student identity number and are identical attributes. (Another possibility is that these are both candidate keys, and only one of them should be selected as the primary key.) One possible resolution would be to standardize on one of the two attribute names, such as StudentID. Another option is to use a new attribute name, such as StudentNo, to replace both synonyms. Assuming the latter approach, merging the two relations would produce the following result:

STUDENT(<u>StudentNo</u>, Name, Address)

Often when there are synonyms, there is a need to allow some database users to refer to the same data by different names. Users may need to use familiar names that are consistent with terminology in their part of the organization. An **alias** is an alternative name used for an attribute. Many database management systems allow the definition of an alias that may be used interchangeably with the primary attribute label.

Alias
An alternative name used for an attribute.

HOMONYMS An attribute name that may have more than one meaning is called a **homonym.** For example, the term *account* might refer to a bank's checking account, savings account, loan account, or other type of account (and therefore *account* refers to different data, depending on how it is used).

Homonym
An attribute that may have more than one meaning.

You should be on the lookout for homonyms when merging relations. Consider the following example:

STUDENT1(<u>StudentID</u>, Name, Address)
STUDENT2(<u>StudentID</u>, Name, PhoneNo, Address)

In discussions with users, an analyst may discover that the attribute Address in STUDENT1 refers to a student's campus address, whereas in STUDENT2 the same attribute refers to a student's permanent (or home) address. To resolve this conflict, we would probably need to create new attribute names, so that the merged relation would become

STUDENT(<u>StudentID</u>, Name, PhoneNo, CampusAddress, PermanentAddress)

TRANSITIVE DEPENDENCIES When two 3NF relations are merged to form a single relation, transitive dependencies (described earlier in this chapter) may result. For example, consider the following two relations:

STUDENT1(<u>StudentID</u>, MajorName)
STUDENT2(<u>StudentID</u>, Advisor)

Because STUDENT1 and STUDENT2 have the same primary key, the two relations can be merged:

STUDENT(StudentID, MajorName, Advisor)

However, suppose that each major has exactly one advisor. In this case, Advisor is functionally dependent on MajorName:

MajorName → Advisor

If the preceding functional dependency exists, then STUDENT is in 2NF but not in 3NF, because it contains a transitive dependency. The analyst can create 3NF relations by removing the transitive dependency. Major Name becomes a foreign key in STUDENT:

STUDENT(StudentID, MajorName)
MAJOR (MajorName, Advisor)

SUPERTYPE/SUBTYPE RELATIONSHIPS   These relationships may be hidden in user views or relations. Suppose that we have the following two hospital relations:

PATIENT1(PatientID, Name, Address)
PATIENT2(PatientID, RoomNo)

Initially, it appears that these two relations can be merged into a single PATIENT relation. However, the analyst correctly suspects that there are two different types of patients: resident patients and outpatients. PATIENT1 actually contains attributes common to all patients. PATIENT2 contains an attribute (RoomNo) that is a characteristic only of resident patients. In this situation, the analyst should create supertype/subtype relationships for these entities:

PATIENT(PatientID, Name, Address)
RESIDENTPATIENT(PatientID, RoomNo)
OUTPATIENT(PatientID, DateTreated)

We have created the OUTPATIENT relation to show what it might look like if it were needed, but it is not necessary, given only PATIENT1 and PATIENT2 user views. For an extended discussion of view integration in database design, see Navathe et al. (1986).

A FINAL STEP FOR DEFINING RELATIONAL KEYS

In Chapter 2, we provided some criteria for selecting identifiers: They do not change values over time and must be unique and known, nonintelligent, and use a single attribute surrogate for composite identifier. Actually, none of these criteria must apply until the database is implemented (i.e., when the identifier becomes a primary key and is defined as a field in the physical database). Before the relations are defined as tables, the primary keys of relations should, if necessary, be changed to conform to these criteria.

Database experts (e.g., Johnston, 2000) have strengthened the criteria for primary key specification. Experts now also recommend that a primary key be unique across *the whole database* (a so-called **enterprise key**), not just unique within the relational table to which it applies. This criterion makes a primary key more like what in object-oriented databases is called an *object identifier* (see online Chapter 14). With this recommendation, the primary key of a relation becomes a value internal to the database system and has no business meaning.

Enterprise key

A primary key whose value is unique across all relations.

A candidate primary key, such as EmpID in the EMPLOYEE1 relation of Figure 4-1 or CustomerID in the CUSTOMER relation (Figure 4-29), if ever used in the organization, is called a *business key* or *natural key* and would be included in the relation as a nonkey attribute. The EMPLOYEE1 and CUSTOMER relations (and every other relation in the database) then have a new enterprise key attribute (called, say, ObjectID), which has no business meaning.

Why create this extra attribute? One of the main motivations for using an enterprise key is database evolvability—merging new relations into a database after the database is created. For example, consider the following two relations:

EMPLOYEE(EmpID, EmpName, DeptName, Salary)
CUSTOMER(CustID, CustName, Address)

In this example, without an enterprise key, EmpID and CustID may or may not have the same format, length, and data type, whether they are intelligent or non-intelligent. Suppose the organization evolves its information processing needs and recognizes that employees can also be customers, so employee and customer are simply two subtypes of the same PERSON supertype. (You saw this in Chapter 3, when studying universal data modeling.) Thus, the organization would then like to have three relations:

PERSON(PersonID, PersonName)
EMPLOYEE(PersonID, DeptName, Salary)
CUSTOMER(PersonID, Address)

In this case, PersonID is supposed to be the same value for the same person throughout all roles. But if values for EmpID and CustID were selected before relation PERSON was created, the values for EmpID and CustID probably will not match. Moreover, if we change the values of EmpID and CustID to match the new PersonID, how do we ensure that all EmpIDs and CustIDs are unique if another employee or customer already has the associated PersonID value? Even worse, if there are other tables that relate to, say, EMPLOYEE, then foreign keys in these other tables have to change, creating a ripple effect of foreign key changes. The only way to guarantee that each primary key of a relation is unique across the database is to create an enterprise key from the very beginning so primary keys never have to change.

In our example, the original database (without PERSON) with an enterprise key is shown in Figures 4-31a (the relations) and 4-31b (sample data). In this figure, EmpID and CustID are now business keys, and OBJECT is the supertype of all other relations. OBJECT can have attributes such as the name of the type of object (included in this example as attribute ObjectType), date created, date last changed, or any other internal system attributes for an object instance. Then, when PERSON is needed, the database evolves to the design shown in Figures 4-31c (the relations) and 4-31d (sample data). Evolution to the database with PERSON still requires some alterations to existing tables, but not to primary key values. The name attribute is moved to PERSON because it is common to both subtypes, and a foreign key is added to EMPLOYEE and CUSTOMER to point to the common person instance. As you will see in Chapter 6, it is easy to add and delete nonkey columns, even foreign keys, to table definitions. In contrast, changing the primary key of a relation is not allowed by most database management systems because of the extensive cost of the foreign key ripple effects.

FIGURE 4-31   Enterprise key

(a) Relations with enterprise key

OBJECT (OID, ObjectType)
EMPLOYEE (OID, EmpID, EmpName, DeptName, Salary)
CUSTOMER (OID, CustID, CustName, Address)

(b) Sample data with enterprise key

EMPLOYEE

OID	EmpID	EmpName	DeptName	Salary
1	100	Jennings, Fred	Marketing	50000
4	101	Hopkins, Dan	Purchasing	45000
5	102	Huber, Ike	Accounting	45000

OBJECT

OID	ObjectType
1	EMPLOYEE
2	CUSTOMER
3	CUSTOMER
4	EMPLOYEE
5	EMPLOYEE
6	CUSTOMER
7	CUSTOMER

CUSTOMER

OID	CustID	CustName	Address
2	100	Fred's Warehouse	Greensboro, NC
3	101	Bargain Bonanza	Moscow, ID
6	102	Jasper's	Tallahassee, FL
7	103	Desks 'R Us	Kettering, OH

(c) Relations after adding PERSON relation

OBJECT (OID, ObjectType)
EMPLOYEE (OID, EmpID, DeptName, Salary, PersonID)
CUSTOMER (OID, CustID, Address, PersonID)
PERSON (OID, Name)

Summary

Logical database design is the process of transforming the conceptual data model into a logical data model. The emphasis in this chapter has been on the relational data model, because of its importance in contemporary database systems. The relational data model represents data in the form of tables called relations. A relation is a named, two-dimensional table of data. A key property of relations is that they cannot contain multivalued attributes.

In this chapter, we described the major steps in the logical database design process. This process is based on transforming EER diagrams into normalized relations. This process has three steps: Transform EER diagrams into relations, normalize the relations, and merge the relations. The result of this process is a set of relations in third normal form that can be implemented using any contemporary relational database management system.

Each entity type in the EER diagram is transformed into a relation that has the same primary key as the entity type. A one-to-many relationship is represented by adding a foreign key to the relation that represents the entity on the many side of the relationship. (This foreign key is the primary key of the entity on the one side of the relationship.) A many-to-many relationship is represented by creating a separate relation. The primary

FIGURE 4-31   *(continued)*

(d) Sample data after adding the PERSON relation

OBJECT

OID	ObjectType
1	EMPLOYEE
2	CUSTOMER
3	CUSTOMER
4	EMPLOYEE
5	EMPLOYEE
6	CUSTOMER
7	CUSTOMER
8	PERSON
9	PERSON
10	PERSON
11	PERSON
12	PERSON
13	PERSON
14	PERSON

PERSON

OID	Name
8	Jennings, Fred
9	Fred's Warehouse
10	Bargain Bonanza
11	Hopkins, Dan
12	Huber, Ike
13	Jasper's
14	Desks 'R Us

EMPLOYEE

OID	EmpID	DeptName	Salary	PersonID
1	100	Marketing	50000	8
4	101	Purchasing	45000	11
5	102	Accounting	45000	12

CUSTOMER

OID	CustID	Address	PersonID
2	100	Greensboro, NC	9
3	101	Moscow, ID	10
6	102	Tallahassee, FL	13
7	103	Kettering, OH	14

key of this relation is a composite key, consisting of the primary key of each of the entities that participate in the relationship.

The relational model does not directly support supertype/subtype relationships, but we can model these relationships by creating a separate table (or relation) for the supertype and for each subtype. The primary key of each subtype is the same (or at least from the same domain) as for the supertype. The supertype must have an attribute called the subtype discriminator that indicates to which subtype (or subtypes) each instance of the supertype belongs.

The purpose of normalization is to derive well-structured relations that are free of anomalies (inconsistencies or errors) that would otherwise result when the relations are updated or modified. Normalization is based on the analysis of functional dependencies, which are constraints between two attributes (or two sets of attributes). It may be accomplished in several stages. Relations in first normal form (1NF) contain no multivalued attributes or repeating groups. Relations in second normal form (2NF) contain no partial dependencies, and relations in third normal form (3NF) contain no transitive dependencies. We can use diagrams that show the functional dependencies in a relation to help decompose that relation (if necessary) to obtain relations in 3NF. Higher normal forms (beyond 3NF) have also been defined; we discuss these normal forms in Appendix B, available on the book's Web site.

We must be careful when combining relations to deal with problems such as synonyms, homonyms, transitive dependencies, and supertype/subtype relationships. In addition, before relations are defined to the database management system, all primary keys should be described as single-attribute nonintelligent keys and, preferably, as enterprise keys.

Chapter Review

Key Terms

Alias *189*
Anomaly *164*
Candidate key *181*
Composite key *157*
Determinant *181*
Enterprise key *191*
Entity integrity rule *162*
First normal form
  (1NF) *183*

Foreign key *158*
Functional
  dependency *179*
Homonym *189*
Normal form *179*
Normalization *179*
Null *161*
Partial functional
  dependency *185*

Primary key *157*
Recursive foreign key *173*
Referential integrity
  constraint *162*
Relation *157*
Second normal form
  (2NF) *185*
Surrogate primary
  key *168*

Synonyms *189*
Third normal form
  (3NF) *186*
Transitive
  dependency *186*
Well-structured
  relation *164*

Review Questions

4-1. Define each of the following terms:
  a. determinant
  b. functional dependency
  c. transitive dependency
  d. recursive foreign key
  e. normalization
  f. composite key
  g. relation
  h. normal form
  i. partial functional dependency
  j. enterprise key
  k. surrogate primary key

4-2. Match the following terms to the appropriate definitions:

____ well-structured relation
____ anomaly
____ functional dependency
____ determinant
____ composite key
____ 1NF
____ 2NF
____ 3NF
____ recursive foreign key
____ relation
____ transitive dependency

  a. constraint between two attributes
  b. functional dependency between the primary key and a nonkey attribute via another nonkey attribute
  c. references the primary key in the same relation
  d. multivalued attributes removed
  e. inconsistency or error
  f. contains little redundancy
  g. contains two (or more) attributes
  h. contains no partial functional dependencies
  i. transitive dependencies eliminated
  j. attribute on left side of functional dependency
  k. named two-dimensional table of data

4-3. Contrast the following terms:
  a. normal form; normalization
  b. candidate key; primary key
  c. partial dependency; transitive dependency
  d. composite key; recursive foreign key
  e. determinant; candidate key
  f. foreign key; primary key
  g. natural primary key; surrogate primary key
  h. enterprise key; surrogate key

4-4. Describe the primary differences between the conceptual and logical data models.

4-5. Summarize six important properties of relations.

4-6. Describe two properties that each candidate key must satisfy.

4-7. Describe three types of anomalies that can arise in a table and the negative consequences of each.

4-8. Demonstrate each of the anomaly types with an example.

4-9. Fill in the blanks in each of the following statements:
  a. A relation that has no partial functional dependencies is in _____ normal form.
  b. A relation that has no transitive dependencies is in _____ normal form.
  c. A relation that has no multivalued attributes is in _____ normal form.

4-10. What is a well-structured relation? Why are well-structured relations important in logical database design?

4-11. Describe the most common way in which relationships in an E-R diagram are expressed in a corresponding relational data model.

4-12. Describe how the following components of an E-R diagram are transformed into relations:
  a. regular entity type
  b. relationship (1:*M*)
  c. relationship (*M:N*)
  d. multivalued attribute
  e. weak entity
  f. composite attribute

4-13. What is the primary purpose of normalization?

4-14. Briefly describe four typical problems that often arise in merging relations and common techniques for addressing those problems.

4-15. List three conditions that you can apply to determine whether a relation that is in first normal form is also in second normal form.

4-16. Explain how each of the following types of integrity constraints is enforced in the SQL CREATE TABLE commands:
  a. entity integrity
  b. referential integrity

4-17. What are the benefits of enforcing the integrity constraints as part of the database design and implementation process (instead of doing it in application design)?

4-18. How do you represent a 1:*M* unary relationship in a relational data model?

4-19. How do you represent an *M:N* ternary relationship in a relational data model?

4-20. How do you represent an associative entity in a relational data model?

4-21. What is the relationship between the primary key of a relation and the functional dependencies among all attributes within that relation?

4-22. Under what conditions must a foreign key not be null?

4-23. Explain what can be done with primary keys to eliminate key ripple effects as a database evolves.

4-24. What are the benefits of the use of a surrogate key?

4-25. Why is Relational Data Model emphasized more than any other model? What are the advantages of this model?

4-26. What are multi-valued attributes? How does one eliminate them?

4-27. What is the purpose of Integrity Constraints? Explain the different types of Integrity Constraints their need?

4-28. What is a well-structured relation? How do anomalies dictate the constitution of a well-structured relation?

4-29. a. What is attribute inheritance? How does this affect a subtype?
   b. What conditions govern the usage of supertype/subtype relationships? What are the processes that aid in the development of these relationships and explain the same in brief?
   c. Discuss the role of constraints on supertype/subtype relationships
   d. What are the different types of business rules and how do they differs from each other?
   e. Explain the various types of action assertions and explain their classification.

Problems and Exercises

4-30. For each of the following E-R diagrams from Chapter 2:
   I. Transform the diagram to a relational schema that shows referential integrity constraints (see Figure 4-5 for an example of such a schema):
   II. For each relation, diagram the functional dependencies (see Figure 4-23 for an example).
   III. If any of the relations are not in 3NF, transform them to 3NF.
   a. Figure 2-8
   b. Figure 2-9b
   c. Figure 2-11a
   d. Figure 2-11b
   e. Figure 2-15a (relationship version)
   f. Figure 2-15b (attribute version)
   g. Figure 2-16b
   h. Figure 2-19

4-31. For each of the following EER diagrams from Chapter 3:
   I. Transform the diagram into a relational schema that shows referential integrity constraints (see Figure 4-5 for an example of such a schema).
   II. For each relation, diagram the functional dependencies (see Figure 4-23 for an example).
   III. If any of the relations are not in 3NF, transform them to 3NF.
   a. Figure 3-6b
   b. Figure 3-7a
   c. Figure 3-9
   d. Figure 3-10
   e. Figure 3-11

4-32. For each of the following relations, indicate the normal form for that relation. If the relation is not in third normal form, decompose it into 3NF relations. Functional dependencies (other than those implied by the primary key) are shown where appropriate.
   a. CLASS(CourseNo, SectionNo)
   b. CLASS(CourseNo, SectionNo, Room)
   c. CLASS(CourseNo, SectionNo, Room, Capacity) [FD: Room → Capacity]
   d. CLASS(CourseNo, SectionNo, CourseName, Room, Capacity) [FD: CourseNo → CourseName; FD: Room → Capacity]

4-33. For your answers to the following Problems and Exercises from prior chapters, transform the EER diagrams into a set of relational schemas, diagram the functional dependencies, and convert all the relations to third normal form:

a. Chapter 2, Problem and Exercise 2-37b
b. Chapter 2, Problem and Exercise 2-37g
c. Chapter 2, Problem and Exercise 2-37h
d. Chapter 2, Problem and Exercise 2-37i
e. Chapter 2, Problem and Exercise 2-43
f. Chapter 2, Problem and Exercise 2-46

MILLENNIUM COLLEGE
CLASS LIST
FALL SEMESTER 2015

COURSE NO.: IS 460
COURSE TITLE: DATABASE
INSTRUCTOR NAME: NORMAL. FORM
INSTRUCTOR LOCATION: B 104

STUDENT NO.	STUDENT NAME	MAJOR	GRADE
38214	Bright	IS	A
40875	Cortez	CS	B
51893	Edwards	IS	A

FIGURE 4-32 Class list (Millennium College)

4-34. Figure 4-32 shows a class list for Millennium College. Convert this user view to a set of 3NF relations using an enterprise key. Assume the following:
   • An instructor has a unique location.
   • A student has a unique major.
   • A course has a unique title.

4-35. Figure 4-33 (page 196) shows an EER diagram for a simplified credit card environment. There are two types of card accounts: debit cards and credit cards. Credit card accounts accumulate charges with merchants. Each charge is identified by the date and time of the charge as well as the primary keys of merchant and credit card.
   a. Develop a relational schema.
   b. Show the functional dependencies.
   c. Develop a set of 3NF relations using an enterprise key.

4-36. Table 4-3 (page 196) contains sample data for parts and for vendors who supply those parts. In discussing these data with users, we find that part numbers (but not descriptions) uniquely identify parts and that vendor names uniquely identify vendors.

FIGURE 4-33 EER diagram for
bank cards

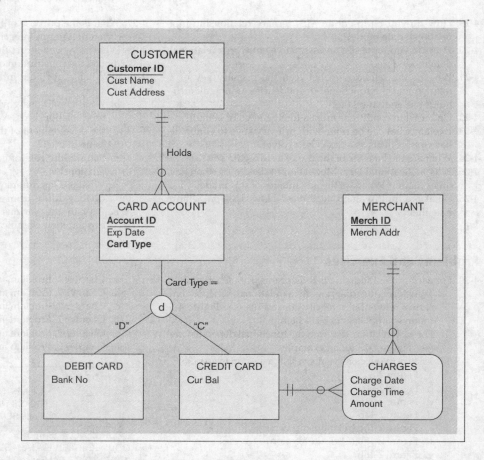

TABLE 4-3 Sample Data for Parts and Vendors

Part No	Description	Vendor Name	Address	Unit Cost
1234	Logic chip	Fast Chips	Cupertino	10.00
		Smart Chips	Phoenix	8.00
5678	Memory chip	Fast Chips	Cupertino	3.00
		Quality Chips	Austin	2.00
		Smart Chips	Phoenix	5.00

a. Convert this table to a relation (named PART SUPPLIER) in first normal form. Illustrate the relation with the sample data in the table.

b. List the functional dependencies in PART SUPPLIER and identify a candidate key.

c. For the relation PART SUPPLIER, identify each of the following: an insert anomaly, a delete anomaly, and a modification anomaly.

d. Draw a relational schema for PART SUPPLIER and show the functional dependencies.

e. In what normal form is this relation?

f. Develop a set of 3NF relations from PART SUPPLIER.

g. Show the 3NF relations using Microsoft Visio (or any other tool specified by your instructor).

4-37. Figure 4-34 (page 197) shows an EER diagram for a restaurant, its tables, and the waiters and waiting staff managers who work at the restaurant. Your assignment is to:

a. Develop a relational schema.

b. Show the functional dependencies.

c. Develop a set of 3NF relations using an enterprise key.

4-38. Table 4-4 shows a relation called GRADE REPORT for a university. Your assignment is as follows:

a. Draw a relational schema and diagram the functional dependencies in the relation.

b. In what normal form is this relation?

c. Decompose GRADE REPORT into a set of 3NF relations.

d. Draw a relational schema for your 3NF relations and show the referential integrity constraints.

e. Draw your answer to part d using Microsoft Visio (or any other tool specified by your instructor).

4-39. Table 4-5 shows a shipping manifest. Your assignment is as follows:

a. Draw a relational schema and diagram the functional dependencies in the relation.

FIGURE 4-34 EER diagram for a restaurant

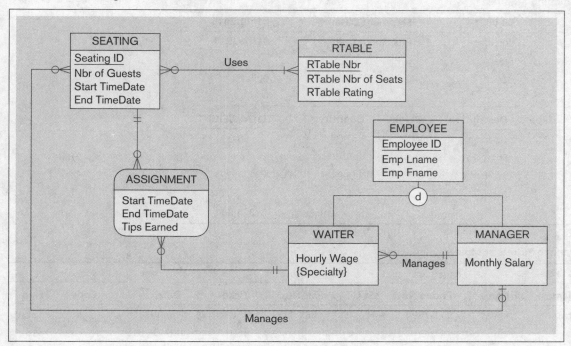

TABLE 4-4 Grade Report Relation

Grade Report

StudentID	StudentName	CampusAddress	Major	CourseID	CourseTitle	Instructor Name	Instructor Location	Grade
168300458	Williams	208 Brooks	IS	IS 350	Database Mgt	Codd	B 104	A
168300458	Williams	208 Brooks	IS	IS 465	Systems Analysis	Parsons	B 317	B
543291073	Baker	104 Phillips	Acctg	IS 350	Database Mgt	Codd	B 104	C
543291073	Baker	104 Phillips	Acctg	Acct 201	Fund Acctg	Miller	H 310	B
543291073	Baker	104 Phillips	Acctg	Mkgt 300	Intro Mktg	Bennett	B 212	A

b. In what normal form is this relation?

c. Decompose MANIFEST into a set of 3NF relations.

d. Draw a relational schema for your 3NF relations and show the referential integrity constraints.

e. Draw your answer to part d using Microsoft Visio (or any other tool specified by your instructor).

4-40. Transform the relational schema developed in Problem and Exercise 4-39 into an EER diagram. State any assumptions that you have made.

4-41. For your answers to the following Problems and Exercises from prior chapters, transform the EER diagrams into a set of relational schemas, diagram the functional dependencies, and convert all the relations to third normal form.

a. Chapter 3, Problem and Exercise 3-35

b. Chapter 3, Problem and Exercise 3-40

TABLE 4-5   Shipping Manifest

Shipment ID:	00-0001	Shipment Date:	01/10/2015
Origin:	Boston	Expected Arrival:	01/14/2015
Destination:	Brazil		
Ship Number:	39	Captain:	002-15
			Henry Moore

Item Number	Type	Description	Weight	Quantity	TOTALWEIGHT
3223	BM	Concrete Form	500	100	50,000
3297	BM	Steel Beam	87	2,000	174,000
				Shipment Total:	224,000

TABLE 4-6   Parking Tickets at Millennium College

Parking Ticket Table

St ID	L Name	F Name	Phone No	St Lic	Lic No	Ticket #	Date	Code	Fine
38249	Brown	Thomas	111-7804	FL	BRY 123	15634	10/17/2015	2	$25
						16017	11/13/2015	1	$15
82453	Green	Sally	391-1689	AL	TRE 141	14987	10/05/2015	3	$100
						16293	11/18/2015	1	$15
						17892	12/13/2015	2	$25

4-42. Transform Figure 2-15a, attribute version, to 3NF relations. Transform Figure 2-15b, relationship version, to 3NF relations. Compare these two sets of 3NF relations with those in Figure 4-10. What observations and conclusions do you reach by comparing these different sets of 3NF relations?

4-43. The Public Safety office at Millennium College maintains a list of parking tickets issued to vehicles parked illegally on the campus. Table 4-6 shows a portion of this list for the fall semester. (Attribute names are abbreviated to conserve space.)

   a. Convert this table to a relation in first normal form by entering appropriate data in the table. What are the determinants in this relation?

   b. Draw a dependency diagram that shows all functional dependencies in the relation, based on the sample data shown.

   c. Give an example of one or more anomalies that can result in using this relation.

   d. Develop a set of relations in third normal form. Include a new column with the heading Violation in the appropriate table to explain the reason for each ticket. Values in this column are: expired parking meter (ticket code 1), no parking permit (ticket code 2), and handicap violation (ticket code 3).

   e. Develop an E-R diagram with the appropriate cardinality notations.

4-44. The materials manager at Pine Valley Furniture Company maintains a list of suppliers for each of the material items purchased by the company from outside vendors. Table 4-7 shows the essential data required for this application.

TABLE 4-7   Pine Valley Furniture Company Purchasing Data

Attribute Name	Sample Value
Material ID	3792
Material Name	Hinges 3" locking
Unit of Measure	each
Standard Cost	$5.00
Vendor ID	V300
Vendor Name	Apex Hardware
Unit Price	$4.75
Terms Code	1
Terms	COD

   a. Draw a dependency diagram for this data. You may assume the following:
   • Each material item has one or more suppliers. Each supplier may supply one or more items or may not supply any items.
   • The unit price for a material item may vary from one vendor to another.
   • The terms code for a supplier uniquely identifies the terms of the sale (e.g., code 2 means 10 percent net 30 days). The terms for a supplier are the same for all material items ordered from that supplier.

   b. Decompose this diagram into a set of diagrams in 3NF.

   c. Draw an E-R diagram for this situation.

4-45. Table 4-8 shows a portion of a shipment table for a large manufacturing company. Each shipment (identified by Shipment#) uniquely identifies the shipment Origin, Destination, and Distance. The shipment Origin and Destination pair also uniquely identifies the Distance.

a. Develop a diagram that shows the functional dependencies in the SHIPMENT relation.

b. In what normal form is SHIPMENT? Why?

c. Convert SHIPMENT to third normal form if necessary. Show the resulting table(s) with the sample data presented in SHIPMENT.

4-46. Figure 4-35 shows an EER diagram for Vacation Property Rentals. This organization rents preferred properties in several states. As shown in the figure, there are two basic types of properties: beach properties and mountain properties.

a. Transform the EER diagram to a set of relations and develop a relational schema.

b. Diagram the functional dependencies and determine the normal form for each relation.

c. Convert all relations to third normal form, if necessary, and draw a revised relational schema.

d. Suggest an integrity constraint that would ensure that no property is rented twice during the same time interval.

TABLE 4-8 Shipment Relation

Shipment#	Origin	Destination	Distance
409	Seattle	Denver	1,537
618	Chicago	Dallas	1,058
723	Boston	Atlanta	1,214
824	Denver	Los Angeles	975
629	Seattle	Denver	1,537

FIGURE 4-35 EER diagram for Vacation Property Rentals

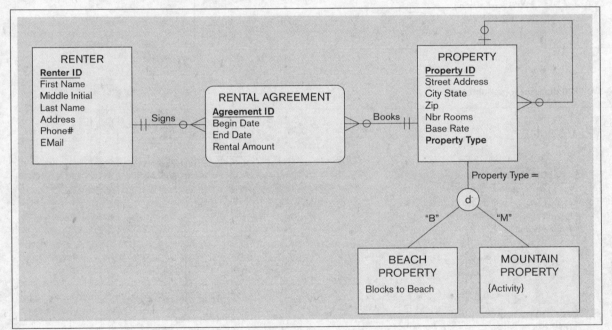

4-47. For your answers to Problem and Exercise 3-36 from Chapter 3, transform the EER diagrams into a set of relational schemas, diagram the functional dependencies, and convert all the relations to third normal form.

4-48. Figure 4-36 includes an EER diagram describing a car racing league. Transform the diagram into a relational schema that shows referential integrity constraints (see Figure 4-5 for an example of such a schema). In addition, verify that the resulting relations are in 3NF.

4-49. Figure 4-37 includes an EER diagram describing a publisher specializing in large edited works. Transform the diagram into a relational schema that shows referential integrity constraints (see Figure 4-5 for an example of such

a schema). In addition, verify that the resulting relations are in 3NF.

4-50. Figure 4-38 includes an EER diagram for a medium-size software vendor. Transform the diagram into a relational schema that shows referential integrity constraints (see Figure 4-5 for an example of such a schema). In addition, verify that the resulting relations are in 3NF.

4-51. Examine the set of relations in Figure 4-39. What normal form are these in? How do you know this? If they are in 3NF, convert the relations into an EER diagram. What assumptions did you have to make to answer these questions?

FIGURE 4-36 EER diagram for a car racing league

FIGURE 4-37 EER diagram for a publisher

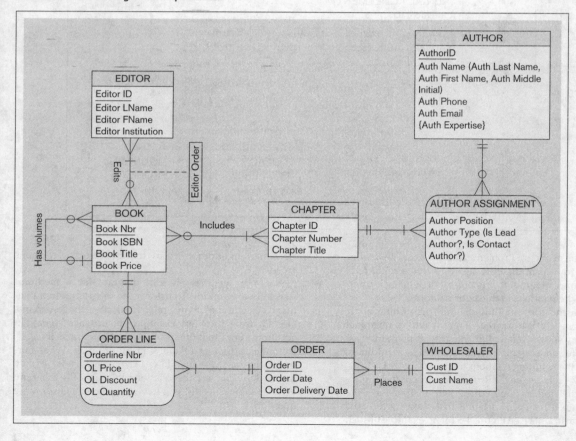

FIGURE 4-38 EER diagram for a middle-size software vendor

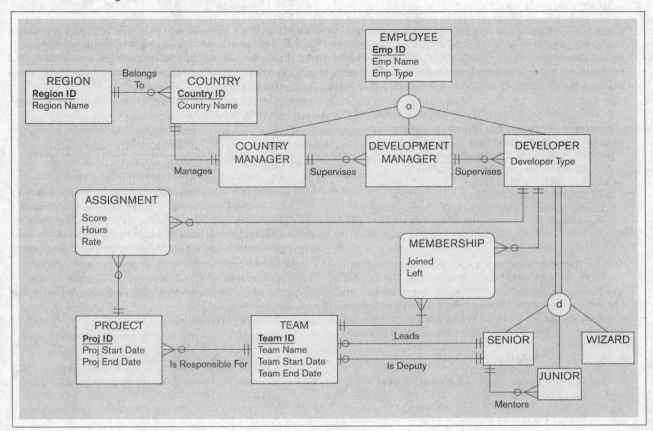

FIGURE 4-39 Relations for Problem and Exercise 4-51

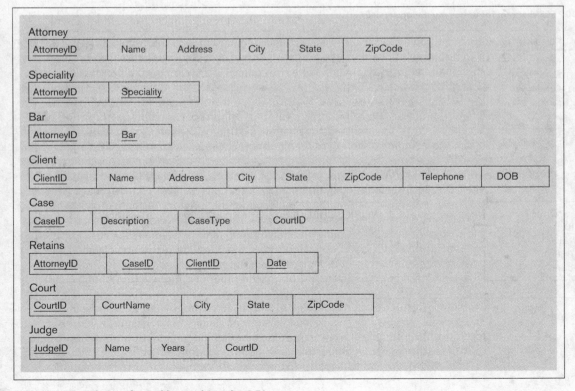

4-52. A pet store currently uses a legacy flat file system to store all of its information. The owner of the store, Peter Corona, wants to implement a Web-enabled database application. This would enable branch stores to enter data regarding inventory levels, ordering, and so on. Presently, the data for inventory and sales tracking are stored in one file that has the following format:

StoreName, PetName, Pet Description, Price, Cost, SupplierName, ShippingTime, QuantityOnHand, DateOfLastDelivery, DateOfLastPurchase, DeliveryDate1, DeliveryDate2, DeliveryDate3, DeliveryDate4, PurchaseDate1, PurchaseDate2, PurchaseDate3, PurchaseDate4, LastCustomerName, CustomerName1, CustomerName2, CustomerName3, CustomerName4

Assume that you want to track all purchase and inventory data, such as who bought the fish, the date that it was purchased, the date that it was delivered, and so on. The present file format allows only the tracking of the last purchase and delivery as well as four prior purchases and deliveries. You can assume that a type of fish is supplied by one supplier.
a. Show all functional dependencies.
b. What normal form is this table in?
c. Design a normalized data model for these data. Show that it is in 3NF.

4-53. For Problem and Exercise 4-52, draw the ER diagram based on the normalized relations.

4-54. How would Problems and Exercises 4-52 and 4-53 change if a type of fish could be supplied by multiple suppliers?

4-55. Figure 4-40 shows an EER diagram for a university dining service organization that provides dining services to a major university.
a. Transform the EER diagram to a set of relations and develop a relational schema.
b. Diagram the functional dependencies and determine the normal form for each relation.
c. Convert all relations to third normal form, if necessary, and draw a revised relational schema.

4-56. Explore the data included in Table 4-9.
Assume that the primary key of this relation consists of two components: Author's ID (AID) and Book number (BNbr). The relation includes data regarding authors, books, and publishers. In addition, it tells what an individual author's per book royalty amount is in the case of multi-authored books.

Your task is to:
a. Identify the functional dependencies between the attributes.
b. Identify the normal form in which the relation currently is.
c. Identify the errors in the data that have been made possible by its poor structural characteristics.
d. Take the actions (if any) necessary to convert the relation into the third normal form. Identify all intermediate steps.

FIGURE 4-40 EER diagram for university dining services

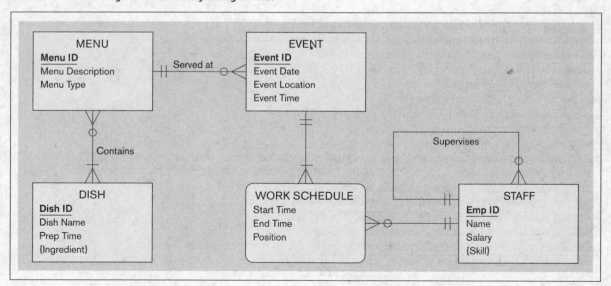

TABLE 4-9 Author Book Royalties

AID	ALname	AFname	AInst	BNbr	BName	BPublish	PubCity	BPrice	AuthBRoyalty
10	Gold	Josh	Sleepy Hollow U	106	JavaScript and HTML5	Wall & Vintage	Chicago, IL	$62.75	$6.28
				102	Quick Mobile Apps	Gray Brothers	Boston, MA	$49.95	$2.50
24	Shippen	Mary	Green Lawns U	104	Innovative Data Management	Smith and Sons	Dallas, TX	$158.65	$15.87
				106	JavaScript and HTML5	Wall & Vintage	Indianapolis, IN	$62.75	$6.00
32	Oswan	Jan	Middlestate College	126	Networks and Data Centers	Grey Brothers	Boston, NH	$250.00	$12.50
				180	Server Infrastructure	Gray Brothers	Boston, MA	$122.85	$12.30
				102	Quick Mobile Apps	Gray Brothers	Boston, MA	$45.00	$2.25

4-57. The following attributes form a relation that includes information about individual computers, their vendors, software packages running on the computers, computer users, and user authorizations. Users are authorized to use a specific software package on a specific computer during a specific time frame (characterized with attributes UserAuthorization Starts and UserAuthorizationEnds and secured with UserAuthorizationPassword). Software is licensed to be used on specific computers (potentially multiple software packages at the same time) until an expiration time (SoftwareLicensePrice) at a specific price. Computers are sold by vendors, and each vendor has a support person with an ID, name, and phone extension. Each individual computer has a specific purchase price. The attributes are as follows:

ComputerSerialNbr, VendorID, VendorName, VendorPhone, VendorSupportID, VendorSupportName, VendorSupportExtension, SoftwareID, SoftwareName, SoftwareVendor, SoftwareLicenseExpires, SoftwareLicensePrice, UserID, UserName, UserAuthorizationStarts, UserAuthorizationEnds, UserAuthorizationPassword, PurchasePrice

Based on this information,
a. Identify the functional dependencies between the attributes.
b. Identify the reasons why this relation is not in 3NF.
c. Present the attributes organized so that the resulting relations are in 3NF.

4-58. The following attributes represent data about a movie copy at an online video rental service. Each movie is identified by a movie number and has a title and information about the director and the studio that produced the movie. Each movie has one or several characters, and there is exactly one actor playing the role of each of the characters (but one actor can play multiple roles in each of the movies). The video rental service has multiple licenses for the same movie, and the service differentiates the licenses with a movie copy number, which is unique within a single movie but not unique between different movies. Each movie license has a rental

status and return date; in addition, each license has a type (Regular or HD). The rental price depends on the movie and the license type, but the price is the same for all licenses of the same type. The attributes are as follows:

Movie Nbr, Title, Director ID, Director Name, Studio ID, Studio Name, Studio Location, Studio CEO, Character, Actor ID, Name, Movie License Nbr, Movie License Type, Movie Rental Price, License Rental Status, License Return Date

A sample data set regarding a movie would be as follows (the data in the curly brackets are character/actor data, in this case for four different characters):

567, "It's a Wonderful Life", 25, "Frank Capra", 234, "Liberty Films", "Hollywood, CA", "Orson Wells", {"George Bailey", 245, "James Stewart" | "Mary Bailey", 236, "Donna Reed" | "Clarence Oddbody", 765, "Henry Travers" | "Henry F. Potter", 325, "Lionel Barrymore" }, 5434, "HD", 3.95, "Rented", "12/15/2015"

Based on this information,
a. Identify the functional dependencies between the attributes.
b. Identify the reasons why this set of data items is not in 3NF and tell what normal form (if any) it is in.
c. Present the attributes organized into 3NF relations that have been named appropriately.

4-59. A start-up is working on an online personal financial management system. The goal of the system is to provide the users an opportunity to obtain item-level purchase data from as many sources as possible in order to improve the accuracy of budget management and control activities (instead of only at the level of the total of each purchase). For example, let's assume a customer purchases three books from a major online bookseller. For most financial management software systems, the system only receives the total of the purchase from a bank or other financial institution. In the case of this start-up, the intent is to create a link between the financial transaction and the vendor's system data so that the financial management system retrieves product details from the vendor. Now it will be easy for the customer to classify one book as self-help, the other one as a business expense, and the third one as entertainment without having to resort to an analysis of receipts.

To provide this capability, the system maintains the following data regarding the transactions:

TransactionID, CustomerID, CustomerName, CustomerEmail, TransactionDate, TransactionTime, TransactionTotalAmount, TransactionTax, ProductID, ProductDescription, ProductCategory, ProductManufacturerID, ManufacturerName, ProductListPrice, ProductPurchasePrice, ProductQuantity, TransactionProductTotal

Sample data for this set of attributes is as follows:

823434434582, 2434254, Silver Patrick, psilver@mail.net, 9/2/2015, 10.28.34, $167.23, $10.37, {78234, "Achieving One's Fullest Potential," self-help, 145432, Brown and Gray, $29.95, $24.75, 1, $24.75 | 4782349, "Programming Server-side Solutions with Python," Programming, 63453632, Green & Yellow, $47.95, $39.99, 2, $79.98 | 2342343, "Murder at Eleven," fiction, 145432, Brown and Gray, $14.95, $12.50, 5, $62.50}. Note that information regarding specific products is repeated multiple times in the sample data set and each repeated set is separated by the "|" symbol.

Based on the facts stated above,
a. Identify the functional dependencies between the attributes.
b. Identify the reasons why this set of data is not in 3NF and indicate the normal form (if any) it is in.
c. Including all intermediate stages, organize the attributes into a set of 3NF relations.
d. Draw an ER diagram based on the normalized relations.

4-60. A bus company is responsible for offering public transportation in the suburbs of a large metropolitan area. The company has significant data management requirements: It needs to keep track of its 150 vehicles, 400 drivers, 60 bus routes, and hundreds of scheduled departures every day. In addition, it is essential for the company to know which drivers are certified to drive which buses.
The data that the company has available include the following attributes:

RouteID, RouteStartPoint, RouteEndPoint, RouteStandardDrivingTime, ScheduleDate,

ScheduledDepTime, ScheduledArrTime, DriverID, DriverFName, DriverLName, DateDriverJoinedCompany, DriverDOB, VehicleID, VehicleMake, VehicleModel, VehiclePassangerCapacity, DriverCertStartDate, DriverCertEndDate.

Sample data for this set of attributes are as follows:

28, Grand Avenue, Madison Street, 38, {9/12/2015, 8.30, 9.18, 8273, Mary, Smith, 5/2/2007, 3/23/1974, 1123, GreatTrucks, CityCoach, 58, 6/10/2015, 6/9/2016 | 9/12/2015, 9.30, 10.12, 7234, John, Jones, 10/12/2011, 12/15/1991, 5673, GreatTrucks, CityCoach 2, 62, 4/12/2015, 4/11/2016 | 9/12/2015, 10.30, 11.08, 2343, Pat, Moore, 2/24/1982, 1/19/1958, 4323, PowerTransport, MidiBus, 32, 8/20/2015, 8/19/2016}

Note that the information for specific bus schedules (starting with the attribute ScheduleDate) is repeated three times in the sample data set and is separated by the "|" symbol. Also, take into account that in this case, the certification is specific to a particular vehicle driver pair.

Based on the facts stated above,
a. Identify the functional dependencies between the attributes.
b. Identify the reasons why this set of data is not in 3NF and indicate the normal form (if any) it is in.
c. Including all intermediate stages, organize the attributes into a set of 3NF relations.
d. Draw an ER diagram based on the normalized relations.
e. Based on the ER diagram you just drew and the case narrative, explore the areas in which there could be opportunities to expand the data model to achieve better tracking of the company's operations or improved clarity, such as maintaining more detailed route information.

4-61. Develop an EER model for the following situation. Identify which of these statements are Attributes, Entities and Business Rules:
A B-School offers Elective courses to its students in their second year. After talking to the P G P Chairperson, the basic list of Entities, Attributes and Business Rules identified are:

• The Elective courses are made available in respective areas such as Marketing, HR, Systems, Finance, and Operations. In future newer areas could be added depending on the Academic Council decisions. The Elective courses could be of 1, 2 or 3 credits. Each credit entails 10 hours of contact sessions.
• The second year has 3 terms of 3 months each.
• Students have a cap on the number of credits they can opt for in each term
• Also the total number of credits for all the terms put together should not exceed a particular number

- Students specialize in a particular area on the basis of a predetermined number of credits opted in that area
- Course has course code as identifier and attributes such as its title, evaluation components, the number of credits, the faculty delivering the course and course description

Student has Roll No. as identifier and has attributes such as Name, courses opted, total credits, credits in each term and specialization area on the basis of the course credits opted in the area.

4-62. The table below contains the sales data at the West Side Store

TABLE 4-10 West Side Store Sales Data

Sl. No.	Bill No.	Credit Card No.	Customer Name	Customer Contact	Bill Date	Item Rate	Qty	Total Cost
1.	100034	447756130	Seema Das	9448961021	30/06/2010	S101	15.00	6
						N110	45.00	3
						T14	110.00	2
						S102	25.00	3
2.	100035	Cash payment	Nikunj Patel	9310756667	02/07/2010	B16	450.00	2
						C108	140.00	5
3.	100036	Cash payment	Aditya Bhandari		02/07/2010	A111	566.00	1

a. Convert the table details into the first normal form.
b. What are the functional dependencies that you can identify? List at least two.
c. Develop the final 3NF for this table enumerating the total number of tables needed for a well-structured relation.

4-63. A local Car Dealer "Friendly Dealers" sells cars from 2–3 different automobile companies. "Friendly Dealers" maintains the details of manufacturers, so that its employees can interact with the manufacturers in case of need. "Friendly Dealers" also keeps information related to the models of cars it deals with. The information maintained is list price; price of the dealership paid, model name, series (ex. Maruti 800, DX etc). They keep information of the sales that they make with the details of the buyers (such as name, address, contact details etc). Create an ERD and apply the rules of Normalization to arrive at a compact database structure.

4-64. Table below shows an Invoice for a Sales Company.
a. Convert the table details into the first normal form.
b. What are the functional dependencies that you can identify? List at least two.
c. Develop the final 3NF for this table enumerating the total number of tables needed for a well-structured relation.

TABLE 4-11 Invoice of ABC Sales Company, Bangalore

ABC Sales Company, Bangalore

Invoice

Invoice Date: Invoice No.:

Sl. No.	Item Code	Item Name	Rate	Quantity	Amount
1.	I-234	Noodles	25.00	5	125.00
2.	I-765	Mayonnaise	32.00	1 pkt	32.00
3.	I-541	Brown Bread	19.00	2 loaves	38.00
				Total	195.00
				Tax @ 2%	3.90
				Grand total	198.90

Field Exercises

4-65. Interview system designers and database designers at several organizations. Ask them to describe the process they use for logical design. How do they transform their conceptual data models (e.g., E-R diagrams) to relational schema? What is the role of CASE tools in this process? Do they use normalization? If they do, how far in the process do they go, and for what purpose?

4-66. Obtain a common document such as a sales slip, customer invoice from an auto repair shop, credit card statement, and so on. Use the normalization steps (Steps 0 through 4) described in this chapter to convert this user view to a set of relations in third normal form. Also draw a relational schema. List several integrity rules that you would recommend to ensure the quality of the data in this application.

4-67. Using the online Appendix B, available on the book's Web site, as a resource, interview a database analyst/designer to determine whether he or she normalizes relations to higher than 3NF. Why or why not does he or she use normal forms beyond 3NF?

4-68. Find a form or report from a business organization, possibly a statement, bill, or document you have received. Draw an EER diagram of the data in this form or report. Transform the diagram into a set of 3NF relations.

References

Chouinard, P. 1989. "Supertypes, Subtypes, and DB2." *Database Programming & Design* 2,10 (October): 50–57.

Codd, E. F. 1970. "A Relational Model of Data for Large Shared Data Banks." *Communications of the ACM* 13,6 (June): 77–87.

Codd, E. F. 1990. *The Relational Model for Database Management*, Version 2. Reading, MA: Addison-Wesley.

Date, C. J. 2003. *An Introduction to Database Systems*. 8th ed. Reading, MA: Addison-Wesley.

Dutka, A. F., and H. H. Hanson. 1989. *Fundamentals of Data Normalization*. Reading, MA: Addison-Wesley.

Fleming, C. C., and B. von Halle. 1989. *Handbook of Relational Database Design*. Reading, MA: Addison-Wesley.

Hoberman, S. 2006. "To Surrogate Key or Not." *DM Review* 16,8 (August): 29.

Johnston, T. 2000. "Primary Key Reengineering Projects: The Problem" and "Primary Key Reengineering Projects: The Solution." Available at **www.information-management.com.**

Navathe, S., R. Elmasri, and J. Larson. 1986. "Integrating User Views in Database Design." *Computer* 19,1 (January): 50–62.

Further Reading

Elmasri, R., and S. Navathe. 2010. *Fundamentals of Database Systems*. 6th ed. Reading, MA: Addison Wesley.

Hoffer, J. A., J. F. George, and J. S. Valacich. 2014. *Modern Systems Analysis and Design*. 7th ed. Upper Saddle River, NJ: Prentice Hall.

Russell, T., and R. Armstrong. 2002. "13 Reasons Why Normalized Tables Help Your Business." *Database Administrator*, April 20, 2002. Available at **http://searchoracle.techtarget.com/tip/13-reasons-why-normalized-tables-help-your-business**

Storey, V. C. 1991. "Relational Database Design Based on the Entity-Relationship Model." *Data and Knowledge Engineering* 7,1 (November): 47–83.

Web Resources

http://en.wikipedia.org/wiki/Database_normalization Wikipedia entry that provides a thorough explanation of first, second, third, fourth, fifth, and Boyce-Codd normal forms.

www.bkent.net/Doc/simple5.htm Web site that presents a summary paper by William Kent titled "A Simple Guide to Five Normal Forms in Relational Database Theory."

http://www.stevehoberman.com Web site where Steve Hoberman, a leading consultant and lecturer on database design, presents and analyzes database design (conceptual and logical) problem. These are practical (based on real experiences or questions sent to him) situations that make for interesting puzzles to solve.

www.troubleshooters.com/codecorn/norm.htm Web page on normalization on Steve Litt's site that contains various troubleshooting tips for avoiding programming and systems development problems.

CASE

Forondo Artist Management Excellence Inc.

Case Description

Having reviewed your conceptual models (from Chapters 2 and 3) with the appropriate stakeholders and gaining their approval, you are now ready to move to the next phase of the project, logical design. Your next deliverable is the creation of a relational schema.

Project Questions

4-69. Map the EER diagram you developed in Chapter 3, 3-48 to a relational schema using the techniques described in this chapter. Be sure to appropriately identify the primary and foreign keys as well as clearly state referential integrity constraints.

4-70. Analyze and document the functional dependencies in each relation identified in 4-69 above. If any relation is not in 3NF, decompose it into 3NF, using the steps described in this chapter. Revise your relational schema accordingly.

4-71. Does it make sense for FAME to use enterprise keys? If so, create the appropriate enterprise keys and revise the relational schema accordingly.

4-72. If necessary, revisit and modify the EER diagram you created in Chapter 3, 3-48 to reflect any changes made in answering 4-70 and 4-71 above.

CHAPTER 5

Physical Database Design and Performance

LEARNING OBJECTIVES

After studying this chapter, you should be able to:

- Concisely define each of the following key terms: **field, data type, denormalization, horizontal partitioning, vertical partitioning, physical file, tablespace, extent, file organization, sequential file organization, indexed file organization, index, secondary key, join index, hashed file organization, hashing algorithm, pointer,** and **hash index table.**
- Describe the physical database design process, its objectives, and its deliverables.
- Choose storage formats for attributes from a logical data model.
- Select an appropriate file organization by balancing various important design factors.
- Describe three important types of file organization.
- Describe the purpose of indexes and the important considerations in selecting attributes to be indexed.
- Translate a relational data model into efficient database structures, including knowing when and how to denormalize the logical data model.

INTRODUCTION

In Chapters 2 through 4, you learned how to describe and model organizational data during the conceptual data modeling and logical database design phases of the database development process. You learned how to use EER notation, the relational data model, and normalization to develop abstractions of organizational data that capture the meaning of data. However, these notations do not explain how data will be processed or stored. The purpose of physical database design is to translate the logical description of data into the technical specifications for storing and retrieving data. The goal is to create a design for storing data that will provide adequate performance and ensure database integrity, security, and recoverability.

Physical database design does not include implementing files and databases (i.e., creating them and loading data into them). Physical database design produces the technical specifications that programmers, database administrators, and others involved in information systems construction will use during the implementation phase, which we discuss in Chapters 6 through 9.

In this chapter, you study the basic steps required to develop an efficient and high-integrity physical database design; security and recoverability are addressed in Chapter 12. We concentrate in this chapter on the design of a single, centralized database. Chapter 13, available on the book's Web site, will focus on the design of databases that are stored at multiple, distributed sites. In this chapter, you learn how to estimate the amount of data that will be stored in the database and determine how data are likely to be used. You learn about choices for storing attribute values and how to select from among these choices to achieve efficiency and data quality. Because of recent U.S. and international regulations (e.g., Sarbanes-Oxley) on financial reporting by organizations, proper controls specified in physical database design are required as a sound foundation for compliance. Hence, we place special emphasis on data quality measures you can implement within the physical design. You will also learn why normalized tables are not always the basis for the best physical data files and how you can denormalize the data to improve the speed of data retrieval. Finally, you learn about the use of indexes, which are important in speeding up the retrieval of data. In essence, you learn in this chapter how to make databases really "hum."

You must carefully perform physical database design, because the decisions made during this stage have a major impact on data accessibility, response times, data quality, security, user friendliness, and similarly important information system design factors. Database administration (described in Chapter 12) plays a major role in physical database design, so we return to some advanced design issues in that chapter. Finally, this chapter focuses on issues related to relational databases. Foundational issues related to a set of technologies under the general title NoSQL and big data/Hadoop will be discussed in Chapter 11.

THE PHYSICAL DATABASE DESIGN PROCESS

To make life a little easier for you, many physical database design decisions are implicit or eliminated when you choose the database management technologies to use with the information system you are designing. Because many organizations have standards for operating systems, database management systems, and data access languages, you must deal only with those choices not implicit in the given technologies. Thus, this chapter covers those decisions that you will make most frequently, as well as other selected decisions that may be critical for some types of applications, such as online data capture and retrieval.

The primary goal of physical database design is data processing efficiency. Today, with ever-decreasing costs for computer technology per unit of measure (both speed and space), it is typically very important to design a physical database to minimize the time required by users to interact with the information system. Thus, we concentrate on how to make processing of physical files and databases efficient, with less attention on minimizing the use of space.

Designing physical files and databases requires certain information that should have been collected and produced during prior systems development phases. The information needed for physical file and database design includes these requirements:

- Normalized relations, including estimates for the range of the number of rows in each table
- Definitions of each attribute, along with physical specifications such as maximum possible length
- Descriptions of where and when data are used in various ways (entered, retrieved, deleted, and updated, including typical frequencies of these events)
- Expectations or requirements for response time and data security, backup, recovery, retention, and integrity
- Descriptions of the technologies (database management systems) used for implementing the database

Physical database design requires several critical decisions that will affect the integrity and performance of the application system. These key decisions include the following:

- Choosing the storage format (called *data type*) for each attribute from the logical data model. The format and associated parameters are chosen to maximize data integrity and to minimize storage space.

- Giving the database management system guidance regarding how to group attributes from the logical data model into *physical records*. You will discover that although the columns of a relational table as specified in the logical design are a natural definition for the contents of a physical record, this does not always form the foundation for the most desirable grouping of attributes in the physical design.
- Giving the database management system guidance regarding how to arrange similarly structured records in secondary memory (primarily hard disks), using a structure (called a *file organization*) so that individual and groups of records can be stored, retrieved, and updated rapidly. Consideration must also be given to protecting data and recovering data if errors are found.
- Selecting structures (including *indexes* and the overall *database architecture*) for storing and connecting files to make retrieving related data more efficient.
- Preparing strategies for handling queries against the database that will optimize performance and take advantage of the file organizations and indexes that you have specified. Efficient database structures will be beneficial only if queries and the database management systems that handle those queries are tuned to intelligently use those structures.

Physical Database Design as a Basis for Regulatory Compliance

One of the primary motivations for strong focus on physical database design is that it forms a foundation for compliance with new national and international regulations on financial reporting. Without careful physical design, an organization cannot demonstrate that its data are accurate and well protected. Laws and regulations such as the Sarbanes-Oxley Act (SOX) in the United States and Basel II for international banking are reactions to recent cases of fraud and deception by executives in major corporations and partners in public accounting firms. The purpose of SOX is to protect investors by improving the accuracy and reliability of corporate disclosures made pursuant to the securities laws, and for other purposes. SOX requires that every annual financial report include an internal control report. This is designed to show that not only are the company's financial data accurate, but also that the company has confidence in them because adequate controls are in place to safeguard financial data. Among these controls are ones that focus on database integrity.

SOX is the most recent regulation in a stream of efforts to improve financial data reporting. The Committee of Sponsoring Organizations (COSO) of the Treadway Commission is a voluntary private-sector organization dedicated to improving the quality of financial reporting through business ethics, effective internal controls, and corporate governance. COSO was originally formed in 1985 to sponsor the National Commission on Fraudulent Financial Reporting, an independent private-sector initiative that studied the factors that can lead to fraudulent financial reporting. Based on its research, COSO developed recommendations for public companies and their independent auditors, for the SEC and other regulators, and for educational institutions. The Control Objectives for Information and Related Technology (COBIT) is an open standard published by the IT Governance Institute and the Information Systems Audit and Control Association (ISACA). It is an IT control framework built in part upon the COSO framework. The IT Infrastructure Library (ITIL), published by the Office of Government Commerce in Great Britain, focuses on IT services and is often used to complement the COBIT framework.

These standards, guidelines, and rules focus on corporate governance, risk assessment, and security and controls of data. Although laws such as SOX and Basel II require comprehensive audits of all procedures that deal with financial data, compliance can be greatly enhanced by a strong foundation of basic data integrity controls. If designed into the database and enforced by the DBMS, such preventive controls are applied consistently and thoroughly. Therefore, field-level data integrity controls can be viewed very positively in compliance audits. Other DBMS features, such as triggers and stored procedures, discussed in Chapter 7, as well as audit trails and activity logs, discussed in Chapter 12, provide even further ways to ensure that only legitimate data values are stored in the database. However, even these control mechanisms are only as good as the underlying field-level data controls. Further, for full compliance, all data integrity controls must be thoroughly documented; defining these controls for the DBMS is a form of documentation. Finally, changes to these controls must occur through well-documented change control procedures (so that temporary changes cannot be used to bypass well-designed controls).

Data Volume and Usage Analysis

As mentioned previously, data volume and frequency-of-use statistics are important inputs to the physical database design process, particularly in the case of very large-scale database implementations. Thus, it is beneficial to maintain a good understanding of the size and usage patterns of the database throughout its life cycle. In this section, we discuss data volume and usage analysis as if it were a one-time static activity. In practice, you should continuously monitor significant changes in usage and data volumes.

An easy way to show the statistics about data volumes and usage is by adding notation to the EER diagram that represents the final set of normalized relations from logical database design. Figure 5-1 shows the EER diagram (without attributes) for a simple inventory database for Pine Valley Furniture Company. This EER diagram represents the normalized relations constructed during logical database design for the original conceptual data model of this situation depicted in Figure 3-5b.

Both data volume and access frequencies are shown in Figure 5-1. For example, there are 3,000 PARTs in this database. The supertype PART has two subtypes, MANUFACTURED (40 percent of all PARTs are manufactured) and PURCHASED (70 percent are purchased; because some PARTs are of both subtypes, the percentages sum to more than 100 percent). The analysts at Pine Valley estimate that there are typically 150 SUPPLIERs, and Pine Valley receives, on average, 40 SUPPLIES instances from each SUPPLIER, yielding a total of 6,000 SUPPLIES. The dashed arrows represent access frequencies. So, for example, across all applications that use this database, there are on average 20,000 accesses per hour of PART data, and these yield, based on subtype percentages, 14,000 accesses per hour to PURCHASED PART data.

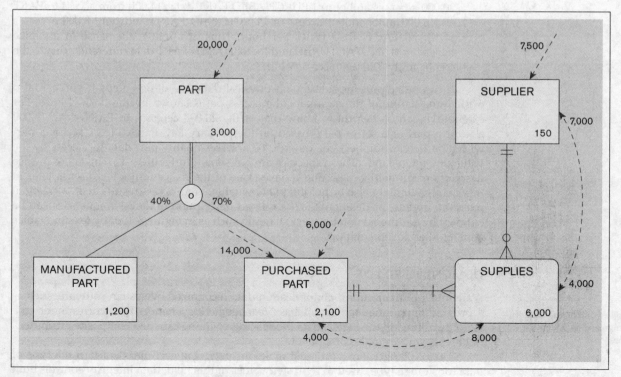

FIGURE 5-1   Composite usage map (Pine Valley Furniture Company)

There are an additional 6,000 direct accesses to PURCHASED PART data. Of this total of 20,000 accesses to PURCHASED PART, 8,000 accesses then also require SUPPLIES data and of these 8,000 accesses to SUPPLIES, there are 7,000 subsequent accesses to SUPPLIER data. For online and Web-based applications, usage maps should show the accesses per second. Several usage maps may be needed to show vastly different usage patterns for different times of day. Performance will also be affected by network specifications.

The volume and frequency statistics are generated during the systems analysis phase of the systems development process when systems analysts are studying current and proposed data processing and business activities. The data volume statistics represent the size of the business and should be calculated assuming business growth over a period of at least several years. The access frequencies are estimated from the timing of events, transaction volumes, the number of concurrent users, and reporting and querying activities. Because many databases support ad hoc accesses, and such accesses may change significantly over time, and known database access can peak and dip over a day, week, or month, the access frequencies tend to be less certain and even than the volume statistics. Fortunately, precise numbers are not necessary. What is crucial is the relative size of the numbers, which will suggest where the greatest attention needs to be given during physical database design in order to achieve the best possible performance. For example, in Figure 5-1, notice the following:

- There are 3,000 PART instances, so if PART has many attributes and some, like description, are quite long, then the efficient storage of PART might be important.
- For each of the 4,000 times per hour that SUPPLIES is accessed via SUPPLIER, PURCHASED PART is also accessed; thus, the diagram would suggest possibly combining these two co-accessed entities into a database table (or file). This act of combining normalized tables is an example of denormalization, which we discuss later in this chapter.
- There is only a 10 percent overlap between MANUFACTURED and PURCHASED parts, so it might make sense to have two separate tables for these entities and redundantly store data for those parts that are both manufactured and purchased; such planned redundancy is acceptable if purposeful. Further, there are a total of 20,000 accesses an hour of PURCHASED PART data (14,000 from access to PART and 6,000 independent access of PURCHASED PART) and only 8,000 accesses of MANUFACTURED PART per hour. Thus, it might make sense to organize tables for MANUFACTURED and PURCHASED PART data differently due to the significantly different access volumes.

It can be helpful for subsequent physical database design steps if you can also explain the nature of the access for the access paths shown by the dashed lines. For example, it can be helpful to know that of the 20,000 accesses to PART data, 15,000 ask for a part or a set of parts based on the primary key, PartNo (e.g., access a part with a particular number); the other 5,000 accesses qualify part data for access by the value of QtyOnHand. (These specifics are not shown in Figure 5-1.) This more precise description can help in selecting indexes, one of the major topics we discuss later in this chapter. It might also be helpful to know whether an access results in data creation, retrieval, update, or deletion. Such a refined description of access frequencies can be handled by additional notation on a diagram such as in Figure 5-1, or by text and tables kept in other documentation.

DESIGNING FIELDS

Field
The smallest unit of application data recognized by system software.

A **field** is the smallest unit of application data recognized by system software, such as a programming language or database management system. A field corresponds to a simple attribute in the logical data model, and so in the case of a composite attribute, a field represents a single component.

The basic decisions you must make in specifying each field concern the type of data (or storage type) used to represent values of this field, data integrity controls built into the database, and the mechanisms that the DBMS uses to handle missing values for the field. Other field specifications, such as display format, also must be made as part of the total specification of the information system, but we will not be concerned here with those specifications that are often handled by applications rather than the DBMS.

Choosing Data Types

A **data type** is a detailed coding scheme recognized by system software, such as a DBMS, for representing organizational data. The bit pattern of the coding scheme is usually transparent to you, but the space to store data and the speed required to access data are of consequence in physical database design. The specific DBMS you will use will dictate which choices are available to you. For example, Table 5-1 lists some of the data types available in the Oracle 12c DBMS, a typical DBMS that uses the SQL data definition and manipulation language. Additional data types might be available for currency, voice, image, and user defined for some DBMSs.

Selecting a data type involves four objectives that will have different relative levels of importance for different applications:

1. Represent all possible values.
2. Improve data integrity.
3. Support all data manipulations.
4. Minimize storage space.

An optimal data type for a field can, in minimal space, represent every possible value (while eliminating illegal values) for the associated attribute and can support the required data manipulation (e.g., numeric data types for arithmetic operations and character data types for string manipulation). Any attribute domain constraints from the conceptual data model are helpful in selecting a good data type for that attribute. Achieving these four objectives can be subtle. For example, consider a DBMS for which a data type has a maximum width of 2 bytes. Suppose this data type is sufficient to represent a QuantitySold field. When QuantitySold fields are summed, the sum may require a number larger than 2 bytes. If the DBMS uses the field's data type for results of any mathematics on that field, the 2-byte length will not work. Some data types have special manipulation capabilities; for example, only the DATE data type allows true date arithmetic.

Data type

A detailed coding scheme recognized by system software, such as a DBMS, for representing organizational data.

TABLE 5-1	Commonly Used Data Types in Oracle 12c
Data Type	Description
VARCHAR2	Variable-length character data with a maximum length of 4,000 characters; you must enter a maximum field length (e.g., VARCHAR2(30) specifies a field with a maximum length of 30 characters). A string that is shorter than the maximum will consume only the required space. A corresponding data type for Unicode character data allowing for the use of a rich variety of national character sets is NVARCHAR2.
CHAR	Fixed-length character data with a maximum length of 2,000 characters; default length is 1 character (e.g., CHAR(5) specifies a field with a fixed length of 5 characters, capable of holding a value from 0 to 5 characters long). There is also a data type called NCHAR, which allows the use of Unicode character data.
CLOB	Character large object, capable of storing up to 4 gigabytes of one variable-length character data field (e.g., to hold a medical instruction or a customer comment).
NUMBER	Positive or negative number in the range 10^{-130} to 10^{126}; can specify the precision (total number of digits to the left and right of the decimal point to a maximum of 38) and the scale (the number of digits to the right of the decimal point). For example, NUMBER(5) specifies an integer field with a maximum of 5 digits, and NUMBER(5,2) specifies a field with no more than 5 digits and exactly 2 digits to the right of the decimal point.
DATE	Any date from January 1, 4712 B.C., to December 31, 9999 A.D.; DATE stores the century, year, month, day, hour, minute, and second.
BLOB	Binary large object, capable of storing up to 4 gigabytes of binary data (e.g., a photograph or sound clip).

FIGURE 5-2   Example of a code lookup table (Pine Valley Furniture Company)

PRODUCT Table

ProductNo	Description	ProductFinish	...
B100	Chair	C	
B120	Desk	A	
M128	Table	C	
T100	Bookcase	B	
...	...	...	

PRODUCT FINISH Lookup Table

Code	Value
A	Birch
B	Maple
C	Oak

PINE VALLEY FURNITURE

CODING TECHNIQUES   Some attributes have a sparse set of values or are so large that, given data volumes, considerable storage space will be consumed. A field with a limited number of possible values can be translated into a code that requires less space. Consider the example of the ProductFinish field illustrated in Figure 5-2. Products at Pine Valley Furniture come in only a limited number of woods: Birch, Maple, and Oak. By creating a code or translation table, each ProductFinish field value can be replaced by a code, a cross-reference to the lookup table, similar to a foreign key. This will decrease the amount of space for the ProductFinish field and hence for the PRODUCT file. There will be additional space for the PRODUCT FINISH lookup table, and when the ProductFinish field value is needed, an extra access (called a join) to this lookup table will be required. If the ProductFinish field is infrequently used or if the number of distinct ProductFinish values is very large, the relative advantages of coding may outweigh the costs. Note that the code table would not appear in the conceptual or logical model. The code table is a physical construct to achieve data processing performance improvements, not a set of data with business value.

Controlling Data Integrity   For many DBMSs, data integrity controls (i.e., controls on the possible value a field can assume) can be built into the physical structure of the fields and controls enforced by the DBMS on those fields. The data type enforces one form of data integrity control because it may limit the type of data (numeric or character) and the length of a field value. The following are some other typical integrity controls that a DBMS may support:

- *Default value*   A default value is the value a field will assume unless a user enters an explicit value for an instance of that field. Assigning a default value to a field can reduce data entry time because entry of a value can be skipped. It can also help to reduce data entry errors for the most common value.
- *Range control*   A range control limits the set of permissible values a field may assume. The range may be a numeric lower-to-upper bound or a set of specific values. Range controls must be used with caution because the limits of the range may change over time. A combination of range controls and coding led to the year 2000 problem that many organizations faced, in which a field for year was represented by only the numbers 00 to 99. It is better to implement any range controls through a DBMS because range controls in applications may be inconsistently enforced. It is also more difficult to find and change them in applications than in a DBMS.
- *Null value control*   A null value was defined in Chapter 4 as an empty value. Each primary key must have an integrity control that prohibits a null value. Any other required field may also have a null value control placed on it if that is the policy of the organization. For example, a university may prohibit adding a course

to its database unless that course has a title as well as a value of the primary key, CourseID. Many fields legitimately may have a null value, so this control should be used only when truly required by business rules.

- *Referential integrity*   The term *referential integrity* was defined in Chapter 4. Referential integrity on a field is a form of range control in which the value of that field must exist as the value in some field in another row of the same or (most commonly) a different table. That is, the range of legitimate values comes from the dynamic contents of a field in a database table, not from some pre-specified set of values. Note that referential integrity only guarantees that some existing cross-referencing value is used, not that it is the correct one. A coded field will have referential integrity with the primary key of the associated lookup table.

HANDLING MISSING DATA   When a field may be null, simply entering no value may be sufficient. For example, suppose a customer zip code field is null and a report summarizes total sales by month and zip code. How should sales to customers with unknown zip codes be handled? Two options for handling or preventing missing data have already been mentioned: using a default value and not permitting missing (null) values. Missing data are inevitable. According to Babad and Hoffer (1984), the following are some other possible methods for handling missing data:

- Substitute an estimate of the missing value. For example, for a missing sales value when computing monthly product sales, use a formula involving the mean of the existing monthly sales values for that product indexed by total sales for that month across all products. Such estimates must be marked so that users know that these are not actual values.
- Track missing data so that special reports and other system elements cause people to resolve unknown values quickly. This can be done by setting up a trigger in the database definition. A trigger is a routine that will automatically execute when some event occurs or time period passes. One trigger could log the missing entry to a file when a null or other missing value is stored, and another trigger could run periodically to create a report of the contents of this log file.
- Perform sensitivity testing so that missing data are ignored unless knowing a value might significantly change results (e.g., if total monthly sales for a particular salesperson are almost over a threshold that would make a difference in that person's compensation). This is the most complex of the methods mentioned and hence requires the most sophisticated programming. Such routines for handling missing data may be written in application programs. All relevant modern DBMSs now have more sophisticated programming capabilities, such as case expressions, user-defined functions, and triggers, so that such logic can be available in the database for all users without application-specific programming.

DENORMALIZING AND PARTITIONING DATA

Modern database management systems have an increasingly important role in determining how the data are actually stored on the storage media. The efficiency of database processing is, however, significantly affected by how the logical relations are structured as database tables. The purpose of this section is to discuss denormalization as a mechanism that is often used to improve efficient processing of data and quick access to stored data. It first describes the best-known denormalization approach: combining several logical tables into one physical table to avoid the need to bring related data back together when they are retrieved from the database. Then the section will discuss another form of denormalization called *partitioning*, which also leads to differences between the logical data model and the physical tables, but in this case one relation is implemented as multiple tables.

Denormalization

With the rapid decline in the costs of secondary storage per unit of data, the efficient use of storage space (reducing redundancy)—while still a relevant consideration—has become less important than it has been in the past. In most cases, the primary goal of physical record design—efficient data processing—dominates the design process. In other words, speed, not style, matters. As in your dorm room, as long as you can find your favorite sweatshirt when you need it, it doesn't matter how tidy the room looks.

Efficient processing of data, just like efficient accessing of books in a library, depends on how close together related data (books or indexes) are. Often all the attributes that appear within a relation are not used together, and data from different relations are needed together to answer a query or produce a report. Thus, although normalized relations solve data maintenance anomalies and minimize redundancies (and storage space), they may not yield efficient data processing, if implemented one for one as physical records.

A fully normalized database usually creates a large number of tables. For a frequently used query that requires data from multiple, related tables, the DBMS can spend considerable computer resources each time the query is submitted in matching up (called *joining*) related rows from each table required to build the query result. Because this joining work is so time-consuming, the processing performance difference between totally normalized and partially normalized databases can be dramatic.

Denormalization

The process of transforming normalized relations into non-normalized physical record specifications.

Denormalization is the process of transforming normalized relations into non-normalized physical record specifications. We will review various forms of, reasons for, and cautions about denormalization in this section. In general, denormalization may partition a relation into several physical records, may combine attributes from several relations together into one physical record, or may do a combination of both.

OPPORTUNITIES FOR AND TYPES OF DENORMALIZATION Rogers (1989) introduces several common denormalization opportunities (Figures 5-3 through 5-5 show examples of normalized and denormalized relations for each of these three situations):

1. *Two entities with a one-to-one relationship* Even if one of the entities is an optional participant, it may be wise to combine these two relations into one record definition if the matching entity exists most of the time (especially if the access frequency between these two entity types is high). Figure 5-3 shows student data with

FIGURE 5-3 A possible denormalization situation: two entities with a one-to-one relationship

(*Note:* We assume that ApplicationID is not necessary when all fields are stored in one record, but this field can be included if it is required application data.)

FIGURE 5-4   A possible denormalization situation: a many-to-many relationship with nonkey attributes

optional data from a standard scholarship application a student may complete. In this case, one record could be formed with four fields from the STUDENT and SCHOLARSHIP APPLICATION normalized relations (assuming that ApplicationID is no longer needed). (Note: In this case, fields from the optional entity must have null values allowed.)

2. *A many-to-many relationship (associative entity) with nonkey attributes*   Rather than join three files to extract data from the two basic entities in the relationship, it may be advisable to combine attributes from one of the entities into the record representing the many-to-many relationship, thus avoiding one of the join operations. Again, this would be most advantageous if this joining occurs frequently. Figure 5-4 shows price quotes for different items from different vendors. In this case, fields from ITEM and PRICE QUOTE relations might be combined into one record to avoid having to join all three tables together. (Note: This may create considerable duplication of data; in the example, the ITEM fields, such as Description, would repeat for each price quote. This would necessitate excessive updating if duplicated data changed. Careful analysis of a composite usage map to study access frequencies and the number of occurrences of PRICE QUOTE per associated VENDOR or ITEM would be essential to understand the consequences of such denormalization.)

3. *Reference data*   Reference data exist in an entity on the one side of a one-to-many relationship, and this entity participates in no other database relationships. You should seriously consider merging the two entities in this situation into one record definition when there are few instances of the entity on the many side for each entity instance on the one side. See Figure 5-5, in which several ITEMs have the same STORAGE INSTRUCTIONS, and STORAGE INSTRUCTIONS relates only to ITEMs. In this case, the storage instructions data could be stored in the ITEM record to create, of course, redundancy and potential for extra data maintenance. (InstrID is no longer needed.)

FIGURE 5-5 A possible denormalization situation: reference data

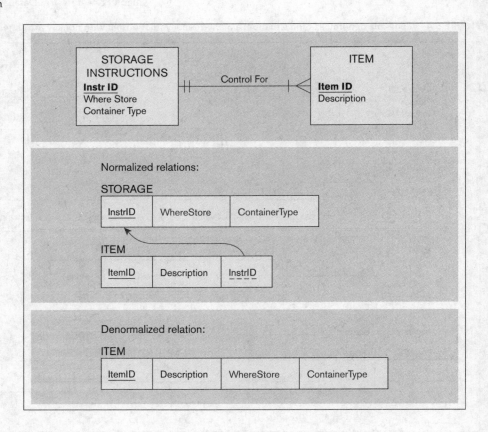

DENORMALIZE WITH CAUTION Denormalization has its critics. As Finkelstein (1988) and Hoberman (2002) discuss, denormalization can increase the chance of errors and inconsistencies (caused by reintroducing anomalies into the database) and can force the reprogramming of systems if business rules change. For example, redundant copies of the same data caused by a violation of second normal form are often not updated in a synchronized way. And, if they are, extra programming is required to ensure that all copies of exactly the same business data are updated together. Further, denormalization optimizes certain data processing at the expense of other data processing, so if the frequencies of different processing activities change, the benefits of denormalization may no longer exist. Denormalization almost always leads to more storage space for raw data and maybe more space for database overhead (e.g., indexes). Thus, denormalization should be an explicit act to gain significant processing speed when other physical design actions are not sufficient to achieve processing expectations.

Pascal (2002a, 2002b) passionately reports of the many dangers of denormalization. The motivation for denormalization is that a normalized database often creates many tables, and joining tables slows database processing. Pascal argues that this is not necessarily true, so the motivation for denormalization may be without merit in some cases. Overall, performance does not depend solely on the number of tables accessed but rather also on how the tables are organized in the database (what we later call *file organizations* and *clustering*), the proper design and implementation of queries, and the query optimization capabilities of the DBMS. Thus, to avoid problems associated with the data anomalies in denormalized databases, Pascal recommends first attempting to use these other means to achieve the necessary performance. This often will be sufficient, but in cases when further steps are needed, you must understand the opportunities for applying denormalization.

Hoberman (2002) has written a very useful two-part "denormalization survival guide," which summarizes the major factors (those outlined previously and a few others) in deciding whether to denormalize.

Partitioning

The opportunities just listed all deal with combining tables to avoid doing joins. Another form of denormalization involves the creation of more tables by partitioning a relation into multiple physical tables. Either horizontal or vertical partitioning, or a combination, is possible. **Horizontal partitioning** implements a logical relation as multiple physical tables by placing different rows into different tables, based on common column values. (In a library setting, horizontal partitioning is similar to placing the business journals in a business library, the science books in a science library, and so on.) Each table created from the partitioning has the same columns. For example, a customer relation could be broken into four regional customer tables based on the value of a column Region.

Horizontal partitioning makes sense when different categories of rows of a table are processed separately (e.g., for the Customer table just mentioned, if a high percentage of the data processing needs to work with only one region at a time). Two common methods of horizontal partitioning are to partition on (1) a single column value (e.g., CustomerRegion) and (2) date (because date is often a qualifier in queries, so just the needed partitions can be quickly found). (See Bieniek, 2006, for a guide to table partitioning.) Horizontal partitioning can also make maintenance of a table more efficient because fragmenting and rebuilding can be isolated to single partitions as storage space needs to be reorganized. Horizontal partitioning can also be more secure because file-level security can be used to prohibit users from seeing certain rows of data. Also, each partitioned table can be organized differently, appropriately for the way it is individually used. In many cases, it is also faster to recover one of the partitioned files than one file with all the rows. In addition, taking one of the partitioned files out of service so it can be recovered still allows processing against the other partitioned files to continue. Finally, each of the partitioned files can be placed on a separate disk drive to reduce contention for the same drive and hence improve query and maintenance performance across the database. These advantages of horizontal partitioning (actually, all forms of partitioning), along with the disadvantages, are summarized in Table 5-2.

Note that horizontal partitioning is very similar to creating a supertype/subtype relationship because different types of the entity (where the subtype discriminator is the field used for segregating rows) are involved in different relationships, hence different processing. In fact, when you have a supertype/subtype relationship, you need to decide whether you will create separate tables for each subtype or combine them in various combinations. Combining makes sense when all subtypes are used about the

Horizontal partitioning
Distribution of the rows of a logical relation into several separate tables.

TABLE 5-2 Advantages and Disadvantages of Data Partitioning

Advantages of Partitioning

1. *Efficiency*:   Data queried together are stored close to one another and separate from data not used together. Data maintenance is isolated in smaller partitions.
2. *Local optimization*:   Each partition of data can be stored to optimize performance for its own use.
3. *Security*:   Data not relevant to one group of users can be segregated from data those users are allowed to use.
4. *Recovery and uptime*:   Smaller files take less time to back up and recover, and other files are still accessible if one file is damaged, so the effects of damage are isolated.
5. *Load balancing*:   Files can be allocated to different storage areas (disks or other media), which minimizes contention for access to the same storage area or even allows for parallel access to the different areas.

Disadvantages of Partitioning

1. *Inconsistent access speed*:   Different partitions may have different access speeds, thus confusing users. Also, when data must be combined across partitions, users may have to deal with significantly slower response times than in a non-partitioned approach.
2. *Complexity*:   Partitioning is usually not transparent to programmers, who will have to write more complex programs when combining data across partitions.
3. *Extra space and update time*:   Data may be duplicated across the partitions, taking extra storage space compared to storing all the data in normalized files. Updates that affect data in multiple partitions can take more time than if one file were used.

same way, whereas partitioning the supertype entity into multiple files makes sense when the subtypes are handled differently in transactions, queries, and reports. When a relation is partitioned horizontally, the whole set of rows can be reconstructed by using the SQL UNION operator (described in Chapter 6). With it, for example, all customer data can be viewed together when desired.

The Oracle DBMS supports several forms of horizontal partitioning, designed in particular to deal with very large tables (Brobst et al., 1999). A table is partitioned when it is defined to the DBMS using the SQL data definition language (you will learn about the CREATE TABLE command in Chapter 6); that is, in Oracle, there is one table with several partitions rather than separate tables per se. Oracle 12c has three data distribution methods as basic partitioning approaches:

1. *Range partitioning,* in which each partition is defined by a range of values (lower and upper key value limits) for one or more columns of the normalized table. A table row is inserted in the proper partition, based on its initial values for the range fields. Because partition key values may follow patterns, each partition may hold quite a different number of rows. A partition key may be generated by the database designer to create a more balanced distribution of rows. A row may be restricted from moving between partitions when key values are updated.
2. *Hash partitioning,* in which data are evenly spread across partitions independent of any partition key value. Hash partitioning overcomes the uneven distribution of rows that is possible with range partitioning. It works well if the goal is to distribute data evenly across devices.
3. *List partitioning,* in which the partitions are defined based on predefined lists of values of the partitioning key. For example, in a table partitioned based on the value of the column State, one partition might include rows that have the value "CT," "ME," "MA," "NH," "RI," or "VT," and another partition rows that have the value "NJ" or "NY."

If a more sophisticated form of partitioning is needed, Oracle 12c also offers composite (or two-level) partitioning, which combines aspects of two of the three single-level partitioning approaches.

Partitions are in many cases transparent to the database user. (You need to refer to a partition only if you want to force the query processor to look at one or more partitions.) The part of the DBMS that optimizes the processing of a query will look at the definition of partitions for a table involved in a query and will automatically decide whether certain partitions can be eliminated when retrieving the data needed to form the query results, which can drastically improve query processing performance.

For example, suppose a transaction date is used to define partitions in range partitioning. A query asking for only recent transactions can be more quickly processed by looking at only the one or few partitions with the most recent transactions rather than scanning the database or even using indexes to find rows in the desired range from a non-partitioned table. A partition on date also isolates insertions of new rows to one partition, which may reduce the overhead of database maintenance, and dropping "old" transactions will require simply dropping a partition. Indexes can still be used with a partitioned table and can improve performance even more than partitioning alone. See Brobst et al. (1999) for more details on the pros and cons of using dates for range partitioning.

In hash partitioning, rows are more evenly spread across the partitions. If partitions are placed in different storage areas that can be processed in parallel, then query performance will improve noticeably compared to when all the data have to be accessed sequentially in one storage area for the whole table. As with range partitioning, the existence of partitions typically is transparent to a programmer of a query.

Vertical partitioning distributes the columns of a logical relation into separate tables, repeating the primary key in each of the tables. An example of vertical partitioning would be breaking apart a PART relation by placing the part number along with accounting-related part data into one record specification, the part number along with engineering-related part data into another record specification, and the part number along with sales-related part data into yet another record specification. The advantages

Vertical partitioning

Distribution of the columns of a logical relation into several separate physical tables.

and disadvantages of vertical partitioning are similar to those for horizontal partitioning. When, for example, accounting-, engineering-, and sales-related part data need to be used together, these tables can be joined. Thus, neither horizontal nor vertical partitioning prohibits the ability to treat the original relation as a whole.

Combinations of horizontal and vertical partitioning are also possible. This form of denormalization—record partitioning—is especially common for a database whose files are distributed across multiple computers.

A single physical table can be logically partitioned or several tables can be logically combined by using the concept of a user view, which will be demonstrated in Chapter 6. With a user view, users can be given the impression that the database contains tables other than what are physically defined; you can create these logical tables through horizontal or vertical partitioning or other forms of denormalization. However, the purpose of any form of user view, including logical partitioning via views, is to simplify query writing and to create a more secure database, not to improve query performance. One form of a user view available in Oracle is called a partition view. With a partition view, physically separate tables with similar structures can be logically combined into one table using the SQL UNION operator. There are limitations to this form of partitioning. First, because there are actually multiple separate physical tables, there cannot be any global index on all the combined rows. Second, each physical table must be separately managed, so data maintenance is more complex (e.g., a new row must be inserted into a specific table). Third, the query optimizer has fewer options with a partition view than with partitions of a single table for creating the most efficient query processing plan.

The final form of denormalization we introduce is data replication. With data replication, the same data are purposely stored in multiple places in the database. For example, consider again Figure 5-1. You learned earlier in this section that relations can be denormalized by combining data from an associative entity with data from one of the simple entities with which it is associated. So, in Figure 5-1, SUPPLIES data might be stored with PURCHASED PART data in one expanded PURCHASED PART physical record specification. With data duplication, the same SUPPLIES data might also be stored with its associated SUPPLIER data in another expanded SUPPLIER physical record specification. With this data duplication, once either a SUPPLIER or PURCHASED PART record is retrieved, the related SUPPLIES data will also be available without any further access to secondary memory. This improved speed is worthwhile only if SUPPLIES data are frequently accessed with SUPPLIER and with PURCHASED PART data and if the costs for extra secondary storage and data maintenance are not great.

DESIGNING PHYSICAL DATABASE FILES

A **physical file** is a named portion of secondary memory (such as a magnetic tape, hard disk, or solid state disk) allocated for the purpose of storing physical records. Some computer operating systems allow a physical file to be split into separate pieces, sometimes called *extents*. In subsequent sections, we will assume that a physical file is not split and that each record in a file has the same structure. That is, subsequent sections address how to store and link relational table rows from a single database in physical storage space. In order to optimize the performance of the database processing, the person who administers a database, the database administrator, often needs to know extensive details about how the database management system manages physical storage space. This knowledge is very DBMS specific, but the principles described in subsequent sections are the foundation for the physical data structures used by most relational DBMSs.

Most database management systems store many different kinds of data in one operating system file. By an *operating system file*, we mean a named file that would appear on a disk directory listing (e.g., a listing of the files in a folder on the C: drive of your personal computer). For example, an important logical structure for storage space in Oracle is a tablespace. A **tablespace** is a named logical storage unit in which data from one or more database tables, views, or other database objects may be stored. An instance of Oracle 12c includes many tablespaces—for example, two (SYSTEM and SYSAUX) for system data (data dictionary or data about data), one (TEMP) for temporary work space, one (UNDOTBS1) for undo operations, and one or several to hold user business data.

Physical file

A named portion of secondary memory (such as a hard disk) allocated for the purpose of storing physical records.

Tablespace

A named logical storage unit in which data from one or more database tables, views, or other database objects may be stored.

A tablespace consists of one or several physical operating system files. Thus, Oracle has responsibility for managing the storage of data inside a tablespace, whereas the operating system has many responsibilities for managing a tablespace, but they are all related to its responsibilities related to the management of operating system files (e.g., handling file-level security, allocating space, and responding to disk read and write errors).

Because an instance of Oracle usually supports many databases for many users, a database administrator usually will create many user tablespaces, which helps achieve database security because the administrator can give each user selected rights to access each tablespace. Each tablespace consists of logical units called *segments* (consisting of one table, index, or partition), which, in turn, are divided into **extents.** These, finally, consist of a number of contiguous *data blocks*, which are the smallest unit of storage. Each table, index, or other so-called schema object belongs to a single tablespace, but a tablespace may contain (and typically contains) one or more tables, indexes, and other schema objects. Physically, each tablespace can be stored in one or multiple data files, but each operating system data file is associated with only one tablespace and only one database. Please note that there are only two physical storage structures: an operating system file and an operating system block (fundamental element of a file). Otherwise, all these concepts are logical concepts managed by the DBMS.

Modern database management systems have an increasingly active role in managing the use of the physical devices and files on them; for example, the allocation of schema objects (e.g., tables and indexes) to data files is typically fully controlled by the DBMS. A database administrator does, however, have the ability to manage the disk space allocated to tablespaces and a number of parameters related to the way free space is managed within a database. Because this is not a text on Oracle, we do not cover specific details on managing tablespaces; however, the general principles of physical database design apply to the design and management of Oracle tablespaces as they do to whatever the physical storage unit is for any database management system. Figure 5-6 is an EER model that shows the relationships between various physical and logical database terms related to physical database design in an Oracle environment.

Extent

A contiguous section of disk storage space.

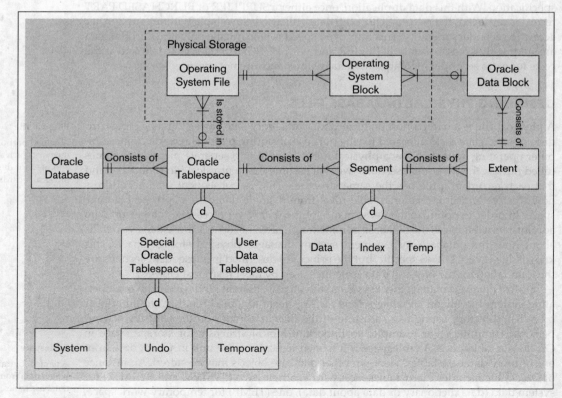

FIGURE 5-6   DBMS terminology in an Oracle 12c environment

File Organizations

A **file organization** is a technique for physically arranging the records of a file on secondary storage devices. With modern relational DBMSs, you do not have to design file organizations, but you may be allowed to select an organization and its parameters for a table or physical file. In choosing a file organization for a particular file in a database, you should consider seven important factors:

File organization

A technique for physically arranging the records of a file on secondary storage devices.

1. Fast data retrieval
2. High throughput for processing data input and maintenance transactions
3. Efficient use of storage space
4. Protection from failures or data loss
5. Minimizing need for reorganization
6. Accommodating growth
7. Security from unauthorized use

Often these objectives are in conflict, and you must select a file organization that provides a reasonable balance among the criteria within resources available.

In this chapter, we consider the following families of basic file organizations: sequential, indexed, and hashed. Figure 5-7 illustrates each of these organizations, with the nicknames of some university sports teams.

HEAP FILE ORGANIZATION   In a heap file organization, the records in the file are not stored in any particular order. For example, in Oracle 12c heap organized is the default table structure. It is, however, seldom used as such because the other organization types provide important advantages for various use scenarios.

SEQUENTIAL FILE ORGANIZATIONS   In a **sequential file organization,** the records in the file are stored in sequence according to a primary key value (see Figure 5-7a). To locate a particular record, a program must normally scan the file from the beginning until the desired record is located. A common example of a sequential file is the alphabetical list of persons in the white pages of a telephone directory (ignoring any index that may be included with the directory). A comparison of the capabilities of sequential files with the other two types of files appears later in Table 5-3. Because of their inflexibility, sequential files are not used in a database but may be used for files that back up data from a database.

Sequential file organization

The storage of records in a file in sequence according to a primary key value.

INDEXED FILE ORGANIZATIONS   In an **indexed file organization,** the records are stored either sequentially or nonsequentially, and an index is created that allows the application software to locate individual records (see Figure 5-7b). Like a card catalog in a library, an **index** is a table that is used to determine in a file the location of records that satisfy some condition. Each index entry matches a key value with one or more records. An index can point to unique records (a primary key index, such as on the ProductID field of a product record) or to potentially more than one record. An index that allows each entry to point to more than one record is called a **secondary key** index. Secondary key indexes are important for supporting many reporting requirements and for providing rapid ad hoc data retrieval. An example would be an index on the ProductFinish column of a Product table. Because indexes are extensively used with relational DBMSs, and the choice of what index and how to store the index entries matters greatly in database processing performance, we review indexed file organizations in more detail than the other types of file organizations.

Indexed file organization

The storage of records either sequentially or nonsequentially with an index that allows software to locate individual records.

Index

A table or other data structure used to determine in a file the location of records that satisfy some condition.

Secondary key

One field or a combination of fields for which more than one record may have the same combination of values. Also called a nonunique key.

Some index structures influence where table rows are stored, and other index structures are independent of where rows are located. Because the actual structure of an index does not influence database design and is not important in writing database queries, we will not address the actual physical structure of indexes in this chapter. Thus, Figure 5-7b should be considered a logical view of how an index is used, not a physical view of how data are stored in an index structure.

FIGURE 5-7   Comparison of file organizations

FIGURE 5-7 *(continued)*

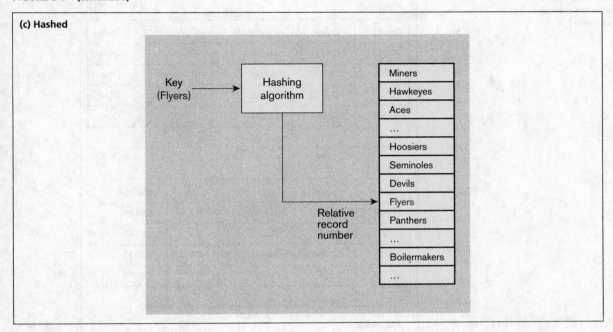

(c) Hashed

Transaction-processing applications require rapid response to queries that involve one or a few related table rows. For example, to enter a new customer order, an order entry application needs to rapidly find the specific customer table row, a few product table rows for the items being purchased, and possibly a few other product table rows based on the characteristics of the products the customer wants (e.g., product finish). Consequently, the application needs to add one customer order and order line rows to the respective tables. The types of indexes discussed so far work very well in an application that is searching for a few specific table rows.

Another increasingly popular type of index, especially in data warehousing and other decision support applications (see Chapter 9), is a join index. In decision support applications, the data accessing tends to want all rows that are related to one another (e.g., all the customers who have bought items from the same store) from very large tables. A **join index** is an index on columns from two or more tables that come from the same domain of values. For example, consider Figure 5-8a, which shows two tables, Customer and Store. Each of these tables has a column called City. The join index of the City column indicates the row identifiers for rows in the two tables that have the same City value. Because of the way many data warehouses are designed, there is a high frequency for queries to find data (facts) in common to a store and a customer in the same city (or similar intersections of facts across multiple dimensions). Figure 5-8b shows another possible application for a join index. In this case, the join index precomputes the matching of a foreign key in the Order table with the associated customer in the Customer table (i.e., the result of a relational join operator, which will be discussed in Chapter 6). Simply stated, a join says find rows in the same or different tables that have values that match some criterion.

A join index is created as rows are loaded into a database, so the index, like all other indexes previously discussed, is always up-to-date. Without a join index in the database of Figure 5-8a, any query that wants to find stores and customers in the same city would have to compute the equivalent of the join index each time the query is run. For very large tables, joining all the rows of one table with matching rows in another possibly large table can be very time consuming and can significantly delay responding to an online query. In Figure 5-8b, the join index provides one place for the DBMS to find information about related table rows. A join index, similar to any other index, saves query processing time by finding data meeting a prespecified qualification at the

Join index
An index on columns from two or more tables that come from the same domain of values.

**FIGURE 5-8   Join indexes
(a) Join index for common
nonkey columns**

Customer

RowID	Cust#	CustName	City	State
10001	C2027	Hadley	Dayton	Ohio
10002	C1026	Baines	Columbus	Ohio
10003	C0042	Ruskin	Columbus	Ohio
10004	C3861	Davies	Toledo	Ohio
. . .				

Store

RowID	Store#	City	Size	Manager
20001	S4266	Dayton	K2	E2166
20002	S2654	Columbus	K3	E0245
20003	S3789	Dayton	K4	E3330
20004	S1941	Toledo	K1	E0874
. . .				

Join Index

CustRowID	StoreRowID	Common Value*
10001	20001	Dayton
10001	20003	Dayton
10002	20002	Columbus
10003	20002	Columbus
10004	20004	Toledo
. . .		

*This column may or may not be included, as
needed. Join index could be sorted on any of the
three columns. Sometimes two join indexes are
created, one as above and one with the two RowID
columns reversed.

expense of the extra storage space and maintenance of the index. The use of databases
for new applications, such as data warehousing and online decision support, is leading to the development of new types of indexes. We encourage you to investigate the
indexing capabilities of the database management system you are using to understand
fully when to apply each type of index and how to tune the performance of the index
structures.

Hashed file organization

A storage system in which
the address for each record is
determined using a hashing
algorithm.

Hashing algorithm

A routine that converts a primary
key value into a relative record
number or relative file address.

HASHED FILE ORGANIZATIONS   In a **hashed file organization,** the address of
each record is determined using a hashing algorithm (see Figure 5-7c). A **hashing
algorithm** is a routine that converts a primary key value into a record address.
Although there are several variations of hashed files, in most cases the records are
located nonsequentially, as dictated by the hashing algorithm. Thus, sequential data
processing is impractical.

A typical hashing algorithm uses the technique of dividing each primary key
value by a suitable prime number and then using the remainder of the division as
the relative storage location. For example, suppose that an organization has a set
of approximately 1,000 employee records to be stored on magnetic disk. A suitable

Order

RowID	Order#	Order Date	Cust#(FK)
30001	O5532	10/01/2015	C3861
30002	O3478	10/01/2015	C1062
30003	O8734	10/02/2015	C1062
30004	O9845	10/02/2015	C2027
...			

Customer

RowID	Cust#(PK)	CustName	City	State
10001	C2027	Hadley	Dayton	Ohio
10002	C1062	Baines	Columbus	Ohio
10003	C0042	Ruskin	Columbus	Ohio
10004	C3861	Davies	Toledo	Ohio
...				

Join Index

CustRowID	OrderRowID	Cust#
10001	30004	C2027
10002	30002	C1062
10002	30003	C1062
10004	30001	C3861
...		

FIGURE 5-8 *(continued)*
(b) Join index for matching a foreign key (FK) and a primary key (PK)

prime number would be 997, because it is close to 1,000. Now consider the record for employee 12,396. When we divide this number by 997, the remainder is 432. Thus, this record is stored at location 432 in the file. Another technique (not discussed here) must be used to resolve duplicates (or overflow) that can occur with the division/remainder method when two or more keys hash to the same address (known as a "hash clash").

One of the severe limitations of hashing is that because data table row locations are dictated by the hashing algorithm, only one key can be used for hashing-based (storage and) retrieval. Hashing and indexing can be combined into what is called a hash index table to overcome this limitation. A **hash index table** uses hashing to map a key into a location in an index (sometimes called a *scatter index table*), where there is a **pointer** (a field of data indicating a target address that can be used to locate a related field or record of data) to the actual data record matching the hash key. The index is the target of the hashing algorithm, but the actual data are stored separately from the addresses generated by hashing. Because the hashing results in a position in an index, the table rows can be stored independently of the hash address, using whatever file organization for the data table makes sense (e.g., sequential or first available space). Thus, as with other indexing schemes but unlike most pure hashing schemes, there can be several primary and secondary keys, each with its own hashing algorithm and index table, sharing one data table.

Also, because an index table is much smaller than a data table, the index can be more easily designed to reduce the likelihood of key collisions, or overflows,

Hash index table

A file organization that uses hashing to map a key into a location in an index, where there is a pointer to the actual data record matching the hash key.

Pointer

A field of data indicating a target address that can be used to locate a related field or record of data.

than can occur in the more space-consuming data table. Again, the extra storage space for the index adds flexibility and speed for data retrieval, along with the added expense of storing and maintaining the index space. Another use of a hash index table is found in some data warehousing database technologies that use parallel processing. In this situation, the DBMS can evenly distribute data table rows across all storage devices to fairly distribute work across the parallel processors, while using hashing and indexing to rapidly find on which processor desired data are stored. Not all DBMSs offer the option of using hash indexes, including Oracle 12c. MySQL, now owned with Oracle, is an example of a DBMS that allows the use of a hash index.

As stated earlier, the DBMS will handle the management of any hashing file organization. You do not have to be concerned with handling overflows, accessing indexes, or the hashing algorithm. What is important for you, as a database designer, is to understand the properties of different file organizations so that you can choose the most appropriate one for the type of database processing required in the database and application you are designing. Also, understanding the properties of the file organizations used by the DBMS can help a query designer write a query in a way that takes advantage of the file organization's properties. As you will see in Chapters 6 and 7, many queries can be written in multiple ways in SQL; different query structures, however, can result in vastly different steps by the DBMS to answer the query. If you know how the DBMS thinks about using a file organization (e.g., what indexes it uses when and how and when it uses a hashing algorithm), you can design better databases and more efficient queries.

The three families of file organizations cover most of the file organizations you will have at your disposal as you design physical files and databases. Although more complex structures can be built using the data structures outlined in Appendix C (available on the book's Web site), you are unlikely to be able to use these with a database management system.

Table 5-3 summarizes the comparative features of sequential, indexed, and hashed file organizations. You should review this table and study Figure 5-7 to see why each comparative feature is true.

TABLE 5-3   Comparative Features of Different File Organizations

Factor	File Organization			
	Heap	Sequential	Indexed	Hashed
Storage space	No wasted space	No wasted space	No wasted space for data but extra space for index	Extra space may be needed to allow for addition and deletion of records after the initial set of records is loaded
Sequential retrieval on primary key	Requires sorting	Very fast	Moderately fast	Impractical, unless using a hash index
Random retrieval on primary key	Impractical	Impractical	Moderately fast	Very fast
Multiple-key retrieval	Possible but requires scanning whole file	Possible but requires scanning whole file	Very fast with multiple indexes	Not possible unless using a hash index
Deleting records	Can create wasted space or requires reorganization	Can create wasted space or require reorganizing	If space can be dynamically allocated, this is easy but requires maintenance of indexes	Very easy
Adding new records	Very easy	Requires rewriting a file	If space can be dynamically allocated, this is easy but requires maintenance of indexes	Very easy, but multiple keys with the same address require extra work
Updating records	Usually requires rewriting a file.	Usually requires rewriting a file	Easy but requires maintenance of indexes	Very easy

Clustering Files

Some database management systems allow adjacent secondary memory space to contain rows from several tables. For example, in Oracle, rows from one, two, or more related tables that are often joined together can be stored so that they share the same data blocks (the smallest storage units). A cluster is defined by the tables and the column or columns by which the tables are usually joined. For example, a Customer table and a customer Order table would be joined by the common value of CustomerID, or the rows of a PriceQuote table (which contains prices on items purchased from vendors) might be clustered with the Item table by common values of ItemID. Clustering reduces the time to access related records compared to the normal allocation of different files to different areas of a disk. Time is reduced because related records will be closer to each other than if the records are stored in separate files in separate areas of the disk. Defining a table to be in only one cluster reduces retrieval time for only those tables stored in the same cluster.

The following Oracle database definition commands show how a cluster is defined and tables are assigned to the cluster. First, the cluster (adjacent disk space) is specified, as in the following example:

```
CREATE CLUSTER Ordering (CustomerID CHAR(25));
```

The term Ordering names the cluster space; the attribute CustomerID specifies the attribute with common values.

Then tables are assigned to the cluster when the tables are created, as in the following example:

```
CREATE TABLE Customer_T(
   CustomerID                      VARCHAR2(25) NOT NULL,
   CustomerAddress                 VARCHAR2(15)
   )
   CLUSTER Ordering (CustomerID);
CREATE TABLE Order_T (
   OrderID                         VARCHAR2(20) NOT NULL,
   CustomerID                      VARCHAR2(25) NOT NULL,
   OrderDate                       DATE
   )
   CLUSTER Ordering (CustomerID);
```

Access to records in a cluster can be specified in Oracle to be via an index on the cluster key or via a hashing function on the cluster key. Reasons for choosing an indexed versus a hashed cluster are similar to those for choosing between indexed and hashed files (see Table 5-3). Clustering records is best used when the records are fairly static. When records are frequently added, deleted, and changed, wasted space can arise, and it may be difficult to locate related records close to one another after the initial loading of records, which defines the clusters. Clustering is, however, one option a file designer has to improve the performance of tables that are frequently used together in the same queries and reports.

Designing Controls for Files

One additional aspect of a database file about which you may have design options is the types of controls you can use to protect the file from destruction or contamination or to reconstruct the file if it is damaged. Because a database file is stored in a proprietary format by the DBMS, there is a basic level of access control. You may require additional security controls on fields, files, or databases. We address these options in detail in Chapter 12. It is likely that files will be damaged at some point during their lifetime, and, therefore, it is essential to be able to rapidly restore a damaged file. Backup procedures provide a copy of a file and of the transactions that have changed the file. When a file is damaged, the file copy or current file, along with the log of transactions, is used to recover the file to an uncontaminated state. In terms of security, the most effective method is to encrypt the contents of the file so that only programs with access to the decryption routine will be able to see the file contents. Again, these important topics will be covered later, when you study the activities of data and database administration in Chapter 12.

USING AND SELECTING INDEXES

Most database manipulations require locating a row (or collection of rows) that satisfies some condition. Given the terabyte size of modern databases, locating data without some help would be like looking for the proverbial "needle in a haystack"; or, in more contemporary terms, it would be like searching the Internet without a powerful search engine. For example, we might want to retrieve all customers in a given zip code or all students with a particular major. Scanning every row in a table, looking for the desired rows, may be unacceptably slow, particularly when tables are large, as they often are in real-world applications. Using indexes, as described earlier, can greatly speed up this process, and defining indexes is an important part of physical database design.

As described in the section on indexes, indexes on a file can be created for either a primary or a secondary key or both. It is typical that an index would be created for the primary key of each table. The index is itself a table with two columns: the key and the address of the record or records that contain that key value. For a primary key, there will be only one entry in the index for each key value.

Creating a Unique Key Index

The Customer table defined in the section on clustering has the primary key CustomerID. A unique key index would be created on this field using the following SQL command:

```
CREATE UNIQUE INDEX CustIndex_PK ON Customer_T(CustomerID);
```

In this command, CustIndex_PK is the name of the index file created to store the index entries. The ON clause specifies which table is being indexed and the column (or columns) that forms the index key. When this command is executed, any existing records in the Customer table would be indexed. If there are duplicate values of CustomerID, the CREATE INDEX command will fail. Once the index is created, the DBMS will reject any insertion or update of data in the CUSTOMER table that would violate the uniqueness constraint on CustomerIDs. Notice that every unique index creates overhead for the DBMS to validate uniqueness for each insertion or update of a table row on which there are unique indexes. We will return to this point later, when we review when to create an index.

When a composite unique key exists, you simply list all the elements of the unique key in the ON clause. For example, a table of line items on a customer order might have a composite unique key of OrderID and ProductID. The SQL command to create this index for the OrderLine_T table would be as follows:

```
CREATE UNIQUE INDEX LineIndex_PK ON OrderLine_T(OrderID, ProductID);
```

Creating a Secondary (Nonunique) Key Index

Database users often want to retrieve rows of a relation based on values for various attributes other than the primary key. For example, in a Product table, users might want to retrieve records that satisfy any combination of the following conditions:

- All table products (Description = "Table")
- All oak furniture (ProductFinish = "Oak")

- All dining room furniture (Room = "DR")
- All furniture priced below $500 (Price < 500)

To speed up such retrievals, we can define an index on each attribute that we use to qualify a retrieval. For example, we could create a nonunique index on the Description field of the Product table with the following SQL command:

```
CREATE INDEX DescIndex_FK ON Product_T(Description);
```

Notice that the term UNIQUE should not be used with secondary (nonunique) key attributes, because each value of the attribute may be repeated. As with unique keys, a secondary key index can be created on a combination of attributes.

When to Use Indexes

During physical database design, you must choose which attributes to use to create indexes. There is a trade-off between improved performance for retrievals through the use of indexes and degraded performance (because of the overhead for extensive index maintenance) for inserting, deleting, and updating the indexed records in a file. Thus, indexes should be used generously for databases intended primarily to support data retrieval, such as for decision support and data warehouse applications. Indexes should be used judiciously for databases that support transaction processing and other applications with heavy updating requirements, because the indexes impose additional overhead.

Following are some rules of thumb for choosing indexes for relational databases:

1. Indexes are most useful on larger tables.
2. Specify a unique index for the primary key of each table.
3. Indexes are most useful for columns that frequently appear in WHERE clauses of SQL commands either to qualify the rows to select (e.g., WHERE ProductFinish = "Oak," for which an index on ProductFinish would speed retrieval) or to link (join) tables (e.g., WHERE Product_T.ProductID = OrderLine_T.ProductID, for which a secondary key index on ProductID in the OrderLine_T table and a primary key index on ProductID in the Product_T table would improve retrieval performance). In the latter case, the index is on a foreign key in the OrderLine_T table that is used in joining tables.
4. Use an index for attributes referenced in ORDER BY (sorting) and GROUP BY (categorizing) clauses. You do have to be careful, though, about these clauses. Be sure that the DBMS will, in fact, use indexes on attributes listed in these clauses (e.g., Oracle uses indexes on attributes in ORDER BY clauses but not GROUP BY clauses).
5. Use an index when there is significant variety in the values of an attribute. Oracle suggests that an index is not useful when there are fewer than 30 different values for an attribute, and an index is clearly useful when there are 100 or more different values for an attribute. Similarly, an index will be helpful only if the results of a query that uses that index do not exceed roughly 20 percent of the total number of records in the file (Schumacher, 1997).
6. Before creating an index on a field with long values, consider first creating a compressed version of the values (coding the field with a surrogate key) and then indexing on the coded version (Catterall, 2005). Large indexes, created from long index fields, can be slower to process than small indexes.
7. If the key for the index is going to be used for determining the location where the record will be stored, then the key for this index should be a surrogate key so that the values cause records to be evenly spread across the storage space (Catterall, 2005). Many DBMSs create a sequence number so that each new row added to a table is assigned the next number in sequence; this is usually sufficient for creating a surrogate key.
8. Check your DBMS for the limit, if any, on the number of indexes allowable per table. Some systems permit no more than 16 indexes and may limit the size of an

index key value (e.g., no more than 2,000 bytes for each composite value). If there is such a limit in your system, you will have to choose those secondary keys that will most likely lead to improved performance.

9. Be careful of indexing attributes that have null values. For many DBMSs, rows with a null value will not be referenced in the index (so they cannot be found from an *index search* based on the attribute value NULL). Such a search will have to be done by scanning the file.

Selecting indexes is arguably the most important physical database design decision, but it is not the only way you can improve the performance of a database. Other ways address such issues as reducing the costs to relocate records, optimizing the use of extra or so-called free space in files, and optimizing query processing algorithms. (See Lightstone, Teorey, and Nadeau, 2010, for a discussion of additional ways to enhance physical database design and efficiency.) We briefly discuss the topic of query optimization in the following section of this chapter because such optimization can be used to overrule how the DBMS would use certain database design options included because of their expected improvement in data processing performance in most instances.

DESIGNING A DATABASE FOR OPTIMAL QUERY PERFORMANCE

The primary purpose of physical database design is to optimize the performance of database processing. Database processing includes adding, deleting, and modifying a database, as well as a variety of data retrieval activities. For databases that have greater retrieval traffic than maintenance traffic, optimizing the database for query performance (producing online or off-line anticipated and ad hoc screens and reports for end users) is the primary goal. This chapter has already covered most of the decisions you can make to tune the database design to meet the need of database queries (clustering, indexes, file organizations, etc.). In this final section of this chapter, we introduce parallel query processing as an additional advanced database design and processing option now available in many DBMSs.

The amount of work a database designer needs to put into optimizing query performance depends greatly on the DBMS. Because of the high cost of expert database developers, the less database and query design work developers have to do, the less costly the development and use of a database will be. Some DBMSs give very little control to the database designer or query writer over how a query is processed or the physical location of data for optimizing data reads and writes. Other systems give the application developers considerable control and often demand extensive work to tune the database design and the structure of queries to obtain acceptable performance. When the workload is fairly focused—say, for data warehousing, where there are a few batch updates and very complex queries requiring large segments of the database—performance can be well tuned either by smart query optimizers in the DBMS or by intelligent database and query design or a combination of both. For example, the Teradata DBMS is highly tuned for parallel processing in a data warehousing environment. In this case, only seldom can a database designer or query writer improve on the capabilities of the DBMS to store and process data. This situation is, however, rare, and therefore it is important for a database designer to consider options for improving database processing performance. Chapter 7 will provide additional guidelines for writing efficient queries.

Parallel Query Processing

One of the major computer architectural changes over the past few years is the increased use of multiple processors and processor cores in database servers. Database servers frequently use one of several parallel processing architectures. To take advantage of these capabilities, some of the most sophisticated DBMSs include strategies for breaking apart a query into modules that can be processed in parallel by each of the related processors. The most common approach is to replicate the query so that each copy works against a portion of the database, usually a horizontal partition (i.e., a set of rows). The partitions need to be defined in advance by the database designer. The same query is run against each portion in parallel on separate processors, and the intermediate results from each processor are combined to create the final query result as if the query were run against the whole database.

Suppose you have an Order table with several million rows for which query performance has been slow. To ensure that subsequent scans of this table are performed in parallel, using at least three processors, you would alter the structure of the table with the SQL command:

```
ALTER TABLE Order_T PARALLEL 3;
```

You need to tune each table to the best degree of parallelism, so it is not uncommon to alter a table several times until the right degree is found.

Parallel query processing speed can be impressive. Schumacher (1997) reports on a test in which the time to perform a query was cut in half with parallel processing compared to using a normal table scan. Because an index is a table, indexes can also be given the parallel structure, so that scans of an index are also faster. Again, Schumacher (1997) shows an example where the time to create an index by parallel processing was reduced from approximately seven minutes to five seconds!

Besides table scans, other elements of a query can be processed in parallel, such as certain types of joining related tables, grouping query results into categories, combining several parts of a query result together (called *union*), sorting rows, and computing aggregate values. Row update, delete, and insert operations can also be processed in parallel. In addition, the performance of some database creation commands can be improved by parallel processing; these include creating and rebuilding an index and creating a table from data in the database. The Oracle environment must be preconfigured with a specification for the number of virtual parallel database servers to exist. Once this is done, the query processor will decide what it thinks is the best use of parallel processing for any command.

Sometimes the parallel processing is transparent to the database designer or query writer. With some DBMSs, the part of the DBMS that determines how to process a query, the query optimizer, uses physical database specifications and characteristics of the data (e.g., a count of the number of different values for a qualified attribute) to determine whether to take advantage of parallel processing capabilities.

Overriding Automatic Query Optimization

Sometimes, the query writer knows (or can learn) key information about the query that may be overlooked or unknown to the query optimizer module of the DBMS. With such key information in hand, a query writer may have an idea for a better way to process a query. But before you as the query writer can know you have a better way, you have to know how the query optimizer (which usually picks a query processing plan that will minimize expected query processing time, or cost) will process the query. This is especially true for a query you have not submitted before. Fortunately, with most relational DBMSs, you can learn the optimizer's plan for processing the query before running the query. A command such as EXPLAIN or EXPLAIN PLAN (the exact command varies by DBMS) will display how the query optimizer intends to access indexes, use parallel servers, and join tables to prepare the query result. If you preface the actual relational command with the explain clause, the query processor displays the logical steps to process the query and stops processing before actually accessing the database. The query optimizer chooses the best plan based on statistics about each table, such as average row length and number of rows. It may be necessary to force the DBMS to calculate up-to-date statistics about the database (e.g., the Analyze command in Oracle) to get an accurate estimate of query costs. You may submit several EXPLAIN commands with your query, written in different ways, to see if the optimizer predicts different performance. Then, you can submit for actual processing the form of the query that had the best predicted processing time, or you may decide not to submit the query because it will be too costly to run.

You may even see a way to improve query processing performance. With some DBMSs, you can force the DBMS to do the steps differently or to use the capabilities of the DBMS, such as parallel servers, differently than the optimizer thinks is the best plan.

For example, suppose we wanted to count the number of orders processed by a particular sales representative, Smith. Let's assume we want to perform this query with a full table scan in parallel. The SQL command for this query would be as follows:

```
SELECT /*+ FULL(Order_T) PARALLEL(Order_T,3) */ COUNT(*)
FROM Order_T
WHERE Salesperson = "Smith";
```

The clause inside the /* */ delimiters is a hint to Oracle. This hint overrides whatever query plan Oracle would naturally create for this query. Thus, a hint is specific to each query, but the use of such hints must be anticipated by altering the structure of tables to be handled with parallel processing.

Summary

During physical database design, you, the designer, translate the logical description of data into the technical specifications for storing and retrieving data. The goal is to create a design for storing data that will provide adequate performance and ensure database integrity, security, and recoverability. In physical database design, you consider normalized relations and data volume estimates, data definitions, data processing requirements and their frequencies, user expectations, and database technology characteristics to establish the specifications that are used to implement the database using a database management system.

A field is the smallest unit of application data, corresponding to an attribute in the logical data model. You must determine the data type and integrity controls and how to handle missing values for each field, among other factors. A data type is a detailed coding scheme for representing organizational data. Data may be coded to reduce storage space. Field integrity control includes specifying a default value, a range of permissible values, null value permission, and referential integrity.

A process of denormalization transforms normalized relations into non-normalized implementation specifications. Denormalization is done to improve the efficiency of input-output operations by specifying the database implementation structure so that data elements that are required together are also accessed together on the physical medium. Partitioning is also considered a form of denormalization. Horizontal partitioning breaks a relation into multiple record specifications by placing different rows into different tables, based on common column values. Vertical partitioning distributes the columns of a relation into separate files, repeating the primary key in each of the files.

A physical file is a named portion of secondary memory allocated for the purpose of storing physical records. Data within a physical file are organized through a combination of sequential storage and pointers. A pointer is a field of data that can be used to locate a related field or record of data.

A file organization arranges the records of a file on a secondary storage device. The four major categories of file organizations are (1) heap, which stores records or rows in no particular order; (2) sequential, which stores records in sequence according to a primary key value; (3) indexed, in which records are stored sequentially or nonsequentially and an index is used to keep track of where the records are stored; and (4) hashed, in which the address of each record is determined using an algorithm that converts a primary key value into a record address. Physical records of several types can be clustered together into one physical file in order to place records frequently used together close to one another in secondary memory.

The indexed file organization is one of the most popular in use today. An index may be based on a unique key or a secondary (nonunique) key, which allows more than one record to be associated with the same key value. A join index indicates rows from two or more tables that have common values for related fields. A hash index table makes the placement of data independent of the hashing algorithm and permits the same data to be accessed via several hashing functions on different fields. Indexes are important in speeding up data retrieval, especially when multiple conditions are used for selecting, sorting, or relating data. Indexes are useful in a wide variety of situations, including for large tables, for columns that are frequently used to qualify the data to be retrieved, when a field has a large number of distinct values, and when data processing is dominated by data retrieval rather than data maintenance.

The introduction of multiprocessor database servers has made possible new capabilities in database management systems. One major new feature is the ability to break apart a query and process the query in parallel against segments of a table. Such parallel query processing can greatly improve the speed of query processing. Also, database programmers can improve database processing performance by providing the DBMS with hints about the sequence in which to perform table operations. These hints override the cost-based optimizer of the DBMS. Both the DBMS and programmers can look at statistics about the database to determine how to process a query. A wide variety of guidelines for good query design were included in the chapter.

This chapter concludes the database design section of this book. Having developed complete physical data specifications, you are now ready to begin implementing the database with database technology. Implementation means defining the database and programming client and server routines to handle queries, reports, and transactions against the database. These are primary topics of the next four chapters, which cover relational database implementation and use with the SQL language database, application development, and data warehouse technologies.

Chapter Review

Key Terms

Data type 213	Hashed file	Indexed file	Sequential file
Denormalization 216	organization 226	organization 223	organization 223
Extent 222	Hashing algorithm 226	Join index 225	Tablespace 221
Field 212	Horizontal	Physical file 221	Vertical partitioning 220
File organization 223	partitioning 219	Pointer 227	
Hash index table 227	Index 223	Secondary key 223	

Review Questions

5-1. Define each of the following terms:
  a. file organization
  b. heap file organization
  c. sequential file organization
  d. indexed file organization
  e. hashed file organization
  f. denormalization
  g. composite key
  h. secondary key
  i. data type
  j. join index

5-2. Match the following terms to the appropriate definitions:

  _____ extent
  _____ hashing algorithm
  _____ index
  _____ physical record
  _____ pointer
  _____ data type
  _____ physical file

  a. a detailed coding scheme for representing organizational data
  b. a data structure used to determine in a file the location of a record/records
  c. a named area of secondary memory
  d. a contiguous section of disk storage space
  e. a field not containing business data
  f. converts a key value into an address
  g. adjacent fields

5-3. Contrast the following terms:
  a. horizontal partitioning; vertical partitioning
  b. physical file; tablespace
  c. normalization; denormalization
  d. range control; null control
  e. secondary key; primary key

5-4. What are the major inputs into physical database design?

5-5. What are the key decisions in physical database design?

5-6. What decisions have to be made to develop a field specification?

5-7. Explain how physical database design has an important role in forming a foundation for regulatory compliance.

5-8. What are the objectives of selecting a data type for a field?

5-9. Explain why you sometimes have to reserve much more space for a numeric field than any of the initial stored values require.

5-10. Why are field values sometimes coded?

5-11. What options are available for controlling data integrity at the field level?

5-12. Describe three ways to handle missing field values.

5-13. Explain why normalized relations may not comprise an efficient physical implementation structure.

5-14. Explain why it makes sense to first go through the normalization process and then denormalize.

5-15. List three common situations that suggest that relations be denormalized before database implementation.

5-16. Explain the reasons why some experts are against the practice of denormalization.

5-17. What are the advantages and disadvantages of horizontal and vertical partitioning?

5-18. List seven important criteria for selecting the best file organization.

5-19. What are the benefits of a hash index table?

5-20. What is the purpose of clustering of data in a file?

5-21. What is the most important mechanism that database designers can use to impact database performance in specific use situations?

5-22. State nine rules of thumb for choosing indexes.

5-23. One of the recommendations regarding indexes is to specify a unique index for each primary key. Explain the justification for this recommendation.

5-24. Explain why an index is useful only if there is sufficient variety in the values of an attribute.

5-25. Indexing can clearly be very beneficial. Why should you *not* create an index for every column of every table of your database?

5-26. Explain the reasons underlying the significant performance gains in query performance that can be achieved with parallel processing.

5-27. a. What are the salient properties of relations?
 b. What are business rules? Name and explain the major types of integrity constraints?
 c. What is a well structured relation? How do anomalies dictate the constitution of a well structured relation?

5-28. Give a roadmap of the steps involved in the transformation of an E-R diagram into a relation.

5-29. What is Normalization? What are the goals of Normalization? What are the steps involved in Normalization? How do functional dependencies affect Normalization?

5-30. How does a DBMS control data integrity? Discuss the various forms of Integrity Control that may be supported by a DBMS? How is missing data in a field handled by the DBMS?

Problems and Exercises

5-31. Consider the following two relations for Millennium College:

STUDENT(StudentID, StudentName, CampusAddress, GPA)
REGISTRATION(StudentID, CourseID, Grade) •

Following is a typical query against these relations:

SELECT Student_T.StudentID, StudentName, CourseID, Grade
FROM Student_T, Registration_T
  WHERE Student_T.StudentID =
    Registration_T.StudentID
    AND GPA > 3.0
ORDER BY StudentName;

a. On what attributes should indexes be defined to speed up this query? Give the reasons for each attribute selected.
b. Write SQL commands to create indexes for each attribute you identified in part a.

Problems and Exercises 5-32—5-35 have been written assuming that the DBMS you are using is Oracle. If that is not the case, feel free to modify the question for the DBMS environment that you are familiar with. You can al--so compare and contrast answers for different DBMSs.

5-32. Choose Oracle data types for the attributes in the normalized relations in Figure 5-4b.

5-33. Choose Oracle data types for the attributes in the normalized relations that you created in Problem and Exercise 4-49 in Chapter 4.

5-34. Explain in your own words what the precision (p) and scale (s) parameters for the Oracle data type NUMBER mean.

5-35. Say that you are interested in storing the numeric value 3,456,349.2334. What will be stored, with each of the following Oracle data types:
a. NUMBER(11)
b. NUMBER(11,1)
c. NUMBER(11,-2)
d. NUMBER(11,6)
e. NUMBER(6)
f. NUMBER

5-36. Suppose you are designing a default value for the age field in a student record at your university. What possible values would you consider, and why? How might the default vary by other characteristics about the student, such as school within the university or degree sought?

5-37. When a student has not chosen a major at a university, the university often enters a value of "Undecided" for the major field. Is "Undecided" a way to represent the null value? Should it be used as a default value? Justify your answer carefully.

5-38. Consider the following normalized relations from a database in a large retail chain:

STORE (StoreID, Region, ManagerID, SquareFeet)
EMPLOYEE (EmployeeID, WhereWork, EmployeeName, EmployeeAddress)
DEPARTMENT (DepartmentID, ManagerID, SalesGoal)
SCHEDULE (DepartmentID, EmployeeID, Date)

What opportunities might exist for denormalizing these relations when defining the physical records for this database? Under what circumstances would you consider creating such denormalized records?

5-39. Consider the following set of normalized relations from a database used by a mobile service provide to keep track of its users and advertiser customers.

USER(UserID, UserLName, UserFName, UserEmail, UserYearOfBirth, UserCategoryID, UserZip)
ADVERTISERCLIENT(ClientID, ClientName, ClientContactID, ClientZip)
CONTACT(ContactID, ContactName, ContactEmail, ContactPhone)
USERINTERESTAREA(UserID, InterestID, UserInterestIntensity)
INTEREST(InterestID, InterestLabel)
CATEGORY(CategoryID, CategoryName, CategoryPriority)
ZIP(ZipCode, City, State)

Assume that the mobile service provider has frequent need for the following information:
• List of users sorted by zip code
• Access to a specific client with the client's contact person's name, e-mail address, and phone number
• List of users sorted by interest area and within each interest area user's estimated intensity of interest
• List of users within a specific age range sorted by their category and within the category by zip code.
• Access to a specific user based on their e-mail address.
Based on these needs, specify the types of indexes you would recommend for this situation. Justify your decisions based on the list of information needs above.

5-40. Consider the relations in Problem and Exercise 5-39. Please identify possible opportunities for denormalizing these relations as part of the physical design of the database. Which ones would you be most likely to implement?

5-41. Consider the following normalized relations for a sports league:

TEAM(<u>TeamID</u>, TeamName, TeamLocation, TeamManager)
PLAYER(<u>PlayerID</u>, PlayerFirstName, PlayerLastName, PlayerDateOfBirth, PlayerSpecialtyCode)
SPECIALTY(<u>SpecialtyCode</u>, SpecialtyDescription) Salary)
LOCATION(<u>LocationID</u>, CityName, CityState, CityCountry, CityPopulation)
MANAGER(<u>ManagerID</u>, ManagerName)

What recommendations would you make regarding opportunities for denormalization? What additional information would you need to make fully informed denormalization decisions?

5-42. What problems might arise from vertically partitioning a relation? Given these potential problems, what general conditions influence when to partition a relation vertically?

5-43. Is it possible with a sequential file organization to permit sequential scanning of the data, based on several sorted orders? If not, why not? If it is possible, how?

5-44. Suppose each record in a file were connected to the prior record and the next record in key sequence using pointers. Thus, each record might have the following format: Primary key, other attributes, pointer to prior record, pointer to next record
  a. What would be the advantages of this file organization compared with a sequential file organization?
  b. In contrast with a sequential file organization, would it be possible to keep the records in multiple sequences? Why or why not?

5-45. Assume that a student table in a university database had an index on StudentID (the primary key) and indexes on Major, Age, MaritalStatus, and HomeZipCode (all secondary keys). Further, assume that the university wanted a list of students majoring in MIS or computer science, over age 25, and married OR students majoring in computer engineering, single, and from the 45462 zip code. How could indexes be used so that only records that satisfy this qualification are accessed?

5-46. Consider the relations specified in Problem and Exercise 5-41. Assume that the database has been implemented without denormalization. Further assume that the database is global in scope and covers thousands of leagues, tens of thousands of teams, and hundreds of thousands of players. In order to accommodate this, a new relation has been added:

LEAGUE(<u>LeagueID</u>, LeagueName, LeagueLocation)

In addition, TEAM has an additional attribute TeamLeague. The following database operations are typical:
• Adding new players
• Adding new player contracts
• Updating player specialty codes
• Updating city populations
• Reporting players by team

• Reporting players by team and specialty
• Reporting players ordered by salary
• Reporting teams and their players by city.
  a. Identify the foreign keys.
  b. Specify the types of indexes you would recommend for this situation. Explain how you used the list of operations described above to arrive at your recommendation.

5-47. Consider Figure 5-7b. Assuming that the empty rows in the leaves of this index show space where new records can be stored, explain where the record for Sooners would be stored. Where would the record for Flashes be stored? What might happen when one of the leaves is full and a new record needs to be added to that leaf?

5-48. Consider Figure 4-38 and your answer to Problem and Exercise 4-50 in Chapter 4. Assume that the most important reports that the organization needs are as follows:
• A list of the current developer's project assignments
• A list of the total costs for all projects
• For each team, a list of its membership history
• For each country, a list of all projects, with projected end dates, in which the country's developers are involved
• For each year separately, a list of all developers, in the order of their average assignment scores for all the assignments that were completed during that year

Based on this (admittedly limited) information, make a recommendation regarding the indexes that you would create for this database. Choose two of the indexes and provide the SQL command that you would use to create those indexes.

5-49. Can clustering of files occur after the files are populated with records? Why or why not?

5-50. Parallel query processing, as described in this chapter, means that the same query is run on multiple processors and that each processor accesses in parallel a different subset of the database. Another form of parallel query processing, not discussed in this chapter, would partition the query so that each part of the query runs on a different processor, but that part accesses whatever part of the database it needs. Most queries involve a qualification clause that selects the records of interest in the query. In general, this qualification clause is of the following form:

  (condition OR condition OR…) AND (condition OR condition OR…) AND…

Given this general form, how might a query be broken apart so that each parallel processor handles a subset of the query and then combines the subsets together after each part is processed?

5-51. Consider the EER diagram in Figure 4-33. Let's make the following assumptions:
• There are 12,500,000 customers.
• These customers have altogether 40,000,000 card accounts. Of these 80 percent are credit card accounts and 20 percent are debit card accounts.
• There are 3,200,000 merchants who accept these cards.
• There are, on average, 30 charges per merchant per day. The range is very large.

- Customers are making, on average, 2,000,000 requests per day to view their account balances and transactions.
- Merchants are making, on average, 5,000,000 requests per day to view the transactions they have submitted to the bank.
a. Based on these assumptions, draw a usage map for this portion of the EER diagram.
b. Create a set of normalized relations based on this EER diagram.

c. What opportunities for denormalization can identify in this case (if any)?

Problems and Exercises 5-52—5-55 refer to the large Pine Valley Furniture Company data set provided with the text.

PINE VALLEY FURNITURE

5-52. Create a join index on the CustomerID fields of the Customer_T and Order_T tables in Figure 4-4.

FIGURE 5-9 Figure for Problem and Exercise 5-54

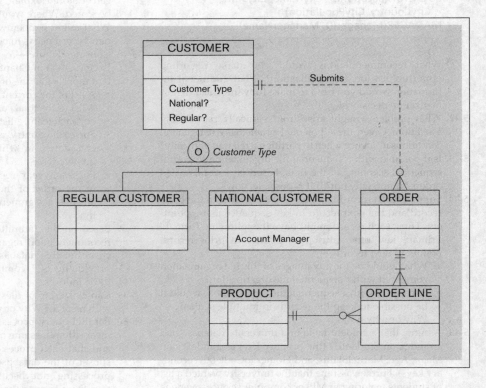

5-53. Consider the composite usage map in Figure 5-1. After a period of time, the assumptions for this usage map have changed, as follows:
- There is an average of 50 supplies (rather than 40) for each supplier.
- Manufactured parts represent only 30 percent of all parts, and purchased parts represent 75 percent.
- The number of direct access to purchased parts increases to 7,500 per hour (rather than 6,000).

Draw a new composite usage map reflecting this new information to replace Figure 5-1.

5-54. Consider the EER diagram for Pine Valley Furniture shown in Figure 3-12. Figure 5-9 looks at a portion of that EER diagram.

Let's make a few assumptions about the average usage of the system:
- There are 50,000 customers, and of these, 80 percent represent regular accounts and 20 percent represent national accounts.
- Currently, the system stores 2,200,000 orders, although this number is constantly changing.
- Each order has an average of 25 products.

- There are 4,000 products.
- Approximately 1,300 orders are placed per hour.
a. Based on these assumptions, draw a usage map for this portion of the EER diagram.
b. Management would like employees only to use this database. Do you see any opportunities for denormalization?

5-55. Refer to Figure 4-5. For each of the following reports (with sample data), indicate any indexes that you feel would help the report run faster as well as the type of index:
a. State, by products (user-specified period)

State, by Products Report, January 1, 2015, to March 31, 2015

State	Product Description	Total Quantity Ordered
CO	8-Drawer Dresser	1
CO	Entertainment Center	0
CO	Oak Computer Desk	1
CO	Writer's Desk	2
NY	Writer's Desk	1

State	Product Description	Total Quantity Ordered
VA	Writer's Desk	5

b. Most frequently sold product finish in a user-specified month

Most Frequently Sold Product Finish Report, March 1, 2015, to March 31, 2015

Product Finish	Units Sold
Cherry	13

c. All orders placed last month

Monthly Order Report, March 1, 2015, to March 31, 2015

Order ID	Order Date	Customer ID	Customer Name
19	3/5/15	4	Eastern Furniture

Associated Order Details:

Product Description	Quantity Ordered	Price	Extended Price
Cherry End Table	10	$75.00	$750.00
High Back Leather Chair	5	$362.00	$1,810.00

Order ID	Order Date	Customer IDs	Customer Name
24	3/10/15	1	Contemporary Casuals

Associated Order Details:

Product Description	Quantity Ordered	Price	Extended Price
Bookcase	4	$69.00	$276.00

d. Total products sold, by product line (user-specified period)

Products Sold by Product Line, March 1, 2015, to March 31, 2015

Product Line	Quantity Sold
Basic	200
Antique	15
Modern	10
Classical	75

5-56. a. What are the major categories of File organizations?
   b. What are the significant points of Parallel Query Processing? Why is it important in the contemporary times?
   c. Explain how Indexing a Table on a DBMS platform ensure data integrity features?
   d. How are Constraints enforced on a Table?

Field Exercises

5-57. Find out which database management systems are available at your university for student use. Investigate which data types these DBMSs support. Compare these DBMSs based on the data types supported and suggest which types of applications each DBMS is best suited for, based on this comparison.

5-58. Using the Web site for this text and other Internet resources, investigate the parallel processing capabilities of several leading DBMSs. How do their capabilities differ?

5-59. Denormalization can be a controversial topic among database designers. Some believe that any database should be fully normalized (even using all the normal forms discussed in Appendix B, available on the book's Web site). Others look for ways to denormalize to improve processing performance. Contact a database designer or administrator in an organization with which you are familiar. Ask whether he or she believes in fully normalized or denormalized physical databases. Ask the person why he or she has this opinion.

5-60. Contact a database designer or administrator in an organization with which you are familiar. Ask what file organizations are available in the various DBMSs used in that organization. Interview this person to learn what factors he or she considers when selecting an organization for database files. For indexed files, ask how he or she decides what indexes to create. Are indexes ever deleted? Why or why not?

References

Babad, Y. M., and J. A. Hoffer. 1984. "Even No Data Has a Value." *Communications of the ACM* 27,8 (August): 748–56.

Bieniek, D. 2006. "The Essential Guide to Table Partitioning and Data Lifecycle Management." *Windows IT Pro* (March), accessed at **www.windowsITpro.com.**

Brobst, S., S. Gant, and F. Thompson. 1999. "Partitioning Very Large Database Tables with Oracle8." *Oracle Magazine* 8,2 (March–April): 123–26.

Catterall, R. 2005. "The Keys to the Database." *DB2 Magazine* 10,2 (Quarter 2): 49–51.

Finkelstein, R. 1988. "Breaking the Rules Has a Price." *Database Programming & Design* 1,6 (June): 11–14.

Hoberman, S. 2002. "The Denormalization Survival Guide—Parts I and II." Published in the online journal *The Data Administration Newsletter*, found in the April and July issues of Tdan.com; the two parts of this guide are available at **www.tdan.com/i020fe02.htm** and **www.tdan.com/i021ht03.htm,** respectively.

Inmon, W. H. 1988. "What Price Normalization." *ComputerWorld* (October 17): 27, 31.

Lightstone, S., T. Teorey, and T. Nadeau. 2010. *Physical Database Design: The Database Professional's Guide to Exploiting Indexes, Views, Storage, and More.* San Francisco, CA: Morgan Kaufmann.

Pascal, F. 2002a. "The Dangerous Illusion: Denormalization, Performance and Integrity, Part 1." *DM Review* 12,6 (June): 52–53, 57.

Pascal, F. 2002b. "The Dangerous Illusion: Denormalization, Performance and Integrity, Part 2." *DM Review* 12,6 (June): 16, 18.

Rogers, U. 1989. "Denormalization: Why, What, and How?" *Database Programming & Design* 2,12 (December): 46–53.

Schumacher, R. 1997. "Oracle Performance Strategies." *DBMS* 10,5 (May): 89–93.

Further Reading

Ballinger, C. 1998. "Introducing the Join Index." *Teradata Review* 1,3 (Fall): 18–23. (Note: *Teradata Review* is now *Teradata Magazine.*)

Bontempo, C. J., and C. M. Saracco. 1996. "Accelerating Indexed Searching." *Database Programming & Design* 9,7 (July): 37–43.

DeLoach, A. 1987. "The Path to Writing Efficient Queries in SQL/DS." *Database Programming & Design* 1,1 (January): 26–32.

Elmasri, R., and S. Navathe. 2010. *Fundamentals of Database Systems*, 6th ed. Reading, MA: Addison Wesley.

Loney, K., E. Aronoff, and N. Sonawalla. 1996. "Big Tips for Big Tables." *Database Programming & Design* 9,11 (November): 58–62.

Oracle. 2014. *Oracle Database Parallel Execution Fundamentals.* An Oracle White Paper, December 2014. Available at **www.oracle.com/technetwork/articles/datawarehouse/twp-parallel-execution-fundamentals-133639.pdf**

Roti, S. 1996. "Indexing and Access Mechanisms." *DBMS* 9,5 (May): 65–70.

Viehman, P. 1994. "Twenty-four Ways to Improve Database Performance." *Database Programming & Design* 7,2 (February): 32–41.

Web Resources

www.SearchOracle.com and **www.SearchSQLServer.com** *Sites* that contain a wide variety of information about database management and DBMSs. New "tips" are added daily, and you can subscribe to an alert service for new postings to the site. Many tips deal with improving the performance of queries through better database and query design.

www.tdan.com Web site of *The Data Administration Newsletter*, which frequently publishes articles on all aspects of database development and design.

www.teradatamagazine.com A journal for Teradata data warehousing products that includes articles on database design. You can search the site for key terms from this chapter, such as *join index*, and find many articles on these topics.

CASE

Forondo Artist Management Excellence Inc.

Case Description

In Chapter 4, you created the relational schema for the FAME system. Your next step is to create a detailed specification that will allow you to implement the database. Specifically, you need to identify and document choices regarding the properties of each data element in the database, using information from the case descriptions and the options available to you in the DBMS that you have chosen for implementation (or that has been selected for you by your instructor).

Project Questions

5-62. Do you see any justifiable opportunities to denormalize the tables? If so, provide appropriate justification and create a new denormalized schema. Do you need to update your ER diagram based on these decisions? Why or why not?

5-63. Create a data dictionary similar to the metadata table shown in Table 1-1 in Chapter 1 to document your choices.

For each table in the relational schema you developed earlier, provide the following information for each field/data element: field name, definition/description, data type, format, allowable values, whether the field is required or optional, whether the field is indexed and the type of index, whether the field is a primary key, whether the field is a foreign key, and the table that is referenced by the foreign key field.

5-64. Create the physical data model for the relational schema you developed in Chapter 4 (and potentially modified in 5-56 above), clearly indicating data types, primary keys, and foreign keys.

5-65. Create a strategy for reviewing your deliverables generated so far with the appropriate stakeholders. Which stakeholders should you meet with? What information would you bring to this meeting? Would you conduct the reviews separately or together? Who do you think should sign off on your logical and physical schemas before you move to the next phase of the project?

Implementation

AN OVERVIEW OF PART FOUR

Part IV considers topics associated with implementing relational systems, including Web-enabled Internet applications and data warehouses. Database implementation, as indicated in Chapter 1, includes coding and testing database processing programs, completing database documentation and training materials, and installing databases and converting data, as necessary, from prior systems. Here, at last, is the point in the systems development life cycle for which we have been preparing. Our prior activities—enterprise modeling, conceptual data modeling, and logical and physical database design—are necessary previous stages. At the end of implementation, we expect a functioning system that meets users' information requirements. After that, the system will be put into production use, and database maintenance will be necessary for the life of the system. The chapters in Part IV help develop an initial understanding of the complexities and challenges of implementing a database system.

Chapter 6 describes Structured Query Language (SQL), which has become a standard language (especially on database servers) for creating and processing relational databases. In addition to a brief history of SQL that includes a thorough introduction to SQL:1999, currently used by most DBMSs, along with discussion of the SQL:2011 standard that is implemented by many relational systems, the syntax of SQL is explored. Data definition language (DDL) commands used to create a database are included, as are single-table data manipulation language (DML) commands used to query a database. Dynamic and materialized views, which constrain a user's environment to relevant tables necessary to complete the user's work, are also covered.

Chapter 7 continues the explanation of more advanced SQL syntax and constructs. Multiple-table queries, along with subqueries and correlated subqueries, are demonstrated. These capabilities provide SQL with much of its power. Transaction integrity issues and an explanation of data dictionary construction place SQL within a wider context. Additional programming capabilities, including triggers and stored procedures, and embedding SQL in other programming language programs (such as Oracle's PL/SQL) further demonstrate the capabilities of SQL. Online transaction processing (OLTP) is contrasted with online analytical processing (OLAP) features of SQL:1999 and SQL:2011; OLAP queries, necessary for accessing data warehouses, are introduced. Strategies for writing and testing queries, from simple to more complex, are offered.

Chapter 8 provides a discussion of the concepts of client/server architecture, applications, middleware, and database access in contemporary database environments. Technologies that are commonly used in creating two- and three-tier applications are presented, and sample application programs are used to demonstrate how to access databases from popular programming languages such as Java, VB.NET, ASP.NET, JSP, and PHP. The impact of cloud computing on database applications is also explored. The chapter also presents expanded coverage of the emerging role of Extensible Markup Language (XML) and related technologies in data storage and retrieval. Topics covered include basics of XML schemas, XQuery, XSLT, Web services, and service-oriented architecture (SOA).

Chapter 9 describes the basic concepts of data warehousing, the reasons data warehousing is regarded as critical to competitive advantage in many organizations, and the database design activities and structures unique to data warehousing. Topics include alternative data warehouse architectures, types of data warehouse data, and the dimensional data model (star schema) for data marts. Database design for data marts, including surrogate keys, fact table grain, modeling dates and time, conformed dimensions, factless fact tables, and helper/hierarchy/reference tables, is explained and illustrated.

As indicated by this brief synopsis of the chapters, Part IV provides both a conceptual understanding of the issues involved in implementing database applications and an initial practical understanding of the procedures necessary to construct a database prototype. The introduction of common strategies, such as client/server, Web enabled, Web services, and data warehousing, equip you to understand expected future developments in databases.

CHAPTER 6

Introduction to SQL

LEARNING OBJECTIVES

After studying this chapter, you should be able to:

- Concisely define each of the following key terms: **relational DBMS (RDBMS)**, **catalog**, **schema**, **data definition language (DDL)**, **data manipulation language (DML)**, **data control language (DCL)**, **scalar aggregate**, **vector aggregate**, **base table**, **virtual table**, **dynamic view**, and **materialized view**.
- Interpret the history and role of SQL in database development.
- Define a database using the SQL data definition language.
- Write single-table queries using SQL commands.
- Establish referential integrity using SQL.
- Discuss the SQL:1999 and SQL:2011 standards.

Visit www.pearsonhighered.com/ hoffer to view the accompanying video for this chapter.

INTRODUCTION

Pronounced "S-Q-L" by some and "sequel" by others, SQL has become the de facto standard language for creating and querying relational databases. (Can the next standard be the sequel to SQL?) The primary purpose of this chapter is to introduce SQL, the most common language for relational systems. It has been accepted as a U.S. standard by the American National Standards Institute (ANSI) and is a Federal Information Processing Standard (FIPS). It is also an international standard recognized by the International Organization for Standardization (ISO). ANSI has accredited the International Committee for Information Technology Standards (INCITS) as a standards development organization; INCITS is working on the next version of the SQL standard to be released.

The SQL standard is like afternoon weather in Florida (and maybe where you live, too)—wait a little while, and it will change. The ANSI SQL standards were first published in 1986 and updated in 1989, 1992 (SQL-92), 1999 (SQL:1999), 2003 (SQL:2003), 2006 (SQL:2006), 2008 (SQL:2008), and 2011 (SQL:2011). (See **http:// en.wikipedia.org/wiki/SQL** for a summary of this history.) The standard is now generally referred to as SQL:2011.

SQL-92 was a major revision and was structured into three levels: Entry, Intermediate, and Full. SQL:1999 established the core-level conformance, which must be met before any other level of conformance can be achieved; core-level conformance requirements are unchanged in SQL:2011. In addition to fixes and enhancements of SQL:1999, SQL:2003 introduced a new set of SQL/XML standards, three new data types, various new built-in functions, and improved methods for generating values automatically. SQL:2006 refined these additions and made them more compatible with XQuery, the XML query language published by the World Wide Web Consortium (W3C). SQL:2008 improved analytics query capabilities and enchanced MERGE for combining tables. The most important new additions to SQL:2011 are related to temporal databases, that is, databases that are able to capture the change in the data values over time. At the time of this writing, most database management systems claim SQL-92 compliance and partial compliance with SQL:1999 and SQL:2011.

Except where noted as a particular vendor's syntax, the examples in this chapter conform to the SQL standard. Concerns have been expressed about SQL:1999 and SQL:2003/SQL:2008/SQL:2011 being true standards because conformance with the standard is no longer certified by the U.S. Department of Commerce's National Institute of Standards and Technology (NIST) (Gorman, 2001). "Standard SQL" may be considered an oxymoron (like safe investment or easy payments)! Vendors' interpretations of the SQL standard differ from one another, and vendors extend their products' capabilities with proprietary features beyond the stated standard. This makes it difficult to port SQL from one vendor's product to another. One must become familiar with the particular version of SQL being used and not expect that SQL code will transfer exactly as written to another vendor's version. Table 6-1 demonstrates differences in handling date and time values to illustrate discrepancies one encounters across SQL vendors (IBM DB2, Microsoft SQL Server, MySQL [an open source DBMS owned by Oracle], and Oracle).

SQL has been implemented in both mainframe and personal computer systems, so this chapter is relevant to both computing environments. Although many of the PC-database packages use a query-by-example (QBE) interface, they also include SQL coding as an option. QBE interfaces use graphic presentations and translate the QBE actions into SQL code before query execution occurs. In Microsoft Access, for example, it is possible to switch back and forth between the two interfaces; a query that has been built using a QBE interface can be viewed in SQL by clicking a button. This feature may aid you in learning SQL syntax. In client/server architectures, SQL commands are executed on the server, and the results are returned to the client workstation.

The first commercial DBMS that supported SQL was Oracle in 1979. Oracle is now available in mainframe, client/server, and PC-based platforms for many operating systems, including various UNIX, Linux, and Microsoft Windows operating systems. IBM's DB2, Informix, and Microsoft SQL Server are available for this range of operating systems also. See Kulkarni and Michels (2012) and Zemke (2012) for descriptions of the latest features added to SQL.

TABLE 6-1 Handling Date and Time Values

TIMESTAMP data type: A core feature, the standard requires that this data type store year, month, day, hour, minute, and second (with fractional seconds; default is six digits).

TIMESTAMP WITH TIME ZONE data type: Extension to TIMESTAMP also stores the time zone.

Product	Follows Standard?	Implementation: Comments
DB2	TIMESTAMP only	DB2's TIMESTAMP data type includes the capability to include time zone information, but the full expression TIMESTAMP WITH TIME ZONE is not implemented.
Transact-SQL (SQL Server)	No	DateTimeOffset data type offers functional equivalency to TIMESTAMP WITH TIME ZONE.
MySQL	TIMESTAMP only with limited range	TIMESTAMP captures also the time zone information; TIMESTAMP values are stored in UTC (coordinated universal time) and converted back to the local time for use. TIMESTAMP range is very limited (1-1-1970 to 1-19-2038).
Oracle	TIMESTAMP and TIMESTAMP WITH TIME ZONE	TIMESTAMP WITH TIME ZONE is fully supported in Oracle 12c.

ORIGINS OF THE SQL STANDARD

The concepts of relational database technology were first articulated in 1970, in E. F. Codd's classic paper "A Relational Model of Data for Large Shared Data Banks." Workers at the IBM Research Laboratory in San Jose, California, undertook development of System R, a project whose purpose was to demonstrate the feasibility of implementing the relational model in a database management system. They used a language called Sequel, also developed at the San Jose IBM Research Laboratory. Sequel was renamed SQL during the project, which took place from 1974 to 1979. The knowledge gained was applied in the development of SQL/DS, the first relational database management system available commercially (from IBM). SQL/DS was first available in 1981, running on the DOS/VSE operating system. A VM version followed in 1982, and the MVS version, DB2, was announced in 1983.

When System R was well received at the user sites where it was installed, other vendors began developing relational products that used SQL. One product, Oracle, from Relational Software, was actually on the market before SQL/DS (1979). Other products included INGRES from Relational Technology (1981), IDM from Britton-Lee (1982), DG/SQL from Data General Corporation (1984), and Sybase from Sybase, Inc. (1986). To provide some directions for the development of relational DBMSs, ANSI and the ISO approved a standard for the SQL relational query language (functions and syntax) that was originally proposed by the X3H2 Technical Committee on Database (Technical Committee X3H2—Database, 1986; ISO, 1987), often referred to as SQL/86. For a more detailed history of the SQL standard, see the documents available at **www.wiscorp.com**.

The following were the original purposes of the SQL standard:

1. To specify the syntax and semantics of SQL data definition and manipulation languages
2. To define the data structures and basic operations for designing, accessing, maintaining, controlling, and protecting an SQL database
3. To provide a vehicle for portability of database definition and application modules between conforming DBMSs
4. To specify both minimal (Level 1) and complete (Level 2) standards, which permit different degrees of adoption in products
5. To provide an initial standard, although incomplete, that will be enhanced later to include specifications for handling such topics as referential integrity, transaction management, user-defined functions, join operators beyond the equi-join, and national character sets

In terms of SQL, when is a standard not a standard? As explained earlier, most vendors provide unique, proprietary features and commands for their SQL database management system. So what are the advantages and disadvantages of having an SQL standard, when there are such variations from vendor to vendor? The benefits of such a standardized relational language include the following (although these are not pure benefits because of vendor differences):

- *Reduced training costs* Training in an organization can concentrate on one language. A large labor pool of IS professionals trained in a common language reduces retraining for newly hired employees.
- *Productivity* IS professionals can learn SQL thoroughly and become proficient with it from continued use. An organization can afford to invest in tools to help IS professionals become more productive. Because they are familiar with the language in which programs are written, programmers can more quickly maintain existing programs.
- *Application portability* Applications can be moved from one context to another when each environment uses SQL. Further, it is economical for the computer software industry to develop off-the-shelf application software when there is a standard language.
- *Application longevity* A standard language tends to remain so for a long time; hence there will be little pressure to rewrite old applications. Rather, applications

will simply be updated as the standard language is enhanced or new versions of DBMSs are introduced.

- *Reduced dependence on a single vendor* When a nonproprietary language is used, it is easier to use different vendors for the DBMS, training and educational services, application software, and consulting assistance; further, the market for such vendors will be more competitive, which may lower prices and improve service.
- *Cross-system communication* Different DBMSs and application programs can more easily communicate and cooperate in managing data and processing user programs.

On the other hand, a standard can stifle creativity and innovation; one standard is never enough to meet all needs, and an industry standard can be far from ideal because it may be the offspring of compromises among many parties. A standard may be difficult to change (because so many vendors have a vested interest in it), so fixing deficiencies may take considerable effort. Another disadvantage of standards that can be extended with proprietary features is that using special features added to SQL by a particular vendor may result in the loss of some advantages, such as application portability.

The original SQL standard has been widely criticized, especially for its lack of referential integrity rules and certain relational operators. Date and Darwen (1997) expressed concern that SQL seems to have been designed without adhering to established principles of language design, and "as a result, the language is filled with numerous restrictions, ad hoc constructs, and annoying special rules" (p. 8). They believe that the standard is not explicit enough and that the problem of standard SQL implementations will continue to exist. Some of these limitations will be noticeable in this chapter.

Many products are available that support SQL, and they run on machines of all sizes, from small personal computers to large mainframes. The database market is maturing, and the rate of significant changes in products may slow, but they will continue to be SQL based. The number of relational database vendors with significant market share has continued to consolidate. Gartner Group reports that Oracle controlled almost 49 percent of the overall relational database management system market in 2011, IBM was in second place, and Microsoft came in a close third. SAP/Sybase and Teradata also had significant—albeit much smaller—shares, and open source products, such as MySQL, PostgreSQL, and Ingres, combined for about 10 percent market share. MySQL, an open source version of SQL that runs on Linux, UNIX, Windows, and Mac OS X operating systems, has achieved considerable popularity. (Download MySQL for free from **www.mysql.com**.) The market position of MySQL changed surprisingly little even though Oracle acquired MySQL as part of its purchase of Sun Microsystems. Opportunities still exist for smaller vendors to prosper through industry-specific systems or niche applications. Upcoming product releases may change the relative strengths of the database management systems by the time you read this book. But all of them will continue to use SQL, and they will follow, to a certain extent, the standard described here.

In Chapter 11, you will learn about new technologies that are not based on the relational model, including big data technologies such as Hadoop and so-called NoSQL ("Not Only SQL") database management systems. SQL's dominant role as a query and data manipulation language has, however, led to the creation of a wide variety of mechanisms that allow data stored on these new platforms to be accessed with SQL or an SQL-like language. See Yegulalp (2014) for details of products such as Hive, Stinger, Drill, and Spark (no, we did not make these up).

Because of its significant market share, we most often illustrate SQL in this text using Oracle 12c syntax. We illustrate using a specific relational DBMS not to promote or endorse Oracle but rather so we know that the code we use will work with some DBMS. In the vast majority of the cases, the code will, in fact, work with many relational DBMSs because it complies with standard ANSI SQL. In some cases, we include illustrations using several or other relational DBMSs when there are interesting differences; however, there are only a few such cases, because we are not trying to compare systems, and we want to be parsimonious.

THE SQL ENVIRONMENT

With today's relational DBMSs and application generators, the importance of SQL within the database architecture is not usually apparent to the application users. Many users who access database applications have no knowledge of SQL at all. For example, sites on the Web allow users to browse their catalogs. The information about an item that is presented, such as size, color, description, and availability, is stored in a database. The information has been retrieved using an SQL query, but the user has not issued an SQL command. Rather, the user has used a prewritten program (written in, e.g., PHP, Python, or Java) with embedded SQL commands for database processing.

An SQL-based relational database application involves a user interface, a set of tables in the database, and a relational database management system (RDBMS) with an SQL capability. Within the RDBMS, SQL will be used to create the tables, translate user requests, maintain the data dictionary and system catalog, update and maintain the tables, establish security, and carry out backup and recovery procedures. A **relational DBMS (RDBMS)** is a data management system that implements a relational data model, one where data are stored in a collection of tables, and the data relationships are represented by common values, not links. This view of data was illustrated in Chapter 2 for the Pine Valley Furniture Company database system and will be used throughout this chapter's SQL query examples.

Figure 6-1 is a simplified schematic of an SQL environment, consistent with SQL:2011 standard. As depicted, an SQL environment includes an instance of an SQL database management system along with the databases accessible by that DBMS and the users and programs that may use that DBMS to access the databases. Each database is contained in a **catalog**, which describes any object that is a part of the database, regardless of which user created that object. Figure 6-1 shows two catalogs: DEV_C and PROD_C. Most companies keep at least two versions of any database they are using. The production version, PROD_C here, is the live version, which captures real business data and thus must be very tightly controlled and monitored. The development version, DEV_C here, is used when the database is being built and continues to serve as a development tool where enhancements and maintenance efforts can be thoroughly tested before being applied to the production database. Typically this database is not as tightly controlled or monitored, because it does not contain live business data. Each database will have a named schema(s) associated with a catalog. A **schema** is a collection of related objects, including but not limited to base tables and views, domains, constraints, character sets, triggers, and roles.

Relational DBMS (RDBMS)

A database management system that manages data as a collection of tables in which all data relationships are represented by common values in related tables.

Catalog

A set of schemas that, when put together, constitute a description of a database.

Schema

A structure that contains descriptions of objects created by a user, such as base tables, views, and constraints, as part of a database.

FIGURE 6-1 A simplified schematic of a typical SQL environment, as described by the SQL:2011 standards

If more than one user has created objects in a database, combining information about all users' schemas will yield information for the entire database. Each catalog must also contain an information schema, which contains descriptions of all schemas in the catalog, tables, views, attributes, privileges, constraints, and domains, along with other information relevant to the database. The information contained in the catalog is maintained by the DBMS as a result of the SQL commands issued by the users and can be rebuilt without conscious action by the user. It is part of the power of the SQL language that the issuance of syntactically simple SQL commands may result in complex data management activities being carried out by the DBMS software. Users can browse the catalog contents by using SQL SELECT statements.

SQL commands can be classified into three types. First, there are **data definition language (DDL)** commands. These commands are used to create, alter, and drop tables, views, and indexes, and they are covered first in this chapter. There may be other objects controlled by the DDL, depending on the DBMS. For example, many DBMSs support defining synonyms (abbreviations) for database objects or a field to hold a specified sequence of numbers (which can be helpful in assigning primary keys to rows in tables). In a production database, the ability to use DDL commands will generally be restricted to one or more database administrators in order to protect the database structure from unexpected and unapproved changes. In development or student databases, DDL privileges will be granted to more users.

Next, there are **data manipulation language (DML)** commands. Many consider the DML commands to be the core commands of SQL. These commands are used for updating, inserting, modifying, and querying the data in the database. They may be issued interactively, so that a result is returned immediately following the execution of the statement, or they may be included within programs written in a procedural programming language, such as C, Java, PHP, or COBOL, or with a GUI tool (e.g., Oracle's SQL Developer, SQL Assistant with Teradata, or MySQL Query Browser). Embedding SQL commands may provide the programmer with more control over timing of report generation, interface appearance, error handling, and database security (see Chapter 8 on embedding SQL in Web-based programs). Most of this chapter is devoted to covering basic DML commands, in interactive format. The general syntax of the SQL SELECT command used in DML is shown in Figure 6-2.

Finally, **data control language (DCL)** commands help a DBA control the database; they include commands to grant or revoke privileges to access the database or particular objects within the database and to store or remove transactions that would affect the database.

Each DBMS has a defined list of data types that it can handle. All contain numeric, string, and date/time-type variables. Some also contain graphic data types, spatial data types, or image data types, which greatly increase the flexibility of data manipulation. When a table is created, the data type for each attribute must be specified. Selection of a particular data type is affected by the data values that need to be stored and the expected uses of the data. A unit price will need to be stored in a numeric format because mathematical manipulations such as multiplying unit price by the number of units ordered are expected. A phone number may be stored as string data, especially if foreign phone numbers are going to be included in the data set. Even though a phone number contains only digits, no mathematical operations, such as adding or multiplying phone numbers, make sense with a phone number. And because character data will process more quickly, numeric data should be stored as character data if no arithmetic calculations are expected. Selecting a date field rather than a string field will allow the developer to take advantage

---

Data definition language (DDL)
Commands used to define a database, including those for creating, altering, and dropping tables and establishing constraints.

Data manipulation language (DML)
Commands used to maintain and query a database, including those for updating, inserting, modifying, and querying data.

Data control language (DCL)
Commands used to control a database, including those for administering privileges and committing (saving) data.

FIGURE 6-2 General syntax of the SELECT statement used in DML

```
SELECT [ALL/DISTINCT] column_list
FROM table_list
[WHERE conditional expression]
[GROUP BY group_by_column_list]
[HAVING conditional expression]
[ORDER BY order_by_column_list]
```

TABLE 6-2   Sample SQL Data Types

String	CHARACTER (CHAR)	Stores string values containing any characters in a character set. CHAR is defined to be a fixed length.
	CHARACTER VARYING (VARCHAR or VARCHAR2)	Stores string values containing any characters in a character set but of definable variable length.
	BINARY LARGE OBJECT (BLOB)	Stores binary string values in hexadecimal format. BLOB is defined to be a variable length. (Oracle also has CLOB and NCLOB, as well as BFILE for storing unstructured data outside the database.)
Number	NUMERIC	Stores exact numbers with a defined precision and scale.
	INTEGER (INT)	Stores exact numbers with a predefined precision and scale of zero.
Temporal	TIMESTAMP TIMESTAMP WITH LOCAL TIME ZONE	Stores a moment an event occurs, using a definable fraction-of-a-second precision. Value adjusted to the user's session time zone (available in Oracle and MySQL).
Boolean	BOOLEAN	Stores truth values: TRUE, FALSE, or UNKNOWN.

of date/time interval calculation functions that cannot be applied to a character field. See Table 6-2 for a few examples of SQL data types. SQL:2008 introduced three new data types: BIGINT, MULTISET, and XML. Watch for these new data types to be added to RDBMSs that had not previously introduced them as an enhancement of the existing standard.

Given the wealth of graphic and image data types, it is necessary to consider business needs when deciding how to store data. For example, color may be stored as a descriptive character field, such as "sand drift" or "beige." But such descriptions will vary from vendor to vendor and do not contain the amount of information that could be contained in a spatial data type that includes exact red, green, and blue intensity values. Such data types are now available in universal servers, which handle data warehouses, and can be expected to appear in RDBMSs as well. In addition to the predefined data types included in Table 6-2, SQL:1999 and SQL:2011 support constructed data types and user-defined types. There are many more predefined data types than those shown in Table 6-2. It will be necessary to familiarize yourself with the available data types for each RDBMS with which you work to achieve maximum advantage from its capabilities.

We are almost ready to illustrate sample SQL commands. The sample data that we will be using are shown in Figure 6-3 (which was captured in Microsoft Access). The data model corresponds to that shown in Figure 2-22. The PVFC database files are available for your use on this text's Web site; the files are available in several formats, for use with different DBMSs, and the database is also available on Teradata University Network. Instructions for locating them are included inside the front cover of the book. There are two PVFC files. The one used here is named BookPVFC (also called Standard PVFC), and you can use it to work through the SQL queries demonstrated in Chapters 6 and 7. Another file, BigPVFC, contains more data and does not always correspond to Figure 2-22, nor does it always demonstrate good database design. Big PVFC is used for some of the exercises at the end of the chapter.

PINE VALLEY FURNITURE

Each table name follows a naming standard that places an underscore and the letter T (for table) at the end of each table name, such as Order_T or Product_T. (Most DBMSs do not permit a space in the name of a table nor typically in the name of an attribute.) When looking at these tables, note the following:

1. Each order must have a valid customer ID included in the Order_T table.
2. Each item in an order line must have both a valid product ID and a valid order ID associated with it in the OrderLine_T table.
3. These four tables represent a simplified version of one of the most common sets of relations in business database systems—the customer order for products. SQL commands necessary to create the Customer_T table and the Order_T table were included in Chapter 2 and are expanded here.

FIGURE 6-3 Sample Pine Valley
Furniture Company data

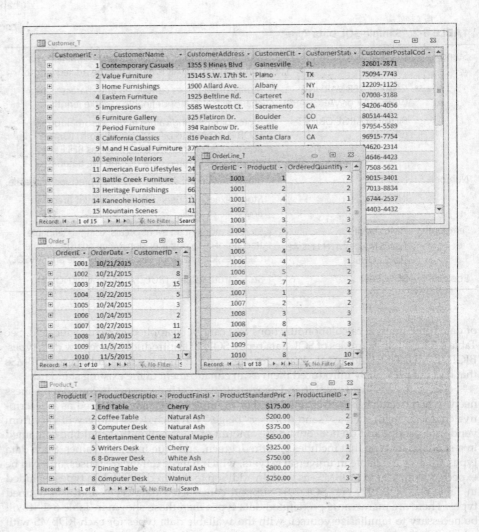

The remainder of the chapter will illustrate DDL, DML, and DCL commands.
Figure 6-4 gives an overview of where the various types of commands are used
throughout the database development process. We will use the following notation in
the illustrative SQL commands:

1. All-capitalized words denote commands. Type them exactly as shown, though
   capitalization may not be required by the RDBMS. Some RDBMSs will always
   show data names in output using all capital letters, even if they can be entered
   in mixed case. (This is the style of Oracle, which is what we follow except where
   noted.) Tables, columns, named constraints, and so forth are shown in mixed
   case. Remember that table names follow the "underscore T" convention. SQL
   commands do not have an "underscore" and so should be easy to distinguish
   from table and column names. Also, RDBMSs do not like embedded spaces in
   data names, so multiple-word data names from ERDs are entered with the words
   together, without spaces between them (following our logical data model convention). A consequence is that, for example, a column named QtyOnHand will
   become QTYONHAND when it is displayed by many RDBMSs. (You can use the
   ALIAS clause in a SELECT to rename a column name to a more readable value
   for display.)
2. Lowercase and mixed-case words denote values that must be supplied by the user.
3. Brackets enclose optional syntax.
4. An ellipsis (...) indicates that the accompanying syntactic clause may be repeated
   as necessary.

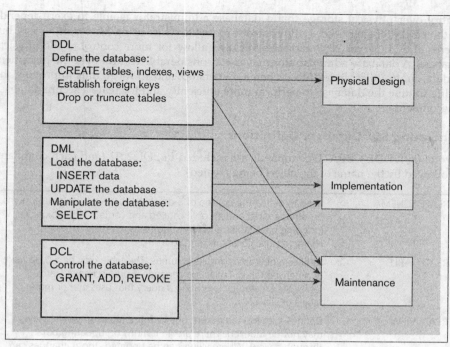

FIGURE 6-4 DDL, DML, DCL, and the database development process

5. Each SQL command ends with a semicolon (;). In interactive mode, when the user presses Enter, the SQL command will execute. Be alert for alternate conventions, such as typing GO or having to include a continuation symbol such as a hyphen at the end of each line used in the command. The spacing and indentations shown here are included for readability and are not a required part of standard SQL syntax.

We will start our discussion with coverage of how to create a database, create and modify its structure, and insert and modify data. After that we will move to a conversation on queries, which allow data retrieval with SQL. This is a natural order because it would be difficult to perform queries without a database, tables, and data in them. If, however, you want to review the simpler material on queries first, feel free to jump ahead to the section on "PROCESSING SINGLE TABLES" on p. 261 and return back here once you have studied that material first.

DEFINING A DATABASE IN SQL

Because most systems allocate storage space to contain base tables, views, constraints, indexes, and other database objects when a database is created, you may not be allowed to create a database. Because of this, the privilege of creating databases may be reserved for the database administrator, and you may need to ask to have a database created. Students at a university may be assigned an account that gives access to an existing database, or they may be allowed to create their own database in a limited amount of allocated storage space (sometimes called *perm space* or *table space*). In any case, the basic syntax for creating a database is

CREATE SCHEMA database_name; AUTHORIZATION owner_user id

The database will be owned by the authorized user, although it is possible for other specified users to work with the database or even to transfer ownership of the database. Physical storage of the database is dependent on both the hardware and software environment and is usually the concern of the system administrator. The amount of control over physical storage that a database administrator is able to exert depends on the RDBMS being used. Little control is possible when using Microsoft Access, but Microsoft SQL Server 2008 and later versions allow for more control of the physical database. A database administrator may exert considerable control over the placement of data, control files, index files, schema ownership, and so forth, thus improving the ability to tune the database to perform more efficiently and to create a secure database environment.

Generating SQL Database Definitions

Several SQL DDL CREATE commands are included in SQL:2011 (and each command is followed by the name of the object being created):

CREATE SCHEMA	Used to define the portion of a database that a particular user owns. Schemas are dependent on a catalog and contain schema objects, including base tables and views, domains, constraints, assertions, character sets, collations, and so forth.
CREATE TABLE	Defines a new table and its columns. The table may be a base table or a derived table. Tables are dependent on a schema. Derived tables are created by executing a query that uses one or more tables or views.
CREATE VIEW	Defines a logical table from one or more tables or views. Views may not be indexed. There are limitations on updating data through a view. Where views can be updated, those changes can be transferred to the underlying base tables originally referenced to create the view.

You don't have to be perfect when you create these objects, and they don't have to last forever. Each of these CREATE commands can be reversed by using a DROP command. Thus, DROP TABLE *tablename* will destroy a table, including its definition, contents, and any constraints, views, or indexes associated with it. Usually only the table creator may delete the table. DROP SCHEMA or DROP VIEW will also destroy the named schema or view. ALTER TABLE may be used to change the definition of an existing base table by adding, dropping, or changing a column or by dropping a constraint. Some RDBMSs will not allow you to alter a table in a way that the current data in that table will violate the new definitions (e.g., you cannot create a new constraint when current data will violate that constraint, or if you change the precision of a numeric column you may lose the extra precision of more precise existing values).

There are also five other CREATE commands included in the SQL standards; we list them here but do not cover them in this text:

CREATE CHARACTER SET	Allows the user to define a character set for text strings and aids in the globalization of SQL by enabling the use of languages other than English. Each character set contains a set of characters, a way to represent each character internally, a data format used for this representation, and a collation, or way of sorting the character set.
CREATE COLLATION	A named schema object that specifies the order that a character set will assume. Existing collations may be manipulated to create a new collation.
CREATE TRANSLATION	A named set of rules that maps characters from a source character set to a destination character set for translation or conversion purposes.
CREATE ASSERTION	A schema object that establishes a CHECK constraint that is violated if the constraint is false.
CREATE DOMAIN	A schema object that establishes a domain, or set of valid values, for an attribute. Data type will be specified, and a default value, collation, or other constraint may also be specified, if desired.

Creating Tables

Once the data model is designed and normalized, the columns needed for each table can be defined, using the SQL CREATE TABLE command. The general syntax for CREATE TABLE is shown in Figure 6-5. Here is a series of steps to follow when preparing to create a table:

1. Identify the appropriate data type, including length, precision, and scale, if required, for each attribute.
2. Identify the columns that should accept null values, as discussed in Chapter 5. Column controls that indicate a column cannot be null are established when a table is created and are enforced for every update of the table when data are entered.
3. Identify the columns that need to be unique. When a column control of UNIQUE is established for a column, the data in that column must have a different value for each row of data within that table (i.e., no duplicate values). Where a column or set of columns is designated as UNIQUE, that column or set of columns is a candidate key, as discussed in Chapter 4. Although each base table may have multiple candidate keys, only one candidate key may be designated as a PRIMARY KEY. When a column(s) is specified as the PRIMARY KEY, that column(s) is also assumed to be NOT NULL, even if NOT NULL is not explicitly stated. UNIQUE and PRIMARY KEY are both column constraints. Note that a table with a composite primary key, OrderLine_T, is defined in Figure 6-6. The OrderLine_PK constraint includes both OrderID and ProductID in the primary key constraint, thus creating a composite key. Additional attributes may be included within the parentheses as needed to create the composite key.
4. Identify all primary key–foreign key mates, as presented in Chapter 4. Foreign keys can be established immediately, as a table is created, or later by altering the table. The parent table in such a parent–child relationship should be created first so that the child table will reference an existing parent table when it is created. The column constraint REFERENCES can be used to enforce referential integrity (e.g., the Order_FK constraint on the Order_T table).
5. Determine values to be inserted in any columns for which a default value is desired. DEFAULT can be used to define a value that is automatically inserted when no value is inserted during data entry. In Figure 6-6, the command that creates the Order_T table has defined a default value of SYSDATE (Oracle's name for the current date) for the OrderDate attribute.
6. Identify any columns for which domain specifications may be stated that are more constrained than those established by data type. Using CHECK as a column constraint, it may be possible to establish validation rules for values to be inserted into the database. In Figure 6-6, creation of the Product_T table includes a check constraint, which lists the possible values for Product_Finish. Thus, even though an entry of 'White Maple' would meet the VARCHAR2 data type constraints, it would be rejected because 'White Maple' is not in the checklist.

FIGURE 6-5 General syntax of the CREATE TABLE statement used in data definition language

```
CREATE TABLE tablename
( {column definition    [table constraint] } . , . .
[ON COMMIT {DELETE | PRESERVE} ROWS] );

where column definition ::=
column_name
        {domain name | datatype [(size)] }
        [column_constraint_clause. . .]
        [default value]
        [collate clause]

and table constraint ::=
        [CONSTRAINT constraint_name]
        Constraint_type [constraint_attributes]
```

FIGURE 6-6 SQL database definition commands for Pine Valley Furniture Company (Oracle 12c)

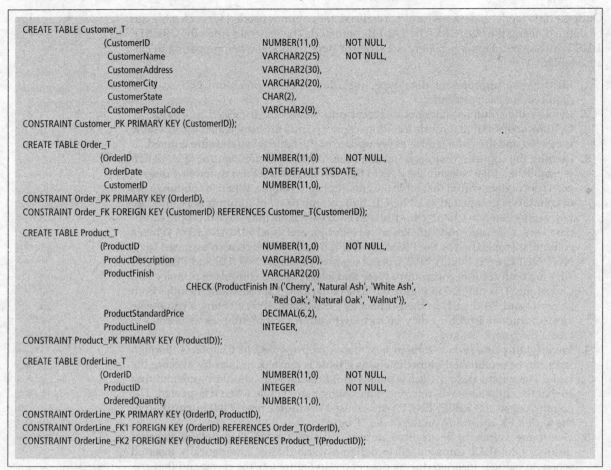

```
CREATE TABLE Customer_T
            (CustomerID                NUMBER(11,0)        NOT NULL,
             CustomerName              VARCHAR2(25)        NOT NULL,
             CustomerAddress           VARCHAR2(30),
             CustomerCity              VARCHAR2(20),
             CustomerState             CHAR(2),
             CustomerPostalCode        VARCHAR2(9),
CONSTRAINT Customer_PK PRIMARY KEY (CustomerID));

CREATE TABLE Order_T
            (OrderID                   NUMBER(11,0)        NOT NULL,
             OrderDate                 DATE DEFAULT SYSDATE,
             CustomerID                NUMBER(11,0),
CONSTRAINT Order_PK PRIMARY KEY (OrderID),
CONSTRAINT Order_FK FOREIGN KEY (CustomerID) REFERENCES Customer_T(CustomerID));

CREATE TABLE Product_T
            (ProductID                 NUMBER(11,0)        NOT NULL,
             ProductDescription        VARCHAR2(50),
             ProductFinish             VARCHAR2(20)
                            CHECK (ProductFinish IN ('Cherry', 'Natural Ash', 'White Ash',
                                        'Red Oak', 'Natural Oak', 'Walnut')),
             ProductStandardPrice      DECIMAL(6,2),
             ProductLineID             INTEGER,
CONSTRAINT Product_PK PRIMARY KEY (ProductID));

CREATE TABLE OrderLine_T
            (OrderID                   NUMBER(11,0)        NOT NULL,
             ProductID                 INTEGER             NOT NULL,
             OrderedQuantity           NUMBER(11,0),
CONSTRAINT OrderLine_PK PRIMARY KEY (OrderID, ProductID),
CONSTRAINT OrderLine_FK1 FOREIGN KEY (OrderID) REFERENCES Order_T(OrderID),
CONSTRAINT OrderLine_FK2 FOREIGN KEY (ProductID) REFERENCES Product_T(ProductID));
```

7. Create the table and any desired indexes, using the CREATE TABLE and CREATE INDEX statements. (CREATE INDEX is not a part of the SQL:2011 standard because indexing is used to address performance issues, but it is available in most RDBMSs.)

PINE VALLEY FURNITURE

Figure 6-6 shows database definition commands using Oracle 12c that include additional column constraints, as well as primary and foreign keys given names. For example, the Customer table's primary key is CustomerID. The primary key constraint is named Customer_PK. In Oracle, for example, once a constraint has been given a meaningful name by the user, a database administrator will find it easy to identify the primary key constraint on the customer table because its name, Customer_PK, will be the value of the constraint_name column in the DBA_CONSTRAINTS table. If a meaningful constraint name were not assigned, a 16-byte system identifier would be assigned automatically. These identifiers are difficult to read and even more difficult to match up with user-defined constraints. Documentation about how system identifiers are generated is not available, and the method can be changed without notification. Bottom line: Give all constraints names or be prepared for extra work later.

When a foreign key constraint is defined, referential integrity will be enforced. This is good: We want to enforce business rules in the database. Fortunately, you are still allowed to have a null value for the foreign key (signifying a zero cardinality of the relationship) as long as you do not put the NOT NULL clause on the foreign key column. For example, if you try to add an order with an invalid CustomerID value (every order has to be related to some customer, so the minimum cardinality is one next to Customer for the Submits relationship in Figure 2-22), you will receive an error message. Each DBMS vendor generates its own error messages, and these messages may be difficult to interpret. Microsoft Access, being intended for both personal and professional use, provides simple error messages in dialog boxes. For example, for a referential integrity violation, Access displays the following error message: "You cannot add or change a record because a related record is required in table Customer_T." No record will be added to Order_T until that record references an existing customer in the Customer_T table.

Sometimes a user will want to create a table that is similar to one that already exists. SQL:1999 introduced the capability of adding a LIKE clause to the CREATE TABLE statement to allow for the copying of the existing structure of one or more tables into a new table. For example, a table can be used to store data that are questionable until the questionable data can be reviewed by an administrator. This exception table has the same structure as the verified transaction table, and missing or conflicting data will be reviewed and resolved before those transactions are appended to the transaction table. SQL:2008 expanded the CREATE...LIKE capability by allowing additional information, such as table constraints, from the original table to be easily ported to the new table when it is created. The new table exists independently of the original table. Inserting a new instance into the original table will have no effect on the new table. However, if the attempt to insert the new instance triggers an exception, the trigger can be written so that the data are stored in the new table to be reviewed later.

Oracle, MySQL, and some other RDBMSs have an interesting "dummy" table that is automatically defined with each database—the Dual table. The Dual table is used to run an SQL command against a system variable. For example,

```
SELECT Sysdate FROM Dual;
```

displays the current date, and

```
SELECT 8 + 4 FROM Dual;
```

displays the result of this arithmetic.

Creating Data Integrity Controls

We have seen the syntax that establishes foreign keys in Figure 6-6. To establish referential integrity constraint between two tables with a 1:*M* relationship in the relational data model, the primary key of the table on the one side will be referenced by a column in the table on the many side of the relationship. Referential integrity means that a value in the matching column on the many side must correspond to a value in the primary key for some row in the table on the one side or be NULL. The SQL REFERENCES clause prevents a foreign key value from being added if it is not already a valid value in the referenced primary key column, but there are other integrity issues.

If a CustomerID value is changed, the connection between that customer and orders placed by that customer will be ruined. The REFERENCES clause prevents making such a change in the foreign key value, but not in the primary key value. This problem could be handled by asserting that primary key values cannot be changed once they are established. In this case, updates to the customer table will be handled in most systems by including an ON UPDATE RESTRICT clause. Then, any updates that would delete or change a primary key value will be rejected unless no foreign key references that value in any child table. See Figure 6-7 for the syntax associated with updates.

Another solution is to pass the change through to the child table(s) by using the ON UPDATE CASCADE option. Then, if a customer ID number is changed, that change will flow through (cascade) to the child table, Order_T, and the customer's ID will also be updated in the Order_T table.

A third solution is to allow the update on Customer_T but to change the involved CustomerID value in the Order_T table to NULL by using the ON UPDATE SET NULL

FIGURE 6-7 Ensuring data
integrity through updates

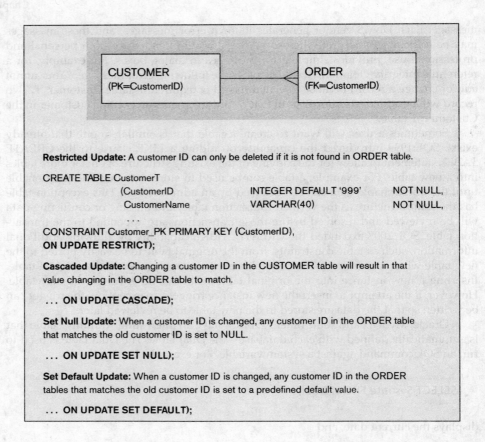

Restricted Update: A customer ID can only be deleted if it is not found in ORDER table.

CREATE TABLE CustomerT
                (CustomerID   INTEGER DEFAULT '999'   NOT NULL,
                 CustomerName   VARCHAR(40)   NOT NULL,
                 . . .
CONSTRAINT Customer_PK PRIMARY KEY (CustomerID),
ON UPDATE RESTRICT);

Cascaded Update: Changing a customer ID in the CUSTOMER table will result in that value changing in the ORDER table to match.

   . . . **ON UPDATE CASCADE);**

Set Null Update: When a customer ID is changed, any customer ID in the ORDER table that matches the old customer ID is set to NULL.

   . . . **ON UPDATE SET NULL);**

Set Default Update: When a customer ID is changed, any customer ID in the ORDER tables that matches the old customer ID is set to a predefined default value.

   . . . **ON UPDATE SET DEFAULT);**

option. In this case, using the SET NULL option would result in losing the connection between the order and the customer, which is not a desired effect. The most flexible option to use would be the CASCADE option. If a customer record were deleted, ON DELETE RESTRICT, CASCADE, or SET NULL would also be available. With DELETE RESTRICT, the customer record could not be deleted unless there were no orders from that customer in the Order_T table. With DELETE CASCADE, removing the customer would remove all associated order records from Order_T. With DELETE SET NULL, the order records for that customer would be set to null before the customer's record was deleted. With DELETE SET DEFAULT, the order records for that customer would be set to a default value before the customer's record was deleted. DELETE RESTRICT would probably make the most sense. Not all SQL RDBMSs provide for primary key referential integrity. In that case, update and delete permissions on the primary key column may be revoked.

Changing Table Definitions

Base table definitions may be changed by using ALTER on the column specifications. The ALTER TABLE command can be used to add new columns to an existing table. Existing columns may also be altered. Table constraints may be added or dropped. The ALTER TABLE command may include keywords such as ADD, DROP, or ALTER and allow the column's names, data type, length, and constraints to be changed. Usually, when adding a new column, its status will be NULL so that data that have already been entered in the table can be dealt with. When the new column is created, it is added to all of the instances in the table, and a value of NULL would be the most reasonable. The ALTER command cannot be used to change a view.

Syntax:

ALTER TABLE table_name alter_table_action;

Some of the alter_table_actions available are:

ADD [COLUMN] column_definition
ALTER [COLUMN] column_name **SET DEFAULT** default-value
ALTER [COLUMN] column_name **DROP DEFAULT**
DROP [COLUMN] column_name **[RESTRICT] [CASCADE]**
ADD table_constraint

Command: To add a customer type column named CustomerType to the Customer table.

ALTER TABLE CUSTOMER_T
ADD COLUMN CustomerType VARCHAR2 (10) DEFAULT "Commercial";

The ALTER command is invaluable for adapting a database to inevitable modifications due to changing requirements, prototyping, evolutionary development, and mistakes. It is also useful when performing a bulk data load into a table that contains a foreign key. The constraint may be temporarily dropped. Later, after the bulk data load has finished, the constraint can be enabled. When the constraint is reenabled, it is possible to generate a log of any records that have referential integrity problems. Rather than have the data load balk each time such a problem occurs during the bulk load, the database administrator can simply review the log and reconcile the few (hopefully few) records that were problematic.

Removing Tables

To remove a table from a database, the owner of the table may use the DROP TABLE command. Views are dropped by using the similar DROP VIEW command.

Command: To drop a table from a database schema.

DROP TABLE Customer_T;

This command will drop the table and save any pending changes to the database. To drop a table, you must either own the table or have been granted the DROP ANY TABLE system privilege. Dropping a table will also cause associated indexes and privileges granted to be dropped. The DROP TABLE command can be qualified by the keywords RESTRICT or CASCADE. If RESTRICT is specified, the command will fail, and the table will not be dropped if there are any dependent objects, such as views or constraints, that currently reference the table. If CASCADE is specified, all dependent objects will also be dropped as the table is dropped. Many RDBMSs allow users to retain the table's structure but remove all of the data that have been entered in the table with its TRUNCATE TABLE command. Commands for updating and deleting part of the data in a table are covered in the next section.

INSERTING, UPDATING, AND DELETING DATA

Once tables have been created, it is necessary to populate them with data and maintain those data before queries can be written. The SQL command that is used to populate tables is the INSERT command. When entering a value for every column in the table, you can use a command such as the following, which was used to add the first row of data to the Customer_T table for Pine Valley Furniture Company. Notice that the data values must be ordered in the same order as the columns in the table.

PINE
VALLEY
FURNITURE

Command: To insert a row of data into a table where a value will be inserted for every attribute.

INSERT INTO Customer_T VALUES
(001, 'Contemporary Casuals', '1355 S. Himes Blvd.', 'Gainesville', 'FL', 32601);

When data will not be entered into every column in the table, either enter the value NULL for the empty fields or specify those columns to which data are to be added. Here, too, the data values must be in the same order as the columns have been specified in the INSERT command. For example, the following statement was used to insert one row of data into the Product_T table, because there was no product line ID for the end table.

Command: To insert a row of data into a table where some attributes will be left null.

```
INSERT INTO Product_T (ProductID,
ProductDescription, ProductFinish, ProductStandardPrice)
    VALUES (1, 'End Table', 'Cherry', 175, 8);
```

In general, the INSERT command places a new row in a table, based on values supplied in the statement, copies one or more rows derived from other database data into a table, or extracts data from one table and inserts them into another. If you want to populate a table, CaCustomer_T, that has the same structure as CUSTOMER_T, with only Pine Valley's California customers, you could use the following INSERT command.

Command: Populating a table by using a subset of another table with the same structure.

```
INSERT INTO CaCustomer_T
SELECT * FROM Customer_T
    WHERE CustomerState = 'CA';
```

In many cases, we want to generate a unique primary identifier or primary key every time a row is added to a table. Customer identification numbers are a good example of a situation where this capability would be helpful. SQL:2008 added a new feature, identity columns, that removes the previous need to create a procedure to generate a sequence and then apply it to the insertion of data. To take advantage of this, the CREATE TABLE Customer_T statement displayed in Figure 6-6 may be modified (emphasized by bold print) as follows:

```
CREATE TABLE Customer_T
(CustomerID INTEGER GENERATED ALWAYS AS IDENTITY
    (START WITH 1
    INCREMENT BY 1
    MINVALUE 1
    MAXVALUE 10000
    NO CYCLE),
CustomerName              VARCHAR2(25) NOT NULL,
CustomerAddress           VARCHAR2(30),
CustomerCity              VARCHAR2(20),
CustomerState             CHAR(2),
CustomerPostalCode        VARCHAR2(9),
CONSTRAINT Customer_PK PRIMARY KEY (CustomerID));
```

Only one column can be an identity column in a table. When a new customer is added, the CustomerID value will be assigned implicitly if the vendor has implemented identity columns.

Thus, the command that adds a new customer to Customer_T will change from this:

```
INSERT INTO Customer_T VALUES
(001, 'Contemporary Casuals', '1355 S. Himes Blvd.', 'Gainesville',
    'FL', 32601);
```

to this:

```
INSERT INTO Customer_T VALUES
('Contemporary Casuals', '1355 S. Himes Blvd.', 'Gainesville', 'FL', 32601);
```

The primary key value, 001, does not need to be entered, and the syntax to accomplish the automatic sequencing has been simplified in SQL:2008. This capability is available in Oracle starting with version 12c.

Batch Input

The INSERT command is used to enter one row of data at a time or to add multiple rows as the result of a query. Some versions of SQL have a special command or utility for entering multiple rows of data as a batch: the INPUT command. For example, Oracle includes a program, SQL*Loader, which runs from the command line and can be used to load data from a file into the database. SQL Server includes a BULK INSERT command with Transact-SQL for importing data into a table or view. (These powerful and feature rich programs are not within the scope of this text.)

Deleting Database Contents

Rows can be deleted from a database individually or in groups. Suppose Pine Valley Furniture decides that it will no longer deal with customers located in Hawaii. Customer_T rows for customers with addresses in Hawaii could all be eliminated using the next command.

Command: Deleting rows that meet a certain criterion from the Customer table.

```
DELETE FROM Customer_T
WHERE CustomerState = 'HI';
```

The simplest form of DELETE eliminates all rows of a table.

Command: Deleting all rows from the Customer table.

```
DELETE FROM Customer_T;
```

This form of the command should be used very carefully!

Deletion must also be done with care when rows from several relations are involved. For example, if we delete a Customer_T row, as in the previous query, before deleting associated Order_T rows, we will have a referential integrity violation, and the DELETE command will not execute. (Note: Including the ON DELETE clause with a field definition can mitigate such a problem. Refer to the "Creating Data Integrity Controls" section in this chapter if you've forgotten about the ON clause.) SQL will actually eliminate the records selected by a DELETE command. Therefore, always execute a SELECT command first to display the records that would be deleted and visually verify that only the desired rows are included.

Updating Database Contents

To update data in SQL, we must inform the DBMS which relation, columns, and rows are involved. If an incorrect price is entered for the dining table in the Product_T table, the following SQL UPDATE statement would establish the correction.

Command: To modify standard price of product 7 in the Product table to 775.

```
UPDATE Product_T
SET ProductStandardPrice = 775
    WHERE ProductID = 7;
```

The SET command can also change a value to NULL; the syntax is SET column-name = NULL. As with DELETE, the WHERE clause in an UPDATE command may contain a subquery, but the table being updated may not be referenced in the subquery. Subqueries are discussed in Chapter 7.

Since SQL:2008, the SQL standard has included a new keyword, MERGE, that makes updating a table easier. Many database applications need to update master tables with new data. A Purchases_T table, for example, might include rows with data about new products and rows that change the standard price of existing products. Updating Product_T can be accomplished by using INSERT to add the new products and UPDATE to modify StandardPrice in an SQL:1999 DBMS. SQL:2008 compliant DBMSs can accomplish the update and the insert in one step by using MERGE:

```
MERGE INTO Product_T AS PROD
USING
(SELECT ProductID, ProductDescription, ProductFinish,
ProductStandardPrice, ProductLineID FROM Purchases_T) AS PURCH
     ON (PROD.ProductID = PURCH.ProductID)
WHEN MATCHED THEN UPDATE
     PROD.ProductStandardPrice = PURCH.ProductStandardPrice
WHEN NOT MATCHED THEN INSERT
     (ProductID, ProductDescription, ProductFinish, ProductStandardPrice,
     ProductLineID)
     VALUES(PURCH.ProductID, PURCH.ProductDescription,
     PURCH.ProductFinish, PURCH.ProductStandardPrice,
       PURCH.ProductLineID);
```

INTERNAL SCHEMA DEFINITION IN RDBMSS

The internal schema of a relational database can be controlled for processing and storage efficiency. The following are some techniques used for tuning the operational performance of the relational database internal data model:

1. Choosing to index primary and/or secondary keys to increase the speed of row selection, table joining, and row ordering. You can also drop indexes to increase speed of table updating. You may want to review the section in Chapter 5 on selecting indexes.
2. Selecting file organizations for base tables that match the type of processing activity on those tables (e.g., keeping a table physically sorted by a frequently used reporting sort key).
3. Selecting file organizations for indexes, which are also tables, appropriate to the way the indexes are used and allocating extra space for an index file so that an index can grow without having to be reorganized.
4. Clustering data so that related rows of frequently joined tables are stored close together in secondary storage to minimize retrieval time.
5. Maintaining statistics about tables and their indexes so that the DBMS can find the most efficient ways to perform various database operations.

Not all of these techniques are available in all SQL systems. Indexing and clustering are typically available, however, so we discuss these in the following sections.

Creating Indexes

Indexes are created in most RDBMSs to provide rapid random and sequential access to base-table data. Because the ISO SQL standards do not generally address performance issues, no standard syntax for creating indexes is included. The examples given here use Oracle syntax and give a feel for how indexes are handled in most RDBMSs. Note that although users do not directly refer to indexes when writing any SQL command, the DBMS recognizes which existing indexes would improve query performance. Indexes can usually be created for both primary and secondary keys and both single and concat-enated (multiple-column) keys. In some systems, users can choose between ascending and descending sequences for the keys in an index.

For example, an alphabetical index on CustomerName in the Customer_T table in Oracle is created here.

Command: To create an alphabetical index on customer name in the Customer table.

```
CREATE INDEX Name_IDX ON Customer_T (CustomerName);
```

RDBMs usually support several different types of indexes, each of which assists in different kinds of keyword searches. For example, in MySQL you can create the fol-lowing index types: unique (appropriate for primary keys), nonunique (secondary keys), fulltext (used for full-text searches), spatial (used for spatial data types), and hash (which is used for in-memory tables).

Indexes can be created or dropped at any time. If data already exist in the key column(s), index population will automatically occur for the existing data. If an index is defined as UNIQUE (using the syntax CREATE UNIQUE INDEX...) and the existing data violate this condition, the index creation will fail. Once an index is created, it will be updated as data are entered, updated, or deleted.

When we no longer need tables, views, or indexes, we use the associated DROP statements. For example, the NAME_IDX index from the previous example is dropped here.

Command: To remove the index on the customer name in the Customer table.

```
DROP INDEX Name_IDX;
```

Although it is possible to index every column in a table, use caution when decid-ing to create a new index. Each index consumes extra storage space and also requires overhead maintenance time whenever indexed data change value. Together, these costs may noticeably slow retrieval response times and cause annoying delays for online users. A system may use only one index even if several are available for keys in a complex qualification. A database designer must know exactly how indexes are used by the particular RDBMS in order to make wise choices about indexing. Oracle includes an explain plan tool that can be used to look at the order in which an SQL statement will be processed and at the indexes that will be used. The output also includes a cost estimate that can be compared with estimates from running the statement with different indexes to determine which is most efficient.

PROCESSING SINGLE TABLES

"Processing single tables" may seem like Friday night at the hottest club in town, but we have something else in mind. Sorry, no dating suggestions (and sorry for the pun).

Four data manipulation language commands are used in SQL. We have talked briefly about three of them (UPDATE, INSERT, and DELETE) and have seen several examples of the fourth, SELECT. Although the UPDATE, INSERT, and DELETE commands allow mod-ification of the data in the tables, it is the SELECT command, with its various clauses, that allows users to query the data contained in the tables and ask many different questions or create ad hoc queries. The basic construction of an SQL command is fairly simple and easy to learn. Don't let that fool you; SQL is a powerful tool that enables users to specify com-plex data analysis processes. However, because the basic syntax is relatively easy to learn, it is also easy to write SELECT queries that are syntactically correct but do not answer the exact question that is intended. Before running queries against a large production data-base, always test them carefully on a small test set of data to be sure that they are returning the correct results. In addition to checking the query results manually, it is often possible to parse queries into smaller parts, examine the results of these simpler queries, and then recombine them. This will ensure that they act together in the expected way. We begin by exploring SQL queries that affect only a single table. In Chapter 7, we join tables and use queries that require more than one table.

Clauses of the SELECT Statement

Most SQL data retrieval statements include the following three clauses:

SELECT	Lists the columns (including expressions involving columns) from base tables, derived tables, or views to be projected into the table that will be the result of the command. (That's the technical way of saying it lists the data you want to display.)
FROM	Identifies the tables, derived tables, or views from which columns can be chosen to appear in the result table and includes the tables, derived tables, or views needed to join tables to process the query.
WHERE	Includes the conditions for row selection within the items in the FROM clause and the conditions between tables, derived tables, or views for joining. Because SQL is considered a set manipulation language, the WHERE clause is important in defining the set of rows being manipulated.

PINE
VALLEY
FURNITURE

The first two clauses are required, and the third is necessary when only certain table rows are to be retrieved or multiple tables are to be joined. (Most examples for this section are drawn from the data shown in Figure 6-3.) For example, we can display product name and quantity on hand from the PRODUCT table for all Pine Valley Furniture Company products that have a standard price of less than $275.

Query: Which products have a standard price of less than $275?

```
SELECT ProductDescription, ProductStandardPrice
  FROM Product_T
    WHERE ProductStandardPrice < 275;
```

Result:

PRODUCTDESCRIPTION	PRODUCTSTANDARDPRICE
End Table	175
Computer Desk	250
Coffee Table	200

As stated before, in this text, we show results (except where noted) in the style of Oracle, which means that column headings are in all capital letters. If this is too annoying for users, then the data names should be defined with an underscore between the words rather than run-on words, or you can use an alias (described later in this section) to redefine a column heading for display.

Every SELECT statement returns a result table (a set of rows) when it executes. So, SQL is consistent—tables in, tables out of every query. This becomes important with more complex queries because we can use the result of one query (a table) as part of another query (e.g., we can include a SELECT statement as one of the elements in the FROM clause, creating a derived table, which we illustrate later in this chapter).

Two special keywords can be used along with the list of columns to display: DISTINCT and *. If the user does not wish to see duplicate rows in the result, SELECT DISTINCT may be used. In the preceding example, if the other computer desk carried by Pine Valley Furniture also had a cost of $250, the results of the query would have had duplicate rows. SELECT DISTINCT ProductDescription would display a result table without the duplicate rows. SELECT *, where * is used as a wildcard to indicate all columns, displays all columns from all the items in the FROM clause.

Also, note that the clauses of a SELECT statement must be kept in order, or syntax error messages will occur and the query will not execute. It may also be necessary to qualify the names of the database objects according to the SQL version being used. If there is any ambiguity in an SQL command, you must indicate exactly from which table, derived table, or view the requested data are to come. For example, in Figure 6-3 CustomerID is a column in both Customer_T and Order_T. When you own the database being used (i.e., the user created the tables) and you want CustomerID to come from Customer_T, specify it by asking for Customer_T.CustomerID. If you want CustomerID to come from Order_T, then ask for Order_T.CustomerID. Even if you don't care which table CustomerID comes from, it must be specified because SQL can't resolve the ambiguity without user direction. When you are allowed to use data created by someone else, you must also specify the owner of the table by adding the owner's user ID. Now a request to SELECT the CustomerID from Customer_T may look like this: <OWNER_ID>.Customer_T.CustomerID. The examples in this text assume that the reader owns the tables or views being used, as the SELECT statements will be easier to read without the qualifiers. Qualifiers will be included where necessary and may always be included in statements if desired. Problems may occur when qualifiers are left out, but no problems will occur when they are included.

If typing the qualifiers and column names is wearisome (computer keyboards aren't, yet, built to accommodate the two-thumb cellphone texting technique), or if the column names will not be meaningful to those who are reading the reports, establish aliases for data names that will then be used for the rest of the query. Although the SQL standard does not include aliases or synonyms, they are widely implemented and aid in readability and simplicity in query construction.

Query: What is the address of the customer named Home Furnishings? Use an alias, Name, for the customer name. (The AS clauses are bolded for emphasis only.)

```
SELECT CUST.CustomerName AS Name, CUST.CustomerAddress
   FROM ownerid.Customer_T AS Cust
      WHERE Name = 'Home Furnishings';
```

This retrieval statement will give the following result in many versions of SQL, but not in all of them. In Oracle's SQL*Plus, the alias for the column cannot be used in the rest of the SELECT statement, except in a HAVING clause, so in order for the query to run, CustomerName would have to be used in the last line rather than Name. Notice that the column header prints as Name rather than CustomerName and that the table alias may be used in the SELECT clause even though it is not defined until the FROM clause.

Result:

NAME	CUSTOMERADDRESS
Home Furnishings	1900 Allard Ave.

You've likely concluded that SQL generates pretty plain output. Using an alias is a good way to make column headings more readable. (Aliases also have other uses, which we'll address later.) Many RDBMSs have other proprietary SQL clauses to improve the display of data. For example, Oracle has the COLUMN clause of the SELECT statement, which can be used to change the text for the column heading, change alignment of the column heading, reformat the column value, or control wrapping of data in a column, among other properties. You may want to investigate such capabilities for the RDBMS you are using.

When you use the SELECT clause to pick out the columns for a result table, the columns can be rearranged so that they will be ordered differently in the result table than in the original table. In fact, they will be displayed in the same order as they are included in the SELECT statement. Look back at Product_T in Figure 6-3 to see the different ordering of the base table from the result table for this query.

Query: List the unit price, product name, and product ID for all products in the Product table.

```
SELECT ProductStandardPrice, ProductDescription, ProductID
FROM Product_T;
```

Result:

PRODUCTSTANDARDPRICE	PRODUCTDESCRIPTION	PRODUCTID
175	End Table	1
200	Coffee Table	2
375	Computer Desk	3
650	Entertainment Center	4
325	Writer's Desk	5
750	8-Drawer Desk	6
800	Dining Table	7
250	Computer Desk	8

Using Expressions

The basic SELECT...FROM...WHERE clauses can be used with a single table in a number of ways. You can create expressions, which are mathematical manipulations of the data in the table, or take advantage of stored functions, such as SUM or AVG, to manipulate the chosen rows of data from the table. Mathematical manipulations can be constructed by using the + for addition, – for subtraction, * for multiplication, and / for division. These operators can be used with any numeric columns. Expressions are computed for each row of the result table, such as displaying the difference between the standard price and unit cost of a product, or they can involve computations of columns and functions, such as standard price of a product multiplied by the amount of that product sold on a particular order (which would require summing OrderedQuantities). Some systems also have an operand called modulo, usually indicated by %. A modulo is the integer remainder that results from dividing two integers. For example, 14 % 4 is 2 because 14/4 is 3, with a remainder of 2. The SQL standard supports year-month and day-time intervals, which makes it possible to perform date and time arithmetic (e.g., to calculate someone's age from today's date and a person's birthday).

Perhaps you would like to know the current standard price of each product and its future price if all prices were increased by 10 percent. Using SQL*Plus, here are the query and the results.

Query: What are the standard price and standard price if increased by 10 percent for every product?

```
SELECT ProductID, ProductStandardPrice, ProductStandardPrice*1.1 AS
Plus10Percent
  FROM Product_T;
```

Result:

PRODUCTID	PRODUCTSTANDARDPRICE	PLUS10PERCENT
2	200.0000	220.00000
3	375.0000	412.50000
1	175.0000	192.50000
8	250.0000	275.00000
7	800.0000	880.00000
5	325.0000	357.50000
4	650.0000	715.00000
6	750.0000	825.00000

The precedence rules for the order in which complex expressions are evaluated are the same as those used in other programming languages and in algebra. Expressions in parentheses will be calculated first. When parentheses do not establish order, multiplication and division will be completed first, from left to right, followed by addition and subtraction, also left to right. To avoid confusion, use parentheses to establish order. Where parentheses are nested, the innermost calculations will be completed first.

Using Functions

Standard SQL identifies a wide variety of mathematical, string and date manipulation, and other functions. We will illustrate some of the mathematical functions in this section. You will want to investigate what functions are available with the DBMS you are using, some of which may be proprietary to that DBMS. The standard functions include the following:

Mathematical	MIN, MAX, COUNT, SUM, ROUND (to round up a number to a specific number of decimal places), TRUNC (to truncate insignificant digits), and MOD (for modular arithmetic)
String	LOWER (to change to all lower case), UPPER (to change to all capital letters), INITCAP (to change to only an initial capital letter), CONCAT (to concatenate), SUBSTR (to isolate certain character positions), and COALESCE (finding the first not NULL values in a list of columns)
Date	NEXT_DAY (to compute the next date in sequence), ADD_MONTHS (to compute a date a given number of months before or after a given date), and MONTHS_BETWEEN (to compute the number of months between specified dates)
Analytical	TOP (find the top n values in a set, e.g., the top 5 customers by total annual sales)

Perhaps you want to know the average standard price of all inventory items. To get the overall average value, use the AVG stored function. We can name the resulting expression with an alias, AveragePrice. Using SQL*Plus, here are the query and the results.

Query: What is the average standard price for all products in inventory?

```
SELECT AVG (ProductStandardPrice) AS AveragePrice
FROM Product_T;
```

Result:

```
AVERAGEPRICE
     440.625
```

SQL:1999 stored functions include ANY, AVG, COUNT, EVERY, GROUPING, MAX, MIN, SOME, and SUM. SQL:2008 added LN, EXP, POWER, SQRT, FLOOR, CEILING, and WIDTH_BUCKET. New functions tend to be added with each new SQL standard, and more functions were added in SQL:2003 and SQL:2008, many of which are for advanced analytical processing of data (e.g., calculating moving averages and statistical sampling of data). As seen in the above example, functions such as COUNT, MIN, MAX, SUM, and AVG of specified columns in the column list of a SELECT command may be used to specify that the resulting answer table is to contain aggregated data instead of row-level data. Using any of these aggregate functions will give a one-row answer.

Query: How many different items were ordered on order number 1004?

```
SELECT COUNT (*)
  FROM OrderLine_T
    WHERE OrderID = 1004;
```

Result:

```
COUNT (*)
    2
```

It seems that it would be simple enough to list order number 1004 by changing the query.

Query: How many different items were ordered on order number 1004, and what are they?

```
SELECT ProductID, COUNT (*)
  FROM OrderLine_T
    WHERE OrderID = 1004;
```

In Oracle, here is the result.

Result:

```
ERROR at line 1:
ORA-00937: not a single-group group function
```

And in Microsoft SQL Server, the result is as follows.

Result:

```
Column 'OrderLine_T.ProductID' is invalid in the select list because
it is not contained in an Aggregate function and there is no
GROUP BY clause.
```

The problem is that ProductID returns two values, 6 and 8, for the two rows selected, whereas COUNT returns one aggregate value, 2, for the set of rows with ID = 1004. In most implementations, SQL cannot return both a row value and a set value; users must run two separate queries, one that returns row information and one that returns set information.

A similar issue arises if we try to find the difference between the standard price of each product and the overall average standard price (which we calculated above). You might think the query would be

```
SELECT ProductStandardPrice – AVG(ProductStandardPrice)
  FROM Product_T;
```

However, again we have mixed a column value with an aggregate, which will cause an error. Remember that the FROM list can contain tables, derived tables, and views. One approach to developing a correct query is to make the aggregate the result of a derived table, as we do in the following sample query.

Query: Display for each product the difference between its standard price and the overall average standard price of all products.

```
SELECT ProductStandardPrice – PriceAvg AS Difference
  FROM Product_T, (SELECT AVG(ProductStandardPrice) AS PriceAvg
    FROM Product_T);
```

Result:

```
DIFFERENCE
  –240.63
   –65.63
  –265.63
  –190.63
   359.38
  –115.63
   209.38
   309.38
```

Also, it is easy to confuse the functions COUNT (*) and COUNT. The function COUNT (*), used in the previous query, counts all rows selected by a query, regardless of whether any of the rows contain null values. COUNT tallies only rows that contain values; it ignores all null values.

SUM and AVG can only be used with numeric columns. COUNT, COUNT (*), MIN, and MAX can be used with any data type. Using MIN on a text column, for example, will find the lowest value in the column, the one whose first column is closest to the beginning of the alphabet. SQL implementations interpret the order of the alphabet differently. For example, some systems may start with A–Z, then a–z, and then 0–9 and special characters. Others treat upper- and lowercase letters as being equivalent. Still others start with some special characters, then proceed to numbers, letters, and other special characters. Here is the query to ask for the first ProductName in Product_T alphabetically, which was done using the AMERICAN character set in Oracle 12c.

Query: Alphabetically, what is the first product name in the Product table?

```
SELECT MIN (ProductDescription)
   FROM Product_T;
```

It gives the following result, which demonstrates that numbers are sorted before letters in this character set. [Note: The following result is from Oracle. Microsoft SQL Server returns the same result but labels the column (No column name) in SQL Query Analyzer, unless the query specifies a name for the result.]

Result:

MIN(PRODUCTDESCRIPTION)
8-Drawer Desk

Using Wildcards

The use of the asterisk (*) as a wildcard in a SELECT statement has been previously shown. Wildcards may also be used in the WHERE clause when an exact match is not possible. Here, the keyword LIKE is paired with wildcard characters and usually a string containing the characters that are known to be desired matches. The wildcard character, %, is used to represent any collection of characters. Thus, using LIKE '%Desk' when searching ProductDescription will find all different types of desks carried by Pine Valley Furniture Company. The underscore (_) is used as a wildcard character to represent exactly one character rather than any collection of characters. Thus, using LIKE '_-drawer' when searching ProductName will find any products with specified drawers, such as 3-, 5-, or 8-drawer dressers.

Using Comparison Operators

With the exception of the very first SQL example in this section, we have used the equality comparison operator in our WHERE clauses. The first example used the greater (less) than operator. The most common comparison operators for SQL implementations are listed in Table 6-3. (Different SQL DBMSs can use different comparison operators.) You are used to thinking about using comparison operators with numeric data, but you can also use them with character data and dates in SQL. The query shown here asks for all orders placed after 10/24/2015.

Query: Which orders have been placed since 10/24/2015?

```
SELECT OrderID, OrderDate
   FROM Order_T
      WHERE OrderDate > '24-OCT-2015';
```

Notice that the date is enclosed in single quotes and that the format of the date is different from that shown in Figure 6-3, which was taken from Microsoft Access. The

TABLE 6-3 Comparison Operators in SQL

Operator	Meaning
=	Equal to
>	Greater than
>=	Greater than or equal to
<	Less than
<=	Less than or equal to
<>	Not equal to
!=	Not equal to

query was run in SQL*Plus. You should check the reference manual for the SQL language you are using to see how dates are to be formatted in queries and for data input.

Result:

ORDERID	ORDERDATE
1007	27-OCT-15
1008	30-OCT-15
1009	05-NOV-15
1010	05-NOV-15

Query: What furniture does Pine Valley carry that isn't made of cherry?

```
SELECT ProductDescription, ProductFinish
  FROM Product_T
    WHERE ProductFinish != 'Cherry';
```

Result:

PRODUCTDESCRIPTION	PRODUCTFINISH
Coffee Table	Natural Ash
Computer Desk	Natural Ash
Entertainment Center	Natural Maple
8-Drawer Desk	White Ash
Dining Table	Natural Ash
Computer Desk	Walnut

Using Null Values

Columns that are defined without the NOT NULL clause may be empty, and this may be a significant fact for an organization. You will recall that a null value means that a column is missing a value; the value is not zero or blank or any special code—there simply is no value. We have already seen that functions may produce different results when null values are present than when a column has a value of zero in all qualified rows. It is not uncommon, then, to first explore whether there are null values before deciding how to write other commands, or it may be that you simply want to see data about table rows where there are missing values. For example, before undertaking a postal mail advertising campaign, you might want to pose the following query.

Query: Display all customers for whom we do not know their postal code.

```
SELECT * FROM Customer_T WHERE CustomerPostalCode IS NULL;
```

Result:

Fortunately, this query returns 0 rows in the result in our sample database, so we can mail advertisements to all our customers because we know their postal codes. The term IS NOT NULL returns results for rows where the qualified column has a non-null value. This allows us to deal with rows that have values in a critical column, ignoring other rows.

Using Boolean Operators

You probably have taken a course or part of a course on finite or discrete mathematics—logic, Venn diagrams, and set theory, oh my! Remember we said that SQL is a set-oriented language, so there are many opportunities to use what you learned in finite math to write complex SQL queries. Some complex questions can be answered by adjusting the WHERE clause further. The Boolean or logical operators AND, OR, and NOT can be used to good purpose:

AND	Joins two or more conditions and returns results only when all conditions are true.
OR	Joins two or more conditions and returns results when any conditions are true.
NOT	Negates an expression.

If multiple Boolean operators are used in an SQL statement, NOT is evaluated first, then AND, then OR. For example, consider the following query.

Query A: List product name, finish, and standard price for all desks and all tables that cost more than $300 in the Product table.

```
SELECT ProductDescription, ProductFinish, ProductStandardPrice
    FROM Product_T
        WHERE ProductDescription LIKE '%Desk'
        OR ProductDescription LIKE '%Table'
        AND ProductStandardPrice > 300;
```

Result:

PRODUCTDESCRIPTION	PRODUCTFINISH	PRODUCTSTANDARDPRICE
Computer Desk	Natural Ash	375
Writer's Desk	Cherry	325
8-Drawer Desk	White Ash	750
Dining Table	Natural Ash	800
Computer Desk	Walnut	250

All of the desks are listed, even the computer desk that costs less than $300. Only one table is listed; the less expensive ones that cost less than $300 are not included. With this query (illustrated in Figure 6-8), the AND will be processed first, returning all tables with a standard price greater than $300. Then the part of the query before the OR

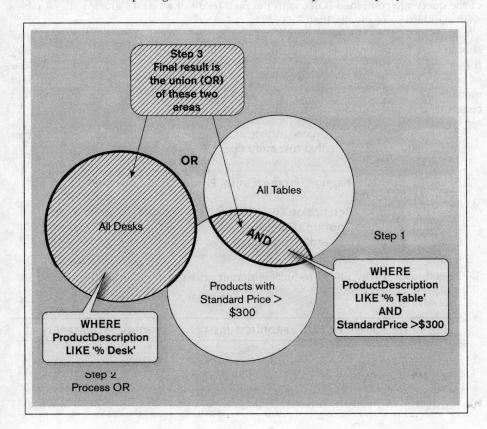

Step 3
Final result is
the union (OR)
of these two
areas

OR

All Tables

All Desks

AND

Step 1

WHERE
ProductDescription
LIKE '% Table'
AND
StandardPrice >$300

Products with
Standard Price >
$300

WHERE
ProductDescription
LIKE '% Desk'

Step 2
Process OR

FIGURE 6-8 Boolean query A without the use of parentheses

FIGURE 6-9 Boolean query B with the use of parentheses

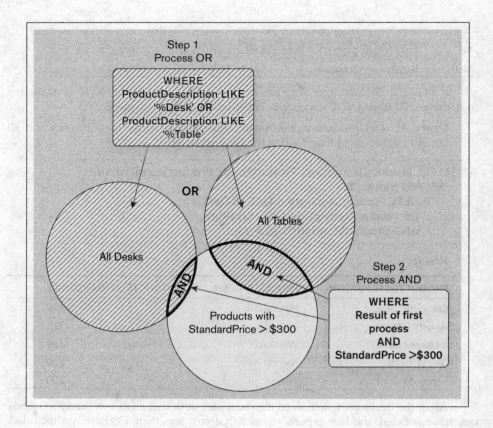

is processed, returning all desks, regardless of cost. Finally the results of the two parts of the query are combined (OR), with the final result of all desks along with all tables with standard price greater than $300.

If we had wanted to return only desks *and* tables costing more than $300, we should have put parentheses after the WHERE and before the AND, as shown in Query B below. Figure 6-9 shows the difference in processing caused by the judicious use of parentheses in the query. The result is all desks and tables with a standard price of more than $300, indicated by the filled area with the darker horizontal lines. The walnut computer desk has a standard price of $250 and is not included.

> *Query B:* List product name, finish, and standard price for all desks and tables in the PRODUCT table that cost more than $300.

```
SELECT ProductDescription, ProductFinish, ProductStandardPrice
  FROM Product_T;
  WHERE (ProductDescription LIKE '%Desk'
    OR ProductDescription LIKE '%Table')
    AND ProductStandardPrice > 300;
```

The results follow. Only products with unit price greater than $300 are included.

Result:

PRODUCTDESCRIPTION	PRODUCTFINISH	PRODUCTSTANDARDPRICE
Computer Desk	Natural Ash	375
Writer's Desk	Cherry	325
8-Drawer Desk	White Ash	750
Dining Table	Natural Ash	800

This example illustrates why SQL is considered a set-oriented, not a record-oriented, language. (C, Java, and Cobol are examples of record-oriented languages because they must process one record, or row, of a table at a time.) To answer this query, SQL will find the set of rows that are Desk products, and then it will union (i.e., merge) that set with the set of rows that are Table products. Finally, it will intersect (i.e., find common rows) the resultant set from this union with the set of rows that have a standard price above $300. If indexes can be used, the work is done even faster, because SQL will create sets of index entries that satisfy each qualification and do the set manipulation on those index entry sets, each of which takes up less space and can be manipulated much more quickly. You will see in Chapter 7 even more dramatic ways in which the set-oriented nature of SQL works for more complex queries involving multiple tables.

Using Ranges for Qualification

The comparison operators < and > are used to establish a range of values. The keywords BETWEEN and NOT BETWEEN can also be used. For example, to find products with a standard price between $200 and $300, the following query could be used.

Query: Which products in the Product table have a standard price between $200 and $300?

```
SELECT ProductDescription, ProductStandardPrice
  FROM Product_T
    WHERE ProductStandardPrice >= 200 AND ProductStandardPrice <= 300;
```

Result:

PRODUCTDESCRIPTION	PRODUCTSTANDARDPRICE
Coffee Table	200
Computer Desk	250

The same result will be returned by the following query.

Query: Which products in the PRODUCT table have a standard price between $200 and $300?

```
SELECT ProductDescription, ProductStandardPrice
  FROM Product_T
    WHERE ProductStandardPrice BETWEEN 200 AND 300;
```

Result: Same as previous query.

Adding NOT before BETWEEN in this query will return all the other products in Product_T because their prices are less than $200 or more than $300.

Using Distinct Values

Sometimes when returning rows that don't include the primary key, duplicate rows will be returned. For example, look at this query and the results that it returns.

Query: What order numbers are included in the OrderLine table?

```
SELECT OrderID
  FROM OrderLine_T;
```

Eighteen rows are returned, and many of them are duplicates because many orders were for multiple items.

Result:

ORDERID
1001
1001
1001
1002
1003
1004
1004
1005
1006
1006
1006
1007
1007
1008
1008
1009
1009
1010

18 rows selected.

Do we really need the redundant OrderIDs in this result? If we add the keyword DISTINCT, then only 1 occurrence of each OrderID will be returned, 1 for each of the 10 orders represented in the table.

Query: What are the distinct order numbers included in the OrderLine table?

```
SELECT DISTINCT OrderID
  FROM OrderLine_T;
```

Result:

ORDERID
1001
1002
1003
1004
1005
1006
1007
1008
1009
1010

10 rows selected.

DISTINCT and its counterpart, ALL, can be used only once in a SELECT statement. It comes after SELECT and before any columns or expressions are listed. If a SELECT statement projects more than one column, only rows that are identical for every column will be eliminated. Thus, if the previous statement also includes OrderedQuantity, 14 rows are returned because there are now only 4 duplicate rows rather than 8. For example, both items ordered on OrderID 1004 were for 2 items, so the second pairing of 1004 and 2 will be eliminated.

Query: What are the unique combinations of order number and order quantity included in the OrderLine table?

SELECT DISTINCT OrderID, OrderedQuantity
  FROM OrderLine_T;

Result:

ORDERID	ORDEREDQUANTITY
1001	1
1001	2
1002	5
1003	3
1004	2
1005	4
1006	1
1006	2
1007	2
1007	3
1008	3
1009	2
1009	3
1010	10

14 rows selected.

Using IN and NOT IN with Lists

To match a list of values, consider using IN.

Query: List all customers who live in warmer states.

SELECT CustomerName, CustomerCity, CustomerState
  FROM Customer_T
    WHERE CustomerState IN ('FL', 'TX', 'CA', 'HI');

Result:

CUSTOMERNAME	CUSTOMERCITY	CUSTOMERSTATE
Contemporary Casuals	Gainesville	FL
Value Furniture	Plano	TX
Impressions	Sacramento	CA
California Classics	Santa Clara	CA
M and H Casual Furniture	Clearwater	FL
Seminole Interiors	Seminole	FL
Kaneohe Homes	Kaneohe	HI

7 rows selected.

IN is particularly useful in SQL statements that use subqueries, which will be covered in Chapter 7. The use of IN is also very consistent with the set nature of SQL. Very simply, the list (set of values) inside the parentheses after IN can be literals, as illustrated here, or can be a SELECT statement with a single result column, the result of which will be plugged in as the set of values for comparison. In fact, some SQL programmers always use IN, even when the set in parentheses after IN includes only one item. Similarly, any "table" of the FROM clause can be itself a derived table defined by including a SELECT statement in parentheses in the FROM clause (as we saw earlier, with the query about the difference between the standard price of each product and the average standard price of all products). The ability to include a SELECT statement anyplace within SQL where a set is involved is a very powerful and useful feature of SQL, and, of course, totally consistent with SQL being a set-oriented language, as illustrated in Figures 6-8 and 6-9.

Sorting Results: The ORDER BY Clause

Looking at the preceding results, it may seem that it would make more sense to list the California customers, followed by the Floridians, Hawaiians, and Texans. That brings us to the other three basic parts of the SQL statement:

ORDER BY	Sorts the final results rows in ascending or descending order.
GROUP BY	Groups rows in an intermediate results table where the values in those rows are the same for one or more columns.
HAVING	Can only be used following a GROUP BY and acts as a secondary WHERE clause, returning only those groups that meet a specified condition.

So, we can order the customers by adding an ORDER BY clause.

Query: List customer, city, and state for all customers in the Customer table whose address is Florida, Texas, California, or Hawaii. List the customers alphabetically by state and alphabetically by customer within each state.

```
SELECT CustomerName, CustomerCity, CustomerState
  FROM Customer_T
    WHERE CustomerState IN ('FL', 'TX', 'CA', 'HI')
      ORDER BY CustomerState, CustomerName;
```

Now the results are easier to read.

Result:

CUSTOMERNAME	CUSTOMERCITY	CUSTOMERSTATE
California Classics	Santa Clara	CA
Impressions	Sacramento	CA
Contemporary Casuals	Gainesville	FL
M and H Casual Furniture	Clearwater	FL
Seminole Interiors	Seminole	FL
Kaneohe Homes	Kaneohe	HI
Value Furniture	Plano	TX
7 rows selected.		

Notice that all customers from each state are listed together, and within each state, customer names are alphabetized. The sorting order is determined by the order in which the columns are listed in the ORDER BY clause; in this case, states were alphabetized first, then customer names. If sorting from high to low, use DESC as a keyword, placed after the column used to sort. Instead of typing the column names in the ORDER BY clause, you can use their column positions in the select list; for example, in the preceding query, we could have written the clause as

```
ORDER BY 3, 1;
```

For cases in which there are many rows in the result table but you need to see only a few of them, many SQL systems (including MySQL) support a LIMIT clause, such as the following, which would show only the first five rows of the result:

```
ORDER BY 3, 1 LIMIT 5;
```

The following would show five rows after skipping the first 30 rows:

```
ORDER BY 3, 1 LIMIT 30, 5;
```

Oracle 12c has added a similar capability to Oracle with a somewhat different syntax. In Oracle, the same outcome could be achieved with the following clauses:

```
ORDER BY 3, 1
OFFSET 30 ROWS
FETCH 5 ROWS ONLY;
```

How are NULLs sorted? Null values may be placed first or last, before or after columns that have values. Where the NULLs will be placed will depend upon the SQL implementation.

Categorizing Results: The GROUP BY Clause

GROUP BY is particularly useful when paired with aggregate functions, such as SUM or COUNT. GROUP BY divides a table into subsets (by groups); then an aggregate function can be used to provide summary information for that group. The single value returned by the previous aggregate function examples is called a **scalar aggregate**. When aggregate functions are used in a GROUP BY clause and several values are returned, they are called **vector aggregates**.

Scalar aggregate

A single value returned from an SQL query that includes an aggregate function.

Vector aggregate

Multiple values returned from an SQL query that includes an aggregate function.

Query: Count the number of customers with addresses in each state to which we ship.

```
SELECT CustomerState, COUNT (CustomerState)
  FROM Customer_T
    GROUP BY CustomerState;
```

Result:

CUSTOMERSTATE	COUNT(CUSTOMERSTATE)
CA	2
CO	1
FL	3
HI	1
MI	1
NJ	2
NY	1
PA	1
TX	1
UT	1
WA	1

11 rows selected.

It is also possible to nest groups within groups; the same logic is used as when sorting multiple items.

Query: Count the number of customers with addresses in each city to which we ship. List the cities by state.

```
SELECT CustomerState, CustomerCity, COUNT (CustomerCity)
  FROM Customer_T
    GROUP BY CustomerState, CustomerCity;
```

Although the GROUP BY clause seems straightforward, it can produce unexpected results if the logic of the clause is forgotten (and this is a common "gotcha" for novice SQL coders). When a GROUP BY is included, the columns allowed to be specified in the SELECT clause are limited. Only a column with a single value for each group can be included. In the previous query, each group is identified by the combination of a city and its state. The SELECT statement includes both the city and state columns. This works because each combination of city and state is one COUNT value. But if the SELECT clause of the first query in this section had also included city, that statement would fail because the GROUP BY is only by state. Because a state can have more than one city, the requirement that each value in the SELECT clause have only one value in the GROUP BY group is not met, and SQL will not be able to present the city information so that it makes sense. *If you write queries using the following rule, your queries will work*: Each column referenced in the SELECT statement must be referenced in the GROUP BY clause, unless the column is an argument for an aggregate function included in the SELECT clause.

Qualifying Results by Categories: The HAVING Clause

The HAVING clause acts like a WHERE clause, but it identifies groups, rather than rows, that meet a criterion. Therefore, you will usually see a HAVING clause following a GROUP BY clause.

Query: Find only states with more than one customer.

```
SELECT CustomerState, COUNT (CustomerState)
  FROM Customer_T
    GROUP BY CustomerState
    HAVING COUNT (CustomerState) > 1;
```

This query returns a result that has removed all states (groups) with one customer. Remember that using WHERE here would not work because WHERE doesn't allow aggregates; further, WHERE qualifies a set of rows, whereas HAVING qualifies a set of groups. As with WHERE, the HAVING qualification can be compared to the result of a SELECT statement, which computes the value for comparison (i.e., a set with only one value is still a set).

Result:

CUSTOMERSTATE	COUNT(CUSTOMERSTATE)
CA	2
FL	3
NJ	2

To include more than one condition in the HAVING clause, use AND, OR, and NOT just as in the WHERE clause. In summary, here is one last command that includes all six clauses; remember that they must be used in this order.

Query: List, in alphabetical order, the product finish and the average standard price for each finish for selected finishes having an average standard price less than 750.

```
SELECT ProductFinish, AVG (ProductStandardPrice)
  FROM Product_T
    WHERE ProductFinish IN ('Cherry', 'Natural Ash', 'Natural Maple',
    'White Ash')
      GROUP BY ProductFinish
        HAVING AVG (ProductStandardPrice) < 750
          ORDER BY ProductFinish;
```

Result:

PRODUCTFINISH	AVG(PRODUCTSTANDARDPRICE)
Cherry	250
Natural Ash	458.333333
Natural Maple	650

Figure 6-10 shows the order in which SQL processes the clauses of a statement. Arrows indicate the paths that may be followed. Remember, only the SELECT and FROM clauses are mandatory. Notice that the processing order is different from the order of the syntax used to create the statement. As each clause is processed, an intermediate results table is produced that will be used for the next clause. Users do not see the intermediate results tables; they see only the final results. A query can be debugged by remembering the order shown in Figure 6-10. Take out the optional clauses and then add them back in one at a time in the order in which they will be processed. In this way, intermediate results can be seen and problems often can be spotted.

Using and Defining Views

The SQL syntax shown in Figure 6-6 demonstrates the creation of four **base tables** in a database schema using Oracle 12c SQL. These tables, which are used to store data physically in the database, correspond to relations in the logical database design. By using SQL queries with any RDBMS, it is possible to create **virtual tables**, or **dynamic views**, whose contents materialize when referenced. These views may often be manipulated

Base table

A table in the relational data model containing the inserted raw data. Base tables correspond to the relations that are identified in the database's conceptual schema.

Virtual table

A table constructed automatically as needed by a DBMS. Virtual tables are not maintained as real data.

Dynamic view

A virtual table that is created dynamically upon request by a user. A dynamic view is not a temporary table. Rather, its definition is stored in the system catalog, and the contents of the view are materialized as a result of an SQL query that uses the view. It differs from a materialized view, which may be stored on a disk and refreshed at intervals or when used, depending on the RDBMS.

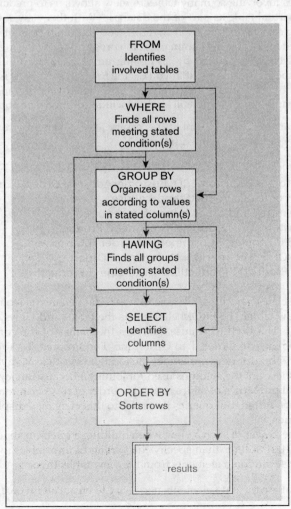

FIGURE 6-10 SQL statement processing order (based on van der Lans, 2006, p. 100)

TABLE 6-4 Pros and Cons of Using Dynamic Views

Positive Aspects	Negative Aspects
Simplify query commands	Use processing time re-creating the view each time it is referenced
Help provide data security and confidentiality	May or may not be directly updateable
Improve programmer productivity	
Contain most current base table data	
Use little storage space	
Provide a customized view for a user	
Establish physical data independence	

Materialized view

Copies or replicas of data, based on SQL queries created in the same manner as dynamic views. However, a materialized view exists as a table and thus care must be taken to keep it synchronized with its associated base tables.

in the same way as a base table can be manipulated, through SQL SELECT queries. **Materialized views**, which are stored physically on a disk and refreshed at appropriate intervals or events, may also be used.

The often-stated purpose of a view is to simplify query commands, but a view may also improve data security and significantly enhance programming consistency and productivity for a database. To highlight the convenience of using a view, consider Pine Valley's invoice processing. Construction of the company's invoice requires access to the four tables from the Pine Valley database of Figure 6-3: Customer_T, Order_T, OrderLine_T, and Product_T. A novice database user may make mistakes or be unproductive in properly formulating queries involving so many tables. A view allows us to predefine this association into a single virtual table as part of the database. With this view, a user who wants only customer invoice data does not have to reconstruct the joining of tables to produce the report or any subset of it. Table 6-4 summarizes the pros and cons of using views.

A view, Invoice_V, is defined by specifying an SQL query (SELECT…FROM… WHERE) that has the view as its result. If you decide to try this query as is, without selecting additional attributes, remove the comma after OrderedQuantity and the following comment. The example assumes you will elect to include additional attributes in the query.

Query: What are the data elements necessary to create an invoice for a customer? Save this query as a view named Invoice_V.

```
CREATE VIEW Invoice_V AS
  SELECT Customer_T.CustomerID, CustomerAddress, Order_T.OrderID,
  Product_T.ProductID,ProductStandardPrice,
  OrderedQuantity, and other columns as required
    FROM Customer_T, Order_T, OrderLine_T, Product_T
      WHERE Customer_T.CustomerID = Order_T.CustomerID
        AND Order_T.OrderID = OrderLine_T.OrderD
        AND Product_T.ProductID = OrderLine_T.ProductID;
```

The SELECT clause specifies, or projects, what data elements (columns) are to be included in the view table. The FROM clause lists the tables and views involved in the view development. The WHERE clause specifies the names of the common columns used to join Customer_T to Order_T to OrderLine_T to Product_T. (You'll learn about joining in Chapter 7, but for now remember the foreign keys that were defined to reference other tables; these are the columns used for joining.) Because a view is a table, and one of the relational properties of tables is that the order of rows is immaterial, the rows in a view may not be sorted. But queries that refer to this view may display their results in any desired sequence.

We can see the power of such a view when building a query to generate an invoice for order number 1004. Rather than specify the joining of four tables, we can have the query include all relevant data elements from the view table, Invoice_V.

Query: What are the data elements necessary to create an invoice for order number 1004?

```
SELECT CustomerID, CustomerAddress, ProductID,
  OrderedQuantity, and other columns as required
    FROM Invoice_V
      WHERE OrderID = 1004;
```

A dynamic view is a virtual table; it is constructed automatically, as needed, by the DBMS and is not maintained as persistent data. Any SQL SELECT statement may be used to create a view. The persistent data are stored in base tables, those that have been defined by CREATE TABLE commands. A dynamic view always contains the most current derived values and is thus superior in terms of data currency to constructing a temporary real table from several base tables. Also, in comparison to a temporary real table, a view consumes very little storage space. A view is costly, however, because its contents must be calculated each time they are requested (that is, each time the view is used in an SQL statement). Materialized views are now available and address this drawback.

A view may join together multiple tables or views and may contain derived (or virtual) columns. For example, if a user of the Pine Valley Furniture database only wants to know the total value of orders placed for each furniture product, a view for this can be created from Invoice_V. The following example in SQL*Plus illustrates how this is done with Oracle, although this can be done with any RDBMS that supports views.

Query: What is the total value of orders placed for each furniture product?

```
CREATE VIEW OrderTotals_V AS
  SELECT ProductID Product, SUM (ProductStandardPrice*OrderedQuantity)
Total
    FROM Invoice_V
    GROUP BY ProductID;
```

We can assign a different name (an alias) to a view column rather than use the associated base table or expression column name. Here, Product is a renaming of ProductID, local to only this view. Total is the column name given the expression for total sales of each product. (Total may not be a legal alias with some relational DBMSs because it might be a reserved word for a proprietary function of the DBMS; you always have to be careful when defining columns and aliases not to use a reserved word.) The expression can now be referenced via this view in subsequent queries as if it were a column rather than a derived expression. Defining views based on other views can cause problems. For example, if we redefine Invoice_V so that StandardPrice is not included, then OrderTotals_V will no longer work because it will not be able to locate standard unit prices.

Views can also help establish security. Tables and columns that are not included will not be obvious to the user of the view. Restricting access to a view with GRANT and REVOKE statements adds another layer of security. For example, granting some users access rights to aggregated data, such as averages, in a view but denying them access to detailed base table data will not allow them to display the base table data. SQL security commands are explained further in Chapter 12.

Privacy and confidentiality of data can be achieved by creating views that restrict users to working with only the data they need to perform their assigned duties. If a clerical worker needs to work with employees' addresses but should not be able to access their compensation rates, they may be given access to a view that does not contain compensation information.

Some people advocate the creation of a view for every single base table, even if that view is identical to the base table. They suggest this approach because views can contribute to greater programming productivity as databases evolve. Consider a situation in which 50 programs all use the Customer_T table. Suppose that the Pine Valley Furniture Company database evolves to support new functions that require the Customer_T table to be renormalized into two tables. If these 50 programs refer directly to the Customer_T base table, they will all have to be modified to refer to one of the two new tables or to joined tables. But if these programs all use the view on this base table, then only the view has to be re-created, saving considerable reprogramming effort. However, dynamic views require considerable run-time computer processing because the virtual table of a view is re-created each time the view is referenced. Therefore, referencing a base table through a view rather than directly can add considerable time to query processing. This additional operational cost must be balanced against the potential reprogramming savings from using a view.

It can be possible to update base table data via update commands (INSERT, DELETE, and UPDATE) against a view as long as it is unambiguous what base table data must change. For example, if the view contains a column created by aggregating base table data, then it would be ambiguous how to change the base table values if an attempt were made to update the aggregate value. If the view definition includes the WITH CHECK OPTION clause, attempts to insert data through the view will be rejected when the data values do not meet the specifications of WITH CHECK OPTION. Specifically, when the CREATE VIEW statement contains any of the following situations, that view may not be used to update the data:

1. The SELECT clause includes the keyword DISTINCT.
2. The SELECT clause contains expressions, including derived columns, aggregates, statistical functions, and so on.
3. The FROM clause, a subquery, or a UNION clause references more than one table.
4. The FROM clause or a subquery references another view that is not updateable.
5. The CREATE VIEW command contains a GROUP BY or HAVING clause.

It could happen that an update to an instance would result in the instance disappearing from the view. Let's create a view named ExpensiveStuff_V, which lists all furniture products that have a StandardPrice over $300. That view will include ProductID 5, a writer's desk, which has a unit price of $325. If we update data using Expensive_Stuff_V and reduce the unit price of the writer's desk to $295, then the writer's desk will no longer appear in the ExpensiveStuff_V virtual table because its unit price is now less than $300. In Oracle, if you want to track all merchandise with an original price over $300, include a WITH CHECK OPTION clause after the SELECT clause in the CREATE VIEW command. WITH CHECK OPTION will cause UPDATE or INSERT statements on that view to be rejected when those statements would cause updated or inserted rows to be removed from the view. This option can be used only with updateable views.

Here is the CREATE VIEW statement for ExpensiveStuff_V.

Query: List all furniture products that have ever had a standard price over $300.

```
CREATE VIEW ExpensiveStuff_V
  AS
    SELECT ProductID, ProductDescription, ProductStandardPrice
      FROM Product_T
        WHERE ProductStandardPrice > 300
        WITH CHECK OPTION;
```

When attempting to update the unit price of the writer's desk to $295 using the following Oracle SQL*Plus syntax:

```
UPDATE ExpensiveStuff_V
SET ProductStandardPrice = 295
  WHERE ProductID = 5;
```

Oracle gives the following error message:

```
ERROR at line 1:
ORA-01402: view WITH CHECK OPTION where-clause violation
```

A price increase on the writer's desk to $350 will take effect with no error message because the view is updateable and the conditions specified in the view are not violated.

Information about views will be stored in the systems tables of the DBMS. In Oracle 12c, for example, the text of all views is stored in DBA_VIEWS. Users with system privileges can find this information.

Query: List some information that is available about the view named EXPENSIVESTUFF_V. (Note that EXPENSIVESTUFF_V is stored in uppercase and must be entered in uppercase in order to execute correctly.)

```
SELECT OWNER,VIEW_NAME,TEXT_LENGTH
  FROM DBA_VIEWS
    WHERE VIEW_NAME = 'EXPENSIVESTUFF_V';
```

Result:

OWNER	VIEW_NAME	TEXT_LENGTH
MPRESCOTT	EXPENSIVESTUFF_V	110

MATERIALIZED VIEWS Like dynamic views, materialized views can be constructed in different ways for various purposes. Tables may be replicated in whole or in part and refreshed on a predetermined time interval or triggered when the table needs to be accessed. Materialized views can be based on queries from one or more tables. It is possible to create summary tables based on aggregations of data. Copies of remote data that use distributed data may be stored locally as materialized views. Maintenance overhead will be incurred to keep the local view synchronized with the remote base tables or data warehouse, but the use of materialized views may improve the performance of distributed queries, especially if the data in the materialized view are relatively static and do not have to be refreshed very often.

Summary

This chapter has introduced the SQL language for relational database definition (DDL), manipulation (DML), and control (DCL) languages, commonly used to define and query relational database management systems (RDBMSs). This standard has been criticized as having many flaws. In reaction to these criticisms and to increase the power of the language, extensions are constantly under review by the ANSI X3H2 committee and International Committee for Information Technology Standards (INCITS). The current generally implemented standard is SQL:1999, but later versions, including SQL:2008 and SQL:2011, are being implemented by some RDBMSs.

The establishment of SQL standards and conformance certification tests has contributed to relational systems being the dominant form of new database development. Benefits of the SQL standards include reduced training costs, improved productivity, application portability and longevity, reduced dependence on single vendors, and improved cross-system communication. SQL has become so dominant as database query and data manipulation language that even the new competitors of the relational model are implementing SQL-like interfaces.

The SQL environment includes an instance of an SQL DBMS along with accessible databases and associated users and programs. Each database is included in a catalog and has a schema that describes the database objects. Information contained in the catalog is maintained by the DBMS itself rather than by the users of the DBMS.

The SQL DDL commands are used to define a database, including its creation and the creation of its tables, indexes, and views. Referential integrity is also established through DDL commands. The SQL DML commands are used to load, update, and query the database through use of the SELECT, INSERT, UPDATE, and DELETE commands. DCL commands are used to establish user access to the database.

SQL commands may directly affect the base tables, which contain the raw data, or they may affect a database view that has been created. Changes and updates made to views may or may not be passed on to the base tables. The basic syntax of an SQL SELECT statement contains the following keywords: SELECT, FROM, WHERE, ORDER BY, GROUP BY, and HAVING. SELECT determines which attributes will be displayed in the query results table. FROM determines which tables or views will be used in the query. WHERE sets the criteria of the query, including any joins of multiple tables that are necessary. ORDER BY determines the order in which the results will be displayed. GROUP BY is used to categorize results and may return either scalar aggregates or vector aggregates. HAVING qualifies results by categories.

Understanding the basic SQL syntax presented in this chapter should enable the reader to start using SQL effectively and to build a deeper understanding of the possibilities for more complex querying with continued practice. Multi-table queries and advanced SQL topics are covered in Chapter 7.

Chapter Review

Key Terms

Base table *279*
Catalog *249*
Data control language
  (DCL) *250*

Data definition language
  (DDL) *250*
Data manipulation
  language (DML) *250*

Dynamic view *279*
Materialized view *280*
Relational DBMS
  (RDBMS) *249*

Scalar aggregate *277*
Schema *249*
Vector aggregate *277*
Virtual table *279*

Review Questions

6-1. Define each of the following terms:
  a. base table
  b. data definition language
  c. data manipulation language
  d. dynamic view
  e. materialized view
  f. referential integrity constraint
  g. relational DBMS (RDBMS)
  h. schema
  i. virtual table

6-2. Match the following terms to the appropriate definitions:

_____ view
_____ referential
  integrity
  constraint
_____ dynamic
  view
_____ materialized
  view
_____ SQL:2011
_____ null value
_____ scalar
  aggregate
_____ vector
  aggregate
_____ catalog
_____ schema
_____ host language

  a. list of values
  b. description of a database
  c. view materialized as a result of
    a SQL query that uses the view
  d. logical table
  e. missing or nonexistent value
  f. descriptions of database
    objects of a database
  g. programming language in
    which SQL commands are
    embedded
  h. established in relational data
    models by use of foreign keys
  i. view that exists as a table
  j. current standard for relational
    query and definition language
  k. single value

6-3. Contrast the following terms:
  a. base table; view
  b. dynamic view; materialized view
  c. catalog; schema

6-4. What are SQL-92, SQL:1999, and SQL:2011? Briefly describe how SQL:2011 differs from SQL:1999.

6-5. Explain what capabilities the new temporal features added to the SQL standard in SQL:2011.

6-6. Describe a relational DBMS (RDBMS), its underlying data model, its data storage structures, and how data relationships are established.

6-7. List six potential benefits of achieving an SQL standard that is widely accepted.

6-8. Describe the components and structure of a typical SQL environment.

6-9. Distinguish among data definition commands, data manipulation commands, and data control commands.

6-10. Explain how referential integrity is established in databases that are SQL:1999 compliant. Explain how the ON UPDATE RESTRICT, ON UPDATE CASCADE, and ON UPDATE SET NULL clauses differ from one another. What happens if the ON DELETE CASCADE clause is set?

6-11. Explain some possible purposes of creating a view using SQL. In particular, explain how a view can be used to reinforce data security.

6-12. Explain why it is necessary to limit the kinds of updates performed on data when referencing data through a view.

6-13. Describe a set of circumstances for which using a view can save reprogramming effort.

6-14. Drawing on material covered in prior chapters, explain the factors to be considered in deciding whether to create a key index for a table in SQL.

6-15. Explain and provide at least one example of how to qualify the ownership of a table in SQL. What has to occur for one user to be allowed to use a table in a database owned by another user?

6-16. How is the order in which attributes appear in a result table changed? How are the column heading labels in a result table changed?

6-17. What is the difference between COUNT, COUNT DISTINCT, and COUNT(*) in SQL? When will these three commands generate the same and different results?

6-18. What is the evaluation order for the Boolean operators (AND, OR, NOT) in an SQL command? How can a query writer be sure that the operators will work in a specific, desired order?

6-19. If an SQL statement includes a GROUP BY clause, the attributes that can be requested in the SELECT statement will be limited. Explain that limitation.

6-20. Describe a situation in which you would need to write a query using the HAVING clause.

6-21. In what clause of a SELECT statement is an IN operator used? What follows the IN operator? What other SQL operator can sometimes be used to perform the same operation as the IN operator? Under what circumstances can this other operator be used?

6-22. How do you determine the order in which the rows in a response to an SQL query appear?

6-23. Explain why SQL is called a set-oriented language.

6-24. When would the use of the LIKE keyword with the CREATE TABLE command be helpful?

6-25. What is an identity column? Explain the benefits of using the identity column capability in SQL.

6-26. SQL:2006 and SQL:2008 introduced a new keyword, MERGE. Explain how using this keyword allows one to accomplish updating and merging data into a table using one command rather than two.

6-27. In what order are the clauses of an SQL statement processed?

6-28. Within which clauses of an SQL statement can a derived table be defined?

6-29. In an ORDER BY clause, what are the two ways to refer to the columns to be used for sorting the results of the query?

6-30. Explain the purpose of the CHECK clause within a CREATE TABLE SQL command. Explain the purpose of the WITH CHECK OPTION in a CREATE VIEW SQL command.

6-31. What can be changed about a table definition, using the SQL command ALTER? Can you identify anything about a table definition that cannot be changed using the ALTER command?

6-32. Explain the difference between the WHERE and HAVING clause.

6-33. Is it possible to use both a WHERE clause and a HAVING clause in the same SQL SELECT statement? If so, what are the different purposes of these two clauses?

6-34. What are the basic operations that can be performed on data that is stored?

6-35. What is the purpose of the GROUP BY clause? Why should the attribute used in the GROUP BY clause also appear in the SELECT statement?

6-36. What is the difference between the following commands:
  a. COUNT( ) and COUNT(*) functions?
  b. DELETE and TRUNCATE commands?
  c. HAVING and WHERE clauses?

6-37. What are the design criteria for efficient physical record design? How does denormalization help in efficient data processing? Explain with examples the types and opportunities for denormalization?

6-38. What is the importance of file organization in a DBMS and what are the relative merits and demerits of different types of file organization?

6-39. How do the different database architecture types impact the design of a DBMS?

6-40. What was the need for a standardized relational language and what are the advantages gained by the adaptation of the same?

6-41. How RAID helps in improving the file access performance and fault tolerance? Which is the best level RAID?

Problems and Exercises

Problems and Exercises 6-42 through 6-52 are based on the class scheduling 3NF relations along with some sample data shown in Figure 6-11. Not shown in this figure are data for an ASSIGNMENT relation, which represents a many-to-many relationship between faculty and sections. Note that values of the SectionNo column do not repeat across semesters.

6-42. Write a database description for each of the relations shown, using SQL DDL (shorten, abbreviate, or change any data names, as needed for your SQL version). Assume the following attribute data types:
  StudentID (integer, primary key)
  StudentName (25 characters)
  FacultyID (integer, primary key)
  FacultyName (25 characters)
  CourseID (8 characters, primary key)
  CourseName (15 characters)
  DateQualified (date)
  SectionNo (integer, primary key)
  Semester (7 characters)

6-43. The database is not fully normalized. Explain how. What problems could this cause?

6-44. Use SQL to define the following view:

StudentID	StudentName
38214	Letersky
54907	Altvater
54907	Altvater
66324	Aiken

6-45. Because of referential integrity, before any row can be entered into the SECTION table, the CourseID to be entered must already exist in the COURSE table. Write an SQL assertion that will enforce this constraint.

6-46. Write SQL data definition commands for each of the following queries:
  a. How would you add an attribute, Class, to the Student table?
  b. How would you remove the Registration table?
  c. How would you change the FacultyName field from 25 characters to 40 characters?

6-47. Write SQL commands for the following:
  a. Create two different forms of the INSERT command to add a student with a student ID of 65798 and last name Lopez to the Student table.
  b. Now write a command that will remove Lopez from the Student table.
  c. Create an SQL command that will modify the name of course ISM 4212 from Database to Introduction to Relational Databases.

6-48. Write SQL queries to answer the following questions:
  a. Which students have an ID number that is less than 50000?
  b. What is the name of the faculty member whose ID is 4756?
  c. What is the smallest section number used in the first semester of 2015?

6-49. Write SQL queries to answer the following questions:
  a. How many students are enrolled in Section 2714 in the first semester of 2015?
  b. Which faculty members have qualified to teach a course since 2008? List the faculty ID, course, and date of qualification.

6-50. Write SQL queries to answer the following questions:
  a. Which students are enrolled in Database and Networking? (Hint: Use SectionNo for each class so you can determine the answer from the Registration table by itself.)
  b. Which instructors cannot teach both Syst Analysis and Syst Design?
  c. Which courses were taught in the first semester of 2015 but not in the second semester of 2015?

6-51. Write SQL queries to answer the following questions:
  a. What are the courses included in the Section table? List each course only once.
  b. List all students in alphabetical order by StudentName.
  c. List the students who are enrolled in each course in Semester I, 2015. Group the students by the sections in which they are enrolled.
  d. List the courses available. Group them by course prefix. (ISM is the only prefix shown, but there are many others throughout the university.)

FIGURE 6-11 Class scheduling relations (missing ASSIGNMENT)

6-52. Write SQL queries to answer the following questions:

  a. List the numbers of all sections of course ISM 3113 that are offered during the semester "I-2015."

  b. List the course IDs and names of all courses that start with the letters "Data."

  c. List the IDs of all faculty members who are qualified to teach both ISM 3112 and ISM 3113.

  d. Modify the query above in part c so that both qualifications must have been earned after the year 2005.

  e. List the ID of the faculty member who has been assigned to teach ISM 4212 during the semester II-2015.

Problems and Exercises 6-53 through 6-61 are based on the relations shown in Figure 6-12. The database tracks an adult literacy program. Tutors complete a certification class offered by the agency. Students complete an assessment interview that results in a report for the tutor and a recorded Read score. When matched with a student, a tutor

meets with the student for one to four hours per week. Some students work with the same tutor for years, some for less than a month. Other students change tutors if their learning style does not match the tutor's tutoring style. Many tutors are retired and are available to tutor only part of the year. Tutor status is recorded as Active, Temp Stop, or Dropped.

6-53. How many tutors have a status of Temp Stop? Which tutors are active?

6-54. What is the average Read score for all students? What are the minimum and maximum Read scores?

6-55. List the IDs of the tutors who are currently tutoring more than one student.

6-56. What are the TutorIDs for tutors who have not yet tutored anyone?

6-57. How many students were matched with someone in the first five months of the year?

TUTOR (TutorID, CertDate, Status)

TutorID	CertDate	Status
100	1/05/2015	Active
101	1/05/2015	Temp Stop
102	1/05/2015	Dropped
103	5/22/2015	Active
104	5/22/2015	Active
105	5/22/2015	Temp Stop
106	5/22/2015	Active

STUDENT (StudentID, Read)

StudentID	Read
3000	2.3
3001	5.6
3002	1.3
3003	3.3
3004	2.7
3005	4.8
3006	7.8
3007	1.5

MATCH HISTORY (MatchID, TutorID, StudentID, StartDate, EndDate)

MatchID	TutorID	StudentID	StartDate	EndDate
1	100	3000	1/10/2015	
2	101	3001	1/15/2015	5/15/2015
3	102	3002	2/10/2015	3/01/2015
4	106	3003	5/28/2015	
5	103	3004	6/01/2015	6/15/2015
6	104	3005	6/01/2015	6/28/2015
7	104	3006	6/01/2015	

FIGURE 6-12   Adult literacy program (for Problems and Exercises 6-53 through 6-61)

6-58. Which student has the highest Read score?
6-59. How long had each student studied in the adult literacy program?
6-60. Which tutors have a Dropped status and have achieved their certification after 4/01/2015?
6-61. What is the average length of time a student stayed (or has stayed) in the program?

Problems and Exercises 6-62 through 6-93 are based on the entire ("big") version) Pine Valley Furniture Company database. Note: Depending on what DBMS you are using, some field names may have changed to avoid using reserved words for the DBMS. When you first use the DBMS, check the

PINE
VALLEY
FURNITURE

table definitions to see what the exact field names are for the DBMS you are using. See the Preface and inside covers of this book for instructions on where to find this database on **www.teradatauniversitynetwork.com.**

6-62. Modify the Product_T table by adding an attribute QtyOnHand that can be used to track the finished goods inventory. The field should be an integer field of five characters and should accept only positive numbers.

6-63. Enter sample data of your own choosing into QtyOnHand in the Product_T table. Test the modification you made in Problem and Exercise 6-62 by attempting to update a product by changing the inventory to 10,000 units. Test it again by changing the inventory for the product to −10 units. If you do not receive error messages and are successful in making these changes, then you did not establish appropriate constraints in Problem and Exercise 6-62.

6-64. Add an order to the Order_T table and include a sample value for every attribute.
  a. First, look at the data in the Customer_T table and enter an order from any one of those customers.
  b. Enter an order from a new customer. Unless you have also inserted information about the new customer in the Customer_T table, your entry of the order data should be rejected. Referential integrity constraints should prevent you from entering an order if there is no information about the customer.

6-65. Use the Pine Valley database to answer the following questions:
  a. How many work centers does Pine Valley have?
  b. Where are they located?

6-66. List the employees whose last names begin with an *L*.

6-67. Which employees were hired during 2005?

6-68. List the customers who live in California or Washington. Order them by zip code, from high to low.

6-69. List the number of customers living at each state that is included in the Customer_T table.

6-70. List all raw materials that are made of cherry and that have dimensions (thickness and width) of 12 by 12.

6-71. List the MaterialID, MaterialName, Material, MaterialStandardPrice, and Thickness for all raw materials made of cherry, pine, or walnut. Order the listing by Material, StandardPrice, and Thickness.

6-72. Display the product line ID and the average standard price for all products in each product line.

6-73. For every product that has been ordered, display the product ID and the total quantity ordered (label this result TotalOrdered). List the most popular product first and the least popular last.

6-74. For each customer, list the CustomerID and total number of orders placed.

6-75. For each salesperson, display a list of CustomerIDs.

6-76. Display the product ID and the number of orders placed for each product. Show the results in decreasing order by the number of times the product has been ordered and label this result column NumOrders.

6-77. For each customer, list the CustomerID and the total number of orders placed in 2015.

6-78. For each salesperson, list the total number of orders.

6-79. For each customer who had more than two orders, list the CustomerID and the total number of orders placed.

6-80. List all sales territories (TerritoryID) that have more than one salesperson.

6-81. Which product is ordered most frequently?

6-82. Measured by average standard price, what is the least expensive product finish?

6-83. Display the territory ID and the number of salespersons in the territory for all territories that have more than one salesperson. Label the number of salespersons NumSalesPersons.

6-84. Display the SalesPersonID and a count of the number of orders for that salesperson for all salespersons except salespersons 3, 5, and 9. Write this query with as few clauses or components as possible, using the capabilities of SQL as much as possible.

6-85. For each salesperson, list the total number of orders by month for the year 2015. (Hint: If you are using Access, use the Month function. If you are using Oracle, convert the date to a string, using the TO_CHAR function, with the format string 'Mon' [i.e., TO_CHAR(order_date,'MON')]. If you are using another DBMS, you will need to investigate how to deal with months for this query.)

6-86. List MaterialName, Material, and Width for raw materials that are *not* cherry or oak and whose width is greater than 10 inches. Show how you constructed this query using a Venn diagram.

6-87. List ProductID, ProductDescription, ProductFinish, and ProductStandardPrice for oak products with a ProductStandardPrice greater than $400 or cherry products with a StandardPrice less than $300. Show how you constructed this query using a Venn diagram.

6-88. For each order, list the order ID, customer ID, order date, and most recent date among all orders. Show how you constructed this query using a Venn diagram.

6-89. For each customer, list the customer ID, the number of orders from that customer, and the ratio of the number of orders from that customer to the total number of orders from all customers combined. (This ratio, of course, is the percentage of all orders placed by each customer.)

6-90. For products 1, 2, and 7, list in one row and three respective columns that product's total unit sales; label the three columns Prod1, Prod2, and Prod7.

6-91. List the average number of customers per state (including only the states that are included in the Customer_T table). Hint: A query can be used as a table specification in the FROM clause.

6-92. Not all versions of this database include referential integrity constraints for all foreign keys. Use whatever commands are available for the RDBMS you are using, investigate if any referential integrity constraints are missing. Write any missing constraints and, if possible, add them to the associated table definitions.

6-93. Tyler Richardson set up a house alarm system when he moved to his new home in Seattle. For security purposes, he has all of his mail, including his alarm system bill, mailed to his local UPS store. Although the alarm system is activated and the company is aware of its physical address, Richardson receives repeated offers mailed to his physical address, imploring him to protect his house with the system he currently uses. What do you think the problem might be with that company's database(s)?

6-94. Write the SQL DDL command descriptions for each of the relations shown below.

EMP Table

Attribute	Data Type	Length	Constraint
EMPNO	INTEGER	NA	NOT NULL, PRIMARY KEY
ENAME	CHARACTER	25	
JOB	CHARACTER	15	
JOINDATE	DATE	NA	
SALARY	INTEGER	NA	
DEPTNO	INTEGER	NA	NOT NULL, FOREIGN KEY

BONUS Table

Attribute	Data Type	Length	Constraint
EMPNO	INTEGER	NA	NOT NULL, FOREIGN KEY
COMM	INTEGER	NA	

DEPT Table

Attribute	Data Type	Length	Constraint
DEPTNO	INTEGER	NA	PRIMARY KEY
DEPTNAME	CHARACTER	15	

Change the data types as needed for your version of SQL.

6-95. Write an SQL command for each of the following queries: (refer to the tables given above for the query to be issued)
   a. How would you list the entire unique JOB in the EMP table?
   b. Find the employees who are earning salaries between 22000 and 30000.
   c. Increase the salary of all the employees by 10%.

6-96. Write an SQL command for each of the following queries: (refer to the tables created in the above question, for the query to be issued)
   a. Find the total amount paid as salary to the employees belonging
   b. List all the employees whose COMM is greater than their SALARY
   c. Define the following view

ENAME	JOB	JOIN DATE
…	…	…
…	…	…

Field Exercises

6-97. Arrange an interview with a database administrator in an organization in your area. When you interview the database administrator, familiarize yourself with one application that is actively used in the organization. Focus your interview questions on determining end users' involvement with the application and understanding the extent to which end users must be familiar with SQL. For example, if end users are using SQL, what training do they receive? Do they use an interactive form of SQL for their work, or do they use embedded SQL? How have the required skills of the end users changed over the past few years, as the database user interfaces have changed?

6-98. Arrange an interview with a database administrator in your area. Focus the interview on understanding the environment within which SQL is used in the organization. Inquire about the version of SQL that is used and determine whether the same version is used at all locations. If different versions are used, explore any difficulties that the DBA has had in administering the database. Also inquire about any proprietary languages, such as Oracle's PL*SQL, that are being used. Learn about possible differences in versions used at different locations and explore any difficulties that occur if different versions are installed.

6-99. Arrange an interview with a database administrator in your area who has at least seven years of experience as a database administrator. Focus the interview on understanding how DBA responsibilities and the way they are completed have changed during the DBA's tenure. Does the DBA have to generate more or less SQL code to administer the databases now than in the past? Has the position become more or less stressful?

References

Codd, E. F. 1970. "A Relational Model of Data for Large Shared Data Banks." *Communications of the ACM* 13,6 (June): 77–87.

Date, C. J., and H. Darwen. 1997. *A Guide to the SQL Standard.* Reading, MA: Addison-Wesley.

Gorman, M. M. 2001. "Is SQL a Real Standard Anymore?" *The Data Administration Newsletter* (July). Available at **www.tdan.com/i016hy01.htm.**

Kulkarni, K.G, and J-E. Michels. 2012. "Temporal features in SQL:2011." *SIGMOD Record*, 41,3,34–43.

van der Lans, R. F. 2006. *Introduction to SQL; Mastering the Relational Database Language*, 4th ed. Workingham, UK: Addison-Wesley.

Yegulalp, S. 2014. "10 ways to query Hadoop with SQL." Available at **http://www.infoworld.com/article/2683729/hadoop/10-ways-to-query-hadoop-with-sql.html**.

Zemke, F. 2012. "What's new in SQL:2011." *SIGMOD Record*, 41,1: 67–73.

Further Reading

Atzeni, P., C. S. Jensen, G. Orsi, S. Ram, L. Tanca, and R. Torlone. 2013. "The relational model is dead, SQL is dead, and I don't feel so good myself." *SIGMOD Record*, 42,2: 64–68.

Beaulieu, A. 2009. *Learning SQL*. Sebastopol, CA: O'Reilly.

Celko, J. 2006. *Joe Celko's SQL Puzzles & Answers*, 2nd ed. San Francisco: Morgan Kaufmann.

Gulutzan, P., and T. Petzer. 1999. *SQL-99 Complete, Really*. Lawrence, KS: R&D Books.

Mistry, R., and S. Misner. 2014. *Introducing Microsoft SQL Server 2014*. Redmond, WA: Microsoft Press.

Nielsen, P., U. Parui, and M. White. 2009. *Microsoft SQL Server 2008 Bible*. Indianapolis, IN: Wiley Publishing.

Price, J. 2012. *Oracle Database 12c SQL*. New Yorks, NY: McGraw Hill Professional.

Web Resources

http://standards.ieee.org The home page of the IEEE Standards Association.

www.1keydata.com/sql/sql.html Web site that provides tutorials on a subset of ANSI standard SQL commands.

www.ansi.org Information on ANSI and the latest national and international standards.

www.fluffycat.com/SQL/ Web site that defines a sample database and shows examples of SQL queries against this database.

www.incits.org The home page of the International Committee for Information Technology Standards, which used to be the National Committee for Information Technology Standards, which used to be the Accredited Standard Committee X3.

http://www.iso.org/iso/home.html International Organization for Standardization Web site, from which copies of current standards may be purchased.

www.itl.nist.gov/div897/ctg/dm/sql_examples.htm Web site that shows examples of SQL commands for creating tables and views, updating table contents, and performing some SQL database administration commands.

www.java2s.com/Code/SQL/CatalogSQL.htm Web site that provides tutorials on SQL in a MySQL environment.

www.mysql.com The official home page for MySQL, which includes many free downloadable components for working with MySQL.

www.paragoncorporation.com/ArticleDetail.aspx?ArticleID=27 Web site that provides a brief explanation of the power of SQL and a variety of sample SQL queries.

www.sqlcourse.com and www.sqlcourse2.com Web sites that provide tutorials for a subset of ANSI SQL, along with a practice database.

www.teradatauniversitynetwork.com Web site where your instructor may have created some course environments for you to use Teradata SQL Assistant, Web Edition, with one or more of the Pine Valley Furniture and Mountain View Community Hospital data sets for this text.

www.tizag.com/sqlTutorial/ A set of tutorials on SQL concepts and commands.

www.wiscorp.com/SQLStandards.html Whitemarsh Information Systems Corp., a good source of information about SQL standards, including SQL:2003 and later standards.

CASE

Forondo Artist Management Excellence Inc.

Case Description

In Chapter 5, you created the physical designs for the database that will support the functionality needed by FAME. You will use this information to actually implement the database in the DBMS of your choice (or as specified by your instructor).

Project Questions

6-100. Write the SQL statements for creating the tables, specifying data types and field lengths, establishing primary keys and foreign keys, and implementing any other constraints you may have identified. Use the examples shown in Chapter 5 to specify indexes, if appropriate.

6-101. Reread the case descriptions in Chapters 1 through 3 with an eye toward identifying the typical types of reports and displays the various stakeholders might want to retrieve from your database. Create a document that summarizes these findings.

6-102. Based on your findings from 6-101 above, populate the tables in your database with sample data that can potentially allow you to test/demonstrate that your database can generate these reports.

6-103. Write and execute a variety of queries to test the functionality of your database based on what you learned in this chapter. Don't panic if you can't write all the queries; many of the queries will require knowledge from Chapter 7. Your instructor may specify for which reports or displays you should write queries.

CHAPTER 7

Advanced SQL

Visit www.pearsonhighered.com/ hoffer to view the accompanying video for this chapter.

LEARNING OBJECTIVES

After studying this chapter, you should be able to:

- Concisely define each of the following key terms: **join, equi-join, natural join, outer join, correlated subquery, user-defined data type, trigger, Persistent Stored Modules (SQL/PSM), function, procedure, embedded SQL,** and **dynamic SQL.**
- Write single- and multiple-table queries using SQL commands.
- Define three types of join commands and use SQL to write these commands.
- Write noncorrelated and correlated subqueries and know when to write each.
- Understand the use of SQL in procedural languages, both standard (e.g., PHP) and proprietary (e.g., PL/SQL).
- Understand common uses of database triggers and stored procedures.
- Discuss the SQL:2011 standard and explain its enhancements and extensions.

INTRODUCTION

The previous chapter introduced SQL and explored its capabilities for querying one table. The real power of the relational model derives from its storage of data in many related entities. Taking advantage of this approach to data storage requires establishing relationships and constructing queries that use data from multiple tables. This chapter examines multiple-table queries in some detail. Different approaches to getting results from more than one table are demonstrated, including the use of subqueries, inner and outer joins, and union joins.

Once an understanding of basic SQL syntax is gained, it is important to understand how SQL is used in the creation of applications. Triggers, small modules of code that include SQL, execute automatically when a particular condition, defined in the trigger, exists. Procedures are similar modules of code but must be called before they execute. SQL commands are often embedded within modules written in a host language, such as C, PHP, .NET, or Java. Dynamic SQL creates SQL statements on the fly, inserting parameter values as needed, and is essential to Web applications. Brief introductions and examples of each of these methods are included in this chapter. Some of the enhancements and extensions to SQL included in SQL:2011 are also covered. Many RDBMS vendors implement SQL:2011 partially but are fully SQL:1999 compliant.

Completion of this chapter gives the student an overview of SQL and some of the ways in which it may be used. Many additional features, often referred to as "obscure" in more detailed SQL texts, will be needed in particular situations. Practice with the syntax included in this chapter will give you a good start toward mastery of SQL.

PROCESSING MULTIPLE TABLES

PINE VALLEY FURNITURE

Now that we have explored some of the possibilities for working with a single table, it's time to bring out the light sabers, jet packs, and tools for heavy lifting: We will work with multiple tables simultaneously. The power of RDBMSs is realized when working with multiple tables. When relationships exist among tables, the tables can be linked together in queries. Remember from Chapter 4 that these relationships are established by including a common column(s) in each table where a relationship is needed. In most cases this is accomplished by setting up a primary key–foreign key relationship, where the foreign key in one table references the primary key in another, and the values in both come from a common domain. We can use these columns to establish a link between two tables by finding common values in the columns. Figure 7-1 carries forward two relations from Figure 6-3, depicting part of the Pine Valley Furniture Company database. Notice that CustomerID values in Order_T correspond to CustomerID values in Customer_T. Using this correspondence, we can deduce that Contemporary Casuals placed orders 1001 and 1010 because Contemporary Casuals's CustomerID is 1, and Order_T shows that OrderID 1001 and 1010 were placed by customer 1. In a relational system, data from related tables are combined into one result table or view and then displayed or used as input to a form or report definition.

The linking of related tables varies among different types of relational systems. In SQL, the WHERE clause of the SELECT command is also used for multiple-table operations. In fact, SELECT can include references to two, three, or more tables in the same command. As illustrated next, SQL has two ways to use SELECT for combining data from related tables.

The most frequently used relational operation, which brings together data from two or more related tables into one resultant table, is called a **join**. Originally, SQL specified a join implicitly by referring in a WHERE clause to the matching of common columns over which tables were joined. Since SQL-92, joins may also be specified in the FROM clause. In either case, two tables may be joined when each contains a column that shares a common domain with the other. As mentioned previously, a primary key from one table and a foreign key that references the table with the primary key will share a common domain and are frequently used to establish a join. In special cases, joins will be established using columns that share a common domain but not the primary-foreign key relationship, and that also works (e.g., we might join customers and salespersons based on common postal codes, for which there is no relationship in the data model for the database). The result of a join operation is a single table. Selected columns from all the tables are included. Each row returned contains data from rows in the different input tables where values for the common columns match.

Explicit JOIN...ON commands are included in the FROM clause. The following join operations are included in the standard, though each RDBMS product is likely to support only a subset of the keywords: INNER, OUTER, FULL, LEFT, RIGHT, CROSS, and UNION. (We'll explain these in a following section.) NATURAL is an optional keyword. No matter what form of join you are using, *there should be one ON or WHERE specification for each pair of tables being joined.* Thus, if two tables are to be combined, one ON or WHERE condition would be necessary, but if three tables (A, B, and C) are to

Join
A relational operation that causes two tables with a common domain to be combined into a single table or view.

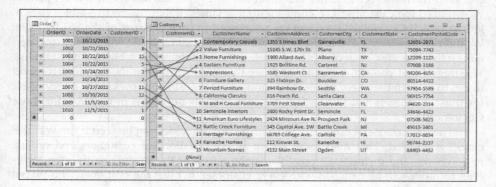

FIGURE 7-1 Pine Valley Furniture Company Customer_T and Order_T tables, with pointers from customers to their orders

be combined, then two ON or WHERE conditions would be necessary because there are 2 pairs of tables (A-B and B-C), and so forth. Most systems support up to 10 pairs of tables within one SQL command. At this time, core SQL does not support CROSS JOIN, UNION JOIN, FULL [OUTER] JOIN, or the keyword NATURAL. Knowing this should help you understand why you may not find these implemented in the RDBMS you are using. Because they are included in the SQL:2011 standard and are useful, expect to find them becoming more widely available.

The various types of joins are described in the following sections.

Equi-join

Equi-join

A join in which the joining condition is based on equality between values in the common columns. Common columns appear (redundantly) in the result table.

With an **equi-join**, the joining condition is based on *equality* between values in the common columns. For example, if we want to know data about customers who have placed orders, we will find that information in two tables, Customer_T and Order_T. It is necessary to match customers with their orders and then collect the information about, for example, customer name and order number in one table in order to answer our question. We call the table created by the query the result or *answer table*.

> *Query:* What are the customer IDs and names of all customers, along with the order IDs for all the orders they have placed?

```
SELECT Customer_T.CustomerID, Order_T.CustomerID,
  CustomerName, OrderID
    FROM Customer_T, Order_T
      WHERE Customer_T.CustomerID = Order_T. CustomerID
      ORDER BY OrderID
```

Result:

CUSTOMERID	CUSTOMERID	CUSTOMERNAME	ORDERID
1	1	Contemporary Casuals	1001
8	8	California Classics	1002
15	15	Mountain Scenes	1003
5	5	Impressions	1004
3	3	Home Furnishings	1005
2	2	Value Furniture	1006
11	11	American Euro Lifestyles	1007
12	12	Battle Creek Furniture	1008
4	4	Eastern Furniture	1009
1	1	Contemporary Casuals	1010

10 rows selected.

The redundant CustomerID columns, one from each table, demonstrate that the customer IDs have been matched and that matching gives one row for each order placed. We prefixed the CustomerID columns with the names of their respective tables so SQL knows which CustomerID column we referenced in each element of the SELECT list. We did not, however, have to prefix CustomerName nor OrderID with their associated table names because each of these columns is found in only one table in the FROM list. We suggest that you study Figure 7-1 to see that the 10 arrows in the figure correspond to the 10 rows in the query result. Also, notice that there are no rows in the query result for those customers with no orders, because there is no match in Order_T for those CustomerIDs.

The importance of achieving the match between tables can be seen if the WHERE clause is omitted. That query will return all combinations of customers and orders, or 150 rows, and includes all possible combinations of the rows from the two tables (i.e., an order will be matched with every customer, not just the customer who placed that order). In this case, this join does not reflect the relationships that exist between the tables and is not a useful or meaningful result. The number of rows is equal to the number of rows in each table, multiplied together (10 orders × 15 customers = 150 rows). This is called a *Cartesian join*. Cartesian joins with spurious results will occur when any joining component of a WHERE clause with multiple conditions is missing or erroneous. In the rare case that a Cartesian join is desired, omit the pairings in the WHERE clause. A Cartesian join may be explicitly created by using the phrase CROSS JOIN in the FROM statement. FROM Customer_T CROSS JOIN Order_T would create a Cartesian product of all customers with all orders. (Use this query only if you really mean to because a cross join against a production database can produce hundreds of thousands of rows and can consume significant computer time—plenty of time to receive a pizza delivery!)

The keywords INNER JOIN...ON are used to establish an equi-join in the FROM clause. While the syntax demonstrated here is Microsoft Access SQL syntax, note that some systems, such as Oracle and Microsoft SQL Server, treat the keyword JOIN by itself without the word INNER to establish an equi-join:

> *Query:*   What are the customer IDs and names of all customers, along with the order IDs for all the orders they have placed?

```
SELECT Customer_T.CustomerID, Order_T.CustomerID,
   CustomerName, OrderID
FROM Customer_T INNER JOIN Order_T ON
   Customer_T.CustomerID = Order_T.CustomerID
ORDER BY OrderID;
```

> *Result:*   Same as the previous query.

Simplest of all would be to use the JOIN...USING syntax, if this is supported by the RDBMS you are using. If the database designer thought ahead and used identical column names for the primary and foreign keys, as has been done with CustomerID in the Customer_T and Order_T tables, the following query could be used:

```
SELECT Customer_T.CustomerID, Order_T.CustomerID,
   CustomerName, OrderID
FROM Customer_T INNER JOIN Order_T USING CustomerID
ORDER BY OrderID;
```

Notice that the WHERE clause now functions only in its traditional role as a filter as needed. Since the FROM clause is generally evaluated prior to the WHERE clause, some users prefer using the newer syntax of ON or USING in the FROM clause. A smaller record set that meets the join conditions is all that must be evaluated by the remaining clauses, and performance may improve. All DBMS products support the traditional method of defining joins within the WHERE clause. Microsoft SQL Server supports the INNER JOIN...ON syntax, Oracle has supported it since 9i, and MySQL has supported it since version 3.23.17.

We again emphasize that SQL is a set-oriented language. Thus, this join example is produced by taking the customer table and the order table as two sets and appending together those rows from Customer_T with rows from Order_T that have equal CustomerID values. This is a set intersection operation, which is followed by appending the selected columns from the matching rows. Figure 7-2 uses set diagrams to display the most common types of two-table joins.

Natural Join

A **natural join** is the same as an equi-join, except that it is performed over matching columns, and one of the duplicate columns is eliminated in the result table. The natural join is the most commonly used form of join operation. (No, a "natural" join is not a more healthy join with more fiber, and there is no unnatural join; but you will find it a

Natural join

A join that is the same as an equi-join except that one of the duplicate columns is eliminated in the result table.

FIGURE 7-2 Visualization of different join types, with the results returned in the shaded area

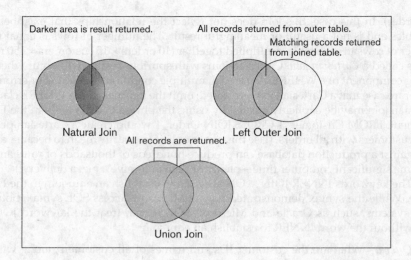

natural and essential function with relational databases.) Notice in the command below that CustomerID must still be qualified because there is still ambiguity; CustomerID exists in both Customer_T and Order_T, and therefore it must be specified from which table CustomerID should be displayed. NATURAL is an optional keyword when the join is defined in the FROM clause.

> *Query:* For each customer who has placed an order, what is the customer's ID, name, and order number?

```
SELECT Customer_T.CustomerID, CustomerName, OrderID
FROM Customer_T NATURAL JOIN Order_T ON
Customer_T.CustomerID = Order_T.CustomerID;
```

Note that the order of table names in the FROM clause is immaterial. The query optimizer of the DBMS will decide in which sequence to process each table. Whether indexes exist on common columns will influence the sequence in which tables are processed, as will which table is on the 1 and which is on the M side of 1:M relationship. If a query takes significantly different amounts of time, depending on the order in which tables are listed in the FROM clause, the DBMS does not have a very good query optimizer.

Outer Join

In joining two tables, we often find that a row in one table does not have a matching row in the other table. For example, several CustomerID numbers do not appear in the Order_T table. In Figure 7-1 pointers have been drawn from customers to their orders. Contemporary Casuals has placed two orders. Furniture Gallery, Period Furniture, M & H Casual Furniture, Seminole Interiors, Heritage Furnishings, and Kaneohe Homes have not placed orders in this small example. We can assume that this is because those customers have not placed orders since 10/21/2015, or their orders are not included in our very short sample Order_T table. As a result, the equi-join and natural join shown previously do not include all the customers shown in Customer_T.

Of course, the organization may be very interested in identifying those customers who have not placed orders. It might want to contact them to encourage new orders, or it might be interested in analyzing these customers to discern why they are not ordering. Using an **outer join** produces this information: Rows that do not have matching values in common columns are also included in the result table. Null values appear in columns where there is not a match between tables.

Outer join

A join in which rows that do not have matching values in common columns are nevertheless included in the result table.

Outer joins can be handled by the major RDBMS vendors, but the syntax used to accomplish an outer join varies across vendors. The example given here uses ANSI standard syntax. When an outer join is not available explicitly, use UNION and NOT EXISTS (discussed later in this chapter) to carry out an outer join. Here is an outer join.

Query: List customer name, identification number, and order number for all customers listed in the Customer table. Include the customer identification number
and name even if there is no order available for that customer.

```
SELECT Customer_T.CustomerID, CustomerName, OrderID
  FROM Customer_T LEFT OUTER JOIN Order_T
  WHERE Customer_T.CustomerID = Order_T. CustomerID;
```

The syntax LEFT OUTER JOIN was selected because the Customer_T table
was named first, and it is the table from which we want all rows returned, regardless of whether there is a matching order in the Order_T table. Had we reversed the
order in which the tables were listed, the same results would be obtained by requesting a RIGHT OUTER JOIN. It is also possible to request a FULL OUTER JOIN. In
that case, all rows from both tables would be returned and matched, if possible,
including any rows that do not have a match in the other table. INNER JOINs are
much more common than OUTER JOINs because outer joins are necessary only when
the user needs to see data from all rows, even those that have no matching row in
another table.

It should also be noted that the OUTER JOIN syntax does not apply easily to a
join condition of more than two tables. The results returned will vary according to the
vendor, so be sure to test any outer join syntax that involves more than two tables until
you understand how it will be interpreted by the DBMS being used.

Also, the result table from an outer join may indicate NULL (or a symbol, such
as ??) as the values for columns in the second table where no match was achieved. If
those columns could have NULL as a data value, you cannot know whether the row
returned is a matched row or an unmatched row unless you run another query that
checks for null values in the base table or view. Also, a column that is defined as NOT
NULL may be assigned a NULL value in the result table of an OUTER JOIN. In the following result, NULL values are shown by an empty value (i.e., a customer without any
orders is listed with no value for OrderID).

Result:

CUSTOMERID	CUSTOMERNAME	ORDERID
1	Contemporary Casuals	1001
1	Contemporary Casuals	1010
2	Value Furniture	1006
3	Home Furnishings	1005
4	Eastern Furniture	1009
5	Impressions	1004
6	Furniture Gallery	
7	Period Furniture	
8	California Classics	1002
9	M & H Casual Furniture	
10	Seminole Interiors	
11	American Euro Lifestyles	1007
12	Battle Creek Furniture	1008
13	Heritage Furnishings	
14	Kaneohe Homes	
15	Mountain Scenes	1003

16 rows selected.

It may help you to glance back at Figures 7-1 and 7-2. In Figure 7-2, customers are represented by the left circle and orders are represented by the right. With a NATURAL JOIN of Customer_T and Order_T, only the 10 rows that have arrows drawn in Figure 7-1 will be returned. The LEFT OUTER JOIN on Customer_T returns all of the customers along with the orders they have placed, and customers are returned even if they have not placed orders. Because Customer 1, Contemporary Casuals, has placed two orders, a total of 16 rows are returned because rows are returned for both orders placed by Contemporary Casuals.

The advantage of an outer join is that information is not lost. Here, all customer names were returned, whether or not they had placed orders. Requesting a RIGHT OUTER join would return all orders. (Because referential integrity requires that every order be associated with a valid customer ID, this right outer join would ensure that only referential integrity is being enforced.) Customers who had not placed orders would not be included in the result.

Query: List customer name, identification number, and order number for all orders listed in the Order table. Include the order number, even if there is no customer name and identification number available.

```
SELECT Customer_T.CustomerID,CustomerName, OrderID
  FROM Customer_T RIGHT OUTER JOIN Order_T ON
    Customer_T.CustomerID = Order_T.CustomerID;
```

Sample Join Involving Four Tables

Much of the power of the relational model comes from its ability to work with the relationships among the objects in the database. Designing a database so that data about each object are kept in separate tables simplifies maintenance and data integrity. The capability to relate the objects to each other by joining the tables provides critical business information and reports to employees. Although the examples provided in Chapter 6 and this chapter are simple and constructed only to provide a basic understanding of SQL, it is important to realize that these commands can be and often are built into much more complex queries that provide exactly the information needed for a report or process.

Here is a sample join query that involves a four-table join. This query produces a result table that includes the information needed to create an invoice for order number 1006. We want the customer information, the order and order line information, and the product information, so we will need to join four tables. Figure 7-3a shows an annotated ERD of the four tables involved in constructing this query; Figure 7-3b shows an abstract instance diagram of the four tables with order 1006 hypothetically having two line items for products Px and Py, respectively. We encourage you to draw such diagrams to help conceive the data involved in a query and how you might then construct the corresponding SQL command with joins.

Query: Assemble all information necessary to create an invoice for order number 1006.

```
SELECT Customer_T.CustomerID, CustomerName, CustomerAddress,
  CustomerCity, CustomerState, CustomerPostalCode, Order_T.OrderID,
  OrderDate, OrderedQuantity, ProductDescription, StandardPrice,
  (OrderedQuantity * ProductStandardPrice)
FROM Customer_T, Order_T, OrderLine_T, Product_T
  WHERE Order_T.CustomerID = Customer_T.CustomerID
    AND Order_T.OrderID = OrderLine_T.OrderID
    AND OrderLine_T.ProductID = Product_T.ProductID
    AND Order_T.OrderID = 1006;
```

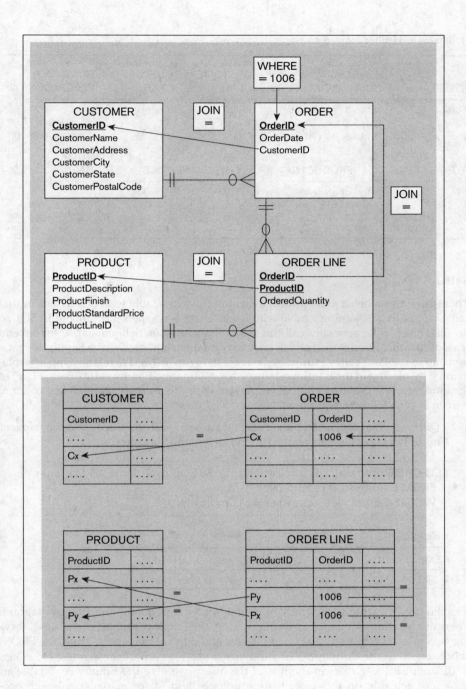

FIGURE 7-3 Diagrams depicting a four-table join (a) Annotated ERD with relations used in a four-table join

(b) Annotated instance diagram of relations used in a four-table join

The results of the query are shown in Figure 7-4. Remember, because the join involves four tables, there are three column join conditions, as follows:

1. Order_T.CustomerID = Customer_T.CustomerID links an order with its associated customer.
2. Order_T.OrderID = OrderLine_T.OrderID links each order with the details of the items ordered.
3. OrderLine_T.ProductID = Product_T.ProductID links each order detail record with the product description for that order line.

FIGURE 7-4   Results from a four-table join (edited for readability)

CUSTOMERID	CUSTOMERNAME	CUSTOMERADDRESS	CUSTOMER CITY	CUSTOMER STATE	CUSTOMER POSTALCODE
2	Value Furniture	15145 S. W. 17th St.	Plano	TX	75094 7743
2	Value Furniture	15145 S. W. 17th St.	Plano	TX	75094 7743
2	Value Furniture	15145 S. W. 17th St.	Plano	TX	75094 7743

ORDERID	ORDERDATE	ORDERED QUANTITY	PRODUCTNAME	PRODUCT STANDARDPRICE	(QUANTITY* STANDARDPRICE)
1006	24-OCT-15	1	Entertainment Center	650	650
1006	24-OCT-15	2	Writer's Desk	325	650
1006	24-OCT-15	2	Dining Table	800	1600

Self-Join

There are times when a join requires matching rows in a table with other rows in that same table—that is, joining a table with itself. There is no special command in SQL to do this, but people generally call this operation a *self-join*. Self-joins arise for several reasons, the most common of which is a unary relationship, such as the Supervises relationship in the Pine Valley Furniture database in Figure 2-22. This relationship is implemented by placing in the EmployeeSupervisor column the EmployeeID (foreign key) of the employee's supervisor, another employee. With this recursive foreign key column, we can ask the following question:

> *Query:*   What are the employee ID and name of each employee and the name of his or her supervisor (label the supervisor's name Manager)?

```
SELECT E.EmployeeID, E.EmployeeName, M.EmployeeName AS Manager
  FROM Employee_T E, Employee_T M
  WHERE E.EmployeeSupervisor = M.EmployeeID;
```

Result:

EMPLOYEEID	EMPLOYEENAME	MANAGER
123-44-347	Jim Jason	Robert Lewis

Figure 7-5 depicts this query in both a Venn diagram and an instance diagram. There are two things to note in this query. First, the Employee table is, in a sense, serving two roles: It contains a list of employees and a list of managers. Thus, the FROM clause refers to the Employee_T table twice, once for each of these roles. However, to distinguish these roles in the rest of the query, we give the Employee_T table an alias for each role (in this case, E for employee and M for manager roles, respectively). Then the columns from the SELECT list are clear: first the ID and name of an employee (with prefix E) and then the name of a manager (with prefix M). Which manager? That then is the second point: The WHERE clause joins the "employee" and "manager" tables based on the foreign key from employee (EmployeeSupervisor) to manager (EmployeeID). As far as SQL is concerned, it considers the E and M tables to be two different tables that have identical column names, so the column names must have a suffix to clarify from which table a column is to be chosen each time it is referenced.

It turns out that there are various interesting queries that can be written using self-joins following unary relationships. For example, which employees have a salary greater than the salary of their manager (not uncommon in professional

FIGURE 7-5 Example of a self-join

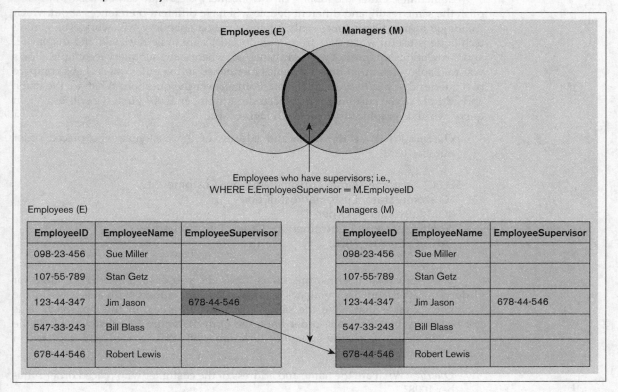

Employees who have supervisors; i.e.,
WHERE E.EmployeeSupervisor = M.EmployeeID

Employees (E)

EmployeeID	EmployeeName	EmployeeSupervisor
098-23-456	Sue Miller	
107-55-789	Stan Getz	
123-44-347	Jim Jason	678-44-546
547-33-243	Bill Blass	
678-44-546	Robert Lewis	

Managers (M)

EmployeeID	EmployeeName	EmployeeSupervisor
098-23-456	Sue Miller	
107-55-789	Stan Getz	
123-44-347	Jim Jason	678-44-546
547-33-243	Bill Blass	
678-44-546	Robert Lewis	

baseball, but generally frowned on in business or government organizations), or (if we had these data in our database) is anyone married to his or her manager (not uncommon in a family-run business but possibly prohibited in many organizations)? Several of the Problems and Exercises at the end of this chapter require queries with a self-join.

As with any other join, it is not necessary that a self-join be based on a foreign key and a specified unary relationship. For example, when a salesperson is scheduled to visit a particular customer, she might want to know all the other customers who are in the same postal code as the customer she is scheduled to visit. Remember, it is possible to join rows on columns from different (or the same) tables as long as those columns come from the same domain of values and the linkage of values from those columns makes sense. For example, even though ProductFinish and EmployeeCity may have the identical data type, they don't come from the same domain of values, and there is no conceivable business reason to link products and employees on these columns. However, one might conceive of some reason to understand the sales booked by a salesperson by looking at order dates of the person's sales relative to his or her hire date. It is amazing what questions SQL can answer (although we have limited control on how SQL displays the results).

Subqueries

The preceding SQL examples illustrate one of the two basic approaches for joining two tables: the joining technique. SQL also provides the subquery technique, which involves placing an inner query (SELECT...FROM...WHERE) within a WHERE or HAVING clause of another (outer) query. The inner query provides a set of one or more values for the search condition of the outer query. Such queries are referred to as subqueries or nested subqueries. Subqueries can be nested multiple times. Subqueries are prime examples of SQL as a set-oriented language.

Sometimes, either the joining or the subquery technique can be used to accomplish the same result, and different people will have different preferences about which technique to use. Other times, only a join or only a subquery will work. The joining technique is useful when data from *several relations* are to be retrieved and displayed, and the relationships are not necessarily nested, whereas the subquery technique allows you to display data from only the tables mentioned in the outer query. Let's compare two queries that return the same result. Both answer the question: What are the name and address of the customer who placed order number 1008? First, we will use a join query, which is graphically depicted in Figure 7-6a.

Query: What are the name and address of the customer who placed order number 1008?

```
SELECT CustomerName, CustomerAddress, CustomerCity,
  CustomerState, CustomerPostalCode
FROM Customer_T, Order_T
WHERE Customer_T.CustomerID = Order_T. CustomerID
  AND OrderID = 1008;
```

In set-processing terms, this query finds the subset of the Order_T table for OrderID = 1008 and then matches the row(s) in that subset with the rows in the Customer_T table that have the same CustomerID values. In this approach, it is not necessary that only one order have the OrderID value 1008. Now, look at the equivalent query using the subquery technique, which is graphically depicted in Figure 7-6b.

Query: What are the name and address of the customer who placed order number 1008?

```
SELECT CustomerName, CustomerAddress, CustomerCity, CustomerState,
CustomerPostalCode
  FROM Customer_T
    WHERE Customer_T.CustomerID =
      (SELECT Order_T.CustomerID
        FROM Order_T
          WHERE OrderID = 1008);
```

Notice that the subquery, shaded in blue and enclosed in parentheses, follows the form learned for constructing SQL queries and could stand on its own as an independent query. That is, the result of the subquery, as with any other query, is a set of rows—in this case, a set of CustomerID values. We know that only one value will be in the result. (There is only one CustomerID for the order with OrderID 1008.) To be safe, we can, and probably should, use the IN operator rather than = when writing subqueries. *The subquery approach may be used for this query because we need to display data from only the table in the outer query.* The value for OrderID does not appear in the query result; it is used as the selection criterion in the inner query. To include data from the subquery in the result, use the join technique, because data from a subquery cannot be included in the final results.

As noted previously, we know in advance that the preceding subquery will return at most one value, the CustomerID associated with OrderID 1008. The result will be empty if an order with that ID does not exist. (It is advisable to check that your query will work if a subquery returns zero, one, or many values.) A subquery can also return a list (set) of values (with zero, one, or many entries) if it includes the keyword IN. *Because the result of the subquery is used to compare with one attribute (CustomerID, in this query), the select list of a subquery may include only one attribute.* For example, which customers have placed orders? Here is a query that will answer that question.

Query: What are the names of customers who have placed orders?

FIGURE 7-6 Graphical depiction of two ways to answer a query with different types of joins

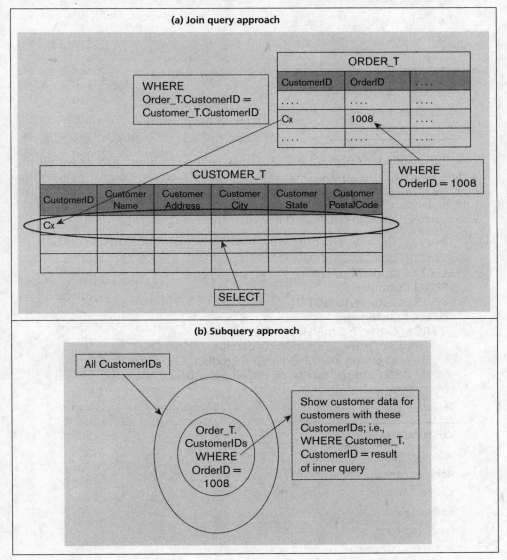

(a) Join query approach

(b) Subquery approach

```
SELECT CustomerName
  FROM Customer_T
    WHERE CustomerID IN
      (SELECT DISTINCT CustomerID
      FROM Order_T);
```

This query produces the following result. As required, the subquery select list contains only the one attribute, CustomerID, needed in the WHERE clause of the outer query. Distinct is used in the subquery because we do not care how many orders a customer has placed, as long as they have placed an order. For each customer identified in the Order_T table, that customer's name has been returned from Customer_T. (You will study this query again in Figure 7-8a.)

Result:

CUSTOMERNAME

Contemporary Casuals

Value Furniture

Home Furnishings

Eastern Furniture

Impressions

California Classics

American Euro Lifestyles

Battle Creek Furniture

Mountain Scenes

9 rows selected.

The qualifiers NOT, ANY, and ALL may be used in front of IN or with logical operators such as = , >, and <. Because IN works with zero, one, or many values from the inner query, many programmers simply use IN instead of = for all queries, even if the equal sign would work. The next example shows the use of NOT, and it also demonstrates that a join can be used in an inner query.

Query: Which customers have not placed any orders for computer desks?

```
SELECT CustomerName
  FROM Customer_T
  WHERE CustomerID NOT IN
  (SELECT CustomerID
    FROM Order_T, OrderLine_T, Product_T
      WHERE Order_T.OrderID = OrderLine_T.OrderID
        AND OrderLine_T.ProductID = Product_T.ProductID
        AND ProductDescription = 'Computer Desk');
```

Result:

CUSTOMERNAME
Value Furniture
Home Furnishings
Eastern Furniture
Furniture Gallery
Period Furniture
M & H Casual Furniture
Seminole Interiors
American Euro Lifestyles
Heritage Furnishings
Kaneohe Homes
10 rows selected.

The result shows that 10 customers have not yet ordered computer desks. The inner query returned a list (set) of all customers who had ordered computer desks. The outer query listed the names of those customers who were not in the list returned by the inner query. Figure 7-7 graphically breaks out the results of the subquery and main query.

Qualifications such as < ANY or >= ALL instead of IN are also useful. For example, the qualification >= ALL can be used to match with the maximum value in a set. But be careful: Some combinations of qualifications may not make sense, such as = ALL (which makes sense only when all the elements of the set have the same value).

Two other conditions associated with using subqueries are EXISTS and NOT EXISTS. These keywords are included in an SQL query at the same location where IN would be, just prior to the beginning of the subquery. EXISTS will take a value of *true* if the subquery returns an intermediate result table that contains one or more rows (i.e.,

FIGURE 7-7   Using the NOT IN qualifier

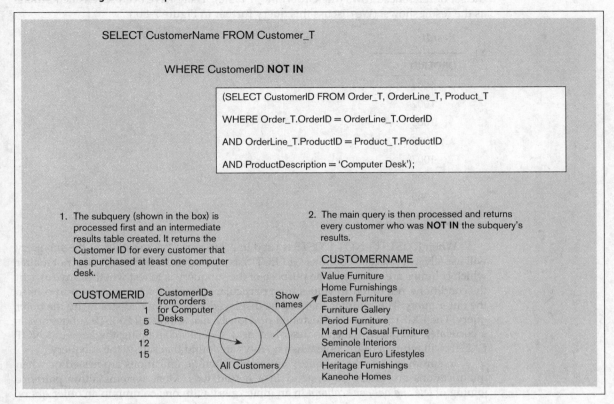

SELECT CustomerName FROM Customer_T

WHERE CustomerID **NOT IN**

(SELECT CustomerID FROM Order_T, OrderLine_T, Product_T

WHERE Order_T.OrderID = OrderLine_T.OrderID

AND OrderLine_T.ProductID = Product_T.ProductID

AND ProductDescription = 'Computer Desk');

1. The subquery (shown in the box) is processed first and an intermediate results table created. It returns the Customer ID for every customer that has purchased at least one computer desk.

CUSTOMERID   CustomerIDs from orders for Computer Desks
    1
    5
    8
   12
   15

All Customers

2. The main query is then processed and returns every customer who was **NOT IN** the subquery's results.

CUSTOMERNAME

Value Furniture
Home Furnishings
Eastern Furniture
Furniture Gallery
Period Furniture
M and H Casual Furniture
Seminole Interiors
American Euro Lifestyles
Heritage Furnishings
Kaneohe Homes

Show names

a nonempty set) and *false* if no rows are returned (i.e., an empty set). NOT EXISTS will take a value of *true* if no rows are returned and *false* if one or more rows are returned.

So, when do you use EXISTS versus IN, and when do you use NOT EXISTS versus NOT IN? You use EXISTS (NOT EXISTS) when your only interest is whether the subquery returns a nonempty (empty) set (i.e., you don't care what is in the set, just whether it is empty), and you use IN (NOT IN) when you need to know what values are (are not) in the set. Remember, IN and NOT IN return a set of values from only one column, which can then be compared to one column in the outer query. EXISTS and NOT EXISTS return only a true or false value depending on whether there are any rows in the answer table of the inner query or subquery.

Consider the following SQL statement, which includes EXISTS.

Query: What are the order IDs for all orders that have included furniture finished in natural ash?

```
SELECT DISTINCT OrderID FROM OrderLine_T
WHERE EXISTS
   (SELECT *
    FROM Product_T
       WHERE ProductID = OrderLine_T.ProductID
       AND ProductFinish = 'Natural Ash');
```

The subquery is different from the subqueries that you have seen before because it will include a reference to a column in a table specified in the outer query. The subquery is executed for each order line in the outer query. The subquery checks for each order line to see if the finish for the product on that order line is natural ash (indicated by the arrow added to the query above). If this is true (EXISTS), the outer query displays the order ID for that order. The outer query checks this one row at a time for every row in the set of referenced rows (the OrderLine_T table). There have been seven such orders, as the result shows. (We discuss this query further in Figure 7-8b.)

Result:

ORDERID
1001
1002
1003
1006
1007
1008
1009
7 rows selected.

When EXISTS or NOT EXISTS is used in a subquery, the select list of the subquery will usually just select all columns (SELECT *) as a placeholder because it does not matter which columns are returned. The purpose of the subquery is to test whether any rows fit the conditions, not to return values from particular columns for comparison purposes in the outer query. The columns that will be displayed are determined strictly by the outer query. The EXISTS subquery illustrated previously, like almost all EXISTS subqueries, is a correlated subquery, which is described next. Queries containing the keyword NOT EXISTS will return a result table when no rows are found that satisfy the subquery.

In summary, use the subquery approach when qualifications are nested or when qualifications are easily understood in a nested way. Most systems allow pairwise joining of *one and only one column* in an inner query with one column in an outer query. An exception to this is when a subquery is used with the EXISTS keyword. Data can be displayed only from the table(s) referenced in the outer query. The number of levels of nesting supported vary depending on the RDBMS but it is seldom a significant constraint. Queries are processed from the inside out, although another type of subquery, a correlated subquery, is processed from the outside in.

Correlated Subqueries

Correlated subquery

In SQL, a subquery in which processing the inner query depends on data from the outer query.

In the first subquery example in the prior section, it was necessary to examine the inner query before considering the outer query. That is, the result of the inner query was used to limit the processing of the outer query. In contrast, **correlated subqueries** use the result of the outer query to determine the processing of the inner query. That is, the inner query is somewhat different for each row referenced in the outer query. In this case, the inner query must be computed for *each* outer row, whereas in the earlier examples, the inner query was computed *only once* for all rows processed in the outer query. The EXISTS subquery example in the prior section had this characteristic, in which the inner query was executed for each OrderLine_T row, and each time it was executed, the inner query was for a different ProductID value—the one from the OrderLine_T row in the outer query. Figures 7-8a and 7-8b depict the different processing order for each of the examples from the previous section on subqueries.

Let's consider another example query that requires composing a correlated subquery.

Query: List the details about the product with the highest standard price.

```
SELECT ProductDescription, ProductFinish, ProductStandardPrice
FROM Product_T PA
  WHERE PA.ProductStandardPrice > ALL
    (SELECT ProductStandardPrice FROM Product_T PB
      WHERE PB.ProductID ! = PA.ProductID);
```

FIGURE 7-8   Subquery processing

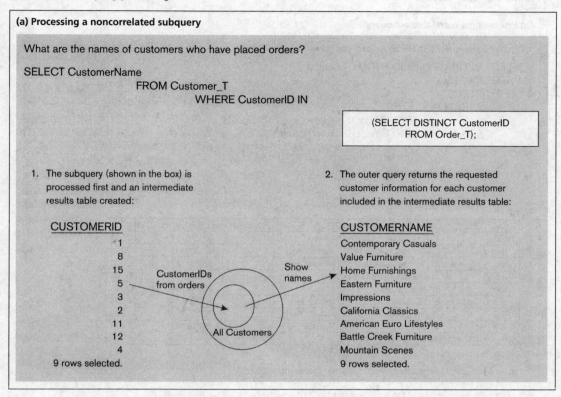

(a) Processing a noncorrelated subquery

What are the names of customers who have placed orders?

SELECT CustomerName

          FROM Customer_T

               WHERE CustomerID IN

                           (SELECT DISTINCT CustomerID
FROM Order_T);

1. The subquery (shown in the box) is processed first and an intermediate results table created:

2. The outer query returns the requested customer information for each customer included in the intermediate results table:

CUSTOMERID
1
8
15
5
3
2
11
12
4
9 rows selected.

CustomerIDs from orders

Show names

All Customers

CUSTOMERNAME
Contemporary Casuals
Value Furniture
Home Furnishings
Eastern Furniture
Impressions
California Classics
American Euro Lifestyles
Battle Creek Furniture
Mountain Scenes
9 rows selected.

As you can see in the following result, the dining table has a higher unit price than any other product.

Result:

PRODUCTDESCRIPTION	PRODUCTFINISH	PRODUCTSTANDARDPRICE
Dining Table	Natural Ash	800

The arrow added to the query above illustrates the cross-reference for a value in the inner query to be taken from a table in the outer query. The logic of this SQL statement is that the subquery will be executed once for each product to be sure that no other product has a higher standard price. Notice that we are comparing rows in a table to themselves and that we are able to do this by giving the table two aliases, PA and PB; you'll recall we identified this earlier as a self-join. First, ProductID 1, the end table, will be considered. When the subquery is executed, it will return a set of values, which are the standard prices of every product except the one being considered in the outer query (product 1, for the first time it is executed). Then, the outer query will check to see if the standard price for the product being considered is greater than all of the standard prices returned by the subquery. If it is, it will be returned as the result of the query. If not, the next standard price value in the outer query will be considered, and the inner query will return a list of all the standard prices for the other products. The list returned by the inner query changes as each product in the outer query changes; that makes it a correlated subquery. Can you identify a special set of standard prices for which this query will not yield the desired result (see Problem and Exercise 7-68)?

FIGURE 7-8 (*continued*)

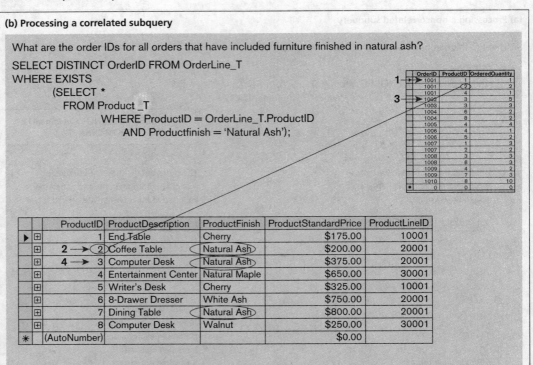

(b) Processing a correlated subquery

What are the order IDs for all orders that have included furniture finished in natural ash?

```
SELECT DISTINCT OrderID FROM OrderLine_T
WHERE EXISTS
        (SELECT *
        FROM Product _T
            WHERE ProductID = OrderLine_T.ProductID
            AND Productfinish = 'Natural Ash');
```

		ProductID	ProductDescription	ProductFinish	ProductStandardPrice	ProductLineID
▶	⊞	1	End Table	Cherry	$175.00	10001
	⊞	2	Coffee Table	Natural Ash	$200.00	20001
	⊞	3	Computer Desk	Natural Ash	$375.00	20001
	⊞	4	Entertainment Center	Natural Maple	$650.00	30001
	⊞	5	Writer's Desk	Cherry	$325.00	10001
	⊞	6	8-Drawer Dresser	White Ash	$750.00	20001
	⊞	7	Dining Table	Natural Ash	$800.00	20001
	⊞	8	Computer Desk	Walnut	$250.00	30001
✳		(AutoNumber)			$0.00	

1. The first order ID is selected from OrderLine_T: OrderID =1001.

2. The subquery is evaluated to see if any product in that order has a natural ash finish. Product 2 does, and is part of the order. EXISTS is valued as true and the order ID is added to the result table.

3. The next order ID is selected from OrderLine_T: OrderID =1002.

4. The subquery is evaluated to see if the product ordered has a natural ash finish. It does. EXISTS is valued as true and the order ID is added to the result table.

5. Processing continues through each order ID. Orders 1004, 1005, and 1010 are not included in the result table because they do not include any furniture with a natural ash finish. The final result table is shown in the text on page 303.

Using Derived Tables

Subqueries are not limited to inclusion in the WHERE clause. As we saw in Chapter 6, they may also be used in the FROM clause to create a temporary derived table (or set) that is used in the query. Creating a derived table that has an aggregate value in it, such as MAX, AVG, or MIN, allows the aggregate to be used in the WHERE clause. Here, pieces of furniture that exceed the average standard price are listed.

Query: Show the product description, product standard price, and overall average standard price for all products that have a standard price that is higher than the average standard price.

```
SELECT ProductDescription, ProductStandardPrice, AvgPrice
  FROM
      (SELECT AVG(ProductStandardPrice) AvgPrice FROM Product_T),
        Product_T
  WHERE ProductStandardPrice > AvgPrice;
```

Result:

PRODUCTDESCRIPTION	PRODUCTSTANDARDPRICE	AVGPRICE
Entertainment Center	650	440.625
8-Drawer Dresser	750	440.625
Dining Table	800	440.625

So, why did this query require a derived table rather than, say, a subquery? The reason is we want to display both the standard price and the average standard price for each of the selected products. The similar query in the prior section on correlated subqueries worked fine to show data from only the table in the outer query, the product table. However, to show both standard price and the average standard price in each displayed row, we have to get both values into the "outer" query, as is done in the query above. The use of derived queries simplifes many solutions and allows you to fulfill complex data requirements.

Combining Queries

Sometimes, no matter how clever you are, you can't get all the rows you want into the single answer table using one SELECT statement. Fortunately, you have a lifeline! The UNION clause is used to combine the output (i.e., union the set of rows) from multiple queries together into a single result table. To use the UNION clause, each query involved must output the same number of columns, and they must be UNION compatible. This means that the output from each query for each column should be of compatible data types. Acceptance as a compatible data type varies among the DBMS products. When performing a union where output for a column will merge two different data types, it is safest to use the CAST command to control the data type conversion yourself. For example, the DATE data type in Order_T might need to be converted into a text data type. The following SQL command would accomplish this:

```
SELECT CAST (OrderDate AS CHAR) FROM Order_T;
```

The following query determines the customer(s) who has in a given line item purchased the largest quantity of any Pine Valley product and the customer(s) who has in a given line item purchased the smallest quantity and returns the results in one table.

Query:

```
SELECT C1.CustomerID, CustomerName, OrderedQuantity,
'Largest Quantity' AS Quantity
FROM Customer_T C1,Order_T O1, OrderLine_T Q1
    WHERE C1.CustomerID = O1.CustomerID
    AND O1.OrderID = Q1.OrderID
    AND OrderedQuantity =
    (SELECT MAX(OrderedQuantity)
    FROM OrderLine_T)
UNION
SELECT C1.CustomerID, CustomerName, OrderedQuantity,
'Smallest Quantity'
FROM Customer_T C1, Order_T O1, OrderLine_T Q1
    WHERE C1.CustomerID = O1.CustomerID
    AND O1.OrderID = Q1.OrderID
    AND OrderedQuantity =
     (SELECT MIN(OrderedQuantity)
     FROM OrderLine_T)
ORDER BY 3;
```

Notice that an expression Quantity has been created in which the strings 'Smallest Quantity' and 'Largest Quantity' have been inserted for readability. The ORDER BY clause has been used to organize the order in which the rows of output are listed. Figure 7-9 breaks the query into parts to help you understand how it processes.

Result:

CUSTOMERID	CUSTOMERNAME	ORDEREDQUANTITY	QUANTITY
1	Contemporary Casuals	1	Smallest Quantity
2	Value Furniture	1	Smallest Quantity
1	Contemporary Casuals	10	Largest Quantity

Did we have to answer this question by using UNION? Could we instead have answered it using one SELECT and a complex, compound WHERE clause with many ANDs and ORs? In general, the answer is sometimes (another good academic answer, like "it depends"). Often, it is simply easiest to conceive of and write a query using several simply SELECTs and a UNION. Or, if it is a query you frequently run, maybe one way will run more efficiently than another. You will learn from experience which approach is most natural for you and best for a given situation.

Now that you remember the union set operation from discrete mathematics, you may also remember that there are other set operations—intersect (to find the elements in common between two sets) and minus (to find the elements in one set that are not in another set). These operations—INTERSECT and MINUS—are also available in SQL, and they are used just as UNION was above to manipulate the result sets created by two SELECT statements.

```
SELECT C1.CustomerID, CustomerName, OrderedQuantity, 'Largest Quantity' AS Quantity
    FROM Customer_T C1, Order_T O1, OrderLine_T Q1
    WHERE C1.CustomerID = O1.CustomerID
        AND O1.OrderID = Q1.OrderID
        AND OrderedQuantity =
                (SELECT MAX(OrderedQuantity)
                FROM OrderLine_T)
```

1. In the above query, the subquery is processed first and an intermediate results table created. It contains the maximum quantity ordered from OrderLine_T and has a value of 10.
2. Next the main query selects customer information for the customer or customers who ordered 10 of any item. Contemporary Casuals has ordered 10 of some unspecified item.

```
SELECT C1.CustomerID, CustomerName, OrderedQuantity, 'Smallest Quantity'
    FROM Customer_T C1, Order_T O1, OrderLine_T Q1
    WHERE C1.CustomerID = O1.CustomerID
        AND O1.OrderID = Q1.OrderID
        AND OrderedQuantity =
                (SELECT MIN(OrderedQuantity)
                FROM OrderLine_T)
ORDER BY 3;
```

1. In the second main query, the same process is followed but the result returned is for the minimum order quantity.
2. The results of the two queries are joined together using the UNION command.
3. The results are then ordered according to the value in OrderedQuantity. The default is ascending value, so the orders with the smallest quantity, 1, are listed first.

FIGURE 7-9 Combining queries using UNION

Conditional Expressions

Establishing IF-THEN-ELSE logical processing within an SQL statement can now be accomplished by using the CASE keyword in a statement. Figure 7-10 gives the CASE syntax, which actually has four forms. The CASE form can be constructed using either an expression that equates to a value or a predicate. The predicate form is based on three-value logic (true, false, don't know) but allows for more complex operations. The value-expression form requires a match to the value expression. NULLIF and COALESCE are the keywords associated with the other two forms of the CASE expression.

CASE could be used in constructing a query that asks "What products are included in Product Line 1?" In this example, the query displays the product description for each product in the specified product line and a special text, '####' for all other products, thus displaying a sense of the relative proportion of products in the specified product line.

Query:

```
SELECT CASE
    WHEN ProductLine = 1 THEN ProductDescription
    ELSE '####'
END AS ProductDescription
FROM Product_T;
```

Result:

PRODUCTDESCRIPTION
End Table
####
####
####
Writers Desk
####
####
####

Gulutzan and Pelzer (1999, p. 573) indicate that "It's possible to use CASE expressions this way as retrieval substitutes, but the more common applications are (a) to make up for SQL's lack of an enumerated <data type>, (b) to perform complicated if/then calculations, (c) for translation, and (d) to avoid exceptions. We find CASE expressions to be indispensable."

More Complicated SQL Queries

We have kept the examples used in Chapter 6 and this chapter very simple in order to make it easier for you to concentrate on the piece of SQL syntax being introduced. It is important to understand that production databases may contain hundreds and even

```
{CASE expression
{WHEN expression
THEN {expression      |  NULL}} ...
 |  {WHEN predicate
THEN {expression      |  NULL}} ...
[ELSE {expression      NULL}]
END }
 |  ( NULLIF (expression, expression)      }
 |  ( COALESCE (expression      . . .) }
```

FIGURE 7-10 CASE conditional syntax

thousands of tables, and many of those contain hundreds of columns. While it is difficult to come up with complicated queries from the four tables used in Chapter 6 and this chapter, the text comes with a larger version of the Pine Valley Furniture Company database, which allows for somewhat more complex queries. This version is available at **www.pearsonhighered.com/hoffer** and at **www.teradatauniversitynetwork.com;** here are two samples drawn from that database:

Question 1:   For each salesperson, list his or her biggest-selling product.

Query: First, we will define a view called TSales, which computes the total sales of each product sold by each salesperson. We create this view to simplify answering this query by breaking it into several easier-to-write queries.

```
CREATE VIEW TSales AS
SELECT SalespersonName,
    ProductDescription,
    SUM(OrderedQuantity) AS Totorders
FROM Salesperson_T, OrderLine_T, Product_T, Order_T
    WHERE Salesperson_T.SalespersonID=Order_T.SalespersonID
    AND Order_T.OrderID=OrderLine_T.OrderID
    AND OrderLine_T.ProductID=Product_T.ProductID
    GROUP BY SalespersonName, ProductDescription;
```

Next we write a correlated subquery using the view (Figure 7-11 depicts this subquery):

```
SELECT SalespersonName, ProductDescription
    FROM TSales AS A
        WHERE Totorders = (SELECT MAX(Totorders) FROM TSales B
        WHERE B.SalesperssonName = A.SalespersonName);
```

Notice that once we had the TSales view, the correlated subquery was rather simple to write. Also, it was simple to conceive of the final query once all the data needed to display were all in the set created by the virtual table (set) of the view. Our thought

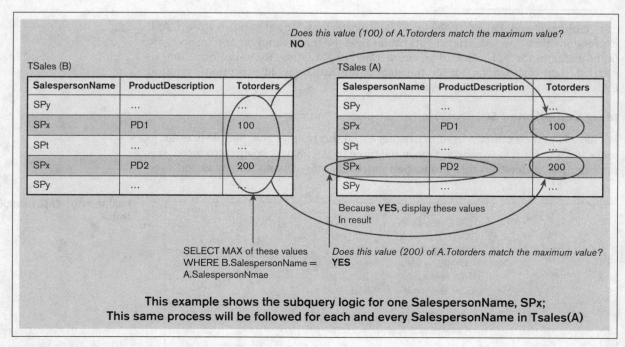

FIGURE 7-11   Correlated subquery involving TSales view

process was if we could create a set of information about the total sales for each salesperson, we could then find the maximum value of total sales in this set. Then it is simply a matter of scanning that set to see which salesperson(s) has total sales equal to that maximum value. There are likely other ways to write SQL statements to answer this question, so use whatever approach works and is most natural for you. We suggest that you draw diagrams, like those you have seen in figures in this chapter, to represent the sets you think you could manipulate to answer the question you face.

Question 2:   Write an SQL query to list all salespersons who work in the territory where the most end tables have been sold.

Query: First, we will create a query called TopTerritory, using the following SQL statement:

```
SELECT TOP 1 Territory_T.TerritoryID,
SUM(OrderedQuantity) AS TopTerritory
    FROM Territory_T INNER JOIN (Product_T INNER JOIN
        (((Customer_T INNER JOIN DoesBusinessIn_T ON
        Customer_T.CustomerID = DoesBusinessIn_T.CustomerID)
        INNER JOIN Order_T ON Customer_T.CustomerID =
        Order_T.CustomerID) INNER JOIN OrderLine_T ON
        Order_T.OrderID = OrderLine_T.OrderID) ON
        Product_T.ProductID = OrderLine_T.ProductID) ON
        Territory_T.TerritoryID = DoesBusinessIn_T.TerritoryID
        WHERE ((ProductDescription)='End Table')
        GROUP BY Territory_T.TerritoryID
        ORDER BY TotSales DESC;
```

This query joins six tables (Territory_T, Product_T, Customer_T, DoesBusinesIn_T, Order_T, and OrderLine_T) based on a chain of common columns between related pairs of these tables. It then limits the result to rows for only End Table products. Then it computes an aggregate of the total of End Table sales for each territory in descending order by this total, and then it produces as the final result the territory ID for only the top (largest) values of total sales of end tables. Sometimes it is helpful to use a graphical representation of the relationships between the tables to create and/or understand the joins (such as the conceptual model from which the table were derived, in this case Figure 2-22).

Next, we will write a query using this query as a derived table. (To save space, we simply insert the name we used for the above query, but SQL requires that the above query be inserted as a derived table where its name appears in the query below. Alternatively, TopTerritory could have been created as a view.) This is a simple query that shows the desired salesperson information for the salesperson in the territory found from the TOP query above.

```
SELECT Salesperson_T.SalespersonID, SalesperspmName
    FROM Territory_T INNER JOIN Salesperson_T ON
        Territory_T.TerritoryID = Salesperson_T.TerritoryID
        WHERE Salesperson_T.TerritoryID IN
            (SELECT TerritoryID FROM TopTerritory);
```

You probably noticed the use of the TOP operator in the TopTerritory query above. TOP, which is compliant with the SQL:2003 standard, specifies a given number or percentage of the rows (with or without ties, as indicated by a subclause) to be returned from the ordered query result set.

TIPS FOR DEVELOPING QUERIES

SQL's simple basic structure results in a query language that is easy for a novice to use to write simple ad hoc queries. At the same time, it has enough flexibility and syntax options to handle complicated queries used in a production system. Both characteristics, however, lead to potential difficulties in query development. As with any other computer programming, you are likely not to write a query correctly the first time. Be sure you have access to an explanation of the error codes generated by the RDBMS. Work initially with a test set of data, usually small, for which you can compute the desired answer by hand as a way to check your coding. This is especially true if you are writing INSERT, UPDATE, or DELETE commands, and it is why organizations have test, development, and production versions of a database, so that inevitable development errors do not harm production data.

As a novice query writer, you might find it easy to write a query that runs without error. Congratulations, but the results may not be exactly what you intended. Sometimes it will be obvious to you that there is a problem, especially if you forget to define the links between tables with a WHERE clause and get a Cartesian join of all possible combinations of records. Other times, your query will appear to be correct, but close inspection using a test set of data may reveal that your query returns 24 rows when it should return 25. Sometimes it will return duplicates you don't want or just a few of the records you want, and sometimes it won't run because you are trying to group data that can't be grouped. Watch carefully for these types of errors before you turn in your final product. Working through a well-thought-out set of test data by hand will help you catch your errors. When you are constructing a set of test data, include some examples of common data values. Then think about possible exceptions that could occur. For example, real data might unexpectedly include null data, out-of-range data, or impossible data values.

Certain steps are necessary in writing any query. The graphical interfaces now available make it easier to construct queries and to remember table and attribute names as you work. Here are some suggestions to help you (we assume that you are working with a database that has been defined and created):

- Familiarize yourself with the data model and the entities and relationships that have been established. The data model expresses many of the business rules that may be idiosyncratic for the business or problem you are considering. It is very important to have a deep understanding of the data model and a good grasp of the data that are available with which to work. As demonstrated in Figures 7-8a and 7-8b, you can draw the segment of the data model you intend to reference in the query and then annotate it to show qualifications and joining criteria. Alternatively you can draw figures such as Figures 7-6 and 7-7 with sample data and Venn diagrams to also help conceive of how to construct subqueries or derived tables that can be used as components in a more complex query.
- Be sure that you understand what results you want from your query. Often, a user will state a need ambiguously, so be alert and address any questions you have after working with users.
- Figure out what attributes you want in your query result. Include each attribute after the SELECT keyword.
- Locate within the data model the attributes you want and identify the entity where the required data are stored. Include these after the FROM keyword.
- Review the ERD and all the entities identified in the previous step. Determine what columns in each table will be used to establish the relationships. Consider what type of join you want between each set of entities.
- Construct a WHERE equality for each link. Count the number of entities involved and the number of links established. Usually there will be one more entity than there are WHERE clauses. When you have established the basic result set, the query may be complete. In any case, run it and inspect your results.
- When you have a basic result set to work with, you can begin to fine-tune your query by adding GROUP BY and HAVING clauses, DISTINCT, NOT IN, and so forth. Test your query as you add keywords to it to be sure you are getting the results you want.
- Until you gain query writing experience, your first draft of a query will tend to work with the data you expect to encounter. Now, try to think of exceptions to the usual data that may be encountered and test your query against a set of test data that includes unusual data, missing data, impossible values, and so forth. If you can handle those, your query is almost complete. Remember that checking by hand will be necessary; just because an SQL query runs doesn't mean it is correct.

As you start to write more complicated queries using additional syntax, debugging queries may be more difficult for you. If you are using subqueries, errors of logic can often be located by running each subquery as a freestanding query. Start with the subquery that is nested most deeply. When its results are correct, use that tested subquery with the outer query that uses its result. You can follow a similar process with derived tables. Follow this procedure until you have tested the entire query. If you are having syntax trouble with a simple query, try taking apart the query to find the problem. You may find it easier to spot a problem if you return just a few crucial attribute values and investigate one manipulation at a time.

As you gain more experience, you will be developing queries for larger databases. As the amount of data that must be processed increases, the time necessary to successfully run a query may vary noticeably, depending on how you write the query. Query optimizers are available in the more powerful database management systems such as Oracle, but there are also some simple strategies for writing queries that may prove helpful for you. The following are some common strategies to consider if you want to write queries that run more efficiently:

- Rather than use the SELECT * option, take the time to include the column names of the attributes you need in a query. If you are working with a wide table and need only a few of the attributes, using SELECT * may generate a significant amount of unnecessary network traffic as unnecessary attributes are fetched over the network. Later, when the query has been incorporated into a production system, changes in the base table may affect the query results. Specifying the attribute names will make it easier to notice and correct for such events.
- Try to build your queries so that your intended result is obtained from one query. Review your logic carefully to reduce the number of subqueries in the query as much as possible. Each subquery you include requires the DBMS to return an interim result set and integrate it with the remaining subqueries, thus increasing processing time.
- Sometimes data that reside in one table will be needed for several separate reports. Rather than obtain those data in several separate queries, create a single query that retrieves all the data that will be needed; you reduce the overhead by having the table accessed once rather than repeatedly. It may help you recognize such a situation by thinking about the data that are typically used by a department and creating a view for the department's use.

Guidelines for Better Query Design

Now you have some strategies for developing queries that will give you the results you want. But will these strategies result in efficient queries, or will they result in the "query from hell," giving you plenty of time for the pizza to be delivered, to watch the *Star Trek* anthology, or to organize your closet? Various database experts, such as DeLoach (1987) and Holmes (1996), provide suggestions for improving query processing in a variety of settings. Also see the Web Resources at the end of this chapter and prior chapters for links to sites where query design suggestions are continually posted. We summarize here some of these suggestions that apply to many situations:

1. *Understand how indexes are used in query processing* Many DBMSs will use only one index per table in a query—often the one that is the most discriminating (i.e., has the most key values). Some will never use an index with only a few values compared to the number of table rows. Others may balk at using an index for which the column has many null values across the table rows. Monitor accesses to indexes and then drop indexes that are infrequently used. This will improve the performance of database update operations. In general, queries that have equality criteria for selecting table rows (e.g., WHERE Finish = "Birch" OR "Walnut") will result in faster processing than queries involving more complex qualifications do (e.g., WHERE Finish NOT = "Walnut") because equality criteria can be evaluated via indexes.
2. *Keep optimizer statistics up-to-date* Some DBMSs do not automatically update the statistics needed by the query optimizer. If performance is degrading, force the running of an update-statistics-like command.

3. *Use compatible data types for fields and literals in queries* Using compatible data types will likely mean that the DBMS can avoid having to convert data during query processing.

4. *Write simple queries* Usually the simplest form of a query will be the easiest for a DBMS to process. For example, because relational DBMSs are based on set theory, write queries that manipulate sets of rows and literals.

5. *Break complex queries into multiple simple parts* Because a DBMS may use only one index per query, it is often good to break a complex query into multiple, simpler parts (which each use an index) and then combine together the results of the smaller queries. For example, because a relational DBMS works with sets, it is very easy for the DBMS to UNION two sets of rows that are the result of two simple, independent queries.

6. *Don't nest one query inside another query* Usually, nested queries, especially correlated subqueries, are less efficient than a query that avoids subqueries to produce the same result. This is another case where using UNION, INTERSECT, or MINUS and multiple queries may produce results more efficiently.

7. *Don't combine a table with itself* Avoid, if possible, using self-joins. It is usually better (i.e., more efficient for processing the query) to make a temporary copy of a table and then to relate the original table with the temporary one. Temporary tables, because they quickly get obsolete, should be deleted soon after they have served their purpose.

8. *Create temporary tables for groups of queries* When possible, reuse data that are used in a sequence of queries. For example, if a series of queries all refer to the same subset of data from the database, it may be more efficient to first store this subset in one or more temporary tables and then refer to those temporary tables in the series of queries. This will avoid repeatedly combining the same data together or repeatedly scanning the database to find the same database segment for each query. The trade-off is that the temporary tables will not change if the original tables are updated when the queries are running. Using temporary tables is a viable substitute for derived tables, and they are created only once for a series of references.

9. *Combine update operations* When possible, combine multiple update commands into one. This will reduce query processing overhead and allow the DBMS to seek ways to process the updates in parallel.

10. *Retrieve only the data you need* This will reduce the data accessed and transferred. This may seem obvious, but there are some shortcuts for query writing that violate this guideline. For example, in SQL the command SELECT * from EMP will retrieve all the fields from all the rows of the EMP table. But, if the user needs to see only some of the columns of the table, transferring the extra columns increases the query processing time.

11. *Don't have the DBMS sort without an index* If data are to be displayed in sorted order and an index does not exist on the sort key field, then sort the data outside the DBMS after the unsorted results are retrieved. Usually a sort utility will be faster than a sort without the aid of an index by the DBMS.

12. *Learn!* Track query processing times, review query plans with the EXPLAIN command, and improve your understanding of the way the DBMS determines how to process queries. Attend specialized training from your DBMS vendor on writing efficient queries, which will better inform you about the query optimizer.

13. *Consider the total query processing time for ad hoc queries* The total time includes the time it takes the programmer (or end user) to write the query as well as the time to process the query. Many times, for ad hoc queries, it is better to have the DBMS do extra work to allow the user to more quickly write a query. And isn't that what technology is supposed to accomplish—to allow people to be more productive? So, don't spend too much time, especially for ad hoc queries, trying to write the most efficient query. Write a query that is logically correct (i.e., produces the desired results) and let the DBMS do the work. (Of course, do an EXPLAIN first to be sure you haven't written "the query from hell" so that all other users will see a serious delay in query processing time.) This suggests a corollary: When possible, run your query when there is a light load on the database, because the total query processing time includes delays induced by other load on the DBMS and database.

All options are not available with every DBMS, and each DBMS has unique options due to its underlying design. You should refer to reference manuals for your DBMS to know which specific tuning options are available to you.

ENSURING TRANSACTION INTEGRITY

RDBMSs are no different from other types of database managers in that one of their primary responsibilities is to ensure that data maintenance is properly and completely handled. Even with extensive testing, as suggested in the prior section, bad things can happen to good data managers: A data maintenance program may not work correctly because someone submitted the job twice, some unanticipated anomaly in the data occurred, or there was a computer hardware, software, or power malfunction during the transaction. Data maintenance is defined in units of work called *transactions*, which involve one or more data manipulation commands. A transaction is a complete set of closely related update commands that must all be done, or none of them done, for the database to remain valid. Consider Figure 7-12, for example. When an order is entered into the Pine Valley database, all of the items ordered should be entered at the same time. Thus, either all OrderLine_T rows from this form are to be entered, along with all the information in Order_T, or none of them should be entered. Here, the business transaction is the complete order, not the individual items that are ordered. What we need are commands to define the boundaries of a transaction, to commit the work of a transaction as a permanent change to the database, and to abort a transaction on purpose and correctly, if necessary. In addition, we need data recovery services to clean up after abnormal termination of database processing in the middle of a transaction. Perhaps the order form is accurate, but in the middle of entering the order, the computer system malfunctions or loses power. In this case, we do not want some of the changes made and not others. It's all or nothing at all if we want a valid database.

When a single SQL command constitutes a transaction, some RDBMSs will automatically commit or roll back after the command is run. With a user-defined transaction, however, where multiple SQL commands need to be run and either entirely committed or entirely rolled back, commands are needed to manage the transaction explicitly. Many systems will have BEGIN TRANSACTION and END TRANSACTION

FIGURE 7-12 An SQL transaction sequence (in pseudocode)

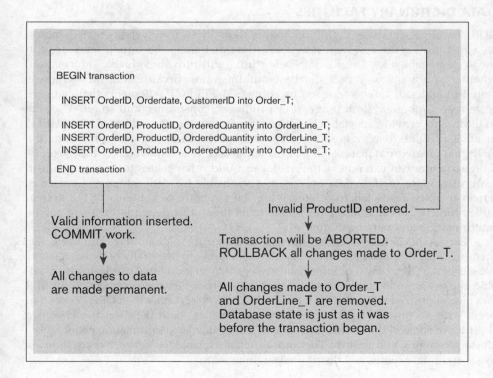

BEGIN transaction

  INSERT OrderID, Orderdate, CustomerID into Order_T;

  INSERT OrderID, ProductID, OrderedQuantity into OrderLine_T;
  INSERT OrderID, ProductID, OrderedQuantity into OrderLine_T;
  INSERT OrderID, ProductID, OrderedQuantity into OrderLine_T;

END transaction

Valid information inserted.
COMMIT work.

All changes to data
are made permanent.

Invalid ProductID entered.

Transaction will be ABORTED.
ROLLBACK all changes made to Order_T.

All changes made to Order_T
and OrderLine_T are removed.
Database state is just as it was
before the transaction began.

commands, which are used to mark the boundaries of a logical unit of work. BEGIN TRANSACTION creates a log file and starts recording all changes (insertions, deletions, and updates) to the database in this file. END TRANSACTION or COMMIT takes the contents of the log file and applies them to the database, thus making the changes permanent, and then empties the log file. ROLLBACK asks SQL to empty the log file. Some RDBMSs also have an AUTOCOMMIT (ON/OFF) command that specifies whether changes are made permanent after each data modification command (ON) or only when work is explicitly made permanent (OFF) by the COMMIT command.

User-defined transactions can improve system performance because transactions will be processed as sets rather than as individual transactions, thus reducing system overhead. When AUTOCOMMIT is set to OFF, changes will not be made automatically until the end of a transaction is indicated. When AUTOCOMMIT is set to ON, changes will be made automatically at the end of each SQL statement; this would not allow for user-defined transactions to be committed or rolled back only as a whole.

SET AUTOCOMMIT is an interactive command; therefore, a given user session can be dynamically controlled for appropriate integrity measures. Each SQL INSERT, UPDATE, and DELETE command typically works on only one table at a time. Some data maintenance requires updating of multiple tables for the work to be complete. Therefore, these transaction-integrity commands are important in clearly defining whole units of database changes that must be completed in full for the database to retain integrity.

Further, some SQL systems have concurrency controls that handle the updating of a shared database by concurrent users. These can journalize database changes so that a database can be recovered after abnormal terminations in the middle of a transaction. They can also undo erroneous transactions. For example, in a banking application, the update of a bank account balance by two concurrent users should be cumulative. Such controls are transparent to the user in SQL; no user programming is needed to ensure proper control of concurrent access to data. To ensure the integrity of a particular database, be sensitive to transaction integrity and recovery issues and make sure that application programmers are appropriately informed of when these commands are to be used.

DATA DICTIONARY FACILITIES

RDBMSs store database definition information in secure system-created tables; we can consider these system tables as a data dictionary. Becoming familiar with the systems tables for any RDBMS being used will provide valuable information, whether you are a user or a database administrator. Because the information is stored in tables, it can be accessed by using SQL SELECT statements that can generate reports about system usage, user privileges, constraints, and so on. Also, the RDBMS will provide special SQL (proprietary) commands, such as SHOW, HELP, or DESCRIBE, to display predefined contents of the data dictionary, including the DDL that created database objects. Further, a user who understands the systems-table structure can extend existing tables or build other tables to enhance built-in features (e.g., to include data on who is responsible for data integrity). A user is, however, often restricted from modifying the structure or contents of the system tables directly, because the DBMS maintains them and depends on them for its interpretation and parsing of queries.

Each RDBMS keeps various internal tables for these definitions. In Oracle 12c, there are more than 500 data dictionary views for DBAs to use. Many of these views, or subsets of the DBA view (i.e., information relevant to an individual user), are also available to users who do not possess DBA privileges. Those view names begin with USER (anyone authorized to use the database) or ALL (any user) rather than DBA. Views that begin with V$ provide updated performance statistics about the database. Here is a short list of some of the tables (accessible to DBAs) that keep information about tables, clusters, columns, and security. There are also tables related to storage, objects, indexes, locks, auditing, exports, and distributed environments.

Table	Description
DBA_TABLES	Describes all tables in the database
DBA_TAB_COMMENTS	Comments on all tables in the database
DBA_CLUSTERS	Describes all clusters in the database
DBA_TAB_COLUMNS	Describes columns of all tables, views, and clusters
DBA_COL_PRIVS	Includes all grants on columns in the database
DBA_COL_COMMENTS	Comments on all columns in tables and views
DBA_CONSTRAINTS	Constraint definitions on all tables in the database
DBA_USERS	Information about all users of the database

To give an idea of the type of information found in the system tables, consider DBA_USERS. DBA_USERS contains information about the valid users of the database; its 12 attributes include user name, user ID, encrypted password, default tablespace, temporary tablespace, date created, and profile assigned. DBA_TAB_COLUMNS has 31 attributes, including owner of each table, table name, column name, data type, data length, precision, and scale, among others. An SQL query against DBA_TABLES to find out who owns PRODUCT_T follows. (Note that we have to specify PRODUCT_T, not Product_T, because Oracle stores data names in all capital letters.)

Query: Who is the owner of the PRODUCT_T table?

```
SELECT OWNER, TABLE_NAME
  FROM DBA_TABLES
     WHERE TABLE_NAME = 'PRODUCT_T';
```

Result:

OWNER	TABLE_NAME
MPRESCOTT	PRODUCT_T

Every RDBMS contains a set of tables in which metadata of the sort described for Oracle 12c is contained. Microsoft SQL Server 2014 divides the system tables (or views) into different categories, based on the information needed:

- *Catalog views,* which return information that is used by the SQL Server database engine. All user-available catalog metadata are exposed through catalog views.
- *Compatibility views,* which are implementations of the system tables from earlier releases of SQL Server. These views expose the same metadata available in SQL Server 2000.
- *Dynamic management views and functions,* which return server state information that can be used to monitor the health of a server instance, diagnose problems, and tune performance. There are two types of dynamic management views and functions:
  - *Server-scoped dynamic management views and functions,* which require VIEW SERVER STATE permission on the server.
  - *Database-scoped dynamic management views and functions,* which require VIEW DATABASE STATE permission on the database.
- *Information schema views,* which provide an internal system table–independent view of the SQL Server metadata. The information schema views included in SQL Server comply with the ISO standard definition for the INFORMATION_SCHEMA.
- *Replication views,* which contain information that is used by data replication in Microsoft SQL Server.

SQL Server metadata tables begin with sys, just as Oracle tables begin with DBA, USER, or ALL.

Here are a few of the Microsoft SQL Server 2014 catalog views:

View	Description
sys.columns	Table and column specifications
sys.computed_columns	Specifications about computed columns
sys.foreign_key_columns	Details about columns in foreign key constraints
sys.indexes	Table index information
sys.objects	Database objects listing
sys.tables	Tables and their column names
sys.synonyms	Names of objects and their synonyms

These metadata views can be queried just like a view of base table data. For example, the following query displays specific information about objects in an SQL Server database that have been modified in the past 10 days:

```
SELECT name as object_name, SCHEMA_NAME (schema_id) AS
  schema_name, type_desc, create_date, modify_date
FROM sys.objects
WHERE modify_date > GETDATE() – 10
ORDER BY modify_date;
```

You will want to investigate the system views and metadata commands available with the RDBMS you are using. They can be life savers when you need critical information to solve a homework assignment or to work exam exercises. (Is this enough motivation?)

RECENT ENHANCEMENTS AND EXTENSIONS TO SQL

Chapter 6 and this chapter have demonstrated the power and simplicity of SQL. However, readers with a strong interest in business analysis may have wondered about the limited set of statistical functions available. Programmers familiar with other languages may have wondered how variables will be defined, flow control established, or **user-defined data types (UDTs)** created. And, as programming becomes more object oriented, how is SQL going to adjust? SQL:1999 extended SQL by providing more programming capabilities. SQL:2008 standardized additional statistical functions. With time, the SQL standard will be modified to encompass object-oriented concepts. Other notable additions in SQL:2008 included three new data types and a new part, SQL/XML. The first two areas, additional statistical functions within the WINDOW clause, and the new data types, are discussed here. SQL:2011 introduced multiple refinements to the changes implemented in SQL:2008. In addition, the most important new elements in SQL:2011 are the temporal features, which allow a significantly more sophisticated treatment of time-variant data. They will be covered briefly after the coverage of the analytical features of SQL:2008. SQL/XML is discussed briefly in Chapter 8.

User-defined data type (UDT)

A data type that a user can define by making it a subclass of a standard type or creating a type that behaves as an object. UDTs may also have defined functions and methods.

Analytical and OLAP Functions

SQL:2008 added a set of analytical functions, referred to as OLAP (online analytical processing) functions, as SQL language extensions. Most of the functions have already been implemented in Oracle, DB2, Microsoft SQL Server, and Teradata. Including these functions in the SQL standard addresses the need for analytical capabilities within the database engine. Linear regressions, correlations, and moving averages can now be calculated without moving the data outside the database. As SQL:2008 is implemented, vendor implementations will adhere strictly to the standard and become more similar. We discuss OLAP further in Chapter 9, as part of the discussion of data warehousing.

Table 7-1 lists a few of the newly standardized functions. Both statistical and numeric functions are included. Functions such as ROW_NUMBER and RANK will allow the developer to work much more flexibly with an ordered result. For database marketing or customer relationship management applications, the ability to consider only the top n rows or to subdivide the result into groupings by percentile is a welcome addition. Users can expect to achieve more efficient processing, too, as the functions are brought into the database engine and optimized. Once they are standardized, application vendors can depend on them, including their use in their applications and avoiding the need to create their own functions outside of the database.

SQL:1999 was amended to include an additional clause, the WINDOW clause. The WINDOW clause improves SQL's numeric analysis capabilities. It allows a query to specify that an action is to be performed over a set of rows (the window). This clause consists of a list of window definitions, each of which defines a name and specification for the window. Specifications include partitioning, ordering, and aggregation grouping.

Here is a sample query from the paper that proposed the amendment (Zemke et al., 1999, p. 4):

```
SELECT SH.Territory, SH.Month, SH.Sales,
AVG (SH.Sales) OVER W1 AS MovingAverage
    FROM SalesHistory AS SH
        WINDOW W1 AS (PARTITION BY (SH.Territory)
            ORDER BY (SH.Month ASC)
            ROWS 2 PRECEDING);
```

The window name is W1, and it is defined in the WINDOW clause that follows the FROM clause. The PARTITION clause partitions the rows in SalesHistory

TABLE 7-1   Some Built-in Functions Added in SQL:2008

Function	Description
CEILING	Computes the least integer greater than or equal to its argument—for example, CEIL(100) or CEILING(100).
FLOOR	Computes the greatest integer less than or equal to its argument—for example, FLOOR(25).
SQRT	Computes the square root of its argument—for example, SQRT(36).
RANK	Computes the ordinal rank of a row within its window. Implies that if duplicates exist, there will be gaps in the ranks assigned. The rank of the row is defined as 1 plus the number of rows preceding the row that are not peers of the row being ranked.
DENSE_RANK	Computes the ordinal rank of a row within its window. Implies that if duplicates exist, there will be no gaps in the ranks assigned. The rank of the row is the number of distinct rows preceding the row and itself.
ROLLUP	Works with GROUP BY to compute aggregate values for each level of the hierarchy specified by the group by columns, (The hierarchy is assumed to be left to right in the list of GROUP BY columns.)
CUBE	Works with GROUP BY to create a subtotal of all possible columns for the aggregate specified.
SAMPLE	Reduces the number of rows by returning one or more random samples (with or without replacement). (This function is not ANSI SQL-2003 compliant but is available with many RDBMSs.)
OVER or WINDOW	Creates partitions of data, based on values of one or more columns over which other analytical functions (e.g., RANK) can be computed.

by Territory. Within each territory partition, the rows will be ordered in ascending order, by month. Finally, an aggregation group is defined as the current row and the two preceding rows of the partition, following the order imposed by the ORDER BY clause. Thus, a moving average of the sales for each territory will be returned as MovingAverage. Although proposed, MOVING_AVERAGE has not been included in any of the SQL standards. It has, however, been implemented by many RDBMS vendors, especially those supporting data warehousing and business intelligence. Though using SQL might not be the preferred way to perform numeric analyses on data sets, inclusion of the WINDOW clause has made many OLAP analyses easier. Several new WINDOW functions were approved in SQL:2008. Of these new window functions, RANK and DENSE_RANK are included in Table 7-1. Previously included aggregate functions, such as AVG, SUM, MAX, and MIN, can also be used in the WINDOW clause.

New Data Types

SQL:2008 introduced three new data types and removed two traditional data types. The data types that were removed are BIT and BIT VARYING. Eisenberg et al. (2004) indicate that BIT and BIT VARYING were removed because they had not been widely supported by RDBMS products and were not expected to be supported.

The three new data types are BIGINT, MULTISET, and XML. BIGINT is an exact numeric type of scale 0, meaning it is an integer. The precision of BIGINT is greater than that of either INT or SMALLINT, but its exact definition is implementation specific. However, BIGINT, INT, and SMALLINT must have the same radix, or base system. All operations that can be performed using INT and SMALLINT can be performed using BIGINT, too.

MULTISET is a new collection data type. The previous collection data type is ARRAY, a noncore SQL data type. MULTISET differs from ARRAY because it can contain duplicates. This also distinguishes a table defined as MULTISET data from a relation, which is a set and cannot contain duplicates. MULTISET is unordered, and all elements are of the same element type. The elements can be any other supported data type. INTEGER MULTISET, for example, would define a multiset where all the elements are INTEGER data type. The values in a multiset may be created through INSERT or through a SELECT statement. An example of the INSERT approach would be MULTISET (2,3,5,7) and of the SELECT approach MULTISET (SELECT ProductDescription FROM Product_T WHERE ProductStandardPrice > 200;. MULTISET) reflects the real-world circumstance that some relations may contain duplicates that are acceptable when a subset is extracted from a table.

New Temporal Features in SQL

Kulkarni and Michels (2012) describe the new temporal (time-related) extensions introduced to SQL in SQL:2011 (together with many other changes, as discussed in Zemke, 2012). The importance of providing support for time-specific data has been recognized for a long time, and there were earlier efforts to introduce elements of the SQL language to deal with time-variant data. Unfortunately, these efforts failed to produce a widely acceptable result; thus, this important set of features was not introduced to the standard until 2011.

The importance of values that change over time can be demonstrated with a relatively simple example. Imagine, for example, a long-time employee of a company. During the time of this employee's tenure with the firm, a number of important characteristics of the employee vary over time: position, department, salary, performance ratings, etc. Some of these can be dealt with easily with separating Position characteristics from Employee characteristics and giving each instance of Position attributes StartTime and EndTime.

Let's, however, assume that an employee's department is not dependent on the employee's position and we would like to track the department over time as an attribute of Employee. We would not be able to do this properly with SQL without the temporal extensions. With them, however, we can add to a relational table a *period definition* (which creates an *application-time period* table). Adapting an example from Kulkarni and Michels (2012), we could specify a table as follows:

```
CREATE TABLE Employee_T(
    EmpNbr          NUMBER(11,0),
    EmpStart        DATE,
    EmpEnd          DATE,
    EmpDept         NUMBER(11,0),
    PERIOD for EmpPeriod (EmpStart, EmpEnd))
```

This would allow us to specify the time period (using EmpStart and EmpEnd) when the rest of the attributes are valid. This will, in practice, require that EmpStart and EmpEnd are added to the primary key. Once this is done, we can use a number of new time-related predicates (CONTAINS, OVERLAPS, EQUALS, PRECEDES, SUCCEEDS, IMMEDIATELY PRECEDES, and IMMEDIATELY SUCCEEDS) in query operations.

In addition to the application-time period tables described above, SQL:2011 adds *system-versioned* tables, which provide capabilities to keep system-maintained data regarding the history of all changes (insertions, updates, and deletions) to the database contents. With increased auditing and regulatory requirements, it is particularly important that the DBMS, not the applications, is maintaining the time-related data (Kulkarni and Michels, 2012, p. 39). SQL:2011 also supports so-called *bi-temporal* tables, which combine the characteristics of application-time period tables and system-versioned tables.

Other Enhancements

In addition to the enhancements to windowed tables described previously, the CREATE TABLE command was enhanced by the expansion of CREATE TABLE LIKE options. CREATE TABLE LIKE allows one to create a new table that is similar to an existing table, but in SQL:1999 information such as default values, expressions used to generate a calculated column, and so forth, could not be copied to the new table. In SQL:2008, a general syntax of CREATE TABLE LIKE...INCLUDING was approved. INCLUDING COLUMN DEFAULTS, for example, will pick up any default values defined in the original CREATE TABLE command and transfer it to the new table by using CREATE TABLE LIKE...INCLUDING. It should be noted that this command creates a table that seems similar to a materialized view. However, tables created using CREATE TABLE LIKE are independent of the table that was copied. Once the table is populated, it will not be automatically updated if the original table is updated.

An additional approach to updating a table was enabled in SQL:2008 with the new MERGE command. In a transactional database, it is an everyday need to be able to add new orders, new customers, new inventory, and so forth, to existing order, customer, and inventory tables. If changes that require updating information about customers and adding new customers are stored in a transaction table, to be added to the base customer table at the end of the business day, adding a new customer used to require an INSERT command, and changing information about an existing customer used to require an UPDATE command. The MERGE command allows both actions to be accomplished using only one query. Consider the following example from Pine Valley Furniture Company:

```
MERGE INTO Customer_T as Cust
    USING (SELECT CustomerID, CustomerName, CustomerAddress,
    CustomerCity, CustomerState, CustomerPostalCode
      FROM CustTrans_T)
      AS CT
    ON (Cust.CustomerID = CT.CustomerID)
```

PINE VALLEY FURNITURE

```
WHEN MATCHED THEN UPDATE
   SET Cust.CustomerName = CT.CustomerName,
       Cust.CustomerAddress = CT.CustomerAddress,
       Cust.CustomerCity = CT.CustomerCity,
       Cust.CustomerState = CT.CustomerState,
       Cust.CustomerPostalCode = CT.CustomerPostalCode
WHEN NOT MATCHED THEN INSERT
   (CustomerID, CustomerName, CustomerAddress, CustomerCity,
   CustomerState, CustomerPostalCode)
       VALUES (CT.CustomerID, CT.CustomerName, CT.CustomerAddress,
       CT.CustomerCity, CT.CustomerState, CT.CustomerPostalCode);
```

TRIGGERS AND ROUTINES

Prior to the issuance of SQL:1999, no support for user-defined functions or procedures was included in the SQL standards. Commercial products, recognizing the need for such capabilities, have provided them for some time, and we expect to see their syntax change over time to be in line with the SQL:1999 and SQL:2011.

Trigger

A named set of SQL statements that are considered (triggered) when a data modification (i.e., INSERT, UPDATE, DELETE) occurs or if certain data definitions are encountered. If a condition stated within a trigger is met, then a prescribed action is taken.

Triggers and routines are very powerful database objects because they are stored in the database and controlled by the DBMS. Thus, the code required to create them is stored in only one location and is administered centrally. As with table and column constraints, this promotes stronger data integrity and consistency of use within the database; it can be useful in data auditing and security to create logs of information about data updates. Not only can triggers be used to prevent unauthorized changes to the database, they can also be used to evaluate changes and take actions based on the nature of the changes. Because triggers are stored only once, code maintenance is also simplified (Mullins, 1995). Also, because they can contain complex SQL code, they are more powerful than table and column constraints; however, constraints are usually more efficient and should be used instead of the equivalent triggers, if possible. A significant advantage of a trigger over a constraint to accomplish the same control is that the processing logic of a trigger can produce a customized user message about the occurrence of a special event, whereas a constraint will produce a standardized, DBMS error message, which often is not very clear about the specific event that occurred.

Both triggers and routines consist of blocks of procedural code. Routines are stored blocks of code that must be called to operate (see Figure 7-13). They do not run automatically. In contrast, trigger code is stored in the database and runs automatically whenever the triggering event, such as an UPDATE, occurs. Triggers are a special type of stored procedure and may run in response to either DML or DDL commands. Trigger syntax and functionality vary from RDBMS to RDBMS. A trigger written to work with an Oracle database will need to be rewritten if the database is ported to Microsoft SQL Server and vice versa. For example, Oracle triggers can be written to fire once per INSERT, UPDATE, or DELETE command or to fire once per row affected by the command. Microsoft SQL Server triggers can fire only once per DML command, not once per row.

Triggers

Because triggers are stored and executed in the database, they execute against all applications that access the database. Triggers can also cascade, causing other triggers to fire. Thus, a single request from a client can result in a series of integrity or logic checks being performed on the server without causing extensive network traffic between client and server. Triggers can be used to ensure referential integrity, enforce business rules, create audit trails, replicate tables, or activate a procedure (Rennhackkamp, 1996).

Constraints can be thought of as a special case of triggers. They also are applied (triggered) automatically as a result of data modification commands, but their precise syntax is determined by the DBMS, and they do not have the flexibility of a trigger.

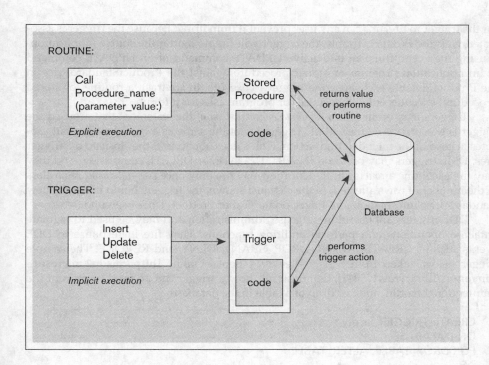

FIGURE 7-13 Triggers
contrasted with stored
procedures
Source: Based on Mullins (1995).

Triggers are used when you need to perform, under specified conditions, a certain action as the result of some database event (e.g., the execution of a DML statement such as INSERT, UPDATE, or DELETE or the DDL statement ALTER TABLE). Thus, a trigger has three parts—the *event*, the *condition*, and the *action*—and these parts are reflected in the coding structure for triggers. (See Figure 7-14 for a simplified trigger syntax.) Consider the following example from Pine Valley Furniture Company: Perhaps the manager in charge of maintaining inventory needs to know (the action of being informed) when an inventory item's standard price is updated in the Product_T table (the event). After creating a new table, PriceUpdates_T, a trigger can be written that enters each product when it is updated, the date that the change was made, and the new standard price that was entered. The trigger is named StandardPriceUpdate, and the code for this trigger follows:

```
CREATE TRIGGER StandardPriceUpdate
AFTER UPDATE OF ProductStandardPrice ON Product_T
FOR EACH ROW
INSERT INTO PriceUpdates_T VALUES (ProductDescription, SYSDATE,
ProductStandardPrice);
```

In this trigger, the *event* is an update of ProductStandardPrice, the *condition* is FOR EACH ROW (i.e., not just certain rows), and the *action after the event* is to insert the specified values in the PriceUpdates_T table, which stores a log of when (SYSDATE) the change occurred and important information about changes made to the ProductStandardPrice of any row in the table. More complicated conditions are possible, such as taking the action for rows where the new ProductStandardPrice meets some limit or the product is associated with only a certain product line. It is important to remember that the procedure in the trigger is performed every time the event occurs; no user has to ask

FIGURE 7-14 Simplified trigger
syntax in SQL:2008

```
CREATE TRIGGER trigger_name
    {BEFORE| AFTER | INSTEAD OF} {INSERT | DELETE | UPDATE} ON
    table_name
    [FOR EACH {ROW | STATEMENT}] [WHEN (search condition)]
    <triggered SQL statement here>;
```

for the trigger to fire, nor can any user prevent it from firing. Because the trigger is associated with the Product_T table, the trigger will fire no matter the source (application) causing the event; thus, an interactive UPDATE command or an UPDATE command in an application program or stored procedure against the ProductStandardPrice in the Product_T table will cause the trigger to execute. In contrast, a routine (or stored procedure) executes only when a user or program asks for it to run.

Triggers may occur either *before*, *after*, or *instead of* the statement that aroused the trigger is executed. An "instead of" trigger is not the same as a before trigger but executes instead of the intended transaction, which does not occur if the "instead of" trigger fires. DML triggers may occur on INSERT, UPDATE, or DELETE commands. And they may fire each time a *row* is affected, or they may fire only once per *statement*, regardless of the number of rows affected. In the case just shown, the trigger should insert the new standard price information into PriceUpdate_T after Product_T has been updated.

DDL triggers are useful in database administration and may be used to regulate database operations and perform auditing functions. They fire in response to DDL events such as CREATE, ALTER, DROP, GRANT, DENY, and REVOKE. The sample trigger below, taken from SQL Server 2014 Books Online [**http://msdn2.microsoft. com/en-us/library/ms175941**], demonstrates how a trigger can be used to prevent the unintentional modification or drop of a table in the database:

```
CREATE TRIGGER safety
ON DATABASE
FOR DROP_TABLE, ALTER_TABLE
AS
     PRINT 'You must disable Trigger "safety" to drop or alter tables!'
     ROLLBACK;
```

A developer who wishes to include triggers should be careful. Because triggers fire automatically, unless a trigger includes a message to the user, the user will be unaware that the trigger has fired. Also, triggers can cascade and cause other triggers to fire. For example, a BEFORE UPDATE trigger could require that a row be inserted in another table. If that table has a BEFORE INSERT trigger, it will also fire, possibly with unintended results. It is even possible to create an endless loop of triggers! So, while triggers have many possibilities, including enforcement of complex business rules, creation of sophisticated auditing logs, and enforcement of elaborate security authorizations, they should be included with care.

Triggers can be written that provide little notification when they are triggered. A user who has access to the database but not the authority to change access permissions might insert the following trigger, also taken from SQL Server 2014 Books Online [**http://msdn2.microsoft.com/en-us/library/ms191134**]:

```
CREATE TRIGGER DDL_trigJohnDoe
ON DATABASE
FOR ALTER_TABLE
AS
GRANT CONTROL SERVER TO JohnDoe;
```

When an administrator with appropriate permissions issues any ALTER _TABLE command, the trigger DDL_trigJohnDoe will fire without notifying the administrator, and it will grant CONTROL SERVER permissions to John Doe.

Routines and other Programming Extensions

In contrast to triggers, which are automatically run when a specified event occurs, routines must be explicitly called, just as the built-in functions (such as MIN and MAX) are called. The routines have been developed to address shortcomings of SQL as an application development language—originally, SQL was only a data retrieval and manipulation language. Therefore, SQL is still typically used in conjunction with computationally more complete languages, such as traditional 3G languages (e.g., Java, C#, or C) or scripting languages (e.g., PHP or Python), to create business applications, procedures, or functions. SQL:1999 did, however, extend SQL by adding programmatic capabilities in core SQL, SQL/PSM, and SQL/OLB. These capabilities have been carried forward and included in SQL:2011.

The extensions that make SQL computationally complete include flow control capabilities, such as IF-THEN, FOR, WHILE statements, and loops, which are contained in a package of extensions to the essential SQL specifications. This package, called **Persistent Stored Modules (SQL/PSM)**, is so named because the capabilities to create and drop program modules are stored in it. *Persistent* means that a module of code will be stored until dropped, thus making it available for execution across user sessions, just as the base tables are retained until they are explicitly dropped. Each module is stored in a schema as a schema object. A schema does not have to have any program modules, or it may have multiple modules.

Using SQL/PSM introduces procedurality to SQL, because statements are processed sequentially. Remember that SQL by itself is a nonprocedural language and that no statement execution sequence is implied. SQL/PSM includes several SQL control statements:

Persistent Stored Modules
Extensions defined originally in SQL:1999 that include the capability to create and drop modules of code stored in the database schema across user sessions.

STATEMENT	DESCRIPTION
CASE	Executes different sets of SQL sequences, according to a comparison of values or the value of a WHEN clause, using either search conditions or value expressions. The logic is similar to that of an SQL CASE expression, but it ends with END CASE rather than END and has no equivalent to the ELSE NULL clause.
IF	If a predicate is TRUE, executes an SQL statement. The statement ends with an ENDIF and contains ELSE and ELSEIF statements to manage flow control for different conditions.
LOOP	Causes a statement to be executed repeatedly until a condition exists that results in an exit.
LEAVE	Sets a condition that results in exiting a loop.
FOR	Executes once for each row of a result set.
WHILE	Executes as long as a particular condition exists. Incorporates logic that functions as a LEAVE statement.
REPEAT	Similar to the WHILE statement, but tests the condition after execution of the SQL statement.
ITERATE	Restarts a loop.

SQL/PSM can be used to create applications or to incorporate procedures or functions directly into SQL. In this section we will focus on these procedures or functions, jointly called *routines*. The terms *procedure* and *function* are used in the same manner as they are in other programming languages. A **function** returns one value and has only input parameters. You have already seen the many built-in functions included in SQL, including the newest functions listed in Table 7-1. A **procedure** may have input parameters, output parameters, and parameters that are both input and output parameters. You may declare and name a unit of procedural code using proprietary code of the RDBMS product being used or invoke (via a CALL to an external procedure) a host-language library routine.

SQL products had developed their own versions of routines prior to the issuance of SQL:1999 and the later revisions to SQL/PSM in SQL:2003, so be sure to become familiar with the syntax and capabilities of any product you use. The implementations by major vendors closest to the standard are stored procedures in MySQL, SQL PL in DB2, and the procedural language of PostgreSQL (Vanroose, 2012). Some of the proprietary languages further away from SQL/PSM, such as Microsoft SQL Server's Transact-SQL and Oracle's PL/SQL, are in wide use and will continue to be available. To give you an idea of how much stored procedure syntax has varied across products, Table 7-2 examines the CREATE PROCEDURE syntax used by three RDBMS vendors; this is the syntax for a procedure stored with the database. This table comes from **www.tdan.com/i023fe03.htm** by Peter Gulutzan (accessed June 6, 2007, but no longer accessible).

Function
A stored subroutine that returns one value and has only input parameters.

Procedure
A collection of procedural and SQL statements that are assigned a unique name within the schema and stored in the database.

TABLE 7-2   Comparison of Vendor Syntax Differences in Stored Procedures

The vendors' syntaxes differ in stored procedures more than in ordinary SQL. For an illustration, here is a chart that shows what CREATE PROCEDURE looks like in three dialects. We use one line for each significant part, so you can compare dialects by reading across the line.

SQL:1999/IBM	MICROSOFT/SYBASE	ORACLE (PL/SQL)
CREATE PROCEDURE	CREATE PROCEDURE	CREATE PROCEDURE
Sp_proc1	Sp_proc1	Sp_proc1
(param1 INT)	@param1 INT	(param1 IN OUT INT)
MODIFIES SQL DATA BEGIN DECLARE num1 INT;	AS DECLARE @num1 INT	AS num1 INT; BEGIN
IF param1 <> 0	IF @param1 <> 0	IF param1 <> 0
THEN SET param1 = 1;	SELECT @param1 = 1;	THEN param1:=1;
END IF		END IF;
UPDATE Table1 SET column1 = param1;	UPDATE Table1 SET column1 = @param1	UPDATE Table1 SET column1 = param1;
END		END

Source: Data from *SQL Performance Tuning* (Gulutzan and Pelzer, Addison-Wesley, 2002). Viewed at **www.tdan.com/i023fe03.htm,** June 6, 2007 (no longer available from this site).

The following are some of the advantages of SQL-invoked routines:

- *Flexibility*   Routines may be used in more situations than constraints or triggers, which are limited to data-modification circumstances. Just as triggers have more code options than constraints, routines have more code options than triggers.
- *Efficiency*   Routines can be carefully crafted and optimized to run more quickly than slower, generic SQL statements.
- *Sharability*   Routines may be cached on the server and made available to all users so that they do not have to be rewritten.
- *Applicability*   Routines are stored as part of the database and may apply to the entire database rather than be limited to one application. This advantage is a corollary to sharability.

The SQL:2011 syntax for procedure and function creation is shown in Figure 7-15. As you can see, the syntax is complicated, and we will not go into the details about each clause here.

Example Routine in Oracle's PL/SQL

In this section, we show an example of a procedure using Oracle's PL/SQL. PL/SQL is an extensive programming language for hosting SQL. We have space here to show only this one simple example.

FIGURE 7-15   Syntax for creating a routine, SQL:2011

```
{CREATE PROCEDURE | CREATE FUNCTION} routine_name
([parameter [{,parameter} . . .]])
[RETURNS data_type result_cast]    /* for functions only */
[LANGUAGE {ADA | C | COBOL | FORTRAN | MUMPS | PASCAL | PLI | SQL}]
[PARAMETER STYLE {SQL | GENERAL}]
[SPECIFIC specific_name]
[DETERMINISTIC | NOT DETERMINISTIC]
[NO SQL | CONTAINS SQL | READS SQL DATA | MODIFIES SQL DATA]
[RETURNS NULL ON NULL INPUT | CALLED ON NULL INPUT]
[DYNAMIC RESULT SETS unsigned_integer]      /* for procedures only */
[STATIC DISPATCH]                           /* for functions only */
[NEW SAVEPOINT LEVEL | OLD SAVEPOINT LEVEL]
routine_body
```

To build a simple procedure that will set a sale price, the existing Product_T table in Pine Valley Furniture Company is altered by adding a new column, SalePrice, that will hold the sale price for the products:

```
ALTER TABLE Product_T
ADD (SalePrice DECIMAL (6,2));
```

Result:

Table altered.

This simple PL/SQL procedure will execute two SQL statements, and there are no input or output parameters; if present, parameters are listed and given SQL data types in a parenthetical clause after the name of the procedure, similar to the columns in a CREATE TABLE command. The procedure scans all rows of the Product_T table. Products with a ProductStandardPrice of $400 or higher are discounted 10 percent, and products with a ProductStandardPrice of less than $400 are discounted 15 percent. As with other database objects, there are SQL commands to create, alter, replace, drop, and show the code for procedures. The following is an Oracle code module that will create and store the procedure named ProductLineSale:

```
CREATE OR REPLACE PROCEDURE ProductLineSale
    AS BEGIN
        UPDATE Product_T
            SET SalePrice =.90 * ProductStandardPrice
            WHERE ProductStandardPrice > = 400;
        UPDATE Product_T
            SET SalePrice =.85 * ProductStandardPrice
            WHERE ProductStandardPrice < 400;
END;
```

Oracle returns the comment "Procedure created" if the syntax has been accepted.

To run the procedure in Oracle, use this command (which can be run interactively, as part of an application program, or as part of another stored procedure):

```
SQL > EXEC ProductLineSale
```

Oracle gives this response:

PL/SQL procedure successfully completed.

Now Product_T contains the following:

PRODUCTLINE	PRODUCTID	PRODUCTDESCRIPTION	PRODUCTFINISH	PRODUCTSTANDARDPRICE	SALEPRICE
10001	1	End Table	Cherry	175	148.75
20001	2	Coffee Table	Natural Ash	200	170
20001	3	Computer Desk	Natural Ash	375	318.75
30001	4	Entertainment Center	Natural Maple	650	585
10001	5	Writer's Desk	Cherry	325	276.25
20001	6	8-Drawer Dresser	White Ash	750	675
20001	7	Dining Table	Natural Ash	800	720
30001	8	Computer Desk	Walnut	250	212.5

We have emphasized numerous times that SQL is a set-oriented language, meaning that, in part, the result of an SQL command is a set of rows. You probably noticed in Figure 7-15 that procedures can be written to work with many different host languages, most of which are record-oriented languages, meaning they are designed to manipulate one record, or row, at a time. This difference is often called an *impedance mismatch* between SQL and the host language that uses SQL commands. When SQL calls an SQL procedure, as in the example above, this is not an issue, but when the procedure is called, for example, by a Java program, it can be an issue. In the next section, we consider embedding SQL in host languages and some of the additional capabilities needed to allow SQL to work seamlessly with languages not designed to communicate with programs written in other, set-oriented languages.

EMBEDDED SQL AND DYNAMIC SQL

We have been using the interactive, or direct, form of SQL. With interactive SQL, one SQL command is entered and executed at a time. Each command constitutes a logical unit of work, or a transaction. The commands necessary to maintain a valid database, such as ROLLBACK and COMMIT, are transparent to the user in most interactive SQL situations. SQL was originally created to handle database access alone and did not have flow control or the other structures necessary to create an application. SQL/PSM, introduced in SQL:1999, provides for the types of programmatic extensions needed to develop a database application.

Prior to SQL/PSM, two other forms of SQL were widely used in creating applications on both clients and servers; they are referred to as **embedded SQL** and **dynamic SQL**. SQL commands can be embedded in third-generation langagues (3GLs), such as Ada, and COBOL, as well as in C, PHP, .NET, and Java if the commands are placed at appropriate locations in a 3GL host program. As we saw in the prior section, Oracle also offers PL/SQL, or SQL Procedural Language, a proprietary language that extends SQL by adding some procedural language features such as variables, types, control structures (including IF-THEN-ELSE loops), functions, and procedures. PL/SQL blocks of code can also be embedded within 3GL programs.

Dynamic SQL derives the precise SQL statement at run time. Programmers write to an application programming interface (API) to achieve the interface between languages. Embedded SQL and dynamic SQL will continue to be used. Programmers are used to them, and in many cases they are still an easier approach than attempting to use SQL as an application language in addition to using it for database creation, administration, and querying.

There are several reasons to consider embedding SQL in a 3GL:

1. It is possible to create a more flexible, accessible interface for the user. Using interactive SQL requires a good understanding of both SQL and the database structure—understanding that a typical application user may not have. Although many RDBMSs come with form, report, and application generators (or such capabilities available as add-ons), developers frequently envision capabilities that are not easily accomplished with these tools but that can be easily accomplished using a 3GL. Large, complex programs that require access to a relational database may best be programmed in a 3GL with embedded SQL calls to an SQL database.

2. It may be possible to improve performance by using embedded SQL. Using interactive SQL requires that each query be converted to executable machine code each time the query is processed. Or, the query optimizer, which runs automatically in a direct SQL situation, may not successfully optimize the query, causing it to run slowly. With embedded SQL, the developer has more control over database access and may be able to create significant performance improvements. Knowing when to rely on the SQL translator and optimizer and when to control it through the program depends on the nature of the problem, and making this trade-off is best accomplished through experience and testing.

Embedded SQL

Hard-coded SQL statements included in a program written in another language, such as C or Java.

Dynamic SQL

Specific SQL code generated on the fly while an application is processing.

3. Database security may be improved by using embedded SQL. Restricted access can be achieved by a DBA through the GRANT and REVOKE permissions in SQL and through the use of views. These same restrictions can also be invoked in an embedded SQL application, thus providing another layer of protection. Complex data integrity checks also may be more easily accomplished, including cross-field consistency checks.

A program that uses embedded SQL will consist of the host program written in a 3GL such as C, Java, or COBOL, and there will also be sections of SQL code sprinkled throughout. Each section of SQL code will begin with EXEC SQL, keywords used to indicate an embedded SQL command that will be converted to the host source code when run through the precompiler. You will need a separate precompiler for each host language that you plan to use. Be sure to determine that the 3GL compiler is compatible with your RDBMS's precompiler for each language.

When the precompiler encounters an EXEC SQL statement, it will translate that SQL command into the host program language. Some, but not all, precompilers will check for correct SQL syntax and generate any required error messages at this point. Others will not generate an error message until the SQL statement actually attempts to execute. Some products' precompilers (DB2, SQL/DS, Ingres) create a separate file of SQL statements that is then processed by a separate utility called a binder, which determines that the referenced objects exist, that the user possesses sufficient privileges to run the statement, and the processing approach that will be used. Other products (Oracle, Informix) interpret the statements at run time rather than compiling them. In either case, the resulting program will contain calls to DBMS routines, and the link/editor programs will link these routines into the program.

Here is a simple example, using C as the host language, that will give you an idea of what embedded SQL looks like in a program. This example uses a prepared SQL statement named GETCUST, which will be compiled and stored as executable code in the database. CustID is the primary key of the customer table. GETCUST, the prepared SQL statement, returns customer information (cname, caddress, city, state, postcode) for an order number. A placeholder is used for the order information, which is an input parameter. Customer information is output from the SQL query and stored into host variables using the *into* clause. This example assumes that only one row is returned from the query, what is often called a singleton SELECT. (We'll discuss below how to handle the situation in which it is possible to return more than one row.)

```
exec sql prepare getcust from
"select cname, c_address, city, state, postcode
from customer_t, order_t
where customer_t.custid = order_t.custid and orderid =?";
.
.
.
./* code to get proper value in theOrder */
exec sql execute getcust into :cname, :caddress, :city, :state,
:postcode using theOrder;
.
.
.
```

If a prepared statement returns multiple rows, it is necessary to write a program loop using cursors to return a row at a time to be stored. A cursor is a data structure, internal to the programming environment, that points to a result table row (similarly to how a display screen cursor points to where data would be inserted in a form if you began entering data). Cursors help eliminate the impedance mismatch between SQL's set-at-a-time processing and procedural languages' record-at-a-time processing. Record-at-a-time languages have to be able to move cursor values forward and backward in the set (FETCH NEXT or FETCH PRIOR), to find the first or last row in a result set (FETCH FIRST and FETCH LAST), to move the cursor to a specific row or one relative to the current position (FETCH ABSOLUTE or FETCH RELATIVE), and to know the number of rows to process and when the end of the result set is reached, which often triggers the end of a programming loop (FOR…END FOR). There are different types of cursors, and the number of types and how they are each handled varies by RDBMS. Thus, this topic is beyond the scope of this text, although you are now aware of this important aspect of embedded SQL.

Dynamic SQL is used to generate appropriate SQL code on the fly while an application is processing. Most programmers write to an API, such as ODBC, which can then be passed through to any ODBC-compliant database. Dynamic SQL is central to most Internet applications. The developer is able to create a more flexible application because the exact SQL query is determined at run time, including the number of parameters to be passed, which tables will be accessed, and so forth. Dynamic SQL is very useful when an SQL statement shell will be used repeatedly, with different parameter values being inserted each time it executes. Dynamic SQL will be discussed further in Chapter 8.

Embedded and dynamic SQL code is vulnerable to malicious modification. Any procedure that has or especially constructs SQL statements should be reviewed for such vulnerabilities. A common form of such an attack involves insertion of the malicious code into user input variables that are concatenated with SQL commands and then executed. Alternatively, malicious code can be included in text stored in the database. As long as the malicious code is syntactically correct, the SQL database engine will process it. Preventing and detecting such attacks can be complicated, and this is beyond the scope of this text. The reader is encouraged to do an Internet search on the topic of SQL injection for recommendations. At a minimum, user input should be carefully validated, strong typing of columns should be used to limit exposure, and input data can be filtered or modified so that special SQL characters (e.g., ;) or words (e.g., DELETE) are put in quotes so they cannot be executed.

Currently, the Open Database Connectivity (ODBC) standard is the most commonly used API. SQL:1999 includes the SQL Call Level Interface (SQL/CLI). Both are written in C, and both are based on the same earlier standard. Java Database Connectivity (JDBC) is an industry standard used for connecting from Java. It is not yet an ISO standard. No new functionality has been added in SQL:2011.

As SQL:2011 becomes implemented more completely, the use of embedded and dynamic SQL will become more standardized because the standard creates a computationally complete SQL language for the first time. Because most vendors have created these capabilities independently, though, the next few years will be a period in which SQL:2011-compliant products will exist side by side with older, but entrenched, versions. The user will need to be aware of these possibilities and deal with them.

Summary

This chapter continues from Chapter 6, which introduced the SQL language. Equi-joins, natural joins, outer joins, and union joins have been considered. Equi-joins are based on equal values in the common columns of the tables that are being joined and will return all requested results including the values of the common columns from each table included in the join. Natural joins return all requested results, but values of the common columns are included only once. Outer joins return all the values in one of the tables included in the join, regardless of whether or not a match exists in the other table. Union joins return a table that includes all data from each table that was joined.

Nested subqueries, where multiple SELECT statements are nested within a single query, are useful for more complex query situations. A special form of the subquery, a correlated subquery, requires that a value be known from the outer query before the inner query can be processed. Other subqueries process the inner query, return a result to the next outer query, and then process that outer query.

Other advanced SQL topics include the use of embedded SQL and the use of triggers and routines. SQL can be included within the context of many third-generation languages including COBOL, C, C#, and Java scripting languages such as PHP and Python. The use of embedded

SQL allows for the development of more flexible interfaces, improved performance, and improved database security. User-defined functions that run automatically when records are inserted, updated, or deleted are called triggers. Procedures are user-defined code modules that can be called to execute. OLTP and OLAP are used for operational transaction processing and data analysis, respectively.

New analytical functions introduced in SQL:2008 and SQL:2011 are shown. Extensions already included in SQL:1999 made SQL computationally complete and included flow control capabilities in a set of SQL specifications known as Persistent Stored Modules (SQL/PSM).

SQL/PSM can be used to create applications or to incorporate procedures and functions using SQL data types directly. Triggers were also introduced in SQL:1999. Users must realize that these capabilities have been included as vendor-specific extensions and will continue to exist for some time.

Dynamic SQL is an integral part of Web-enabling databases and will be demonstrated in more detail in Chapter 8. This chapter has presented some of the more complex capabilities of SQL and has created awareness of the extended and complex capabilities of SQL that must be mastered to build database application programs.

Chapter Review

Key Terms

Correlated subquery 306
Dynamic SQL 330
Embedded SQL 330
Equi-join 294

Function 327
Join 293
Natural join 295
Outer join 296

Persistent Stored Modules (SQL/PSM) 327
Procedure 327
Trigger 324

User-defined data type (UDT) 320

Review Questions

7-1. Define each of the following terms:
   a. dynamic SQL
   b. correlated subquery
   c. embedded SQL
   d. procedure
   e. join
   f. equi-join
   g. self join
   h. outer join
   i. function
   j. Persistent Stored Modules (SQL/PSM)

7-2. Match the following terms to the appropriate definition:

_____ equi-join
_____ natural join
_____ outer join
_____ trigger
_____ procedure
_____ embedded SQL
_____ UDT
_____ COMMIT
_____ SQL/PSM
_____ Dynamic SQL
_____ ROLLBACK

   a. undoes changes to a table
   b. user-defined data type
   c. SQL:1999 extension
   d. returns all records of designated table
   e. keeps redundant columns
   f. makes changes to a table permanent
   g. process that includes SQL statements within a host language
   h. process of making an application capable of generating specific SQL code on the fly
   i. does not keep redundant columns
   j. set of SQL statements that execute under stated conditions
   k. stored, named collection of procedural and SQL statements

7-3. When is an outer join used instead of a natural join?
7-4. Explain the processing order of a correlated subquery.
7-5. What are some of the purposes for which you would use correlated subqueries?

7-6. Explain the relationship between EXISTS and correlated subqueries.
7-7. Explain the following statement regarding SQL: Any query that can be written using the subquery approach can also be written using the joining approach but not vice versa.
7-8. What is the purpose of the COMMIT command in SQL? How does commit relate to the notion of a business transaction (e.g., entering a customer order or issuing a customer invoice)?
7-9. Care must be exercised when writing triggers for a database. What are some of the problems that could be encountered?
7-10. Explain the structure of a module of code that defines a trigger.
7-11. Under what conditions can a UNION clause be used?
7-12. Discuss the differences between triggers and stored procedures.
7-13. Explain the purpose of SQL/PSM.
7-14. List four advantages of SQL-invoked routines.
7-15. When would you consider using embedded SQL? When would you use dynamic SQL?
7-16. When do you think that the CASE keyword in SQL would be useful?
7-17. Explain the use of derived tables.
7-18. Describe an example in which you would want to use a derived table.
7-19. What is PL/SQL, and what does it include in addition to SQL?
7-20. If two queries involved in a UNION operation contained columns that were data type incompatible, how would you recommend fixing this?
7-21. Can an outer join be easily implemented when joining more than two tables? Why or why not?

7-22. What is the purpose of the temporal extensions to SQL that were introduced in SQL:2011?

7-23. Discuss some of the mechanisms that were used for the same purposes as the temporal extensions before they were introduced.

7-24. This chapter discusses the data dictionary views for Oracle 12c. Research another RDBMS, such as Microsoft SQL Server, and report on its data dictionary facility and how it compares with Oracle.

7-25. What was the need for a standardized relational language and what are the advantages gained by the adaptation of the same?

7-26. Explain the differences between static and dynamic SQL?

7-27. 'Views created from the join of multiple tables cannot be updated, whereas views created from a single table is sometimes updatable'.—Qualify the statement above, with appropriate explanations?

Problems and Exercises

Problems and Exercises 7-28 through 7-33 are based on the class schedule 3NF relations along with some sample data in Figure 7-16. For Problems and Exercises 7-28 through 7-33, draw a Venn or ER diagram and mark it to show the data you expect your query to use to produce the results.

7-28. Write SQL retrieval commands for each of the following queries:
   a. Display the course ID and course name for all courses with an ISM prefix.
   b. Display all courses for which Professor Berndt has been qualified.
   c. Display the class roster, including student name, for all students enrolled in section 2714 of ISM 4212.

7-29. Write an SQL query to answer the following question: Which instructors are qualified to teach ISM 3113?

7-30. Write an SQL query to answer the following question: Is any instructor qualified to teach ISM 3113 and not qualified to teach ISM 4930?

7-31. Write SQL queries to answer the following questions:
   a. What are the names of the course(s) that student Altvater took during the semester I-2015?
   b. List names of the students who have taken at least one course that Professor Collins is qualified to teach.
   c. How many students did Professor Collins teach during the semester I-2015?

STUDENT (StudentID, StudentName)

StudentID	StudentName
38214	Letersky
54907	Altvater
66324	Aiken
70542	Marra
...	

QUALIFIED (FacultyID, CourseID, DateQualified)

FacultyID	CourseID	DateQualified
2143	ISM 3112	9/2005
2143	ISM 3113	9/2005
3467	ISM 4212	9/2012
3467	ISM 4930	9/2013
4756	ISM 3113	9/2008
4756	ISM 3112	9/2008
...		

FACULTY (FacultyID, FacultyName)

FacultyID	FacultyName
2143	Birkin
3467	Berndt
4756	Collins
...	

SECTION (SectionNo, Semester, CourseID)

SectionNo	Semester	CourseID
2712	I-2015	ISM 3113
2713	I-2015	ISM 3113
2714	I-2015	ISM 4212
2715	I-2015	ISM 4930
...		

COURSE (CourseID, CourseName)

CourseID	CourseName
ISM 3113	Syst Analysis
ISM 3112	Syst Design
ISM 4212	Database
ISM 4930	Networking
...	

REGISTRATION (StudentID, SectionNo)

StudentID	SectionNo
38214	2714
54907	2714
54907	2715
66324	2713
...	

FIGURE 7-16 Class scheduling relations (for Problems and Exercises 7-28—7-33)

FIGURE 7-17 **Adult literacy program (for Problems and Exercises 7-34–7-44)**

TUTOR (TutorID, CertDate, Status)

TutorID	CertDate	Status
100	1/05/2015	Active
101	1/05/2015	Temp Stop
102	1/05/2015	Dropped
103	5/22/2015	Active
104	5/22/2015	Active
105	5/22/2015	Temp Stop
106	5/22/2015	Active

MATCH HISTORY (MatchID, TutorID, StudentID, StartDate, EndDate)

MatchID	TutorID	StudentID	StartDate	EndDate
1	100	3000	1/10/2015	
2	101	3001	1/15/2015	5/15/2015
3	102	3002	2/10/2015	3/01/2015
4	106	3003	5/28/2015	
5	103	3004	6/01/2015	6/15/2015
6	104	3005	6/01/2015	6/28/2015
7	104	3006	6/01/2015	

STUDENT (StudentID, Read)

StudentID	Read
3000	2.3
3001	5.6
3002	1.3
3003	3.3
3004	2.7
3005	4.8
3006	7.8
3007	1.5

TUTOR REPORT (MatchID, Month, Hours, Lessons)

MatchID	Month	Hours	Lessons
1	6/15	8	4
4	6/15	8	6
5	6/15	4	4
4	7/15	10	5
1	7/15	4	2

7-32. Write SQL queries to answer the following questions:
   a. How many students were enrolled in section 2714 during semester I-2015?
   b. How many students were enrolled in ISM 3113 during semester I-2015?

7-33. Write an SQL query to answer the following question: Which students were not enrolled in any courses during semester I-2015?

Problems and Exercises 7-34 through 7-44 are based on Figure 7-17. This problem set continues from Chapter 6, Problems and Exercises 6-53 through 6-61, which were based on Figure 6-12.

7-34. Determine the relationships among the four relations in Figure 7-17. List primary keys for each relation and any foreign keys necessary to establish the relationships and maintain referential integrity. Pay particular attention to the data contained in TUTOR REPORTS when you set up its primary key.

7-35. Write the SQL command to add column MATH SCORE to the STUDENT table.

7-36. Write the SQL command to add column SUBJECT to TUTOR. The only values allowed for SUBJECT will be Reading, Math, and ESL.

7-37. What do you need to do if a tutor signs up and wants to tutor in both reading and math? Draw the new ERD, create new relations, and write any SQL statements that would be needed to handle this development.

7-38. Write the SQL command to find any tutors who have not submitted a report for July.

7-39. Where do you think student and tutor information such as name, address, phone, and e-mail should be kept? Write the necessary SQL commands to capture this information.

7-40. Write an SQL query to determine the total number of hours and the total number of lessons Tutor 106 taught in June and July 2015.

7-41. Write an SQL query to list the Read scores of students who were ever taught by tutors whose status is Dropped.

7-42. List all active students in June by name. (Make up names and other data if you are actually building a prototype database.) Include the number of hours students received tutoring and how many lessons they completed.

7-43. Which tutors, by name, are available to tutor? Write the SQL command.

7-44. Which tutor needs to be reminded to turn in reports? Write the SQL command. Show how you constructed this query using a Venn or other type of diagram.

Problems and Exercises 7-45 through 7-79 are based on the entire ("big") version Pine Valley Furniture Company database. Note: Depending on what DBMS you are using, some field names may have changed to avoid conflicting with reserved words for the DBMS. When you first use the DBMS, check the table definitions to see what the field names are for

the DBMS you are using. See the Preface and inside covers of this book for instructions on where to find this database, including on **www. teradatauniversitynetwork.com**.

7-45. Write an SQL command that will find any customers who have not placed orders.

7-46. List the names and number of employees supervised (label this value HeadCount) for each supervisor who supervises more than two employees.

7-47. List the name of each employee, his or her birth date, the name of his or her manager, and the manager's birth date for those employees who were born before their manager was born; label the manager's data Manager and ManagerBirth. Show how you constructed this query using a Venn or other type of diagram.

7-48. Write an SQL command to display the order number, customer number, order date, and items ordered for some particular customer.

7-49. Write an SQL command to display each item ordered for order number 1, its standard price, and the total price for each item ordered.

7-50. Write an SQL command to total the cost of order number 1.

7-51. Calculate the total raw material cost (label TotCost) for each product compared to its standard product price. Display product ID, product description, standard price, and the total cost in the result.

7-52. For every order that has been received, display the order ID, the total dollar amount owed on that order (you'll have to calculate this total from attributes in one or more tables; label this result TotalDue), and the amount received in payments on that order (assume that there is only one payment made on each order). To make this query a little simpler, you don't have to include those orders for which no payment has yet been received. List the results in decreasing order of the difference between total due and amount paid.

7-53. Write an SQL query to list each customer who has bought computer desks and the number of units sold to each customer. Show how you constructed this query using a Venn or other type of diagram.

7-54. Write an SQL query to list each customer who bought at least one product that belongs to product line Basic in March 2015. List each customer only once.

7-55. Modify Problem and Exercise 7-54 so that you include the number of products in product line Basic that the customer ordered in March 2015.

7-56. Modify Problem and Exercise 7-55 so that the list includes the number of products each customer bought in each product line in March 2015.

7-57. List, in alphabetical order, the names of all employees (managers) who are now managing people with skill ID BS12; list each manager's name only once, even if that manager manages several people with this skill.

7-58. Display the salesperson name, product finish, and total quantity sold (label as TotSales) for each finish by each salesperson.

7-59. Write a query to list the number of products produced in each work center (label as TotalProducts). If a work center does not produce any products, display the result with a total of 0.

7-60. The production manager at PVFC is concerned about support for purchased parts in products owned by customers. A simple analysis he wants done is to determine for each customer how many vendors are in the same state

as that customer. Develop a list of *all* the PVFC customers by name with the number of vendors in the same state as that customer. (Label this computed result NumVendors.)

7-61. Display the order IDs for customers who have not made any payment, yet, on that order. Use the set command UNION, INTERSECT, or MINUS in your query.

7-62. Display the names of the states in which customers reside but for which there is no salesperson residing in that state. There are several ways to write this query. Try to write it without any WHERE clause. Write this query two ways, using the set command UNION, INTERSECT, or MINUS and not using any of these commands. Which was the most natural approach for you, and why?

7-63. Write an SQL query to produce a list of all the products (i.e., product description) and the number of times each product has been ordered. Show how you constructed this query using a Venn or other type of diagram.

7-64. Display the customer ID, name, and order ID for all customer orders. For those customers who do not have any orders, include them in the display once.

7-65. Display the EmployeeID and EmployeeName for those employees who do not possess the skill Router. Display the results in order by EmployeeName. Show how you constructed this query using a Venn or other type of diagram.

7-66. Display the name of customer 16 and the names of all the customers that are in the same zip code as customer 16. (Be sure this query will work for any customer.)

7-67. Rewrite your answer to Problem and Exercise 7-66 for each customer, not just customer 16.

7-68. Display the customer ID, name, and order ID for all customer orders. For those customers who do not have any orders, include them in the display once by showing order ID 0.

7-69. Show the customer ID and name for all the customers who have ordered both products with IDs 3 and 4 on the same order.

7-70. Display the customer names of all customers who have ordered (on the same or different orders) both products with IDs 3 and 4.

7-71. Review the first query in the "Correlated Subqueries" section. Can you identify a special set of standard prices for which this query will not yield the desired result? How might you rewrite the query to handle this situation?

7-72. List the IDs and names of all products that cost less than the average product price in their product line.

7-73. List the IDs and names of those sales territories that have at least 50 percent more customers as the average number of customers per territory.

7-74. Write an SQL query to list the order number and order quantity for all customer orders for which the order quantity is greater than the average order quantity of that product. (Hint: This involves using a correlated subquery.)

7-75. Write an SQL query to list the salesperson who has sold the most computer desks.

7-76. Display in product ID order the product ID and total amount ordered of that product by the customer who has bought the most of that product; use a derived table in a FROM clause to answer this query.

7-77. Display employee information for all the employees in each state who were hired before the most recently hired person in that state.

7-78. The head of marketing is interested in some opportunities for cross-selling of products. She thinks that the way to identify cross-selling opportunities is to know for each product how many other products are sold to the same customer on the same order (e.g., a product that is bought by a customer in the same order with lots of other products is a better candidate for cross-selling than a product bought by itself).

  a. To help the marketing manager, first list the IDs for all the products that have sold in total more than 20 units across all orders. (These are popular products, which are the only products she wants to consider as triggers for potential cross-selling.)

  b. Make a new query that lists all the IDs for the orders that include products that satisfy the first query, along with the number of products on those orders. Only orders with three or more products on them are of interest to the marketing manager. Write this query as general as possible to cover any answer to the first query, which might change over time. To clarify, if product X is one of the products that is in the answer set from part a, then in part b we want to see the desired order information for orders that include product X.

  c. The marketing manager needs to know what other products were sold on the orders that are in the result for part b. (Again, write this query for the general, not specific, result to the query in part b.) These are products that are sold, for example, with product X from part a, and these are the ones that if people buy that product, we'd want to try to cross-sell them product X because history says they are likely to buy it along with what else they are buying. Write a query to identify these other products by ID and description. It is okay to include "product X" in your result (i.e., you don't need to exclude the products in the result of part a.).

7-79. For each product, display in ascending order, by product ID, the product ID and description, along with the customer ID and name for the customer who has bought the most of that product; also show the total quantity ordered by that customer (who has bought the most of that product). Use a correlated subquery.

Field Exercises

7-80. Conduct a search of the Web to locate as many links as possible that discuss SQL standards.

7-81. Compare two versions of SQL to which you have access, such as Microsoft Access and Oracle SQL*Plus. Identify at least five similarities and three dissimilarities in the SQL code from these two SQL systems. Do the dissimilarities cause results to differ?

References

DeLoach, A. 1987. "The Path to Writing Efficient Queries in SQL/DS." *Database Programming & Design* 1,1 (January): 26–32.

Eisenberg, A., J. Melton, K. Kulkarni, J. E. Michels, and F. Zemke. 2004. "SQL:2003 Has Been Published." *SIGMOD Record* 33,1 (March): 119–26.

Gulutzan, P., and T. Pelzer. 1999. *SQL-99 Complete, Really!* Lawrence, KS: R&D Books.

Holmes, J. 1996. "More Paths to Better Performance." *Database Programming & Design* 9, 2 (February): 47–48.

Kulkarni, K., and J-E. Michels. 2012. "Temporal Features in SQL:2011." *SIGMOD Record* 41,3: 34–43.

Mullins, C. S. 1995. "The Procedural DBA." *Database Programming & Design* 8,12 (December): 40–45.

Rennhackkamp, M. 1996. "Trigger Happy." *DBMS* 9,5 (May): 89–91, 95.

Vanroose, P. 2012. "MySQL: Stored Procedures and SQL/PSM." Available at **http://www.abis.be/html/en2012-10_MySQL_procedures.html**.

Zemke, F. 2012. "What's New in SQL:2011." *SIGMOD Record* 41,1: 67–73.

Zemke, F., K. Kulkarni, A. Witkowski, and B. Lyle. 1999. "Introduction to OLAP Functions." ISO/IEC JTC1/SC32 WG3: YGJ.068 ANSI NCITS H2–99–154r2.

Further Reading

American National Standards Institute. 2000. *ANSI Standards Action* 31,11 (June 2): 20.

Celko, J. 2006. *Analytics and OLAP in SQL*. San Francisco: Morgan Kaufmann.

Codd, E. F. 1970. "A Relational Model of Data for Large Shared Data Banks." *Communications of the ACM* 13,6 (June): 77–87.

Date, C. J., and H. Darwen. 1997. *A Guide to the SQL Standard*. Reading, MA: Addison-Wesley.

Date, C. J., and H. Darwen. 2014. *Time and Relational Theory. Temporal Databases in the Relational Model and SQL*. Waltham, MA: Morgan Kaufmann.

Itzik, B., L. Kollar, and D. Sarka. 2009. *Inside Microsoft SQL Server 2008 T-SQL Querying*. Redmond, WA: Microsoft Press.

Itzik B., D. Sarka, and R. Wolter. 2010. *Inside Microsoft SQL Server 2008: T-SQL Programming*. Redmond, WA: Microsoft Press.

Kulkarni, K. 2004. "Overview of SQL:2003." Accessed at **www.wiscorp.com/SQLStandards.html#keyreadings**.

Melton, J. 1997. "A Case for SQL Conformance Testing." *Database Programming & Design* 10,7 (July): 66–69.

van der Lans, R. F. 2006. *Introduction to SQL*, 4th ed. Workingham, UK: Addison-Wesley.

Winter, R. 2000. "SQL-99's New OLAP Functions." *Intelligent Enterprise* 3,2 (January 20): 62, 64–65.

Winter, R. 2000. "The Extra Mile." *Intelligent Enterprise* 3,10 (June 26): 62–64.

See also "Further Reading" in Chapter 6.

Web Resources

www.ansi.org Web site of the American National Standards Institute. Contains information on the ANSI federation and the latest national and international standards.

www.fluffycat.com/SQL/ Web site that defines a sample database and shows examples of SQL queries against this database.

www.iso.ch The International Organization for Standardization's (ISO's) Web site, which provides information about the ISO. Copies of current standards may be purchased here.

richardfoote.wordpress.com A Web site with expert commentary particularly on issues related to indexing.

www.sqlcourse.com and **www.sqlcourse2.com** Web sites that provide tutorials for a subset of ANSI SQL with a practice database.

standards.ieee.org The home page of the IEEE standards organization.

www.tizag.com/sqlTutorial/ Web site that provides a set of tutorials on SQL concepts and commands.

http://troelsarvin.blogspot.com/ Blog that provides a detailed comparison of different SQL implementations, including DB2, Microsoft SQL, MySQL, Oracle, and PostGreSQL

www.teradatauniversitynetwork.com Web site where your instructor may have created some course environments for you to use Teradata SQL Assistant, Web Edition, with one or more of the Pine Valley Furniture and Mountain View Community Hospital data sets for this text.

CASE

Forondo Artist Management Excellence Inc.

Case Description

In Chapter 6, you implemented the database for FAME and populated it with sample data. You will use the same database to complete the exercises below.

Project Questions

7-82. Write and execute queries for the various reports and displays you identified as being required by the various stakeholders in 6-101 in Chapter 6. Make sure you use both subqueries and joins. Your instructor may

specify for which reports or displays you should write queries, how many queries you are to write, and their complexity.

7-83. Identify opportunities for using triggers in your database and write the appropriate DDL queries for them.

7-84. Create a strategy for reviewing your database implementation with the appropriate stakeholders. Which stakeholders should you meet with? What information would you bring to this meeting? Who do you think should sign off on your database implementation before you move to the next phase of the project?

CHAPTER 8

Database Application Development

LEARNING OBJECTIVES

After studying this chapter, you should be able to:

- Concisely define each of the following key terms: **client/server systems, fat client, database server, three-tier architecture, thin client, application partitioning, middleware, application program interface (API), Extensible Markup Language (XML), XML Schema Definition (XSD), Extensible Stylesheet Language Transformation (XSLT), XPath, XQuery, Java servlet, Web services, Universal Description, Discovery, and Integration (UDDI), Web Services Description Language (WSDL), Simple Object Access Protocol (SOAP), and Service-oriented architecture (SOA).**

- Explain the three components of client/server systems: data presentation services, processing services, and storage services.

- Distinguish between two-tier and three-tier architectures.

- Describe how to connect to databases in a two-tier application in VB.NET and Java.

- Describe the key components of a Web application and the information flow between the various components.

- Describe how to connect to databases in a three-tier Web application using Java Server Pages (JSP), PHP, and ASP.NET.

- Explain the purpose of XML and its uses in standardizing data exchange across the Internet.

- Understand how XQuery can be used to query XML documents.

- Explain how XML has led to the spread of Web services and the emergence of service-oriented architectures.

LOCATION, LOCATION, LOCATION!

When looking for property to buy, at least one of your friends will say, "It's all about location, location, location." Storing data and applications comes down to making location decisions, too. No, we aren't talking about giving data an ocean view with a hot tub and proximity to good schools. But good database design is built on picking the right location to store data.

You studied the location concept for storing data on storage devices in Chapter 5, with such concepts as denormalization and partitioning. In addition, multitiered computer architectures offer storage possibilities at each tier, and there is no right answer for all situations. That's the beauty of the client/server approach: It can be tailored to optimize performance. As with most other major steps forward in computerization, the first client/server applications were tried in noncritical situations. By the mid-1990s, success stories began to be publicized, and the client/server approach moved up to handle business-critical applications. Now client/server has become old hat, and you may feel that this chapter is the most mundane one in the whole book. That may be, but you are urged to pay close attention anyway because the client/server approach continues to drive the newest directions in database computing. You will read about Web-enabled databases and learn about some of the newest acronyms, including service-oriented architecture (SOA) and Web services. Some authors will write as though these newest approaches are somehow different and beyond client/server technology. Actually, the clients may be fat or thin, and the servers can be connected in different ways, but the basic concepts included in this chapter underlie the newest approaches to distributed computing (for Web applications here and distributed databases in Chapter 13), available on the book's Web site).

And it's mostly about location: what must be located on the client (think smartphone), what is stored on the server, and how much information should be moved from the server to the smartphone when a request for data (think SQL query) is made (think about locating a restaurant when you're traveling). Part of the answer to optimizing a particular architecture lies not in location but in quickly moving the information from one location to another location. These issues are critically important to mobile applications, such as those for smartphones. In addition to transmitting voice data, most phone services now include text messaging, Web browsing, object/image uploading/downloading, and a whole variety of business and personal applications. Just as we can make a voice phone call from any phone in the world to any other phone, we expect to use these newer services in the same way, and we want immediate response times. Addressing these problems requires a good understanding of the client/server principles you will learn in this chapter.

INTRODUCTION

Client/server systems operate in networked environments, splitting the processing of an application between a front-end client and a back-end processor. Generally, the client process requires some resource, which the server provides to the client. Clients and servers can reside in the same computer, or they can be on different computers that are networked together. Both clients and servers are intelligent and programmable, so the computing power of both can be used to devise effective and efficient applications.

It is difficult to overestimate the impact that client/server applications have had in the past 25 years. Advances in personal computing, smartphone, and tablet technology and the corresponding rapid evolution of graphical user interfaces (GUIs), networking, and communications have changed the way businesses use computing systems to meet ever more demanding business needs. Electronic commerce requires that clients (PCs or smartphones) be able to access dynamic Web pages attached to databases that provide real-time information. Mainframe applications have been rewritten to run in client/server environments and take advantage of the greater cost-effectiveness of advances in networking, personal computers, smartphones, and tablets. The need for strategies that fit specific business environments is being filled by client/server solutions because they offer flexibility, scalability (the ability to upgrade a system without having to redesign it), and extensibility (the ability to define new data types and operations).

Client/server system

A networked computing model that distributes processes between clients and servers, which supply the requested services. In a database system, the database generally resides on a server that processes the DBMS. The clients may process the application systems or request services from another server that holds the application programs.

CLIENT/SERVER ARCHITECTURES

Client/server architectures can be distinguished by how application logic components are distributed across clients and servers. There are three components of application logic (see Figure 8-1). The first is the input/output (I/O), or presentation logic, component. This component is responsible for formatting and presenting data on the user's screen or other output device and for managing user input from a keyboard or other input device

FIGURE 8-1 Application logic components

Application partitioning

The process of assigning portions of application code to client or server partitions after it is written to achieve better performance and interoperability (ability of a component to function on different platforms).

Fat client

A client PC that is responsible for processing presentation logic, extensive application and business rules logic, and many DBMS functions.

(such as your phone or tablet's screen). Presentation logic often resides on the client and is the mechanism with which the user interacts with the system. The second component is the processing logic. This handles data processing logic, business rules logic, and data management logic. Data processing logic includes such activities as data validation and identification of processing errors. Business rules that have not been coded at the DBMS level may be coded in the processing component. Data management logic identifies the data necessary for processing the transaction or query. Processing logic resides on both the client and servers. The third component is storage, the component responsible for data storage and retrieval from the physical storage devices associated with the application. Storage logic usually resides on the database server, close to the physical location of the data. Activities of a DBMS occur in the storage logic component. For example, data integrity control activities, such as constraint checking, are typically placed there. Triggers, which will always fire when appropriate conditions are met, are associated with insert, modify, update, and delete commands, are also placed here. Stored procedures that use the data directly are usually also stored on the database server.

Client/server architectures are normally categorized into three types: two-, three-, or *n*-tier architectures, depending on the placement of the three types of application logic. There is no one optimal client/server architecture that is the best solution for all business problems. Rather, the flexibility inherent in client/server architectures offers organizations the possibility of tailoring their configurations to fit their particular processing needs. **Application partitioning** helps in this tailoring.

Figure 8-2a depicts three commonly found configurations of two-tier systems based on the placement of the processing logic. In the **fat client**, the application processing occurs entirely on the client, whereas in the thin client, this processing occurs primarily on the server. In the distributed example, application processing is partitioned between the client and the server.

Figure 8-2b presents the typical setup of three-tier and *n*-tier architectures. These types of architectures are most prevalent in Web-based systems. As in two-tier systems, some processing logic could be placed on the client, if desired. But a typical client in a Web-enabled client/server environment will be a thin client, using a browser or a smartphone app for its presentation logic. The middle tiers are typically coded in a portable language such as C or Java. The flexibility and easier manageability of the *n*-tier approaches account for its increasing popularity, in spite of the increased complexity of managing the communication among the tiers. The fast-paced, distributed, and heterogeneous environment of the Internet and e-commerce initiatives have also led to the development of many *n*-tier architectures.

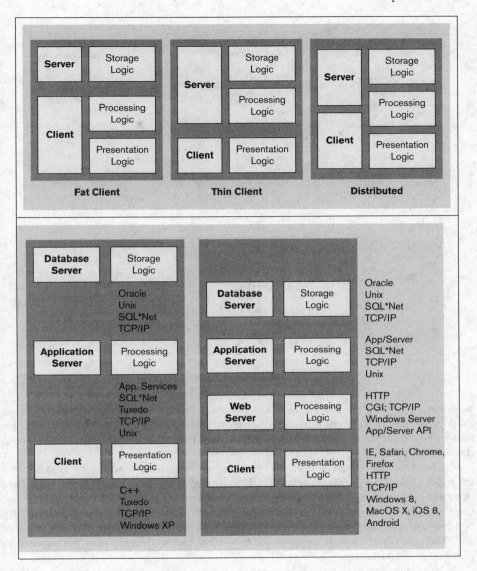

FIGURE 8-2   Common logic distributions
(a) Two-tier client/server environments

(b) Three-tier and *n*-tier client/server environments

Now that we have examined the different types of client/server architectures and their advantages and disadvantages in general, in the next two sections, we show specific examples of the role of databases in these types of architectures.

DATABASES IN A TWO-TIER ARCHITECTURE

In a two-tier architecture, a client workstation is responsible for managing the user interface, including presentation logic, data processing logic, and business rules logic, and a **database server** is responsible for database storage, access, and processing. Figure 8-3 shows a typical database server architecture. With the DBMS placed on the database server, LAN traffic is reduced because only those records that match the requested criteria are transmitted to the client station, rather than entire data files. Some people refer to the central DBMS functions as the *back-end functions*, whereas they call the application programs on the client PCs/smartphones/tablets *front-end programs*.

With this architecture, only the database server requires processing power adequate to handle the database, and the database is stored on the server, not on the clients. Therefore, the database server can be tuned to optimize database-processing

Database server

A computer that is responsible for database storage, access, and processing in a client/server environment. Some people also use this term to describe a two-tier client/server application.

FIGURE 8-3 Database server architecture (two-tier architecture)

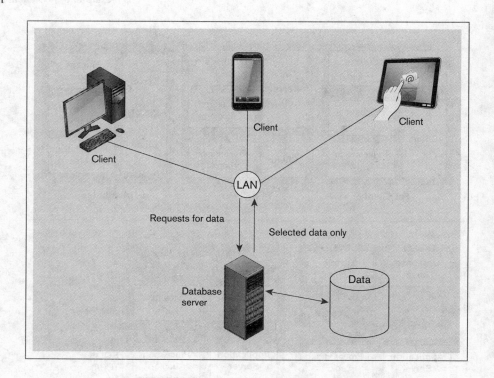

performance. Because fewer data are sent across the LAN, the communication load is reduced. User authorization, integrity checking, data dictionary maintenance, and query and update processing are all performed at one location, on the database server.

Client/server projects that use two-tier architectures tend to be departmental applications, supporting a relatively small number of users. Such applications are not mission critical and have been most successful when transaction volumes are low, immediate availability is not critical, and security is not of the highest concern. As companies have sought to gain expected benefits from client/server projects, such as scalability, flexibility, and lowered costs, they have had to develop new approaches to client/server architectures.

Most two-tier applications are written in a programming language such as Java, VB.NET, or C#. Connecting an application written in a common programming language, such as Java, VB.NET, or C#, to a database is achieved through the use of special software called *database-oriented middleware*. Middleware is often referred to as the glue that holds together client/server applications. It is a term that is commonly used to describe any software component between the PC client and the relational database in *n*-tier architectures. Simply put, **middleware** is any of several classes of software that allow an application to interoperate with other software without requiring the user to understand and code the low-level operations required to achieve interoperability (Hurwitz, 1998). The database-oriented middleware needed to connect an application to a database consists of two parts: an **application programming interface (API)** and a database driver to connect to a specific type database (e.g., SQL Server or Oracle). The most common APIs are **Open Database Connectivity (ODBC)** and ADO.NET for the Microsoft platform (VB.NET and C#) and Java Database Connectivity (JDBC) for use with Java programs.

No matter which API or language is used, the basic steps for accessing a database from an application remain surprisingly similar:

1. Identify and register a database driver.
2. Open a connection to a database.
3. Execute a query against the database.

Middleware

Software that allows an application to interoperate with other software without requiring the user to understand and code the low-level operations necessary to achieve interoperability.

Application programming interface (API)

Sets of routines that an application program uses to direct the performance of procedures by the computer's operating system.

Open Database Connectivity (ODBC)

An application programming interface that provides a common language for application programs to access and process SQL databases independent of the particular DBMS that is accessed.

4. Process the results of the query.
5. Repeat steps 3–4 as necessary.
6. Close the connection to the database.

A VB.NET Example

Let us take a look at these steps in action in the context of a simple VB.NET application. The purpose of the code snippet shown in Figure 8-4 is to insert a new record into a student database. For simplicity, we will not show code related to error handling. Also, while we show the password embedded in the code below, in commercial applications, other mechanisms to retrieve passwords are used.

The VB.NET code shown in Figure 8-4 uses the ADO.NET data access framework and .NET data providers to connect to the database. The .NET Framework has different data providers (or database drivers) that allow you to connect a program written in a .NET programming language to a database. Common data providers available in the framework are for SQL Server and Oracle.

The VB.NET code illustrates how a simple INSERT query can be executed against the Oracle database. Figure 8-4a shows the VB.NET code needed to create a simple form that allows the user input to a name, department number, and student ID. Figure 8-4b shows the detailed steps to connect to a database and issue an INSERT query. By reading the explanations presented in the text boxes in the figure, you can see how the generic steps for accessing a database described in the previous section are implemented in the context of a VB.NET program. Figure 8-4c shows how you would access the database and process the results for a SELECT query. The main difference is that you use the ExecuteReader() method instead of the ExecuteNonQuery() method. The latter is used for INSERT, UPDATE, and DELETE queries. The table that results from running a SELECT query is captured inside an OracleDataReader object. You can access each row in the result by traversing the object, one row at a time. Each column in the object can be accessed by a Get method and by referring to the column's position in the query result (or by name). ADO.NET provides two main choices with respect to handling the result of the query: DataReader (e.g., OracleDataReader in Figure 8-4c) and DataSet. The

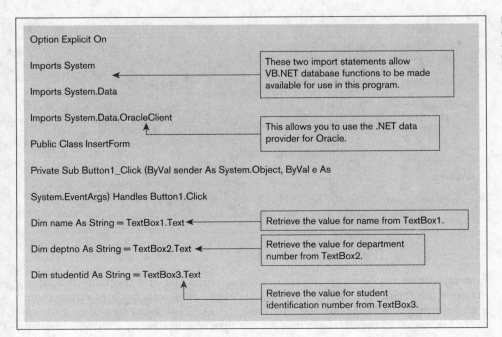

FIGURE 8-4 Sample VB.NET code that demonstrates an INSERT in a database (a) Setup form for receiving user input

FIGURE 8-4 (*continued*)
(b) Connecting to a database and issuing an INSERT query

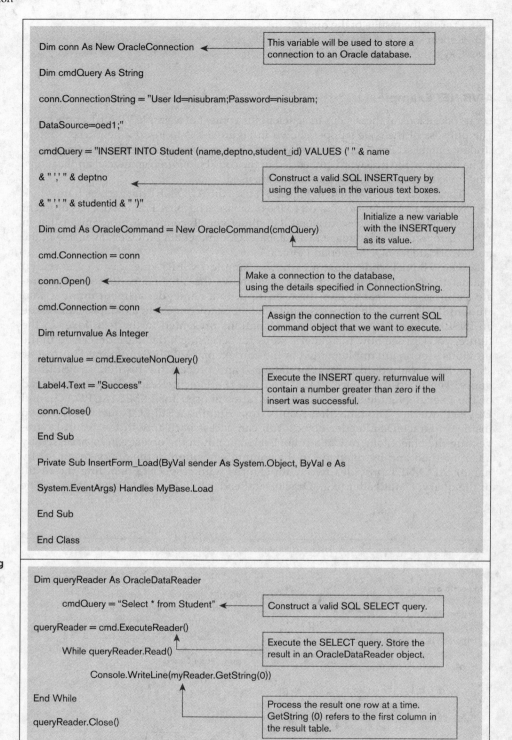

(c) Sample code snippet for using a SELECT query

primary difference between the two options is that the first limits us to looping through the result of a query one row at a time. This can be very cumbersome if the result has a large number of rows. The DataSet object provides a disconnected snapshot of the database that we can then manipulate in our program using the features available in the programming language. Later in this chapter, we will see how .NET data controls (which use DataSet objects) can provide a cleaner and easier way to manipulate data in a program.

A Java Example

Let us now look at an example of how to connect to a database from a Java application (see Figure 8-5). This Java application is actually connecting to the same database as the VB.NET application in Figure 8-4. Its purpose is to retrieve and print the names of all students in the Student table. In this example, the Java program is using the JDBC API and an Oracle thin driver to access the Oracle database.

Notice that unlike the INSERT query shown in the VB.NET example, running an SQL SELECT query requires us to capture the data inside an object that can appropriately handle the tabular data. JDBC provides two key mechanisms for this: the ResultSet and RowSet objects. The difference between these two is somewhat similar to the difference between the DataReader and DataSet objects described in the VB.NET example.

The ResultSet object has a mechanism, called the cursor, that points to its current row of data. When the ResultSet object is first initialized, the cursor is positioned before the first row. This is why we need to first call the next() method before retrieving data. The ResultSet object is used to loop through and process each row of data and retrieve the column values that we want to access. In this case, we access the value in the name column using the rec.getString method, which is a part of the JDBC API. For each of the common database types, there is a corresponding *get* and *set* method that allows for retrieval and storage of data in the database. Table 8-1 provides some common examples of SQL-to-Java mappings.

It is important to note that while the ResultSet object maintains an active connection to the database, depending on the size of the table, the entire table (i.e., the result of the query) may or may not actually be in memory on the client machine. How and when data are transferred between the database and client is handled by the Oracle driver. By default, a ResultSet object is read-only and can be traversed only in one direction (forward). However, advanced versions of the ResultSet object allow scrolling in both directions and can be updateable as well.

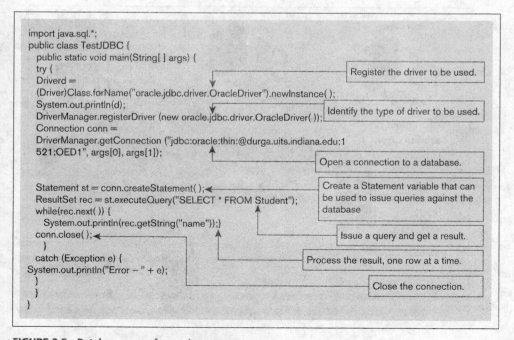

FIGURE 8-5 Database access from a Java program

TABLE 8-1 Common Java-to-SQL Mappings

SQL Type	Java Type	Common Get/Set Methods
INTEGER	int	getInt(), setInt()
CHAR	String	getString, setString()
VARCHAR	String	getString, setString()
DATE	java.util.Date	getDate(), setDate()
TIME	java.sql.Time	getTime(), setTime()
TIMESTAMP	java.sql.Timestamp	getTimestamp(), setTimestamp()

THREE-TIER ARCHITECTURES

Three-tier architecture

A client/server configuration that includes three layers: a client layer and two server layers. Although the nature of the server layers differs, a common configuration contains an application server and a database server.

In general, a **three-tier architecture** includes another server layer in addition to the client and database server layers previously mentioned (see Figure 8-6a). Such configurations are also referred to as *n*-tier, multitier, or enhanced client/server architectures. The additional server in a three-tier architecture may be used for different purposes. Often, application programs reside and are run on the additional server, in which case it is referred to as an application server. Or the additional server may hold a local database while another server holds the enterprise database. Each of these configurations is likely to be referred to as a three-tier architecture, but the functionality of each differs, and each is appropriate for a different situation. Advantages of the three-tier compared with the two-tier architecture, such as increased scalability, flexibility, performance, and reusability, have made three-layer architectures a popular choice for Internet applications and net-centric information systems. These advantages are discussed in more detail later.

In some three-tier architectures, most application code is stored on the application server. This case realizes the same benefits as those that come from putting stored procedures on the database server in a two-tier architecture. Using an application server can also improve performance through the use of true machine code, easier portability of the application code to other platforms, and less reliance on proprietary languages

FIGURE 8-6 Three-tier architecture
(a) Generic three-tier architecture

FIGURE 8-6 (*continued*)
(b) Sample PeopleSoft Financials three-tier configuration

such as SQL*Plus (Quinlan, 1995). In many situations, most business processing occurs on the application server rather than on the client (workstation or tablet/phone) or database server, resulting in a **thin client**. The use of Internet browsers for accessing the Web is an example of a thin client. Applications that reside on a server and execute on that server without downloading to the client are becoming more common. Thus, upgrading application programs requires loading the new version only on the application server, rather than on client workstations.

The most common type of three-tier application in use in modern organizations is a Web-based application. Such applications can be accessed from either the Internet or an intranet. Figure 8-7 depicts the basic environment needed to set up both intranet and Internet database-enabled connectivity. In the box on the right side of the diagram is a depiction of an intranet. The client/server nature of the architecture is evident from the labeling. The network that connects the client (workstations, tablets, smartphones, etc.), Web server, and database server uses TCP/IP. While multitier intranet structures are also used, Figure 8-7 depicts a simpler architecture, where a request from a client browser will be sent through the network to the Web server, which stores pages scripted in HTML to be returned and displayed through the client browser. If the request requires that data be obtained from the database, the Web server constructs a query and sends it to the database server, which processes the query and returns the results set when the query is run against the database. Similarly, data entered at the client station can be passed through and stored in the database by sending it to the Web server, which passes it on to the database server, which commits the data to the database.

The processing flow described here is similar when connecting from outside the company. This is the case whether the connection is available only to a particular customer or supplier or to any workstation connected to the Internet. However, opening up the Web server to the outside world requires that additional data security measures be in place. Security is central to the deployment of Web services and will be discussed in more detail in Chapter 12.

Thin client

An application where the client (PC) accessing the application primarily provides the user interfaces and some application processing, usually with no or limited local data storage.

FIGURE 8-7   A database-enabled intranet/Internet environment

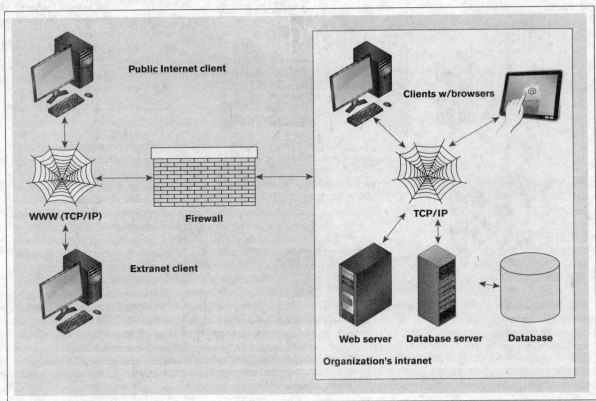

Internally, access to data is typically controlled by the database management system, with the database administrator setting the permissions that determine employee access to data. Firewalls limit external access to the company's data and the movement of company data outside the company's boundaries. All communication is routed through a proxy server outside of the organization's network. The proxy server controls the passage of messages or files through to the organization's network. It can also improve a site's performance by caching frequently requested pages that can then be displayed without having to attach to the Web server.

Given that the most common type of three-tier application is a Web application, in the next section we take a closer look at the key components of a Web application. We then present examples of simple Web applications written in three common languages: Java Server Pages (JSP), ASP.NET, and PHP.

WEB APPLICATION COMPONENTS

Figure 8-2 shows the various components of a typical Web application. Four key components must be used together to create a Web application site:

1. *A database server*   This server hosts the storage logic for the application and hosts the DBMS. You have read about many of them, including Oracle, Microsoft SQL Server, Informix, Sybase, DB2, Microsoft Access, and MySQL. The DBMS may reside either on a separate machine or on the same machine as the Web server.
2. *A Web server*   The Web server provides the basic functionality needed to receive and respond to requests from browser clients. These requests use HTTP or HTTPS as a protocol. The most common Web server software in use is Apache, but you are also likely to encounter Microsoft's Internet Information Server (IIS) Web server. Apache can run on different operating systems, such as Windows, UNIX, or Linux. IIS is primarily intended to run on Windows servers.

3. *An application server* This software provides the building blocks for creating dynamic Web sites and Web-based applications. Examples include the .NET Framework from Microsoft; Java Platform, Enterprise Edition (Java EE); and ColdFusion. Also, while technically not considered an application server platform, software that enables you to write applications in languages such as PHP, Python, and Perl also belong to this category.
4. *A Web browser* Microsoft's Internet Explorer, Mozilla's Firefox, Apple's Safari, and Google's Chrome are examples.

As you can see, a bewildering collection of tools are available to use for Web application development. Although Figure 8-7 gives an overview of the architecture required, there is no one right way to put together the components. Rather, there are many possible configurations, using redundant tools. Often, Web technologies within the same category can be used interchangeably. One tool may solve the same problem as well as another tool. However, the following are the most common combinations you will encounter:

- IIS Web server, SQL Server/Oracle as the DBMS, and applications written in ASP.NET
- Apache Web server, Oracle/IBM as the DBMS, and applications written using Java
- Apache Web server, Oracle/IBM/SQL Server as the DBMS, and applications written using ColdFusion
- The Linux operating system, Apache Web server, a MySQL database, and applications written in PHP/Python or Perl (also sometimes referred to as the LAMP stack).

Your development environment is likely to be determined by your employer. When you know what environment you will be using, there are many alternatives available for becoming familiar and proficient with the tools. Your employer may send you to training classes or even hire a subject matter expert to work with you. You will find one or more books specific to each tool when you search online or in a bookstore. Figure 8-8 presents a visual depiction of the components necessary to create a dynamic Web site.

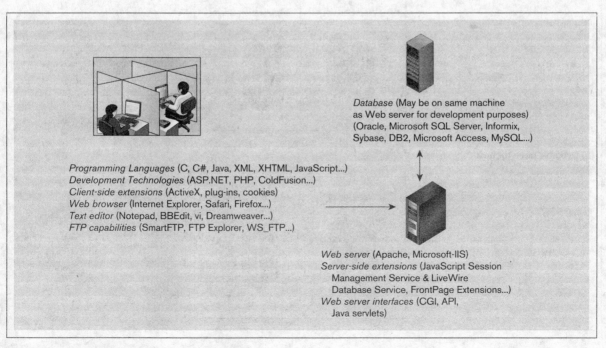

Programming Languages (C, C#, Java, XML, XHTML, JavaScript...)
Development Technologies (ASP.NET, PHP, ColdFusion...)
Client-side extensions (ActiveX, plug-ins, cookies)
Web browser (Internet Explorer, Safari, Firefox...)
Text editor (Notepad, BBEdit, vi, Dreamweaver...)
FTP capabilities (SmartFTP, FTP Explorer, WS_FTP...)

Database (May be on same machine as Web server for development purposes) (Oracle, Microsoft SQL Server, Informix, Sybase, DB2, Microsoft Access, MySQL...)

Web server (Apache, Microsoft-IIS)
Server-side extensions (JavaScript Session Management Service & LiveWire Database Service, FrontPage Extensions...)
Web server interfaces (CGI, API, Java servlets)

FIGURE 8-8 Dynamic Web development environment

DATABASES IN THREE-TIER APPLICATIONS

Figure 8-9a presents a general overview of the information flow in a Web application. A user submitting a Web page request is unaware of whether the request being submitted is returning a static Web page or a Web page whose content is a mixture of static information and dynamic information retrieved from the database. The data returned from the Web server is always in a format that can be rendered by the browser (i.e., HTML or XML).

As shown in Figure 8-9a, if the Web server determines that the request from the client can be satisfied without passing the request on to the application server, it will process the request and then return the appropriately formatted information to the client machine. This decision is most often based on the file suffix. For example, all .html and .htm files can be processed by the Web server itself.

However, if the request has a suffix that requires application server intervention, the information flow shown in Figure 8-9b is invoked. The application invokes the database, as necessary, using one of the mechanisms described previously (ADO.NET or JDBC) or a proprietary one. While the internal details of how each of the popular platforms (JSP/Java servlets, ASP.NET, ColdFusion, and PHP) handles the requests are likely very different, the general logic for creating Web applications is very similar to what is shown in Figure 8-9b.

A JSP Web Application

As indicated previously, there are several suitable languages and development tools available with which to create dynamic Web pages. One of the most popular languages in use is Java Server Pages (JSP). JSP pages are a mixture of HTML and Java. The HTML parts are used to display information on the browser. The Java parts are used to process information sent from an HTML form.

FIGURE 8-9   Information flow in a three-tier architecture

FIGURE 8-10 Sample JSP application

(a) Validation and database connection code

```
<%@ page import="java.sql.*" %>
<%

// Create an empty new variable
String message = null;

// Handle the form
if (request.getParameter("submit") != null)
{
  String firstName = null;
  String lastName = null;
  String email = null;
  String userName = null;
  String password = null;

  // Check for a first name
  if (request.getParameter("first_name")=="") {
    message = "<p>You forgot to enter your first name!</p>";
    firstName = null;
  }
  else {
    firstName = request.getParameter("first_name");
  }

  // Check for a last name
  if (request.getParameter("last_name")=="") {
    message = "<p>You forgot to enter your last name!</p>";
    lastName = null;
  }
  else {
    lastName = request.getParameter("last_name");
  }

  // Check for an email address
  if (request.getParameter("email")=="") {
    message = "<p>You forgot to enter your email address!</p>";
    email = null;
  }
  else {
    email = request.getParameter("email");
  }

  // Check for a username
  if (request.getParameter("username")=="") {
    message = "<p>You forgot to enter your username!</p>";
    userName = null;
  }
  else {
    userName = request.getParameter("username");
  }

  // Check for a password and match against the confirmed password
  if (request.getParameter("password1")=="") {
    message = "<p>You forgot to enter your password!</p>";
    password = null;
  }
```

Annotations:
- The <%@ page %>directive applies to the entire JSP page. The import attribute specifies the Java packages that should be included within the JSP file.
- Check whether the form needs to be processed.
- Validate first name
- Validate last name
- Validate e-mail address
- Validate username
- Validate the password

The code in Figure 8-10 shows a sample JSP application whose purpose is to capture user registration information and store the data in a database. Let us assume that the name of the page is registration.jsp. This JSP page performs the following functions:

- Displays the registration form
- Processes the user's filled-in form and checks it for common errors, such as missing items and matching password fields

FIGURE 8-10 (*continued*)

(a) Validation and database connection code

```
else {
  if(request.getParameter("password1").equals(request.getParameter("password2"))) {
  password = request.getParameter("password1");
  }
  else {
  password = null;
  message = "<p>Your password did not match the confirmed password!</p>";
  }
}

// If everything's OK
PreparedStatement stmt = null;
Connection conn = null;
if (firstName!=null && lastName!=null && email!=null && userName!=null && password!=null) {

// Call method to register student
try {

// Connect to the db
DriverManager.registerDriver(new oracle.jdbc.driver.OracleDriver( ));
conn=DriverManager.getConnection("jdbc:oracle:thin:@localhost:1521:xe","scott","tiger");

// Make the query
String ins_query="INSERT INTO users VALUES ('"+firstName+"','"+lastName+"',"
+email+"','"+userName+"','"+password+"')";
stmt=conn.prepareStatement(ins_query);

// Run the query
int result = stmt.executeUpdate(ins_query);
conn.commit();
message = "<p><b> You have been registered ! </b></p>";

// Close the database connection
stmt.close();
conn.close();
}
catch (SQLException ex) {

message = "<p><b> You could not be registered due to a system error. We apologize
for any inconvenience. </b></p>"+ex.getMessage()+"</p>";
stmt.close();
conn.close();
}
}
else {
  message = message+"<p>.Please try again</p>";
}
}
%>
```

Boxes:
- If all user information has been validated, the data will be inserted into the database (an Oracle Database in this case)
- Connect to the Database : Connection String : jdbc:oracle:thin:@localhost:1521:xe Username : scott Password : tiger
- Prepare and Execute INSERT query
- If the INSERT was successful print message
- Close Connection and Statement
- If the INSERT was not successful print error message
- End of JSP code

- If there is an error, redisplays the entire form, with an error message in red
- If there is no error, enters the user's information into a database and sends the user to a "success" screen.

Let us examine the various pieces of the code to see how it accomplishes the above functions. All Java code is found between <% and %> and is not displayed in the browser. The only items displayed in the browser are the ones enclosed in

FIGURE 8-10 *(continued)*

(b) HTML code to create a form in the JSP application

```
HTML code to create a form in the JSP application
<html>                                    ←—————— Beginning of HTML form
<head><title> Register </title></head>
<body>
<% if (message!=null) {%>
<font color ='red'><%=message%></font>
<%}%>
<form method="post">
<fieldset>
<legend>Enter your information in the form below:</legend>
<p><b> First Name:       </b>
      <input type="text"    name="first_name"  size="15" maxlength ="15" value=""/></p>
<p><b> Last Name:       </b>
      <input type="text"    name="last_name"   size="30" maxlength ="30" value=""/></p>
<p><b> Email Address:   </b>
      <input type="text"    name="email"       size="40" maxlength ="40" value=""/></p>
<p><b> User Name:       </b>
      <input type="text"    name="username"    size="10" maxlength ="20" value=""/></p>
<p><b> Password:        </b>
      <input type="password" name="password1"  size="20" maxlength ="20" value=""/></p>
<p><b> Confirm Password: </b>
      <input type="password" name="password2"  size="20" maxlength ="20" value=""/></p>
</fieldset>
<div align="center"><input type="submit" name="submit" value="Register"/></div>
</form><!-- End of Form -->
</body>
</html>
```

(c) Sample form output from the JSP application

Enter your information in the form below.

First Name: [   ]

Last Name: [   ]

Email Address: [   ]

User Name: [   ]

Password: [   ]

Confirm Password: [   ]

[Register]

HTML tags. It is worthwhile noting that both browsers on PCs and smartphones/tablets are capable of displaying HTML.

When a user accesses the registration.jsp page in a browser by typing in a URL similar to **http://myserver.mydomain.edu/regapp/registration.jsp**, the value of the message Web parameter is NULL. Because the IF condition fails, the HTML form is displayed without an error message. Notice that this form has a submit button and that the action value in the form indicates that the page that is going to process the data is also registration.jsp.

After the user fills in the details and clicks the submit button, the data are sent to the Web server. The Web server passes on the data (called parameters) to the application server, which in turn invokes the code in the page specified in the actions parameter (i.e., the registration.jsp page). This is the code in the page that is enclosed in the <% and %> and is written in Java. This code has several IF-ELSE statements for error checking purposes as well as a portion that contains the logic to store the user form data in a database.

If any of the user entries are missing or if the passwords don't match, the Java code sets the message value to something other than NULL. At the end of that check, the original form is displayed, but now an error message in red will be displayed at the top of the form because of the very first IF statement.

On the other hand, if the form has been filled correctly, the code segment for inserting the data into the database is executed. Notice that this code segment is very similar to the code we showed in the Java example before. After the user information is inserted into the database, <jsp:forward> causes the application server to execute a new JSP page called success.jsp. Notice that the message that should be displayed by this page is the value that is in the message variable and is passed to it in the form of a Web parameter. It is worthwhile to note that all JSP pages are actually compiled into **Java servlets** on the application server before execution.

Java servlet

A Java program that is stored on the server and contains the business and database logic for a Java-based application.

If you examine the segments of the application from a database access perspective (starting from the try block), you will notice that there is nothing fundamentally different about how the code inside a JSP page looks compared to the code in a Java application, as described earlier. It still follows the same six steps identified earlier in the chapter. The primary difference is that in this case, the database access code is now part of a Java servlet that runs on the application server instead of the client.

A PHP Example

Java, C, C++, C#, and Perl are APIs that can be used with MySQL. PHP is one of the most popular APIs for several reasons. Support for MySQL has been built into PHP since PHP4. It has a reputation for ease of use, short development time, and high performance. PHP5, recently released, is more object oriented than PHP4 and includes several class libraries. It is considered to be relatively easy to learn. Intermediate-level programmers will learn it quickly.

Figure 8-11 includes a sample script from Ullman (2003) that demonstrates the integration of PHP with a MySQL database and HTML code. The script accepts a guest's registration on a Web site, including first name, last name, e-mail address, user name, and password. Once this information has been stored in the MySQL database, the database owner will want to retrieve it. Ullman also includes a sample script for retrieving the results and displaying them in good form. Reviewing Figure 8-11 will give you an overview of one approach to building a dynamic Web site with an attached database, as well as an appreciation for PHP's use of other languages' syntax conventions that will make the script relatively easy for you to understand. As you review the figure, look for the embedded SQL code, necessary to establish a dynamic Web site.

The JSP and PHP examples presented above have several drawbacks associated with them. First, the HTML code, Java code, and SQL code are all mixed in together. Because the same person is unlikely to possess expertise in all three areas, creating large applications using this paradigm will be challenging. Further, even small changes to one part of an application can have a ripple effect and require that many pages be rewritten, which is inherently error prone. For example, if the name of the database needs to be changed from xe to oed1, then every page that makes a connection to a database will need to be changed.

To overcome this problem, most Web applications are designed using a concept known as the Model-View-Controller (MVC). Using this architecture, the presentation logic (view), the business logic (controller/model), and the database logic (model) are separated.

FIGURE 8-11 Sample PHP script that accepts user registration input

(a) PHP script initiation and input validation

```
<?php # Script 6.6 - register.php

// Set the page title and include the HTML header.
$page_title = 'Register';
include ('templates/header.inc');

//Handle the form.
if (isset($_POST['submit'])) {

        // Create an empty new variable.
        $message = NULL;

        // Check for a first name.
        if (empty($_POST['first_name'])) {
                $fn = FALSE;
                $message = '<p>You forgot to enter your first name!</p>';
        } else {
                $fn = $_POST['first_name'];
        }

        // Check for a last name.
        if (empty($_POST['last_name'])) {
                $ln = FALSE;
                $message = '<p>You forgot to enter your last name!</p>';
        } else {
                $ln = $_POST['last_name'];
        }

        // Check for an email address.
        if (empty($_POST['email'])) {
                $e = FALSE;
                $message = '<p>You forgot to enter your email address!</p>';
        } else {
                $e = $_POST['email'];
        }

        // Check for a username.
        if (empty($_POST['username'])) {
                $u = FALSE;
                $message = '<p>You forgot to enter your username!</p>';
        } else {
                $u = $_POST['username'];
        }

        // Check for a password and match against the confirmed password.
        if (empty($_POST['password1'])) {
                $p = FALSE;
                $message = '<p>You forgot to enter your password!</p>';
        } else {
                if ($_POST['password1'] == $_POST['password2']) {
                        $p = $_POST['password1'];
                } else {
                        $p = FALSE;
                        $message .= '<p>Your password did not match
                                the confirmed password!</p>';
                }
        }
}
```

Annotations: PHP file named register.php begins. This file contains HTML code to set up a generic page, including its page title and header. Check whether to process form. Validate first name. Validate last name. Validate e-mail address. Validate username. Validate the password.

FIGURE 8-11 (continued)

(b) Adding user information to the database

```
//If everything's OK.
     if ($fn && $ln && $e && $u && $p) {

          // Register the user in the database.          ◄─── If all user information has been
                                                               validated, the data will be inserted
          // Connect to the db.   ◄───                         into the MySQL database.
          require_once ('../mysql_connect.php');

                                                        ◄─── Establish connection to database.
          // Make the query.   ◄───                     SQL query with encrypted password and current date.
          $query = "INSERT INTO users (username, first_name, last_name, email, password,
          registration_date) VALUES ('$u', '$fn', '$ln', '$e', PASSWORD('$p'), NOW( ))";

          //Run the query.   ◄───                        mysql_query( ) function sends SQL to MySQL.
          $result = @mysql_query ($query);
                                                         $result contains value returned by mysql_query.
          //If it ran OK.   ◄───                         If TRUE, message is displayed, footer is required,
          if ($result) {                                 script is halted.

                    // Send an email, if desired.
                    echo '<p><b>You have been registered!</b></p>';

                    //Include the HTML footer.
                    include ('templates/footer.inc');

                    //Quit the script.
                    exit();

          // If it did not run OK.   ◄───               If $result FALSE, assign value to $message.
          } else {

                    $message = '<p>You could not be registered due to a system error.
                    We apologize for any inconvenience.</p><p>' . mysql_error() . '</p>';

          }

          //Close the database connection.   ◄───       Close connection to MySQL database.
          mysql_close();

     } else {

          $message = '<p>Please try again.</p>';
                                                         ◄─── Completion of registration conditional.
     }

// End of the main Submit conditional.
}                                            ◄─── Completion of submit conditional.
```

An ASP.NET Example

A final code segment that we will examine (Figure 8-12, page 357) shows how the registration page can be written in ASP.NET.

Notice that the ASP.NET code is considerably shorter than either the PHP or JSP code. This is partially because we have not included all the error checking aspects in this code. Further, we have used some powerful built-in controls available in ASP.NET to perform the majority of the functions that we were writing code for ourselves in the other two languages. The DetailsView control, for example, automatically grabs data from the various text fields in the Web page and assigns the values to the corresponding data field variable in the control (e.g., the User Name form field is stored in the username data field). Further, the SqlDataSource control hides the details of the steps needed to connect to the database, issue SQL queries, and retrieve the results.

FIGURE 8-11 *(continued)*

(c) Closing the PHP script and displaying the HTML form

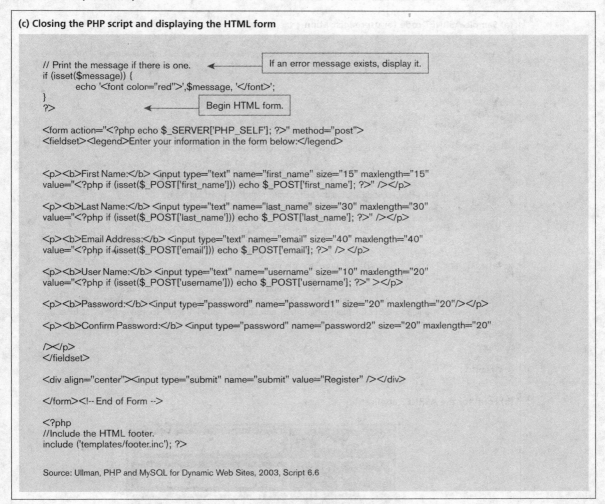

```
// Print the message if there is one.    ◄────  If an error message exists, display it.
if (isset($message)) {
        echo '<font color="red">',$message, '</font>';
}
?>                              ◄────  Begin HTML form.

<form action="<?php echo $_SERVER['PHP_SELF']; ?>" method="post">
<fieldset><legend>Enter your information in the form below:</legend>

<p><b>First Name:</b> <input type="text" name="first_name" size="15" maxlength="15"
value="<?php if (isset($_POST['first_name'])) echo $_POST['first_name']; ?>" /></p>

<p><b>Last Name:</b> <input type="text" name="last_name" size="30" maxlength="30"
value="<?php if (isset($_POST['last_name'])) echo $_POST['last_name']; ?>" /></p>

<p><b>Email Address:</b> <input type="text" name="email" size="40" maxlength="40"
value="<?php if (isset($_POST['email'])) echo $_POST['email']; ?>" /> </p>

<p><b>User Name:</b> <input type="text" name="username" size="10" maxlength="20"
value="<?php if (isset($_POST['username'])) echo $_POST['username']; ?>" ></p>

<p><b>Password:</b><input type="password" name="password1" size="20" maxlength="20"/></p>

<p><b>Confirm Password:</b> <input type="password" name="password2" size="20" maxlength="20"

/></p>
</fieldset>

<div align="center"><input type="submit" name="submit" value="Register" /></div>

</form><!-- End of Form -->

<?php
//Include the HTML footer.
include ('templates/footer.inc'); ?>
```

Source: Ullman, PHP and MySQL for Dynamic Web Sites, 2003, Script 6.6

KEY CONSIDERATIONS IN THREE-TIER APPLICATIONS

In describing the database component of the applications in the preceding sections, we observed that the basics of connecting, retrieving, and storing data in a database do not change substantially when we move from a two-tier application to a three-tier application. In fact, what changes is where the code for accessing the database is located. However, there are several key considerations that application developers need to keep in mind in order to be able to create a stable high-performance application.

Stored Procedures

Stored procedures (same as procedures; see Chapter 7 for a definition) are modules of code that implement application logic and are included on the database server. As pointed out by Quinlan (1995), stored procedures have the following advantages:

- Performance improves for compiled SQL statements.
- Network traffic decreases as processing moves from the client to the server.
- Security improves if the stored procedure rather than the data is accessed and code is moved to the server, away from direct end-user access.
- Data integrity improves as multiple applications access the same stored procedure.
- Stored procedures result in a thinner client and a fatter database server.

FIGURE 8-12 A registration page written in ASP.NET

(a) Sample ASP.NET code for user registration

```
<%@ Page Language="C#" AutoEventWireup="true" CodeFile="users.aspx.cs" Inherits="users" %>
<html xmlns="http://www.w3.org/1999/xhtml" >
<head runat="server">
  <title>Register</title>
</head>
<body>
<form id="form1" runat="server">
<div>
<asp:DetailsView ID="manageUsers" runat="server" DataSourceID="usersDataSource">
    <Fields>
            <asp:BoundField DataField="username" HeaderText="User Name" />
            <asp:BoundField DataField="first_name" HeaderText="First Name" />
            <asp:BoundField DataField="last_name" HeaderText="Last Name" />
            <asp:BoundField DataField="email" HeaderText="Email Address" />
            <asp:BoundField DataField="password" HeaderText="Password" />
            <asp:CommandField ShowInsertButton="True" ButtonType="Button" />
    </Fields>
    </asp:DetailsView>
<asp:SqlDataSource ID="usersDataSource" runat="server"
    ConnectionString="<%$ ConnectionStrings:StudentConnectionString %>"
    InsertCommand="INSERT INTO users(username, first_name, last_name, email, password,
    registration_date) VALUES (@username, @first_name, @last_name, @email, @password, GETDATE())"
    SelectCommand="SELECT [username], [first_name], [last_name], [email], [password] FROM [users]">
</asp:SqlDataSource>
</div>
</form>
</body>
</html>
```

(b) Form for the ASP.NET application

User Name	
First Name	
Last Name	
Email Address	
Password	
Insert	Cancel

However, writing stored procedures can also take more time than using Visual Basic or Java to create an application. Also, the proprietary nature of stored procedures reduces their portability and may make it difficult to change DBMSs without having to rewrite the stored procedures. However, using stored procedures appropriately can lead to more efficient processing of database code.

Figure 8-13a shows an example of a stored procedure written in Oracle's PL/SQL that is intended to check whether a user name already exists in the database. Figure 8-13b shows a sample code segment that illustrates that this stored procedure can be called from a Java program.

FIGURE 8-13 Example Oracle PL/SQL stored procedure

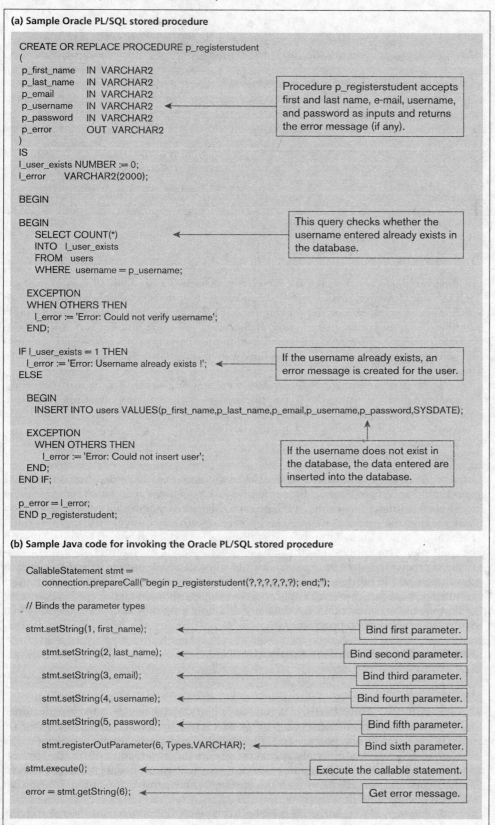

(a) Sample Oracle PL/SQL stored procedure

```
CREATE OR REPLACE PROCEDURE p_registerstudent
(
p_first_name    IN  VARCHAR2
p_last_name     IN  VARCHAR2
p_email         IN  VARCHAR2
p_username      IN  VARCHAR2
p_password      IN  VARCHAR2
p_error            OUT  VARCHAR2
)
IS
l_user_exists NUMBER := 0;
l_error      VARCHAR2(2000);

BEGIN

BEGIN
    SELECT COUNT(*)
    INTO  l_user_exists
    FROM  users
    WHERE  username = p_username;

  EXCEPTION
  WHEN OTHERS THEN
    l_error := 'Error: Could not verify username';
  END;

IF l_user_exists = 1 THEN
    l_error := 'Error: Username already exists !';
ELSE

    BEGIN
      INSERT INTO users VALUES(p_first_name,p_last_name,p_email,p_username,p_password,SYSDATE);

    EXCEPTION
      WHEN OTHERS THEN
        l_error := 'Error: Could not insert user';
    END;
END IF;

p_error = l_error;
END p_registerstudent;
```

Procedure p_registerstudent accepts first and last name, e-mail, username, and password as inputs and returns the error message (if any).

This query checks whether the username entered already exists in the database.

If the username already exists, an error message is created for the user.

If the username does not exist in the database, the data entered are inserted into the database.

(b) Sample Java code for invoking the Oracle PL/SQL stored procedure

```
CallableStatement stmt =
    connection.prepareCall("begin p_registerstudent(?,?,?,?,?,?); end;");

// Binds the parameter types

stmt.setString(1, first_name);
    stmt.setString(2, last_name);
    stmt.setString(3, email);
    stmt.setString(4, username);
    stmt.setString(5, password);
    stmt.registerOutParameter(6, Types.VARCHAR);
stmt.execute();
error = stmt.getString(6);
```

Bind first parameter.

Bind second parameter.

Bind third parameter.

Bind fourth parameter.

Bind fifth parameter.

Bind sixth parameter.

Execute the callable statement.

Get error message.

FIGURE 8-14   Sample Java code snippet for an SQL transaction

Transactions

In the examples shown so far, we have only examined code that consists of a single SQL action. However, most business applications require several SQL queries to complete a business transaction (refer to Figure 7-10). By default, most database connections assume that you would like to commit the results of executing a query to the database immediately. However, it is possible to define the notion of a business transaction in your program. Figure 8-14 shows how a Java program would execute a database transaction.

Given that there might be thousands of users simultaneously trying to access and/or update a database through a Web application at any given point time (think **Amazon.com** or eBay), application developers need to be well versed in the concepts of database transactions and need to use them appropriately when developing applications.

Database Connections

In most three-tier applications, while it is very common to have the Web servers and application servers located on the same physical machine, the database server is often located on a different machine. In this scenario, the act of making a database connection and keeping the connection alive can be very resource intensive. Further, most databases allow only a limited number of connections to be open at any given time. This can be challenging for applications that are being accessed via the Internet because it is difficult to predict the number of users. Luckily, most database drivers relieve application developers of the burden of managing database connections by using the concept of connection pooling. However, application developers should still be careful about how often they make connections to a database and how long they keep a connection open within their application program.

Key Benefits of Three-Tier Applications

The appropriate use of three-tier applications can lead to several benefits in organizations (Thompson, 1997):

- *Scalability*   Three-tier architectures are more scalable than two-tier architectures. For example, the middle tier can be used to reduce the load on a database server by using a transaction processing (TP) monitor to reduce the number of connections to a server, and additional application servers can be added to distribute application processing. A TP monitor is a program that controls data transfer between clients and servers to provide a consistent environment for online transaction processing (OLTP).
- *Technological flexibility*   It is easier to change DBMS engines, although triggers and stored procedures will need to be rewritten, with a three-tier architecture.

The middle tier can even be moved to a different platform. Simplified presentation services make it easier to implement various desired interfaces such as Web browsers or kiosks.

- *Lower long-term costs* Use of off-the-shelf components or services in the middle tier can reduce costs, as can substitution of modules within an application rather than an entire application.
- *Better match of systems to business needs* New modules can be built to support specific business needs rather than building more general, complete applications.
- *Improved customer service* Multiple interfaces on different clients can access the same business processes.
- *Competitive advantage* The ability to react to business changes quickly by changing small modules of code rather than entire applications can be used to gain a competitive advantage.
- *Reduced risk* Again, the ability to implement small modules of code quickly and combine them with code purchased from vendors limits the risk assumed with a large-scale development project.

Cloud Computing and Three-Tier Applications

An emerging trend that is likely to have an effect on the development of three-tier applications is cloud computing. Cloud computing advertisements are even prevalent on primetime TV and in major airports around the world!

So what exactly is cloud computing? According to Mell and Grance (2011), the phrase *cloud computing* refers to a model for providing "ubiquitous, convenient and on-demand network access" to a set of shared computing resources (networks, servers, applications, and services).

All cloud technologies share the following characteristics (Mell and Grance, 2011):

1. On-demand self-service—IT capabilities can be created or released with minimal interaction with the service provider.
2. Broad network access—IT capabilities can be accessed via commonly used network technologies using a wide variety of devices (mobile phones, desktops, etc.).
3. Resource pooling—The service provider is capable of serving multiple consumer organizations and pools their resources (storage, servers etc.) so as to be able to deal with varying consumer demand for the services.
4. Rapid elasticity—The consumer is able to easily (and often automatically) scale up or down the capabilities needed from the service provider.
5. Measured service—Consumers are able to control how much capability they need to use and pay only for the services they use. To achieve this, the service provider should be able to measure the usage of its services by consumers at an appropriate level.

Mell and Grance (2011) also present a popular categorization of cloud technologies:

1. Infrastructure-as-a Service: This category of cloud computing refers to the use of technologies such as servers, storage, and networks from external service providers. The primary benefit to organizations is that the tasks of buying, running, and maintaining the equipment and software are borne by the service providers. Popular examples of the IaaS model are Microsoft's Azure and Rackspace.
2. Platform-as-a Service: This category of cloud computing refers to the provision of building blocks of key technological solutions on the cloud. Examples include application servers, Web servers, and database technologies. Popular databases such as SQL Server, MySQL, Oracle, and IBM's DB2 are all available through this model and offered by the vendors directly, for example, Microsoft's SQL Azure/ Oracle's Public cloud, or through cloud services such as Amazon's EC^2.
3. Software-as-a Service: This refers to an entire application or application suite being run on the cloud via the Internet instead of on an organization's own infrastructure. A popular example of this model is **Salesforce.com's** CRM system. Companies such as SAP and Oracle have also recently announced "cloud ready" versions of their enterprise applications.

From your perspective as a database applications development professional, the proliferation of cloud computing is likely to affect you in two key ways. First, when developing three (or more) tier applications, it is likely that one or more of the tiers—Web, application and/or database—might be hosted by a cloud service provider. Second, the ubiquitous availability of cloud database/application platforms will make it easier for you to develop and deploy applications using a variety of databases/application platforms because the tasks of buying, installing, configuring, and maintaining the various components of the typical *n*-tier application will now be much simplified. This would be particularly beneficial for those working in organizations with limited IT budgets/resources. It is worthwhile noting that cloud computing does not substantially change the core principles around developing three-tier applications that were discussed earlier in this chapter. However, databases hosted in the cloud will have substantial implications for database administrators. We discuss these in more detail in Chapter 12.

EXTENSIBLE MARKUP LANGUAGE (XML)

Extensible Markup Language (XML)

A text-based scripting language used to describe data structures hierarchically, using HTML-like tags.

Extensible Markup Language (XML) is a key development that is likely to continue to revolutionize the way data are exchanged over the Internet. XML addresses the issue of representing data in a structure and format that can both be exchanged over the Internet and be interpreted by different components (i.e., browsers, Web servers, application servers). XML does not replace Hyptertext Markup Language (HTML), but it works with HTML to facilitate the transfer, exchange, and manipulation of data.

XML uses tags, short descriptions enclosed in angle brackets (< >), to characterize data. The use of angle brackets in XML is similar to their use for HTML tags. But whereas HTML tags are used to describe the appearance of content, XML tags are used to describe the content, or data, itself. Consider the following XML document stored in a file called PVFC.xml that is intended to provide the description of a product in PVFC:

```
<?xml version = "1.0"/>
<furniturecompany>
    <product ID="1">
        <description>End Table</description>
        <finish>Cherry</finish>
        <standard price>175.00</standard price>
        <line>1</line>
    </product>
</furniturecompany>
```

The notations <description>, <finish>, and so on are examples of XML tags; <description>End Table</description> is an example of an element. Hence, an XML document consists of a series of nested elements. There are few restrictions on what can and cannot constitute tags in an XML element. However, an XML document itself must conform to a set of rules in terms of its structure. Three main techniques are used to validate that an XML document is structured correctly (i.e., follows all the rules for what constitutes a valid XML document): document structure declarations (DSDs), **XML Schema Definition (XSD)**, and Relax NG. All of these are alternatives to document type declarations (DTDs). DTDs were included in the first version XML but have some limitations. They cannot specify data types and are written in their own language, not in XML. In addition, DTDs do not support some newer features of XML, such as namespaces.

XML Schema Definition (XSD)

Language used for defining XML databases that has been recommended by the W3C.

To overcome these difficulties, the World Wide Web Consortium (W3C) published the XML Schema standard in May 2001. It defines the data model and establishes data types for the document data. The W3C XML Schema Definition (XSD) language uses a custom XML vocabulary to describe XML documents. It represents a step forward from using DTDs because it allows data types to be denoted. The following is a very simple XSD schema that describes the structure, data typing, and validation of a salesperson record.

```
<?xml version="1.0" encoding="utf-8"?>
<xsd:schema id="salespersonSchema"
xmlns:xsd="http://www.w3.org/2001/XMLSchema">
   <xsd:element name="Salesperson" type ="SalespersonType" />
   <xsd:complexType name="SalespersonType">
       <xsd:sequence>
           <xsd:elementname="SalespersonID"
                        type="xsd:integer"/>
           <xsd:elementname="SalespersonName"
                        type="xsd:string" />
           <xsd:element name="SalespersonTelephone"
                        type="PhoneNumberType">
           <xsd:element name="SalespersonFax"
                        type="PhoneNumber" minOccurs="0" />
           </xsd:element>
       </xsd:sequence>
   </xsd:complexType>
   <xsd:simpleType name="PhoneNumberType">
       <xsd:restriction base="xsd:string">
           <xsd:length value="12" />
           <xsd:pattern value="\d{3}-\d{3}-\d{4}" />
       </xsd:restriction>
   </xsd:simpleType>
</xsd:schema>
```

The following XML document conforms to the schema listed previously.

```
<?xml version="1.0" encoding="utf-8"?>
<Salesperson xmlns:xsi=http://www.w3.org/2001/XMLSchema-instance
xsi:noNamespaceSchemaLocation="salespersonSchema.xsd">
    <SalespersonID>1</SalespersonID>
    <SalespersonName>Doug Henny</SalespersonName>
    <SalespersonTelephone>813-444-5555></SalespersonTelephone>
</Salesperson>
```

While it is possible to set up your own XML vocabulary, as we have just done, a wide variety of public XML vocabularies already exist and can be used to mark up your data. Many of them are listed at **http://wdvl.com/Authoring/Languages/XML/ Specifications.html** and **www.service-architecture.com/xml/articles/xml_vocabularies. html**. Such vocabularies make it easier for an organization to exchange data with other organizations without having to engage in individual agreements with each business partner. Selecting the best XML vocabulary to use to describe a database is very important. As XML gains popularity, more libraries of external XML schemas should become available, but for now, Web searches and word of mouth are the most likely mechanisms for you to find the appropriate schemas for your application.

New XML-based vocabularies, such as Extensible Business Reporting Language (XBRL) and Structured Product Labeling (SPL), have emerged as open standards that allow meaningful and unambiguous comparisons that could not be made easily previously. Financial organizations that adhere to XBRL may record up to 2,000 financial data points, such as cost, assets, and net income, using standard XBRL tag definitions. These data points may then be combined or compared across institutions' financial reports. As products that enable easier use of XBRL come to market, large financial institutions expect to spend much less time cleansing and normalizing their data and exchanging data with business partners. Smaller institutions can anticipate improved and more affordable access to financial analysis (Henschen, 2005). The FDA is also beginning to require the use of Structured Product Labeling (SPL), to record the information provided on drug labels, for both prescription and over-the-counter drugs.

Now that you have a basic understanding of what constitutes an XML document, we can turn our attention to how XML data can be used in the modern computing environment and the unique challenges they bring to the table.

Storing XML Documents

One of the biggest questions that needs to be answered as XML data becomes more prevalent is "Where do we store these data?" While it is possible to store XML data as a series of files, doing so brings back into play the same disadvantages with file processing systems that we discussed in Chapter 1. Luckily, we have several choices when it comes to storing XML data:

1. *Store XML data in a relational database by shredding the XML document* Shredding an XML document essentially means that we store each element of an XML schema independently in a relational table and use other tables to store the relationships among the elements. Modern databases such as Microsoft SQL Server and Oracle provide capabilities beyond standard SQL to help store and retrieve XML data.
2. *Store an entire XML document in a field capable of storing large objects, such as a binary large object (BLOB) or a character large object (CLOB)* This technique is not very useful if you have to actually search for data within the XML document.
3. *Store the XML document using special XML columns that are made available as part of database* These columns can be associated with an XSD, for example, to ensure that the XML document that is being inserted is a valid document.
4. *Store the XML document using a native XML database* These are non-relational databases designed specifically to store XML documents.

In general, the latter two options are used when the majority of the information being processed is originally in XML format. For example, many academic and practitioner conferences are beginning to require that authors submit their presentations and papers in XML format. On the other hand, the first two options are used primarily if XML is used as a data exchange format between a browser and an application server.

Retrieving XML Documents

XPath

One of a set of XML technologies that supports XQuery development. XPath expressions are used to locate data in XML documents.

Modern databases provide extensive support for retrieving information from databases in XML format. The key technologies behind XML data retrieval are **XPath** and XQuery. Each of the storage options listed above provides specific mechanisms by which you can retrieve data in XML format. For the first three options, these take the form of extensions to the SQL language (based on XPath and XQuery). In the case of a native XML database, the most likely choice is XQuery itself. XQuery helps in locating and extracting elements from XML documents; it can be used to accomplish such activities as transforming XML data to XHTML, providing information for use by Web services, generating summary reports, and searching Web documents.

XQuery

An XML transformation language that allows applications to query both relational databases and XML data.

The XML Query Working Group describes **XQuery** most simply in these words, published at **www.w3c.org/XML/Query**: "XQuery is a standardized language for combining documents, databases, Web pages and almost anything else. It is very widely implemented. It is powerful and easy to learn. XQuery is replacing proprietary middleware languages and Web application development languages. XQuery is replacing complex Java or C++ programs with a few lines of code. XQuery is simpler to work with and easier to maintain than many other alternatives.

Built on XPath expressions, XQuery is now supported by the major relational database engines, including those from IBM, Oracle, and Microsoft.

FIGURE 8-15   XML code segments
(a) XML schema

```
<?xml version = "1.0"?>
<furniture company>
    <product ID="1">
        <description>End Table</description>
        <finish>Cherry</finish>
        <standard price>175.00</standard price>
        <line>1</line>
    </product>
    <product ID="2">
        <description>Coffee Table</description>
        <finish>Natural Ash</finish>
        <standard price>200.00</standard price>
        <line>2</line>
    </product>
    <product ID="3">
        <description>Computer Desk</description>
        <finish>Natural Ash</finish>
        <standard price>375.00</standard price>
        <line>2</line>
    </product>
    <product ID="4">
        <description>Entertainment Center</description>
        <finish>Natural Maple</finish>
        <standard price>650.00</standard price>
        <line>3</line>
    </product>
    <product ID="5">
        <description>Writers Desk</description>
        <finish>Cherry</finish>
        <standard price>325.00</standard price>
        <line>1</line>
    </product>
    <product ID="6">
        <description>8-Drawer Desk</description>
        <finish>White Ash</finish>
        <standard price>750.00</standard price>
        <line>2</line>
    </product>
    <product ID="7">
        <description>Dining Table</description>
        <finish>Natural Ash</finish>
        <standard price>800.00</standard price>
        <line>2</line>
    </product>
    <product ID="8">
        <description>Computer Desk</description>
        <finish>Walnut</finish>
        <standard price>250.00</standard price>
        <line>3</line>
    </product>
</furniture company>
```

Take a look at the XML document shown in Figure 8-15a. Now, consider the following XQuery expression that returns all product elements that have a standard price > 300.00:

```
for $p in doc("PVFC.xml")/furniture company/product
where $p/standardprice>300.00
order by $p/description
return $p/description
```

You can see the similarities between XQuery and SQL in this example. It is often said that XQuery is to XML as SQL is to relational databases. This example demonstrates the ease with which you will become fluent in XQuery as your understanding of

FIGURE 8-15 *(continued)*
(b) XSLT code

```
<?xml version = "1.0"?>
<xsl:stylesheet version="1.0" xmlns:xsl="http://www.w3.org/1999/XSL/Transform">
<xsl:template match="/">
    <html>
        <body>
        <h2>Product Listing</h2>
        <table border="1">
        <tr bgcolor="orange">
                <th>Description</th>
                <th>Finish</th>
                <th>Price</th>
        </tr>
        <xsl:for-each select="furniturecompany/product">
        <tr>
            <td><xsl:value-of select="description"/></td>
            <td><xsl:value-of select="finish"/></td>
            <td><xsl:value-of select="price"/></td>
        </tr>
        </xsl:for-each>
        </table>
        </body>
    </html>
</xsl:template>
</xsl:stylesheet>
```

(c) Output of XSLT transformation

Product Listing

Description	Finish	Price
End Table	Cherry	175.00
Coffee Table	Natural Ash	200.00
Computer Desk	Natural Ash	375.00
Entertainment Center	Natural Maple	650.00
Writers Desk	Cherry	325.00
8-Drawer Desk	White Ash	750.00
Dining Table	Natural Ash	800.00
Computer Desk	Walnut	250.00

SQL increases. The XQuery expression shown previously is called a FLWOR expression. FLWOR is an acronym for For, LET, Where, Order by, and Return:

- The FOR clause selects all product elements from furniture company into the variable named $p.
- The WHERE clause selects all product elements with a standard price greater than $300.00.
- The ORDER BY clause sets the sorting order of the results to be by the description element.
- The RETURN clause specifies that the description elements should be returned.

The results of the above XQuery are as follows:

```
<description>8-Drawer Desk</description>
<description>Computer Desk</description>
<description>Dining Table</description>
<description>Entertainment Center</description>
<description>Writer's Desk</description>
```

This example shows how to query data that is in XML format. Given the importance of XML as a data exchange format, many relational databases also provide mechanisms to return data from relational tables in an XML format. In Microsoft SQL Server, this can be achieved by adding the statement FOR XML AUTO or PATH to the end of a typical SELECT query. Essentially, the result table from the SELECT is converted into an XML form and returned to the calling program. Behind the scenes, many of these additional features use XPath as the basis for the queries.

Displaying XML Data

Notice that in the XML examples so far, we have provided little information about what to do with XML data. In fact, the separation of how data are formatted from how the data are displayed is one of the key reasons XML is gaining popularity over HTML, where the data and formatting are intermingled. The display of XML data on a Web browser is controlled by a stylesheet specified using the **Extensible Stylesheet Language Transformation (XSLT)**. Most modern browsers and programming languages provide support for XSLT. Thus, the transformation of the XML can happen either at the Web server layer or the application server layer. Figure 8-15b shows a sample XSLT specification for displaying the Salesperson data in the form of an HTML table. The resultant output is shown in Figure 8-15c.

> **Extensible Stylesheet Language Transformation (XSLT)**
> A language used to transform complex XML documents and also used to create HTML pages from XML documents.

One of the advantages of XSLT is that it can be used to handle the myriad devices that now use the Internet. For example, smartphones and tablets have built-in browsers that allow a user to access the Internet. Most of these browsers are capable of interpreting HTML5, the newest version of HTML. HTML5 has built-in support for features important for mobile devices, such as audio and video streaming, offline support, and geolocation support. Others can handle HTML, as long as it has been appropriately transformed for optimal viewing on the screen size of a mobile device. By using XSLT, XML, and other technologies, the same set of data can be rendered onto the different devices without having to write a separate page for each device type.

XML and Web Services

The Internet has served as a powerful driver to encourage the integration of communication between the providers of software applications and the users of those applications. As the Internet evolves as a distributed computing platform, a set of emerging standards is affecting software development and distribution practices. Easing the automatic communication of software programs through the use of XML coding and Internet protocols such as HTTP and e-mail protocols, a new class of applications called **Web services** is improving the ability of computers to communicate over the Internet automatically, thus aiding the development and deployment of applications within a company or across an industry. Existing methods of establishing communication, such as electronic data interchange (EDI), are still being used, but the widespread availability of XML means that the Web services approach promises to make it much easier to create program application modules that execute in a distributed environment.

> **Web services**
> A set of emerging standards that define protocols for automatic communication between software programs over the Web. Web services are XML based and usually run in the background to establish transparent communication among computers.

The promise of Web services is the development of a standardized communication system among different applications, using XML based technologies at their core. Easier integration of applications is possible because developers need not be familiar with the technical details associated with the applications being integrated, nor must they learn the programming language of the application being integrated. Anticipation of increased business agility derived from significant reductions in the time and effort needed to establish enterprise application integration and B2B relationships is driving the interest in the Web services approach. Figure 8-16 is a very simple diagram of an order entry system that includes both internal Web services (Order Entry and Accounting) and Web services that are outsourced to companies that provide authentication and credit validation services over the Web (Newcomer, 2002).

There are some key additional terms that are associated with using Web services. Figure 8-17 depicts a common database/Web services protocol stack. The transformation

FIGURE 8-16 A typical order entry system that uses Web services
Source: Based on Newcomer (2002).

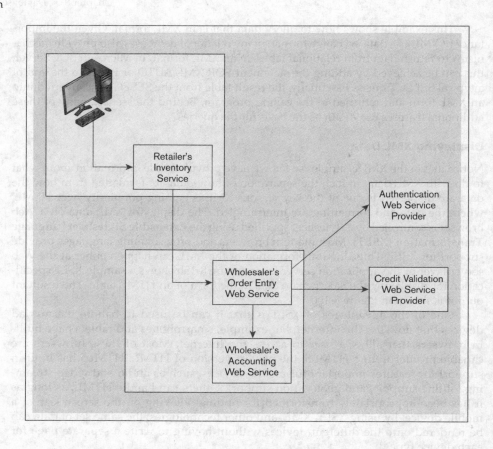

FIGURE 8-17 Web services protocol stack

Publish, Find, Use Services	UDDI	**U**niversal **D**escription, **D**iscovery, **I**ntegration
Describe Services	WSDL	**W**eb **S**ervices **D**escription **L**anguage
Service Interactions	SOAP	**S**imple **O**bject **A**ccess **P**rotocol
Data Format	XML	e**X**tensible **M**arkup **L**anguage
Open Communications	Internet	

Universal Description, Discovery, and Integration (UDDI)

A technical specification for creating a distributed registry of Web services and businesses that are open to communicating through Web services.

Web Services Description Language (WSDL)

An XML-based grammar or language used to describe a Webservice and specify a public interface for that service.

and communication of data into and out of application programs and databases rely on a set of XML-based protocols. **Universal Description, Discovery, and Integration (UDDI)** is a technical specification for creating a distributed registry of Web services and businesses that are open to communicating through Web services. **Web Services Description Language (WSDL)** is an XML-based grammar or language used to describe what a Web service can do and to specify a public interface for how to use that service. WSDL is used to create a file that automatically generates a client interface, allowing a developer to attend to the business logic rather than the communications requirements of an application. The definition of the public interface may indicate data types for XML messages, message format, location information for the specified Web service, the transport protocol to be used (HTTP, HTTPS, or e-mail), and so forth. These descriptions are stored in a UDDI repository.

Simple Object Access Protocol (SOAP) is an XML-based communication protocol used for sending messages between applications via the Internet. Because it is a language-independent platform, it enables communication between diverse applications. As SOAP moves toward becoming a W3C standard, it generalizes a capability that was previously established on an ad hoc basis between specific programs. Many view it as the most important Web service. SOAP structures a message into three parts: an optional header, a required body, and optional attachments. The header can support in-transit processing and can thus deal with firewall security issues.

The following is an example, adapted from an example displayed at **http://en.wikipedia.org/wiki/SOAP**, of how Pine Valley Furniture Company might format a SOAP message requesting product information from one of its suppliers. PVFC needs to know which product corresponds to the supplier's product ID 32879.

> **Simple Object Access Protocol (SOAP)**
>
> An XML-based communication protocol used for sending messages between applications via the Internet.

```
<soap:Envelope xmlns:soap=http://schemas.xmlsoap.org/soap/envelope/>
  <soap:Body>
    <getProductDetails xmlns=http://supplier.example.com/ws
      <productID>32879</productID>
    </getProductDetails>
  </soap:Body>
</soap:Envelope>
```

The supplier's Web service could format its reply message, which contains the requested information about the product, in this way:

```
<soap:Envelope xmlns:soap=http://schemas.xmlsoap.org/soap/envelope/>
  <soap:Body>
    <getProductDetailsResponse xmlns="suppliers.example.com/ws">
      <getProductDetailsResult>
        <productName>Dining Table</productName>
        <Finish>Natural Ash</Finish>
        <Price>800</Price>
        <inStock>True</inStock>
      </getProductDetailsResult>
    </getProductDetailsResponse>
  </soap:Body>
</soap:Envelope>
```

Figure 8-18 shows the interaction of applications and systems with Web services. Note that as a transaction flows from one business to another or from a customer to a business, a SOAP processor creates a message envelope that allows the exchange of formatted XML data across the Web. Because SOAP messages connect remote sites, appropriate security measures must be implemented in order to maintain data integrity.

Web services, with their promise of automatic communication between businesses and customers, whether they are other businesses or individual retail customers, have generated much discussion and anticipation in the past few years. Concerns about adopting a Web services approach focus on transaction speed, security, and reliability. The open system implied in establishing automatic communication among computers attached to the Web must be further developed before the security and reliability match those of traditional business applications.

However, it is clear that Web services are here to stay. Several organizations have already attracted attention by their use of Web services. Both Amazon.com and Google,

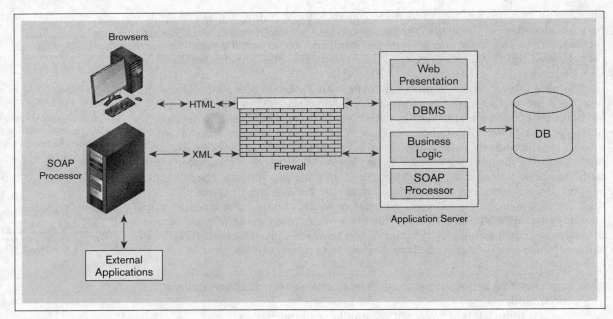

FIGURE 8-18 **Web services deployment**

Source: Based on Newcomer (2002).

two companies with high-profile Web presence, use Web services extensively. Google began its program in April 2002, allowing developers to access its search database directly for noncommercial uses and to create their own interfaces to the data. Access to Amazon.com's inventory database was made available in July 2002. Combining the service with a blog tool, an API allows bloggers to create a link to a relevant Amazon.com product in one step. Programmers benefit from improved ease of access, customers conduct more efficient searches, and Amazon.com and Google continue to spread and support their brands. Google "Amazon Web services documentation" or "Google Web services" to become more familiar with these free opportunities.

The growing popularity and availability of Web services is also leading to a change in the way organizations think about developing their IT applications and capabilities. A new paradigm called **service-oriented architecture (SOA)** is gaining a foothold. An SOA is a collection of services that communicate with each other in some manner, usually passing data or coordinating a business activity. While these services do not have to be Web services, Web services are the predominant mechanism used. SOAs differ from traditional object-oriented approaches in that the services are loosely coupled and very interoperable. The software components are very reusable and operate across different development platforms, such as Java and .NET. Using XML, SOAP, and WSDL eases the establishment of necessary connections.

Using an SOA approach leads to the establishment of a modeling, design, and software development process that supports the efficient development of applications. Organizations that have adopted such an approach have found their development time reduced by at least 40 percent. Not only are the organizations experiencing shorter development time, they also hope to demonstrate more flexibility in responding to the rapidly changing business environment.

Service-oriented architecture (SOA)

A collection of services that communicate with each other in some manner, usually by passing data or coordinating a business activity.

Summary

Client/server architectures have offered businesses opportunities to better fit their computer systems to their business needs. Establishing the appropriate balance between client/server and mainframe DBMSs is a matter of much current discussion. Client/server architectures are prominent in providing Internet applications, including dynamic data access. Application partitioning assigns portions of application code to client or server partitions after it is written in order to achieve better performance and interoperability. Application developer productivity is expected to increase as a result of using application partitioning, but the developer must understand each process intimately to place it correctly.

In a two-tier architecture, the client manages the user interface and business logic, while the database server manages database storage and access. This architecture reduces network traffic, reduces the power required for each client, and centralizes user authorization, integrity checking, data dictionary maintenance, and query and update processing on the database server. We looked at examples of a two-tier application written in VB.NET and Java and examined the six key steps needed to retrieve data from a database.

Three-tier architectures, which include another server in addition to the client and database server layers, allow application code to be stored on the additional server. This approach allows business processing to be performed on the additional server, resulting in a thin client. Advantages of the three-tier architecture can include scalability, technological flexibility, lower long-term costs, better matching of systems to business needs, improved customer service, competitive advantage, and reduced risk. But higher short-term costs, advanced tools and training, shortages of experienced personnel, incompatible standards, and lack of end-user tools are some of the challenges related to using three-tier or *n*-tier architectures.

The most common type of three-tier application is the Internet-based Web application. In its simplest form, a request from a client (workstation, smartphone or tablet) browser is sent through the network to the Web server. If the request requires that data be obtained from the database, the Web server constructs a query and sends it to the database server, which processes the query and returns the results. Firewalls are used to limit external access to the company's data. Cloud computing is likely to become a popular paradigm for three-tier applications in the coming years.

Common components of Internet architecture are certain programming and markup languages, Web servers, applications servers, database servers, and database drivers and other middleware that can be used to connect the various components together. To aid in our understanding of how to create a Web application, we looked at examples of three-tier applications written in JSP, PHP, and ASP.NET and examined some of the key database-related issues in such applications.

Finally, we discussed the role of XML as a data exchange standard on the Internet. We examined issues related to the storage of XML documents in databases, retrieval of XML using languages such as XQuery and XPath, as well as transformation of XML data into presentation formats such as HTML. We also examined various XML-based technologies, UDDI, WSDL, and SOAP, which are all fueling the interest in SOA and Web services. These allow disparate applications within a company or around the globe to be able to talk to each other.

Chapter Review

Key Terms

Application partitioning *342*
Application program interface (API) *344*
Client/server system *341*
Database server *343*
Extensible Markup Language (XML) *364*
Extensible Stylesheet Language

Transformation (XSLT) *369*
Fat client *342*
Java servlet *356*
Middleware *344*
Open Database Connectivity (ODBC) *344*
Service-oriented architecture (SOA) *372*

Simple Object Access Protocol (SOAP) *371*
Thin client *349*
Three-tier architecture *348*
Universal Description, Discovery, and Integration (UDDI) *370*
Web services *369*
Web Services Description Language (WSDL) *370*

XML Schema Definition (XSD) *364*
XPath *366*
XQuery *366*

Review Questions

8-1. Define each of the following terms:
  a. application partitioning
  b. application program interface (API)
  c. client/server system
  d. middleware
  e. stored procedure

  f. three-tier architecture
  g. Open Database Connectivity (ODBC)
  h. XML Schema
  i. Web services
  j. XSLT
  k. SOAP

8-2. Match each of the following terms with the most appropriate definition:

_____ client/server system

_____ application program interface (API)

_____ fat client

_____ database server

_____ middleware

_____ three-tier architecture

_____ thin client

_____ XSD

_____ SOA

a. a client that is responsible for processing, including application logic and presentation logic

b. a PC configured for handling the presentation layer and some business logic processing for an application

c. a collection of services that communicate with each other in some manner

d. software that facilitates interoperability, reducing programmer coding effort

e. device responsible for database storage and access

f. systems where the application logic components are distributed

g. software that facilitates communication between front-end programs and back-end database servers

h. three-layer client/server configuration

i. language used for defining XML databases

8-3. List several major advantages of the client/server architecture compared with other computing approaches.

8-4. Contrast the following terms:
   a. two-tier architecture; three-tier architecture
   b. fat client; thin client
   c. ODBC; JDBC
   d. SOAP; XSLT
   e. SQL; XQuery
   f. Web services; SOA

8-5. Describe the advantages and disadvantages of two-tier architectures.

8-6. Describe the advantages and disadvantages of three-tier architectures.

8-7. Describe the common components needed to create a Web-based application.

8-8. What database APIs are commonly used to access databases from various programming languages?

8-9. What are the six common steps needed to access databases from a typical program?

8-10. If you were charged with developing a client/server application, how would you ensure success?

8-11. What are the three common types of cloud computing services?

8-12. What are the four common approaches to storing XML data?

8-13. What components must a PHP program that enables a dynamic Web site contain?

8-14. Explain why using XML Schema is a step forward from using document type declarations (DTDs).

8-15. What is XSLT, and how does it differ from XML? What role does it play in the creation of a Web application?

8-16. Why is HTML5 beneficial for developing mobile applications?

8-17. What is SOA? How would you in your view point, logical relate it to Database Application Development?

8-18. What are the XML-based protocols that used in Web Services?

8-19. Explain why eXtensible Markup Language is a major development that has happened for data exchange over the Internet?

8-20. How are triggers different from routines? When are constraints thought of as special constraints?

8-21. Contrast Dynamic SQL with Embedded SQL? Explain why and when would one be preferred over another?

8-22. Explain the life cycle of embedded SQL.

Problems and Exercises

8-23. You have been asked to prepare a report that evaluates possible client/server solutions to handle a new customer application system for all branch offices. What business characteristics would you evaluate? What technology characteristics would you evaluate? Why?

8-24. Explain the difference between a static Web site and a dynamic one. What are the characteristics of a dynamic Web site that enable it to better support the development of e-business?

8-25. Historically, what types of applications have moved quickly to client/server database systems? What types have moved more slowly, and why? What do you think will happen in the future to the ratio of client/server database systems versus mainframe database systems?

8-26. Discuss some of the languages that are associated with Internet application development. Classify these languages according to the functionality they provide for each application. It is not necessary that you use the same classification scheme used in the chapter.

8-27. Find some dynamic Web site code such as that included in Figures 8-10, 8-11, and 8-12. Annotate the code, as is done in these figures, to explain each section, especially the elements that involve interaction with the database. (Hint: Google "JSP," "ASP.NET," or "PHP MySQL Examples" to find a rich set of sample code to explore.)

8-28. Rewrite the example shown in Figure 8-5 using VB.NET.

8-29. Rewrite the example shown in Figure 8-4 using Java.

8-30. Consider the example code shown in Figure 8-10. Assume that instead of accessing data from a local server, you are going to access data from a cloud provider that offers the appropriate application server (i.e., JSP) and database technologies. What changes, if any, do you have to make to the example code segment(s)?

8-31. Consider the example code shown in Figure 8-10. What changes would you need to make to ensure that the application works on mobile phone browsers?

8-32. Visit the Web sites of at least two cloud service providers that offer cloud database services. What are some of the common benefits of using cloud database services listed on these Web sites? If you are not sure where to start, try **aws.amazon.com** or **cloud.oracle.com**.

8-33. Construct a simple XML schema that describes a tutor. Include the tutor's last name, first name, phone, e-mail address, and certification date as child elements of the TUTOR element.

8-34. Using your schema from Problem and Exercise 8-33 write an FLWOR XQuery expression that lists only the tutors' names and lists them alphabetically by last name.

8-35. Using your schema from Problem and Exercise 8-23 write an XSLT program to display the tutor information in the form of an HTML table.

8-36. Discuss how Web services can be used to effectively integrate business applications and data. Search the Web for resources on current Web services that employ XML, SOAP, and WSDL. Find at least three and discuss how each is used, including examples from industry.

Field Exercises

8-37. Investigate the computing architecture of your university. Trace the history of computing at your university and determine what path the university followed to get to its present configurations. Some universities started early with mainframe environments; others started when PCs became available. Can you tell how your university's initial computing environment has affected today's computing environment?

8-38. On a smaller scale than in Field Exercise 8-31 investigate the computing architecture of a department within your university. Try to find out how well the current system is meeting the department's information-processing needs.

8-39. Locate three sites on the Web that have interactive database systems attached to them. Evaluate the functionality of each site and discuss how its interactive database system is likely to affect that functionality. If you're not sure where to start, try **www.amazon.com**.

8-40. Determine what you would have to do to use PHP, JSP, or ASP.NET on a public Web site owned either by you or by the organization for which you work.

8-41. Outline the steps you would take to conduct a risk assessment for your place of employment with regard to attaching a database to your public site. If possible, help with the actual implementation of the risk assessment.

8-42. According to your own personal interests, use one of the common combinations PHP and MySQL, JSP and Oracle, or ASP.NET and Microsoft Access to attach a database to your personal Web site. Test it locally and then move it to your public site.

8-43. Identify a Web site that extensively describes XML technologies. What other XML technologies besides the ones described in this chapter do you see being discussed? What purpose do they serve? If you're not sure where to start, try **www.xml.com** or **www.w3.org**.

References

Henschen, D. 2005. "XBRL Offers a Faster Route to Intelligence." *Intelligent Enterprise 8,8* (August): 12.

Hurwitz, J. 1998. "Sorting Out Middleware." *DBMS* 11,1 (January): 10–12.

Mell, P., and T. Grance. 2011. "The NIST Definition of Cloud Computing" *National Institute of Standards and Technology*, **http://csrc.nist.gov/publications/nistpubs/800-145/SP800-145.pdf**, accessed 12/18/2011.

Newcomer, E. 2002. *Understanding Web Services, XML, WSDL, SOAP, and UDDI*. Boston: Addison-Wesley.

Quinlan, T. 1995. "The Second Generation of Client/Server." *Database Programming & Design* 8,5 (May): 31–39.

Thompson, C. 1997. "Committing to Three-Tier Architecture." *Database Programming & Design* 10,8 (August): 26–33.

Ullman, L. 2003. *PHP and MySQL for Dynamic Web Sites*. Berkeley, CA: Peachpit Press.

Further Reading

Anderson, G., and B. Armstrong. 1995. "Client/Server: Where Are We Really?" *Health Management Technology* 16,6 (May): 34, 36, 38, 40, 44.

Cerami, E. 2002. *Web Services Essentials*. Sebastopol, CA: O'Reilly & Associates, Inc.

Frazer, W. D. 1998. "Object/Relational Grows Up." *Database Programming & Design* 11,1 (January): 22–28.

Innocenti, C. 2006. "XQuery Levels the Data Integration Playing Field." *DM Review* accessed at *DM Direct*, **http://www.information-management.com/infodirect/20061201/1069184-1.html** (December).

Koenig, D., A. Glover, P. King, G. Laforge, and J. Skeet. 2007. *Groovy in Action*. Greenwich, CT: Manning Publications.

Mason, J. N., and M. Hofacker. 2001. "Gathering Client-Server Data." *Internal Auditor* 58:6 (December): 27–29.

Melton, J., and S. Buxton. 2006. *Querying XML, XQuery, XPath, and SQL/XML in Context*. Morgan Kaufmann Series in Data Management Systems. San Francisco: Morgan Kaufmann.

Morrison, M., and J. Morrison. 2003. *Database-Driven Web Sites*, 2nd ed. Cambridge, MA: Thomson-Course Technologies.

Richardson, L., S. Ruby, and D. H. Hansson. 2007. *RESTful Web Services*. Sebastopol, CA: O'Reilly Media, Inc.

Valade, J. 2006. *PHP & MySQL: Your Visual Blueprint for Creating Dynamic, Database-Driven Web Sites*. Hoboken, NJ: Wiley & Sons.

Wamsley, P. 2007. *XQuery*. Sebastopol, CA: O'Reilly Media, Inc.

Web Resources

www.javacoffeebreak.com/articles/jdbc/index.html "Getting Started with JDBC" by David Reilly.

http://www.w3schools.com/ASPNET/default.asp Tutorial on ASP.NET.

www.w3.org/html/wg W3C's home page for HTML.

www.w3.org/MarkUp W3C's home page for XHTML.

www.w3.org/XML/Query W3C's home page for XQuery.

www.w3.org/XML/1999/XML-in-10-points The W3C article "XML in 10 points," which presents basic XML concepts.

www.netcraft.com The Netcraft Web Server survey, which tracks the market share of different Web servers and SSL site operating systems.

www.w3schools.com/default.asp A Web developers' site that provides Web-building tutorials on topics from basic HTML and HTML5 to advanced XML, and SQL.

www.oasis-open.org/home/index.php The home page of the Organization for the Advancement of Structured Information Standards (OASIS).

xml.apache.org/cocoon The Cocoon project, a Java Web publishing framework that separates document content, style, and logic, allowing the independent design, creation, and management of each.

CASE

Forondo Artist Management Excellence Inc.

Case Description

You are now ready to create to a proof of concept system for FAME.

Project Questions

8-44. Revisit your deliverable for question 1-59, Chapter 1, and reread the case descriptions in Chapters 1 through 3 with an eye towards identifying the functionality you want to provide to the various stakeholders. Document the subset of functionality (with your instructor's guidance, if appropriate) that you want to incorporate into your system.

8-45. Provide a document that provides your recommendation on the set of technologies (DBMS, programming language, Web server [if appropriate]) that you believe are best suited for FAME. Ensure that this document has some information on the options you considered and provides a solid justification for your recommendation. In particular, Martin wants to know whether you considered cloud-based solutions and whether they are appropriate for FAME.

8-46. Create your proof of concept using your technological recommendations (or using the environment that your instructor asks you to use).

8-47. Create a testing strategy (including user acceptance testing) for your proof of concept. Which stakeholders should you involve in the phase? Who do you think should sign off on the testing phase before you move to full-fledged deployment?

8-48. Create a deployment/rollout strategy for your system within FAME. Ensure that your deployment strategy includes a plan for training, conversion/loading of existing data into the new system, and post-implementation support.

CHAPTER 9

Data Warehousing

LEARNING OBJECTIVES

After studying this chapter, you should be able to:

- Concisely define each of the following key terms: **data warehouse, operational system, informational system, data mart, independent data mart, dependent data mart, enterprise data warehouse (EDW), operational data store (ODS), logical data mart, real-time data warehouse, reconciled data, derived data, transient data, periodic data, star schema, grain, conformed dimension, snowflake schema**

- Give two important reasons why an "information gap" often exists between an information manager's need and the information generally available.

- List two major reasons most organizations today need data warehousing.

- Name and briefly describe the three levels in a data warehouse architecture.

- Describe the two major components of a star schema.

- Estimate the number of rows and total size, in bytes, of a fact table, given reasonable assumptions concerning the database dimensions.

- Design a data mart using various schemes to normalize and denormalize dimensions and to account for fact history, hierarchical relationships between dimensions, and changing dimension attribute values.

- Develop the requirements for a data mart from questions supporting decision making.

- Understand the trends that are likely to affect the future of data warehousing in organizations.

INTRODUCTION

Everyone agrees that readily available high-quality information is vital in business today. Consider the following actual critical situation:

> PMPL is a pioneer in the perfumery industry in India. The company began in 1940s, as a cottage industry and has now grown into ₹300 crores annual turnover company. It is headquartered in Hassan, Karnataka. The company has over 2,500 employees and has operations in 7 countries and in all the states of India. The company has different business units for manufacturing, packaging marketing and sales.

Its marketing and sales unit operated independently and is responsible for sales plan, budget, advertising, sales promotion and invoicing. This Business unit is supported by a state-of-art data warehouse running of MS-SQL Analysis Services. The data warehouse incorporates daily sales from the company depots to its wholesalers, and its inventory data, plus country—wise data and data from external sources regarding finance and market data. It provides decision support milieu to the sales managers who manage regional sales territories to re-align the territories in case needed. The market specialists need the data warehouse for analyzing market potential. The data warehouse is also used as an Executive information system by the corporate managers to create reports of the company quarterly results.

In light of this strong emphasis on information and the recent advances in information technology, you might expect most organizations to have highly developed systems for delivering information to managers and other users. Yet this is often not the case. In fact, despite having mountains of data (as in petabytes—1000 terabytes, or 1000^5 bytes), and often many databases, few organizations have more than a fraction of the information they need. The increase in the types of data being generated by various devices, such as, social media feeds, RFID tags, GPS location information etc., is only adding to this complexity. Managers are often frustrated by their inability to access or use the data and information they need. This situation contributes to why some people claim that "business intelligence" is an oxymoron.

Modern organizations are said to be drowning in data but starving for information. Despite the mixed metaphor, this statement seems to portray quite accurately the situation in many organizations. What is the reason for this state of affairs? Let's examine two important (and related) reasons why an information gap has been created in most organizations.

The first reason for the information gap is the fragmented way in which organizations have developed information systems—and their supporting databases—for many years. The emphasis in this text is on a carefully planned, architectural approach to systems development that should produce a compatible set of databases. However, in reality, constraints on time and resources cause most organizations to resort to a "one-thing-at-a-time" approach to developing islands of information systems. This approach inevitably produces a hodgepodge of uncoordinated and often inconsistent databases. Usually databases are based on a variety of hardware, software platforms, and purchased applications and have resulted from different organizational mergers, acquisitions, and reorganizations. Under these circumstances, it is extremely difficult, if not impossible, for managers to locate and use accurate information, which must be synthesized across these various systems of record.

The second reason for the information gap is that most systems are developed to support operational processing, with little or no thought given to the information or analytical tools needed for decision making. *Operational processing*, also called transaction processing, captures, stores, and manipulates data to support daily operations of the organization. It tends to focus database design on optimizing access to a small set of data related to a transaction (e.g., a customer, order, and associated product data). *Informational processing* is the analysis of data or other forms of information to support decision making. It needs large "swatches" of data from which to derive information (e.g., sales of all products, over several years, from every sales region). Most systems that are developed internally or purchased from outside vendors are designed to support operational processing, with little thought given to informational processing.

Bridging the information gap are *data warehouses* that consolidate and integrate information from many internal and external sources and arrange it in a meaningful format for making accurate and timely business decisions. They support executives, managers, and business analysts in making complex business decisions through applications such as the analysis of trends, target marketing, competitive analysis, customer relationship management, and so on. Data warehousing has evolved to meet these needs without disturbing existing operational processing.

The proliferation of Web-based customer interactions has made the situation much more interesting and more real time. The activities of customers and suppliers on an organization's Web site provide a wealth of new clickstream data to help understand behaviors and preferences and create a unique opportunity to communicate the right message (e.g., product cross-sales message). Extensive details, such as time, IP address, pages visited, context from where the page request was made, links taken, elapsed time on page, and so forth, can be captured unobtrusively. These data, along with customer transaction, payment, product return, inquiry, and other history consolidated into the data warehouse from a variety of transaction systems, can be used to personalize pages. Such reasoned and active interactions can lead to satisfied customers and business partners and more profitable business relationships. A similar proliferation of data for decision making is resulting from the growing use of RFID and GPS-generated data to track the movement of packages, inventory, or people.

This chapter provides an overview of data warehousing. This exceptionally broad topic normally requires an entire text, especially when the expansive topic of business intelligence is the focus. This is why most texts on the topic are devoted to just a single aspect, such as data warehouse design or administration, data quality and governance, or business intelligence. We focus on the two areas relevant to a text on database management: data architecture and database design for data warehousing. You will learn first how a data warehouse relates to databases in existing operational systems. Described next is the three-tier data architecture, which characterizes most data warehouse environments. Then, we show special database design elements frequently used in data warehousing. In Chapter 11, you will see how users interact with the data warehouse, including online analytical processing, data mining, and data visualization. This chapter provides the bridge from this text to the broader context in which data warehousing is most often applied—business intelligence and analytics.

Data warehousing requires extracting data from existing operational systems, cleansing and transforming data for decision making, and loading them into a data warehouse—what is often called the extract–transform–load (ETL) process. An inherent part of this process are activities to ensure data quality, which is of special concern when data are consolidated across disparate systems. Data warehousing is not the only method organizations use to integrate data to gain greater reach to data across the organization. Thus, we devote Chapter 10, the first chapter in the next section of this text, to issues of data quality, which apply to data warehousing as well as other forms of data integration, which are also introduced in Chapter 10.

BASIC CONCEPTS OF DATA WAREHOUSING

Data warehouse

A subject-oriented, integrated, time-variant, nonupdateable collection of data used in support of management decision-making processes.

A **data warehouse** is a subject-oriented, integrated, time-variant, nonupdateable collection of data used in support of management decision-making processes and business intelligence (Inmon and Hackathorn, 1994). The meaning of each of the key terms in this definition follows:

- *Subject-oriented* A data warehouse is organized around the key subjects (or high-level entities) of the enterprise. Major subjects may include customers, patients, students, products, and time.
- *Integrated* The data housed in the data warehouse are defined using consistent naming conventions, formats, encoding structures, and related characteristics

gathered from several internal systems of record and also often from sources external to the organization. This means that the data warehouse holds the one version of "the truth."

- **Time-variant** Data in the data warehouse contain a time dimension so that they may be used to study trends and changes.
- **Nonupdateable** Data in the data warehouse are loaded and refreshed from operational systems but cannot be updated by end users.

A data warehouse is not just a consolidation of all the operational databases in an organization. Because of its focus on business intelligence, external data, and time-variant data (not just current status), a data warehouse is a unique kind of database. Fortunately, you don't need to learn a different set of database skills to work with a data warehouse. Most data warehouses are relational databases designed in a way optimized for decision support, not operational data processing. Thus, everything you have learned so far in this text still applies. In this chapter you will learn the additional features, database design structures, and concepts that make a data warehouse unique.

Data warehousing is the process whereby organizations create and maintain data warehouses and extract meaning from and help inform decision making through the use of data in the data warehouses. Successful data warehousing requires following proven data warehousing practices, sound project management, strong organizational commitment, as well as making the right technology decisions.

A Brief History of Data Warehousing

The key discovery that triggered the development of data warehousing was the recognition (and subsequent definition) of the fundamental differences between operational (or transaction processing) systems (sometimes called *systems of record* because their role is to keep the official, legal record of the organization) and informational (or decision-support) systems. Devlin and Murphy (1988) published the first article describing the architecture of a data warehouse, based on this distinction. In 1992, Inmon published the first book describing data warehousing, and he has subsequently become one of the most prolific authors in this field.

The Need for Data Warehousing

Two major factors drive the need for data warehousing in most organizations today:

1. A business requires an integrated, company-wide view of high-quality information.
2. The information systems department must separate informational from operational systems to improve performance dramatically in managing company data.

NEED FOR A COMPANY-WIDE VIEW Data in operational systems are typically fragmented and inconsistent, so-called silos, or islands, of data. They are also generally distributed on a variety of incompatible hardware and software platforms. For example, one source of customer data may be located on a UNIX-based server running an Oracle DBMS, whereas another may be located on a SAP system. Yet, for decision-making purposes, it is often necessary to provide a single, corporate view of that information.

To understand the difficulty of deriving a single corporate view, look at the simple example shown in Figure 9-1. This figure shows three tables from three separate systems of record, each containing similar student data. The STUDENT DATA table is from the class registration system, the STUDENT EMPLOYEE table is from the personnel system, and the STUDENT HEALTH table is from a health center system. Each table contains some unique data concerning students, but even common data (e.g., student names) are stored using different formats.

FIGURE 9-1   Examples
of heterogeneous data

STUDENT DATA

StudentNo	LastName	MI	FirstName	Telephone	Status	• • •
123-45-6789	Enright	T	Mark	483-1967	Soph	
389-21-4062	Smith	R	Elaine	283-4195	Jr	

STUDENT EMPLOYEE

StudentID	Address	Dept	Hours	• • •
123-45-6789	1218 Elk Drive, Phoenix, AZ 91304	Soc	8	
389-21-4062	134 Mesa Road, Tempe, AZ 90142	Math	10	

STUDENT HEALTH

StudentName	Telephone	Insurance	ID	• • •
Mark T. Enright	483-1967	Blue Cross	123-45-6789	
Elaine R. Smith	555-7828	?	389-21-4062	

Suppose you want to develop a profile for each student, consolidating all data into a single file format. Some of the issues that you must resolve are as follows:

- *Inconsistent key structures*   The primary key of the first two tables is some version of the student Social Security number, whereas the primary key of STUDENT HEALTH is StudentName.
- *Synonym*   In STUDENT DATA, the primary key is named StudentNo, whereas in STUDENT EMPLOYEE it is named StudentID. (We discussed how to deal with synonyms in Chapter 4.)
- *Free-form fields versus structured fields*   In STUDENT HEALTH, StudentName is a single field. In STUDENT DATA, StudentName (a composite attribute) is broken into its component parts: LastName, MI, and FirstName.
- *Inconsistent data values*   Elaine Smith has one telephone number in STUDENT DATA but a different number in STUDENT HEALTH. Is this an error, or does this person have two telephone numbers?
- *Missing data*   The value for Insurance is missing (or null) for Elaine Smith in the STUDENT HEALTH table. How will this value be located?

This simple example illustrates the nature of the problem of developing a single corporate view but fails to capture the complexity of that task. A real-life scenario would likely have dozens (if not hundreds) of tables and thousands (or millions) of records.

Why do organizations need to bring data together from various systems of record? Ultimately, of course, the reason is to be more profitable, to be more competitive, or to grow by adding value for customers. This can be accomplished by increasing the speed and flexibility of decision making, improving business processes, or gaining a clearer understanding of customer behavior. For the previous student example, university administrators may want to investigate if the health or number of hours students work on campus is related to student academic performance; if taking certain courses is related to the health of students; or whether poor academic performers cost more to support, for example, due to increased health care as well as other costs. In general, certain trends in organizations encourage the need for data warehousing; these trends include the following:

- *No single system of record*   Almost no organization has only one database. Seems odd, doesn't it? Remember our discussion in Chapter 1 about the reasons for using a database compared to using separate file-processing systems? Because of the heterogeneous needs for data in different operational settings, because of corporate mergers and acquisitions, and because of the sheer size of many organizations, multiple operational databases exist.

- *Multiple systems are not synchronized*   It is difficult, if not impossible, to make separate databases consistent. Even if the metadata are controlled and made the same by one data administrator (see Chapter 12), the data values for the same attributes will not agree. This is because of different update cycles and separate places where the same data are captured for each system. Thus, to get one view of the organization, the data from the separate systems must be periodically consolidated and synchronized into one additional database. We will see that there can be actually two such consolidated databases—an operational data store and an enterprise data warehouse, both of which we include under the topic of data warehousing.

- *Organizations want to analyze the activities in a balanced way*   Many organizations have implemented some form of a balanced scorecard—metrics that show organization results in financial, human, customer satisfaction, product quality, and other terms simultaneously. To ensure that this multidimensional view of the organization shows consistent results, a data warehouse is necessary. When questions arise in the balanced scorecard, analytical software working with the data warehouse can be used to "drill down," "slice and dice," visualize, and in other ways mine business intelligence.

- *Customer relationship management*   Organizations in all sectors are realizing that there is value in having a total picture of their interactions with customers across all touch points. Different touch points (e.g., for a bank, these touch points include ATMs, online banking, tellers, electronic funds transfers, investment portfolio management, and loans) are supported by separate operational systems. Thus, without a data warehouse, a teller may not know to try to cross-sell a customer one of the bank's mutual funds if a large, atypical automatic deposit transaction appears on the teller's screen. Having a total picture of the activity with a given customer requires a consolidation of data from various operational systems.

- *Supplier relationship management*   Managing the supply chain has become a critical element in reducing costs and raising product quality for many organizations. Organizations want to create strategic supplier partnerships based on a total picture of their activities with suppliers, from billing, to meeting delivery dates, to quality control, to pricing, to support. Data about these different activities can be locked inside separate operational systems (e.g., accounts payable, shipping and receiving, production scheduling, and maintenance). ERP systems have improved this situation by bringing many of these data into one database. However, ERP systems tend to be designed to optimize operational, not informational or analytical, processing, which we discuss next.

NEED TO SEPARATE OPERATIONAL AND INFORMATIONAL SYSTEMS   An **operational system** is a system that is used to run a business in real time, based on current data. Examples of operational systems are sales order processing, reservation systems, and patient registration systems. Operational systems must process large volumes of relatively simple read/write transactions and provide fast response. Operational systems are also called *systems of record*.

Operational system
A system that is used to run a business in real time, based on current data. Also called a system of record.

TABLE 9-1   Comparison of Operational and Informational Systems

Characteristic	Operational Systems	Informational Systems
Primary purpose	Run the business on a current basis	Support managerial decision making
Type of data	Current representation of state of the business	Historical point-in-time (snapshots) and predictions
Primary users	Clerks, salespersons, administrators	Managers, business analysts, customers
Scope of usage	Narrow, planned, and simple updates and queries	Broad, ad hoc, complex queries and analysis
Design goal	Performance: throughput, availability	Ease of flexible access and use
Volume	Many constant updates and queries on one or a few table rows	Periodic batch updates and queries requiring many or all rows

Informational system

A system designed to support decision making based on historical point-in-time and prediction data for complex queries or data-mining applications.

Informational systems are designed to support decision making based on historical point-in-time and prediction data. They are also designed for complex queries or data-mining applications. Examples of informational systems are systems for sales trend analysis, customer segmentation, and human resources planning.

The key differences between operational and informational systems are shown in Table 9-1. These two types of processing have very different characteristics in nearly every category of comparison. In particular, notice that they have quite different communities of users. Operational systems are used by clerks, administrators, salespersons, and others who must process business transactions. Informational systems are used by managers, executives, business analysts, and (increasingly) by customers who are searching for status information or who are decision makers.

The need to separate operational and informational systems is based on three primary factors:

1. A data warehouse centralizes data that are scattered throughout disparate operational systems and makes them readily available for decision support applications.
2. A properly designed data warehouse adds value to data by improving their quality and consistency.
3. A separate data warehouse eliminates much of the contention for resources that results when informational applications are confounded with operational processing.

DATA WAREHOUSE ARCHITECTURES

The architecture for data warehouses has evolved, and organizations have considerable latitude in creating variations. We will review here two core structures that form the basis for most implementations. The first is a three-level architecture that characterizes a bottom-up, incremental approach to evolving the data warehouse; the second is also a three-level data architecture that appears usually from a more top-down approach that emphasizes more coordination and an enterprise-wide perspective. Even with their differences, there are many common characteristics to these approaches.

Independent Data Mart Data Warehousing Environment

The independent data mart architecture for a data warehouse is shown in Figure 9-2. Building this architecture requires four basic steps (moving left to right in Figure 9-2):

1. Data are extracted from the various internal and external source system files and databases. In a large organization, there may be dozens or even hundreds of such files and databases.
2. The data from the various source systems are transformed and integrated before being loaded into the data marts. Transactions may be sent to the source systems to correct errors discovered in data staging. The data warehouse is considered to be the collection of data marts.

FIGURE 9-2 Independent data mart data warehousing architecture

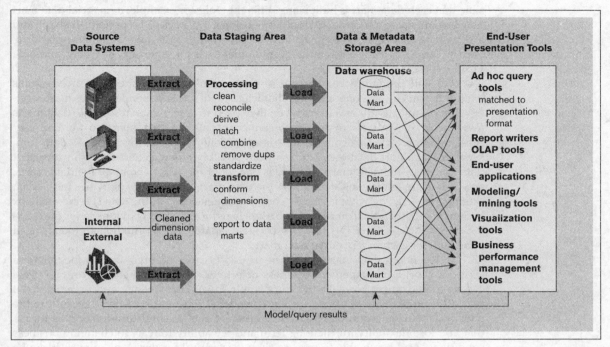

3. The data warehouse is a set of physically distinct databases organized for decision support. It contains both detailed and summary data.

4. Users access the data warehouse by means of a variety of query languages and analytical tools. Results (e.g., predictions, forecasts) may be fed back to data warehouse and operational databases.

We will discuss the important processes of extracting, transforming, and loading (ETL) data from the source systems into the data warehouse in more detail in Chapter 10. We will also overview in a subsequent section various end-user presentation tools.

Extraction and loading happen periodically—sometimes daily, weekly, or monthly. Thus, the data warehouse often does not have, nor does it need to have, current data. Remember, the data warehouse is not (directly) supporting operational transaction processing, although it may contain transactional data (but more often summaries of transactions and snapshots of status variables, such as account balances and inventory levels). For most data warehousing applications, users are not looking for a reaction to an individual transaction but rather for trends and patterns in the state of the organization across a large subset of the data warehouse. At a minimum, five fiscal quarters of data are kept in a data warehouse so that at least annual trends and patterns can be discerned. Older data may be purged or archived. We will see later that one advanced data warehousing architecture, real-time data warehousing, is based on a different assumption about the need for current data.

Contrary to many of the principles discussed so far in this chapter, the independent data marts approach does not create one data warehouse. Instead, this approach creates many separate data marts, each based on data warehousing, not transaction processing database technologies. A **data mart** is a data warehouse that is limited in scope, customized for the decision-making applications of a particular end-user group. Its contents either are obtained from independent ETL processes, as shown in Figure 9-2 for an **independent data mart,** or are derived from the data warehouse, which we will discuss in the next two sections. A data mart is designed to optimize the performance for well-defined and predicable uses, sometimes as few as a single or a couple of queries. For example, an organization may have a marketing data mart, a finance data mart,

Data mart

A data warehouse that is limited in scope, whose data are obtained by selecting and summarizing data from a data warehouse or from separate extract, transform, and load processes from source data systems.

Independent data mart

A data mart filled with data extracted from the operational environment, without the benefit of a data warehouse.

a supply chain data mart, and so on to support known analytical processing. It is possible that each data mart is built using different tools; for example, a financial data mart may be built using a proprietary multidimensional tool such as Hyperion's Essbase, and a sales data mart may be built on a more general-purpose data warehouse platform, such as Teradata, using MicroStrategy and other tools for reporting, querying, and data visualization.

We will provide a comparison of the various data warehousing architectures later, but you can see one obvious characteristic of the independent data mart strategy: the complexity for end users when they need to access data in separate data marts (evidenced by the crisscrossed lines connecting all the data marts to the end-user presentation tools). This complexity comes not only from having to access data from separate data mart databases but also from possibly a new generation of inconsistent data systems—the data marts. If there is one set of metadata across all the data marts, and if data are made consistent across the data marts through the activities in the data staging area (e.g., by what is called "conform dimensions" in the data staging area box in Figure 9-2), then the complexity for users is reduced. Not so obvious in Figure 9-2 is the complexity for the ETL processes, because separate transformation and loads need to be built for each independent data mart.

Independent data marts are often created because an organization focuses on a series of short-term, expedient business objectives. The limited short-term objectives can be more compatible with the comparably lower cost (money and organizational capital) to implement yet one more independent data mart. However, designing the data warehousing environment around different sets of short-term objectives means that you lose flexibility for the long term and the ability to react to changing business conditions. And being able to react to change is critical for decision support. It can be organizationally and politically easier to have separate, small data warehouses than to get all organizational parties to agree to one view of the organization in a central data warehouse. Also, some data warehousing technologies have technical limitations for the size of the data warehouse they can support—what we will call later a scalability issue. Thus, technology, rather than the business, may dictate a data warehousing architecture if you first lock yourself into a particular data warehousing set of technologies before you understand your data warehousing requirements. We discuss the pros and cons of the independent data mart architecture compared with its prime competing architecture in the next section.

Dependent Data Mart and Operational Data Store Architecture: A Three-Level Approach

The independent data mart architecture in Figure 9-2 has several important limitations (Marco, 2003; Meyer, 1997):

1. A separate ETL process is developed for each data mart, which can yield costly redundant data and processing efforts.
2. Data marts may not be consistent with one another because they are often developed with different technologies, and thus they may not provide a clear enterprise-wide view of data concerning important subjects such as customers, suppliers, and products.
3. There is no capability to drill down into greater detail or into related facts in other data marts or a shared data repository, so analysis is limited, or at best very difficult (e.g., doing joins across separate platforms for different data marts). Essentially, relating data across data marts is a task performed by users outside the data warehouse.
4. Scaling costs are excessive because every new application that creates a separate data mart repeats all the extract and load steps. Usually, operational systems have limited time windows for batch data extracting, so at some point, the load on the operations systems may mean that new technology is needed, with additional costs.
5. If there is an attempt to make the separate data marts consistent, the cost to do so is quite high.

The value of independent data marts has been hotly debated. Kimball (1997) strongly supports the development of independent data marts as a viable strategy for a phased development of decision support systems. Armstrong (1997), Inmon (1997, 2000), and Marco (2003) point out the five fallacies previously mentioned and many more. There are two debates as to the actual value of independent data marts:

1. One debate deals with the nature of the phased approach to implementing a data warehousing environment. The essence of this debate is whether each data mart should or should not evolve in a bottom-up fashion from a subset of enterprise-wide decision support data.
2. The other debate deals with the suitable database architecture for analytical processing. This debate centers on the extent to which a data mart database should be normalized.

The essences of these two debates are addressed throughout this chapter. We provide an exercise at the end of the chapter for you to explore these debates in more depth.

One of the most popular approaches to addressing the independent data mart limitations raised earlier is to use a three-level approach represented by the dependent data mart and operational data store architecture (see Figure 9-3). Here the new level is the operational data store, and the data and metadata storage level is reconfigured. The first and second limitations are addressed by loading the **dependent data marts** from an **enterprise data warehouse (EDW)**, which is a central, integrated data warehouse that is the control point and single "version of the truth" made available to end users for decision support applications. Dependent data marts still have a purpose to provide a simplified and high-performance environment that is tuned to the decision-making needs of user groups. A data mart may be a separate physical database (and different data marts may be on different platforms) or can be a logical (user view) data mart instantiated on the fly when accessed. We explain logical data marts in the next section.

A user group can access its data mart, and then when other data are needed, users can access the EDW. Redundancy across dependent data marts is planned, and redundant data are consistent because each data mart is loaded in a synchronized way from one common source of data (or is a view of the data warehouse). Integration of data is the responsibility of the IT staff managing the enterprise data warehouse; it is not the

Dependent data mart

A data mart filled exclusively from an enterprise data warehouse and its reconciled data.

Enterprise data warehouse (EDW)

A centralized, integrated data warehouse that is the control point and single source of all data made available to end users for decision support applications.

FIGURE 9-3   Dependent data mart and operational data store: A three-level architecture

Operational data store (ODS)

An integrated, subject-oriented, continuously updateable, current-valued (with recent history), enterprise-wide, detailed database designed to serve operational users as they do decision support processing.

end users' responsibility to integrate data across independent data marts for each query or application. The dependent data mart and operational data store architecture is often called a "hub and spoke" approach, in which the EDW is the hub and the source data systems and the data marts are at the ends of input and output spokes.

The third limitation is addressed by providing an integrated source for all the operational data in an operational data store. An **operational data store (ODS)** is an integrated, subject-oriented, continuously updateable, current-valued (with recent history), organization-wide, detailed database designed to serve operational users as they do decision support processing (Imhoff, 1998; Inmon, 1998). An ODS is typically a relational database and normalized like databases in the systems of record, but it is tuned for decision-making applications. For example, indexes and other relational database design elements are tuned for queries that retrieve broad groups of data, rather than for transaction processing or querying individual and directly related records (e.g., a customer order). Because it has volatile, current, and only recent history data, the same query against an ODS very likely will yield different results at different times. An ODS typically does not contain "deep" history, whereas an EDW typically holds a multiyear history of snapshots of the state of the organization. An ODS may be fed from the database of an ERP application, but because most organizations do not have only one ERP database and do not run all operations against one ERP, an ODS is usually different from an ERP database. The ODS also serves as the staging area for loading data into the EDW. The ODS may receive data immediately or with some delay from the systems of record, whichever is practical and acceptable for the decision-making requirements that it supports.

The dependent data mart and operational data store architecture is also called a *corporate information factory (CIF)* (see Imhoff, 1999). It is considered to be a comprehensive view of organizational data in support of all user data requirements.

Different leaders in the field endorse different approaches to data warehousing. Those who endorse the independent data mart approach argue that this approach has two significant benefits:

1. It allows for the concept of a data warehouse to be demonstrated by working on a series of small projects.
2. The length of time until there is some benefit from data warehousing is reduced because the organization is not delayed until all data are centralized.

The advocates of the CIF (Armstrong, 2000 Inmon, 1999) raise serious issues with the independent approach; these issues include the five limitations of independent data marts outlined earlier. Inmon suggests that an advantage of physically separate *dependent* data marts is that they can be tuned to the needs of each community of users. In particular, he suggests the need for an *exploration warehouse*, which is a special version of the EDW optimized for data mining and business intelligence using advanced statistical, mathematical modeling, and visualization tools. Armstrong (2000) and others go further to argue that the benefits claimed by the independent data mart advocates really are benefits of taking a phased approach to data warehouse development. A phased approach can be accomplished within the CIF framework as well and is facilitated by the final data warehousing architecture we review in the next section.

Logical Data Mart and Real-Time Data Warehouse Architecture

The logical data mart and real-time data warehouse architecture is practical for only moderate-sized data warehouses or when using high-performance data warehousing technology, such as the Teradata system. As can be seen in Figure 9-4, this architecture has the following unique characteristics:

Logical data mart

A data mart created by a relational view of a data warehouse.

1. **Logical data marts** are not physically separate databases but rather different relational views of one physical, slightly denormalized relational data warehouse. (Refer to Chapter 6 to review the concept of views.)
2. Data are moved into the data warehouse rather than to a separate staging area to utilize the high-performance computing power of the warehouse technology to perform the cleansing and transformation steps.

FIGURE 9-4 Logical data mart and real-time data warehouse architecture

3. New data marts can be created quickly because no physical database or database technology needs to be created or acquired and no loading routines need to be written.
4. Data marts are always up to date because data in a view are created when the view is referenced; views can be materialized if a user has a series of queries and analysis that need to work off the same instantiation of the data mart.

Whether logical or physical, data marts and data warehouses play different roles in a data warehousing environment; these different roles are summarized in Table 9-2. Although limited in scope, a data mart may not be small. Thus, scalable technology is often critical. A significant burden and cost are placed on users when they themselves need to integrate the data across separate physical data marts (if this is even possible). As data marts are added, a data warehouse can be built in phases; the easiest way for this to happen is to follow the logical data mart and real-time data warehouse architecture.

The **real-time data warehouse** aspect of the architecture in Figure 9-4 means that the source data systems, decision support services, and the data warehouse *exchange* data and business rules at a *near*-real-time pace because there is a need for rapid response (i.e., action) to a current, comprehensive picture of the organization. The purpose of real-time data warehousing is to know what is happening, when it is happening, and to make desirable things happen through the operational systems. For example, a help desk professional answering questions and logging problem tickets will have a total picture of the customer's most recent sales contacts, billing and payment transactions, maintenance activities, and orders. With this information, the system supporting the help desk can, based on operational decision rules created from a continuous analysis of up-to-date warehouse data, automatically generate a script for the professional to sell what the analysis has shown to be a likely and profitable maintenance contract, an upgraded product, or another product bought by customers with a similar profile. A critical event, such as entry of a new product order, can be considered immediately so that the organization knows at least as much about the relationship with its customer as does the customer.

Real-time data warehouse

An enterprise data warehouse that accepts near-real-time feeds of transactional data from the systems of record, analyzes warehouse data, and in near-real-time relays business rules to the data warehouse and systems of record so that immediate action can be taken in response to business events.

TABLE 9-2 Data Warehouse Versus Data Mart

Data Warehouse	Data Mart
Scope	**Scope**
• Application independent	• Specific DSS application
• Centralized, possibly enterprise-wide	• Decentralized by user area
• Planned	• Organic, possibly not planned
Data	**Data**
• Historical, detailed, and summarized	• Some history, detailed, and summarized
• Lightly denormalized	• Highly denormalized
Subjects	**Subjects**
• Multiple subjects	• One central subject of concern to users
Sources	**Sources**
• Many internal and external sources	• Few internal and external sources
Other Characteristics	**Other Characteristics**
• Flexible	• Restrictive
• Data oriented	• Project oriented
• Long life	• Short life
• Large	• Starts small, becomes large
• Single complex structure	• Multi, semi-complex structures, together complex

Another example of real-time data warehousing (with real-time analytics) would be an express mail and package delivery service using frequent scanning of parcels to know exactly where a package is in its transportation system. Real-time analytics, based on this package data, as well as pricing, customer service–level agreements, and logistics opportunities, could automatically reroute packages to meet delivery promises for their best customers. RFID technologies are allowing these kinds of opportunities for real-time data warehousing (with massive amounts of data) coupled with real-time analytics to be used to greatly reduce the latency between event data capture and appropriate actions being taken.

The orientation is that each event with, say, a customer, is a potential opportunity for a customized, personalized, and optimized communication based on a strategic decision of how to respond to a customer with a particular profile. Thus, decision making and the data warehouse are actively involved in guiding operational processing, which is why some people call this active data warehousing. The goal is to shorten the cycle to do the following:

- Capture customer data at the time of a business event (what did happen)
- Analyze customer behavior (why did something happen) and predict customer responses to possible actions (what will happen)
- Develop rules for optimizing customer interactions, including the appropriate response and channel that will yield the best results
- Take immediate *action* with customers at touch points based on best responses to customers as determined by decision rules in order to make desirable results happen

The idea is that the potential value of taking the right action decays the longer the delay from event to action. The real-time data warehouse is where all the intelligence comes together to reduce this delay. Thus, real-time data warehousing moves data warehousing from the back office to the front office. We look at some other trends related to this in a later section.

The following are some beneficial applications for real-time data warehousing:

- Just-in-time transportation for rerouting deliveries based on up-to-date inventory levels
- E-commerce where, for instance, an abandoned shopping cart can trigger an e-mail promotional message before the user signs off

- Salespeople who monitor key performance indicators for important accounts in real time
- Fraud detection in credit card transactions, where an unusual pattern of transactions could alert a sales clerk or online shopping cart routine to take extra precautions

Such applications are often characterized by online user access 24/7. For any of the data warehousing architectures, users may be employees, customers, or business partners.

With high-performance computers and data warehousing technologies, there may not be a need for a separate ODS from the enterprise data warehouse. When the ODS and EDW are one and the same, it is much easier for users to drill down and drill up when working through a series of ad hoc questions in which one question leads to another. It is also a simpler architecture, because one layer of the dependent data mart and operational data store architecture has been eliminated.

Three-Layer Data Architecture

Figure 9-5 shows a three-layer data architecture for a data warehouse. This architecture is characterized by the following:

1. Operational data are stored in the various operational systems of record throughout the organization (and sometimes in external systems).
2. Reconciled data are the type of data stored in the enterprise data warehouse and an operational data store. **Reconciled data** are detailed, current data intended to be the single, authoritative source for all decision support applications.
3. Derived data are the type of data stored in each of the data marts. **Derived data** are data that have been selected, formatted, and aggregated for end-user decision support applications.

We discuss reconciled data in the next chapter because the processes for reconciling data across source systems are a part of a topic larger than simply data warehousing: data quality and integration. Pertinent to data warehousing is derived data, which we cover in a subsequent section of the current chapter. Two components shown in Figure 9-5 play critical roles in the data architecture: the enterprise data model and metadata.

Reconciled data

Detailed, current data intended to be the single, authoritative source for all decision support applications.

Derived data

Data that have been selected, formatted, and aggregated for end-user decision support applications.

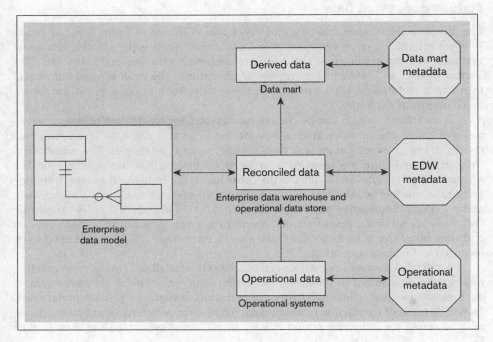

FIGURE 9-5 Three-layer data architecture for a data warehouse

ROLE OF THE ENTERPRISE DATA MODEL   In Figure 9-5, we show the reconciled data layer linked to the enterprise data model. Recall from Chapter 1 that the enterprise data model presents a total picture explaining the data required by an organization. If the reconciled data layer is to be the single, authoritative source for all data required for decision support, it must conform to the design specified in the enterprise data model. Thus, the enterprise data model controls the phased evolution of the data warehouse. Usually the enterprise data model evolves as new problems and decision applications are addressed. It takes too long to develop the enterprise data model in one step, and the dynamic needs for decision making will change before the warehouse is built.

ROLE OF METADATA   Figure 9-5 also shows a layer of metadata linked to each of the three data layers. Recall from Chapter 1 that metadata are technical and business data that describe the properties or characteristics of other data. Following is a brief description of the three types of metadata shown in Figure 9-5.

1. *Operational metadata*   describe the data in the various operational systems (as well as external data) that feed the enterprise data warehouse. Operational metadata typically exist in a number of different formats and unfortunately are often of poor quality.
2. *Enterprise data warehouse (EDW) metadata*   are derived from (or at least consistent with) the enterprise data model. EDW metadata describe the reconciled data layer as well as the rules for extracting, transforming, and loading operational data into reconciled data.
3. *Data mart metadata*   describe the derived data layer and the rules for transforming reconciled data to derived data.

For a thorough review of data warehouse metadata, see Marco (2000).

SOME CHARACTERISTICS OF DATA WAREHOUSE DATA

To understand and model the data in each of the three layers of the data architecture for a data warehouse, you need to learn some basic characteristics of data as they are stored in data warehouse databases. The characteristics of data for a data warehouse are different from those of data for operational databases.

Status Versus Event Data

The difference between status data and event data is shown in Figure 9-6. The figure shows a typical log entry recorded by a DBMS when processing a business transaction for a banking application. This log entry contains both status and event data: The "before image" and "after image" represent the status of the bank account before and then after a withdrawal. Data representing the withdrawal (or update event) are shown in the middle of the figure.

Transactions, which are discussed further in Chapter 12, are business activities that cause one or more business events to occur at a database level. An event results in one or more database actions (create, update, or delete). The withdrawal transaction in Figure 9-6 leads to a single update, which is the reduction in the account balance from 750 to 700. On the other hand, the transfer of money from one account to another would lead to two actions: two updates to handle a withdrawal and a deposit. Sometimes nontransactions, such as an abandoned online shopping cart, busy signal or dropped network connection, or an item put in a shopping cart and then taken out before checkout, can also be important activities that need to be recorded in the data warehouse.

Both status data and event data can be stored in a database. However, in practice, most of the data stored in databases (including data warehouses) are status data. A data warehouse likely contains a history of snapshots of status data or a summary (say, an hourly total) of transaction or event data. Event data, which represent transactions, may be stored for a defined period but are then deleted or archived to save storage

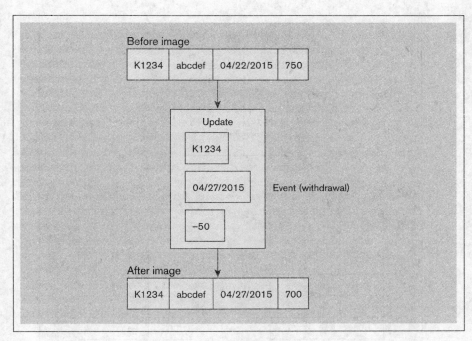

FIGURE 9-6 Example of a DBMS log entry

space. Both status and event data are typically stored in database logs (as represented in Figure 9-6) for backup and recovery purposes. As will be explained later, the database log plays an important role in filling the data warehouse.

Transient Versus Periodic Data

In data warehouses, it is typical to maintain a record of when events occurred in the past. This is necessary, for example, to compare sales or inventory levels on a particular date or during a particular period with the previous year's sales on the same date or during the same period.

Most operational systems are based on the use of transient data. **Transient data** are data in which changes to existing records are written over previous records, thus destroying the previous data content. Records are deleted without preserving the previous contents of those records.

You can easily visualize transient data by again referring to Figure 9-6. If the after image is written over the before image, the before image (containing the previous balance) is lost. However, because this is a database log, both images are normally preserved.

Periodic data are data that are never physically altered or deleted once added to the store. The before and after images in Figure 9-6 represent periodic data. Notice that each record contains a time stamp that indicates the date (and time, if needed) when the most recent update event occurred. (We introduced the use of time stamps in Chapter 2.)

An Example of Transient and Periodic Data

A more detailed example comparing transient and periodic data is shown in Figures 9-7 and 9-8.

TRANSIENT DATA Figure 9-7 shows a relation (Table X) that initially contains four rows. The table has three attributes: a primary key and two nonkey attributes, A and B. The values for each of these attributes on the date 10/09 are shown in the figure. For example, for record 001, the value of attribute A on this date is a.

On date 10/10, three changes are made to the table (changes to rows are indicated by arrows to the left of the table). Row 002 is updated, so the value of A is changed from c to r. Row 004 is also updated, so the value of A is changed from g to y. Finally, a new row (with key 005) is inserted into the table.

Transient data

Data in which changes to existing records are written over previous records, thus destroying the previous data content.

Periodic data

Data that are never physically altered or deleted once they have been added to the store.

FIGURE 9-7 Transient operational data

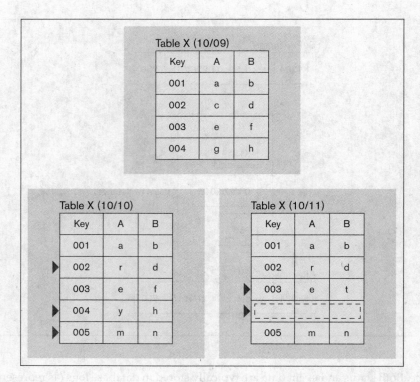

Table X (10/09)

Key	A	B
001	a	b
002	c	d
003	e	f
004	g	h

Table X (10/10)

Key	A	B
001	a	b
▶ 002	r	d
003	e	f
▶ 004	y	h
▶ 005	m	n

Table X (10/11)

Key	A	B
001	a	b
002	r	d
▶ 003	e	t
▶ _ _ _	_ _ _	_ _ _
005	m	n

Table X (10/09)

Key	Date	A	B	Action
001	10/09	a	b	C
002	10/09	c	d	C
003	10/09	e	f	C
004	10/09	g	h	C

Table X (10/10)

Key	Date	A	B	Action
001	10/09	a	b	C
002	10/09	c	d	C
▶ 002	10/10	r	d	U
003	10/09	e	f	C
004	10/09	g	h	C
▶ 004	10/10	y	h	U
▶ 005	10/10	m	n	C

Table X (10/11)

Key	Date	A	B	Action
001	10/09	a	b	C
002	10/09	c	d	C
002	10/10	r	d	U
003	10/09	e	f	C
▶ 003	10/11	e	t	U
004	10/09	g	h	C
004	10/10	y	h	U
▶ 004	10/11	y	h	D
005	10/10	m	n	C

FIGURE 9-8 Periodic warehouse data

Notice that when rows 002 and 004 are updated, the new rows replace the previous rows. Therefore, the previous values are lost; there is no historical record of these values. This is characteristic of transient data.

More changes are made to the rows on date 10/11 (to simplify the discussion, we assume that only one change can be made to a given row on a given date). Row 003 is updated, and row 004 is deleted. Notice that there is no record to indicate that row 004 was ever stored in the database. The way the data are processed in Figure 9-7 is characteristic of the transient data typical in operational systems.

PERIODIC DATA   One typical objective for a data warehouse is to maintain a historical record of key events or to create a time series for particular variables such as sales. This often requires storing periodic data, rather than transient data. Figure 9-8 shows the table used in Figure 9-7, now modified to represent periodic data. The following changes have been made in Figure 9-8:

1. Two new columns have been added to Table X:
   a. The column named Date is a time stamp that records the most recent date when a row has been modified.
   b. The column named Action is used to record the type of change that occurred. Possible values for this attribute are C (Create), U (Update), and D (Delete).
2. Once a record has been stored in the table, that record is never changed. When an update operation occurs on a record, both the before image and the after image are stored in the table. Although a record may be *logically* deleted, a historical version of the deleted record is maintained in the database for as much history (at least five quarters) as needed to analyze trends.

Now let's examine the same set of actions that occurred in Figure 9-7. Assume that all four rows were created on the date 10/09, as shown in the first table.

In the second table (for 10/10), rows 002 and 004 have been updated. The table now contains both the old version (for 10/09) and the new version (for 10/10) for these rows. The table also contains the new row (005) that was created on 10/10.

The third table (for 10/11) shows the update to row 003, with both the old and new versions. Also, row 004 is deleted from this table. This table now contains three versions of row 004: the original version (from 10/09), the updated version (from 10/1010), and the deleted version (from 10/11). The D in the last row for record 004 indicates that this row has been logically deleted, so that it is no longer available to users or their applications.

If you examine Figure 9-8, you can see why data warehouses tend to grow very rapidly. Storing periodic data can impose large storage requirements. Therefore, users must choose very carefully the key data that require this form of processing.

OTHER DATA WAREHOUSE CHANGES   Besides the periodic changes to data values outlined previously, six other kinds of changes to a warehouse data model must be accommodated by data warehousing:

1. *New descriptive attributes*   For example, new characteristics of products or customers that are important to store in the warehouse must be accommodated. Later in the chapter, we call these attributes of dimension tables. This change is fairly easily accommodated by adding columns to tables and allowing null values for existing rows (if historical data exist in source systems, null values do not have to be stored).
2. *New business activity attributes*   For example, new characteristics of an event already stored in the warehouse, such as a column C for the table in Figure 9-8, must be accommodated. This can be handled as in item 1, but it is more difficult when the new facts are more refined, such as data associated with days of the week, not just month and year, as in Figure 9-8.
3. *New classes of descriptive attributes*   This is equivalent to adding new tables to the database.
4. *Descriptive attributes become more refined*   For example, data about stores must be broken down by individual cash register to understand sales data. This change

is in the grain of the data, an extremely important topic, which we discuss later in the chapter. This can be a very difficult change to accommodate.

5. *Descriptive data are related to one another*   For example, store data are related to geography data. This causes new relationships, often hierarchical, to be included in the data model.

6. *New source of data*   This is a very common change, in which some new business need causes data feeds from an additional source system or some new operational system is installed that must feed the warehouse. This change can cause almost any of the previously mentioned changes, as well as the need for new extract, transform, and load processes.

It is usually not possible to go back and reload a data warehouse to accommodate all of these kinds of changes for the whole data history maintained. But it is critical to accommodate such changes smoothly to enable the data warehouse to meet new business conditions and information and business intelligence needs. Thus, designing the warehouse for change is very important.

THE DERIVED DATA LAYER

We turn now to the derived data layer. This is the data layer associated with logical or physical data marts (see Figure 9-5). It is the layer with which users normally interact for their decision support applications. Ideally, the reconciled data level is designed first and is the basis for the derived layer, whether data marts are dependent, independent, or logical. In order to derive any data mart we might need, it is necessary that the EDW be a fully normalized relational database accommodating transient and periodic data; this gives us the greatest flexibility to combine data into the simplest form for all user needs, even those that are unanticipated when the EDW is designed. In this section, we first discuss the characteristics of the derived data layer. We then introduce the star schema (or dimensional model), which is the data model most commonly used today to implement this data layer. A star schema is a specially designed, denormalized relational data model. We emphasize that the derived data layer can use normalized relations in the enterprise data warehouse; however, most organizations still build many data marts.

Characteristics of Derived Data

Earlier we defined *derived data* as data that have been selected, formatted, and aggregated for end-user decision support applications. In other words, derived data are information instead of raw data. As shown in Figure 9-5, the source of the derived data is the reconciled data, created from what can be a rather complex data process to integrate and make consistent data from many systems of record inside and outside the organization. Derived data in a data mart are generally optimized for the needs of particular user groups, such as departments, workgroups, or even individuals, to measure and analyze business activities and trends. A common mode of operation is to select the relevant data from the enterprise data warehouse on a daily basis, format and aggregate those data as needed, and then load and index those data in the target data marts. A data mart typically is accessed via online analytical processing (OLAP) tools, which we describe and illustrate in Chapter 11.

The objectives that are sought with derived data are quite different from the objectives of reconciled data. Typical objectives are the following:

- Provide ease of use for decision support applications
- Provide fast response for predefined user queries or requests for information (information usually in the form of metrics used to gauge the health of the organization in areas such as customer service, profitability, process efficiency, or sales growth)
- Customize data for particular target user groups
- Support ad hoc queries and data mining and other analytical applications

To satisfy these needs, we usually find the following characteristics in derived data:

- Both detailed data and aggregate data are present:
  a. Detailed data are often (but not always) periodic—that is, they provide a historical record.
  b. Aggregate data are formatted to respond quickly to predetermined (or common) queries.
- Data are distributed to separate data marts for different user groups.
- The data model that is most commonly used for a data mart is a dimensional model, usually in the form of a star schema, which is a relational-like model (such models are used by relational online analytical processing [ROLAP] tools). Proprietary models (which often look like hypercubes) are also sometimes used (such models are used by multidimensional online analytical processing [MOLAP] tools); these tools will be illustrated later in Chapter 11.

The Star Schema

A **star schema** is a simple database design (particularly suited to ad hoc queries) in which dimensional data (describing how data are commonly aggregated for reporting) are separated from fact or event data (describing business activity). A star schema is one version of a dimensional model (Kimball, 1996a). Although the star schema is suited to ad hoc queries (and other forms of informational processing), it is not suited to online transaction processing, and, therefore, it is not generally used in operational systems, operational data stores, or an EDW. It is called a star schema because of its visual appearance, not because it has been recognized on the Hollywood Walk of Fame.

Star schema

A simple database design in which dimensional data are separated from fact or event data. A dimensional model is another name for a star schema.

FACT TABLES AND DIMENSION TABLES A star schema consists of two types of tables: one fact table and one or more dimension tables. *Fact tables* contain factual or quantitative data (measurements that are numerical, continuously valued, and additive) about a business, such as units sold, orders booked, and so on. *Dimension tables* hold descriptive data (context) about the subjects of the business. The dimension tables are usually the source of attributes used to qualify, categorize, or summarize facts in queries, reports, or graphs; thus, dimension data are usually textual and discrete (even if numeric). A data mart might contain several star schemas with similar dimension tables but each with a different fact table. Typical business dimensions (subjects) are Product, Customer, and Period. Period, or time, is always one of the dimensions. This structure is shown in Figure 9-9, which contains four dimension tables. As we will see shortly, there are variations on this basic star structure that provide further abilities to summarize and categorize the facts.

Each dimension table has a one-to-many relationship to the central fact table. Each dimension table generally has a simple primary key, as well as several nonkey attributes. The primary key, in turn, is a foreign key in the fact table (as shown in Figure 9-9). The primary key of the fact table is a composite key that consists of the concatenation of all of the foreign keys (four keys in Figure 9-9), plus possibly other components that do not correspond to dimensions. The relationship between each dimension table and the fact table provides a join path that allows users to query the database easily, using SQL statements for either predefined or ad hoc queries.

By now you have probably recognized that the star schema is not a new data model, but instead a denormalized implementation of the relational data model. The fact table plays the role of a normalized *n*-ary associative entity that links the instances of the various dimensions, which are in second, but possibly not third, normal form. To review associative entities, see Chapter 2, and for an example of the use of an associative entity, see Figures 2-11 and 2-14. The dimension tables are denormalized. Most experts view this denormalization as acceptable because dimensions are not updated and avoid costly joins; thus, the star is optimized around certain facts and business objects to respond to specific information needs. Relationships between dimensions are not allowed; although such a relationship might exist in the organization (e.g., between

**FIGURE 9-9 Components
of a star schema**

employees and departments), such relationships are outside the scope of a star schema. As we will see later, there may be other tables related to dimensions, but these tables are never related directly to the fact table.

EXAMPLE STAR SCHEMA A star schema provides answers to a domain of business questions. For example, consider the following questions:

1. Which cities have the highest sales of large products?
2. What is the average monthly sales for each store manager?
3. In which stores are we losing money on which products? Does this vary by quarter?

A simple example of a star schema that could provide answers to such questions is shown in Figure 9-10. This example has three dimension tables: PRODUCT, PERIOD, and STORE, and one fact table, named SALES. The fact table is used to record three

**FIGURE 9-10 Star schema
example**

business facts: total units sold, total dollars sold, and total dollars cost. These totals are recorded for each day (the lowest level of PERIOD) a product is sold in a store.

Could these three questions be answered from a fully normalized data model of transactional data? Sure, a fully normalized and detailed database is the most flexible, able to support answering almost any question. However, more tables and joins would be involved, data need to be aggregated in standard ways, and data need to be sorted in an understandable sequence. These tasks might make it more difficult for the typical business manager to interrogate the data (especially using raw SQL), unless the business intelligence tool he or she uses can mask such complexity from them (see Chapter 11). And sufficient sales history would have to be kept, more than would be needed for transaction processing applications. With a data mart, the work of joining and summarizing data (which can cause extensive database processing) into the form needed to directly answer these questions has been shifted to the reconciliation layer, and processes in which the end user does not need to be involved. However, exactly what range of questions will be asked must be known in order to design the data mart for sufficient, optimal, and easy processing. Further, once these three questions become no longer interesting to the organization, the data mart (if it is physical) can be thrown away, and new ones built to answer new questions, whereas fully normalized models tend to be built for the long term to support less dynamic database needs (possibly with logical data marts that exist to meet transient needs). Later in this chapter, we will show some simple methods to use to decide how to determine a star schema model from such business questions.

Some sample data for this schema are shown in Figure 9-11. From the fact table, we find (for example) the following facts for product number 110 during period 002:

1. Thirty units were sold in store S1. The total dollar sale was 1500, and total dollar cost was 1200.
2. Forty units were sold in store S3. The total dollar sale was 2000, and total dollar cost was 1200.

Additional detail concerning the dimensions for this example can be obtained from the dimension tables. For example, in the PERIOD table, we find that period 002 corresponds to year 2010, quarter 1, month 5. Try tracing the other dimensions in a similar manner.

SURROGATE KEY   Every key used to join the fact table with a dimension table should be a surrogate (nonintelligent, or system-assigned) key, not a key that uses a business value (sometimes called a natural, smart, or production key). That is, in Figure 9-10, Product Code, Store Code, and Period Code should all be surrogate keys in both the fact and dimension tables. If, for example, it is necessary to know the product catalog number, engineering number, or inventory item number for a product, these attributes would be stored along with Description, Color, and Size as attributes of the product dimension table. The following are the main reasons for this surrogate-key rule (Kimball, 1998a):

- Business keys change, often slowly, over time, and we need to remember old and new business key values for the same business object. As we will see in a later section on slowly changing dimensions, a surrogate key allows us to handle changing and unknown keys with ease.
- Using a surrogate key also allows us to keep track of different nonkey attribute values for the same production key over time. Thus, if a product package changes in size, we can associate the same product production key with several surrogate keys, each for the different package sizes.
- Surrogate keys are often simpler and shorter, especially when the production key is a composite key.
- Surrogate keys can be of the same length and format for all keys, no matter what business dimensions are involved in the database, even dates.

The primary key of each dimension table is its surrogate key. The primary key of the fact table is the composite of all the surrogate keys for the related dimension tables, and each of the composite key attributes is obviously a foreign key to the associated dimension table.

FIGURE 9-11 Star schema
sample data

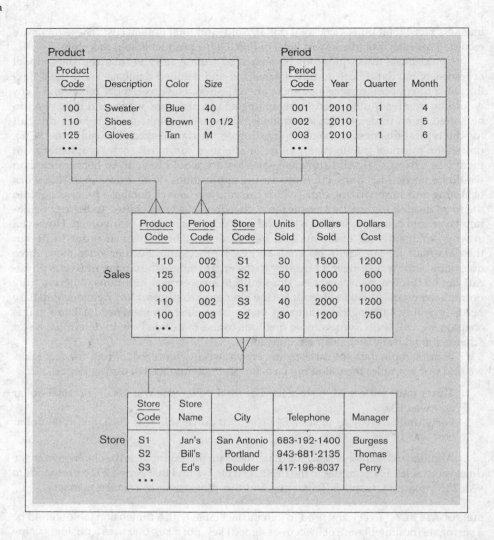

GRAIN OF THE FACT TABLE The raw data of a star schema are kept in the fact table. All the data in a fact table are determined by the same combination of composite key elements; so, for example, if the most detailed data in a fact table are daily values, then all measurement data must be daily in that fact table, and the lowest level of characteristics for the period dimension must also be a day. Determining the lowest level of detailed fact data stored is arguably the most important and difficult data mart design step. The level of detail of this data is specified by the intersection of all of the components of the primary key of the fact table. This intersection of primary keys is called the **grain** of the fact table. Determining the grain is critical and must be determined from business decision-making needs (i.e., the questions to be answered from the data mart). There is always a way to summarize fact data by aggregating using dimension attributes, but there is no way in the data mart to understand business activity at a level of detail finer than the fact table grain.

A common grain would be each business transaction, such as an individual line item or an individual scanned item on a product sales receipt, a personnel change order, a line item on a material receipt, a claim against an insurance policy, a boarding pass, or an individual ATM transaction. A transactional grain allows users to perform analytics such as a market basket analysis, which is the study of buying behavior of individual customers. A grain higher than the transaction level might be all sales of a product on a given day, all receipts of a raw material in a given month at a specific warehouse, or the net effect of all ATM transactions for one ATM session. The finer the grain of the fact table, the more dimensions exist, the more fact rows exist, and often the closer the data mart model is to a data model for the operational data store.

Grain

The level of detail in a fact table, determined by the intersection of all the components of the primary key, including all foreign keys and any other primary key elements.

With the explosion of Web-based commerce, clicks become the possible lowest level of granularity. An analysis of Web site buying habits requires clickstream data (e.g., time spent on page, pages migrated from and to). Such an analysis may be useful to understand Web site usability and to customize messages based on navigational paths taken. However, this very fine level of granularity actually may be too low to be useful. It has been estimated that 90 percent or more of clickstream data are worthless (Inmon, 2006); for example, there is no business value to knowing a user moved a cursor when such movements are due to irrelevant events such as exercising the wrist, bumping a mouse, or moving a mouse to get it out of the way of something on the person's desk.

Kimball (2001) and others recommend using the smallest grain possible, given the limitations of the data mart technology. Even when data mart user information requirements imply a certain level of aggregated grain, often after some use, users ask more detailed questions (drill down) as a way to explain why certain aggregated patterns exist. You cannot "drill down" below the grain of the fact tables (without going to other data sources, such as the EDW, ODS, or the original source systems, which may add considerable effort to the analysis).

DURATION OF THE DATABASE   As in the case of the EDW or ODS, another important decision in the design of a data mart is the amount of history to be kept, that is, the duration of the database. The natural duration is about 13 months or 5 calendar quarters, which is sufficient to see annual cycles in the data. Some businesses, such as financial institutions, have a need for longer durations. Older data may be difficult to source and cleanse if additional attributes are required from data sources. Even if sources of old data are available, it may be most difficult to find old values of dimension data, which are less likely than fact data to have been retained. Old fact data without associated dimension data at the time of the fact may be worthless.

SIZE OF THE FACT TABLE   As you would expect, the grain and duration of the fact table have a direct impact on the size of that table. We can estimate the number of rows in the fact table as follows:

1. Estimate the number of possible values for each dimension associated with the fact table (in other words, the number of possible values for each foreign key in the fact table).
2. Multiply the values obtained in the first step after making any necessary adjustments.

Let's apply this approach to the star schema shown in Figure 9-11. Assume the following values for the dimensions:

> Total number of stores = 1000
> Total number of products = 10,000
> Total number of periods = 24 (2 years' worth of monthly data)

Although there are 10,000 total products, only a fraction of these products are likely to record sales during a given month. Because item totals appear in the fact table only for items that record sales during a given month, we need to adjust this figure. Suppose that on average 50 percent (or 5000) items record sales during a given month. Then an estimate of the number of rows in the fact table is computed as follows:

> Total rows = 1000 stores × 5000 active products × 24 months
>   = 120,000,000 rows (!)

Thus, in our relatively small example, the fact table that contains two years' worth of monthly totals can be expected to have well over 100 million rows. This example clearly illustrates that the size of the fact table is many times larger than the dimension tables. For example, the STORE table has 1000 rows, the PRODUCT table 10,000 rows, and the PERIOD table 24 rows.

If we know the size of each field in the fact table, we can further estimate the size (in bytes) of that table. The fact table (named SALES) in Figure 9-11 has six fields. If each of these fields averages four bytes in length, we can estimate the total size of the fact table as follows:

Total size = 120,000,000 rows × 6 fields × 4 bytes/field
= 2,880,000,000 bytes (or 2.88 gigabytes)

The size of the fact table depends on both the number of dimensions and the grain of the fact table. Suppose that after using the database shown in Figure 9-11 for a short period of time, the marketing department requests that *daily* totals be accumulated in the fact table. (This is a typical evolution of a data mart.) With the grain of the table changed to daily item totals, the number of rows is computed as follows:

Total rows = 1000 stores × 2000 active products × 720 days (2 years)
= 1,440,000,000 rows

In this calculation, we have assumed that 20 percent of all products record sales on a given day. The database can now be expected to contain well over 1 *billion* rows. The database size is calculated as follows:

Total size = 1,440,000,000 rows × 6 fields × 4 bytes/field
= 34,560,000,000 bytes (or 34.56 gigabytes)

MODELING DATE AND TIME Because data warehouses and data marts record facts about dimensions over time, date and time (henceforth simply called *date*) is always a dimension table, and a date surrogate key is always one of the components of the primary key of any fact table. Because a user may want to aggregate facts on many different aspects of date or different kinds of dates, a date dimension may have many nonkey attributes. Also, because some characteristics of dates are country or event specific (e.g., whether the date is a holiday or there is some standard event on a given day, such as a festival or football game), modeling the date dimension can be more complex than illustrated so far.

Figure 9-12 shows a typical design for the date dimension. As we have seen before, a date surrogate key appears as part of the primary key of the fact table and is the primary key of the date dimension table. The nonkey attributes of the date dimension table include all of the characteristics of dates that users use to categorize, summarize, and group facts that do not vary by country or event. For an organization doing business in several countries (or several geographical units in which dates have different

FIGURE 9-12 Modeling dates

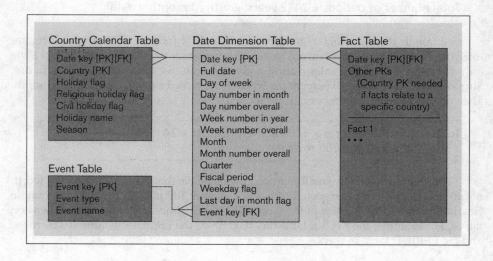

characteristics), we have added a Country Calendar table to hold the characteristics of each date in *each country*. Thus, the Date key is a foreign key in the Country Calendar table, and each row of the Country Calendar table is unique by the combination of Date key and Country, which form the composite primary key for this table. A special event may occur on a given date. (We assume here, for simplicity, no more than one special event may occur on a given date.) We have normalized the Event data by creating an Event table, so descriptive data on each event (e.g., the "Strawberry Festival" or the "Homecoming Game") are stored only once.

It is possible that there will be several kinds of dates associated with a fact, including the date the fact occurred, the date the fact was reported, the date the fact was recorded in the database, and the date the fact changed values. Each of these may be important in different analyses.

Variations of the Star Schema

The simple star schema introduced earlier is adequate for many applications. However, various extensions to this schema are often required to cope with more complex modeling problems. In this section, we briefly describe several such extensions: multiple fact tables with conformed dimensions and factless fact tables. For a discussion of additional extensions and variations, see subsequent sections, Poe (1996), and **www.kimballgroup.com.**

MULTIPLE FACT TABLES   It is often desirable for performance or other reasons to define more than one fact table in a given star schema. For example, suppose that various users require different levels of aggregation (in other words, a different table grain). Performance can be improved by defining a different fact table for each level of aggregation. The obvious trade-off is that storage requirements may increase dramatically with each new fact table. More commonly, multiple fact tables are needed to store facts for different combinations of dimensions, possibly for different user groups.

Figure 9-13 illustrates a typical situation of multiple fact tables with two related star schemas. In this example, there are two fact tables, one at the center of each star:

1. Sales—facts about the sale of a product to a customer in a store on a date
2. Receipts—facts about the receipt of a product from a vendor to a warehouse on a date

As is common, data about one or more business subjects (in this case, Product and Date) need to be stored in dimension tables for each fact table, Sales and Receipts. Two approaches have been adopted in this design to handle shared dimension tables. In one

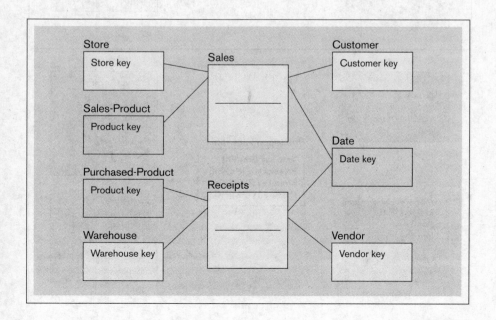

FIGURE 9-13   Conformed dimensions

case, because the description of product is quite different for sales and receipts, two separate product dimension tables have been created. On the other hand, because users want the same descriptions of dates, one date dimension table is used. In each case, we have created a **conformed dimension**, meaning that the dimension means the same thing with each fact table and, hence, uses the same surrogate primary keys. Even when the two star schemas are stored in separate physical data marts, if dimensions are conformed, there is a potential for asking questions across the data marts (e.g., Do certain vendors recognize sales more quickly, and are they able to supply replenishments with less lead time?). In general, conformed dimensions allow users to do the following:

- Share nonkey dimension data
- Query across fact tables with consistency
- Work on facts and business subjects for which all users have the same meaning

FACTLESS FACT TABLES As strange as it may seem, there are applications for fact tables that do not have nonkey (fact) data but do have foreign keys for the associated dimensions. The two general situations in which factless fact tables may apply are tracking events (see Figure 9-14a) and taking inventory of the set of possible occurrences (called coverage) (see Figure 9-14b). The star schema in Figure 9-14a tracks which students attend

Conformed dimension

One or more dimension tables associated with two or more fact tables for which the dimension tables have the same business meaning and primary key with each fact table.

FIGURE 9-14 Factless fact tables
(a) Factless fact table showing occurrence of an event

(b) Factless fact table showing coverage

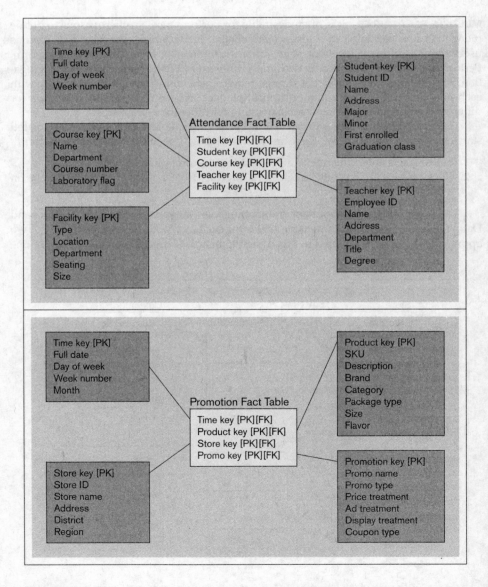

which courses at which time in which facilities with which instructors. All that needs to be known is whether this event occurs, represented by the intersection of the five foreign keys. The star schema in Figure 9-14b shows the set of possible sales of a product in a store at a particular time under a given promotion. A second sales fact table, not shown in Figure 9-14b, could contain the dollar and unit sales (facts) for this same combination of dimensions (i.e., with the same four foreign keys as the Promotion fact table plus these two nonkey facts). With these two fact tables and four conformed dimensions, it is possible to discover which products that were on a specific promotion at a given time in a specific store did not sell (i.e., had zero sales), which can be discovered by finding a combination of the four key values in the promotion fact table, which are not in the sales fact table. The sales fact table, alone, is not sufficient to answer this question because it is missing rows for a combination of the four key values, which has zero sales.

Normalizing Dimension Tables

Fact tables are fully normalized because each fact depends on the whole composite primary key and nothing but the composite key. However, dimension tables may not be normalized. Most data warehouse experts find this acceptable for a data mart optimized and simplified for a given user group, so that all the dimension data are only one join away from associated facts. (Remember that this can be done with logical data marts, so duplicate data do not need to be stored.) Sometimes, as with any other relational database, the anomalies of a denormalized dimension table cause add, update, and delete problems. In this section, we address various situations in which it makes sense or is essential to further normalize dimension tables.

MULTIVALUED DIMENSIONS There may be a need for facts to be qualified by a set of values for the same business subject. For example, consider the hospital example in Figure 9-15. In this situation, a particular hospital charge and payment for a patient on a date (e.g., for all foreign keys in the Finances fact table) is associated with one or more diagnoses. (We indicate this with a dashed *M:N* relationship line between the Diagnosis and Finances tables.) We could pick the most important diagnosis as a component key for the Finances table, but that would mean we lose potentially important information about other diagnoses associated with a row. Or, we could design the Finances table with a fixed number of diagnosis keys, more than we think is ever possible to associate with one row of the Finances table, but this would create null components of the primary key for many rows, which violates a property of relational databases.

The best approach (the normalization approach) is to create a table for an associative entity between Diagnosis and Finances, in this case the Diagnosis group table. (Thus, the dashed relationship in Figure 9-15 is not needed.) In the data warehouse

FIGURE 9-15 Multivalued dimension

database world, such an associative entity table is called a "helper table," and we will see more examples of helper tables as we progress through subsequent sections. A helper table may have nonkey attributes (as can any table for an associative entity); for example, the weight factor in the Diagnosis group table of Figure 9-15 indicates the relative role each diagnosis plays in each group, presumably normalized to a total of 100 percent for all the diagnoses in a group. Also note that it is not possible for more than one Finances row to be associated with the same Diagnosis group key; thus, the Diagnosis group key is really a surrogate for the composite primary key of the Finances fact table.

HIERARCHIES Many times a dimension in a star schema forms a natural, fixed depth hierarchy. For example, there are geographical hierarchies (e.g., markets with in a state, states within a region, and regions within a country) and product hierarchies (packages or sizes within a product, products within bundles, and bundles within product groups). When a dimension participates in a hierarchy, a database designer has two basic choices:

1. Include all the information for each level of the hierarchy in a single denormalized dimension table for the most detailed level of the hierarchy, thus creating considerable redundancy and update anomalies. Although it is simple, this is usually not the recommended approach.
2. Normalize the dimension into a nested set of a fixed number of tables with 1:*M* relationships between them. Associate only the lowest level of the hierarchy with the fact table. It will still be possible to aggregate the fact data at any level of the hierarchy, but now the user will have to perform nested joins along the hierarchy or be given a view of the hierarchy that is prejoined.

When the depth of the hierarchy can be fixed, each level of the hierarchy is a separate dimensional entity. Some hierarchies can more easily use this scheme than can others. Consider the product hierarchy in Figure 9-16. Here each product is part of a product family (e.g., Crest with Tartar Control is part of Crest), and a product family is part of a product category (e.g., toothpaste), and a category is part of a product group (e.g., health and beauty). This works well if every product follows this same hierarchy. Such hierarchies are very common in data warehouses and data marts.

Now, consider the more general example of a typical consulting company that invoices customers for specified time periods on projects. A revenue fact table in this situation might show how much revenue is billed and for how many hours on each invoice, which is for a particular time period, customer, service, employee, and project. Because consulting work may be done for different divisions of the same organization, if we want to understand the total role of consulting in any level of a customer organization, we need a customer hierarchy. This hierarchy is a recursive relationship between

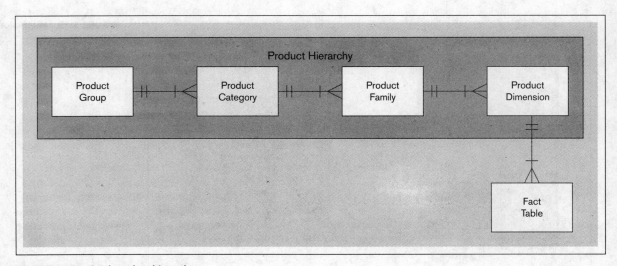

FIGURE 9-16 Fixed product hierarchy

organizational units. As shown in Figure 4-17 for a supervisory hierarchy, the standard way to represent this in a normalized database is to put into the company row a foreign key of the Company key for its parent unit.

Recursive relationships implemented in this way are difficult for the typical end user because specifying how to aggregate at any arbitrary level of the hierarchy requires complex SQL programming. One solution is to transform the recursive relationship into a fixed number of hierarchical levels by combining adjacent levels into general categories; for example, for an organizational hierarchy, the recursive levels above each unit could be grouped into enterprise, division, and department. Each instance of an entity at each hierarchical level gets a surrogate primary key and attributes to describe the characteristics of that level needed for decision making. Work done in the reconciliation layer will form and maintain these instances.

Another simple but more general alternative appears in Figure 9-17. Figure 9-17a shows how this hierarchy is typically modeled in a data warehouse using a helper table (Chisholm, 2000; Kimball, 1998b). Each customer organizational unit the consulting firm serves is assigned a different surrogate customer key and row in the Customer dimension table, and the customer surrogate key is used as a foreign key in the Revenue fact table; this foreign key relates to the Sub customer key in the Helper table because the revenue facts are associated at the lowest possible level of the organizational hierarchy. The problem with joining in a recursive relationship of arbitrary depth is that the user has to write code to join an arbitrary number of times (once for each level of subordination) and these joins in a data warehouse, because of its massive size, can be very time-consuming

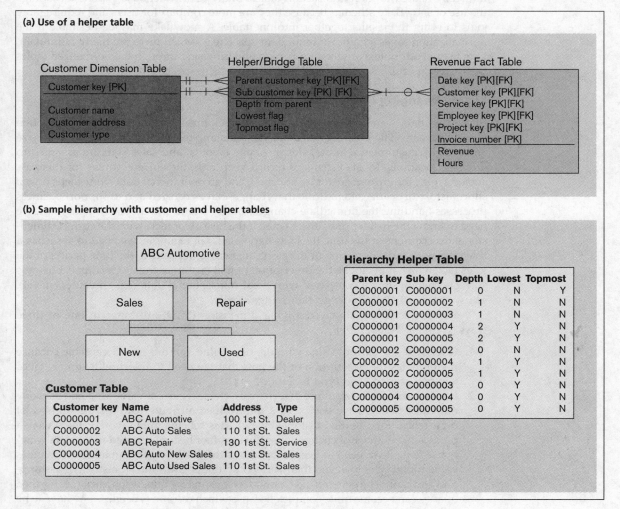

FIGURE 9-17   Representing hierarchical relationships within a dimension

(except for some high-performance data warehouse technologies that use parallel processing). To avoid this problem, the helper table flattens out the hierarchy by recording a row for each organizational subunit and each of its parent organizational units (including itself) all the way up to the top unit of the customer organization. Each row of this helper table has three descriptors: the number of levels the subunit is from its parent unit for *that* table row, a flag indicating whether this subunit is the lowest in the hierarchy, and a flag indicating whether this subunit is the highest in the hierarchy. Figure 9-17b depicts an example customer organizational hierarchy and the rows that would be in the helper table to represent that total organization. (There would be other rows in the helper table for the subunit-parent unit relationships within other customer organizations.)

The Revenue fact table in Figure 9-17a includes a primary key attribute of Invoice number. Invoice number is an example of a *degenerative dimension*, which has no interesting dimension attributes. (Thus, no dimension table exists and Invoice number is not part of the table's primary key.) Invoice number also is not a fact that will be used for aggregation because mathematics on this attribute has no meaning. This attribute may be helpful if there is a need to explore an ODS or source systems to find additional details about the invoice transaction or to group together related fact rows (e.g., all the revenue line items on the same invoice).

Snowflake schema

An expanded version of a star schema in which dimension tables are normalized into several related tables.

When the dimension tables are further normalized by using helper tables (sometimes called *bridge tables*, or *reference tables*), the simple star schema turns into a **snowflake schema**. A snowflake schema resembles a segment of an ODS or source database centered on the transaction tables summarized into the fact table and all of the tables directly and indirectly related to these transaction tables. Many data warehouse experts discourage the use of snowflake schemas because they are more complex for users and require more joins to bring the results together into one table. A snowflake may be desirable if the normalization saves significant redundant space (e.g., when there are many redundant, long textual attributes) or when users may find browsing through the normalized tables themselves useful.

Slowly Changing Dimensions

Recall that data warehouses and data marts track business activities over time, often for many years. The business does not remain static over time; products change size and weight, customers relocate, stores change layouts, and sales staff are assigned to different locations. Most systems of record keep only the current values for business subjects (e.g., the current customer address), and an operational data store keeps only a short history of changes to indicate that changes have occurred and to support business processes handling the immediate changes. But in a data warehouse or data mart, we need to know the history of values to match the history of facts with the correct dimensional descriptions at the time the facts happened. For example, we need to associate a sales fact with the description of the associated customer during the time period of the sales fact, which may not be the description of that customer today. Of course, business subjects change slowly compared with most transactional data (e.g., inventory level). Thus, dimensional data change, but change slowly.

We might handle slowly changing dimension (SCD) attributes in one of three ways (Kimball, 1996b, 1999):

1. Overwrite the current value with the new value, but this is unacceptable because it eliminates the description of the past that we need to interpret historical facts. Kimball calls this the Type 1 method.
2. For each dimension attribute that changes, create a current value field and as many old value fields as we wish (i.e., a multivalued attribute with a fixed number of occurrences for a limited historical view). This schema might work if there were a predictable number of changes over the length of history retained in the data warehouse (e.g., if we need to keep only 24 months of history and an attribute changes value monthly). However, this works only under this kind of restrictive assumption and cannot be generalized to any slowly changing dimension attribute. Further, queries can become quite complex because which column is needed may have to be determined within the query. Kimball calls this the Type 3 method.

3. Create a new dimension table row (with a new surrogate key) each time the dimension object changes; this new row contains all the dimension characteristics at the time of the change; the new surrogate key is the original surrogate key plus the start date for the period when these dimension values are in effect. A fact row is associated with the surrogate key whose attributes apply at the date/time of the fact (i.e., the fact date/time falls between the start and end dates of a dimension row for the same original surrogate key). We likely also want to store in a dimension row the date/ time the change ceases being in effect (which will be the maximum possible date or null for the current row for each dimension object) and a reason code for the change. This approach allows us to create as many dimensional object changes as necessary. However, it becomes unwieldy if rows frequently change or if the rows are very long. Kimball calls this the Type 2 method, and it is the one most often used.

Changes in some dimensional attributes may not be important. Hence, the first policy can be used for these attributes. The Type 2 scheme is the most frequently used approach for handling slowly changing dimensions for which changes matter. Under this scheme, we likely also store in a dimension row the surrogate key value for the original object; this way, we can relate all changes to the same object. In fact, the primary key of the dimension table becomes a composite of the original surrogate key plus the date of the change, as depicted in Figure 9-18. In this example, each time an attribute of Customer changes, a new customer row is written to the Customer dimension table; the PK of that row is the original surrogate key for that customer plus the date of the change. The nonkey elements are the values for all the nonkey attributes at the time of the change (i.e., some attributes will have new values due to the change, but probably most will remain the same as for the most recent row for the same customer). Finding the dimension row for a fact row is a little more complex; the SQL WHERE clause would include the following:

```
WHERE Fact.CustomerKey = Customer.CustomerKey
AND Fact.DateKey BETWEEN Customer.StartDate and Customer.EndDate
```

For this to work, EndDate for the last change to the customer dimension data must be the largest date possible. If not, the EndDate for the last change could be null, and the WHERE clause can be modified to handle this possibility. Another common feature of the Type 2 approach is to include a reason code (Kimball, 2006) with each new dimension row to document why the change occurred; in some cases, the reason code itself is useful for decision making (e.g., to see trends in correcting errors, resolve recurring issues, or see patterns in the business environment).

As noted, however, this schema can cause an excessive number of dimension table rows when dimension objects frequently change or when dimension rows are large "monster dimensions." Also, if only a small portion of the dimension row has changing values, there are excessive redundant data created. Figure 9-19 illustrates one approach, dimension segmentation, which handles this situation as well as the more general case of subsets of dimension attributes that change at different frequencies. In this example, the Customer dimension is segmented into two dimension tables; one segment may hold nearly constant or very slowly changing dimensions and other segments (we show only two in this example) hold clusters of attributes that change more rapidly and,

FIGURE 9-18 Example of Type 2 SCD Customer dimension table

FIGURE 9-19 Dimension segmentation

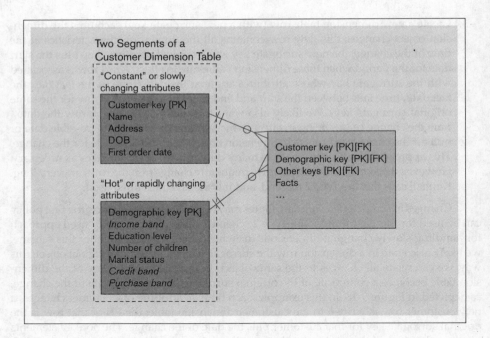

for attributes in the same cluster, often change at the same time. These more rapidly changing attributes are often called "hot" attributes by data warehouse designers.

Another aspect of this segmentation is that for hot attributes, we changed individual dimension attributes, such as customer income (e.g., $75,400/year), into an attribute for a band, or range, of income values (e.g., $60,000–$89,999/year). Bands are defined as required by users and are as narrow or wide as can be useful, but certainly some precision is lost. Bands make the hot attributes less hot, because a change within a band does not cause a new row to be written. This design is more complex for users because they now may have to join facts with multiple dimension segments, depending on the analysis.

One other common variation for handling slowly changing dimensions is to segment the dimension table horizontally into two tables, one to hold only the current values for the dimension entities and the other table to hold all the history, possibly including the current row. The logic to this approach is that many queries need to access only the current values, which can be done quickly from a smaller table of only current rows; when a query needs to look at history, the full dimension history table is used. Another version of this same kind of approach is to use only the one dimension table but to add a column (a flag attribute) to indicate whether that row contains the most current or out-of-date values. See Kimball (2002) for additional ideas on handling slowly changing dimensions.

Determining Dimensions and Facts

Which dimensions and facts are required for a data mart is driven by the context for decision making. Each decision is based on specific metrics to monitor the status of some important factor (e.g., inventory turns) or to predict some critical event (e.g., customer churn). Many decisions are based on a mixture of metrics, balancing financial, process efficiency, customer, and business growth factors. Decisions usually start with questions such as how much did we sell last month, why did we sell what we did, how much do we think we will sell next month, and what can we do to sell the amount we want to sell?

The answers to questions often cause us to ask new questions. Consequently, although for a given domain we can anticipate the initial questions someone might ask of a data mart, we cannot perfectly predict everything the users will want to know. This is why independent data marts are discouraged. With dependent data marts, it is much easier to expand an existing data mart or for the user to be given access to other data marts or to the EDW when their new questions require data in addition to what is in the current data mart.

The starting point for determining what data should be in a data mart is the initial questions the users want answered. Each question can be broken down into discrete items of business information the user wants to know (facts) and the criteria used to access, sort, group, summarize, and present the facts (dimension attributes). An easy way to model the questions is through a matrix, such as that illustrated in Figure 9-20a. In this figure, the rows are the qualifiers (dimension or dimension attributes) and the columns are the metrics (facts) referenced in the questions. The cells of the matrix contain codes to indicate which qualifiers and metrics are included in each question. For example, question 3 uses the fact number of complaints and the dimension attributes

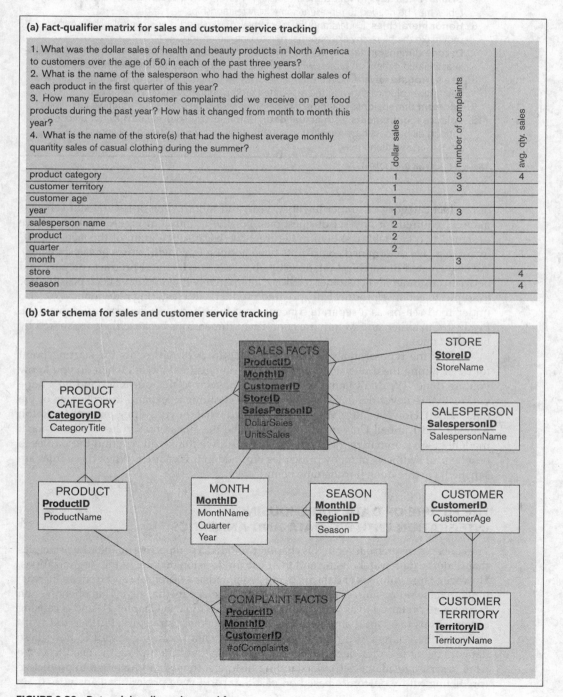

(a) Fact-qualifier matrix for sales and customer service tracking

1. What was the dollar sales of health and beauty products in North America to customers over the age of 50 in each of the past three years?
2. What is the name of the salesperson who had the highest dollar sales of each product in the first quarter of this year?
3. How many European customer complaints did we receive on pet food products during the past year? How has it changed from month to month this year?
4. What is the name of the store(s) that had the highest average monthly quantity sales of casual clothing during the summer?

	dollar sales	number of complaints	avg. qty. sales
product category	1	3	4
customer territory	1	3	
customer age	1		
year	1	3	
salesperson name	2		
product	2		
quarter	2		
month		3	
store			4
season			4

(b) Star schema for sales and customer service tracking

FIGURE 9-20 Determining dimensions and facts

TABLE 9-3 Ten Essential Rules of Dimensional Modeling

1. **Use atomic facts:** Eventually, users want detailed data, even if their initial requests are for summarized facts.
2. **Create single-process fact tables:** Each fact table should address the important measurements for one business process, such as taking a customer order or placing a material purchase order.
3. **Include a date dimension for every fact table:** A fact should be described by the characteristics of the associated day (or finer) date/time to which that fact is related.
4. **Enforce consistent grain:** Each measurement in a fact table must be atomic for the same combination of keys (the same grain).
5. **Disallow null keys in fact tables:** Facts apply to the combination of key values, and helper tables may be needed to represent some *M:N* relationships.
6. **Honor hierarchies:** Understand the hierarchies of dimensions and carefully choose to snowflake the hierarchy or denormalize into one dimension.
7. **Decode dimension tables:** Store descriptions of surrogate keys and codes used in fact tables in associated dimension tables, which can then be used to report labels and query filters.
8. **Use surrogate keys:** All dimension table rows should be identified by a surrogate key, with descriptive columns showing the associated production and source system keys.
9. **Conform dimensions:** Conformed dimensions should be used across multiple fact tables.
10. **Balance requirements with actual data:** Unfortunately, source data may not precisely support all business requirements, so you must balance what is technically possible with what users want and need.

Source: Based on Ross (2009).

of product category, customer territory, year, and month. One or several star schemas may be required for any set of questions. For the example in Figure 9-20a, we have designed two fact tables, shown in Figure 9-20b because the grain of the facts are different (e.g., we determined complaints have nothing to do with stores or salespersons). We also created hierarchical relationships between product and product category and between customer and customer territory; alternatively it would have been possible, for example, to collapse product category into product, with resulting redundancy. We also understood season as a separate concept from month, and to be territory dependent. Product, Customer, and Month are conformed dimensions because they are shared by two fact tables.

So, if the type of analysis depicted in Figure 9-20 represents the starting point for determining the dimensions and facts of a dimensional model, when do you know you are done? We don't know of a definitive answer to this question (and let's hope you really are never done, but simply need to continue to expand the coverage of the data model). However, Ross (2009) has identified what the consulting practice for Ralph Kimball and Kimball University considers to be the 10 essential rules of dimensional modeling. We summarize these rules in Table 9-3; we think you will find these rules to be a helpful synthesis of many principles outlined in this chapter. When these rules are satisfied, you are done (for the time being).

THE FUTURE OF DATA WAREHOUSING: INTEGRATION WITH BIG DATA AND ANALYTICS

The concepts covered earlier in this chapter provided a perspective on the core principles that underlie data warehousing and their use for decision making within organizations. However, large volumes of data are being generated at a faster rate and from an increasingly diverse set of sources (e.g., mobile devices, social media, etc.). This phenomenon is commonly referred to as "big data" (we cover this topic in Chapter 11) and is causing organizations to adapt their enterprise data management strategies. Further, the availability of these larger and more diverse types of data is causing a shift in how these data are being used for decision making. Organizations are finding the need to move from descriptive analytics (understanding historical trends and patterns) to predictive (predicting future outcomes based on past data) and even prescriptive analytics (how to ensure desired outcomes will happen). We cover the different types of analytics and their applications to business in Chapter 11. Data warehousing 2.0 (Inmon et al., 2008) is a term that is commonly used to describe the characteristics of data warehouses that will be needed to support the emerging trends identified above.

In the following section, we highlight three key business needs that have emerged: speed of processing, cost of storage, and variety of data, and discuss the technological advances in data warehousing that are enabling organizations to meet these needs.

Speed of Processing

Organizations need to invest in upgrading their data warehouse infrastructure to handle the volume and variety of data. A key trend in this regard is that of engineered systems wherein the storage, database, and networking aspects of the warehouse are designed and purchased in tandem to provide better performance and flexibility. One example of such a platform is SAP HANA (**www.saphana.com**), a dedicated in-memory database (see below) that can meet the transactional, reporting, and analytical needs of an organization. To gain optimal performance, the software runs on Intel-based hardware (processor and memory) configurations specifically engineered to support the analytical processing needs of enterprises.

Another related trend is in-memory databases. These differ from traditional databases in that the majority of the data in the database (even terabytes of data) is stored in RAM instead of on disks. This, in turn, makes retrieving data significantly faster than disk-based access. This trend is, of course, made possible by the significant cost reduction for RAM storage that has occurred over the past few years. These databases have the ability to seamlessly and efficiently move data between RAM, solid state, and traditional disk-based access based on predicted patterns of access. In other words, the most frequently used data are stored in memory and some information is still kept on disk. Most database vendors such as Microsoft, IBM, and Oracle now provide an in-memory option that is part of their DBMS.

Finally, as the need for advanced analytics capabilities such as data mining, predictive analytics, etc. (covered in Chapter 11) becomes the norm, one way to increase the speed of processing is by adding the analytical capabilities closer to where the data are, that is, the database software itself. By doing this, the time spent in moving the data (this can be terabytes of data) from the warehouse to the analytical processing software is reduced or eliminated. This is referred to as in-database analytics and is becoming a part of the database offering of many vendors (e.g., Teradata, Oracle, SAP Hana, etc.).

Cost of Storing Data

A consequence of having large amounts of data being generated at a fast rate is that the need to store this data in a cost-effective manner becomes critical. A very attractive option in this regard is to simply move the data warehouse into the cloud and thus enjoy the benefits of lower total cost of ownership (TCO). Moving the warehouse into the cloud also allows organizations to use a pay-as-you-go model and grow the size of their data warehouses dynamically as demand arises. Almost all major vendors, such as IBM, Oracle, Microsoft, Teradata, and SAP (HANA), have a cloud-based data warehousing offering. In addition, Amazon Web Services recently entered this market with a product named Redshift. Behind the scenes, many of these cloud-based offerings use advanced techniques such as columnar databases, massively parallel processing, and in-memory databases to help achieve faster processing times.

Dealing with Unstructured Data

Unstructured data, for example, data from Twitter feeds, are inherently not in a form that can be stored in relational databases. This means that new approaches to data transformation and storage are needed to handle the variety of data that is being generated. Technologies such as Hadoop play a critical role in helping achieve this transformation and storage in a cost-efficient and timely fashion. Another key technology that is helping handle the variety of data is NoSQL (Not only SQL). We cover both these technologies in detail in Chapter 11.

Irrespective of the actual technologies in play, what is clear is that the next generation of data warehouses will deal with data that are in different stages of their life cycle (real-time data to archival data), are of different types (structured and unstructured), and will be used for a variety of analytical decision-making purposes.

Summary

Despite the vast quantities of data collected in organizations today, most managers have difficulty obtaining the information they need for decision making. Two major factors contribute to this "information gap." First, data are often heterogeneous and inconsistent as a result of the piecemeal systems development approaches that have commonly been used. Second, systems are developed (or acquired) primarily to satisfy operational objectives, with little thought given to the information needs of managers.

There are major differences between operational and informational systems and between the data that appear in those systems. Operational systems are used to run the business on a current basis, and the primary design goal is to provide high performance to users who process transactions and update databases. Informational systems are used to support managerial decision making, and the primary design goal is to provide ease of access and use for information workers.

The purpose of a data warehouse is to consolidate and integrate data from a variety of sources and to format those data in a context for making accurate business decisions. A data warehouse is an integrated and consistent store of subject-oriented data obtained from a variety of sources and formatted into a meaningful context to support decision making in an organization.

Most data warehouses today follow a three-layer architecture. The first layer consists of data distributed throughout the various operational systems. The second layer is an enterprise data warehouse, which is a centralized, integrated data warehouse that is the control point and single source of all data made available to end users for decision support applications. The third layer is a series of data marts. A data mart is a data warehouse whose data are limited in scope for the decision-making needs of a particular user group. A data mart can be independent of an enterprise data warehouse (EDW), derived from the EDW, or a logical subset of the EDW.

The data layer in an enterprise data warehouse is called the reconciled data layer. The characteristics of this data layer (ideally) are the following: It is detailed, historical, normalized, comprehensive, and quality controlled. Reconciled data are obtained by filling the enterprise data warehouse or operational data store from the various operational systems. Reconciling the data requires four steps: capturing the data from the source systems, scrubbing the data (to remove inconsistencies), transforming the data (to convert it to the format required in the data warehouse), and loading and indexing the data in the data warehouse. Reconciled data are not normally accessed directly by end users.

The data layer in the data marts is referred to as the derived data layer. These are the data that are accessed by end users for their decision support applications.

Data are most often stored in a data mart using a variation of the relational model called the star schema, or dimensional model. A star schema is a simple database design where dimensional data are separated from fact or event data. A star schema consists of two types of tables: dimension tables and fact tables. The size of a fact table depends, in part, on the grain (or level of detail) in that table. Fact tables with more than 1 billion rows are common in data warehouse applications today. There are several variations of the star schema, including models with multiple fact tables and snowflake schemas that arise when one or more dimensions have a hierarchical structure.

The nature of data warehousing in organizations is shifting to accommodate the need to handle larger amounts and different types of data for various analytical purposes. Technologies such as in-memory databases, columnar databases, in-database analytics, cloud data warehouses, etc., deployed individually or in tandem, are all expected to help organizations with their future data and analytics needs.

Chapter Review

Key Terms

Conformed dimension *404*
Data mart *385*
Data warehouse *380*
Dependent data mart *387*
Derived data *391*

Enterprise data warehouse (EDW) *387*
Grain *400*
Independent data mart *385*
Informational system *384*

Logical data mart *388*
Operational data store (ODS) *388*
Operational system *383*
Periodic data *393*

Real-time data warehouse *389*
Reconciled data *391*
Snowflake schema *408*
Star schema *397*
Transient data *393*

Review Questions

9-1. Define each of the following terms:
   a. data warehouse
   b. data mart
   c. reconciled data
   d. derived data
   e. enterprise data warehouse
   f. real-time data warehouse
   g. star schema
   h. snowflake schema
   i. grain
   j. conformed dimension

9-2. Match the following terms and definitions:

_____ periodic data	a. lost previous data content
_____ data mart	b. detailed historical data
_____ star schema	c. data not altered or deleted
_____ grain	d. data warehouse of limited scope
_____ reconciled data	e. dimension and fact tables
	f. level of detail in a fact table
_____ dependent data mart	g. data filled from a data warehouse
_____ real-time data warehouse	h. structure that results from hierarchical dimensions
_____ transient data	i. a warehouse that accepts near real-time feeds of data
_____ snowflake schema	

9-3. Contrast the following terms:
   a. transient data; periodic data
   b. data warehouse; data mart; operational data store
   c. reconciled data; derived data
   d. fact table; dimension table
   e. star schema; snowflake schema
   f. independent data mart; dependent data mart; logical data mart
   g. status versus event data

9-4. List the five major trends that necessitate data warehousing in many organizations today.

9-5. Briefly describe the major components of a data warehouse architecture.

9-6. List the three types of metadata that appear in a three-layer data warehouse architecture and briefly describe the purpose of each.

9-7. List four characteristics of a data warehouse.

9-8. List five claimed limitations of independent data marts.

9-9. List two claimed benefits of independent data marts.

9-10. List the ten essential rules for dimensional modeling.

9-11. List four objectives of derived data.

9-12. Is a star schema a relational data model? Why or why not?

9-13. Explain how the volatility of a data warehouse is different from the volatility of a database for an operational information system.

9-14. Explain the pros and cons of logical data marts.

9-15. What is a helper table, and why is it often used to help organize derived data?

9-16. Describe the characteristics of a surrogate key as used in a data warehouse or data mart.

9-17. Why is time almost always a dimension in a data warehouse or data mart?

9-18. What is the purpose of conformed dimensions for different star schemas within the same data warehousing environment?

9-19. In what ways are dimension tables often not normalized?

9-20. What is a hierarchy as it relates to a dimension table?

9-21. What is the meaning of the phrase "slowly changing dimension"?

9-22. Explain the most common approach used to handle slowly changing dimensions.

9-23. One of the claimed characteristics of a data warehouse is that it is nonupdateable. What does this mean?

9-24. In what ways are a data staging area and an enterprise data warehouse different?

9-25. Describe the current key trends in data warehousing.

9-26. How and when stored procedures are used? What are the likely merits and demerits of using a stored procedure?

9-27. How are logical data marts more helpful under circumstances?

9-28. What are the applications for real-time data warehouses? What factors characterize the usage of real-time Data Warehouses?

9-29. How is Dimension modeling different from E-R Modeling? Can E-R modeling system be applied Data Warehouse?

Problems and Exercises

9-30. Examine the three tables with student data shown in Figure 9-1. Design a single-table format that will hold all of the data (nonredundantly) that are contained in these three tables. Choose column names that you believe are most appropriate for these data.

9-31. The following table shows some simple student data as of the date 06/20/2015:

Key	Name	Major
001	Amy	Music
002	Tom	Business
003	Sue	Art
004	Joe	Math
005	Ann	Engineering

The following transactions occur on 06/21/2015:
- Student 004 changes major from Math to Business.
- Student 005 is deleted from the file.
- New student 006 is added to the file: Name is Jim, Major is Phys Ed.

The following transactions occur on 06/22/2015:
- Student 003 changes major from Art to History.
- Student 006 changes major from Phys Ed to Basket Weaving.

Your assignment involves two parts:

a. Construct tables for 06/21/2015 and 06/22/2015, reflecting these transactions; assume that the data are transient (refer to Figure 9-7).

b. Construct tables for 06/21/2015 and 06/22/2015, reflecting these transactions; assume that the data are periodic (refer to Figure 9-8).

9-32. Millennium College wants you to help design a star schema to record grades for courses completed by students. There are four dimension tables, with attributes as follows:

CourseSection	Attributes: CourseID, SectionNumber, CourseName, Units, RoomID, and RoomCapacity. During a given semester, the college offers an average of 500 course sections.
Professor	Attributes: ProfID, ProfName, Title, DepartmentID, and DepartmentName. There are typically 200 professors at Millennium at any given time.
Student	Attributes: StudentID, StudentName, and Major. Each course section has an average of 40 students, and students typically take five courses per period.
Period	Attributes: SemesterID and Year. The database will contain data for 30 periods (a total of 10 years).

The only fact that is to be recorded in the fact table is CourseGrade.
a. Design a star schema for this problem. See Figure 9-10 for the format you should follow.
b. Estimate the number of rows in the fact table, using the assumptions stated previously.
c. Estimate the total size of the fact table (in bytes), assuming that each field has an average of 5 bytes.
d. If you didn't want to or didn't have to stick with a strict star schema for this data mart, how would you change the design? Why?
e. Various characteristics of sections, professors, and students change over time. How do you propose designing the star schema to allow for these changes? Why?

9-33. Having mastered the principles of normalization described in Chapter 4, you recognize immediately that the star schema you developed for Millennium College (Problem and Exercise 4-32) is not in third normal form. Using these principles, convert the star schema to a snowflake schema. What impact (if any) does this have on the size of the fact table for this problem?

9-34. You are to construct a star schema for Simplified Automobile Insurance Company (see Kimball, 1996b, for a more realistic example). The relevant dimensions, dimension attributes, and dimension sizes are as follows:

InsuredParty	Attributes: InsuredPartyID and Name. There is an average of two insured parties for each policy and covered item.
CoverageItem	Attributes: CoverageKey and Description. There is an average of 10 covered items per policy.
Agent	Attributes: AgentID and AgentName. There is one agent for each policy and covered item.
Policy	Attributes: PolicyID and Type. The company has approximately 1 million policies at the present time.
Period	Attributes: DateKey and FiscalPeriod.

Facts to be recorded for each combination of these dimensions are PolicyPremium, Deductible, and NumberOfTransactions.
a. Design a star schema for this problem. See Figure 9-10 for the format you should follow.
b. Estimate the number of rows in the fact table, using the assumptions stated previously.
c. Estimate the total size of the fact table (in bytes), assuming an average of 5 bytes per field.

9-35. Simplified Automobile Insurance Company would like to add a Claims dimension to its star schema (see Problem and Exercise 9-34). Attributes of Claim are ClaimID, ClaimDescription, and ClaimType. Attributes of the fact table are now PolicyPremium, Deductible, and MonthlyClaimTotal.
a. Extend the star schema from Problem and Exercise 9-34 to include these new data.
b. Calculate the estimated number of rows in the fact table, assuming that the company experiences an average of 2000 claims per month.

9-36. Millennium College (see Problem and Exercise 9-32) now wants to include new data about course sections: the department offering the course, the academic unit to which the department reports, and the budget unit to which the department is assigned. Change your answer to Problem and Exercise 9-32 to accommodate these new data requirements. Explain why you implemented the changes in the star schema the way you did.

9-37. As mentioned in the chapter, Kimball (1997), Inmon (1997, 2000), and Armstrong (2000) have debated the merits of independent and dependent data marts and normalized versus denormalized data marts. Obtain copies of these articles from your library or from online sources and summarize the arguments made by each side of this debate.

9-38. A food manufacturing company needs a data mart to summarize facts about orders to move goods. Some orders transfer goods internally, some are sales to customers, some are purchases from vendors, and some are returns of goods from customers. The company needs to treat customers, vendors, plants, and storage locations as distinct dimensions that can be involved at both ends of a movement event. For each type of destination or origin, the company wants to know the type of location (i.e., customer, vendor, etc.), name, city, and state. Facts about each movement include dollar volume moved, cost of movement, and revenue collected from the move (if any, and this can be negative for a return). Design a star-type schema to represent this data mart. Hint: After you design a typical star schema, think about how you might simplify the design through the use of generalization.

9-39. Visit **www.kimballgroup.com** and locate Kimball University Design Tip 37. Study this design tip and draw the dimensional model for the recommended design for a "pipeline" application for university admissions.

9-40. Visit **www.teradatauniversitynetwork.com** and download the dimensional modeling tool located under the downloadable software section. (Your instructor will have to give you the current password to access this site.) Use this tool to draw your answers to Problems and Exercises 9-32, 9-34, 9-35, and 9-38. Write a report that comments on the usefulness of this modeling tool. What other features would you like the tool to have? Is this tool better or worse than other database diagramming tools you've used (such as Visio, SmartDraw, ERWin, or others)? Why or why not?

9-41. Pine Valley Furniture wants you to help design a data mart for analysis of sales. The subjects of the data mart are as follows:

PINE VALLEY FURNITURE

Salesperson	Attributes: SalespersonID, Years with PVFC, SalespersonName, and SupervisorRating.
Product	Attributes: ProductID, Category, Weight, and YearReleasedToMarket.
Customer	Attributes: CustomerID, CustomerName, CustomerSize, and Location. Location is also a hierarchy over which they want to be able to aggregate data. Each Location has attributes LocationID, AverageIncome, PopulationSize, and NumberOfRetailers. For any given customer, there is an arbitrary number of levels in the Location hierarchy.
Period	Attributes: DayID, FullDate, WeekdayFlag, and LastDay of MonthFlag.

Data for this data mart come from an enterprise data warehouse, but there are many systems of record that feed this data to the data warehouse. The only fact that is to be recorded in the fact table is Dollar Sales.

a. Design a typical multidimensional schema to represent this data mart.

b. Among the various dimensions that change is Customer information. In particular, over time, customers may change their location and size. Redesign your answer to part a to accommodate keeping the history of these changes so that the history of DollarSales can be matched with the precise customer characteristics at the time of the sales.

c. As was stated, a characteristic of Product is its category. It turns out that there is a hierarchy of product categories, and management would like to be able to summarize sales at any level of category. Change the design of the data mart to accommodate product hierarchies.

Problems 9-42 through 9-45 are based upon the Fitchwood Insurance Company case study, which is described next.

Fitchwood Insurance Company, which is primarily involved in the sale of annuity products, would like to design a data mart for its sales and marketing organization. Presently, the OLTP system is a legacy system residing on a shared network drive consisting of approximately 600 different flat files. For the purposes of our case study, we can assume that 30 different flat files are going to be used for the data mart. Some of these flat files are transaction files that change constantly. The OLTP system is shut down overnight on Friday evening beginning at 6 P.M. for backup. During that time, the flat files are copied to another server, an extraction process is run, and the extracts are sent via FTP to a UNIX server. A process is run on the UNIX server to load the extracts into Oracle and rebuild the star schema. For the initial loading of the data mart, all information from the 30 files was extracted and loaded. On a weekly basis, only additions and updates will be included in the extracts.

Although the data contained in the OLTP system are broad, the sales and marketing organization would like to focus on the sales data only. After substantial analysis, the ERD shown in Figure 9-21 was developed to describe the data to be used to populate the data mart.

From this ERD, we get the set of relations shown in Figure 9-22. Sales and marketing is interested in viewing all sales data by territory, effective date, type of policy, and face value. In addition, the data mart should be able to provide reporting by individual agent on sales as well as commissions earned. Occasionally, the sales territories are revised (i.e., zip codes are added or deleted). The Last Redistrict attribute of the Territory table is used to store the date of the last revision. Some sample queries and reports are listed here:

- Total sales per month by territory, by type of policy
- Total sales per quarter by territory, by type of policy
- Total sales per month by agent, by type of policy
- Total sales per month by agent, by zip code
- Total face value of policies by month of effective date
- Total face value of policies by month of effective date, by agent
- Total face value of policies by quarter of effective date
- Total number of policies in force, by agent
- Total number of policies not in force, by agent
- Total face value of all policies sold by an individual agent
- Total initial commission paid on all policies to an agent
- Total initial commission paid on policies sold in a given month by agent
- Total commissions earned by month, by agent
- Top-selling agent by territory, by month

Commissions are paid to an agent upon the initial sale of a policy. The InitComm field of the policy table contains the percentage of the face value paid as an initial commission. The Commission field contains a percentage that is paid each month as long as a policy remains active or in force. Each month, commissions are calculated by computing the sum of the commission on each individual policy that is in force for an agent.

9-42. Create a star schema for this case study. How did you handle the time dimension?

9-43. Would you prefer to normalize (snowflake) the star schema of your answer to Problem and Exercise 9-42? If so, how and why? Redesign the star schema to accommodate your recommended changes.

9-44. Agents change territories over time. If necessary, redesign your answer to Problem and Exercise 9-43 to handle this changing dimensional data.

9-45. Customers may have relationships with one another (e.g., spouses, parents and children). Redesign your answer to Problem and Exercise 9-44 to accommodate these relationships.

*Problems and Exercises 9-46 through 9-53 deal with the Sales Analysis Module data mart available on Teradata University Network (**www.teradatauniversitynetwork.com**). To use Teradata University Network, you will need to obtain the current TUN password from your instructor. Go to the Assignments section of Teradata University Network or to this textbook's Web site to find the document "MDBM 10e SAM Assignment Instructions" in order to prepare to do the following Problems and Exercises. When requested, use course password MDBM10e to set up your SQL Assistant account.*

9-46. Review the metadata file for the db_samwh database and the definitions of the database tables. (You can use SHOW TABLE commands to display the DDL for tables.) Explain the methods used in this database for modeling hierarchies. Are hierarchies modeled as described in this chapter?

FIGURE 9-21 Fitchwood
Insurance Company ERD

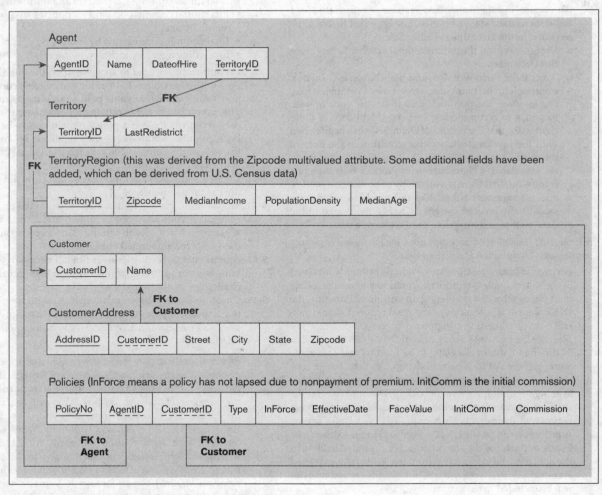

FIGURE 9-22 Relations for Fitchwood Insurance Company

9-47. Review the metadata file for the db_samwh database and the definitions of the database tables. (You can use SHOW TABLE commands to display the DDL for tables.) Explain what dimension data, if any, are maintained to support slowly changing dimensions. If there are slowly changing dimension data, are they maintained as described in this chapter?

9-48. Review the metadata file for the db_samwh database and the definitions of the database tables. (You can use SHOW TABLE commands to display the DDL for tables.) Are dimension tables conformed in this data mart? Explain.

9-49. The database you are using was developed by MicroStrategy, a leading business intelligence software vendor. The MicroStrategy software is also available on TUN. Most business intelligence tools generate SQL to retrieve the data they need to produce the reports and charts and to run the models users want. Go to the Apply & Do area on the Teradata University Network main screen and select MicroStrategy, then select MicroStrategy Application Modules, and then the Sales Force Analysis Module. Then make the following selections: Shared Reports → Sales Performance Analysis → Quarterly Revenue Trend by Sales Region → 2005 → Run Report. Go to the File menu and select the Report Details option. You will then see the SQL statement that was used, along with some MicroStrategy functionality, to produce the chart in the report. Cut and paste this SQL code into SQL Assistant and run this query in SQL Assistant. (You may want to save the code as an intermediate step to a Word file so you don't lose it.) Produce a file with the code and the SQL Assistant query result (answer set) for your instructor. You have now done what is called *screen scrapping* the SQL. This is often necessary to create data for analysis that is beyond the capabilities of a business intelligence package.

9-50. Take the query you scrapped from Problem and Exercise 9-45 and modify it to show only the U.S. region grouped by each quarter, not just for 2005 but for all years available, in order by quarter. Label the total orders by quarter with the heading TOTAL and the region ID simply as ID in the result. Produce a file with the revised SQL code and the answer set for your instructor.

9-51. Using the MDIFF "ordered analytical function" in Teradata SQL (see the Functions and Operators manual), show the differences (label the difference CHANGE) in TOTAL (which you calculated in the previous Problem and Exercise) from quarter to quarter. Hint: You will likely create a derived table based on your query above, similar to what is shown in examples in the Functions and Operators manual; when you do so, you will need to give the derived table an alias name and then use that alias name in the outer select statement when you ask to display the results of the query. Save your query and answer set to a file to give your instructor. (By the way, MDIFF is not standard SQL; this is an analytical SQL function proprietary to Teradata.)

9-52. Because data warehouses and even data marts can become very large, it may be sufficient to work with a subset of data for some analyses. Create a sample of orders from 2004 using the SAMPLE SQL command (which is standard SQL); put a randomized allocation of 10 percent of the rows into the sample. Include in the sample results the order ID, product ID, sales rep region ID, month description, and order amount. Show the results, in sequence, by month. Run the query two times to check that the sample is actually random. Put your SQL query and a portion of the two answer sets (enough to show that they are different) into a file for your instructor.

9-53. GROUP BY by itself creates subtotals by category, and the ROLLUP extension to GROUP BY creates even more categories for subtotals. Using all the orders, do a rollup to get total order amounts by product, sales region, and month and all combinations, including a grand total. Display the results sorted by product, region, and month. Put your query and the first portion of the answer set, including all of product 1 and a few rows for product 2, into a file for your instructor. Also, do a regular GROUP BY and put this query and the similar results from it into the file and then place an explanation in the file of how GROUP BY and GROUP BY with ROLLUP are different.

9-54. How will the database client/server solution suggested to a nationalized bank differ from the one that is suggested to a Sales and Marketing company? Elucidate with enough information in your answer to bring out the similarities and differences.

9-55. Describe the advantages and disadvantages of three tier and n-tier architecture. Under which circumstance these architectures are selected.

9-56. The Marketing arm of PMPL, a FMCG company needs Data Warehousing for its Sales data. The company's Sales Distribution Channel is mainly with pre-identified Wholesalers. The company has several depots all over the country, from where the sales data is collated over their country-wise enterprise intranet over VPN, at their Corporate Office in Bangalore. The following are the dimension tables with their attributes:

Product Attributes:
ProdID, ProductName, ProdCategory, ProdCostPrice, ProdSellPrice
(There typical 25 products on offer)

Invoice Attributes:
Invno, InvDate, WholesalerID, DepotID, Qty, ProdID, ProdRate, TotalAmount, PriceDiscount
(Around 700-800 invoices are generated country-wide across depots)

Wholesaler Attributes:
WholesalerID, Wholesaler_Owner, WS_Address, WS_Phone, WS_DepotID
(The FMCG has around 500 distributors spread across the country and depots)

Depot Attributes:
DepotID, DepotRegion, DepotManager
(There are around 15 depots in different regions of the country)
a. Design a star schema for this problem.
b. Describe the OLAP uses of this data warehouse.
c. Estimate the numbers of rows in the fact table.

Field Exercises

9-57. Visit an organization that has developed a data warehouse and interview the data administrator or other key participant. Discuss the following issues:
   a. How satisfied are users with the data warehouse? In what ways has it improved their decision making?
   b. Does the warehouse employ a three-tier architecture?
   c. Does the architecture employ one or more data marts? If so, are they dependent or independent?
   d. What end-user tools are employed?
   e. What were the main obstacles or difficulties overcome in developing the data warehouse environment?

9-58. Visit the following Web sites. Browse these sites for additional information on data warehouse topics, including case examples of warehouse implementations, descriptions of the latest warehouse-related products, and announcements of conferences and other events.
   a. The Data Warehousing Institute: **www.tdwi.org**
   b. Knowledge Discovery Mine: **www.kdnuggets.com**
   c. An electronic data warehousing journal: **www.tdan.com**

9-59. Visit **www.teradatauniversitynetwork.com** and use the various business intelligence software products available on this site. Compare the different products, based on the types of business intelligence problems for which they are most appropriate. Also, search the content of this Web site for articles, case studies, podcasts, training materials, and other items related to data warehousing. Select one item, study it, and write an executive briefing on its contents.

References

Armstrong, R. 1997. "A Rebuttal to the Dimensional Modeling Manifesto." A white paper produced by NCR Corporation.

Armstrong, R. 2000. "Avoiding Data Mart Traps." *Teradata Review* (Summer): 32–37.

Chisholm, M. 2000. "A New Understanding of Reference Data." *DM Review* 10,10 (October): 60, 84–85.

Devlin, B., and P. Murphy. 1988. "An Architecture for a Business Information System." *IBM Systems Journal* 27,1 (March): 60–80.

Hays, C. 2004. "What They Know About You." *New York Times*. November 14: section 3, page 1.

Imhoff, C. 1998. "The Operational Data Store: Hammering Away." *DM Review* 8,7 (July) available at **http://www.information-management.com/issues/19980701/470-1.html**.

Imhoff, C. 1999. "The Corporate Information Factory." *DM Review* 9,12 (December), available at **http://www.information-management.com/issues/19991201/1667-1.html**.

Inmon, B. 1997. "Iterative Development in the Data Warehouse." *DM Review* 7,11 (November): 16, 17.

Inmon, W. 1998. "The Operational Data Store: Designing the Operational Data Store." *DM Review* 8,7 (July), available at **http://www.information-management.com/issues/19980701/469-1.html**.

Inmon, W. 1999. "What Happens When You Have Built the Data Mart First?" *TDAN* accessed at **www.tdan.com/i012fe02.htm** (no longer available as of June, 2009).

Inmon, W. 2000. "The Problem with Dimensional Modeling." *DM Review* 10,5 (May): 68–70.

Inmon, W. 2006. "Granularity of Data: Lowest Level of Usefulness." *B-Eye Network* (December 14) available at **http://searchdatamanagement.techtarget.com/news/2240034162/Granularity-of-data**.

Inmon, W., and R. D. Hackathorn. 1994. *Using the Data Warehouse*. New York: Wiley.

Inmon, W. H., D. Strauss, G. Neushloss 2008. *DW 2.0: The Architecture for the Next Generation of Data Warehousing.* Morgan Kaufmann Series in Data Management Systems.

Kimball, R. 1996a. *The Data Warehouse Toolkit*. New York: Wiley.

Kimball, R. 1996b. "Slowly Changing Dimensions." *DBMS* 9,4 (April): 18–20.

Kimball, R. 1997. "A Dimensional Modeling Manifesto." *DBMS* 10,9 (August): 59.

Kimball, R. 1998a. "Pipelining Your Surrogates." *DBMS* 11,6 (June): 18–22.

Kimball, R. 1998b. "Help for Hierarchies." *DBMS* 11,9 (September) 12–16.

Kimball, R. 1999. "When a Slowly Changing Dimension Speeds Up." *Intelligent Enterprise* 2,8 (August 3): 60–62.

Kimball, R. 2001. "Declaring the Grain." from Kimball University, Design Tip 21, available at **www.kimballgroup.com.**

Kimball, R. 2002. "What Changed?" *Intelligent Enterprise* 5,8 (August 12): 22, 24, 52.

Kimball, R. 2006. "Adding a Row Change Reason Attribute." from Kimball University, Design Tip 80, available at *www.kimballgroup.com.*

Marco, D. 2000. *Building and Managing the Meta Data Repository: A Full Life-Cycle Guide*. New York: Wiley.

Marco, D. 2003. "Independent Data Marts: Stranded on Islands of Data, Part 1." *DM Review* 13,4 (April): 30, 32, 63.

Meyer, A. 1997. "The Case for Dependent Data Marts." *DM Review* 7,7 (July–August): 17–24.

Poe, V. 1996. *Building a Data Warehouse for Decision Support*. Upper Saddle River, NJ: Prentice Hall.

Ross, M. 2009. "Kimball University: The 10 Essential Rules of Dimensional Modeling." (May 29), available at **http://www.informationweek.com/software/information-management/kimball-university-the-10-essential-rules-of-dimensional-modeling/d/d-id/1080009?**

Further Reading

Gallo, J. 2002. "Operations and Maintenance in a Data Warehouse Environment." *DM Review* 12,12 (2003 Resource Guide): 12–16.

Goodhue, D., M. Mybo, and L. Kirsch. 1992. "The Impact of Data Integration on the Costs and Benefits of Information Systems." *MIS Quarterly* 16,3 (September): 293–311.

Jenks, B. 1997. "Tiered Data Warehouse." *DM Review* 7,10 (October): 54–57.

Mundy, J., W. Thornthwaite, and R. Kimball. 2006. *The Microsoft Data Warehouse Toolkit: With SQL Server 2005 and the Microsoft Business Intelligence Toolset*. Hoboken, NJ: Wiley.

Web Resources

www.teradata.com/tdmo Web site of *Teradata* magazine, which contains articles on the technology and application of the Teradata data warehouse system. (This magazine recently changed its name. Articles under the magazine's new and previous names can be found at **www.teradatamagazine.com**.)

www.information-management.com Web site of *Information Management*, a monthly trade magazine that contains articles and columns about data warehousing.

www.tdan.com An electronic journal on data warehousing.

http://www.inmoncif.com/home/ Web site of Bill Inmon, a leading authority on data management and data warehousing.

www.kimballgroup.com Web site of Ralph Kimball, a leading authority on data warehousing.

www.tdwi.org Web site of The Data Warehousing Institute, an industry group that focuses on data warehousing methods and applications.

www.datawarehousing.org The Data Warehousing Knowledge Center, which contains links to many vendors.

www.teradatauniversitynetwork.com A portal to resources for databases, data warehousing, and business intelligence. Data sets from this textbook are stored on the software site, from which you can use SQL, data mining, dimensional modeling, and other tools. Also, some very large data warehouse databases are available through this site to resources at the University of Arkansas. New articles and Webinars are added to this site all the time, so visit it frequently or subscribe to its RSS feed service to know when new materials are added. You will need to obtain a password to this site from your instructor.

PART V

Advanced Database Topics

AN OVERVIEW OF PART FIVE

Parts II through IV have prepared you to develop useful and efficient databases. Part V introduces some additional important database design and management issues. These issues include preserving data quality (including complying with regulations for accuracy of data reporting) and integrating across decentralized organizational databases (Chapter 10); big data and business analytics (Chapter 11); database security, backup, recovery, and control of concurrent access to data, and advanced topics in database performance tuning (Chapter 12); distributed databases (Chapter 13) and object-oriented databases (Chapter 14). Chapters 10, 11, and 12 are included in their entirety in the printed text; Chapters 13 and 14 are included on the textbook's Web site. Following Part V are three appendices available on the book's Web site, covering alternative E-R notations (Appendix A, complementing Chapters 2 and 3), advanced normal forms (Appendix B, supplementing Chapter 4), and data structures (Appendix C, supplementing Chapter 5).

Modern organizations are quickly realizing that one of their most prized assets is data and that effectively governing and managing data across an enterprise can be a potential source of competitive advantage. Chapter 10 ("Data Quality and Integration") focuses on key topics that are critical to enterprise data management: data governance, data quality, master data management, and data integration. Today data quality has become a major organizational issue for two reasons: Data quality is poor in many organizations, and new U.S. and international regulations impose criminal penalties for reporting erroneous financial and health data. Although data quality has been a theme throughout this book, Chapter 10 gives special attention to processes organizations can use (including data stewardship and governance) to systematically deal with data quality. Another major issue for data management is providing consistent and transparent access for users to data from multiple databases. Data warehousing, covered in the last chapter of Part IV, is one approach to achieving this goal. Other data integration strategies are outlined in Chapter 10. Data quality is a special concern when integrating disparate data sources.

In Chapter 11, we will introduce you to two key concepts that are taking the world of data management by storm: big data and analytics. Big data is a term that is used to refer to large amounts of data that exist in a variety of forms (think data as diverse as Twitter feeds and Facebook posts to operational data about customers, products, etc., and everything in between) and is generated at very high speeds. We will introduce you to technologies such as Hadoop, MapReduce, NoSQL, etc., that make it possible to handle these types of data. Analytics refers to a set of techniques that can be used to draw insights from all the data that is available to an organization. We will introduce you to three categories of analytic techniques:

Chapter 10
Data Quality and Integration

Chapter 11
Big Data and Analytics

Chapter 12
Data and Database Administration

Chapter 13
Distributed Databases

Chapter 14
Object-Oriented Data Modeling

descriptive, predictive, and prescriptive, and how each of these techniques can be used in organizations.

You are likely to conclude from reading this text that data are corporate resources that are too valuable to be managed casually. In Chapter 12 ("Data and Database Administration"), you will learn about the roles of the following:

- *A data administrator*—a person who takes overall responsibility for data, metadata, and policies about data use
- *A database administrator*—a person who is responsible for physical database design and for dealing with the technical issues—such as security enforcement, database performance, and backup and recovery—associated with managing a database

Specialized data and database administrator roles for Web-based data warehouses and mobile systems are also defined in Chapter 12. You will also learn about cloud databases and the opportunities and challenges associated with this emerging paradigm. Finally, in Chapter 12 you will learn about the challenges in managing security of data in a database and techniques that are available to help overcome these challenges. You will learn about views, integrity controls, authorization rules, encryption, and authentication—all key mechanisms to help manage data security. You will also understand the role of databases in Sarbanes-Oxley compliance, a hot topic in publicly traded companies in the United States. Finally, you will learn about open source DBMSs, concurrency control, deadlock, information repositories, locking, database recovery and backup, system catalogs, transactions, and versioning—all core topics today for managing data resources.

CHAPTER 10

Data Quality and Integration

LEARNING OBJECTIVES

After studying this chapter, you should be able to:

- Concisely define each of the following key terms: **data governance, data steward, chief data officer (CDO), master data management (MDM), changed data capture (CDC), data federation, static extract, incremental extract, data scrubbing, refresh mode, update mode, data transformation, selection, joining,** and **aggregation**.

- Describe the importance of data governance and identify key goals of a data governance program.

- Describe the importance of data quality and list several measures to improve quality.

- Define the characteristics of quality data.

- Describe the reasons for poor-quality data in organizations.

- Describe a program for improving data quality in organizations, including data stewardship.

- Describe the purpose and role of master data management.

- Describe the three types of data integration approaches.

- Describe the four steps and activities of the Extract, Transform, and Load (ETL) process for data integration for a data warehouse.

- Explain the various forms of data transformations needed to prepare data for a data warehouse.

INTRODUCTION

Quality data are the foundation for all of information processing and are essential for well-run organizations.

According to Friedman and Smith (2011), "poor data quality is the primary reason for 40 percent of business initiatives failing to achieve their business benefits." Data quality also impacts labor productivity by as much as 20 percent. In 2011, poor data quality is estimated to have cost the U.S. economy almost 3 trillion dollars, almost twice the size of the federal deficit (http://hollistibbetts.sys-con.com/node/1975126).

We have addressed data quality throughout this book, from designing data models that accurately represent the rules by which an organization operates, to including data integrity controls in database definitions, to data security and backup procedures that protect data from loss and contamination. However, with the increased emphasis on accuracy in financial reporting, the burgeoning supply of data inside and outside an organization, and the need to integrate data from disparate data sources for business intelligence, data quality deserves special attention by all database professionals.

Quality data is in the eye of the beholder. Data may be of high quality within one information system, meeting the standards of users of that system. But when users look beyond their system to match, say, their customer data with customer data from other systems, the quality of data can be called into question. Thus, data quality is but one component of a set of highly related enterprise data management topics that also includes data governance, master data management, and data integration. A final key aspect of enterprise data management, data security, is covered in Chapter 12.

This chapter on data quality and integration reviews the major issues related to the four topics identified above. First, we present an overview of data governance and how it lays the foundation for enterprise-wide data management activities. We then review why data quality is important and how to measure data quality, using seven important characteristics of quality data: identity uniqueness, accuracy, consistency, completeness, timeliness, currency, conformance, and referential integrity. Next, we explain why many organizations have difficulty achieving high-quality data, and then we review a program for data quality improvement that can overcome these difficulties. Part of this program involves creating new organizational roles of data stewards and organizational oversight for data quality via a data governance process. We then examine the topic of master data management and its role as a critical asset in enabling sharing of data across applications.

Managers and executives increasingly need data from many data systems and require this data in a consistent and consolidated way that makes the data appear to come from one database. Data integration methods of consolidation, federation, and propagation, along with master data management, make this possible. Data warehousing (see Chapter 9), a significant data management approach used to support decision making and business intelligence, often uses one consolidation approach called extract–transform–load (ETL); we explain ETL in detail in this chapter. First, the four major steps of ETL—mapping source to target and metadata management, extract, load, and finally transformation—are explained. The chapter illustrates the two types of extracts: static and incremental. Data cleansing is the ETL step most related to achieving quality data from the perspective of the data warehouse, so the chapter explains special data quality concerns for data warehousing. Then, different types of data transformations are reviewed at the record and field levels. Finally, we introduce a few selected tools to assist in ETL.

DATA GOVERNANCE

Data governance

High-level organizational groups and processes that oversee data stewardship across the organization. It usually guides data quality initiatives, data architecture, data integration and master data management, data warehousing and business intelligence, and other data-related matters.

Data governance is a set of processes and procedures aimed at managing the data within an organization with an eye toward high-level objectives such as availability, integrity, and compliance with regulations. Data governance oversees data access policies by measuring risk and security exposures (Leon, 2007). Data governance provides a mandate for dealing with data issues. According to a The Data Warehousing Institute (TDWI) 2005 (Russom, 2006) survey, only about 25 to 28 percent of organizations (depending on how the question was asked) have a data governance approach. Certainly, broad-based data governance programs are still emerging. Data governance is a function that has to be jointly owned by IT and the business. Successful data governance will require support from upper management in the firm. A key role in enabling success of data governance in an organization is that of a data steward.

The Sarbanes-Oxley Act of 2002 has made it imperative that organizations undertake actions to ensure data accuracy, timeliness, and consistency (Laurent, 2005). Although not mandated by regulations, many organizations require the CIO as well as the CEO and CFO to sign off on financial statements, recognizing the role of IT in building procedures to ensure data quality. Establishment of a business information advisory committee consisting of representatives from each major business unit who have the authority to make business policy decisions can contribute to the establishment of high data quality (Carlson, 2002; Moriarty, 1996). These committee members act as liaisons between IT and their business unit and consider not only their functional unit's data needs but also enterprise-wide data needs. The members are subject matter experts for the data they steward and hence need to have a strong interest in managing information as a corporate resource, an in-depth understanding of the business of the organization, and good negotiation skills. Such members (typically high-level managers) are sometimes referred to as **data stewards,** people who have the responsibility to ensure that organizational applications properly support the organization's enterprise goals.

Data steward

A person assigned the responsibility of ensuring that organizational applications properly support the organization's enterprise goals for data quality.

A data governance program needs to include the following:

- Sponsorship from both senior management and business units
- A data steward manager to support, train, and coordinate the data stewards
- Data stewards for different business units, data subjects, source systems, or combinations of these elements
- A governance committee, headed by one person, but composed of data steward managers, executives and senior vice presidents, IT leadership (e.g., data administrators), and other business leaders, to set strategic goals, coordinate activities, and provide guidelines and standards for all enterprise data management activities

The goals of data governance are transparency—within and outside the organization to regulators—and increasing the value of data maintained by the organization. The data governance committee measures data quality and availability, determines targets for quality and availability, directs efforts to overcome risks associated with bad or unsecured data, and reviews the results of data audit processes. Data governance is best chartered by the most senior leadership in the organization.

Data governance also provides the key guidelines for the key areas of enterprise data management identified in the introduction section: data quality initiatives, data architecture, master data management, data integration, data warehousing/business intelligence, and other data-related matters (Russom, 2006). We have already examined data warehousing issues in Chapter 9. In the next few sections, we examine the key issues in each of the other areas.

MANAGING DATA QUALITY

The importance of high-quality data cannot be overstated. According to Brauer (2002):

> Critical business decisions and allocation of resources are made based on what is found in the data. Prices are changed, marketing campaigns created, customers are communicated with, and daily operations evolve around whatever data points are churned out by an organization's various systems. The data that serves as the foundation of these systems *must be good data*. Otherwise we fail before we ever begin. It doesn't matter how pretty the screens are, how intuitive the interfaces are, how high the performance rockets, how automated the processes are, how innovative the methodology is, and how far-reaching the access to the system is, *if the data are bad—the systems fail.* Period. And if the systems fail, or at the very least provide inaccurate information, every process, decision, resource allocation, communication, or interaction with the system will have a damaging, if not disastrous impact on the business itself.

This quote is, in essence, a restatement of the old IT adage "garbage-in, garbage-out" (GIGO), but with increased emphasis on the dramatically high stakes in today's environment.

High-quality data—that is, data that are accurate, consistent, and available in a timely fashion—are essential to the management of organizations today. Organizations must strive to identify the data that are relevant to their decision making to develop business policies and practices that ensure the accuracy and completeness of the data, and to facilitate enterprise-wide data sharing. Managing the quality of data is an organization-wide responsibility, with data administration (the topic of Chapter 12) often playing a leading role in planning and coordinating the efforts.

What is your data quality ROI? In this case, we don't mean *return on investment*; rather, we mean *risk of incarceration*. According to Yugay and Klimchenko (2004), "The key to achieving SOX [Sarbanes-Oxley] compliance lies within IT, which is ultimately the single resource capable of responding to the charge to create effective reporting mechanisms, provide necessary data integration and management systems, ensure data quality and deliver the required information on time." Poor data quality can put executives in jail. Specifically, SOX requires organizations to measure and improve metadata quality; ensure data security; measure and improve data accessibility and ease of use; measure and improve data availability, timeliness, and relevance; measure and improve accuracy, completeness, and understandability of general ledger data; and identify and eliminate duplicates and data inconsistencies. According to Informatica (2005), a leading provider of technology for data quality and integration, data quality is important to

- *Minimize IT project risk*   Dirty data can cause delays and extra work on information systems projects, especially those that involve reusing data from existing systems.
- *Make timely business decisions*   The ability to make quick and informed business decisions is compromised when managers do not have high-quality data or when they lack confidence in their data.
- *Ensure regulatory compliance*   Not only is quality data essential for SOX and Basel II (Europe) compliance, quality data can also help an organization in justice, intelligence, and antifraud activities.
- *Expand the customer base*   Being able to accurately spell a customer's name or to accurately know all aspects of customer activity with your organization will help in up-selling and cross-selling new business.

Characteristics of Quality Data

What, then, are quality data? Redman (2004) summarizes data quality as "fit for their intended uses in operations, decision making, and planning." In other words, this means that data are free of defects and possess desirable features (relevant, comprehensive, proper level of detail, easy to read, and easy to interpret). Loshin (2006) and Russom (2006) further delineate the characteristics of quality data:

- *Uniqueness*   Uniqueness means that each entity exists no more than once within the database, and there is a key that can be used to uniquely access each entity. This characteristic requires identity matching (finding data about the same entity) and resolution to locate and remove duplicate entities.
- *Accuracy*   Accuracy has to do with the degree to which any datum correctly represents the real-life object it models. Often accuracy is measured by agreement with some recognized authority data source (e.g., one source system or even some external data provider). Data must be both accurate and precise enough for their intended use. For example, knowing sales accurately is important, but for many decisions, knowing sales only to the nearest $1000 per month for each product is sufficient. Data can be valid (i.e., satisfy a specified domain or range of values) and not be accurate.
- *Consistency*   Consistency means that values for data in one data set (database) are in agreement with the values for related data in another data set (database). Consistency can be within a table row (e.g., the weight of a product should have some relationship to its size and material type), between table rows (e.g., two products with similar characteristics should have about the same prices, or data that are meant to be redundant should have the same values), between the same attributes over time (e.g., the product price should be the same from one month to the next unless there was a price change event), or within some tolerance (e.g., total sales computed from orders filled and orders billed should be roughly the same values). Consistency also relates to attribute inheritance from super- to subtypes. For example, a subtype instance cannot exist without a corresponding supertype, and overlap or disjoint subtype rules are enforced.
- *Completeness*   Completeness refers to data having assigned values if they need to have values. This characteristic encompasses the NOT NULL and foreign key constraints of SQL, but more complex rules might exist (e.g., male employees do not need a maiden name but female employees may have a maiden name).

Completeness also means that all data needed are present (e.g., if we want to know total dollar sales, we may need to know both total quantity sold and unit price, or if an employee record indicates that an employee has retired, we need to have a retirement date recorded). Sometimes completeness has an aspect of precedence. For example, an employee in an employee table who does not exist in an applicant table may indicate a data quality issue.

- *Timeliness* Timeliness means meeting the expectation for the time between when data are expected and when they are readily available for use. As organizations attempt to decrease the latency between when a business activity occurs and when the organization is able to take action on that activity, timeliness is becoming a more important quality of data characteristic (i.e., if we don't know in time to take action, we don't have quality data). A related aspect of timeliness is retention, which is the span of time for which data represent the real world. Some data need to be time-stamped to indicate from when to when they apply, and missing from or to dates may indicate a data quality issue.
- *Currency* Currency is the degree to which data are recent enough to be useful. For example, we may require that customers' phone numbers be up-to-date so we can call them at any time, but the number of employees may not need to be refreshed in real time. Varying degrees of currency across data may indicate a quality issue (e.g., if the salaries of different employees have drastically different updated dates).
- *Conformance* Conformance refers to whether data are stored, exchanged, or presented in a format that is as specified by their metadata. The metadata include both domain integrity rules (e.g., attribute values come from a valid set or range of values) and actual format (e.g., specific location of special characters, precise mixture of text, numbers, and special symbols).
- *Referential integrity* Data that refer to other data need to be unique and satisfy requirements to exist (i.e., satisfy any mandatory one or optional one cardinalities).

These are high standards. Quality data requires more than defect correction; it also requires prevention and reporting. Because data are frequently updated, achieving quality data requires constant monitoring and measurement as well as improvement actions. Quality data are also not perfectly achievable nor absolutely necessary in some situations (there are obvious situations of life and death where perfection is the goal); "just enough quality" may be the best business decision to trade off costs versus returns.

Table 10-1 lists four important reasons why the quality of data in organizational databases has deteriorated in the past few years; we describe these reasons in the following sections.

EXTERNAL DATA SOURCES Much of an organization's data originates outside the organization, where there is less control over the data sources to comply with expectations of the receiving organization. For example, a company receives a flood of data via the Internet from Web forms filled out by users. Such data are often inaccurate or incomplete, or even purposely wrong. (Have you ever entered a wrong phone number in a Web-based form because a phone number was required and you didn't want to divulge your actual phone number?) Other data for B2B transactions arrive via XML channels,

TABLE 10-1 Reasons for Deteriorated Data Quality

Reason	Explanation
External data sources	Lack of control over data quality
Redundant data storage and inconsistent metadata	Proliferation of databases with uncontrolled redundancy and metadata
Data entry problems	Poor data capture controls
Lack of organizational commitment	Not recognizing poor data quality as an organizational issue

and these data may also contain inaccuracies. Also, organizations often purchase data files or databases from external organizations, and these sources may contain data that are out-of-date, inaccurate, or incompatible with internal data.

REDUNDANT DATA STORAGE AND INCONSISTENT METADATA Many organizations have allowed the uncontrolled proliferation of spreadsheets, desktop databases, legacy databases, data marts, data warehouses, and other repositories of data. These data may be redundant and filled with inconsistencies and incompatibilities. Data can be wrong because the metadata are wrong (e.g., a wrong formula to aggregate data in a spreadsheet or an out-of-date data extraction routine to refresh a data mart). Then if these various databases become sources for integrated systems, the problems can cascade further.

DATA ENTRY PROBLEMS According to a TDWI survey (Russom, 2006), user interfaces that do not take advantage of integrity controls—such as automatically filling in data, providing drop-down selection boxes, and other improvements in data entry control—are tied for the number-one cause of poor data. And the best place to improve data entry across all applications is in database definitions, where integrity controls, valid value tables, and other controls can be documented and enforced.

LACK OF ORGANIZATIONAL COMMITMENT For a variety of reasons, many organizations simply have not made the commitment or invested the resources to improve their data quality. Some organizations are simply in denial about having problems with data quality. Others realize they have a problem but fear that the solution will be too costly or that they cannot quantify the return on investment. The situation is improving; in a 2001 TDWI survey (Russom, 2006), about 68 percent of respondents reported no plans or were only considering data quality initiatives, but by 2005 this percentage had dropped to about 58 percent.

Data Quality Improvement

Implementing a successful quality improvement program will require the active commitment and participation of all members of an organization. Following is a brief outline of some of the key steps in such a program (see Table 10-2).

GET THE BUSINESS BUY-IN Data quality initiatives need to be viewed as business imperatives rather than as an IT project. Hence, it is critical that the appropriate level of executive sponsorship be obtained and that a good business case be made for the improvement. A key element of making the business case is being able to identify the impact of poor data quality. Loshin (2009) identifies four dimensions of impacts: increased costs, decreased revenues, decreased confidence, and increased risk. For each of these dimensions, it is important to identify and define key performance indicators and metrics that can quantify the results of the improvement efforts.

TABLE 10-2 Key Steps in a Data Quality Program

Step	Motivation
Get the business buy-in	Show the value of data quality management to executives
Conduct a data quality audit	Understand the extent and nature of data quality problems
Establish a data stewardship program	Achieve organizational commitment and involvement
Improve data capture processes	Overcome the "garbage in, garbage out" phenomenon
Apply modern data management principles and technology	Use proven methods and techniques to make more thorough data quality activities easier to execute
Apply TQM principles and practices	Follow best practices to deal with all aspects of data quality management

With the competing demands for resources today, management must be convinced that a data quality program will yield a sufficient ROI (in this case, we do mean *return on investment*). Fortunately (or unfortunately), this is not difficult to do in most organizations today. There are two general types of benefits from such a program: cost avoidance and avoidance of opportunity losses.

Consider a simple example. Suppose a bank has 500,000 customers in its customer file. The bank plans to advertise a new product to all of its customers by means of a direct mailing. Suppose the error rate in the customer file is 10 percent, including duplicate customer records, obsolete addresses, and so on (such an error rate is not unusual). If the direct cost of mailing is $5.00 (including postage and materials), the expected loss due to bad data is 500,000 customers × .10 × $5, or $250,000.

Often, the opportunity loss associated with bad data is greater than direct costs. For example, assume that the average bank customer generates $2000 in revenue annually from interest charges, service fees, and so on. This equates to $10,000 over a five-year period. Suppose the bank implements an enterprise-wide data quality program that improves its customer relationship management, cross-selling, and other related activities. If this program results in a net increase of only 2 percent new business (an educated guess), the results over five years will be remarkable: 500,000 customers × $10,000 × .02, or $50 million. This is why it is sometimes stated that "quality is free."

CONDUCT A DATA QUALITY AUDIT An organization without an established data quality program should begin with an audit of data to understand the extent and nature of data quality problems. A data quality audit includes many procedures, but one simple task is to statistically profile all files. A profile documents the set of values for each field. By inspection, obscure and unexpected extreme values can be identified. Patterns of data (distribution, outliers, frequencies) can be analyzed to see if the distribution makes sense. (An unexpected high frequency of one value may indicate that users are entering an easy number or a default is often being used, thus accurate data are not being recorded.) Data can be checked against relevant business rules to be sure that controls that are in place are effective and somehow not being bypassed (e.g., some systems allow users to override warning messages that data entered violates some rule; if this happens too frequently, it can be a sign of lax enforcement of business rules). Data quality software, such as the programs mentioned later in this chapter for ETL processes, can be used to check for valid addresses, find redundant records due to insufficient methods for matching customer or other subjects across different sources, and violations of specified business rules.

Business rules to be checked can be as simple as an attribute value must be greater than zero or can involve more complex conditions (e.g., loan accounts with a greater than zero balance and open more than 30 days must have an interest rate greater than zero). Rules can be implemented in the database (e.g., foreign keys), but if there are ways for operators to override rules, there is no guarantee that even these rules will be strictly followed. The business rules are reviewed by a panel of application and database experts, and the data to be checked are identified. Rules often do not have to be checked against all existing data, rather a random but representative sample is usually sufficient. Once the data are checked against the rules, a panel judges what actions should be taken to deal with broken rules, usually addressed in some priority order.

Using specialized tools for data profiling makes a data audit more productive, especially considering that data profiling is not a one-time task. Because of changes to the database and applications, data profiling needs to be done periodically. In fact, some organizations regularly report data profiling results as critical success factors for the information systems organization. Informatica's PowerCenter tool is representative of the capabilities of specialized tools to support data profiling. PowerCenter can profile a wide variety of data sources and supports complex business rules in a business rules library. It can track profile results over time to show improvements and new problem areas. Rules can check on column values (e.g., valid range of values), sources (e.g., row counts and redundancy checks), and multiple tables (e.g., inner versus outer join results). It is also recommended that any new application for a database, which may be analyzing data in new ways, could benefit from a specialized data profile to see if new queries, using previously hidden business rules, would fail because the database was never protected against violations of these rules. With a specialized data profiling tool, new rules can be quickly checked and inventoried against all rules as part of a total data quality audit program.

An audit will thoroughly review all process controls on data entry and maintenance. Procedures for changing sensitive data should likely involve actions by at least two people with separated duties and responsibilities. Primary keys and important financial data fall into this category. Proper edit checks should be defined and implemented for all fields. Error logs from processing data from each source (e.g., user, workstation, or source system) should be analyzed to identify patterns or high frequencies of errors and rejected transactions, and actions should be taken to improve the ability of the sources to provide high-quality data. For example, users should be prohibited from entering data into fields for which they are not intended. Some users who do not have a use for certain data may use that field to store data they need but for which there is not an appropriate field. This can confuse other users who do use these fields and see unintended data.

ESTABLISH A DATA STEWARDSHIP PROGRAM As pointed out in the section on data governance, stewards are held accountable for the quality of the data for which they are responsible. They must also ensure that the data that are captured are accurate and consistent throughout the organization, so that users throughout the organization can rely on the data. Data stewardship is a role, not a job; as such, data stewards do not own the data, and data stewards usually have other duties inside and usually outside the data administration area.

Seiner (2005) outlines a comprehensive set of roles and responsibilities for data stewards. Roles include oversight of the data stewardship program, managers of data subject areas (e.g., customer, product), stewards for data definitions of each data subject, stewards for accurate and efficient production/maintenance of data for each subject, and stewards for proper use of data for each subject area.

There is debate about whether data steward roles should report through the business or IT organizations. Data stewards need to have business acumen, understand data requirements and usage, and understand the finer details of metadata. Business data stewards can articulate specific data uses and understand the complex relationships between data from a grounded business perspective. Business data stewards emphasize the business ownership of data and can represent the business on access rights, privacy, and regulations/policies that affect data. They should know why data are the way they are and can see data reuse possibilities.

But, as Dyché (2007) has discovered, a business data steward often is myopic, seeing data from only the depths of the area or areas of the organization from which he or she comes. If data do not originate in the area of the data steward, the steward will have limited knowledge and may be at a disadvantage in debates with other data stewards. Dyché argues also for source data stewards, who understand the systems of record, lineage, and formatting of different data systems. Source data stewards can help determine the best source for user data requirements by understanding the details of how a source system acquires and processes data.

Chief data officer (CDO)

An executive-level position accountable for all data-related activities in the enterprise.

Another emerging trend is the establishment of the **chief data officer (CDO)** (Lee et al., 2014). The establishment of this executive-level position signifies a commitment to viewing data as a strategic asset and also allows for the successful execution of enterprise-wide data focused projects.

IMPROVE DATA CAPTURE PROCESSES As noted earlier, lax data entry is a major source of poor data quality, so improving data capture processes is a fundamental step in a data quality improvement program. Inmon (2004) identifies three critical points of data entry: where data are (1) originally captured (e.g., a customer order entry screen), (2) pulled into a data integration process (e.g., an ETL process for data warehousing), and (3) loaded into an integrated data store, such as a data warehouse. A database professional can improve data quality at each of these steps. For simplicity, we summarize what Inmon recommends only for the original data capture step (and we discuss the process of cleansing data during ETL in a later section of this chapter):

- Enter as much of the data as possible via automatic, not human, means (e.g., from data stored in a smart card or pulled from a database, such as retrieving current values for addresses, account numbers, and other personal characteristics).
- Where data must be entered manually, ensure that it is selected from preset options (e.g., drop-down menus of selections pulled from the database), if possible.
- Use trained operators when possible (help systems and good prompts/examples can assist end users in proper data entry).
- Follow good user interface design principles (see Hoffer et al., 2014, for guidelines) that create consistent screen layouts, easy to follow navigation paths, clear data entry masks and formats (which can be defined in DDL), minimal use of obscure codes (full values of codes can be looked up and displayed from the database, not in the application programs), and so on.
- Immediately check entered data for quality against data in the database, so use triggers and user-defined procedures liberally to make sure that only high-quality data enter the database; when questionable data are entered (e.g., "T" for gender), immediate and understandable feedback should be given to the operator, questioning the validity of the data.

APPLY MODERN DATA MANAGEMENT PRINCIPLES AND TECHNOLOGY   Powerful software is now available that can assist users with the technical aspects of data quality improvement. This software often employs advanced techniques such as pattern matching, fuzzy logic, and expert systems. These programs can be used to analyze current data for quality problems, identify and eliminate redundant data, integrate data from multiple sources, and so on. Some of these programs are discussed later in this chapter, under the topic of data extract, transform, and load.

Of course, in a database management book, we certainly cannot neglect sound data modeling as a central ingredient in a data quality program. Chapters 3 through 6 introduced the principles of conceptual to physical data modeling and design that are the basis for a high-quality data model. Hay (2005) (drawing on prior work) has summarized these into six principles for high-quality data models.

APPLY TQM PRINCIPLES AND PRACTICES   Data quality improvements should be considered as an ongoing effort and not treated as one-time projects. With this mind, many leading organizations are applying total quality management (TQM) to improve data quality, just as in other business areas. Some of the principles of TQM that apply are defect prevention (rather than correction), continuous improvement of the processes that touch data, and the use of enterprise data standards. For example, where data in legacy systems are found defective, it is better to correct the legacy systems that generate that data than to attempt to correct the data when moving it to a data warehouse.

TQM balances a focus on the customer (in particular, customer satisfaction) and the product or service (in our case, the data resource). Ultimately, TQM results in decreased costs, increased profits, and reduced risks. As stated earlier in this chapter, data quality is in the eye of the beholder, so the right mix of the seven characteristics of quality data will depend on data users. TQM builds on a strong foundation of measurements, such as what we have discussed as data profiling. For an in-depth discussion of applying TQM to data quality improvement, see English (1999a, 1999b, 2004).

Summary of Data Quality

Ensuring the quality of data that enters databases and data warehouses is essential if users are to have confidence in their systems. Users have their own perceptions of the quality of data, based on balancing the characteristics of uniqueness, accuracy, consistency, completeness, timeliness, currency, conformance, and referential integrity. Ensuring data quality is also now mandated by regulations such as the Sarbanes-Oxley Act and the Basel II Accord. Many organizations today do not have proactive data quality programs, and poor-quality data is a widespread problem. We have outlined in this section key steps in a proactive data quality program that employs the use of data audits and profiling, best practices in data capture and entry, data stewards, proven TQM principles and practices, modern data management software technology, and appropriate ROI calculations.

MASTER DATA MANAGEMENT

If one were to examine the data used in applications across a large organization, one would likely find that certain categories of data are referenced more frequently than others across the enterprise in operational and analytical systems. For example, almost all information systems and databases refer to common subject areas of data (people, things, places) and often enhance those common data with local (transactional) data relevant to only the application or database. The challenge for an organization is to ensure that all applications that use common data from these areas, such as customer, product, employee, invoice, and facility, have a "single source of truth" they can use. **Master data management (MDM)** refers to the disciplines, technologies, and methods to ensure the currency, meaning, and quality of reference data within and across various subject areas (Imhoff and White, 2006). MDM ensures that across the enterprise, the current description of a product, the current salary of an employee, and the current billing address of a customer, and so on are consistent. Master data can be as simple as a list of acceptable city names and abbreviations. MDM does not address sharing transactional data, such as customer purchases. MDM can also be realized in specialized forms. One of the most discussed is customer data integration (CDI), which is MDM that focuses just on customer data (Dyché and Levy, 2006). Another is product data integration (PDI).

MDM has become more common due to active mergers and acquisitions and to meet regulations, such as the Sarbanes-Oxley Act. Although many vendors (consultants and technology suppliers) exist to provide MDM approaches and technologies, it is important for firms to acknowledge that master data are a key strategic asset for a firm. It is therefore imperative that MDM projects have the appropriate level of executive buy-in and be treated as enterprise-wide initiatives. MDM projects also need to work closely with ongoing data quality and data governance initiatives.

No one source system usually contains the "golden record" of all relevant facts about a data subject. For example, customer master data might be integrated from customer relationship management, billing, ERP, and purchased data sources. MDM determines the best source for each piece of data (e.g., customer address or name) and makes sure that all applications reference the same virtual "golden record." MDM also provides analysis and reporting services to inform data quality managers about the quality of master data across databases (e.g., what percentage of city data stored in individual databases conforms with the master city values). Finally, because master data are "golden records," no application owns master data. Rather, master data are truly enterprise assets, and business managers must take responsibility for the quality of master data.

There are three popular architectures for master data management: identity registry, integration hub, and persistent. In the *identity registry* approach, the master data remain in their source systems, and applications refer to the registry to determine where the agreed-upon source of particular data (e.g., customer address) resides. The registry helps each system match its master record with corresponding master records in other source systems by using a global identifier for each instance of a subject area. The registry maintains a complete list of all master data elements and knows which source system to access for the best value for each attribute. Thus, an application may have to access several databases to retrieve all the data it needs, and a database may need to allow more applications to access it. This is similar to the federation style of data integration.

In the *integration hub* approach, data changes are broadcast (typically asynchronously) through a central service to all subscribing databases. Redundant data are kept, but there are mechanisms to ensure consistency, yet each application does not have to collect and maintain all of the data it needs. When this style of integration hub is created, it acts like a propagation form of data integration. In some cases, however, a central master data store is also created for some master data; thus, it may be a combination of propagation and consolidation. However, even with consolidation, the systems of

Master data management (MDM)
Disciplines, technologies, and methods used to ensure the currency, meaning, and quality of reference data within and across various subject areas.

record or entry—the distributed transaction systems—still maintain their own databases including the local and propagated data they need for their most frequent processing.

In the *persistent* approach, one consolidated record is maintained, and all applications draw on that one "golden record" for the common data. Thus, considerable work is necessary to push all data captured in each application to the persistent record so that the record contains the most recent values and to go to the persistent record when any system needs common data. Data redundancy is possible with the persistent approach because each application database may also maintain a local version of any data elements at its discretion, even those maintained in the persistent consolidated table. This is a pure consolidated data integration approach for master data.

It is important to realize that MDM is not intended to replace a data warehouse, principally because only master data and usually only current master data are integrated, whereas a data warehouse needs a historical view of both master and transactional data. MDM is strictly about getting a single view of data about each instance for each master data type. A data warehouse, however, might be (and often is) one of the systems that uses master data, either as a source to feed the warehouse or as an extension of the warehouse for the most current data when warehouse users want to drill through to source data. MDM does do data cleansing, similar to what is done with data warehousing. For this reason, MDM also is not an operational data store (see Chapter 9 for a description of ODSs). MDM is also considered by most people to be part of the data infrastructure of an organization, whereas an ODS, and even data warehousing, are considered application platforms.

DATA INTEGRATION: AN OVERVIEW

Many databases, especially enterprise-level databases, are built by consolidating data from existing internal and external data sources possibly with new data to support new applications. Most organizations have different databases for different purposes (see Chapter 1), some for transaction processing in different parts of the enterprise (e.g., production planning, control, and order entry); some for local, tactical, or strategic decision making (e.g., for product pricing and sales forecasting); and some for enterprise-wide coordination and decision making (e.g., for customer relationship management and supply chain management). Organizations are diligently working to break down silos of data, yet allow some degree of local autonomy. To achieve this coordination, at times data must be integrated across disparate data sources.

It is safe to say that you cannot avoid dealing with data integration issues. As a database professional or even a user of a database created from other existing data sources, there are many data integration concepts you should understand to do your job or to understand the issues you might face. This is the purpose of the following sections of this chapter.

We have already studied one such data integration approach, data warehousing, in Chapter 9. Data warehousing creates data stores to support decision making and business intelligence. We will review in a subsequent section how data are brought together through an ETL process into what we called in Chapter 9 the *reconciled data layer* of the data warehousing approach to data integration. But before we dig in to this approach in detail, it is helpful to overview the two other general approaches, data federation and data propagation, that can be used for data integration, each with a different purpose and each being ideal approaches under different circumstances.

General Approaches to Data Integration

Data integration creates a unified view of business data. This view can be created via a variety of techniques, which we will outline in the following subsections. However, data integration is not the only way data can be consolidated across an enterprise. Other ways to consolidate data are as follows (White, 2000):

- *Application integration* Achieved by coordinating the flow of event information between business applications (a service-oriented architecture can facilitate application integration)

- *Business process integration* Achieved by tighter coordination of activities across business processes (e.g., selling and billing) so that applications can be shared and more application integration can occur
- *User interaction integration* Achieved by creating fewer user interfaces that feed different data systems (e.g., using an enterprise portal to interact with different data reporting and business intelligence systems)

Core to any method of data integration are techniques to capture changed data (**changed data capture [CDC]**), so only data that have changed need to be refreshed by the integration methods. Changed data can be identified by flags or a date of last update (which, if it is after the last integration action, indicates new data to integrate). Alternatively, transaction logs can be analyzed to see which data were updated when.

Three techniques form the building blocks of any data integration approach: data consolidation, data federation, and data propagation. Data consolidation is exemplified by the ETL processes used for data warehousing; we devote later sections of this chapter to an extensive explanation of this approach. The other two approaches are overviewed here. A detailed comparison of the three approaches is presented in Table 10-3.

DATA FEDERATION **Data federation** provides a virtual view of integrated data (as if they were all in one database) without actually bringing the data all into one physical, centralized database. Rather, when an application wants data, a federation engine (no, not from the *Starship Enterprise*!) retrieves relevant data from the actual sources (in real time) and sends the result to the requesting application (so the federation engine looks like a database to the requesting application). Data transformations are done dynamically as needed. Enterprise information integration (EII) is one common term used to apply to data federation approaches. XML is often used as the vehicle for transferring data and metadata between data sources and application servers.

A main advantage of the federation approach is access to current data: There is no delay due to infrequent refreshes of a consolidated data store. Another advantage is that this approach hides the intricacies of other applications and the way data

Changed data capture (CDC)
Technique that indicates which data have changed since the last data integration activity.

Data federation
A technique for data integration that provides a virtual view of integrated data without actually creating one centralized database.

TABLE 10-3 Comparison of Consolidation, Federation, and Propagation Forms of Data Integration

Method	Pros	Cons
Consolidation (ETL)	• Users are isolated from conflicting workloads on source systems, especially updates. • It is possible to retain history, not just current values. • A data store designed for specific requirements can be accessed quickly. • It works well when the scope of data needs are anticipated in advance. • Data transformations can be batched for greater efficiency.	• Network, storage, and data maintenance costs can be high. • Performance can degrade when the data warehouse becomes quite large (with some technologies).
Federation (EII)	• Data are always current (like relational views) when requested. • It is simple for the calling application. • It works well for read-only applications because only requested data need to be retrieved. • It is ideal when copies of source data are not allowed. • Dynamic ETL is possible when one cannot anticipate data integration needs in advance or when there is a one-time need.	• Heavy workloads are possible for each request due to performing all integration tasks for each request. • Write access to data sources may not be supported.
Propagation (EAI & EDR)	• Data are available in near real time. • It is possible to work with ETL for real-time data warehousing. • Transparent access is available to the data source.	• There is considerable (but background) overhead associated with synchronizing duplicate data.

are stored in them from a given query or application. However, the workload can be quite burdensome for large amounts of data or for applications that need frequent data integration activities. Federation requires some form of a distributed query to be composed and run, but EII technology will hide this from the query writer or application developer. Federation works best for query and reporting (read-only) applications and when security of data, which can be concentrated at the source of data, is of high importance. The federation approach is also used as a stop-gap technique until more tightly integrated databases and applications can be built.

DATA PROPAGATION   This approach duplicates data across databases, usually with near-real-time delay. Data are pushed to duplicate sites as updates occur (so-called event-driven propagation). These updates can be synchronous (a true distributed database technique in which a transaction does not complete until all copies of the data are updated; see Chapter 13 on the book's Web site) or asynchronous, which decouples the updates to the remote copies. Enterprise application integration (EAI) and enterprise data replication (EDR) techniques are used for data propagation.

The major advantage of the data propagation approach to data integration is the near-real-time cascading of data changes throughout the organization. Very specialized technologies are needed for data propagation in order to achieve high performance and to handle frequent updates. Real-time data warehousing applications, which were discussed in Chapter 9, require data propagation (what are often called "trickle feeds" in data warehousing).

DATA INTEGRATION FOR DATA WAREHOUSING: THE RECONCILED DATA LAYER

Now that you have studied data integration approaches in general, let's look at one approach in detail. Although we detail only one approach, there are many activities in common across all approaches. These common tasks include extracting data from source systems, identity matching to match records from different source systems that pertain to the same entity instance (e.g., the same customer), cleansing data into a value all users agree is the true value for that data, transforming data into the desired format and detail users want to share, and loading the reconciled data into a shared view or storage location.

As indicated in Chapter 9 in Figure 9-5, we use the term *reconciled data* to refer to the data layer associated with the operational data store and enterprise data warehouse. This is the term IBM used in 1993 to describe data warehouse architectures. Although the term is not widely used, it accurately describes the nature of the data that should appear in the data warehouse as the result of the ETL process. An EDW or ODS usually is a normalized, relational database because it needs the flexibility to support a wide variety of decision support needs.

Characteristics of Data After ETL

The goal of the ETL process is to provide a single, authoritative source for data that support decision making. Ideally, this data layer has the following characteristics:

1. *Detailed*   The data are detailed (rather than summarized), providing maximum flexibility for various user communities to structure the data to best suit their needs.
2. *Historical*   The data are periodic (or point-in-time) to provide a historical perspective.
3. *Normalized*   The data are fully normalized (i.e., third normal form or higher). (We discussed normalization in Chapter 4.) Normalized data provide greater integrity and flexibility of use than denormalized data do. Denormalization is not necessary to improve performance because reconciled data are usually accessed periodically using batch processes. We will see, however, that some popular data warehouse data structures are denormalized.

4. *Comprehensive* Reconciled data reflect an enterprise-wide perspective, whose design conforms to the enterprise data model.
5. *Timely* Except for real-time data warehousing, data need not be (near) real time, but data must be current enough that decision making can react in a timely manner.
6. *Quality controlled* Reconciled data must be of unquestioned quality and integrity because they are summarized into the data marts and used for decision making.

Notice that these characteristics of reconciled data are quite different from the typical operational data from which they are derived. Operational data are typically detailed, but they differ strongly in the other four dimensions described earlier:

1. Operational data are transient rather than historical.
2. Operational data are not normalized. Depending on their roots, operational data may never have been normalized or may have been denormalized for performance reasons.
3. Rather than being comprehensive, operational data are generally restricted in scope to a particular application.
4. Operational data are often of poor quality, with numerous types of inconsistencies and errors.

The data reconciliation process is responsible for transforming operational data to reconciled data. Because of the sharp differences between these two types of data, data reconciliation clearly is the most difficult and technically challenging part of building a data warehouse. The Data Warehousing Institute supports this claim, finding that 60 to 80 percent of work on a business intelligence project, often the reason for data warehousing, is spent on ETL activities (Eckerson and White, 2003). Fortunately, several sophisticated software products are available to assist with this activity. (See Krudop, 2005, for a summary of why ETL tools are useful and how to successfully implement them in an organization.)

The ETL Process

Data reconciliation occurs in two stages during the process of filling an enterprise data warehouse:

1. During an initial load, when the EDW is first created
2. During subsequent updates (normally performed on a periodic basis) to keep the EDW current and/or to expand it

Data reconciliation can be visualized as a process, shown in Figure 10-1, consisting of five steps: mapping and metadata management (the result shown as a metadata repository in Figure 10-1), capture, scrub, transform, and load and index. In reality, the steps may be combined in different ways. For example, data capture and scrub might be combined as a single process, or scrub and transform might be combined. Typically, data rejected from the cleansing step cause messages to be sent to the appropriate operational systems to fix the data at the source and to be resent in a later extract. Figure 10-1 actually simplifies ETL considerably. Eckerson (2003) outlines seven components of an ETL process, whereas Kimball (2004) outlines 38 subsystems of ETL. We do not have space to detail all of these subsystems. The fact that there are as many as 38 subsystems highlights why so much time is spent on ETL for data warehousing and why selecting ETL tools can be so important and difficult. We discuss mapping and metadata management, capture, scrub, and load and index next, followed by a thorough discussion of transform.

MAPPING AND METADATA MANAGEMENT ETL begins with a design step in which data (detailed or aggregate) needed in the warehouse are mapped back to the source data to be used to compose the warehouse data. This mapping could be shown graphically or in a simple matrix with rows as source data elements, columns as data warehouse table columns, and the cells as explanations of any reformatting, transformations, and cleansing actions to be done. The process flows take the source data through various steps of

FIGURE 10-1 **Steps in data reconciliation**

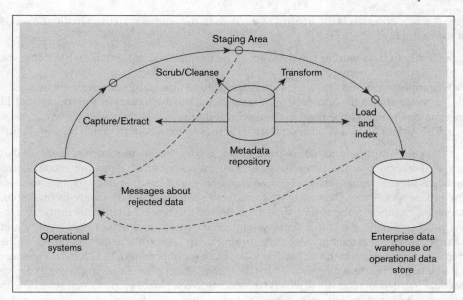

consolidation, merging, de-duping, and simply conversion into one consistent stream of jobs to feed the scrubbing and transformation steps. And to do this mapping, which involves selecting the most reliable source for data, one must have good metadata sufficient to understand fine differences between apparently the same data in multiple sources. Metadata are then created to explain the mapping and job flow process. This mapping and any further information needed (e.g., explanation of why certain sources were chosen, the timing and frequencies of extracts needed to create the desired target data) are documented in a metadata repository. Choosing among several sources for target warehouse data is based on the kinds of data quality characteristics discussed earlier in this chapter.

EXTRACT   Capturing the relevant data from the source files and databases used to fill the EDW is typically called *extracting*. Usually, not all data contained in the various operational source systems are required; just a subset is required. Extracting the subset of data is based on an extensive analysis of both the source and target systems, which is best performed by a team directed by data administration and composed of both end users and data warehouse professionals.

Technically, an alternative to this classical beginning to the ETL process is supported by a newer class of tools called enterprise application integration (EAI), which we outlined earlier in this chapter. EAI tools enable event-driven (i.e., real-time) data to be captured and used in an integrated way across disparate source systems. EAI can be used to capture data when they change not on a periodic basis, which is common of many ETL processes. So-called trickle feeds are important for the real-time data warehouse architecture to support active business intelligence. EAI tools can also be used to feed ETL tools, which often have richer abilities for cleansing and transformation.

The two generic types of data extracts are static extract and incremental extract. Static extract is used to fill the data warehouse initially, and incremental extract is used for ongoing warehouse maintenance. **Static extract** is a method of capturing a snapshot of the required source data at a point in time. The view of the source data is independent of the time at which it was created. **Incremental extract** captures only the changes that have occurred in the source data since the last capture. The most common method is log capture. Recall that the database log contains after images that record the most recent changes to database records (see Figure 9-6). With log capture, only images that are logged after the last capture are selected from the log.

English (1999a) and White (2000) address in detail the steps necessary to qualify which systems of record and other data sources to use for extraction into the staging

Static extract

A method of capturing a snapshot of the required source data at a point in time.

Incremental extract

A method of capturing only the changes that have occurred in the source data since the last capture.

area. A major criterion is the quality of the data in the source systems. Quality depends on the following:

- Clarity of data naming, so the warehouse designers know exactly what data exist in a source system
- Completeness and accuracy of business rules enforced by a source system, which directly affects the accuracy of data; also, the business rules in the source should match the rules to be used in the data warehouse
- The format of data (Common formats across sources help to match related data.)

It is also important to have agreements with the owners of source systems so that they will inform the data warehouse administrators when changes are made in the metadata for the source system. Because transaction systems frequently change to meet new business needs and to utilize new and better software and hardware technologies, managing changes in the source systems is one of the biggest challenges of the extraction process. Changes in the source system require a reassessment of data quality and the procedures for extracting and transforming data. These procedures map data in the source systems to data in the target data warehouse (or data marts). For each data element in the data warehouse, a map says which data from which source systems to use to derive that data; transformation rules, which we address in a separate section, then state how to perform the derivation. For custom-built source systems, a data warehouse administrator has to develop customized maps and extraction routines; predefined map templates can be purchased for some packaged application software, such as ERP systems.

Extraction may be done by routines written with tools associated with the source system, say, a tool to export data. Data are usually extracted in a neutral data format, such as comma-delimited ANSI format. Sometimes the SQL command SELECT...INTO can be used to create a table. Once the data sources have been selected and extraction routines written, data can be moved into the staging area, where the cleansing process begins.

CLEANSE   It is generally accepted that one role of the ETL process (as with any other data integration activity) is to identify erroneous data, not fix them. Experts generally agree that fixes should be made in the appropriate source systems, so such erroneous data, created by systematic procedural mistakes, do not reoccur. Rejected data are eliminated from further ETL steps and will be reprocessed in the next feed from the relevant source system. Some data can be fixed by cleansing so that loading data into the warehouse is not delayed. In any case, messages need to be sent to the offending source system(s) to prevent future errors or confusions.

Poor data quality is the bane of ETL. In fact, it is the bane of all information systems ("garbage in, garbage out"). Unfortunately, this has always been true and remains so. Eckerson and White (2003) found that ensuring adequate data quality was the number-one challenge of ETL, followed closely by understanding source data, a highly related issue. Procedures should be in place to ensure data are captured "correctly" at the source. But what is correct depends on the source system, so the cleansing step of ETL must, at a minimum, resolve differences between what each source believes is quality data. The issue may be timing; that is, one system is ahead of another on updating common or related data. (As you will see later, time is a very important factor in data warehouses, so it is important for data warehousing to understand the time stamp for a piece of data.) So there is a need for further data quality steps to be taken during ETL.

Data in the operational systems are of poor quality or are inconsistent across source systems for many common reasons, including data entry errors by employees and customers, changes to the source systems, bad and inconsistent metadata, and system errors or corrupted data from the extract process. You cannot assume that data are clean even when the source system works fine (e.g., the source system may have used default but inaccurate values). Some of the errors and inconsistencies typical of these data that can be troublesome to data warehousing are as follows:

1. Misspelled names and addresses, odd formats for names and addresses (e.g., leading spaces, multiple spaces between words, missing periods for abbreviations, use of different capitalizations like all caps instead of upper- and lowercase letters)

2. Impossible or erroneous dates of birth
3. Fields used for purposes for which they were not intended or for different purposes in different table rows (essentially, multiple meanings for the same column)
4. Mismatched addresses and area codes
5. Missing data
6. Duplicate data
7. Inconsistencies (e.g., different addresses) in values or formats across sources (e.g., data could be kept at different levels of detail or for different time periods)
8. Different primary keys across sources

Thorough data cleansing involves detecting such errors and repairing them and preventing them from occurring in the future. Some of these types of errors can be corrected during cleansing, and the data can be made ready for loading; in any case, source system owners need to be informed of errors so that processes can be fixed in the source systems to prevent such errors from occurring in the future.

Let's consider some examples of such errors. Customer names are often used as primary keys or as search criteria in customer files. However, these names are often misspelled or spelled in various ways in these files. For example, the name The Coca-Cola Company is the correct name for the soft-drink company. This name may be entered in customer records as Coca-Cola, Coca Cola, TCCC, and so on. In one study, a company found that the name McDonald's could be spelled 100 different ways!

A feature of many ETL tools is the ability to parse text fields to assist in discerning synonyms and misspellings, and also to reformat data. For example, name and address fields, which could be extracted from source systems in varying formats, can be parsed to identify each component of the name and address so they can be stored in the data warehouse in a standardized way and can be used to help match records from different source systems. These tools can also often correct name misspellings and resolve address discrepancies. In fact, matched records can be found through address analysis.

Another type of data pollution occurs when a field is used for purposes for which it was not intended. For example, in one bank, a record field was designed to hold a telephone number. However, branch managers who had no such use for this field instead stored the interest rate in it. Another example, reported by a major UK bank, was even more bizarre. The data-scrubbing program turned up a customer on their files whose occupation was listed as "steward on the *Titanic*" (Devlin, 1997).

You may wonder why such errors are so common in operational data. The quality of operational data is largely determined by the value of data to the organization responsible for gathering them. Unfortunately, it often happens that the data-gathering organization places a low value on some data whose accuracy is important to downstream applications, such as data warehousing.

Given the common occurrence of errors, the worst thing a company can do is simply copy operational data to the data warehouse. Instead, it is important to improve the quality of the source data through a technique called data scrubbing. **Data scrubbing** (also called data cleansing) involves using pattern recognition and other techniques to upgrade the quality of raw data before transforming them and moving the data to a data warehouse. How to scrub each piece of data varies by attribute, so considerable analysis goes into the design of each ETL scrubbing step. Also, the data scrubbing techniques must be reassessed each time changes are made to the source system. Some scrubbing will reject obviously bad data outright, and the source system will be sent a message to fix the erroneous data and get them ready for the next extract. Other results from scrubbing may flag the data for more detailed manual analysis (e.g., why did one salesperson sell more than three times any other salesperson?) before rejecting the data.

Successful data warehousing requires that a formal program in TQM be implemented. TQM focuses on defect prevention rather than defect correction. Although data scrubbing can help upgrade data quality, it is not a long-term solution to the data quality problem. (See the earlier section in this chapter on TQM in data quality management.)

Data scrubbing

A process of using pattern recognition and other artificial intelligence techniques to upgrade the quality of raw data before transforming and moving the data to the data warehouse. Also called data cleansing.

The type of data cleansing required depends on the quality of data in the source system. Besides fixing the types of problems identified earlier, other common cleansing tasks include the following:

- Decoding data to make them understandable for data warehousing applications.
- Parsing text fields to break them into finer components (e.g., breaking apart an address field into its constituent parts).
- Standardizing data, such as in the prior example for variations on customer names; standardization involves even simple actions such as using fixed vocabularies across all values (e.g., Inc. for incorporated and Jr. for junior).
- Reformatting and changing data types and performing other functions to put data from each source into the standard data warehouse format, ready for transformation.
- Adding time stamps to distinguish values for the same attribute over time.
- Converting between different units of measure.
- Generating primary keys for each row of a table. (We discuss the formation of data warehouse table primary and foreign keys later in this chapter.)
- Matching and merging separate extractions into one table or file and matching data to go into the same row of the generated table. (This can be a very difficult process when different keys are used in different source systems, when naming conventions are different, and when the data in the source systems are erroneous.)
- Logging errors detected, fixing those errors, and reprocessing corrected data without creating duplicate entries.
- Finding missing data to complete the batch of data necessary for subsequent loading.

The order in which different data sources are processed may matter. For example, it may be necessary to process customer data from a sales system before new customer demographic data from an external system can be matched to customers.

Once data are cleansed in the staging area, the data are ready for transformation. Before we discuss the transformation process in some detail, however, we briefly review in the next section the procedures used to load data into the data warehouse or data marts. It makes sense to discuss transformation after discussing load. There is a trend in data warehousing to reformulate ETL into ELT, utilizing the power of the data warehouse technology to assist in the cleansing and transformation activities.

LOAD AND INDEX The last step in filling an enterprise data warehouse (see Figure 10-1) is to load the selected data into the target data warehouse and to create the necessary indexes. The two basic modes for loading data to the target EDW are refresh and update.

Refresh mode

An approach to filling a data warehouse that involves bulk rewriting of the target data at periodic intervals.

Update mode

An approach to filling a data warehouse in which only changes in the source data are written to the data warehouse.

Refresh mode is an approach to filling a data warehouse that involves bulk rewriting of the target data at periodic intervals. That is, the target data are written initially to fill the warehouse. Then, at periodic intervals, the warehouse is rewritten, replacing the previous contents. This mode has become less popular than update mode.

Update mode is an approach in which only changes in the source data are written to the data warehouse. To support the periodic nature of warehouse data, these new records are usually written to the data warehouse without overwriting or deleting previous records (see Figure 9-8).

As you would expect, refresh mode is generally used to fill a warehouse when it is first created. Update mode is then generally used for ongoing maintenance of the target warehouse. Refresh mode is used in conjunction with static data capture, whereas update mode is used in conjunction with incremental data capture.

With both refresh and update modes, it is necessary to create and maintain the indexes that are used to manage the warehouse data. Two types of indexing, called *bit-mapped indexing* and *join indexing* (see Chapter 5), are often used in a data warehouse environment.

Because a data warehouse keeps historical data, integrated from disparate source systems, it is often important to those who use the data warehouse to know where the data came from. Metadata may provide this information about specific attributes, but the metadata, too, must show history (e.g., the source may change over time). More detailed procedures may be necessary if there are multiple sources or if knowing which specific extract or load file placed the data in the warehouse or what transformation routine created the data. (This may be necessary for uncovering the source of errors discovered in the warehouse.) Variar (2002) outlines the intricacies of tracing the origins of warehouse data.

Westerman (2001), based on the highly publicized and successful data warehousing at Wal-Mart Corporation, discusses factors in determining how frequently to update the data warehouse. His guideline is to update a data warehouse as frequently as is practical. Infrequent updating causes massive loads and requires users to wait for new data. Near-real-time loads are necessary for active data warehousing but may be inefficient and unnecessary for most data-mining and analysis applications. Westerman suggests that daily updates are sufficient for most organizations. (Statistics show that 75 percent of organizations do daily updates.) However, daily updates make it impossible to react to some changing conditions, such as repricing or changing purchase orders for slow-moving items. Wal-Mart updates its data warehouse continuously, which is practical given the massively parallel data warehouse technology it uses. The industry trend is toward updates several times a day, in near-real-time, and less use of more infrequent refresh intervals, such as monthly (Agosta, 2003).

Loading data into a warehouse typically means appending new rows to tables in the warehouse. It may also mean updating existing rows with new data (e.g., to fill in missing values from an additional data source), and it may mean purging identified data from the warehouse that have become obsolete due to age or that were incorrectly loaded in a prior load operation. Data may be loaded from the staging area into a warehouse by the following:

- SQL commands (e.g., INSERT or UPDATE)
- Special load utilities provided by the data warehouse vendor or a third-party vendor
- Custom-written routines coded by the warehouse administrators (a very common practice, which uses the previously mentioned two approaches)

In any case, these routines must not only update the data warehouse but must also generate error reports to show rejected data (e.g., attempting to append a row with a duplicate key or updating a row that does not exist in a table of the data warehouse).

Load utilities may work in batch or continuous mode. With a utility, you write a script that defines the format of the data in the staging area and which staging area data maps to which data warehouse fields. The utility may be able to convert data types for a field in the staging area to the target field in the warehouse and may be able to perform IF...THEN...ELSE logic to handle staging area data in various formats or to direct input data to different data warehouse tables. The utility can purge all data in a warehouse table (DELETE * FROM *tablename*) before data loading (refresh mode) or can append new rows (update mode). The utility may be able to sort input data so that rows are appended before they are updated. The utility program runs as would any stored procedure for the DBMS, and ideally all the controls of the DBMS for concurrency as well as restart and recovery in case of a DBMS failure during loading will work. Because the execution of a load can be very time-consuming, it is critical to be able to restart a load from a checkpoint in case the DBMS crashes in the middle of executing a load. See Chapter 12 for a thorough discussion of restart and recovery of databases.

DATA TRANSFORMATION

Data transformation (or transform) is at the very center of the data reconciliation process. **Data transformation** involves converting data from the format of the source operational systems to the format of the enterprise data warehouse. Data transformation accepts data from the data capture component (after data scrubbing, if it applies), maps the data to the format of the reconciled data layer, and then passes the data to the load and index component.

Data transformation

The component of data reconciliation that converts data from the format of the source operational systems to the format of the enterprise data warehouse.

Data transformation may range from a simple change in data format or representation to a highly complex exercise in data integration. Following are three examples that illustrate this range:

1. A salesperson requires a download of customer data from a mainframe database to her laptop computer. In this case, the transformation required is simply mapping the data from EBCDIC to ASCII representation, which can easily be performed by off-the-shelf software.
2. A manufacturing company has product data stored in three different legacy systems: a manufacturing system, a marketing system, and an engineering application. The company needs to develop a consolidated view of these product data. Data transformation involves several different functions, including resolving different key structures, converting to a common set of codes, and integrating data from different sources. These functions are quite straightforward, and most of the necessary software can be generated using a standard commercial software package with a graphical interface.
3. A large health-care organization manages a geographically dispersed group of hospitals, clinics, and other care centers. Because many of the units have been obtained through acquisition over time, the data are heterogeneous and uncoordinated. For a number of important reasons, the organization needs to develop a data warehouse to provide a single corporate view of the enterprise. This effort will require the full range of transformation functions described next, including some custom software development.

The functions performed in data scrubbing and the functions performed in data transformation blend together. In general, the goal of data scrubbing is to correct errors in data *values* in the source data, whereas the goal of data transformation is to convert the data *format* from the source to the target system. Note that it is essential to scrub the data before they are transformed because if there are errors in the data before they are transformed, the errors will remain in the data after transformation.

Data Transformation Functions

Data transformation encompasses a variety of different functions. These functions may be classified broadly into two categories: record-level functions and field-level functions. In most data warehousing applications, a combination of some or even all of these functions is required.

RECORD-LEVEL FUNCTIONS   Operating on a set of records, such as a file or table, the most important record-level functions are selection, joining, normalization, and aggregation.

Selection

The process of partitioning data according to predefined criteria.

   Selection (also called subsetting) is the process of partitioning data according to predefined criteria. For data warehouse applications, selection is used to extract the relevant data from the source systems that will be used to fill the data warehouse. In fact, selection is typically a part of the capture function discussed earlier. When the source data are relational, SQL SELECT statements can be used for selection. (See Chapter 6 for a detailed discussion.) For example, recall that incremental capture is often implemented by selecting after images from the database log that have been created since the previous capture. A typical after image was shown in Figure 9-6. Suppose that the after images for this application are stored in a table named AccountHistory_T. Then the after images that have been created after 12/31/2015 can be selected with the following statements:

```
SELECT *
FROM AccountHistory_T
WHERE CreateDate > 12/31/2015;
```

Joining

The process of combining data from various sources into a single table or view.

   Joining combines data from various sources into a single table or view. Data joining is an important function in data warehouse applications because it is often necessary to consolidate data from various sources. For example, an insurance company may have client data spread throughout several different files and databases. When the source data are relational, SQL statements can be used to perform a join operation. (See Chapter 6 for details.)

Joining is often complicated by factors such as the following:

- Often the source data are not relational (the extracts are flat files), in which case SQL statements cannot be used. Instead, procedural language statements must be coded or the data must first be moved into a staging area that uses an RDBMS.
- Even for relational data, primary keys for the tables to be joined are often from different domains (e.g., engineering part number versus catalog number). These keys must then be reconciled before an SQL join can be performed.
- Source data may contain errors, which makes join operations hazardous.

Normalization is the process of decomposing relations with anomalies to produce smaller, well-structured relations. (See Chapter 4 for a detailed discussion.) As indicated earlier, source data in operational systems are often denormalized (or simply not normalized). The data must therefore be normalized as part of data transformation.

Aggregation is the process of transforming data from a detailed level to a summary level. For example, in a retail business, individual sales transactions can be summarized to produce total sales by store, product, date, and so on. Because (in our model) the enterprise data warehouse contains only detailed data, aggregation is not normally associated with this component. However, aggregation is an important function in filling the data marts, as explained next.

Aggregation
The process of transforming data from a detailed level to a summary level.

FIELD-LEVEL FUNCTIONS A field-level function converts data from a given format in a source record to a different format in the target record. Field-level functions are of two types: single-field and multifield functions.

A *single-field* transformation converts data from a single source field to a single target field. Figure 10-2a is a basic representation of this type of transformation (designated by the letter *T* in the diagram). An example of a single-field transformation is converting a textual representation, such as Yes/No, into a numeric 1/0 representation.

As shown in Figures 10-2b and 10-2c, there are two basic methods for performing a single-field transformation: algorithmic and table lookup. An algorithmic transformation is performed using a formula or logical expression. Figure 10-2b shows

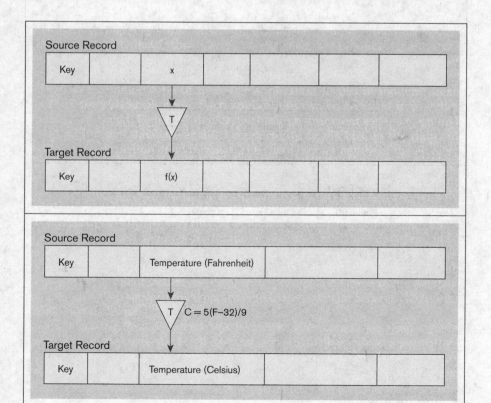

FIGURE 10-2 Single-field transformations
(a) Basic representation

(b) Algorithmic

FIGURE 10-2 (*continued*)
(c) Table lookup

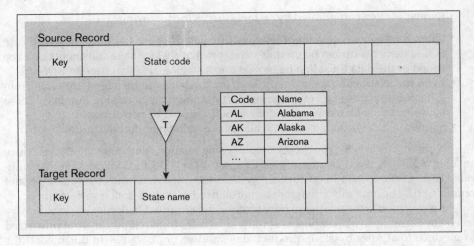

a conversion from Fahrenheit to Celsius temperature using a formula. When a simple algorithm does not apply, a lookup table can be used instead. Figure 10-2c shows the use of a table to convert state codes to state names. (This type of conversion is common in data warehouse applications.)

A *multifield* transformation converts data from one or more source fields to one or more target fields. This type of transformation is very common in data warehouse applications. Two multifield transformations are shown in Figure 10-3.

FIGURE 10-3 Multifield transformations
(a) Many sources to one target

(b) One source to many targets

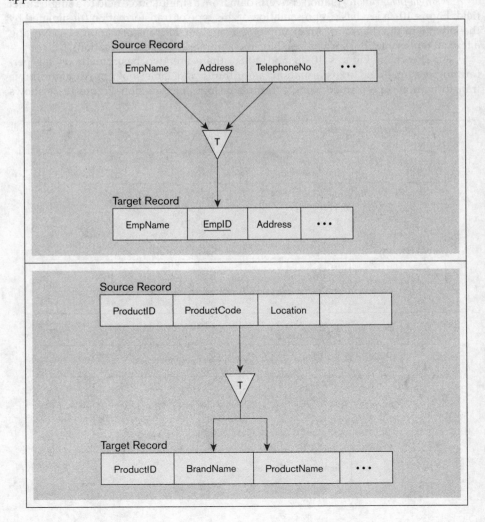

Figure 10-3a is an example of a many-to-one transformation. (In this case, two source fields are mapped to one target field.) In the source record, the combination of employee name and telephone number is used as the primary key. This combination is awkward and may not uniquely identify a person. Therefore, in creating a target record, the combination is mapped to a unique employee ID (EmpID). A lookup table would be created to support this transformation. A data scrubbing program might be employed to help identify duplicates in the source data.

Figure 10-3b is an example of a one-to-many transformation. (In this case, one source field has been converted to two target fields.) In the source record, a product code has been used to encode the combination of brand name and product name. (The use of such codes is common in operational data.) However, in the target record, it is desired to display the full text describing product and brand names. Again, a lookup table would be employed for this purpose.

In Figure 10-3, the multifield transformations shown involve only one source record and one target record. More generally, multifield transformations may involve more than one source record and/or more than one target record. In the most complex cases, these records may even originate in different operational systems and in different time zones (Devlin, 1997).

Summary

Ensuring the quality of data that enter databases and data warehouses is essential if users are to have confidence in their systems. Ensuring data quality is also now mandated by regulations such as the Sarbanes-Oxley Act and the Basel II Accord. Data quality is often a key part of an overall data governance initiative. Data governance is often the backbone of enterprise data management initiatives in an organization. Data integration, master data management, and data security are other activities that are often part of enterprise data management.

Many organizations today do not have proactive data quality programs, and poor quality data are a widespread problem. A proactive data quality program will start with a good business case to address any organizational barriers, be a part of an overall data governance program, employ the use of data stewards, apply proven TQM principles and practices, and use modern data management software technology. Data quality is of special concern when data are integrated across sources from inside and outside the organization. Fairly modern techniques of data integration—consolidation (including ETL for data warehouses), federation, propagation, and master data management—are vastly improving opportunities for sharing data while allowing for local controls and databases optimized for local uses.

Chapter Review

Key Terms

Aggregation 445	Data federation 436	Incremental extract 439	Selection 444
Changed data capture (CDC) 436	Data governance 426	Joining 444	Static extract 439
	Data scrubbing 441	Master data management (MDM) 434	Update mode 442
Chief data officer (CDO) 432	Data steward 427		
	Data transformation 443	Refresh mode 442	

Review Questions

10-1. Define each of the following terms:
   a. static extract
   b. incremental extract
   c. chief data officer
   d. master data management
   e. refresh mode

10-2. Match the following terms and definitions:
   _____ data transformation   a. converts data formats
   _____ data scrubbing   b. corrects errors in source data

   _____ selection

   _____ data steward

   _____ changed data capture

   c. partitioning of data based on predefined criteria
   d. oversees data quality for a particular data subject
   e. information needed in order to integrate updated data

10-3. Contrast the following terms:
   a. static extract; incremental extract
   b. data scrubbing; data transformation

c. consolidation; federation

d. ETL; master data management

10-4. What are the key activities that are often the focus of enterprise data management initiatives?

10-5. What are the key components of a data governance program? How does data stewardship relate to data governance?

10-6. What are four reasons why data quality is important to an organization?

10-7. Explain the effect of the Sarbanes-Oxley Act on the need for organizations to improve data quality.

10-8. Define the eight characteristics of quality data.

10-9. Explain four reasons why the quality of data is poor in many organizations.

10-10. Describe the key steps to improve data quality in an organization.

10-11. What is data profiling, and what role does it play in a data quality program?

10-12. What are the four dimensions along which the impact of poor quality can be measured?

10-13. How can data capture processes be improved to improve data quality?

10-14. Why is master data management important in an organization?

10-15. Describe the three major approaches to master data management.

10-16. What are the major differences between the data federation and data propagation forms of data integration?

10-17. What distinguishes master data management from other forms of data integration?

10-18. List six typical characteristics of reconciled data.

10-19. List and briefly describe five steps in the data reconciliation process.

10-20. List five errors and inconsistencies that are commonly found in operational data.

10-21. Explain how the phrase "extract–transform–load" relates to the data reconciliation process.

10-22. List common tasks performed during data cleansing.

10-23. Describe some field-level and record-level data transformations that often occur during the ETL process for loading a data warehouse.

10-24. How has XML helped in bridging the legacy data with web applications?

10-25. What are the security issues of web related databases? Explain.

10-26. What is the significance of ETL process? Explain Extraction, Transformation, and Loading.

10-27. What are the data quality challenges? Why is data quality critical?

Problems and Exercises

Problems 10-29 through 10-33 are based on the Fitchwood Insurance Company case study, which was described in the Problems and Exercises for Chapter 9, and the associated Figure 9-21.

10-28. The OLTP system data for the Fitchwood Insurance Company is in a series of flat files. What process do you envision would be needed in order to extract the data and create the ERD shown in Figure 9-21? How often should the extraction process be performed? Should it be a static extract or an incremental extract?

10-29. What types of data pollution/cleansing problems might occur with the Fitchwood OLTP system data?

10-30. Research some tools that perform data scrubbing. What tool would you recommend for the Fitchwood Insurance Company?

10-31. What types of data transformations might be needed in order to build the Fitchwood data mart?

10-32. After some further analysis, you discover that the commission field in the Policies table is updated yearly to reflect changes in the annual commission paid to agents on existing policies. Would knowing this information change the way in which you extract and load data into the data mart from the OLTP system?

 PINE VALLEY FURNITURE

10-33. Any successful data governance program needs to address the people ("who"), process ("how"), and technology ("what") aspects. Based on your reading of Chapter 10, provide some examples for each of these categories.

10-34. Examine the set of activities in Table 10-2 and categorize them as belonging to one of the following categories: people ("who"), process ("how"), and technology ("what").

10-35. The Pine Valley databases for this textbook (one small version illustrated in queries throughout the text and a larger version) are available to your instructor to download from the text's Web site. Your instructor can make those databases available to you. Alternatively, these and other databases are available at **www.teradatauniversitynetwork.com** (your instructor will tell you the login password, and you will need to register and then create an SQL Assistant login for the parts of this question). There may actually be another database your instructor wants you to use for this series of questions. Regardless of how you gain access to a database, answer the following exercises for that database.

a. Develop a plan for performing a data profile analysis on this database. Base your plan on the eight characteristics of quality data, on other concepts introduced in the chapter, and on a set of business rules you will need to create for this database. Justify your plan.

b. Perform your data profile plan for one of the tables in the database (pick the table you think might be the most vulnerable to data quality issues). Develop an audit report on the quality of data in this table.

c. Execute your data profile plan for a set of three or four related tables. Develop an audit report on the quality of data in these tables.

d. Based on the potential errors you discover in the data in the previous two exercises (assuming that you find some potential errors), recommend some ways the capture of the erroneous data could be improved to prevent errors in future data entry for this type of data.

e. Evaluate the ERD for the database. (You may have to reverse-engineer the ERD if one is not available with the database.) Is this a high-quality data model? If not, how should it be changed to make it a high-quality data model?

f. Assume that you are working with a Pine Valley Furniture Company (PVFC) database in this exercise. Consider the large and small PVFC databases as two different source systems within PVFC. What type of approach would you recommend (consolidation, federation, propagation, master data management), and why, for data integration across these two databases? Presume that you do not know a specific list of queries or reports that need the integrated database; therefore, design your data integration approach to support any requirements against any data from these databases.

10-36. On page 424, we identified four dimensions along which poor data might impact a business. For a company of your choice, for example, a hospital, identify one or more scenarios that could serve as a good example for each type of impact.

10-37. Perform a search of companies and products that are available to help with data reconciliation and integration. Document your results by filling in the table below. We have provided a sample example:

Product Name	Company	Data Integration Steps Supported
Data Bridger	Taurus Software	Extract, transform, load, and index

10-38. With the kind of mind boggling and bewildering array of tools available for web development, how should one go about choosing the right combination of components to be put together for the development of a e-commerce website.

10-39. a. Refer to the Problems and Exercises given in Chapter 9—PMPL, what could be the problems with respect to data cleansing and data pollution?

b. In case the Finance department of PMPL needs a data mart from the Dimension tables what transformations are required for the data?

Field Exercises

10-40. Master data management and the related specialty customer data integration are rapidly changing disciplines. Find a recent article or book on these topics (or some other specialty area for master data management, such as in health care, operations, or human resources) and prepare a summary of new ideas introduced in that resource that expand on the discussion from this chapter.

10-41. Access the resources at Teradata University Network (**www.teradatauniversitynetwork.com**) for a Webinar or Webcast (produced after 2007) on the topic of data integration or master data management. Prepare a summary of new ideas introduced in that Webcast that expand on the discussion from this chapter.

10-42. Interview data warehouse managers in an organization where you have contacts about their ETL processes. What lessons did you learn from your interviews about the design of sound ETL processes?

10-43. Interview a data administrator in an organization that has established a data governance committee and data stewards. Document the different roles provided by the data administrator(s), data stewards, and data governance committee members. What is the charter for the data governance committee? How are issues about data planning, quality, security, and ownership resolved? What would the data administrator like to change about the data governance process, and why?

References

Agosta, L. 2003. "Data Warehouse Refresh Rates." *DM Review* 13,6 (June): 49.

Brauer, B. 2002. "Data Quality—Spinning Straw into Gold," **www2.sas.com/proceedings/sugi26/p117-26.pdf.**

Carlson, D. 2002. "Data Stewardship Action," *DM Review* 12,5 (May): 37, 62.

Devlin, B. 1997. *Data Warehouse: From Architecture to Implementation.* Reading, MA: Addison-Wesley Longman.

Dyché, J. 2007. "The Myth of the Purebred Data Steward." (February 22) available at **www.b-eye-network.com/view/3971**.

Dyché, J., and E. Levy. 2006. *Customer Data Integration: Reaching a Single Version of the Truth.* Hoboken, NJ: Wiley.

Eckerson, W. 2003. "The Evolution of ETL." *Business Intelligence Journal* (Fall): 4–8.

Eckerson, W., and C. White. 2003. *Evaluating ETL and Data Integration Platforms.* The Data Warehouse Institute, available at **www.tdwi.org**, under "Research Reports."

English, L. 1999a. *Business Information Quality: Methods for Reducing Costs and Improving Profits.* New York: Wiley.

English, L. P. 1999b. *Improving Data Warehouse and Business Information Quality.* New York: Wiley.

English, L. P. 2004. "Six Sigma and Total Information Quality Management (TIQM)." *DM Review* 14,10 (October): 44–49, 73.

Friedman, T., and M. Smith. 2011. "Measuring the Business Value of Data Quality." (October) Gartner.

Hay, D. C. 2005. "Data Model Quality: Where Good Data Begin." Published online at **www.tdan.com** (January).

Hoffer, J., J. George, and J. Valacich. 2014. *Modern Systems Analysis and Design,* 7th ed. Upper Saddle River, NJ. Prentice Hall.

Imhoff, C., and C. White. 2006. "Master Data Management: Creating a Single View of the Business," available at **www.beyeresearch.com/study/3360**.

Informatica. 2005. "Addressing Data Quality at the Enterprise Level." (October).

Inmon, B. 2004. "Data Quality." (June 24) available at **www.b-eye-network.com/view/188**.

Kimball, R. 2004. "The 38 Subsystems of ETL." *Intelligent Enterprise* 8,12 (December 4): 16, 17, 46.

Krudop, M. E. 2005. "Maximizing Your ETL Tool Investment." *DM Review* 15,3 (March): 26–28.

Laurent, W. 2005. "The Case for Data Stewardship." *DM Review* 15,2 (February): 26–28.

Lee, Y., S. Madnick, R. Wang, F. Wang, and H. Zhang. 2014. "A Cubic Framework for the Chief Data Officer: Succeeding in a World of Big Data." *MIS Quarterly Executive* 13,1: 1, 13.

Leon, M. 2007. "Escaping Information Anarchy." *DB2 Magazine* 12,1: 23–26.

Loshin, D. 2001. "The Cost of Poor Data Quality." *DM Review* (June 29) available at **www.information-management.com/infodirect/20010629/3605-1.html**.

Loshin, D. 2006. "Monitoring Data Quality Performance Using Data Quality Metrics." A white paper from Informatica (November).

Loshin, D. 2009. "The Data Quality Business Case: Projecting Return on Investment." available at **http://knowledge-integrity.com/Assets/data_quality_business_case.pdf**.

Moriarty, T. 1996. "Better Business Practices." *Database Programming & Design* 9,7 (September): 59–61.

Redman, T. 2004. "Data: An Unfolding Quality Disaster." *DM Review* 14,8 (August): 21–23, 57.

Russom, P. 2006. "Taking Data Quality to the Enterprise through Data Governance." *TDWI Report Series* (March).

Seiner, R. 2005. "Data Steward Roles & Responsibilities," available at **www.tdan.com**, July 2005.

Variar, G. 2002. "The Origin of Data." *Intelligent Enterprise* 5,2 (February 1): 37–41.

Westerman, P. 2001. *Data Warehousing: Using the Wal-Mart Model.* San Francisco: Morgan Kaufmann.

White, C. 2000. "First Analysis." *Intelligent Enterprise* 3,9 (June): 50–55.

Yugay, I., and V. Klimchenko. 2004. "SOX Mandates Focus on Data Quality & Integration." *DM Review* 14,2 (February): 38–42.

Further Reading

Eckerson, W. 2002. "Data Quality and the Bottom Line: Achieving Business Success Through a Commitment to Data Quality." **www.tdwi.org**.

Weill, P., and J. Ross. 2004. *IT Governance: How Top Performers Manage IT Decision Rights for Superior Results.* Boston: Harvard Business School Press.

Web Resources

www.knowledge-integrity.com Web site of David Loshin, a leading consultant in the data quality and business intelligence fields.

http://mitiq.mit.edu Web site for data quality research done at Massachusetts Institute of Technology.

www.tdwi.org Web site of The Data Warehousing Institute, which produces a variety of white papers, research reports, and Webinars that are available to the general public, as well as a wider array that are available only to members.

www.teradatauniversitynetwork.com The Teradata University Network, a free portal service to a wide variety of journal articles, training materials, Webinars, and other special reports on data quality, data integration, and related topics.

CHAPTER 11

Big Data and Analytics

LEARNING OBJECTIVES

After studying this chapter, you should be able to:

- Concisely define each of the following key terms: **big data, analytics, data lake, NoSQL, MapReduce, Hadoop, HDFS, Pig, Hive, business intelligence, descriptive analytics, predictive analytics, prescriptive analytics, online analytical processing, relational OLAP (ROLAP), multidimensional OLAP (MOLAP), data mining,** and **text mining.**

- Describe the reasons why data management technologies and approaches have expanded beyond relational databases and data warehousing technologies.

- List the main categories of NoSQL database management systems.

- Choose between relational databases and various types of NoSQL databases depending on the organization's data management needs.

- Describe the meaning of big data and the demands big data will place on data management technology.

- List the key technology components of a typical Hadoop environment and describe their uses.

- Articulate the differences between descriptive, predictive, and prescriptive analytics.

- Describe the impact of advances in analytics on data management technologies and practices.

INTRODUCTION

There are few terms in the context of data management that have seen such an explosive growth in interest and commercial hype as "big data," a term that is still elusive and ill-defined but at the same time widely used and applied in practice by businesses, scientists, government agencies, and not-for-profit organizations. **Big data** are data that exist in very large volumes and many different varieties (data types) and that need to be processed at a very high velocity (speed). Not surprisingly, big data analytics refers to analytics that deals with big data. We will discuss the big data concept at a more detailed level later in this chapter (including the introduction of more terms starting with a "*v,*" in addition to volume, variety, and velocity), pointing out that the concept of big data is constantly changing depending on the state of the art in technology. Big data is not a single, separate phenomenon but an umbrella term for a subset of advances in a field that emerged much earlier—analytics (also called data analytics or, in business contexts, business analytics). At its most fundamental level, **analytics** refers to systematic analysis and interpretation of data—typically using mathematical, statistical, and computational tools—to improve our understanding of a real-world domain.

Big data

Data that exist in very large volumes and many different varieties (data types) and that need to be processed at a very high velocity (speed).

Analytics

Systematic analysis and interpretation of data—typically using mathematical, statistical, and computational tools—to improve our understanding of a real-world domain.

451

What makes big data and analytics so important that an entire chapter is justified? Consider the following story (adapted from Laskowski, 2014; this source describes Gartner's Doug Laney's 55 big data success stories):

> One of the top customers of Morton's Steakhouse was on Twitter lamenting a late flight that prevented him from dining at Morton's. The company used the opportunity to create a publicity stunt and surprised the customer with a meal delivered to him prepared exactly the way he typically wanted to have it. This was possible only with sophisticated social media monitoring, detailed customer data, and the ability to bring all of this together and act on it in real time.

The technologies discussed in this chapter help organizations implement solutions that are based on real-time analysis of very large and heterogeneous data sets from a variety of sources. For example, Telefónica UK O2—the number 2 wireless communications provider in the UK—brings together network performance data and customer survey data in order to understand better and faster how to allocate its network upgrade resources in a way that provides the highest value for the company and its customers (TCSET, 2014). None of this would have been possible without big data and analytics.

For a long period of time, the most critical issue of data management was to ensure that an organization's transaction processing systems worked reliably at a reasonable cost. As discussed earlier in this book, well-designed and carefully implemented relational databases allow us to achieve those goals even in very high-volume environments (such as Web-based e-commerce systems). Chapter 9 discussed the second major step in data management—the use of data warehouses that are separate from the transactional databases for two purposes: first, to enable analytics to describe how the organization has performed in the past and second, to make possible modeling of the future based on what we have learned about the history. Data are structured in a different way for data warehousing. Particularly for large companies, the warehouses are implemented with different technical solutions (often using appliances specifically designed to work as data warehouses).

Technologies related to big data have brought us to the third era of data management. These technologies have stringent requirements: They have to (1) process much larger quantities of data than either operational databases or data warehouses do (thus requiring, for example, a high level of scalability using affordable hardware), (2) deal effectively with a broad variety of different data types (and not only textual or numeric data), and (3) adapt much better to changes in the structure of data, and thus not require a strictly predefined schema (data model) as relational databases do. These requirements are addressed with two broad families of technologies: a core big data technology called Hadoop (and its alternatives/competitors) and database management technologies under the umbrella NoSQL (these days typically interpreted as "Not only SQL" instead of "No SQL"). We will discuss both at a more detailed level later in this chapter.

This chapter starts with a brief general overview of big data as a combination of technologies and processes that make it possible for organizations to convert very large amounts of raw data into information and insights for use in business, science, health care, law, and dozens of other fields of practice. We also place the concept of big data in the broader context of analytics. The discussion continues with a central element of this chapter: a section on the data management infrastructure that is required for modern analytics in addition to the technologies that we have covered in earlier chapters. We pay particular attention to alternatives to traditional relational DBMS technologies grouped under the title NoSQL and the technologies that are currently used to implement big data solutions, such as Hadoop. We next discuss typical uses of descriptive, predictive, and prescriptive analytics and provide an in-depth review of data infrastructure technologies for analytics. The chapter ends with a section on the uses and implications of big data analytics.

BIG DATA

Big data has been one of the most frequently covered concepts in the popular business press during the last few years. Even though it is clear that some of the enthusiasm related to big data is overheated, it is equally evident that big data represents something new, interesting, and quite promising. The most common ways to explain what big data is have approached the question from three perspectives labeled with names starting with a "v," including volume, variety, and velocity; these dimensions were originally presented in Laney (2001). As previously described, the concept of big data refers to a lot of data (high volume) that exists in many different forms (high variety) and arrives/ is collected fast (at a high velocity or speed). This gives us a vague definition that is changing all the time: When technology develops, today's high volume, variety, and velocity will be perfectly ordinary tomorrow, and we will probably have new capabilities for processing data that will lead to new types of highly beneficial outcomes. Thus, it is likely to be futile to seek out a specific and detailed definition of big data.

It is still worth our time to discuss briefly the original three Vs and two others that some observers later added. These are summarized in Table 11-1.

- At a time when terabyte-size databases are relatively typical even in small and middle-sized organizations, the *Volume* dimension of big data refers to collections of data that are hundreds of terabytes or more (petabytes) in size. Large data centers can currently store exabytes of data.
- *Variety* refers to the explosion in the types of data that are collected, stored, and analyzed. As we will discuss in the context of the three eras of business intelligence and analytics later in this chapter, the traditional numeric administrative data are now only a small subset of the data that organizations want to maintain. For example, Hortonworks (2014) identifies the following types of data as typical in big data systems: sensor, server logs, text, social, geographic, machine, and clickstream. Missing from this list are still audio and video data.
- *Velocity* refers to the speed at which the data arrives—big data analytics deals with not only large total amounts of data but also data arriving in streams that are very fast, such as sensor data from large numbers of mobile devices, and clickstream data.
- *Veracity* is a dimension of big data that is both a desired characteristic and a challenge that has to be dealt with. Because of the richness of data types and sources of data, traditional mechanisms for ensuring data quality (discussed in detail in Chapter 10) do not necessarily apply; there are sources of data quality problems that simply do not exist with traditional structured data. At the same time, there is nothing inherent in big data that would make it easier to deal with data quality problems; therefore, it is essential that these issues are addressed carefully.
- *Value* is an essential dimension of big data applications and the use of big data to support organizational actions and decisions. Large quantities, high arrival speeds, and a wide variety of types of data together do not guarantee that data genuinely provides value for the enterprise. A large number of contemporary business books have made the case for the potential value that big data technologies bring to a modern enterprise. These include *Analytics at Work* (Davenport, Harris, and Morison, 2010), *Big Data at Work* (Davenport, 2014), and *Taming the Big Data Tidal Wave* (Franks, 2012).

TABLE 11-1   Five Vs of Big Data

Volume	In a big data environment, the amounts of data collected and processed are much larger than those stored in typical relational databases.
Variety	Big data consists of a rich variety of data types.
Velocity	Big data arrives to the organization at high speeds and from multiple sources simultaneously.
Veracity	Data quality issues are particularly challenging in a big data context.
Value	Ultimately, big data is meaningless if it does not provide value toward some meaningful goal.

Another important difference between traditional structured databases and data stored in big data systems is that—as we learned in Chapters 2 to 8—creating high-quality structured databases requires that these databases be based on carefully developed data models (both conceptual and logical) or schemas. This approach is often called *schema on write*—the data model is predefined and changing it later is difficult. The same approach is required for traditional data warehouses. The philosophy of big data systems is different and can be described as *schema on read*—the reporting and analysis organization of the data will be determined at the time of the use of the data. Instead of carefully planning in advance what data will be collected and how the collected data items are related to each other, the big data approach focuses on the collection and storage of data in large quantities even though there might not be a clear idea of how the collected data will be used in the future. The structure of the data might not be fully (or at all) specified, particularly in terms of the relationships between the data items. Technically, the "schema on read" approach is typically based on the use of either JavaScript Object Notation (JSON) or Extensible Markup Language (XML). Both of these specify the structure of each collection of attribute values at the record level (see Figure 11-1 for an example), and thus make it possible to analyze complex and varying record structures at the time of the use of the data. "Schema on read" refers to the fact that there is no predefined schema for the collected data but that the necessary models will be developed when the data are read for utilization.

An integrated repository of data with various types of structural characteristics coming from internal and external sources (Gualtieri and Yuhanna, 2014, p. 3) is called a **data lake**. A white paper by The Data Warehousing Institute calls a data lake a "dumping ground for all kinds of data because it is inexpensive and does not require a schema on write" (Halper, 2014, p. 2). Hortonworks (2014, p. 13) specifies three characteristics of a data lake:

Data lake

A large integrated repository for internal and external data that does not follow a predefined schema.

- *Collect everything*. A data lake includes all collected raw data over a long period of time and any results of processing of data.
- *Dive in anywhere*. Only limited by constraints related to confidentiality and security, data in a data lake can be accessed by a wide variety of organizational actors for a rich set of perspectives.
- *Flexible access*. "Schema on read" allows an adaptive and agile creation of connections among data items.

There are, however, many reasons why the big data approach is not suitable for all data management purposes and why it is not likely to replace the "schema on write" approach universally. As you will learn soon, the most common big data technologies

FIGURE 11-1 Examples of JSON and XML

JSON Example

```
{"products": [
        {"number": 1, "name": "Zoom X", "Price": 10.00},
        {"number": 2, "name": "Wheel Z", "Price": 7.50},
        {"number": 3, "name": "Spring 10", "Price": 12.75}
]}
```

XML Example

```
<products>
        <product>
                <number>1</number> <name>Zoom X</name> <price>10.00</price>
        </product>
        <product>
                <number>2</number> <name>Wheel Z</name> <price>7.50</price>
        </product>
        <product>
                <number>3</number> <name>Spring 10</name> <price>12.75</price>
        </product>
</products>
```

(those based on Hadoop) are based on batch processing—designing an analytical task and the approach for solving it, submitting the job to execute the task to the system, and waiting for the results while the system is processing it. With very large amounts of data the execution of the tasks may last quite a long time (potentially hours). The big data approach is not intended for exploring individual cases or their dependencies when addressing an individual business problem; instead, it is targeted to situations with very large amounts of data, with a variety of data, and very fast streams of data. For other types of data and information needs, relational databases and traditional data warehouses offer well-tested capabilities.

Next, we will discuss two specific categories of technologies that have become known as core infrastructure elements of big data solutions: NoSQL and Hadoop. The first is NoSQL (abbreviated from "Not only SQL"), a category of data storage and retrieval technologies that are not based on the relational model. The second is Hadoop, an open source technology specifically designed for managing large quantities, varieties, and fast streams of data.

NoSQL

NoSQL (abbreviated from "Not only SQL") is a category of recently introduced data storage and retrieval technologies that are not based on the relational model. We will first discuss the general characteristics of these technologies and then analyze them at a more detailed level using a widely used categorization into key-value stores, document stores, wide-column stores, and graph databases.

NoSQL
A category of recently introduced data storage and retrieval technologies that are not based on the relational model.

The need to minimize storage space used to be one of the key reasons underlying the strong focus on avoidance of replication in relational database design. Economics of storage have, however, changed because of a rapid reduction in storage costs, thus minimizing storage space is no longer a key design consideration. Instead, the focus has moved to scalability, flexibility, agility, and versatility. For many purposes, particularly in transaction processing and management reporting, the predictability and stability of databases based on the relational model continue to be highly favorable characteristics. For other purposes, such as complex analytics, other design dimensions are more important. This has led to the emergence of database models that provide an alternative to the relational model. These models, often discussed under the umbrella term of NoSQL, are particularly interesting in contexts that require versatile processing of a rich variety of data types and structures.

NoSQL database management systems allow "scaling out" through the use of a large number of commodity servers that can be easily added to the architectural solution instead of "scaling up," an older model used in the context of the relational model that in many cases required large stepwise investments in larger and larger hardware. The NoSQL systems are designed so that the failure of a single component will not lead to the failure of the entire system. This model can be easily implemented in a cloud environment in which the commodity servers (real or virtual) are located in a service provider's data center environment accessible through the public Internet. Many NoSQL systems enable automated sharding, that is, distributing the data among multiple nodes in a way that allows each server to operate independently on the data located on it. This makes it possible to implement a shared-nothing architecture, a replication architecture that does not have separate master/slave roles.

NoSQL systems also provide opportunities for the use of the "schema on read" model instead of the "schema on write" model that assumes and requires a predefined schema that is difficult to change. As previously discussed and illustrated in Figure 11-2, "schema on read" is built on the idea that every individual collection of individual data items (record) is specified separately using a language such as JSON or XML.

Interestingly, many NoSQL database management systems are based on technologies that have emerged from open source communities; for enterprise use, they are offered with commercial support.

It is important to understand that most NoSQL database management systems do not support ACID (atomicity, consistency, isolation, and durability) properties of transactions, typically considered essential for guaranteeing the consistency of administrative systems and discussed in Chapter 12 (available on the book's Web

FIGURE 11-2 Schema on write vs. schema on read

site). NoSQL database management systems are often used for purposes in which it is acceptable to sacrifice guaranteed consistency for ensure constant availability. Instead of the ACID properties, NoSQL systems are said to have BASE properties: basically available, soft state, and eventually consistent. Eric Brewer's (2000) CAP theorem states that no system can achieve consistency, high availability, and partition tolerance at the same time in case errors occur; in practice, this means that distributed systems cannot achieve high availability and guaranteed consistency at the same time. NoSQL database management systems are choosing high availability over guaranteed consistency whereas relational databases with ACID propertied are offering guaranteed consistency while sacrificing availability in certain situations (Voroshilin, 2012).

Classification of NoSQL Database Management Systems

There are four main types of NoSQL database data models (McKnight, 2014): key-value stores, document stores, wide-column stores, and graph databases.

KEY-VALUE STORES Key-value stores (illustrated in Figure 11-3a) consist of a simple pair of a key and an associated collection of values. A key-value store database maintains a structure that allows it to store and access "values" (number, name, and price in our example) based on a "key" (with value "Prod_1" in our example). The "key" is typically a string, with or without specific meaning, and in many ways it is similar to a primary key in a relational table. The database does not care or even know about the contents of the individual "value" collections; if some part of the "value" needs to be changed, the entire collection will need to be updated. For the database, the "value" is an arbitrary collection of bytes, and any processing of the contents of the "value" is left for the application. The only operations a typical key-value store offers are *put* (for storing the "value"), *get* (for retrieving the "value" based on the "key"), and *delete* (for deleting a specific key-value pair). As you see, no update operation exists.

DOCUMENT STORES Document stores (illustrated in Figure 11-3b) do not deal with "documents" in a typical sense of the word; they are not intended for storing, say, word-processing or spreadsheet documents. Instead, a document in this context is a structured set of data formatted using a standard such as JSON. The key difference between key-value stores and document stores is that a document store has the capability of accessing and modifying the contents of a specific document based on its structure; each

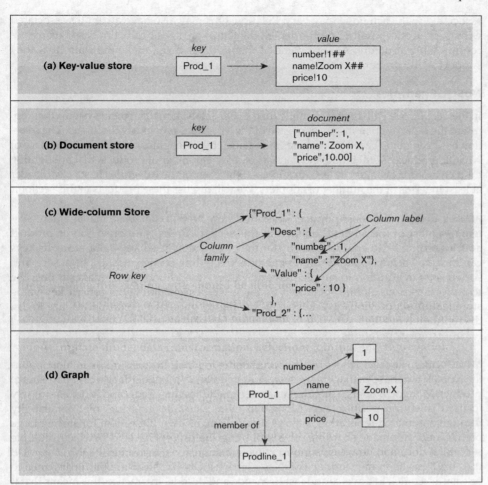

FIGURE 11-3 Four-part figure illustrating NoSQL databases

Some of the example structures have been adapted from Kauhanen (2010).

"document" is still accessed based on a "key." In addition to this, the internal structure of the "document" (specified within it using JSON) can be used to access and manipulate its contents. In our example, the key "Prod_1" is used to access the document consisting of components "number," "name," and "price." Each of these can be manipulated separately in a document store context. The "documents" may have a hierarchical structure, and they do not typically reference each other.

WIDE-COLUMN STORES Wide-column stores or extensible record stores (illustrated in Figure 11-3c) consist of rows and columns, and their characteristic feature is the distribution of data based on both key values (records) and columns, using "column groups" or "column families" to indicate which columns are best to be stored together. They allow each row to have a different column structure (there are no constraints defined by a shared schema), and the length of the rows varies. Edjladi and Beyer (2013) suggest that wide-column stores are particularly good for storing semi-structured data in a distributed environment.

GRAPH-ORIENTED DATABASES Graph-oriented databases (illustrated in Figure 11-3d) have been specifically designed for purposes in which it is critically important to be able to maintain information regarding the relationships between data items (which, in many cases, represent real-world instances of entities). Data in a graph-oriented database is stored in nodes with properties (named attribute values), and the connections between the nodes represent relationships between the real-world instances. As with other forms of NoSQL database management systems, the collections of attributes associated with each node may vary. Relationships may also have attributes associated with them. Conceptually, graph-oriented databases are specifically not based on a row-column table structure. At least some of them do, however, make the claim that they support ACID properties (Neo4j).

NoSQL Examples

In this section, we will discuss examples of NoSQL database management systems that represent the most popular instances of each of the categories previously discussed. The selection has been made based on rankings maintained by db-engines.com. The marketplace of NoSQL products is still broad and consists of a large number of products that are fighting for a chance for eventual long-term success. Still, each of the categories has a clear leader at least in terms of the number of adopters. We will discuss these products in this section.

REDIS   Redis is the most popular key-value store NoSQL database management system. As most of the others discussed in this section, Redis is an open source product and, according to db-engines.com, by far the most widely used key-value store. Its keys can include various complex data structures (including strings, hashes, lists, sets, and sorted sets) in addition to simple numeric values. In addition, Redis makes it possible to perform various atomic operations on the key types, extending the generic key-value store feature set previously discussed. Many highly popular Web properties use Redis, the reputation of which is largely based on its high performance, enabled by its support for in-memory operations.

MONGODB   The clear leader in the document store category (and also the most popular NoSQL database management system in general) is MongoDB, also an open source product. MongoDB offers a broader range of capabilities than Redis and is not as strongly focused solely on performance. MongoDB offers versatile indexing, high availability through automated replication, a query mechanism, its own file system for storing large objects, and automatic sharding for distributing the processing load between multiple servers. It does not, however, support joins or transactions. Instead of JSON, MongoDB uses BSON as its storage format. BSON is a binary JSON-like structure that is designed to be easy and quick to traverse and fast to encode and decode. In practice, this means that it is easier and faster to find things within a BSON structure than within a JSON structure.

APACHE CASSANDRA   The main player in the wide-column store category is Apache Cassandra, which also competes with MongoDB for the leading NoSQL DBMS position (although Cassandra still has a much smaller user base than MongoDB). Google's BigTable algorithm was a major inspiration underlying Cassandra, as was also Amazon's Dynamo; thus, some call Cassandra a marriage between BigTable and Dynamo. Cassandra uses a row/column structure, but as with other wide-column stores, rows are extensible (i.e., they do not necessarily follow the same structure), and it has multiple column grouping levels (columns, supercolumns, and column families).

NEO4J   Finally, Neo4j is a graph database that was originated by Neo Technologies in 2003, before the NoSQL concept was coined. As previously mentioned, Neo4j supports ACID properties. It is highly scalable, enabling the storage of billions of nodes and relationships, and fast for the purposes for which it has been designed, that is, understanding complex relationships specified as graphs. It has its own declarative query language called Cypher; in addition to the queries, Cypher is used to create new nodes and relationships and manage indexes and constraints (in the same way SQL is used for inserting data and managing relational database indexes and constraints).

Impact of NoSQL on Database Professionals

From the perspective of a database professional, it is truly exciting that the introduction of NoSQL database management systems has made a rich variety of new tools available for the management of complex and variable data. Relational database management systems and SQL will continue to be very important for many purposes, particularly

TABLE 11-2 Comparison of NoSQL Database Characteristics (Based on Scofield, 2010)

	Key-Value Store	Document Store	Column Oriented	Graph
Performance	high	high	high	variable
Scalability	high	variable/high	high	variable
Flexibility	high	high	moderate	high
Complexity	none	low	low	high
Functionality	variable	variable (low)	minimal	graph theory

Source: http://www.slideshare.net/bscofield/nosql-codemash-2010. Courtesy of Ben Scofield.

in the context of administrative systems that require a high level of predictability and structure. In addition, SQL will continue to be an important foundation for new data manipulation and definition languages that are created for different types of contexts because of SQL's very large existing user base. The exciting new tools under the NoSQL umbrella add a significant set of capabilities to an expert data management professional's toolkit. For a long time, relational DBMSs were the primary option for managing organizational data; the NoSQL database management systems discussed in this section provide the alternatives that allow organizations to make informed decisions regarding the composition of their data management arsenal. Table 11-2 provides an example of a comparative review of these four categories of NoSQL technologies.

Hadoop

There is probably no current data management product or platform discussed as broadly as Hadoop. At times it seems that the entire big data discussion revolves around Hadoop, and it is easy to get the impression that there would be no big data analytics without Hadoop. The truth is not, of course, this simple. The purpose of this section is to give you an overview of Hadoop and help you understand its true importance and the purposes for which it can be effectively used. It is an important technology that provides significant benefits for many (big) data management tasks, and Hadoop has helped organizations achieve important analytics results that would not have been possible without it. However, it is also important to understand that Hadoop is not a solution for all data management problems; instead, it is a tool in the data management toolbox that needs to be used for the right purposes.

The foundation of Hadoop is **MapReduce**, an algorithm for massive parallel processing of various types of computing tasks originally published in a paper by two Google employees in the early 2000s (Dean and Ghemawat, 2004). The key purpose of MapReduce is to automate the parallelization of large-scale tasks so that they can be performed on a large number of low-cost commodity servers in a fault-tolerant way. **Hadoop**, in turn, is an open-source implementation framework of MapReduce that makes it easier (but not easy) to apply the algorithm to a number of real-world problems. As will be discussed below, Hadoop consists of a large number of components integrated with each other. It is also important to understand that Hadoop is fundamentally a batch-processing tool. That is, it has been designed for tasks that can be scheduled for execution without human intervention at a specific time or under specific conditions (e.g., low processing load or a specific time of the day).

Thus, Hadoop is not a tool that you would run on a local area network to address the administrative data processing needs of a small or middle-sized company. It is also not a tool that you can easily demonstrate on a single computer (however powerful its processing capabilities might be). Hadoop's essence is in processing very large amounts (terabytes or petabytes) of data by distributing the data (using Hadoop Distributed File System or HDFS) and processing task(s) among a large number of low-cost commodity servers.

A large number of projects powered by Hadoop are described in **http://wiki. apache.org/hadoop/PoweredBy**; the smallest of them have only a few nodes but most of them dozens and some hundreds or more (for example, Facebook describes an 1100-machine (8800 core) system with 12 petabytes of storage). Hadoop is also not a tool

MapReduce

An algorithm for massive parallel processing of various types of computing tasks.

Hadoop

An open source implementation framework of MapReduce.

FIGURE 11-4 Hortonworks
Enterprise Hadoop Data Platform

Adapted from http://
hortonworks.com/hdp.
Courtesy of HortonWorks, Inc.

that you manage and use with a high-level point-and-drag interface; submitting even a simple MapReduce job to Hadoop typically requires the use of the Java programming language and specific Hadoop libraries. Fortunately, many parties have built tools that make it easier to use the capabilities of Hadoop.

Components of Hadoop

The Hadoop framework consists of a large number of components that together form an implementation environment that enables the use of the MapReduce algorithm to solve practical large-scale analytical problems. These components will be the main focus of this section. Figure 11-4 includes a graphical representation of a Hadoop component architecture for an implementation by Hortonworks.

HDFS

HDFS or Hadoop Distributed File System is a file system designed for managing a large number of potentially very large files in a highly distributed environment.

THE HADOOP DISTRIBUTED FILE SYSTEM (HDFS) **HDFS** is the foundation of the data management infrastructure of Hadoop. It is not a relational database management system or any type of DBMS; instead, it is a file system designed for managing a large number of potentially very large files in a highly distributed environment (up to thousands of servers). HDFS breaks data into small chunks called blocks and distributes them on various computers (nodes) throughout the Hadoop cluster. This distribution of data forms the foundation for Hadoop's processing and storage model: Because data are divided between various nodes in the cluster, it can be processed by all those nodes at the same time.

Data in HDFS files cannot be updated; instead, it can only be added at the end of the file. HDFS does not provide indexing; thus HDFS is not usable in applications that require real-time sequential or random access to the data (White, 2012). HDFS assumes that hardware failure is a norm in a massively distributed environment; with thousands of servers, some hardware elements are always in a state of failure and thus HDFS has been designed to quickly discover the component failures and recover from them (HDFSDesign, 2014). Another important principle underlying HDFS is that it is cheaper to move the execution of computation to the data than to move the data to computation.

A typical HDFS cluster consists of a single master server (NameNode) and a large number of slaves (DataNodes). The NameNode is responsible for the management of the file system name space and regulating the access to files by clients (HDFSDesign, 2014). Replication of data is an important characteristic of HDFS. By default, HDFS maintains three copies of data (both the number of copies and the size of data blocks can be configured). An interesting special characteristic of HDFS is that it is aware of the positioning of nodes in racks and can take this information into account when designing its replication policy. Since Hadoop 2.0, it has been possible to maintain two redundant NameNodes in the same cluster to avoid the NameNode becoming a single point of failure. See Figure 11-5 for an illustration of a HDFS Cluster associated with MapReduce.

A highly distributed system requires a traffic cop that controls the allocation of various resources available in the system. In the current version of Hadoop (Hadoop 2), this component is called YARN (Yet Another Resource Allocator, also called MapReduce 2.0). YARN consists of a global ResourceManager and a per-application ApplicationMaster, and its fundamental role is to provide access to the files stored on HDFS and to organize the processes that utilize this data (see also Figure 11-4).

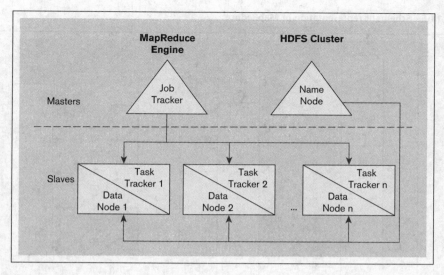

FIGURE 11-5 MapReduce and HDFS

MAPREDUCE MapReduce is a core element of Hadoop; as discussed earlier, Hadoop is a MapReduce implementation framework that makes the capabilities of this algorithm available for other applications. The problem that MapReduce helps solve is the parallelization of data storage and computational problem solving in an environment that consists of a large number of commodity servers. MapReduce has been designed so that it can provide its capabilities in a fault-tolerant way. The authors of the original MapReduce article (Dean and Ghemawat, 2004) specifically state that MapReduce is intended to allow "programmers without any experience with parallel and distributed systems to easily utilize the resources of a large distributed system" (Dean and Ghemawat, 2004, p. 1). MapReduce intends to make the power of parallel processing available to a large number of users so that (programmer) users can focus on solving the domain problem instead of having to worry about complex details related to the management of parallel systems. In the component architecture represented in Figure 11-4, MapReduce is integrated with YARN.

The core idea underlying the MapReduce algorithm is dividing the computing task so that multiple nodes of a computing cluster can work on the same problem at the same time. Equally important is that each node is working on local data and only the results of processing are moved across the network, saving both time and network resources. The name of MapReduce comes from the names of the components of this distribution process. The first part, *map*, performs a computing task in parallel on multiple subsets of the entire data, returning a result for each subset separately. The second part, *reduce*, integrates the results of each of the *map* processes, creating the final result. It is up to the developer to define the mapper and the reducer so that they together get the work done. See Figure 11-6 for a schematic representation.

Let's look at an example. Imagine that you have a very large number of orders and associated orderline data (with attributes productID, price, and quantity), and your goal is to count the number of orders in which each productID exists and the average price for each productID. Let's assume that the volumes are so high that using a traditional RDBMS to perform the task is too slow. If you used the MapReduce algorithm to perform this task, you would define the mapper so that it would produce the following (key → value) pairs: (productID → [1, price]) where productID is the key and the [1, price] pair is the value. The mapper on each of the nodes could independently produce these pairs that, in turn, would be used as input by the reducer. The reducer would create a set of different types of (key → value) pairs: For each productID, it would produce a count of orders and the average of all the prices in the form of (productID → [countOrders, avgPrice].

In this case, the mapper and reducer algorithms are very simple. Sometimes this is the case with real-world applications; sometimes those algorithms are quite complex. For example, **http://highlyscalable.wordpress.com/2012/02/01/mapreduce-patterns/** presents a number of interesting and relevant uses for MapReduce. It is important to note that in many cases these types of tasks can be performed easily and without any extra effort with

FIGURE 11-6 Schematic representation of MapReduce

MapReduce: Simplified Data Processing on Large Clusters, Jeff Dean, Sanjay Ghemawat, Google, Inc., http://research.google.com/archive/mapreduce-osdi04-slides/index-auto-0007.html. Courtesy of the authors.

a RDBMS—only when the amounts of data are very large, data types are highly varied, and/or the speeds of arrival of data are very high (i.e., we are dealing with real big data) do massively distributed approaches, such as Hadoop, produce real advantages that justify the additional cost in complexity and the need for an additional technology platform.

In addition to HDFS, MapReduce, and YARN, other components of the Hadoop framework have been developed to automate the computing tasks and raise the abstraction level so that Hadoop users can focus on organizational problem solving. These tools also have unusual names, such as Pig, Hive, and Zookeeper. The rest of the section provides an overview of these remaining components.

Pig

A tool that integrates a scripting language and an execution environment intended to simplify the use of MapReduce.

PIG MapReduce programming is difficult, and multiple tools have been developed to address the challenges associated with it. One of the most important of them is called **Pig**. This platform integrates a scripting language (appropriately called PigLatin) and an execution environment. Its key purpose is to translate execution sequences expressed in PigLatin into multiple sequenced MapReduce programs. The syntax of Pig is familiar to those who know some of the well-known scripting languages. In some contexts it is also called SQL-like (**http://hortonworks.com/hadoop-tutorial/how-to-use-basic-pig-commands/**), although it is not a declarative language.

Pig can automate important data preparation tasks (such as filter rows that do not include useful data), transform data for processing (e.g., convert text data into all lower case or extract only needed data elements), execute analytic functions, store results, define processing sequences, etc. All this is done at a much higher level of abstraction than would be possible with Java and direct use of MapReduce libraries. Not surprisingly, Pig is quite useful for ETL (extract–transform–load) processes (discussed in Chapter 10), but it can also be used for studying the characteristics of raw data and for iterative processing of data (**http://hortonworks.com/hadoop/pig/**). Pig can be extended with custom functions (UDFs or user defined functions). See Figure 11-4 for an illustration of how Pig fits the overall Hadoop architecture.

Hive

An Apache project that supports the management and querying of large data sets using HiveQL, an SQL-like language that provides a declarative interface for managing data stored in Hadoop.

HIVE I am sure you are happy to hear that the SQL skills you've learned earlier are also applicable in the big data context. Another Apache project called **Hive** (which Apache calls "data warehouse software") supports the management of large data sets and querying them. HiveQL is an SQL-like language that provides a declarative interface for managing data stored in Hadoop. HiveQL includes DDL operations (CREATE TABLE,

SHOW TABLES, ALTER TABLE, and DROP TABLE), DML operations, and SQL operations, including SELECT, FROM, WHERE, GROUP BY, HAVING, ORDER BY, JOIN, UNION, and subqueries. HiveQL also supports limiting the answer to top [x] rows with LIMIT [x] and using regular expressions for column selection.

At runtime, Hive creates MapReduce jobs based on the HiveQL statements and executes them on a Hadoop cluster. As with Hadoop in general, HiveQL is intended for very large scale data retrieval tasks primarily for data analysis purposes; it is specifically not a language for transaction processing or fast retrieval of single values.

Gates (2010) discusses the differences between Pig and Hive (and, consequently, PigLatin and HiveQL) at Yahoo!, and illustrates well the different uses for the two technologies. Pig is typically used for data preparation (or *data factory*) whereas Hive is the more suitable option for data presentation (or *data warehouse*). The combination of the two has allowed Yahoo! to move a major part of its data factory and data warehouse operations into Hadoop. Figure 11-4 shows also the positioning of Hive in the context of the Hadoop architecture.

HBASE   The final Hadoop component that we will discuss in this text is HBase, a wide-column store database that runs on top of HDFS and is modeled after Google's BigTable (Chang et al., 2008). As discussed earlier in this chapter, another Apache project called Cassandra is more popular in this context. A detailed comparison between HBase and Cassandra is beyond the scope of this text; both products are used to support projects with massive data storage needs. It is, however, important to understand that HBase does not use MapReduce; instead, it can serve as a source of data for MapReduce jobs.

Integrated Analytics and Data Science Platforms

Various vendors offer platforms that are intended to offer integrated data management capabilities for analytics and data science. They bring together traditional data warehousing (discussed in Chapter 9) and the big data–related capabilities discussed earlier. In this section, we will briefly discuss the key characteristics of a few of them in order to demonstrate the environments that organizations are using to make big data work in practice. They include HP's HAVEn, Teradata's Aster, and IBM's Big Data Platform.

HP HAVEn   HP HAVEn is a platform that integrates some core HP technologies with open source big data technologies, promising an ability to derive insights fast from very large amounts of data stored on Hadoop/HDFS and HP's Vertica column-oriented data store. Vertica is based on an academic prototype called C-Store (Lamb et al., 2012) and was acquired by HP in 2011. In addition to Hadoop and Vertica, HAVEn includes an Autonomy analytics engine with a particular focus on unstructured textual information.

TERADATA ASTER   Teradata, one of the long-term leaders in data warehousing, has recently extended its product offerings to cover both big data analytics and marketing applications as two additional pillars of its strategy. In big data, the core of its offering is based on a 2011 acquisition called Aster. One of the core ideas of Aster is to integrate a number of familiar analytics tools (such as SQL, extensions of SQL for graph analysis and access to MapReduce data stores, and the statistical language R) with several different analytical data store options. These, in turn, are connected to a variety of external sources of data. Figure 11-7 shows a schematic representation of the Aster platform.

IBM BIG DATA PLATFORM   IBM brings together in its Big Data Platform a number of components that offer similar capabilities to those previously described in the context of HP and Teradata. IBM's commercial distribution of Hadoop is called InfoSphere BigInsights. In addition to standard Hadoop capabilities IBM offers JSON Query Language (JAQL), a high-level functional, declarative query language for analyzing large-scale semi-structured data that IBM describes as a "blend of Pig and Hive." Moreover, BigInsights offers connectors to IBM's DB2 relational database and analytics data sources such as Netezza, IBM's 2010 acquisition. Netezza is a data warehousing appliance that allows fast parallel processing of query and analytics tasks against

FIGURE 11-7 Teradata Aster Discovery Portfolio

Source: http://www.teradata.com/Teradata-Aster-Discovery-Portfolio/. Courtesy of Teradata Corporation.

large amounts of data. DB2, BigInsights, Netezza, and IBM's enterprise data warehouse Smart Analytics System all are feeding into analytics tools such as Cognos and SPSS.

Putting it All Together: Integrated Data Architecture

To help you understand all of this together, we will be using a framework description from one of the vendors discussed earlier. Teradata has developed a model illustrating how various elements of a modern data management environment belong together. It is called Unified Data Architecture and presented in Figure 11-8.

In this model, the various *Sources* of data are included on the left side. These are the generators of data that the data management environment will collect and store for processing and analysis. They include various enterprise systems (ERP, SCM, CRM) and other similar structured data sources, data collected from the Web and various social media sources, internal and external text documents, and multimedia sources (still images, audio, and video). This version of the model includes machine logs (capturing what takes place in various devices that together comprise the organizational systems). These could be extended with sensor data and other Internet of Things sources (data generated with devices serving various practical purposes both in households, corporations, and public organizations and spaces).

In the middle are the three core activities that are required for transforming the raw data from the sources to actionable insights for the *Users* on the right. They include preparing the *Data*, enabling *Insights*, and driving *Action*. The *Data* category refers to the actions that bring the data into the system from the sources, process it to analyze and ensure its quality, and archive it. *Insights* refer to the activities that are needed for making sense of the data through data discovery, pattern recognition, and development of new models. Finally, the *Action* category produces results that can be put to action as direct recommendations, insights, or rules. Alternatively, action support can be generated through reports and dashboards that users will use to support their decision making. *Insights* and *Action* are achieved through various *Analytic tools* used either by professional analysts and data scientists or directly by managers.

FIGURE 11-8 **Teradata Unified Data Architecture – logical view**

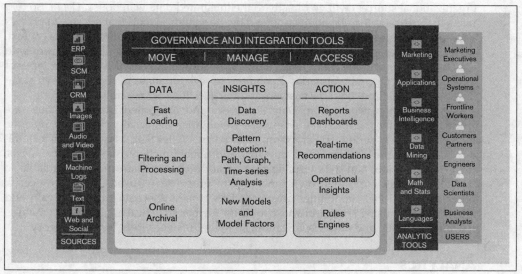

Source: http://www.teradata.com/Resources/White-Papers/Teradata-Unified-Data-Architecture-in-Action. Courtesy of Teradata Corporation.

Figure 11-9 presents an implementation perspective of the same model using Teradata's technologies. For our purposes the most interesting element of this version is the division of labor between the three components. *Data Platform* refers to the capabilities that are required to capture or retrieve the data from the *Sources*, store it for analytical purposes, and prepare it for statistical analysis (by, for example, ensuring the quality of the data to the extent it is possible). The capabilities of Hadoop would be used in this context to manage, distribute, and process in parallel the large amounts of data generated by the sources. *Integrated Data Warehouse* is the primary context for analytics that supports directly ongoing strategic and operational analytics, activities that are often planned and designed to support ongoing business. This element of the model is familiar to you from

FIGURE 11-9 **Teradata Unified Data Architecture – system conceptual view**

Source: http://www.teradata.com/Resources/White-Papers/Teradata-Unified-Data-Architecture-in-Action. Courtesy of Teradata Corporation.

Chapter 9. Please note that some of the data (particularly structured data from traditional organizational sources) will go directly to the integrated data warehouse. *Data Discovery* refers to the exploratory capabilities offered by the analytical tools that are able to process very quickly large amounts of heterogeneous data from multiple sources. In this context, these capabilities are implemented by Teradata Aster, which can utilize data from both the *Data Platform* and *Integrated Data Warehouse* in addition to flat files and other types of databases. *Data Discovery* provides capabilities to seek for answers and insights in situations when sometimes both the answers and the questions are missing.

Many of the results from Data Discovery and Integrated Data Warehouse are readily usable by the analysts. Analytical capabilities increasingly are built into the data management products. For example, Teradata's Aster SQL-MapReduce® technology builds into the familiar SQL framework additional functions for statistical analysis, data manipulation, and data visualization. In addition, the platform is expandable so that analysts can write their own functions for proprietary purposes. In many cases, however, additional capabilities are needed to process the data further to gain and report insights, using special-purpose tools for further statistical analysis, data mining, machine learning, and data visualization, all in the *Analytics Tools & Apps* category.

ANALYTICS

During your earlier studies of Information Systems related topics, you might have encountered several concepts that are related to analytics. One of the earliest is decision support systems (DSS), which was one of the early information system types in a commonly used typology, together with transaction processing systems (TPS), management information systems (MIS), and executive information systems (EIS). Sprague (1980) characterized decision support systems as systems that support less structured and underspecified problems, use models and analytic techniques together with data access, have features that make them accessible by non-technical users, and are flexible and adaptable for different types of questions and problems. In this classification, one of the essential differences between structured and pre-defined MIS systems and DSS systems was that the former produced primarily pre-specified reports. The latter were designed to address many different types of situations and allowed the decision maker to change the nature of the support they received from the system depending on their needs. Earlier we defined analytics as systematic analysis and interpretation of raw data (typically using mathematical, statistical, and computational tools) to improve our understanding of a real-world domain—not that far from the definition of DSS.

Business intelligence

A set of methodologies, processes, architectures, and technologies that transform raw data into meaningful and useful information.

From the DSS concept grew **business intelligence**, which Forrester Research defines as "a set of methodologies, processes, architectures, and technologies that transform raw data into meaningful and useful information" (Evelson and Nicolson, 2008); the term itself was made popular by an analyst working for another major IT research firm, Gartner. This broad definition of business intelligence leads to an entire layered framework of capabilities starting from foundational infrastructure components and data and ending with user interface components that deliver the results of discovery and integration, analytics, supporting applications, and performance management to the users. Analytics is certainly in the core of the model. It provides most of the capabilities that allow the transformation of data into information that enables decision makers to see in a new light the context that they are interested in and change it. Still, in this context, the word analytics is used to refer to a collection of components in whole called business intelligence.

During recent years the meaning of analytics has changed. It has become the new umbrella term that encompasses not only the specific techniques and approaches that transform collected data into useful information but also the infrastructure required to make analytics work, the various sources of data that feed into the analytical systems, the processes through which the raw data are cleaned up and organized for analysis, the user interfaces that make the results easy to view and simple to understand, etc. Analytics has become an even broader term than business intelligence used to be, and it has grown to include a whole range of capabilities that allow an organization to provide analytical insights. The transition from decision support systems to analytics through business intelligence is described in Figure 11-10.

FIGURE 11-10 Moving from decision support systems to analytics

Types of Analytics

Many authors, including Watson (2014), divide analytics into three major categories: descriptive, predictive, and prescriptive. Over the years, there has been a clear progression from relatively simple descriptive analytics to more advanced, forward looking and guiding forms of analytics.

Descriptive analytics is the oldest form of analytics. As the name suggests, it primarily focuses on describing the past status of the domain of interest using a variety of tools through techniques such as reporting, data visualization, dashboards, and scorecards. Online analytical processing (OLAP) is also part of descriptive analytics; it allows users to get a multidimensional view of data and drill down deeper to the details when appropriate and useful. The key emphasis of predictive analytics is on the future. **Predictive analytics** systems apply statistical and computational methods and models to data regarding past and current events to predict what might happen in the future (potentially depending on a number of assumptions regarding various parameters). Finally, **prescriptive analytics** focuses on the question "How can we make it happen?" or "What do we need to do to make it happen?" For prescriptive analysis we need optimization and simulation tools and advanced modeling to understand the dependencies between various actors within the domain of interest. Table 11-3 summarizes these types of analytics.

In addition to the types of outcomes, the types of analytics can also be differentiated based on the type of data used for the analytical processes. Chen et al. (2012) differentiate between three eras of Business Intelligence and Analytics (BI&A) as follows (see also Figure 11-11):

- BI&A 1.0 deals mostly with *structured quantitative data* that originates from an organization's own administrative systems and is at least originally stored in relational database management systems (such as those discussed in Chapters 4–7). The data warehousing techniques described in Chapter 9 are an essential element in preparing and making this type of data available for analysis. Both descriptive and predictive analytics are part of BI&A 1.0.
- BI&A 2.0 refers to the use of the *data that can be collected from Web-based sources*. The Web has become a very rich source of data for understanding customer behavior and

Descriptive analytics

Describes the past status of the domain of interest using a variety of tools through techniques such as reporting, data visualization, dashboards, and scorecards.

Predictive analytics

Applies statistical and computational methods and models to data regarding past and current events to predict what might happen in the future.

Prescriptive analytics

Uses results of predictive analytics together with optimization and simulation tools to recommend actions that will lead to a desired outcome.

TABLE 11-3 Types of Analytics

Type of Analytics	Key Questions
Descriptive Analytics	What happened yesterday/last week/last year?
Predictive Analytics	What might happen in the future? How does this change if we change assumptions?
Prescriptive Analytics	How can we make it happen? What needs to change to make it happen?

FIGURE 11-11 Generations of business intelligence and analytics

Adapted from Chen et al., 2012.

interaction both between organizations and their stakeholders and among various stakeholder groups at a much more detailed level than earlier. From an individual organization's perspective, this data includes data collected from various Web interaction logs, Web-based customer communication platforms, and social media sources. Much of this data is text-based in nature, thus the analytical techniques used to process it are different from those used for BI&A 1.0, including text mining, Web mining, and social network analysis. To achieve the most effective results, these techniques should be integrated with the more traditional approaches.

- BI&A 3.0 is based on an even richer and more individualized data based on the *ubiquitous use of mobile devices* that have the capability of producing literally millions of observations per second from various sensors, capturing measurements such as guaranteed identification, location, altitude, speed, acceleration, direction of movement, temperature, use of specific applications, etc. The number of smartphones is already counted in billions. The Internet of Things (Chui, Löffler, and Roberts, 2010) adds yet another dimension to this: An increasingly large number of technical devices and their components are capable of producing and communicating data regarding their status. The opportunities to improve the effectiveness and efficiency of the way in which we individually and collectively work to achieve our goals are very significant.

As discussed earlier in this section, analytics is often divided into three categories: descriptive analytics, predictive analytics, and prescriptive analysis. We will next discuss these categories at a more detailed level, illustrating how these technologies can be used for analytical purposes.

Use of Descriptive Analytics

Most of the user interface tools associated with traditional data warehouses will provide capabilities for descriptive analytics, which, as we discussed earlier in this section, primarily focuses on describing the status of the domain of interest from the historical perspective. This was also the original meaning of the widely used term *business intelligence*.

Descriptive analytics is the oldest form of analytics. As the name suggests, it primarily focuses on describing the past status of the domain of interest using a variety of tools. The simplest form of descriptive analytics is the *reporting* of aggregate quantitative facts regarding various objects of interest, such as quarterly sales per region, monthly payroll by division, or the average length of a hospital stay per department. Aggregated data can be reported either in a tabular form or using various tools and techniques of *data visualization*. When descriptive data are aggregated in to a few key indicators, each of which integrates and represents an important aspect of the domain of interest, descriptive analytics is said to use a *dashboard*. A *scorecard* might include a broader range of more detailed indicators, but still, a scorecard reports descriptive data regarding past behavior.

Finally, online analytical processing (OLAP) is an important form of descriptive analytics. Key characteristics of OLAP allow its users to get an in-depth multidimensional view of various aspects of interest within a domain. Typical OLAP processes start with high-level aggregated data, which an OLAP user can explore from a number of perspectives. For example, an OLAP system for sales data could start with last month's overall revenue figure compared to both the previous month and the same month a year ago. The user of the system might observe a change in revenue that is either significantly higher or lower than expected. Using an OLAP system, the user could easily ask for the total revenue to be divided by region, salesperson, product, or division. If a report by region demonstrated that the Northeast region is the primary reason underlying the decrease in revenue, the system could easily be used to drill down to the region in question and explore the revenue further by the other dimensions. This could further show that the primary reason for the decrease within the region is a specific product. Within the product, the problem could be narrowed down to a couple of salespeople. OLAP allows very flexible ad hoc queries and analytical approaches that allow quick adaptation of future questions to the findings made previously. Speed of execution is very important with OLAP databases.

Many of the data warehousing products discussed in Chapter 9 are used for various forms of descriptive analytics. According to Gartner (Edjlali and Beyer, 2013), the leaders of the underlying data warehousing products include Teradata (including Aster), Oracle (including Oracle Exadata), IBM (Netezza), SAP (Sybase IQ and Hana), Microsoft (SQL Server 2012 Parallel Data Warehouse), and EMC (Greenplum). Building on these foundational products, specific business intelligence and analytics platforms provide deeper analytical capabilities. In this category, Gartner (Sallam et al., 2014) identified Tableau, Qlik, Microsoft, IBM, SAS, SAP, Tibco, Oracle, MicroStrategy, and Information Builders as leading vendors. The descriptive capabilities that Gartner expected a product to have to do well in this category included reporting, dashboards, ad hoc reports/queries, integration with Microsoft Office, mobile business intelligence, interactive visualization, search-based data discovery, geospatial and location intelligence, and OLAP.

In this section, we will discuss a variety of tools for querying and analyzing data stored in data warehouses and data marts. These tools can be classified, for example, as follows:

- Traditional query and reporting tools
- OLAP, MOLAP, and ROLAP tools
- Data visualization tools
- Business performance management and dashboard tools

Traditional query and reporting tools include spreadsheets, personal computer databases, and report writers and generators. We do not describe these commonly known tools in this chapter. Instead, we assume that you have learned them somewhere else in your program of study.

SQL OLAP QUERYING The most common database query language, SQL (covered extensively in Chapters 6 and 7), has been extended to support some types of calculations and querying needed for a data warehousing environment. In general, however, SQL is not an analytical language (Mundy, 2001). At the heart of analytical queries is the ability to perform categorization (e.g., group data by dimension characteristics), aggregation (e.g., create averages per category), and ranking (e.g., find the customer in some category with the highest average monthly sales). Consider the following business question in the familiar Pine Valley Furniture Company context:

Which customer has bought the most of each product we sell? Show the product ID and description, customer ID and name, and the total quantity sold of that product to that customer; show the results in sequence by product ID.

Even with the limitations of standard SQL, this analytical query can be written without the OLAP extensions to SQL. One way to write this query, using the large version of the Pine Valley Furniture database provided with this textbook, is as follows:

```
SELECT P1.ProductId, ProductDescription, C1.CustomerId,
    CustomerName, SUM(OL1.OrderedQuantity) AS TotOrdered
  FROM Customer_T AS C1, Product_T AS P1, OrderLine_T
    AS OL1, Order_T AS O1
  WHERE C1.CustomerId = O1.CustomerId
    AND O1.OrderId = OL1.OrderId
    AND OL1.ProductId = P1.ProductId
  GROUP BY P1.ProductId, ProductDescription,
    C1.CustomerId, CustomerName
  HAVING TotOrdered >= ALL
  (SELECT SUM(OL2.OrderedQuantity)
  FROM OrderLine_T AS OL2, Order_T AS O2
  WHERE OL2.ProductId = P1.ProductId
    AND OL2.OrderId = O2.OrderId
    AND O2.CustomerId <> C1.CustomerId
  GROUP BY O2.CustomerId)
ORDER BY P1.ProductId;
```

This approach uses a correlated subquery to find the set of total quantity ordered across all customers for each product, and then the outer query selects the customer whose total is greater than or equal to all of these (in other words, equal to the maximum of the set). Until you write many of these queries, this can be very challenging to develop and is often beyond the capabilities of even well-trained end users. Even this query is rather simple because it does not have multiple categories, does not ask for changes over time, or does not want to see the results graphically. Finding the second in rank is even more difficult.

Some versions of SQL support special clauses that make ranking questions easier to write. For example, Microsoft SQL Server and some other RDBMSs support clauses of FIRST n, TOP n, LAST n, and BOTTOM n rows. Thus, the query shown previously could be greatly simplified by adding TOP 1 in front of the SUM in the outer query and eliminating the HAVING and subquery. TOP 1 was illustrated in Chapter 7, in the section on "More Complicated SQL Queries."

Recent versions of SQL include some data warehousing and business intelligence extensions. Because many data warehousing operations deal with categories of objects, possibly ordered by date, the SQL standard includes a WINDOW clause to define dynamic sets of rows. (In many SQL systems, the word OVER is used instead of WINDOW, which is what we illustrate next.) For example, an OVER clause can be used to define three adjacent days as the basis for calculating moving averages. (Think of a window moving between the bottom and top of its window frame, giving you a sliding view of rows of data.) PARTITION BY within an OVER clause is similar to GROUP BY; PARTITION BY tells an OVER clause the basis for each set, an ORDER BY clause sequences the elements of a set, and the ROWS clause says how many rows in sequence to use in a calculation. For example, consider a SalesHistory table (columns TerritoryID, Quarter, and Sales) and the desire to show a three-quarter moving average of sales. The following SQL will produce the desired result using these OLAP clauses:

```
SELECT TerritoryID, Quarter, Sales,
  AVG(Sales) OVER (PARTITION BY TerritoryID
    ORDER BY Quarter ROWS 2 PRECEDING) AS 3QtrAverage
FROM SalesHistory;
```

The PARTITION BY clause groups the rows of the SalesHistory table by TerritoryID for the purpose of computing 3QtrAverage, and then the ORDER BY clause sorts by quarter within these groups. The ROWS clause indicates how many rows over which to calculate the AVG(Sales). The following is a sample of the results from this query:

TerritoryID	Quarter	Sales	3QtrAverage
Atlantic	1	20	20
Atlantic	2	10	15
Atlantic	3	6	12
Atlantic	4	29	15
East	1	5	5
East	2	7	6
East	3	12	8
East	4	11	10
...			

In addition, but not shown here, a QUALIFY clause can be used similarly to a HAVING clause to eliminate the rows of the result based on the aggregate referenced by the OVER clause.

The RANK windowing function calculates something that is very difficult to calculate in standard SQL, which is the row of a table in a specific relative position based on some criteria (e.g., the customer with the third-highest sales in a given period). In the case of ties, RANK will cause gaps (e.g., if there is a two-way tie for third, then there is no rank of 4, rather the next rank is 5). DENSE_RANK works the same as RANK but creates no gaps. The CUME_DIST function finds the relative position of a specified value in a group of values; this function can be used to find the break point for percentiles (e.g., what value is the break point for the top 10 percent of sales or which customers are in the top 10 percent of sales?).

Different DBMS vendors are implementing different subsets of the OLAP extension commands in the standards; some are adding capabilities specific to their products. For example, Teradata supports a SAMPLE clause, which allows samples of rows to be returned for the query. Samples can be random, with or without replacement, a percentage or count of rows can be specified for the answer set, and conditions can be placed to eliminate certain rows from the sample. SAMPLE is used to create subsets of a database that will be, for example, given different product discounts to see consumer behavior differences, or one sample will be used for a trial and another for a final promotion.

ONLINE ANALYTICAL PROCESSING (OLAP) TOOLS A specialized class of tools has been developed to provide users with multidimensional views of their data. Such tools also usually offer users a graphical interface so that they can easily analyze their data. In the simplest case, data are viewed as a three-dimensional cube.

Online analytical processing (OLAP) is the use of a set of query and reporting tools that provides users with multidimensional views of their data and allows them to analyze the data using simple windowing techniques. The term *online analytical processing* is intended to contrast with the more traditional term *online transaction processing (OLTP)*. The differences between these two types of processing were summarized in Table 9-1 in Chapter 9. The term *multidimensional analysis* is often used as a synonym for OLAP.

An example of a "data cube" (or multidimensional view) of data that is typical of OLAP is shown in Figure 11-12. This three-dimensional view corresponds quite closely to the star schema introduced in Chapter 9 in Figure 9-10. Two of the dimensions in Figure 11-12 correspond to the dimension tables (PRODUCT and PERIOD) in Figure 9-10, whereas the third dimension (named measures) corresponds to the data in the fact table (named SALES) in Figure 9-10.

OLAP is actually a general term for several categories of data warehouse and data mart access tools (Dyché, 2000). **Relational OLAP (ROLAP)** tools use variations of SQL and view the database as a traditional relational database, in either a star schema or

Online analytical processing (OLAP)

The use of a set of graphical tools that provides users with multidimensional views of their data and allows them to analyze the data using simple windowing techniques.

Relational OLAP (ROLAP)

OLAP tools that view the database as a traditional relational database in either a star schema or other normalized or denormalized set of tables.

FIGURE 11-12 Slicing a data cube

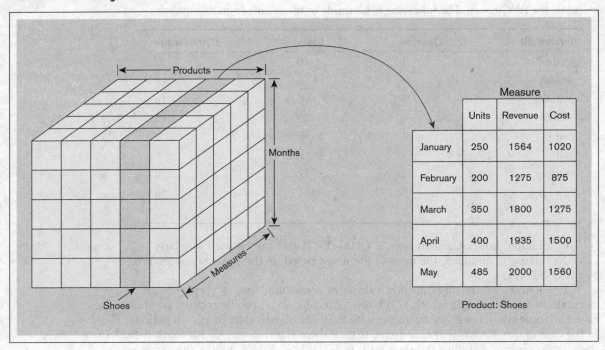

	Measure		
	Units	Revenue	Cost
January	250	1564	1020
February	200	1275	875
March	350	1800	1275
April	400	1935	1500
May	485	2000	1560

Product: Shoes

Multidimensional OLAP (MOLAP)

OLAP tools that load data into an intermediate structure, usually a three- or higher-dimensional array.

another normalized or denormalized set of tables. ROLAP tools access the data warehouse or data mart directly. **Multidimensional OLAP (MOLAP)** tools load data into an intermediate structure, usually a three or higher-dimensional array (hypercube). We illustrate MOLAP in the next few sections because of its popularity. It is important to note with MOLAP that the data are not simply viewed as a multidimensional hypercube, but rather a MOLAP data mart is created by extracting data from the data warehouse or data mart and then storing the data in a specialized separate data store through which data can be viewed only through a multidimensional structure. Other, less-common categories of OLAP tools are database OLAP (DOLAP), which includes OLAP functionality in the DBMS query language (there are proprietary, non-ANSI standard SQL systems that do this), and hybrid OLAP (HOLAP), which allows access via both multidimensional cubes or relational query languages.

Figure 11-12 shows a typical MOLAP operation: slicing the data cube to produce a simple two-dimensional table or view. In Figure 11-12, this slice is for the product named Shoes. The resulting table shows the three measures (units, revenues, and cost) for this product by period (or month). Other views can easily be developed by the user by means of simple "drag and drop" operations. This type of operation is often called *slicing and dicing* the cube. Another operation closely related to slicing and dicing is data pivoting (similar to the pivoting possible in Microsoft Excel). This term refers to rotating the view for a particular data point to obtain another perspective. For example, Figure 11-12 shows sales of 400 units of shoes for April. The analyst could pivot this view to obtain (for example) the sales of shoes by store for the same month.

Another type of operation often used in multidimensional analysis is *drill-down*—that is, analyzing a given set of data at a finer level of detail. An example of drill-down is shown in Figure 11-13. Figure 11-13a shows a summary report for the total sales of three package sizes for a given brand of paper towels: 2-pack, 3-pack, and 6-pack. However, the towels come in different colors, and the analyst wants a further breakdown of sales by color within each of these package sizes. Using an OLAP tool, this breakdown can be easily obtained using a "point-and-click" approach with a pointing device. The result of the drill-down is shown in Figure 11-13b. Notice that a drill-down presentation is equivalent to adding another column to the original report. (In this case, a column was added for the attribute color.)

FIGURE 11-13 Example
of drill-down
a) Summary report

Brand	Package size	Sales
SofTowel	2-pack	$75
SofTowel	3-pack	$100
SofTowel	6-pack	$50

Brand	Package size	Color	Sales
SofTowel	2-pack	White	$30
SofTowel	2-pack	Yellow	$25
SofTowel	2-pack	Pink	$20
SofTowel	3-pack	White	$50
SofTowel	3-pack	Green	$25
SofTowel	3-pack	Yellow	$25
SofTowel	6-pack	White	$30
SofTowel	6-pack	Yellow	$20

Executing a drill-down (as in this example) may require that the OLAP tool "reach back" to the data warehouse to obtain the detail data necessary for the drill-down. This type of operation can be performed by an OLAP tool (without user participation) only if an integrated set of metadata is available to that tool. Some tools even permit the OLAP tool to reach back to the operational data if necessary for a given query.

It is straightforward to show a three-dimensional hypercube in a spreadsheet-type format using columns, rows, and sheets (pages) as the three dimensions. It is possible, however, to show data in more than three dimensions by cascading rows or columns and using drop-down selections to show different slices. Figure 11-14 shows a portion of a report from a Microsoft Excel pivot table with four dimensions, with travel method and number of days in cascading columns. OLAP query and reporting tools usually allow this way to handle sharing dimensions within the limits of two-dimension printing or display space. Data visualization tools, to be shown in the next section, allow using shapes, colors, and other properties of multiples of graphs to include more than three dimensions on the same display.

DATA VISUALIZATION Often the human eye can best discern patterns when data are represented graphically. Data visualization is the representation of data in graphical and multimedia formats for human analysis. Benefits of data visualization include the ability to better observe trends and patterns and to identify correlations and clusters. Data visualization is often used in conjunction with data mining and other analytical techniques.

In essence, data visualization is a way to show multidimensional data not as numbers and text but as graphs. Thus, precise values are often not shown, but rather the intent is

FIGURE 11-14   Sample pivot table with four dimensions: Country (pages), Resort Name (rows), Travel Method, and No. of Days (columns)

Country	(All)														
Average of Price	**Travel Method No. of Days**														
	Coach			Coach Total	Plane									Plane Total
Resort Name	4	5	7		6	7	8	10	14	16	21	32	60	
Aviemore			135	135										
Barcelona														
Black Forest	69			69										
Cork							269							269
Grand Canyon													1128	1128
Great Barrier Reef												750		750
Lake Geneva							699							699
London														
Los Angeles						295			375					335
Lyon									399					399
Malaga										234				234
Nerja					198				255					226.5
Nice						289								289
Paris–Euro Disney														
Prague		95		95										
Seville								199						199
Skiathos											429			429
Grand Total	69	95	135	99.66666667	198	292	484	199	343	234	429	750	1128	424.5384615

to more readily show relationships between the data. As with OLAP tools, the data for the graphs are computed often from SQL queries against a database (or possibly from data in a spreadsheet). The SQL queries are generated automatically by the OLAP or data visualization software simply from the user indicating what he or she wants to see.

Figure 11-15 shows a simple visualization of sales data using the data visualization tool Tableau. This visualization uses a common technique called small multiples, which places many graphs on one page to support comparison. Each small graph plots metrics of SUM(Total Sales) on the horizontal axis and SUM(Gross Profit) on the vertical axis. There is a separate graph for the dimensions region and year; different market segments are shown via different symbols for the plot points. The user simply drags and drops these metrics

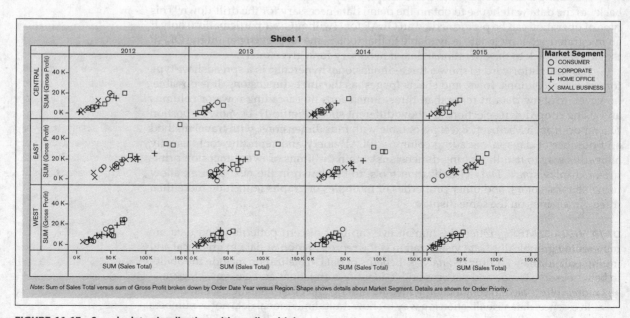

FIGURE 11-15   Sample data visualization with small multiples

and dimensions to a menu and then selects the style of visualization or lets the tool pick what it thinks would be the most illustrative type of graph. The user indicates what he or she wants to see and in what format instead of describing how to retrieve data.

BUSINESS PERFORMANCE MANAGEMENT AND DASHBOARDS A business performance management (BPM) system allows managers to measure, monitor, and manage key activities and processes to achieve organizational goals. Dashboards are often used to provide an information system in support of BPM. Dashboards, just as those in a car or airplane cockpit, include a variety of displays to show different aspects of the organization. Often the top dashboard, an executive dashboard, is based on a balanced scorecard, in which different measures show metrics from different processes and disciplines, such as operations efficiency, financial status, customer service, sales, and human resources. Each display of a dashboard will address different areas in different ways. For example, one display may have alerts about key customers and their purchases. Another display may show key performance indicators for manufacturing, with "stoplight" symbols of red, yellow, and green to indicate if the measures are inside or outside tolerance limits. Each area of the organization may have its own dashboard to determine health of that function. For example, Figure 11-16 is a simple dashboard for one financial measure, revenue. The left panel shows dials about revenue over the past three years, with needles indicating where these measures fall within a desirable range. Other panels show more details to help a manager find the source of out-of-tolerance measures.

Each of the panels is a result of complex queries to a data mart or data warehouse. As a user wants to see more details, there often is a way to click on a graph to get a menu of choices for exploring the details behind the icon or graphic. A panel may be the result of running some predictive model against data in the data warehouse to forecast future conditions (an example of predictive modeling).

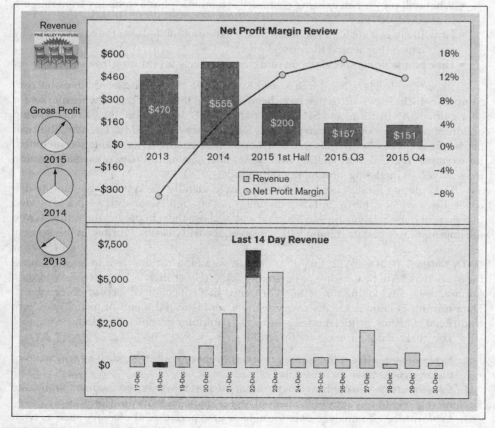

FIGURE 11-16 Sample dashboard

Integrative dashboard displays are possible only when data are consistent across each display, which requires a data warehouse and dependent data marts. Stand-alone dashboards for independent data marts can be developed, but then it is difficult to trace problems between areas (e.g., production bottlenecks due to higher sales than forecast).

Use of Predictive Analytics

If descriptive analytics focuses on the past, the key emphasis of predictive analytics is on the future. Predictive analytics systems use statistical and computational methods that use data regarding past and current events to form models regarding what might happen in the future (potentially depending on a number of assumptions regarding various parameters). The methods for predictive analytics are not new; for example, classification trees, linear and logistic regression analysis, machine learning, and neural networks have existed for quite a while. What has changed recently is the ease with which they can be applied to practical organizational questions and our understanding of the capabilities of various predictive analytics approaches. New approaches are, of course, continuously developed for predictive analytics, such as the golden path analysis for forecasting stakeholder actions based on past behavior (Watson, 2014). Please note that even though predictive analytics focuses on the future, it cannot operate without data regarding the past and the present—predictions have to be built on a firm foundation.

Predictive analytics can be used to improve an organization's understanding of fundamental business questions such as this (adapted from Parr-Rud, 2012):

- What type of an offer will a specific prospective customer need so that she/he will become a new customer?
- What solicitation approaches are most likely to lead to new donations from the patrons of a non-profit organization?
- What approach will increase the probability of a telecommunications company succeeding in making a household switch to their services?
- What will prevent an existing customer of a mobile phone company from moving to another provider?
- How likely is a customer to lease their next automobile from the same company from which they leased their previous car?
- How profitable is a specific credit card customer likely to be during the next five years?

According to Herschel, Linden, and Kart (2014), the leading predictive analytics companies include two firms that have been leaders in the statistical software market for a long time: SAS Institute and SPSS (now part of IBM). In addition, the Gartner leading quadrant consists of open source products RapidMiner and KNIME. The availability of predictive analytics techniques that Gartner used as criteria in its evaluation included, for example, regression modeling, time-series analysis, neural networks, classification trees, Bayesian modeling, and hierarchical models.

Data mining is often used as a mechanism to identify the key variables and to discover the essential patterns, but data mining is not enough: An analyst's work is needed to represent these relationships in a formal way and use them to predict the future. Given the important role of data mining in this process, we will discuss it further in this section.

DATA MINING TOOLS With OLAP, users are searching for answers to specific questions, such as "Are health-care costs greater for single or married persons?" With data mining, users are looking for patterns or trends in a collection of facts or observations. **Data mining** is knowledge discovery using a sophisticated blend of techniques from traditional statistics, artificial intelligence, and computer graphics (Weldon, 1996).

Data mining
Knowledge discovery using a sophisticated blend of techniques from traditional statistics, artificial intelligence, and computer graphics.

The goals of data mining are threefold:

1. *Explanatory* To explain some observed event or condition, such as why sales of pickup trucks have increased in Colorado
2. *Confirmatory* To confirm a hypothesis, such as whether two-income families are more likely to buy family medical coverage than single-income families
3. *Exploratory* To analyze data for new or unexpected relationships, such as what spending patterns are likely to accompany credit card fraud

TABLE 11-4 Data-Mining Techniques

Technique	Function
Regression	Test or discover relationships from historical data
Decision tree induction	Test or discover if…then rules for decision propensity
Clustering and signal processing	Discover subgroups or segments
Affinity	Discover strong mutual relationships
Sequence association	Discover cycles of events and behaviors
Case-based reasoning	Derive rules from real-world case examples
Rule discovery	Search for patterns and correlations in large data sets
Fractals	Compress large databases without losing information
Neural nets	Develop predictive models based on principles modeled after the human brain

Several different techniques are commonly used for data mining. See Table 11-4 for a summary of the most common of these techniques. The choice of an appropriate technique depends on the nature of the data to be analyzed, as well as the size of the data set. Data mining can be performed against all types of data sources in the unified data architecture, including **text mining** of unstructured textual material.

Data-mining techniques have been successfully used for a wide range of real-world applications. A summary of some of the typical types of applications, with examples of each type, is presented in Table 11-5. Data-mining applications are growing rapidly, for the following reasons:

- The amount of data in the organizational data sources is growing exponentially. Users need the type of automated techniques provided by data-mining tools to mine the knowledge in these data.
- New data-mining tools with expanded capabilities are continually being introduced.
- Increasing competitive pressures are forcing companies to make better use of the information and knowledge contained in their data.

Text mining

The process of discovering meaningful information algorithmically based on computational analysis of unstructured textual information.

TABLE 11-5 Typical Data-Mining Applications

Data-Mining Application	Example
Profiling populations	Developing profiles of high-value customers, credit risks, and credit-card fraud.
Analysis of business trends	Identifying markets with above-average (or below-average) growth.
Target marketing	Identifying rustomers (or customer segments) for promotional activity.
Usage analysis	Identifying usage patterns for products and services.
Campaign effectiveness	Comparing campaign strategies for effectiveness.
Product affinity	Identifying products that are purchased concurrently or identifying the characteristics of shoppers for certain product groups.
Customer retention and churn	Examining the behavior of customers who have left for competitors to prevent remaining customers from leaving.
Profitability analysis	Determining which customers are profitable, given the total set of activities the customer has with the organization.
Customer value analysis	Determining where valuable customers are at different stages in their life.
Upselling	Identifying new products or services to sell to a customer based upon critical events and life-style changes.

Source: Based on Dyché (2000).

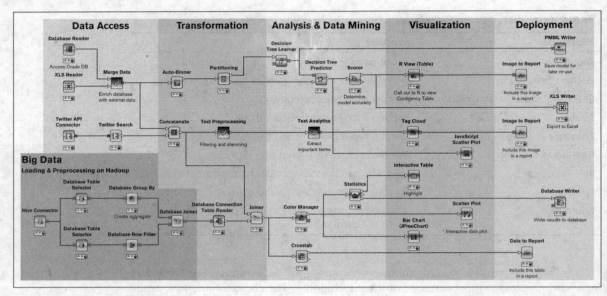

FIGURE 11-17 KNIME architecture

Source: https://www.knime.org/knime. Courtesy of KNIME.

For thorough coverage of data mining and all analytical aspects of business intelligence from a data warehousing perspective, see, for example, Sharda, Delen, and Turban (2013).

EXAMPLES OF PREDICTIVE ANALYTICS Predictive analytics can be used in a variety of ways to analyze past data in order to make predictions regarding the future state of affairs based on mathematical models without direct human role in the process. The underlying models are not new: The core ideas underlying regression analysis, neural networks, and machine learning were developed decades ago, but only the recent tools (such as SAS Enterprise Miner or KNIME) have made them easier to use. Earlier in this chapter we discussed in general terms some of the typical business applications of predictive analytics. In this section we will present some additional examples at a more detailed level.

KNIME's (see Figure 11-17) illustration of use cases includes a wide variety of examples from marketing to finance. In the latter area, credit scoring is a process that takes past financial data at the individual level and develops a model that gives every individual a score describing the probability of a default for that individual. In a KNIME example (**https://www.knime.org/knime-applications/credit-scoring**), the workflow includes three separate methods (decision tree, neural network, and machine learning algorithm called SVM) for developing the initial model. As the second step, the system selects the best model by accuracy and finally writes the best model out in the Predictive Model Markup Language (PMML). PMML is a de facto standard for representing a collection of modeling techniques that together form the foundation for predictive modeling. In addition to modeling, PMML can also be used to specify the transformations that the data has to go through before it is ready to be modeled, demonstrating again the strong linkage between data management and analytics.

In marketing, a frequently used example is the identification of those customers that are predicted to leave the company and go elsewhere (churn). The KNIME example (**https://www.knime.org/knime-applications/churn-analysis**) uses an algorithm called k-Means to divide the cases into clusters, in this case predicting whether or not a particular customer will be likely to leave the company. Finally, KNIME also includes a social media data analysis example (**https://www.knime.org/knime-applications/lastfm-recommodation**), demonstrating how association analysis can be used to identify the performers to whom those listening to a specific artist are also likely to listen.

In addition to the business examples, the KNIME case descriptions illustrate how close the linkage between data management and analytics is in the context of an advanced analytics platform. For example, the churn analysis example includes the use of modules such as XLS Reader, Column Filter, XLS Writer, and Data to Report to get the job done. The social media example utilizes File Reader, Joiner, GroupBy, and Data to Report. Even if you do not know these modules, it is likely that they look familiar as operations, and the names directly refer to operations with data.

Use of Prescriptive Analytics

If the key question in descriptive analytics is "What happened?" and in predictive analytics is "What will happen?" then prescriptive analytics focuses on the question "How can we make it happen?" or "What do we need to do to make it happen?" For prescriptive analysis we need optimization and simulation tools and advanced modeling to understand the dependencies between various actors within the domain of interest. In many contexts, the results of prescriptive analytics are automatically moved to business decision making. For example:

- Automated algorithms make millions or billions of trading decisions daily, buying and selling securities in markets where human actions are far too slow.
- Airlines and hotels are pricing their products automatically using sophisticated algorithms to maximize revenue that can be extracted from these perishable resources.
- Companies like Amazon and Netflix are providing automated product recommendations based on a number of factors, including their customers' prior purchase history and the behavior of the people with whom they are connected.

The tools for prescriptive analytics are less structured and packaged than those for descriptive and predictive analytics. Many of the most sophisticated tools are internally developed. The leading vendors of predictive analytics products do, however, also include modules for enabling prescriptive analytics.

Wu (as cited in Bertolucci, 2013) describes prescriptive analytics as a type of predictive analytics, and this is, indeed, a helpful way to look at the relationship of the two. Without the modeling characteristic of predictive analytics, systems for prescriptive analytics could not perform their task of prescribing an action based on past data. Further, prescriptive analytics systems typically collect data regarding the impact of the action taken so that the models can be further improved in the future. As we discussed in the introduction, prescriptive analytics provides model-based views regarding the impact of various actions on business performance (Underwood, 2013) and often make automated decisions based on the predictive models.

Prescriptive analytics is not new, either, because various technologies have been used for a long time to make automated business decisions based on past data. What has changed recently, however, is the sophistication of the models that support these decisions and the level of granularity related to the decision processes. For example, service businesses can make decisions regarding price/product feature combinations not only at the level of large customer groups (such as business vs. leisure) but at the level of an individual traveler so that recommendation systems can configure individual service offerings addressing a traveler's key needs while keeping the price at a level that is still possible for the traveler (Braun, 2013).

Implementing prescriptive analytics solutions typically requires integration of analytics software from third parties and an organization's operational information systems solutions (whether ERPs, other packaged solutions, or systems specifically developed for the organization). Therefore, there are many fewer analytics packages labeled specifically as "prescriptive analytics" than there are those for descriptive or predictive analytics. Instead, the development of prescriptive analytics solutions requires more sophisticated integration skills, and these solutions often provide more distinctive business value because they are tailored to a specific organization's needs.

Hernandez and Morgan (2014) discuss the reasons underlying the complexity of the systems for prescriptive analytics. Not only do these systems require sophisticated predictive modeling of organizational and external data, they also require in-depth understanding of the processes required for optimal business decisions in a specific context. This is not a simple undertaking; it requires the identification of the potential decisions that need to be made, the interconnections and dependencies between these decisions, and the factors that affect the outcomes of these decisions. In addition to the statistical analysis methods common in predictive analytics, prescriptive analytics relies on advanced simulations, optimization processes, decision-analysis methods, and game theory. This all needs to take place real-time with feedback loops that will analyze the successfulness of each decision/recommendation the system has made and use this information to improve the decision algorithms.

Data Management Infrastructure for Analytics

In this section, we will review the technical infrastructure that is required for enabling the big data approach specified earlier and other forms of data sources for advanced analytics. We will not focus on the analytical processes themselves—other textbooks such as *Business Intelligence: A Managerial Perspective on Analytics* (Sharda, Delen, and Turban, 2013) and *Business Intelligence and Analytics: Systems for Decision Support* (Sharda, Delen, and Turban, 2014) are good sources for those readers interested in the approaches and techniques of analytics. In this text, we will emphasize the foundational technologies that are needed to enable big data and advanced analytics in general, that is, the infrastructure for big data and advanced analytics.

Schoenborn (2014) identified four specific infrastructure capabilities that are required for big data and advanced analytics. They are as follows:

- *Scalability*, which refers to the organization's planned ability to add capacity (processing resources, storage space, and connectivity) based on changes in demand. Highly scalable infrastructure allows an organization to respond to increasing demand quickly without long lead times or huge individual investments.
- *Parallelism*, which is a widely used design principle in modern computing systems. Parallel systems are capable of processing, transferring, and accessing data in multiple chunks at the same time. We will later discuss a particular implementation model of parallelism called massively parallel processing (MPP) systems, which is commonly used, among other contexts, in large data centers run by companies such as Google, Amazon, Facebook, and Yahoo!.
- *Low latency* of various technical components of the system. Low latency refers, in practice, to a high speed in various processing and data access and writing tasks. When designing high-capacity infrastructure systems, it is essential that the components of these systems add as little latency as possible to the system.
- *Data optimization*, which refers to the skills needed to design optimal storage and processing structures.

According to Schoenborn (2014), there are three major infrastructure characteristics that can be measured. All of these are enabled by the capabilities previously discussed: speed, availability, and access.

- *Speed* tells how many units of action (such as certain processing or data access task) the system is able to perform in a time unit (such as a second).
- *Availability* describes how well the system stays available in case of component failure(s). A highly available system can withstand failures of multiple components, such as processor cores or disk drives.
- *Access* illustrates who will have access to the capabilities offered by the system and how this access is implemented. A well-designed architecture provides easy access to all stakeholders based on their needs.

Four specific technology solutions are used in modern data storage systems that enable advanced analytics and allow systems to achieve the infrastructure capabilities previously described (see, e.g., Watson, 2014). These include massively parallel

TABLE 11-6 Technologies Enabling Infrastructure Advances in Data Management

Massively parallel processing (MPP)	Instead of relying on a single processor, MPP divides a computing task (such as query processing) between multiple processors, speeding it up significantly.
In-memory DBMSs	In-memory DBMSs keep the entire database in primary memory, thus enabling significantly faster processing.
In-database analytics	If analytical functions are integrated directly to the DBMS, there is no need to move large quantities of data to separate analytics tools for processing.
Columnar DBMSs	They reorient the data in the storage structures, leading to efficiencies in many data warehousing and other analytics applications.

processing (MPP), in-memory database management systems, in-database analytics, and columnar databases (see summary in Table 11-6).

Massively parallel processing (MPP) is one of the key advances not only in data storage but in computing technologies in general. The principle is simple: A complex and time-consuming computing task will be divided into multiple tasks that are executed simultaneously to increase the speed at which the system achieves the result. Instead of having one unit of computing power (such as a processor) to perform a specific task, the system will be able to use dozens or thousands of units at the same time. In practice, this is a very complex challenge and requires careful design of the computing tasks. Large Web-based service providers have made significant advances in understanding how massively parallel systems can be developed using very large numbers of commodity hardware, that is, standardized, inexpensive processing and storage units.

In-memory database management systems are also based on a simple concept: storing the database(s) in the database server's random access memory instead of storing them on a hard disk or another secondary storage device, such as flash memory. Modern server computers used as database servers can have several terabytes of RAM, an amount that just a few years ago was large even for a disk drive capacity. The primary benefit of storing the databases in-memory (and not just temporarily caching data in-memory) is improved performance specifically with random access: Jacobs (2009) demonstrates how random access reads with a solid-state disk (SSD) are about six times faster than with a mechanical disk drive but random in-memory access is 20,000 times faster than SSD access.

In-database analytics is an interesting architectural development, which is based on the idea of integrating the software that enables analytical work directly with the database management system software. This will make it possible to do the analytical work directly in the database instead of extracting the required data first onto a separate server for analytics. This reduces the number of stages in the process, thus improving overall performance, ensuring that all data available in the database will be available for analysis, and helping to avoid errors. This approach also makes it possible to integrate analytical tools with traditional data retrieval languages (such as SQL).

Columnar or column-oriented database management systems are using an approach to storing data that differs significantly from traditional row-oriented relational database management systems. Traditional RDBM technology is built around the standard relational data model of tables of rows and columns and physical structures that store data as files of records for rows, with columns as fields in each record. This approach has served the needs of RDBMs used for transaction processing and simple management reporting well. Complex analytics with very large and versatile data sets, however, can benefit from a different storage structure for data, one where data are stored on a column basis instead of on a row basis. That is, values are stored in sequence for one column, followed by the values for another column, and so on, thus virtually turning a table of data 90 degrees.

Vendors of column-based products claim to reduce storage space (because data compression techniques are used, for example, to store a value only once) and to speed query processing time because the data are physically organized to support analytical queries. Column database technologies trade off storage space savings (data compression of more than 70 percent is common) for computing time. The conceptual and logical data models for the data warehouse do not change. SQL is still the query language, and you do not write queries any differently; the DBMS simply stores and accesses the data differently than in traditional row-oriented RDBMSs. Data compression and storage depend on the data and queries. For example, with Vertica (a division of HP), one of the leading column database management system providers, the logical relational database is defined in SQL as with any RDBMS. Next, a set of sample queries and data are presented to a database design tool. This tool analyzes the predicates (WHERE clauses) of the queries and the redundancy in the sample data to suggest a data compression scheme and storage of columnar data. Different data compression techniques are used depending on the type of predicate data (numeric, textual, limited versus a wide range of values, etc.).

We will not cover in this text the implementation details of these advances in data management technologies because they are primarily related to the internal technology design and not the design of the database. It is, however, essential that you understand the impact these technological innovations potentially have on the use of data through faster access, better integration of data management and analytics, improved balance between the use of in-memory and on-disk storage, and innovative storage structures that improve performance and reduce storage costs. These new structural and architectural innovations are significantly broadening the options companies have available for implementing technical solutions for making data available for analytics.

IMPACT OF BIG DATA AND ANALYTICS

In this final section of Chapter 11, we will discuss a number of important issues related to the impact of big data, primarily from two perspectives: applications and implications of big data analytics. In the applications section, we will focus on the areas of human activity most affected by the new opportunities created by big data and illustrate some of the ways in which big data analytics has transformed business, government, and not-for-profit organizations.

Applications of Big Data and Analytics

The following categorization of areas of human activity affected by big data analytics is adapted and extended from Chen et al. (2012):

1. Business (originally e-commerce and market intelligence),
2. E-government and politics,
3. Science and technology,
4. Smart health and well-being, and
5. Security and public safety.

The ways in which human activities are conducted and organized in all of these areas have already changed quite significantly because of analytics, and there is potential for much more significant transformation in the future. There are, of course, other areas of human activity that could also have been added to this list, including, for example, arts and entertainment.

From the perspective of the core focus area of this textbook, one of the key lessons to remember is that all of these exciting and very significant changes in important areas of life are only possible if the collection, organizing, quality control, and analysis of data are implemented systematically and with a strong focus on quality. Some of the discussions in the popular press and the marketing materials of the vendor may create the impression that truly insightful results emerge from various systems without human intervention. This is a dangerous fallacy, and it is essential that you as a professional with an in-depth understanding of data management are well-informed of what is needed to enable the truly amazing new applications based on big data analytics and decision making based on it. Sometimes you will need to do a lot of work to educate your colleagues and customers of what is needed to deliver the true benefits of analytics (Lohr, 2014).

Another major lesson to take away from this section is the breadth of current and potential applications of big data analytics. The applications of analytics are not limited to business but extend to a wide range of essential human activities, all of which are going through major changes because of advanced analytics capabilities. These changes are not limited to specific geographic regions, either—applications of analytics will have an impact on countries and areas regardless of their location or economic development status. For example, the relative importance of mobile communication technologies is particularly high in developing countries, and many of the advanced applications of analytics are utilizing data collected by mobile systems.

We will next briefly discuss the areas that big data analytics is changing and the changes it is introducing.

BUSINESS   In business, advanced uses of analytics have the potential to change the relationship between a business and its individual customers dramatically. As already discussed in the context of prescriptive analytics, analytics allows businesses to tailor both products and pricing to the needs of an individual customer, leading to something economists call *first degree* or *complete price discrimination*, that is, extracting from each customer the maximum price they are willing to pay. This is, of course, not beneficial from the customers' perspective. At the same time, customers do benefit from the ability to receive goods and services that are tailored to their specific needs.

Some of the best-known examples of the use of big data analytics in business are related to the targeting of marketing communication to specific customers. The often-told true story (Duhigg, 2012) about how a large U.S. retail chain started to send a female teenager pregnancy-related advertisements, leading to complaints by an irritated father, is a great example of the power and the dangers of the use of analytics. To make a long story short, the father, became even more irritated after finding out that the retail chain had learned about his daughter's pregnancy earlier than he had by using product and other Web search data. Big data analytics gives companies outstanding opportunities to learn a lot about their current and prospective customers. At the same time, it creates a major responsibility for them to understand the appropriate uses of these technologies.

Businesses are also learning a lot about and from their customers by analyzing data that they collect from Web- and mobile-based interactions between them and their customers and social media data. Customers leave a lot of clues about their characteristics and preferences through the actions that they take when navigating a company's Web site, performing searches with external search engines, or making comments regarding the company's products or services on various social media platforms. Many companies are particularly attentive to communication on social media because of the public nature of the communication. Sometimes a complaint on Twitter will lead to a faster response time than using e-mail for the same purpose.

E-GOVERNMENT AND POLITICS   Analytics has also had a significant impact on politics, particularly in terms of how politicians interact with their constituents and how political campaigns are conducted. Again, social media platforms are important sources of data for understanding public opinion regarding general issues and specific positions taken by a politician, and social media forms important communication channels and platforms for interactions between politicians and their stakeholders (Wattal et al., 2010).

One important perspective on analytics in the context of government is that of the role of government as a data source. Governments all over the world both collect huge amounts of data through their own actions and fund the collection of research data. Providing access to the government-owned data through well-defined open interfaces has led to significant opportunities to provide useful new services or create insights regarding possible actions by local governments. Some of these success stories are told on the Web site of The Open Data Institute (**theodi.org/stories**), co-founded by World Wide Web inventor Sir Tim Berners-Lee and others at **opendatastories.org**.

In addition, it was at least originally hoped that data openness would be associated with gains in values associated with democracy (improved transparency of public actions, opportunities for more involved citizen participation, improved ability to evaluate elected officials, etc.); it is not clear whether or not these advances can truly materialize (Chignard, 2013).

SCIENCE AND TECHNOLOGY Big data analytics has already greatly benefited a wide variety of scientific disciplines, from astrophysics to genomics to many of the social sciences. As described in Chen et al. (2012, p. 1170), the U.S. National Science foundation described some of the potential scientific benefits of big data:

> "to accelerate the progress of scientific discovery and innovation; lead to new fields of inquiry that would not otherwise be possible; [encourage] the development of new data analytic tools and algorithms; facilitate scalable, accessible, and sustainable data infrastructure; increase understanding of human and social processes and interactions; and promote economic growth and improved health and quality of life."

We can expect significant advances in a number of scientific disciplines from big data analytics. One of the interesting issues that connects the role of government and the practice of science in the area of big data is the ownership and availability of research data to the broader scientific community. When research is funded by a government agency (such as the U.S. National Science Foundation or National Institutes of Health), should the raw data from that research be made available freely? What rules should govern the access to such data? How should it be organized and secured? These are significant questions that are not easy to answer, and any answers found need significant sophistication in data management before they can be implemented.

SMART HEALTH AND WELL-BEING The opportunities to collect personal health and well-being–related data and benefit from it are increasing dramatically. Not only are typical formal medical tests producing much more data than used to be the case, there are also new types of sources of large amounts of personal medical data (such as mapping of an individual's entire genome, which is soon going to cost a few hundred dollars or less). Furthermore, there are opportunities to integrate large amounts of individual data collected by, for example, insurance companies or national medical systems (where they exist). This data from a variety of sources can, in turn, be used for a variety of research purposes. Individuals are also using a variety of devices to collect and store personal health and well-being data using devices that they are wearing (such as Fitbit, Jawbone, or Nike FuelBand).

Chen et al. (2012) discuss the ways in which all this health and well-being–related data could be used to transform the entire concept of medicine from disease control to an evidence-based, individually focused preventive process with the main goal of maintaining health. Health and wellness is an area that will test the capabilities of the data collection and management infrastructure for analytics in a number of ways, given the continuous nature of the data collection and the highly private nature of the data.

SECURITY AND PUBLIC SAFETY Around the world, concerns regarding security, safety, and fraud have led to the interest in applying big data analytics to the processes of identifying potential security risks in advance and reacting to them before the risks materialize. The methods and capabilities related to the storage and processing of large amounts of data real-time are applicable to fraud detection, screening of individuals of interest from large groups, identifying potential cybersecurity attacks, understanding the behavior of criminal and terrorist networks, and many other similar purposes.

Concerns of security and privacy are particularly important in this area because of the high human cost of false identification of individuals as security risks and the fundamentally important need to maintain a proper balance between security and individual rights. The conversation regarding the appropriate role of government agencies started by the revelations made by Edward Snowden in 2013 and 2014 (Greenwald et al., 2013) has brought many essential questions regarding individual privacy to the forefront of public debate, at the minimum pointing out the importance of making informed decisions regarding the collection of private data by public entities.

Implications of Big Data Analytics and Decision Making

As already tentatively discussed, big data analytics raises a number of important questions regarding possible negative implications. As with any other new technology, it is important that decision makers and experts at various levels have a clear understanding of the possible implications of their choices and actions. Many of the opportunities created by big data analytics are genuinely transformative, but the benefits have to be evaluated in the context of the potentially harmful consequences.

In January 2014, a workshop funded by the U.S. National Science Foundation (Markus, 2014) brought together a large number of experts on big data analytics and decision making to identify the key implications of the technical developments related to big data. This section is built on the key themes that emerged from the workshop conversations.[1]

PERSONAL PRIVACY VS. COLLECTIVE BENEFITS   Personal privacy is probably the most commonly cited concern in various conversations regarding the implications of big data analytics. What mechanisms should be in place to make sure that individual citizens can control the data that various third parties—including businesses, government agencies, and non-profit organizations—maintain about them? What control should an individual customer have over the profiles various companies build about them in order to target marketing communication better? What rights should individuals have to demand that data collected regarding them is protected, corrected, or deleted if they so desire? Should medical providers be allowed to collect detailed personal data in order to advance science and medial practice? How about the role of government agencies—how much should they be allowed to know about a random individual in order to protect national security? Many of these questions are, in practice, about the relationship between personal right to privacy vs. the collective benefits we can gain if detailed individual data are collected and maintained.

The legal and ethical issues that need to be considered in this context are complex and multiple, but no organization or individual manager or designer dealing with large amounts of individual data can ignore them. Legal codes and practices vary across the world, and it is essential that privacy and security questions are carefully built into any process of designing systems that utilize big data.

OWNERSHIP AND ACCESS   Another complex set of questions is related to the ownership of the large collections of data that various organizations put together to gain the benefits previously discussed. What rights should individuals have to data that has been collected about them? Should they have the right to benefit financially about the data they are providing through their actions? Many of the free Web-based services are, in practice, not free: Individuals get access to the services by giving up some of their rights to privacy.

In this category is also the question about ownership of research data, particularly in the context of research projects funded by various government agencies. If research is taxpayer funded, should the data collected in that research be made available to all interested parties? If yes, how is individual privacy of research participants protected?

QUALITY AND REUSE OF DATA AND ALGORITHMS   The fact that big data analytics is based on large amounts of data does not mean that data quality (discussed at a more detailed level in Chapter 10) is any less important. On the contrary, high volumes of poor quality data arriving at high speeds can lead to particularly bad analytical results. Some of the data quality questions related to big data are exactly the same that data management professionals have struggled with for a long time: missing data, incorrect coding, replicated data, missing specifications, etc. Others are specific to the new context particularly because particularly NoSQL-based systems often are not based on careful conceptual and logical modeling (in some contexts by definition).

In addition, often big data systems reuse data and algorithms for purposes for which they were not originally developed. In these situations, it is essential that reuse does not become misuse because of, for example, poor fit between the new purpose and the data that was originally collected for something else or algorithms that work well for one purpose but are not a good fit with a slightly different situation.

---

[1] Acknowledgement: The material in this section is partially based upon work supported by the National Science Foundation under Grant No. 1348929. Any opinions, findings, and conclusions or recommendations expressed in this material are those of the author(s) and do not necessarily reflect the views of the National Science Foundation.

TRANSPARENCY AND VALIDATION   One of the challenges with big data in both business and science is that in many cases it is impossible for anybody else but the party doing the analysis to verify if the analysis is correctly performed or if the data that was used is correct. For example, automated credit rating systems can have a major impact on an individual's ability to get a car loan or a mortgage and also on the interest cost of the borrowed funds. Even if the outcome is negative, it is very difficult for an individual to get access to the specific data that led to the decision and to verify its correctness.

The need for validation and transparency becomes particularly important in the case of entirely automated prescriptive analytics, for example, in the form of automated trading of securities or underwriting of insurance policies. If there is no human intervention, there should be at least processes in place that make a continuous review of the actions taken by the automated system.

CHANGING NATURE OF WORK   Big data analytics will also have an impact on the nature of work. In the same way many jobs requiring manual labor have changed significantly because of robotics, many knowledge work opportunities will be transformed because sophisticated analytical systems will assume at least some of the responsibilities that earlier required expert training and long experience. For example, Frey and Osborne (2013) evaluated the future of employment based on computerization and based on a sophisticated mathematical model calculated probabilities for specific occupations to be significantly impacted by computer-based technologies (in the context of knowledge work, analytics). Their list of occupations suggests that many knowledge work professions will disappear in the relatively near future because of advances in computing.

DEMANDS FOR WORKFORCE CAPABILITIES AND EDUCATION   Finally, big data analytics has already changed the requirements for the capabilities knowledge workers are expected to have and, consequently, for the education that a knowledge professional should have. It will not be long until any professional will be expected to use a wide variety of analytical tools to understand not only numeric data but also textual and multimedia data collected from a variety of sources. This will not be possible without a conscious effort to prepare analysts for these tasks.

For information systems professionals, the additional challenge is that the concept of data management has broadened significantly from the management of well-designed structured data in relational databases and building systems on the top of those. Data management brings together and is required to take care of a wide variety of data from a rich set of internal and external sources, ensuring the quality and security of those resources, and organizing the data so that they are available for the analysts to use.

Summary

The landscape of data management is changing rapidly because of the requirements and opportunities created by new analytics capabilities. In addition to its traditional responsibilities related to managing traditional organizational data resources primarily stored in relational databases, enterprise-wide data warehouses, and data marts, organizational data and information management function now has additional responsibilities. It is responsible for overseeing and partially implementing the processes related to bringing together semi- and unstructured data of various types from many external and internal sources, managing its quality and security, and making it available for a rich set of analytical tools.

Big data has created more excitement and sense of new opportunities than any other organizational data and information-related concept for a decade; therefore this umbrella concept referring to the collection, storage, management, and analysis of very large amounts of heterogeneous data that arrives at very high speeds is an essential area of study. For the purposes of organizational data and information management, the key questions are related to the specific requirements that big data sets for the tools and infrastructure. Two key new technology categories are data management environments under the title NoSQL (Not only SQL) and the massively parallel open source platform Hadoop. Both NoSQL technologies and Hadoop have given organizations tools for storing and analyzing very large amounts of data at unit costs that were not possible earlier. In many cases, NoSQL and Hadoop-based solutions do not have predefined schemas. Instead of the traditional *schema on write* approach, the structures are specified (or even discovered) at the time when the data are explored and analyzed (*schema on read*). Both NoSQL technologies and Hadoop provide important new capabilities for organizational data management.

Hadoop and NoSQL technologies are not, however, useful alone and, in practice, they are used as part of larger organization-wide platforms of data management technologies, which bring together tools for collecting, storing, managing, and analyzing massive amounts of data. Many vendors have introduced their own comprehensive conceptual architectures for bringing together the various tools, such as Teradata's Unified Data Architecture.

Given its recent surge in the ranks of organizational buzzwords, the world of analytics is currently in turmoil, suffering from inconsistent use of concepts. Dividing analytics into descriptive, predictive, and prescriptive variants provides useful structure to this evolving area.

In addition, it also helps to categorize analytics based on the types of sources from which data are retrieved to the organizational analytics systems: traditional administrative systems, the Web, and ubiquitous mobile systems.

Big data and other advanced analytics approaches create truly exciting new opportunities for business, government, civic engagement, not-for-profit organizations, various scientific disciplines, engineering, personal health and well-being, and security. The advantages are not, however, without their potential downsides. Therefore, it is important that decision makers and professionals working with and depending on analytics solutions understand the implications of big data related to personal privacy, data ownership and access, quality and reuse of data and algorithms, openness of the solutions based on big data, changing nature of work, and the requirements for education and workforce capabilities.

Chapter Review

Key Terms

Analytics 451
Big data 451
Business intelligence 466
Data lake 454
Data mining 476
Descriptive analytics 467

Hadoop 459
HDFS 460
Hive 462
MapReduce 459
Multidimensional OLAP (MOLAP) 472

NoSQL 455
Online analytical processing (OLAP) 471
Pig 462
Predictive analytics 467
Prescriptive analytics 467

Relational OLAP (ROLAP) 471
Text mining 477

Review Questions

11-1. Define each of the following terms:
  a. Hadoop
  b. MapReduce
  c. HDFS
  d. NoSQL
  e. Pig
  f. data mining
  g. online analytical processing
  h. business intelligence

11-2. Match the following terms to the appropriate definitions:
  _____ Hive
  _____ text mining
  _____ data lake
  _____ data mining
  _____ descriptive analytics
  _____ analytics
  _____ predictive analytics

  _____ prescriptive analytics

  a. knowledge discovery using a variety of statistical and computational techniques
  b. analytics that suggests mechanisms for achieving desired outcomes
  c. tool that provides an SQL-like interface for managing data in Hadoop
  d. converting textual data into useful information
  e. form of analytics that forecasts future based on past and current events
  f. a large, unstructured collection of data from both internal and external sources
  g. systematic analysis and interpretation of data to improve our understanding of a real-world domain
  h. a form of analytics that provides reports regarding past events

11-3. Contrast the following terms:
  a. Data mining; text mining
  b. Pig; Hive
  c. ROLAP; MOLAP
  d. NoSQL; SQL
  e. Data lake; data warehouse

11-4. Identify and briefly describe the five Vs that are often used to define big data.

11-5. What is a key problem associated with defining big data with the five Vs?

11-6. What are the two main categories of technologies that are used to implement big data solutions?

11-7. What is the difference between "schema on write" and "schema on read"?

11-8. What are the four main types of NoSQL database management systems?

11-9. What is the primary difference between key-value stores and document stores?

11-10. JSON is widely used in the context of NoSQL databases. What is its primary role?

11-11. What are the key capabilities of NoSQL that extend what SQL can do?

11-12. Explain the relationship between Hadoop and MapReduce.

11-13. Why is massively parallel processing very important in the context of big data?

11-14. Identify the main components of the Hadoop architecture and present them in a diagram.

11-15. Describe the roles of HDFS in the Hadoop architecture.

11-16. Explain the core principle of the MapReduce algorithm.

11-17. Pig and Hive share a common purpose. What is it?

11-18. Explain the progression from decision support systems to analytics through business intelligence.

11-19. Describe the differences between descriptive, predictive, and prescriptive analytics.

11-20. Discuss the impact that the emergence of Internet of Things will have on the need for advanced big data and analytics technologies.

11-21. Discuss the role of OLAP in the context of descriptive analytics.

11-22. Briefly describe three types of operations that can easily be performed with OLAP tools.

11-23. Use an example to illustrate the role dashboards play in descriptive analytics.

11-24. What types of skills are essential for competency in predictive modeling?

11-25. State at least seven commonly used data mining techniques.

11-26. Discuss the purposes for which data mining can be used.

11-27. Describe the mechanism through which prescriptive analytics is dependent on descriptive and predictive analytics.

11-28. Describe the core idea underlying in-memory database management systems.

11-29. Describe the core idea underlying in-database analytics.

11-30. Identify at least five categories of human activity that are affected by big data and analytics.

11-31. Identify six broad categories of implications of big data analytics and decision making.

11-32. 'A number of independent data marts together form a Data warehouse'—Explain why or why not this statement is True or False.

11-33. Explain the various characteristics of Data warehouse data. What are the data transformation functions?

11-34. Why is a Data warehouse said to be non-updatable?

11-35. What is concurrency control? What are the repercussions of not having concurrency control? Using your own example (other than the one provided in the text) to explain' inconsistent read'?

11-36. What is pessimistic concurrency control? How does Versioning help in solving the problems of locking?

11-37. What type of problems in which the forward recovery and backward recovery help solve? How does mirroring a database related to these two recovery concepts?

11-38. What is a journal or a log? Explain the different types of logs and their purposes.

Problems and Exercises

11-39. Compare the JSON and XML representations of a record in Figure 11-1. What is the primary difference between these? Can you identify any advantages of one compared to the other?

11-40. Review Figure 11-3. For each of the formats, identify the elements that are data values and those that are labels describing the data.

11-41. Figure 11-5 describes a simple Hadoop architecture. If a real-world system is implemented using this approach, it will suffer from a specific weakness. Identify what this weakness is and find out what the latest versions of Hadoop have done to address it.

11-42. Review Figure 11-6 and answer the following questions based on it.
   a. What has happened between Input and Input'?
   b. Assume that the values associated with each of the keys (k1, k2, etc.) are counts. What is the purpose of the Shuffle stage?
   c. If the overall goal is to count the number of instances per key, what does the role of the Reduce stage have to be?

11-43. For each of the following cases, select the type of NoSQL DBMS that would fit best the needs of the situation.
   a. The database has to support a relatively complex hierarchical internal record structure that may vary for each record.
   b. The key requirement for the database is to access a specific record as quickly as possible without any concern regarding the internal structure of the record.
   c. The data are particularly well suitable to be organized as a network of associations between the data items.
   d. It is important that the DBMS provides quick access to each of the records by a key value, but, in addition, it has to also allow easy access to the components of each record.

11-44. For each of the situations described below, select the type of analytics that would address the specific organizational need and justify your selection.
   a. A mid-sized bank would like to provide as much automated support for its lending decisions as possible.
   b. A large retail chain wants to understand what factors contributed to the overall sales decline it experienced in a specific month in the past.
   c. To support staffing analysis for a holiday season, a clothing store wants to improve its understanding of the number of customers that are likely to visit each of its stores during the November 15–January 15 time frame.
   d. A gaming company wants to provide all of its employees an up-to-date graphical representation of the number of downloads of its game products and in-app revenue associated with them.

11-45. Review the white paper that has been used as a source for Figure 11-9. Which of the following tasks is the responsibility of data platform, integrated data warehouse, and integrated discovery platform, respectively?
   a. Finding new, previously unknown relationships within the data.
   b. Storing very large amounts of heterogeneous data from a variety of sources so that it is available for further analysis and processing.
   c. Storing structured data in a predefined format.
   d. Maintaining data without predefined structural connections.

Problems and Exercises 11-46–11-52 are based on the description of the Fitchwood Insurance Company that was introduced in the context of Problems and Exercises 9-42–9-45 in Chapter 9.

11-46. Fitchwood management would like to use the data mart for drill-down online reporting. For example, a sales manager might want to view a report of total sales for an agent by month and then drill down into the individual types of policies to see how sales are broken down by type of policy. What type of tools would you recommend for this? What additional tables, other than those required by the tool for administration, might need to be added to the data mart?

11-47. Suggest some visualization options that Fitchwood managers might want to use to support their decision making.

11-48. Using a drawing tool such as Microsoft PowerPoint, design a simple prototype of a top management dashboard for Fitchwood Insurance Company.

11-49. Do you see any opportunities for data mining using the Fitchwood data mart? Research data mining tools and recommend one or two for use with the data mart.

11-50. Text mining is an increasingly important subcategory of data mining. Can you identify potential uses of text mining in the context of an insurance company?

11-51. Fitchwood is a relatively small company (annual premium revenues less than $1B per year) that insures slightly more than 500,000 automobiles and about 200,000 homes. For what types of purposes might Fitchwood want to use big data technologies (i.e., either Hadoop or one of the NoSQL products)?

11-52. Read a SAS White Paper (**http://www.sas.com/resources/whitepaper/wp_56343.pdf**) on the use of telematics in car insurance. If Fitchwood started to use one of these technologies, what consequences would it have for its IT infrastructure needs?

*Problems and Exercises 11-53 and 11-54 are based on the use of resources on Teradata University Network (**TUN at** teradatauniversitynetwork.com). To use TUN, you need to obtain the current TUN password from your instructor.*

11-53. Teradata University Network offers access to a tool called SAS Visual Analytics (VA). Use TUN to access SAS VA and complete some of the exercises associated with the tool to become familiar with it. What are your impressions regarding the usefulness of this type of analytical tool?

11-54. Another tool featured on TUN is called Tableau. Tableau offers a student version of its product for free (**www.tableausoftware.com/academic/students**), and TUN offers several assignments and exercises with which you can explore its features. Compare the capabilities of Tableau with those of SAS Visual Analytics. How do these products differ from each other? What are the similarities between them?

11-55. The Indian Railways (IR), is the largest rail network in Asia and the world's second largest under one management. It spans over 6,000 stations, carries 17 million passengers every day. The Indian Railways has a portal for booking passenger tickets and cargo freights online. The Passengers, needless to say, can book their tickets from any source to destination. The passengers are given a login and password to book online. The ticket booking transactions are stored onto a mainframe server at their regional Hub, in Hyderabad and New Delhi. If you were hired as the Database consultant, how would you design
1. An all-inclusive set of data security measures to protect the Railways data
2. A concurrency control mechanism
3. Disaster Recovery techniques from a wide range of failures from natural calamity to human errors.

References

Bertolucci, J. 2013. *Big Data Analytics: Descriptive vs. Predictive vs. Prescriptive,* available at **www.informationweek.com/big-data/big-data-analytics/big-data-analytics-descriptive-vs-predictive-vs-prescriptive/d/d-id/1113279.**

Braun, V. 2013. *Prescriptive Versus Predictive: An IBMer's Guide to Advanced Data Analytics in Travel,* available at **www.tnooz.com/article/prescriptive-vs-predictive-an-ibmers-guide-to-advanced-data-analytics-in-travel/.**

Brewer, E. A. 2000. "Towards Robust Distributed Systems." In the *Proceedings of 19th ACM Symposium on Principles of Distributed Computing,* June 16–19, 2000, Portland, Oregon.

Chang, F., J. Dean, S. Ghemawat, W. C. Hsieh, D. A. Wallach, M. Burrows, T. Chandra, A. Fikes, and R. E. Gruber. 2008. "Bigtable: A Distributed Storage System for Structured Data." *ACM Transactions on Computer Systems* 26,2: 4:1–4:26.

Chen, H., R. H. Chiang, and V. C. Storey. 2012. "Business Intelligence and Analytics: From Big Data to Big Impact." *MIS Quarterly* 36,4: 1165–1188.

Chignard, S. 2013. *A brief history of Open Data.* Available at **www.paristechreview.com/2013/03/29/brief-history-open-data/.**

Chui, M., M. Löffler, and R. Roberts. 2010. "The Internet of Things." *McKinsey Quarterly* 2: 1–9.

Davenport, T. 2014. *Big Data at Work: Dispelling the Myths, Uncovering the Opportunities.* Boston, MA: Harvard Business Review Press.

Davenport, T. H., J. G. Harris, and R. Morison. 2010. *Analytics at Work: Smarter Decisions, Better Results.* Boston, MA: Harvard Business School Publishing.

Dean, J., and S. Ghemawat. 2004. "MapReduce: Simplified Data Processing on Large Clusters," *Proceedings of OSDI'04: Sixth Symposium on Operating System Design and Implementation,* San Francisco, CA, December.

Duhigg, C. 2012. "Psst, You in Aisle 5," *New York Times Magazine,* February 19, 2012, pp. 30–37, 54–55.

Dyché, K. 2000. *e-Data: Turning Data into Information with Data Warehousing.* Reading, MA: Addison-Wesley.

Edjlali, R., and M. A. Beyer. 2013. *Hype Cycle for Information Infrastructure.* Gartner Group research report #G00252518. Gartner Group.

Evelson, B., and N. Nicolson. 2008. *Topic Overview: Business Intelligence.* Forrester Research, available at **www.forrester.com/Topic+Overview+Business+Intelligence/fulltext/-/E-RES39218.**

Franks, B. 2012. *Taming the Big Data Tidal Wave: Finding Opportunities in Huge Data Streams with Advanced Analytics.* Hoboken, NJ: John Wiley & Sons.

Frey, C. B., and M. Osborne. 2013. *The Future of Employment: How Susceptible Are Jobs to Computerization.* Oxford Martin School, Oxford University, available at **www.oxfordmartin.ox.ac.uk/publications/view/1314.**

Gates, A. 2010. *Pig and Hive at Yahoo!* Available at **https://developer.yahoo.com/blogs/hadoop/pig-hive-yahoo-464.html.**

Greenwald, G., E. MacAskill, and L. Poitras. 2013. "Edward Snowden: the Whistleblower Behind the NSA Surveillance Revelations." *The Guardian,* June 9, 2013.

Gualtieri, M., and N. Yuhanna, 2014. *The Forrester Wave™: Big Data Hadoop Solutions*. Cambridge, MA: Forrester Research.

Halper, F. 2014. *Eight Considerations for Utilizing Big Data Analytics with Hadoop*. The Data Warehousing Institute.

HDFSDesign. (2014) HDFS Architecture. Apache Software Foundation. Available at **http://hadoop.apache.org/docs/current/hadoop-project-dist/hadoop-hdfs/HdfsDesign.html**.

Hernandez, A., and K. Morgan. 2014. *Winning in a Competitive Environment*. Grant Thornton research report.

Herschel, G., A. Linden, and L. Kart. 2014. *Magic Quadrant for Advanced Analytics Platforms*. Garner Group research report G00258011. Gartner Group.

Hortonworks. 2014. *A Modern Data Architecture with Apache Hadoop*. Hortonworks White Paper series.

Jacobs, A. 2009. "The Pathologies of Big Data." *Communications of the ACM* 52,8: 36–44.

Kauhanen, H. 2010. *NoSQL Databases*. Available at **www.slideshare.net/harrikauhanen/nosql-3376398**.

Lamb, A., M. Fuller, R. Varadarajan, N. Tran, B. Vandiver, L. Doshi, and C. Bear. 2012. "The Vertica Analytic Database: C-store 7 Years Later," *Proceedings of the VLDB Endowment* 5,12: 1790–1801.

Laney, D. 2001. *3D Data Management: Controlling Data Volume, Velocity, and Variety*. META Group/Gartner. Available at **http://blogs.gartner.com/doug-laney/files/2012/01/ad949-3D-Data-Management-Controlling-Data-Volume-Velocity-and-Variety.pdf**.

Laskowski, N. 2014. *Ten Big Data Case Studies in a Nutshell*. Available at **http://searchcio.techtarget.com/opinion/Ten-big-data-case-studies-in-a-nutshell**.

Lohr, S. 2014. "For Data Scientists, 'Janitor Work' Is Hurdle to Insights," *New York Times*, August 18, 2014.

Markus, M. L. 2014. *Big Data, Big Decisions: A Workshop for a Research Agenda on the Social, Economic, and Workforce Implications of Big Data*. An NSF-funded workshop organized on January 30–31, 2014 (Award #1348929).

McKnight, W. 2014. *NoSQL Evaluator's Guide*. Plano, TX: McKnight Consulting Group.

Mundy, J. 2001. "Smarter Data Warehouses." *Intelligent Enterprise* 4,2 (February 16): 24–29.

Parr-Rud, O. 2012. *Drive Your Business With Predictive Analytics*. SAS Institute, available at **www.sas.com/en_us/whitepapers/drive-your-business-with-predictive-analytics-105620.html**.

Sallam, R. L., J. Tapadinhas, J. Parenteau, D. Yuen, and B. Hostmann. 2014. *Magic Quadrant for Business Intelligence and Analytics Platforms*. Garner Group research report G00257740. Gartner Group.

Schoenborn, B. 2014. *Big Data Infrastructure for Dummies*. Hoboken, NJ: John Wiley & Sons.

Scofield, B. 2010. *NoSQL. Death to Relational Databases(?)*. Available at **www.slideshare.net/bscofield/nosql-codemash-2010**.

Sharda, R., D. Delen, and E. Turban. 2013. *Business Intelligence: A Managerial Perspective on Analytics*. Prentice Hall.

Sharda, R., D. Delen, D., and E. Turban. 2014. *Business Intelligence and Analytics: Systems for Decision Support*. Prentice Hall.

Sprague, R. H. Jr. 1980. "A Framework for the Development of Decision Support Systems." *Management Information Systems Quarterly* 4,4: 1–26.

TCSET (Teradata Customer Success and Engagement Team). 2014. *Communications*. Available at **http://blogs.teradata.com/customers/category/industries/communications/**.

Underwood, J. 2013. *Prescriptive Analytics Takes Analytics Maturity Model to a New Level*. SearchBusinessAnalytics. Available at **http://searchbusinessanalytics.techtarget.com/feature/Prescriptive-analytics-takes-analytics-maturity-model-to-a-new-level**.

Voroshilin, I. 2012. *Brewer's CAP Theorem Explained: BASE versus ACID*. Available at **http://ivoroshilin.com/2012/12/13/brewers-cap-theorem-explained-base-versus-acid**.

Watson, H. 2014. "Tutorial: Big Data Analytics: Concepts, Technologies, and Applications." *Communications of the AIS* 34,65: 1247–1268.

Wattal, S., D. Schuff, M. Mandviwalla, and C. B. Williams. 2010. "Web 2.0 and politics: the 2008 US Presidential Election and an E-Politics Research Agenda." *MIS Quarterly* 34,4: 669–688.

Weldon, J. L. 1996. "Data Mining and Visualization." *Database Programming & Design*, 9,5: 21–24.

White, T. 2012. *Hadoop: The Definitive Guide*. Sebastopol, CA: Yahoo! Press/O'Reilly Media.

Further Reading

Berman, J. J. 2013. *Principles of Big Data. Preparing, Sharing, and Analyzing Complex Information*. Waltham, MA: Morgan Kauffman.

Boyd, D., and K. Crawford. 2011. *Six Provocations for Big Data*, Available at **http://papers.ssrn.com/sol3/papers.cfm?abstract_id=1926431**.

Economist. 2012. *Big Data and the Democratisation of Decisions*. Available at **http://pages.alteryx.com/economist-report.html**.

Jurney, R. 2013. *Agile Data Science: Building Data Analytics Applications with Hadoop*. Sebastopol, CA: O'Reilly Media.

Mayer-Schönenberger, V., and K. Cukier. 2014. *Big Data: A Revolution That Will Transform How We Live, Work, and Think*. New York, NY: Houghton Mifflin Harcourt.

World Economic Forum. 2012. *Big Data, Big Impact: New Possibilities for International Development*. Available at **www3.weforum.org/docs/WEF_TC_MFS_BigDataBigImpact_Briefing_2012.pdf**.

Web Resources

aws.amazon.com/big-data Amazon Web Services is a commercial provider that offers a wide range of services related to big data on the cloud. This material serves as a good example of the opportunities organizations have to implement at least part of their big data operations using cloud-based resources.

bigdatauniversity.com A collection of (mostly free) educational materials related to big data.

datasciencecentral.com A social networking site for professionals interested in data science, analytics, and big data.

db-engines.com A site that collects and integrates information regarding various database management systems.

http://smartdatacollective.com/bernardmarr/235366/big-data-20-free-big-data-sources-everyone-should-know A reference collection of sources of large, publicly available data sources.

CHAPTER 12

Data and Database Administration

LEARNING OBJECTIVES

After studying this chapter, you should be able to:

- Concisely define each of the following key terms: **data administration, database administration, open source DBMS, database security, authorization rules, user-defined procedures, encryption, smart card, database recovery, backup facilities, journalizing facilities, transaction, transaction log, database change log, before image, after image, checkpoint facility, recovery manager, restore/rerun, transaction boundaries, backward recovery (rollback), forward recovery (rollforward), aborted transaction, database destruction, concurrency control, inconsistent read problem, locking, locking level (lock granularity), shared lock (S lock, or read lock), exclusive lock (X lock, or write lock), deadlock, deadlock prevention, two-phase locking protocol, deadlock resolution, versioning, data dictionary, system catalog, information repository, data archiving,** and **heartbeat query.**

- List several major functions of data administration and of database administration.

- Describe the changing roles of the data administrator and database administrator in the current business environment.

- Describe the role of data dictionaries and information repositories and how they are used by data administration.

- Compare the optimistic and pessimistic systems of concurrency control.

- Describe the problem of database security and list five techniques that are used to enhance security.

- Understand the role of databases in Sarbanes-Oxley compliance.

- Describe the problem of database recovery and list four basic facilities that are included with a DBMS to recover databases.

- Describe the problem of tuning a database to achieve better performance, and list five areas where changes may be made when tuning a database.

- Describe the importance of data availability and list several measures to improve availability.

INTRODUCTION

Global Bank has branches world-wide and has many Corporate Accounts. The bank ran into deep problems because of its customers' data being compromised.

While the bank maintains that it servers were not hacked, rather caused by cyber criminals posing are legitimate business houses.

In certain cases the accounts of HNI (High Net-worth Individuals) have been compromised and misused in stock market speculations leading to losses to the HNI. And it is shocking that in most cases the fraud has been perpetuated by the internal staff of Global Bank.

The other HNIs have been alerted of such a fraud happening. The law enforcers have tracked down the criminals, but Global Bank had to bear the brunt of fraud as it had to compensate the HNI quite an large amount running to the tune of several millions of dollars.

The critical importance of data to organizations is widely recognized. Data are a corporate asset, just as personnel, physical resources, and financial resources are corporate assets. Like these other assets, data and information are too valuable to be managed casually. The development of information technology has made effective management of corporate data far more possible, but data are also vulnerable to accidental and malicious damage and misuse. Data and database administration activities have been developed to help achieve organizations' goals for the effective management of data.

Ineffective data administration, on the other hand, leads to poor data quality, security, and availability and can be characterized by the following conditions, which are all too common in organizations:

1. Multiple definitions of the same data entity and/or inconsistent representations of the same data elements in separate databases, making integration of data across different databases hazardous
2. Missing key data elements, whose loss eliminates the value of existing data
3. Low data quality levels due to inappropriate sources of data or timing of data transfers from one system to another, thus reducing the reliability of the data
4. Inadequate familiarity with existing data, including awareness of data location and meaning of stored data, thus reducing the capability to use the data to make effective strategic or planning decisions
5. Poor and inconsistent query response time, excessive database downtime, and either stringent or inadequate controls to ensure agreed upon data privacy and security
6. Lack of access to data due to damaged, sabotaged, or stolen files or due to hardware failures that eliminate paths to data users need
7. Embarrassment to the organization because of unauthorized access to data

Many of these conditions put an organization at risk for failing to comply with regulations, such as the Sarbanes-Oxley Act (SOX), the Health Insurance Portability and Accountability Act (HIPAA), and the Gramm-Leach-Bliley Act for adequate internal controls and procedures in support of financial control, data transparency, and data privacy. Manual processes for data control are discouraged, so organizations need to implement automated controls, in part through a DBMS (e.g., sophisticated data validation controls, security features, triggers, and stored procedures), to prevent and detect accidental damage of data and fraudulent activities. Databases must be backed up and recovered to prevent permanent data loss. The who, what, when, and where of data must be documented in metadata repositories for auditor review. Data stewardship programs, aimed at reviewing data quality control procedures, are becoming popular. Collaboration across the organization is needed so data consolidation across distributed databases is accurate. Breaches of data accuracy or security must be communicated to executives and managers.

THE ROLES OF DATA AND DATABASE ADMINISTRATORS

Morrow (2007) views data as the lifeblood of an organization. Good management of data involves managing data quality (as discussed in Chapter 10) as well as data security and availability (which we cover in this chapter). Organizations have responded to these data management issues with different strategies. Some have created a function called *data administration*. The person who heads this function is called the data administrator (DA), or information resource manager, and he or she takes responsibility for the overall management of data resources. A second function, *database administration*, has been regarded as responsible for physical database design and for dealing with the technical issues, such as security enforcement, database performance, and backup and recovery, associated with managing a database. Other organizations combine the data administration and database administration functions. The rapidly changing pace of business has caused the roles of the data administrator and the database administrator (DBA) to change, in ways that are discussed next.

Traditional Data Administration

Databases are shared resources that belong to the entire enterprise; they are not the property of a single function or individual within the organization. Data administration is the custodian of the organization's data, in much the same sense that the controller is custodian of the financial resources. Like the controller, the data administrator must develop procedures to protect and control the resource. Also, data administration must resolve disputes that may arise when data are centralized and shared among users and must play a significant role in deciding where data will be stored and managed. **Data administration** is a high-level function that is responsible for the overall management of data resources in an organization, including maintaining corporate-wide data definitions and standards.

Selecting the data administrator and organizing the function are extremely important organizational decisions. The data administrator must be a highly skilled manager capable of eliciting the cooperation of users and resolving differences that normally arise when significant change is introduced into an organization. The data administrator should be a respected, senior-level manager selected from within the organization, rather than a technical computer expert or a new individual hired for the position. However, the data administrator must have sufficient technical skills to interact effectively with technical staff members such as database administrators, system administrators, and programmers.

Following are some of the core roles of traditional data administration:

- *Data policies, procedures, and standards* Every database application requires protection established through consistent enforcement of data policies, procedures, and standards. Data policies are statements that make explicit the goals of data administration, such as "Every user must have a valid password." Data procedures are written outlines of actions to be taken to perform a certain activity. Backup and recovery procedures, for example, should be communicated to all involved employees. Data standards are explicit conventions and behaviors that are to be followed and that can be used to help evaluate database quality. Naming conventions for database objects should be standardized for programmers, for example. Increased use of external data sources and increased access to organizational databases from outside the organization have increased the importance of employees' understanding of data policies, procedures, and standards. Such policies and procedures need to be well documented to comply with the transparency requirements of financial reporting, security, and privacy regulations.
- *Planning* A key administration function is providing leadership in developing the organization's information architecture. Effective administration requires both an understanding of the needs of the organization for data and information and the ability to lead the development of an information architecture that will meet the diverse needs of the typical organization.
- *Data conflict resolution* Databases are intended to be shared and usually involve data from several different departments of the organization. Ownership of data is a ticklish issue at least occasionally in every organization. Those in data administration are well placed to resolve data ownership issues because they are not typically associated with a certain department. Establishing procedures for resolving such conflicts is essential. If the administration function has been given sufficient authority to mediate and enforce the resolution of the conflict, it may be very effective in this capacity.
- *Managing the information repository* Repositories contain the metadata that describe an organization's data and data processing resources. Information repositories are replacing data dictionaries in many organizations. Whereas data dictionaries are simple data element documentation tools, information repositories are used by data administrators and other information specialists to manage the total information processing environment. An information repository serves as an essential source of information and functionality for each of the following:
  1. Users who must understand data definitions, business rules, and relationships among data objects

Data administration
A high-level function that is responsible for the overall management of data resources in an organization, including maintaining corporate-wide definitions and standards.

2. Automated data modeling and design tools that are used to specify and develop information systems
3. Applications that access and manipulate data (or business information) in the corporate databases
4. Database management systems, which maintain the repository and update system privileges, passwords, object definitions, and so on

- *Internal marketing* Although the importance of data and information to an organization has become more widely recognized within organizations, it is not necessarily true that an appreciation for data management issues—such as information architecture, data modeling, metadata, data quality, and data standards—has also evolved. The importance of following established procedures and policies must be proactively instituted through data (and database) administrators. Effective internal marketing may reduce resistance to change and data ownership problems.

When the data administration role is not separately defined in an organization, these roles are assumed by database administration and/or others in the IT organization.

Traditional Database Administration

Database administration

A technical function that is responsible for physical database design and for dealing with technical issues, such as security enforcement, database performance, and backup and recovery.

Typically, the role of database administration is taken to be a hands-on, physical involvement with the management of a database or databases. **Database administration** is a technical function responsible for logical and physical database design and for dealing with technical issues, such as security enforcement, database performance, backup and recovery, and database availability. A database administrator (DBA) must understand the data models built by data administration and be capable of transforming them into efficient and appropriate logical and physical database designs (Mullins, 2002). The DBA implements the standards and procedures established by the data administrator, including enforcing programming standards, data standards, policies, and procedures.

Just as a data administrator needs a wide variety of job skills, so does a DBA. Having a broad technical background, including a sound understanding of current hardware and software (operating system and networking) architectures and capabilities and a solid understanding of data processing, is essential. An understanding of the database development life cycle, including traditional and prototyping approaches, is also necessary. Strong design and data modeling skills are essential, especially at the logical and physical levels. But managerial skills are also critical; a DBA must manage other information systems (IS) personnel while the database is analyzed, designed, and implemented, and the DBA must also interact with and provide support for the end users who are involved with the design and use of the database.

Following are some of the core roles assumed by database administration:

- *Analyzing and designing the database* The key role played by a DBA in the database analysis stage is the definition and creation of the data dictionary repository. The key task in database design for a DBA includes prioritizing application transactions by volume, importance, and complexity. Because these transactions are going to be most critical to the application, specifications for them should be reviewed as quickly as the transactions are developed. Logical data modeling, physical database modeling, and prototyping may occur in parallel. DBAs should strive to provide adequate control of the database environment while allowing the developers space and opportunity to experiment.
- *Selecting DBMS and related software tools* The evaluation and selection of hardware and software are critical to an organization's success. The database administration group must establish policies regarding the DBMS and related system software (e.g., compilers, system monitors) that will be supported within the organization. This requires evaluating vendors and their software products, performing benchmarks, and so on.
- *Installing and upgrading the DBMS* Once the DBMS is selected, it must be installed. Before installation, benchmarks of the workload against the database on a computer supplied by the DBMS vendor should be taken. Benchmarking anticipates issues that must be addressed during the actual installation. A DBMS installation can be a complex process of making sure all the correct versions of different

modules are in place, all the proper device drivers are present, and the DBMS works correctly with any third-party software products. DBMS vendors periodically update package modules; planning for, testing, and installing upgrades to ensure that existing applications still work properly can be time-consuming and intricate. Once the DBMS is installed, user accounts must be created and maintained.

- *Tuning database performance*   Because databases are dynamic, it is improbable that the initial design of a database will be sufficient to achieve the best processing performance for the life of the database. The performance of a database (query and update processing time as well as data storage utilization) needs to be constantly monitored. The design of a database must be frequently changed to meet new requirements and to overcome the degrading effects of many content updates. The database must periodically be rebuilt, reorganized, and re-indexed to recover wasted space and to correct poor data allocation and fragmentation with the new size and use of the database.
- *Improving database query processing performance*   The workload against a database will expand over time as more users find more ways to use the growing amount of data in a database. Thus, some queries that originally ran quickly against a small database may need to be rewritten in a more efficient form to run in a satisfactory time against a fully populated database. Indexes may need to be added or deleted to balance performance across all queries. Data may need to be relocated to different devices to allow better concurrent processing of queries and updates. The vast majority of a DBA's time is likely to be spent on tuning database performance and improving database query processing time.
- *Managing data security, privacy, and integrity*   Protecting the security, privacy, and integrity of organizational databases rests with the database administration function. More detailed explanations of the ways in which privacy, security, and integrity are ensured are included later in the chapter. Here it is important to realize that the advent of the Internet and intranets to which databases are attached, along with the possibilities for distributing data and databases to multiple sites, has complicated the management of data security, privacy, and integrity.
- *Performing data backup and recovery*   A DBA must ensure that backup procedures are established that will allow for the recovery of all necessary data should a loss occur through application failure, hardware failure, physical or electrical disaster, or human error or malfeasance. Common backup and recovery strategies are also discussed later in this chapter. These strategies must be fully tested and evaluated at regular intervals.

Reviewing these data administration and database administration functions should convince any reader of the importance of proper administration, at both the organizational and project levels. Failure to take the proper steps can greatly reduce an organization's ability to operate effectively and may even result in its going out of business. Pressures to reduce application development time must always be reviewed to be sure that necessary quality is not being forgone in order to react more quickly, for such shortcuts are likely to have very serious repercussions. Figure 12-1 summarizes how these data administration and database administration functions are typically viewed with respect to the steps of the systems development life cycle.

Trends in Database Administration

Rapidly changing business conditions are leading to the need for DBAs to possess skills that go above and beyond the ones described above. Here we describe four of these trends and the associated new skills needed:

1. *Increased use of procedural logic*   Features such as triggers, stored procedures, and persistent stored modules (all described in Chapter 7) provide the ability to define business rules to the DBMS rather than in separate application programs. Once developers begin to rely on the use of these objects, a DBA must address the issues of quality, maintainability, performance, and availability. A DBA is now responsible for ensuring that all such procedural database logic is effectively planned, tested, implemented, shared, and reused (Mullins, 2002). A person filling such a role will typically need to come from the ranks of application programming and be capable of working closely with that group.

FIGURE 12-1 Functions of data administration and database administration

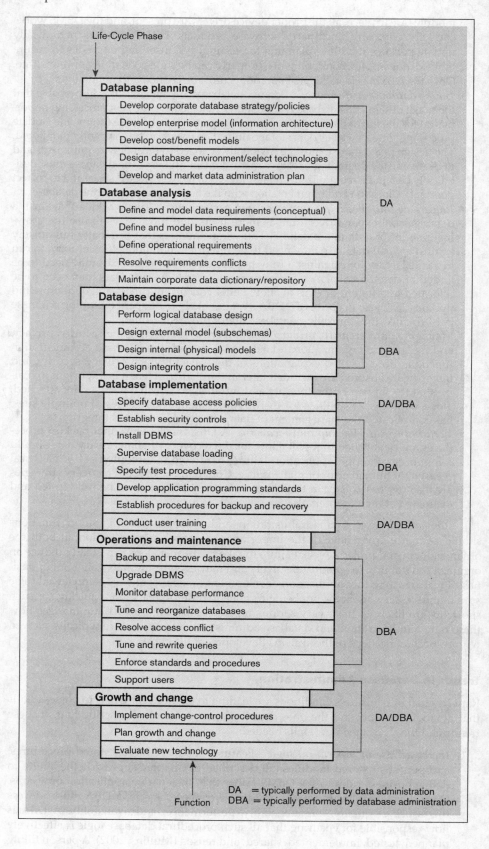

2. **Proliferation of Internet-based applications** When a business goes online, it never closes. People expect the site to be available and fully functional on a 24/7 basis. A DBA in such an environment needs to have a full range of DBA skills and also be capable of managing applications and databases that are Internet enabled (Mullins, 2001). Major priorities in this environment include high data availability (24/7), integration of legacy data with Web-based applications, tracking of Web activity, and performance engineering for the Internet.

3. **Increase use of smart devices** Use of smartphones, tablets, etc. in organizations is exploding. Most DBMS vendors (e.g., Oracle, IBM, and Sybase) offer small-footprint versions of their products to run on these smartphones, typically in support of specific applications. (This is an example of the personal databases described in Chapter 1.) A small amount of critical data is typically stored on a smartphone, which then is periodically synchronized with data stored on the enterprise data servers. In such an environment, DBAs will often be asked questions about how to design these personal databases (or how to rescue users when they get in trouble). A greater issue is how to manage data synchronization from hundreds (or possibly thousands) of such smartphones while maintaining the data integrity and data availability requirements of the enterprise. However, a number of applications are now available on smartphones that enable DBAs to remotely monitor databases and solve minor issues without requiring physical possession of the devices.

4. **Cloud computing and database/data administration** Moving databases to the cloud has several implications for data/database administrators impacting both both operations and governance (Cloud Security Alliance, 2011). From an operations perspective, as databases move to the cloud, several of the activities of the data/database listed under the database implementation, operations, and maintenance headings in Figure 12-1 will be affected. Activities such as installing the DBMS, backup and recovery, and database tuning will be the service provider's responsibility. However, it will still be up to the client organization's data/database administrator to define the parameters around these tasks so that they are appropriate to the organization's needs. These parameters, often documented in a service-level agreement, will include such aspects as uptime requirements, requirements for backup and recovery, and demand planning. Further, several tasks such as establishing security controls and database access policies, planning for growth or change in business needs, and evaluating new technologies will likely remain the primary responsibility of the data/database administrator in the client organization. Data security and complying with regulatory requirements will in particular pose significant challenges to the data/database administrator. From a governance perspective, the data/database administrator will need to develop new skills related to the management of the relationship with the service providers in areas such as monitoring and managing service providers, defining service-level agreements, and negotiating/enforcing contracts.

Data Warehouse Administration

The significant growth in data warehousing (see Chapter 9) in the past five years has caused a new role to emerge: that of a data warehouse administrator (DWA). Two generalizations are true about the DWA role:

1. A DWA plays many of the same roles as do DAs and DBAs for the data warehouse and data mart databases for the purpose of supporting decision-making applications (rather than transaction-processing applications for the typical DA and DBA).

2. The role of a DWA emphasizes integration and coordination of metadata and data (extraction agreements, operational data stores, and enterprise data warehouses) across many data sources, not necessarily the standardization of data across these separately managed data sources outside the control and scope of the DWA. Specifically, Inmon (1999) suggests that a DWA has a unique charter to perform the following functions:

   • Build and administer an environment supportive of decision support applications. Thus, a DWA is more concerned with the time to make a decision than with query response time.

- Build a stable architecture for the data warehouse. A DWA is more concerned with the effect of data warehouse growth (scalability in the amount of data and number of users) than with redesigning existing applications. Inmon refers to this architecture as the *corporate information factory*. For a detailed discussion of this architecture, see Chapter 9 and Inmon et al. (2001).
- Develop service-level agreements with suppliers and consumers of data for the data warehouse. Thus, a DWA works more closely with end users and operational system administrators to coordinate vastly different objectives and to oversee the development of new applications (data marts, ETL procedures, and analytical services) than do DAs and DBAs.

3. These responsibilities are in addition to the responsibilities typical of any DA or DBA, such as selecting technologies, communicating with users about data needs, making performance and capacity decisions, and budgeting and planning data warehouse requirements.

DWAs typically report through the IT unit of an organization but have strong relationships with marketing and other business areas that depend on the EDW for applications, such as customer or supplier relationship management, sales analysis, channel management, and other analytical applications. DWAs should not be part of traditional systems development organizations, as are many DBAs, because data warehousing applications are developed differently than operational systems are and need to be viewed as independent from any particular operational system. Alternatively, DWAs can be placed in the primary end-user organization for the EDW, but this runs the risk of creating many data warehouses or marts, rather than leading to a true, scalable EDW.

Summary of Evolving Data Administration Roles

The DA and DBA roles are some of the most challenging roles in any organization. The DA has renewed visibility with the enactment of financial control regulations and greater interest in data quality. The DBA is always expected to keep abreast of rapidly changing new technologies and is usually involved with mission-critical applications. A DBA must be constantly available to deal with problems, so the DBA is constantly on call. In return, the DBA position ranks among the best compensated in the IS profession.

Many organizations have blended together the data administration and database administration roles. These organizations emphasize the capability to build a database quickly, tune it for maximum performance, and restore it to production quickly when problems develop. These databases are more likely to be departmental, client/server databases that are developed quickly using newer development approaches, such as prototyping, which allow changes to be made more quickly. The blending of data administration and database administration roles also means that DBAs in such organizations must be able to create and enforce data standards and policies.

As the big data and analytics technologies described in Chapter 11 become more pervasive, it is expected that the DBA role will continue to evolve toward increased specialization, with skills such as Hadoop cluster management, Java programming, customization of off-the-shelf packages, and support for data warehousing becoming more important. The ability to work with multiple databases, communication protocols, and operating systems will continue to be highly valued. DBAs who gain broad experience and develop the ability to adapt quickly to changing environments will have many opportunities. It is possible that some current DBA activities, such as tuning, will be replaced by decision support systems able to tune systems by analyzing usage patterns. Some operational duties, such as backup and recovery, can be outsourced and offshored with remote database administration services.

THE OPEN SOURCE MOVEMENT AND DATABASE MANAGEMENT

As mentioned previously, one role of a DBA is to select the DBMS(s) to be used in the organization. Database administrators and systems developers in all types of organizations have new alternatives when selecting a DBMS. Increasingly, organizations of all sizes are seriously considering open source DBMSs, such as MySQL and PostgreSQL, as viable choices along with Oracle, DB2, Microsoft SQL Server, and Teradata. This interest is spurred by the success of the Linux operating system and the Apache Web server. The open source movement began in roughly 1984, with the start of the Free Software Foundation. Today, the Open Source Initiative (**www.opensource.org**) is a nonprofit organization dedicated to managing and promoting the open source movement.

Why has open source software become so popular? It's not all about cost. Advantages of open source software include the following:

- A large pool of volunteer testers and developers facilitates the construction of reliable, low-cost software in a relatively short amount of time. (But be aware that only the most widely used open source software comes close to achieving this advantage; for example, MySQL has more than 11 million installations.)
- The availability of the source code allows people to make modifications to add new features, which are easily inspected by others. (In fact, the agreement is that you do share all modifications for the good of the community.)
- Because the software is not proprietary to one vendor, you do not become locked into the product development plans (i.e., new features, time lines) of a single vendor, which might not be adding the features you need for your environment.
- Open source software often comes in multiple versions, and you can select the version that is right for you (from simple to complex, from totally free to some costs for special features).
- Distributing application code dependent on and working with the open source software does not incur any additional costs for copies or licenses. (Deploying software across multiple servers even within the same organization has no marginal cost for the DBMS.)

There are, however, some risks or disadvantages of open source software:

- Often there is not complete documentation (although for-fee services might provide quite sufficient documentation).
- Systems with specialized or proprietary needs across organizations do not have the commodity nature that makes open source software viable, so not all kinds of software lend themselves to being provided via an open source arrangement. (However, DBMSs are viable.)
- There are different types of open source licenses, and not all open source software is available under the same terms; thus, you have to know the ins and outs of each type of license (see Michaelson, 2004).
- An open source tool may not have all the features needed. For example, early versions of MySQL did not support subqueries (although it has now supported subqueries for several releases). An open source tool may not have options for certain functionality, so it may require that "one size fits all."
- Open source software vendors often do not have certification programs. This may not be a major factor for you, but some organizations (often software development contractors) want staff to be certified as a way to demonstrate competence in competitive bidding.

An **open source DBMS** is free or nearly free database software whose source code is publicly available. (Some people refer to open source as "sharing with rules.") The free DBMS is sufficient to run a database, but vendors provide additional fee-based components and support services that make the product more full featured and comparable to the more traditional product leaders. Because many vendors often provide the additional fee-based components, use of an open source DBMS means that an organization is not tied to one vendor's proprietary product.

A core open source DBMS is not competitive with IBM's DB2, Oracle, or Teradata, but it is more than competitive against Microsoft Access and other PC-oriented packages. However, the cost savings can be substantial. For example, the total cost of ownership over a 3-year period for MySql is $60,000, compared to about $1.5M for Microsoft SQL Server (**www.mysql.com/tcosavings**). The majority of the differential comes from licensing and support/maintenance costs. However, as cloud-based offerings of commercial databases become more popular, this differential will start reducing considerably.

Open source DBMS
Free DBMS source code software that provides the core functionality of an SQL-compliant DBMS.

Open source DBMSs are improving rapidly to include more powerful features, such as the transaction controls described later in this chapter, needed for mission-critical applications. Open source DBMSs are fully SQL compliant and run on most popular operating systems. For organizations that cannot afford to spend a lot on software or staff (e.g., small businesses, nonprofits, and educational institutions), an open source DBMS can be an ideal choice. For example, many Web sites are supported by MySQL or PostgreSQL database back ends. Visit **www.postgresql.org** and **www.mysql.com** for more details on these two leading open source DBMSs.

When choosing an open source (or really any) DBMS, you need to consider the following types of factors:

- *Features* Does the DBMS include capabilities you need, such as subqueries, stored procedures, views, and transaction integrity controls?
- *Support* How widely is the DBMS used, and what alternatives exist for helping you solve problems? Does the DBMS come with documentation and ancillary tools?
- *Ease of use* This often depends on the availability of tools that make any piece of system software, such as a DBMS, easier to use through things such as a GUI interface.
- *Stability* How frequently and how seriously does the DBMS malfunction over time or with high-volume use?
- *Speed* How rapid is the response time to queries and transactions with proper tuning of the database? (Because open source DBMSs are often not as fully loaded with advanced, obscure features, their performance can be attractive.)
- *Training* How easy is it for developers and users to learn to use the DBMS?
- *Licensing* What are the terms of the open source license, and are there commercial licenses that would provide the types of support needed?

MANAGING DATA SECURITY

Consider the following situations:

- At a university, anyone with access to the university's main automated system for student and faculty data can see everyone's Social Security number.
- A previously loyal employee is given access to sensitive documents, and within a few weeks leaves the organization, purportedly with a trove of trade secrets to share with competing firms.
- The FBI reports (Morrow, 2007) that there are 3,000 clandestine organizations in the United States whose sole purpose is to steal secrets and acquire technology for foreign organizations.
- Sarbanes-Oxley requires that companies audit the access of privileged users to sensitive data, and the payment card industry standards require companies to track user identity information whenever credit card data are used.

Database security

Protection of database data against accidental or intentional loss, destruction, or misuse.

The goal of **database security** is to protect data from accidental or intentional threats to their integrity and access. The database environment has grown more complex, with distributed databases located on client/server architectures and personal computers as well as on mainframes. Access to data has become more open through the Internet and corporate intranets and from mobile computing devices. As a result, managing data security effectively has become more difficult and time-consuming. Some security procedures for client/server and Web-based systems were introduced in Chapter 8.

Because data are a critical resource, all persons in an organization must be sensitive to security threats and take measures to protect the data within their domains. For example, computer listings or computer disks containing sensitive data should not be left unattended on desktops. Data administration is often responsible for developing overall policies and procedures to protect databases. Database administration is typically responsible for administering database security on a daily basis. The facilities that database administrators have to use in establishing adequate data security are discussed later, but first it is important to review potential threats to data security.

Threats to Data Security

Threats to data security may be direct threats to the database. For example, those who gain unauthorized access to a database may then browse, change, or even steal the data to which they have gained access. (See the news story at the beginning of this chapter for a good example.) Focusing on database security alone, however, will not ensure a secure database. All parts of the system must be secure, including the database, the network, the operating system, the building(s) in which the database resides physically, and all personnel who have any opportunity to access the system. Figure 12-2 diagrams many of the possible locations for data security threats. Accomplishing this level of security requires careful review, establishment of security procedures and policies, and implementation and enforcement of those procedures and policies. The following threats must be addressed in a comprehensive data security plan:

- *Accidental losses, including human error, software, and hardware-caused breaches*   Creating operating procedures such as user authorization, uniform software installation procedures, and hardware maintenance schedules are examples of actions that may be taken to address threats from accidental losses. As in any effort that involves human beings, some losses are inevitable, but well-thought-out policies and procedures should reduce the amount and severity of losses. Of potentially more serious consequence are the threats that are not accidental.
- *Theft and fraud*   These activities are going to be perpetrated by people, quite possibly through electronic means, and may or may not alter data. Attention here should focus on each possible location shown in Figure 12-2. For example, physical security must be established so that unauthorized persons are unable to gain access to rooms where computers, servers, telecommunications facilities, or computer files are located. Physical security should also be provided for employee offices and any other locations where sensitive data are stored or easily accessed. Establishment of a firewall to protect unauthorized access to inappropriate parts of the database through outside communication links is another example of a security procedure that will hamper people who are intent on theft or fraud.
- *Loss of privacy or confidentiality*   Loss of privacy is usually taken to mean loss of protection of data about individuals, whereas loss of confidentiality is usually

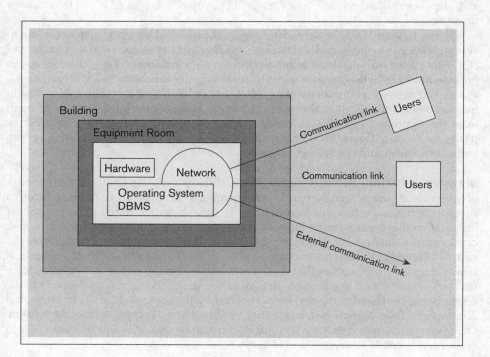

FIGURE 12-2   Possible locations of data security threats

taken to mean loss of protection of critical organizational data that may have strategic value to the organization. Failure to control privacy of information may lead to blackmail, bribery, public embarrassment, or stealing of user passwords. Failure to control confidentiality may lead to loss of competitiveness. State and federal laws now exist to require some types of organizations to create and communicate policies to ensure privacy of customer and client data. Security mechanisms must enforce these policies, and failure to do so can mean significant financial and reputation loss.

- *Loss of data integrity*   When data integrity is compromised, data will be invalid or corrupted. Unless data integrity can be restored through established backup and recovery procedures, an organization may suffer serious losses or make incorrect and expensive decisions based on the invalid data.
- *Loss of availability*   Sabotage of hardware, networks, or applications may cause the data to become unavailable to users, which again may lead to severe operational difficulties. This category of threat includes the introduction of viruses intended to corrupt data or software or to render the system unusable. It is important to counter this threat by always installing the most current antivirus software, as well as educating employees on the sources of viruses. We discuss data availability later in this chapter.

As noted earlier, data security must be provided within the context of a total program for security. Two critical areas that strongly support data security are client/server security and Web application security. We address these two topics next, before outlining approaches aimed more directly at data security.

Establishing Client/Server Security

Database security is only as good as the security of the whole computing environment. Physical security, logical security, and change control security must be established across all components of the client/server environment, including the servers, the client workstations, the network and its related components, and the users.

SERVER SECURITY   In a modern client/server environment, multiple servers, including database servers, need to be protected. Each should be located in a secure area, accessible only to authorized administrators and supervisors. Logical access controls, including server and administrator passwords, provide layers of protection against intrusion.

Most modern DBMSs have database-level password security that is similar to system-level password security. Database management systems, such as Oracle and SQL Server, provide database administrators with considerable capabilities that can provide aid in establishing data security, including the capability to limit each user's access and activity permissions (e.g., *select*, *update*, *insert*, or *delete*) to tables within the database. Although it is also possible to pass authentication information through from the operating system's authentication capability, this reduces the number of password security layers. Thus, in a database server, sole reliance on operating system authentication should not be encouraged.

NETWORK SECURITY   Securing client/server systems includes securing the network between client and server. Networks are susceptible to breaches of security through eavesdropping, unauthorized connections, or unauthorized retrieval of packets of information that are traversing the network. Thus, encryption of data so that attackers cannot read a data packet that is being transmitted is obviously an important part of network security. (We discuss encryption later in the chapter.) In addition, authentication of the client workstation that is attempting to access the server also helps enforce network security, and application authentication gives the user confidence that the server being contacted is the real server needed by the user. Audit trails of attempted accesses can help administrators identify unauthorized attempts to use the system. Other system components, such as routers, can also be configured to restrict access to authorized users, IP addresses, and so forth.

Application Security Issues in Three-Tier Client/Server Environments

The explosion of Web sites that make data accessible to viewers through their Internet connections raises new issues that go beyond the general client/server security issues just addressed. In a three-tier environment, the dynamic creation of a Web page from a database requires access to the database, and if the database is not properly protected, it is vulnerable to inappropriate access by any user. This is a new point of vulnerability that was previously avoided by specialized client access software. Also of interest is privacy. Companies are able to collect information about those who access their Web sites. If they are conducting e-commerce activities, selling products over the Web, they can collect information about their customers that has value to other businesses. If a company sells customer information without those customers' knowledge or if a customer believes that may happen, ethical and privacy issues are raised that must be addressed.

Figure 12-3 illustrates a typical environment for Web-enabled databases. The Web farm includes Web servers and database servers supporting Web-based applications. If an organization wishes to make only static HTML pages available, protection must be established for the HTML files stored on a Web server. Creation of a static Web page with extracts from a database uses traditional application development languages such as Visual Basic.NET or Java, and thus their creation can be controlled by using standard methods of database access control. If some of the HTML files loaded on the Web server are sensitive, they can be placed in directories that are protected using operating system security or they may be readable but not published in the directory. Thus, the user must know the exact file name to access the sensitive HTML page. It is also common to segregate the Web server and limit its contents to publicly browsable Web pages. Sensitive files may be kept on another server accessible through an organization's intranet.

Security measures for dynamic Web page generation are different. Dynamic Web pages are stored as a template into which the appropriate and current data are inserted from the database or user input once any queries associated with the page are run. This means that the Web server must be able to access the database. To function appropriately, the connection usually requires full access to the database. Thus, establishing adequate

FIGURE 12-3 Establishing Internet security

server security is critical to protecting the data. The server that owns the database connection should be physically secure, and the execution of programs on the server should be controlled. User input, which could embed SQL commands, also needs to be filtered so unauthorized scripts are not executed.

Access to data can also be controlled through another layer of security: user-authentication security. Use of an HTML login form will allow the database administrator to define each user's privileges. Each session may be tracked by storing a piece of data, or cookie, on the client machine. This information can be returned to the server and provide information about the login session. Session security must also be established to ensure that private data are not compromised during a session, because information is broadcast across a network for reception by a particular machine and is thus susceptible to being intercepted. TCP/IP is not a very secure protocol, and encryption systems, such as the ones discussed later in this chapter, are essential. A standard encryption method, Secure Sockets Layer (SSL), is used by many developers to encrypt all data traveling between client and server during a session. URLs that begin with https:// use SSL for transmission.

Additional methods of Web security include ways to restrict access to Web servers:

- Restrict the number of users on the Web server as much as possible. Of those users, give as few as possible superuser or administrator rights. Only those given these privileges should also be allowed to load software or edit or add files.
- Restrict access to the Web server, keeping a minimum number of ports open. Try to open a minimum number of ports, and preferably only http and https ports.
- Remove any unneeded programs that load automatically when setting up the server. Demo programs are sometimes included that can provide a hacker with the access desired. Compilers and interpreters such as Perl should not be on a path that is directly accessible from the Internet.

DATA PRIVACY Protection of individual privacy when using the Internet has become an important issue. E-mail, e-commerce and marketing, and other online resources have created new computer-mediated communication paths. Many groups have an interest in people's Internet behavior, including employers, governments, and businesses. Applications that return individualized responses require that information be collected about the individual, but at the same time proper respect for the privacy and dignity of employees, citizens, and customers should be observed.

Concerns about the rights of individuals to not have personal information collected and disseminated casually or recklessly have intensified as more of the population has become familiar with computers and as communications among computers have proliferated. Information privacy legislation generally gives individuals the right to know what data have been collected about them and to correct any errors in those data. As the amount of data exchanged continues to grow, the need is also growing to develop adequate data protection. Also important are adequate provisions to allow the data to be used for legitimate legal purposes so that organizations that need the data can access them and rely on their quality. Individuals need to be given the opportunity to state with whom data retained about them may be shared, and then these wishes must be enforced; enforcement is more reliable if access rules based on privacy wishes are developed by the DBA staff and handled by the DBMS.

Individuals must guard their privacy rights and be aware of the privacy implications of the tools they are using. For example, when using a browser, users may elect to allow cookies to be placed on their machines, or they may reject that option. To make a decision with which they would be comfortable, they must know several things. They must be aware of cookies, understand what they are, evaluate their own desire to receive customized information versus their wish to keep their browsing behavior to themselves, and learn how to set their machine to accept or reject cookies. Browsers and Web sites have not been quick to help users understand all of these aspects. Abuses of privacy, such as selling customer information collected in cookies, have helped increase general awareness of the privacy issues that have developed as use of the Web for communication, shopping, and other uses has developed.

At work, individuals need to realize that communication executed through their employer's machines and networks is not private. Courts have upheld the rights of employers to monitor all employee electronic communication.

On the Internet, privacy of communication is not guaranteed. Encryption products, anonymous remailers, and built-in security mechanisms in commonly used software help preserve privacy. Protecting the privately owned and operated computer networks that now make up a very critical part of our information infrastructure is essential to the further development of electronic commerce, banking, health care, and transportation applications over the Web.

The W3C has created a standard, the Platform for Privacy Preferences (P3P), that will communicate a Web site's stated privacy policies and compare that statement with the user's own policy preferences. P3P uses XML code on Web site servers that can be fetched automatically by any browser or plug-in equipped for P3P. The client browser or plug-in can then compare the site's privacy policy with the user's privacy preferences and inform the user of any discrepancies. P3P addresses the following aspects of online privacy:

- Who is collecting the data?
- What information is being collected, and for what purpose?
- What information will be shared with others, and who are those others?
- Can users make changes in the way their data will be used by the collector?
- How are disputes resolved?
- What policies are followed for retaining data?
- Where can the site's detailed policies be found, in readable form?

Anonymity is another important facet of Internet communication that has come under pressure. Although U.S. law protects a right to anonymity, chat rooms and e-mail forums have been required to reveal the names of people who have posted messages anonymously. A 1995 European Parliament directive that would cut off data exchanges with any country lacking adequate privacy safeguards has led to an agreement that the United States will provide the same protection to European customers as European businesses do. An update to this directive in the form of the General Data Protection Regulation is currently in draft form.

DATABASE SOFTWARE DATA SECURITY FEATURES

A comprehensive data security plan will include establishing administrative policies and procedures, physical protections, and data management software protections. Physical protections, such as securing data centers and work areas, disposing of obsolete media, and protecting portable devices from theft, are not covered here. We discuss administrative policies and procedures later in this section. All the elements of a data security plan work together to achieve the desired level of security. Some industries, for example health care, have regulations that set standards for the security plan and, hence, put requirements on data security. (See Anderson, 2005, for a discussion of the HIPAA security guidelines.) The most important security features of data management software follow:

1. Views or subschemas, which restrict user views of the database
2. Domains, assertions, checks, and other integrity controls defined as database objects, which are enforced by the DBMS during database querying and updating
3. Authorization rules, which identify users and restrict the actions they may take against a database
4. User-defined procedures, which define additional constraints or limitations in using a database
5. Encryption procedures, which encode data in an unrecognizable form
6. Authentication schemes, which positively identify persons attempting to gain access to a database
7. Backup, journaling, and checkpointing capabilities, which facilitate recovery procedures

Views

In Chapter 6, we defined a view as a subset of a database that is presented to one or more users. A view is created by querying one or more of the base tables, producing a dynamic result table for the user at the time of the request. Thus, a view is always based on the current data in the base tables from which it is built. The advantage of a view is that it can be built to present only the data (certain columns and/or rows) to which the user requires access, effectively preventing the user from viewing other data that may be private or confidential. The user may be granted the right to access the view, but not to access the base tables upon which the view is based. So, confining a user to a view may be more restrictive for that user than allowing him or her access to the involved base tables.

 PINE VALLEY FURNITURE

For example, we could build a view for a Pine Valley employee that provides information about materials needed to build a Pine Valley furniture product without providing other information, such as unit price, that is not relevant to the employee's work. This command creates a view that will list the wood required and the wood available for each product:

```
CREATE VIEW MATERIALS_V AS
    SELECT Product_T.ProductID, ProductName, Footage,
        FootageOnHand
    FROM Product_T, RawMaterial_T, Uses_T
    WHERE Product_T.ProductID = Uses_T.ProductID
    AND RawMaterial_T.MaterialID = Uses_T.MaterialID;
```

The contents of the view created will be updated each time the view is accessed, but here are the current contents of the view, which can be accessed with the SQL command:

```
SELECT * FROM MATERIALS_V;
```

ProductID	ProductName	Footage	FootageOnHand
1	End Table	4	1
2	Coffee Table	6	11
3	Computer Desk	15	11
4	Entertainment Center	20	84
5	Writer's Desk	13	68
6	8-Drawer Desk	16	66
7	Dining Table	16	11
8	Computer Desk	15	9

8 rows selected.

The user can write SELECT statements against the view, treating it as though it were a table. Although views promote security by restricting user access to data, they are not adequate security measures because unauthorized persons may gain knowledge of or access to a particular view. Also, several persons may share a particular view; all may have authority to read the data, but only a restricted few may be authorized to update the data. Finally, with high-level query languages, an unauthorized person may gain access to data through simple experimentation. As a result, more sophisticated security measures are normally required.

Integrity Controls

Integrity controls protect data from unauthorized use and update. Often, integrity controls limit the values a field may hold and the actions that can be performed on data, or trigger the execution of some procedure, such as placing an entry in a log to record which users have done what with which data.

One form of integrity control is a domain. In essence, a domain can be used to create a user-defined data type. Once a domain is defined, any field can be assigned that domain as its data type. For example, the following PriceChange domain (defined in SQL) can be used as the data type of any database field, such as PriceIncrease and PriceDiscount, to limit the amount standard prices can be augmented in one transaction:

```
CREATE DOMAIN PriceChange AS DECIMAL
   CHECK (VALUE BETWEEN .001 and .15);
```

Then, in the definition of, say, a pricing transaction table, we might have the following:

```
PriceIncrease PriceChange NOT NULL,
```

One advantage of a domain is that if it ever has to change, it can be changed in one place—the domain definition—and all fields with this domain will be changed automatically. Alternatively, the same CHECK clause could be included in a constraint on both the PriceIncrease and PriceDiscount fields, but in this case, if the limits of the check were to change, a DBA would have to find every instance of this integrity control and change it in each place separately.

Assertions are powerful constraints that enforce certain desirable database conditions. Assertions are checked automatically by the DBMS when transactions are run involving tables or fields on which assertions exist. For example, assume that an employee table has the fields EmpID, EmpName, SupervisorID, and SpouseID. Suppose that a company rule is that no employee may supervise his or her spouse. The following assertion enforces this rule:

```
CREATE ASSERTION SpousalSupervision
   CHECK (SupervisorID < > SpouseID);
```

If the assertion fails, the DBMS will generate an error message.

Assertions can become rather complex. Suppose that Pine Valley Furniture has a rule that no two salespersons can be assigned to the same territory at the same time. Suppose a Salesperson table includes the fields SalespersonID and TerritoryID. This assertion can be written using a correlated subquery, as follows:

```
CREATE ASSERTION TerritoryAssignment
   CHECK (NOT EXISTS
      (SELECT * FROM Salesperson_T SP WHERE SP.TerritoryID IN
         (SELECT SSP.TerritoryID FROM Salesperson_T SSP WHERE
            SSP.SalespersonID < > SP.SalespersonID)));
```

Finally, *triggers* (defined and illustrated in Chapter 7) can be used for security purposes. A trigger, which includes an event, a condition, and an action, is potentially more complex than an assertion. For example, a trigger can do the following:

- Prohibit inappropriate actions (e.g., changing a salary value outside the normal business day)
- Cause special handling procedures to be executed (e.g., if a customer invoice payment is received after some due date, a penalty can be added to the account balance for that customer)
- Cause a row to be written to a log file to echo important information about the user and a transaction being made to sensitive data, so that the log can be reviewed by human or automated procedures for possible inappropriate behavior (e.g., the log can record which user initiated a salary change for which employee)

FIGURE 12-4   Authorization
matrix

Subject	Object	Action	Constraint
Sales Dept.	Customer record	Insert	Credit limit LE $5000
Order trans.	Customer record	Read	None
Terminal 12	Customer record	Modify	Balance due only
Acctg. Dept.	Order record	Delete	None
Ann Walker	Order record	Insert	Order aml LT $2000
Program AR4	Order record	Modify	None

As with domains, a powerful benefit of a trigger, as with any other stored procedure, is that the DBMS enforces these controls for all users and all database activities. The control does not have to be coded into each query or program. Thus, individual users and programs cannot circumvent the necessary controls.

Assertions, triggers, stored procedures, and other forms of integrity controls may not stop all malicious or accidental use or modification of data. Thus, it is recommended (Anderson, 2005) that a change audit process be used in which all user activities are logged and monitored to check that all policies and constraints are enforced. Following this recommendation means that every database query and transaction is logged to record characteristics of all data use, especially modifications: who accessed the data, when it was accessed, what program or query was run, where in the computer network the request was generated, and other parameters that can be used to investigate suspicious activity or actual breaches of security and integrity.

Authorization Rules

Authorization rules

Controls incorporated in a data management system that restrict access to data and also restrict the actions that people may take when they access data.

Authorization rules are controls incorporated in a data management system that restrict access to data and also restrict the actions that people may take when they access data. For example, a person who can supply a particular password may be authorized to read any record in a database but cannot necessarily modify any of those records.

Fernandez et al. (1981) have developed a conceptual model of database security. Their model expresses authorization rules in the form of a table (or matrix) that includes subjects, objects, actions, and constraints. Each row of the table indicates that a particular subject is authorized to take a certain action on an object in the database, perhaps subject to some constraint. Figure 12-4 shows an example of such an authorization matrix. This table contains several entries pertaining to records in an accounting database. For example, the first row in the table indicates that anyone in the Sales Department is authorized to insert a new customer record in the database, provided that the customer's credit limit does not exceed $5,000. The last row indicates that the program AR4 is authorized to modify order records without restriction. Data administration is responsible for determining and implementing authorization rules that are implemented at the database level. Authorization schemes can also be implemented at the operating system level or the application level.

FIGURE 12-5   Implementing
authorization rules
(a) Authorization table
for subjects (salespersons)

	Customer records	Order records
Read	Y	Y
Insert	Y	Y
Modify	Y	N
Delete	N	N

(b) Authorization table
for objects (order records)

	Salespersons (password BATMAN)	Order entry (password JOKER)	Accounting (password TRACY)
Read	Y	Y	Y
Insert	N	Y	N
Modify	N	Y	Y
Delete	N	N	Y

Most contemporary database management systems do not implement an authorization matrix such as the one shown in Figure 12-4; they normally use simplified versions. There are two principal types: authorization tables for subjects and authorization tables for objects. Figure 12-5 shows an example of each type. In Figure 12-5a, for example, we see that salespersons are allowed to modify customer records but not delete these records. In Figure 12-5b, we see that users in Order Entry or Accounting can modify order records, but salespersons cannot. A given DBMS product may provide either one or both of these types of facilities.

Authorization tables, such as those shown in Figure 12-5, are attributes of an organization's data and their environment; they are therefore properly viewed as metadata. Thus, the tables should be stored and maintained in the repository. Because authorization tables contain highly sensitive data, they themselves should be protected by stringent security rules. Normally, only selected persons in data administration have authority to access and modify these tables.

For example, in Oracle, the privileges included in Figure 12-6 can be granted to users at the database level or table level. INSERT and UPDATE can be granted at the column level. Where many users, such as those in a particular job classification, need similar privileges, roles may be created that contain a set of privileges, and then all the privileges can be granted to a user simply by granting the role. To grant the ability to read the product table and update prices to a user with the log in ID of SMITH, the following SQL command may be given:

```
GRANT SELECT, UPDATE (UnitPrice) ON Product_T TO SMITH;
```

There are eight data dictionary views that contain information about privileges that have been granted. In this case, DBA_TAB_PRIVS contains users and objects for every user who has been granted privileges on objects, such as tables. DBA_COL_PRIVS contains users who have been granted privileges on columns of tables.

User-Defined Procedures

Some DBMS products provide user exits (or interfaces) that allow system designers or users to create their own **user-defined procedures** for security, in addition to the authorization rules we have just described. For example, a user procedure might be designed to provide positive user identification. In attempting to log on to the computer, the user might be required to supply a procedure name in addition to a simple password. If valid password and procedure names are supplied, the system then calls the procedure, which asks the user a series of questions whose answers should be known only to that password holder (e.g., mother's maiden name).

User-defined procedures
User exits (or interfaces) that allow system designers to define their own security procedures in addition to the authorization rules.

Encryption

Data encryption can be used to protect highly sensitive data such as customer credit card numbers or account balances. **Encryption** is the coding or scrambling of data so that humans cannot read them. Some DBMS products include encryption routines that automatically encode sensitive data when they are stored or transmitted over

Encryption
The coding or scrambling of data so that humans cannot read them.

FIGURE 12-6   Oracle privileges

Privilege	Capability
SELECT	Query the object.
INSERT	Insert records into the table/view. Can be given for specific columns.
UPDATE	Update records in table/view. Can be given for specific columns.
DELETE	Delete records from table/view.
ALTER	Alter the table.
INDEX	Create indexes on the table.
REFERENCES	Create foreign keys that reference the table.
EXECUTE	Execute the procedure, package, or function.

communications channels. For example, encryption is commonly used in electronic funds transfer (EFT) systems. Other DBMS products provide exits that allow users to code their own encryption routines.

Any system that provides encryption facilities must also provide complementary routines for decoding the data. These decoding routines must be protected by adequate security, or else the advantages of encryption are lost. They also require significant computing resources.

Two common forms of encryption exist: one key and two key. With a one-key method, also called Data Encryption Standard (DES), both the sender and the receiver need to know the key that is used to scramble the transmitted or stored data. A two-key method, also called asymmetric encryption, employs a private and a public key. Two-key methods (see Figure 12-7) are especially popular in e-commerce applications to provide secure transmission and database storage of payment data, such as credit card numbers.

A popular implementation of the two-key method is Secure Sockets Layer (SSL), commonly used by most major browsers to communicate with Web/application servers. It provides data encryption, server authentication, and other services in a TCP/IP connection. For example, the U.S. banking industry uses a 128-bit version of SSL (the most secure level in current use) to secure online banking transactions.

Details about encryption techniques are beyond the scope of this book and are generally handled by the DBMS without significant involvement of a DBA; it is simply important to know that database data encryption is a strong measure available to a DBA.

Authentication Schemes

A long-standing problem in computer circles is how to identify persons who are trying to gain access to a computer or its resources, such as a database or DBMS. In an electronic environment, a user can prove his or her identity by supplying one or more of the following factors:

1. Something the user knows, usually a password or personal identification number (PIN)
2. Something the user possesses, such as a smart card or token
3. Some unique personal characteristic, such as a fingerprint or retinal scan

Authentication schemes are called one-factor, two-factor, or three-factor authentication, depending on how many of these factors are employed. Authentication becomes stronger as more factors are used.

FIGURE 12-7 Basic two-key encryption

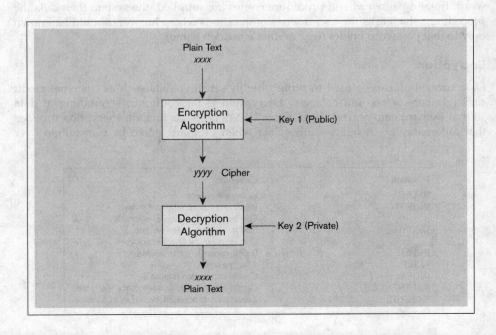

PASSWORDS The first line of defense is the use of passwords, which is a one-factor authentication scheme. With such a scheme, anyone who can supply a valid password can log on to a database system. (A user ID may also be required, but user IDs are typically not secured.) A DBA (or perhaps a system administrator) is responsible for managing schemes for issuing or creating passwords for the DBMS and/or specific applications.

Although requiring passwords is a good starting point for authentication, it is well known that this method has a number of deficiencies. People assigned passwords for different devices quickly devise ways to remember these passwords, ways that tend to compromise the password scheme. The passwords are written down, where others may find them. They are shared with other users; it is not unusual for an entire department to use one common password for access. Passwords are included in automatic logon scripts, which removes the inconvenience of remembering them and typing them but also eliminates their effectiveness. And passwords usually traverse a network in clear-text, not encrypted, so if intercepted they may be easily interpreted. Also, passwords cannot, by themselves, ensure the security of a computer and its databases because they give no indication of who is trying to gain access. Thus, for example, a log should be kept and analyzed of attempted logons with incorrect passwords.

STRONG AUTHENTICATION More reliable authentication techniques have become a business necessity, with the rapid advances in e-commerce and increased security threats in the form of hacking, identity theft, and so on.

Two-factor authentication schemes require two of the three factors: something the user has (usually a card or token) and something the user knows (usually a PIN). You are already familiar with this system from using automated teller machines (ATMs). This scheme is much more secure than using only passwords because (barring carelessness) it is quite difficult for an unauthorized person to obtain both factors at the same time.

Although an improvement over password-only authentication, two-factor schemes are not infallible. Cards can be lost or stolen, and PINs can be intercepted. *Three-factor authentication* schemes add an important third factor: a biometric attribute that is unique for each individual user. Personal characteristics that are commonly used include fingerprints, voiceprints, eye pictures, and signature dynamics.

Three-factor authentication is normally implemented with a high-tech card called a smart card (or smart badge). A **smart card** is a credit card–sized plastic card with an embedded microprocessor chip that can store, process, and output electronic data in a secure manner. Smart cards are replacing the familiar magnetic-stripe-based cards we have used for decades. Using smart cards can be a very strong means to authenticate a database user. In addition, smart cards can themselves be database storage devices; today smart cards can store several gigabytes of data, and this number is increasing rapidly. Smart cards can provide secure storage of personal data such as medical records or a summary of medications taken.

All of the authentication schemes described here, including use of smart cards, can be only as secure as the process that is used to issue them. For example, if a smart card is issued and personalized to an imposter (either carelessly or deliberately), it can be used freely by that person. Thus, before allowing any form of authentication—such as issuing a new card to an employee or other person—the issuing agency must validate beyond any reasonable doubt the identity of that person. Because paper documents are used in this process—birth certificates, passports, driver's licenses, and so on—and these types of documents are often unreliable because they can be easily copied, forged, and so on, significant training of personnel, use of sophisticated technology, and sufficient oversight of the process are needed to ensure that this step is rigorous and well controlled.

Smart card

A credit card–sized plastic card with an embedded microprocessor chip that can store, process, and output electronic data in a secure manner.

SARBANES-OXLEY (SOX) AND DATABASES

The Sarbanes-Oxley Act (SOX) and other similar global regulations were designed to ensure the integrity of public companies' financial statements. A key component of this is ensuring sufficient control and security over the financial systems and IT infrastructure in use within an organization. This has resulted in an increased emphasis on understanding controls around information technology. Given that the focus of SOX is on the integrity of financial statements, controls around the databases and applications that are the source of these data are key.

The key focus of SOX audits is around three areas of control:

1. IT change management
2. Logical access to data
3. IT operations

Most audits start with a walkthrough—that is, a meeting with business owners (of the data that fall under the scope of the audit) and technical architects of the applications and databases. During this walkthrough, the auditors will try to understand how the above three areas are handled by the IT organization.

IT Change Management

IT change management refers to the process by which changes to operational systems and databases are authorized. Typically any change to a production system or database has to be approved by a change control board that is made up of representatives from the business and IT organizations. Authorized changes must then be put through a rigorous process (essentially a mini systems development life cycle) before being put into production. From a database perspective, the most common types of changes are changes to the database schema, changes to database configuration parameters, and patches/updates to the DBMS software itself.

A key issue related to change management that was a top deficiency found by SOX auditors was adequate segregation of duties between people who had access to databases in the three common environments: development, test, and production. SOX mandates that the DBAs who have the ability to modify data in these three environments be different. This is primarily to ensure that changes to the operating environment have been adequately tested before being implemented. When the size of the organization does not allow this, other personnel should be authorized to do periodic reviews of database access by DBAs, using features such as database audits (described in the next section).

Logical Access to Data

Logical access to data is essentially about the security procedures in place to prevent unauthorized access to the data. From a SOX perspective, the two key questions to ask are: Who has access to what? and Who has access to too much? In response to these two questions, organizations must establish administrative policies and procedures that serve as a context for effectively implementing these measures. Two types of security policies and procedures are personnel controls and physical access controls.

PERSONNEL CONTROLS Adequate controls of personnel must be developed and followed, for the greatest threat to business security is often internal rather than external. In addition to the security authorization and authentication procedures just discussed, organizations should develop procedures to ensure a selective hiring process that validates potential employees' representations about their backgrounds and capabilities. Monitoring to ensure that personnel are following established practices, taking regular vacations, working with other employees, and so forth should be done. Employees should be trained in those aspects of security and quality that are relevant to their jobs and encouraged to be aware of and follow standard security and data quality measures. Standard job controls, such as separating duties so no one employee has responsibility for an entire business process or keeping application developers from having access to production systems, should also be enforced. Should an employee need to be let go, there should be an orderly and timely set of procedures for removing authorizations and authentications and notifying other employees of the status change. Similarly, if an employee's job profile changes, care should be taken to ensure that his or her new set of roles and responsibilities does not lead to violations of separation of duties.

PHYSICAL ACCESS CONTROLS   Limiting access to particular areas within a building is usually a part of controlling physical access. Swipe, or proximity access, cards can be used to gain access to secure areas, and each access can be recorded in a database, with a time stamp. Guests, including vendor maintenance representatives, should be issued badges and escorted into secure areas. Access to sensitive equipment, including hardware and peripherals such as printers (which may be used to print classified reports) can be controlled by placing these items in secure areas. Other equipment may be locked to a desk or cabinet or may have an alarm attached. Backup data tapes should be kept in fireproof data safes and/or kept offsite, at a safe location. Procedures that make explicit the schedules for moving media and disposing of media and that establish labeling and indexing of all materials stored must be established.

Placement of computer screens so that they cannot be seen from outside the building may also be important. Control procedures for areas external to the office building should also be developed. Companies frequently use security guards to control access to their buildings or use a card swipe system or handprint recognition system (smart badges) to automate employee access to the building. Visitors should be issued an identification card and required to be accompanied throughout the building.

New concerns are raised by the increasingly mobile nature of work. Laptop computers are very susceptible to theft, which puts data on a laptop at risk. Encryption and multiple-factor authentication can protect data in the event of laptop theft. Antitheft devices (e.g., security cables, geographic tracking chips) can deter theft or help quickly recover stolen laptops on which critical data are stored.

IT Operations

IT operations refers to the policies and procedures in place related to the day-to-day management of the infrastructure, applications, and databases in an organization. Key areas in this regard that are relevant to data and database administrators are database backup and recovery, as well as data availability. These are discussed in detail in later sections.

An area of control that helps maintain data quality and availability but that is often overlooked is vendor management. Organizations should periodically review external maintenance agreements for all hardware and software they are using to ensure that appropriate response rates are agreed to for maintaining system quality and availability. It is also important to consider reaching agreements with the developers of all critical software so that the organization can get access to the source code should the developer go out of business or stop supporting the programs. One way to accomplish this is by having a third party hold the source code, with an agreement that it will be released if such a situation develops. Controls should be in place to protect data from inappropriate access and use by outside maintenance staff and other contract workers.

DATABASE BACKUP AND RECOVERY

Database recovery is database administration's response to Murphy's law. Inevitably, databases are damaged or lost or become unavailable because of some system problem that may be caused by human error, hardware failure, incorrect or invalid data, program errors, computer viruses, network failures, conflicting transactions, or natural catastrophes. It is the responsibility of a DBA to ensure that all critical data in a database are protected and can be recovered in the event of loss. Because an organization depends heavily on its databases, a DBA must be able to minimize downtime and other disruptions while a database is being backed up or recovered. To achieve these objectives, a database management system must provide mechanisms for backing up data with as little disruption of production time as possible and restoring a database quickly and accurately after loss or damage.

Database recovery
Mechanisms for restoring a database quickly and accurately after loss or damage.

Basic Recovery Facilities

A database management system should provide four basic facilities for backup and recovery of a database:

1. *Backup facilities*, which provide periodic backup (sometimes called *fallback*) copies of portions of or the entire database
2. *Journalizing facilities*, which maintain an audit trail of transactions and database changes
3. *A checkpoint facility*, by which the DBMS periodically suspends all processing and synchronizes its files and journals to establish a recovery point
4. *A recovery manager*, which allows the DBMS to restore the database to a correct condition and restart processing transactions

Backup facility

A DBMS COPY utility that produces a backup copy (or save) of an entire database or a subset of a database.

BACKUP FACILITIES A DBMS should provide **backup facilities** that produce a backup copy (or save) of the entire database plus control files and journals. Each DBMS normally provides a COPY utility for this purpose. In addition to the database files, the backup facility should create a copy of related database objects including the repository (or system catalog), database indexes, source libraries, and so on. Typically, a backup copy is produced at least once per day. The copy should be stored in a secured location where it is protected from loss or damage. The backup copy is used to restore the database in the event of hardware failure, catastrophic loss, or damage.

Some DBMSs provide backup utilities for a DBA to use to make backups; other systems assume that the DBA will use the operating system commands, export commands, or SELECT...INTO SQL commands to perform backups. Because performing the nightly backup for a particular database is repetitive, creating a script that automates regular backups will save time and result in fewer backup errors.

With large databases, regular full backups may be impractical because the time required to perform a backup may exceed the time available, or a database may be a critical system that must always remain available; in such a case, a cold backup, where the database is shut down, is not practical. As a result, backups may be taken of dynamic data regularly (a so-called *hot backup*, in which only a selected portion of the database is shut down from use), but backups of static data, which don't change frequently, may be taken less often. Incremental backups, which record changes made since the last full backup, but which do not take so much time to complete, may also be taken on an interim basis, allowing for longer periods of time between full backups. Thus, backup strategies must be based on the demands being placed on the database systems.

Database downtime can be very expensive. The lost revenue from downtime (e.g., inability to take orders or place reservations) needs to be balanced against the cost of additional technology, primarily disk storage, to achieve a desired level of availability. To help achieve the desired level of reliability, some DBMSs will automatically make backup (often called fallback) copies of the database in real time as the database is updated. These fallback copies are usually stored on separate disk drives and disk controllers, and they are used as live backup copies if portions of the database become inaccessible due to hardware failures. As the cost of secondary storages steadily decreases, the cost to make redundant copies becomes more practical in more situations. Fallback copies are different from redundant array of independent disks (RAID) storage because the DBMS is making copies of only the database as database transactions occur, whereas RAID is used by the operating system for making redundant copies of all storage elements as any page is updated.

Journalizing facility

An audit trail of transactions and database changes.

Transaction

A discrete unit of work that must be completely processed or not processed at all within a computer system. Entering a customer order is an example of a transaction.

Transaction log

A record of the essential data for each transaction that is processed against the database.

JOURNALIZING FACILITIES A DBMS must provide **journalizing facilities** to produce an audit trail of **transactions** and database changes. In the event of a failure, a consistent database state can be reestablished, using the information in the journals together with the most recent complete backup. As Figure 12-8 shows, there are two basic journals, or logs. The first is the **transaction log**, which contains a record of the essential data for each transaction that is processed against the database. Data that are typically recorded for each transaction include the transaction code or identification, action or

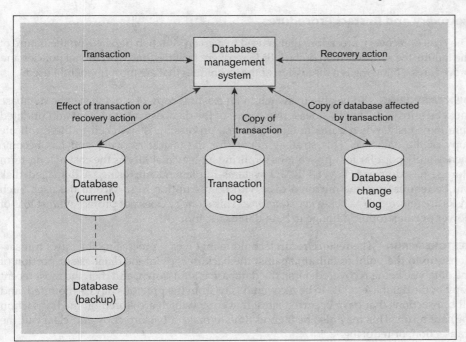

FIGURE 12-8   Database audit trail

type of transaction (e.g., insert), time of the transaction, terminal number or user ID, input data values, table and records accessed, records modified, and possibly the old and new field values.

The second type of log is a **database change log**, which contains before and after images of records that have been modified by transactions. A **before image** is simply a copy of a record before it has been modified, and an **after image** is a copy of the same record after it has been modified. Some systems also keep a security log, which can alert the DBA to any security violations that occur or are attempted. The recovery manager uses these logs to undo and redo operations, which we explain later in this chapter. These logs may be kept on disk or tape; because they are critical to recovery, they, too, must be backed up.

CHECKPOINT FACILITY   A **checkpoint facility** in a DBMS periodically refuses to accept any new transactions. All transactions in progress are completed, and the journal files are brought up-to-date. At this point, the system is in a quiet state, and the database and transaction logs are synchronized. The DBMS writes a special record (called a *checkpoint record*) to the log file, which is like a snapshot of the state of the database. The checkpoint record contains information necessary to restart the system. Any dirty data blocks (i.e., pages of memory that contain changes that have not yet been written out to disk) are written from memory to disk storage, thus ensuring that all changes made prior to taking the checkpoint have been written to long-term storage.

A DBMS may perform checkpoints automatically (which is preferred) or in response to commands in user application programs. Checkpoints should be taken frequently (say, several times an hour). When failures occur, it is often possible to resume processing from the most recent checkpoint. Thus, only a few minutes of processing work must be repeated, compared with several hours for a complete restart of the day's processing.

RECOVERY MANAGER   The **recovery manager** is a module of a DBMS that restores the database to a correct condition when a failure occurs and then resumes processing user requests. The type of restart used depends on the nature of the failure. The recovery manager uses the logs shown in Figure 12-8 (as well as the backup copy, if necessary) to restore the database.

Database change log
A log that contains before and after images of records that have been modified by transactions.

Before image
A copy of a record (or page of memory) before it has been modified.

After image
A copy of a record (or page of memory) after it has been modified.

Checkpoint facility
A facility by which a DBMS periodically refuses to accept any new transactions. The system is in a quiet state, and the database and transaction logs are synchronized.

Recovery manager
A module of a DBMS that restores the database to a correct condition when a failure occurs and then resumes processing user questions.

Recovery and Restart Procedures

The type of recovery procedure that is used in a given situation depends on the nature of the failure, the sophistication of the DBMS recovery facilities, and operational policies and procedures. Following is a discussion of the techniques that are most frequently used.

DISK MIRRORING   To be able to switch to an existing copy of a database, the database must be mirrored. That is, at least two copies of the database must be kept and updated simultaneously. When a media failure occurs, processing is switched to the duplicate copy of the database. This strategy allows for the fastest recovery and has become increasingly popular for applications requiring high availability as the cost of long-term storage has dropped. Level 1 RAID systems implement mirroring. A damaged disk can be rebuilt from the mirrored disk with no disruption in service to the user. Such disks are referred to as being *hot-swappable*. This strategy does not protect against loss of power or catastrophic damage to both databases, though.

Restore/rerun

A technique that involves reprocessing the day's transactions (up to the point of failure) against the backup copy of the database.

RESTORE/RERUN   The **restore/rerun** technique involves reprocessing the day's transactions (up to the point of failure) against the backup copy of the database or portion of the database being recovered. First, the database is shut down, and then the most recent copy of the database or file to be recovered (say, from the previous day) is mounted, and all transactions that have occurred since that copy (which are stored on the transaction log) are rerun. This may also be a good time to make a backup copy and clear out the transaction, or redo, log.

The advantage of restore/rerun is its simplicity. The DBMS does not need to create a database change journal, and no special restart procedures are required. However, there are two major disadvantages. First, the time to reprocess transactions may be prohibitive. Depending on the frequency with which backup copies are made, several hours of reprocessing may be required. Processing new transactions will have to be deferred until recovery is completed, and if the system is heavily loaded, it may be impossible to catch up. The second disadvantage is that the sequencing of transactions will often be different from when they were originally processed, which may lead to quite different results. For example, in the original run, a customer deposit may be posted before a withdrawal. In the rerun, the withdrawal transaction may be attempted first and may lead to sending an insufficient funds notice to the customer. For these reasons, restore/rerun is not a sufficient recovery procedure and is generally used only as a last resort in database processing.

MAINTAINING TRANSACTION INTEGRITY   A database is updated by processing transactions that result in changes to one or more database records. If an error occurs during the processing of a transaction, the database may be compromised, and some form of database recovery is required. Thus, to understand database recovery, we must first understand the concept of transaction integrity.

A business transaction is a sequence of steps that constitute some well-defined business activity. Examples of business transactions are Admit Patient in a hospital and Enter Customer Order in a manufacturing company. Normally, a business transaction requires several actions against the database. For example, consider the transaction Enter Customer Order. When a new customer order is entered, the following steps may be performed by an application program:

1. Input the order data (keyed by the user).
2. Read the CUSTOMER record (or insert record if a new customer).
3. Accept or reject the order. If Balance Due plus Order Amount does not exceed Credit Limit, accept the order; otherwise, reject it.
4. If the order is accepted, increase Balance Due by Order Amount. Store the updated CUSTOMER record. Insert the accepted ORDER record in the database.

When processing transactions, a DBMS must ensure that the transactions follow four well-accepted properties, called the ACID properties:

1. *Atomic,*   meaning that the transaction cannot be subdivided and, hence, it must be processed in its entirety or not at all. Once the whole transaction is processed,

we say that the changes are *committed*. If the transaction fails at any midpoint, we say that it has aborted. For example, suppose that the program accepts a new customer order, increases Balance Due, and stores the updated CUSTOMER record. However, suppose that the new ORDER record is not inserted successfully (perhaps due to a duplicate Order Number key or insufficient physical file space). In this case, we want none of the parts of the transaction to affect the database.

2. *Consistent,* meaning that any database constraints that must be true before the transaction must also be true after the transaction. For example, if the inventory on-hand balance must be the difference between total receipts minus total issues, this will be true both before and after an order transaction, which depletes the on-hand balance to satisfy the order.

3. *Isolated,* meaning that changes to the database are not revealed to users until the transaction is committed. For example, this property means that other users do not know what the on-hand inventory is until an inventory transaction is complete; this property then usually means that other users are prohibited from simultaneously updating and possibly even reading data that are in the process of being updated. We discuss this topic in more detail later under concurrency controls and locking. A consequence of transactions being isolated from one another is that concurrent transactions (i.e., several transactions in some partial state of completion) all affect the database as if they were presented to the DBMS in serial fashion.

4. *Durable,* meaning that changes are permanent. Thus, once a transaction is committed, no subsequent failure of the database can reverse the effect of the transaction.

To maintain transaction integrity, the DBMS must provide facilities for the user or application program to define **transaction boundaries**—that is, the logical beginning and end of a transaction. In SQL, the BEGIN TRANSACTION statement is placed in front of the first SQL command within the transaction, and the COMMIT command is placed at the end of the transaction. Any number of SQL commands may come in between these two commands; these are the database processing steps that perform some well-defined business activity, as explained earlier. If a command such as ROLLBACK is processed after a BEGIN TRANSACTION is executed and before a COMMIT is executed, the DBMS aborts the transaction and undoes the effects of the SQL statements processed so far within the transaction boundaries. The application would likely be programmed to execute a ROLLBACK when the DBMS generates an error message performing an UPDATE or INSERT command in the middle of the transaction. The DBMS thus commits (makes durable) changes for successful transactions (those that reach the COMMIT statement) and effectively rejects changes from transactions that are aborted (those that encounter a ROLLBACK). Any SQL statement encountered after a COMMIT or ROLLBACK and before a BEGIN TRANSACTION is executed as a single statement transaction, automatically committed if it executed without error, aborted if any error occurs during its execution.

Although conceptually a transaction is a logical unit of business work, such as a customer order or receipt of new inventory from a supplier, you may decide to break the business unit of work into several database transactions for database processing reasons. For example, because of the isolation property, a transaction that takes many commands and a long time to process may prohibit other uses of the same data at the same time, thus delaying other critical (possibly read-only) work. Some database data are used frequently, so it is important to complete transactional work on these so-called hotspot data as quickly as possible. For example, a primary key and its index for bank account numbers will likely need to be accessed by every ATM transaction, so the database transaction must be designed to use and release these data quickly. Also, remember, all the commands between the boundaries of a transaction must be executed, even those commands seeking input from an online user. If a user is slow to respond to input requests within the boundaries of a transaction, other users may encounter significant delays. Thus, if possible, collect all user input before beginning a transaction. Also, to minimize the length of a transaction, check for possible errors, such as duplicate keys or insufficient account balance, as early in the transaction as possible, so portions of the

Transaction boundaries

The logical beginning and end of a transaction.

database can be released as soon as possible for other users if the transaction is going to be aborted. Some constraints (e.g., balancing the number of units of an item received with the number placed in inventory less returns) cannot be checked until many database commands are executed, so the transaction must be long to ensure database integrity. Thus, the general guideline is to make a database transaction as short as possible while still maintaining the integrity of the database.

BACKWARD RECOVERY With **backward recovery** (also called **rollback**), the DBMS backs out of or undoes unwanted changes to the database. As Figure 12-9a shows, before images of the records that have been changed are applied to the database. As a result, the database is returned to an earlier state; the unwanted changes are eliminated.

Backward recovery is used to reverse the changes made by transactions that have aborted, or terminated abnormally. To illustrate the need for backward recovery (or UNDO), suppose that a banking transaction will transfer $100 in funds from the account for customer A to the account for customer B. The following steps are performed:

1. The program reads the record for customer A and subtracts $100 from the account balance.
2. The program then reads the record for customer B and adds $100 to the account balance. Now the program writes the updated record for customer A to the database. However, in attempting to write the record for customer B, the program encounters an error condition (e.g., a disk fault) and cannot write the record. Now the database is inconsistent—record A has been updated but record B has not—and the transaction must be aborted. An UNDO command will cause the recovery manager to apply the before image for record A to restore the account balance to its original value. (The recovery manager may then restart the transaction and make another attempt.)

Backward recovery (rollback)

The backout, or undo, of unwanted changes to a database. Before images of the records that have been changed are applied to the database, and the database is returned to an earlier state. Rollback is used to reverse the changes made by transactions that have been aborted, or terminated abnormally.

FIGURE 12-9 Basic recovery techniques
(a) Rollback

(b) Rollforward

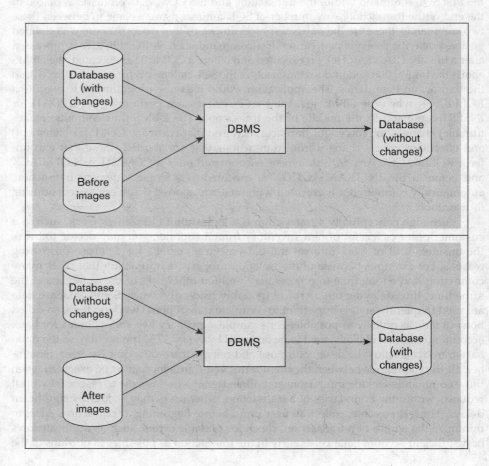

FORWARD RECOVERY With **forward recovery** (also called **rollforward**), the DBMS starts with an earlier copy of the database. Applying after images (the results of good transactions) quickly moves the database forward to a later state (see Figure 12-9b). Forward recovery is much faster and more accurate than restore/rerun, for the following reasons:

- The time-consuming logic of reprocessing each transaction does not have to be repeated.
- Only the most recent after images need to be applied. A database record may have a series of after images (as a result of a sequence of updates), but only the most recent, "good" after image is required for rollforward.

With rollforward, the problem of different sequencing of transactions is avoided, because the results of applying the transactions (rather than the transactions themselves) are used.

Forward recovery (rollforward)
A technique that starts with an earlier copy of a database. After images (the results of good transactions) are applied to the database, and the database is quickly moved forward to a later state.

Types of Database Failure

A wide variety of failures can occur in processing a database, ranging from the input of an incorrect data value to complete loss or destruction of the database. Four of the most common types of problems are aborted transactions, incorrect data, system failure, and database loss or destruction. Each of these types of problems is described in the following sections, and possible recovery procedures are indicated (see Table 12-1).

ABORTED TRANSACTIONS As we noted earlier, a transaction frequently requires a sequence of processing steps to be performed. An **aborted transaction** terminates abnormally. Some reasons for this type of failure are human error, input of invalid data, hardware failure, and deadlock (covered in the next section). A common type of hardware failure is the loss of transmission in a communications link when a transaction is in progress.

Aborted transaction
A transaction in progress that terminates abnormally.

When a transaction aborts, we want to "back out" the transaction and remove any changes that have been made (but not committed) to the database. The recovery manager accomplishes this through backward recovery (applying before images for the transaction in question). This function should be accomplished automatically by the DBMS, which then notifies the user to correct and resubmit the transaction. Other procedures, such as rollforward or transaction reprocessing, could be applied to bring the database to the state it was in just prior to the abort occurrence, but rollback is the preferred procedure in this case.

INCORRECT DATA A more complex situation arises when the database has been updated with incorrect, but valid, data. For example, an incorrect grade may be recorded for a student, or an incorrect amount could be input for a customer payment.

TABLE 12-1 Responses to Database Failure

Type of Failure	Recovery Technique
Aborted transaction	Rollback (preferred)
	Rollforward/return transactions to state just prior to abort
Incorrect data (update inaccurate)	Rollback (preferred)
	Reprocess transactions without inaccurate data updates
	Compensating transactions
System failure (database intact)	Switch to duplicate database (preferred)
	Rollback
	Restart from checkpoint (rollforward)
Database destruction	Switch to duplicate database (preferred)
	Rollforward
	Reprocess transactions

r

Incorrect data are difficult to detect and often lead to complications. To begin with, some time may elapse before an error is detected and the database record (or records) corrected. By this time, numerous other users may have used the erroneous data, and a chain reaction of errors may have occurred as various applications made use of the incorrect data. In addition, transaction outputs (e.g., documents and messages) based on the incorrect data may be transmitted to persons. An incorrect grade report, for example, may be sent to a student or an incorrect statement sent to a customer.

When incorrect data have been processed, the database may be recovered in one of the following ways:

- If the error is discovered soon enough, backward recovery may be used. (However, care must be taken to ensure that all subsequent errors have been reversed.)
- If only a few errors have occurred, a series of compensating transactions may be introduced through human intervention to correct the errors.
- If the first two measures are not feasible, it may be necessary to restart from the most recent checkpoint before the error occurred, and subsequent transactions processed without the error.

Any erroneous messages or documents that have been produced by the erroneous transaction will have to be corrected by appropriate human intervention (letters of explanation, telephone calls, etc.).

SYSTEM FAILURE   In a system failure, some component of the system fails, but the database is not damaged. Some causes of system failure are power loss, operator error, loss of communications transmission, and system software failure.

When a system crashes, some transactions may be in progress. The first step in recovery is to back out those transactions, using before images (backward recovery). Then, if the system is mirrored, it may be possible to switch to the mirrored data and rebuild the corrupted data on a new disk. If the system is not mirrored, it may not be possible to restart because status information in main memory has been lost or damaged. The safest approach is to restart from the most recent checkpoint before the system failure. The database is rolled forward by applying after images for all transactions that were processed after that checkpoint.

DATABASE DESTRUCTION   In the case of **database destruction**, the database itself is lost, destroyed, or cannot be read. A typical cause of database destruction is a disk drive failure (or head crash).

Again, using a mirrored copy of the database is the preferred strategy for recovering from such an event. If there is no mirrored copy, a backup copy of the database is required. Forward recovery is used to restore the database to its state immediately before the loss occurred. Any transactions that may have been in progress when the database was lost are restarted.

Database destruction
The database itself is lost, destroyed, or cannot be read.

Disaster Recovery

Every organization requires contingency plans for dealing with disasters that may severely damage or destroy its data center. Such disasters may be natural (e.g., floods, earthquakes, tornadoes, hurricanes) or human-caused (e.g., wars, sabotage, terrorist attacks). For example, the 2001 terrorist attacks on the World Trade Center resulted in the complete destruction of several data centers and widespread loss of data.

Planning for disaster recovery is an organization-wide responsibility. Database administration is responsible for developing plans for recovering the organization's data and for restoring data operations. Following are some of the major components of a recovery plan (Mullins, 2002):

- Develop a detailed written disaster recovery plan. Schedule regular tests of the plan.
- Choose and train a multidisciplinary team to carry out the plan.
- Establish a backup data center at an offsite location. This site must be located a sufficient distance from the primary site so that no foreseeable disaster will disrupt

both sites. If an organization has two or more data centers, each site may serve as a backup for one of the others. If not, the organization may contract with a disaster recovery service provider.

• Send backup copies of databases to the backup data center on a scheduled basis. Database backups may be sent to the remote site by courier or transmitted by replication software.

CONTROLLING CONCURRENT ACCESS

Databases are shared resources. Database administrators must expect and plan for the likelihood that several users will attempt to access and manipulate data at the same time. With concurrent processing involving updates, a database without **concurrency control** will be compromised due to interference between users. There are two basic approaches to concurrency control: a pessimistic approach (involving locking) and an optimistic approach (involving versioning). We summarize both of these approaches in the following sections.

Concurrency control
The process of managing simultaneous operations against a database so that data integrity is maintained and the operations do not interfere with each other in a multiuser environment.

If users are only reading data, no data integrity problems will be encountered because no changes will be made in the database. However, if one or more users are updating data, then potential problems with maintaining data integrity arise. When more than one transaction is being processed against a database at the same time, the transactions are considered to be concurrent. The actions that must be taken to ensure that data integrity is maintained are called *currency control actions*. Although these actions are implemented by a DBMS, a database administrator must understand these actions and may expect to make certain choices governing their implementation.

Remember that a CPU can process only one instruction at a time. As new transactions are submitted while other processing is occurring against the database, the transactions are usually interleaved, with the CPU switching among the transactions so that some portion of each transaction is performed as the CPU addresses each transaction in turn. Because the CPU is able to switch among transactions so quickly, most users will not notice that they are sharing CPU time with other users.

The Problem of Lost Updates

The most common problem encountered when multiple users attempt to update a database without adequate concurrency control is lost updates. Figure 12-10 shows a common situation. John and Marsha have a joint checking account, and both want to withdraw some cash at the same time, each using an ATM terminal in a different location. Figure 12-10 shows the sequence of events that might occur in the absence of a concurrency control mechanism. John's transaction reads the account balance (which is $1,000) and he proceeds to withdraw $200. Before the transaction writes the new account balance ($800), Marsha's transaction reads the account balance (which is still $1,000). She then withdraws $300, leaving a balance of $700. Her transaction then writes this account balance, which replaces the one written by John's transaction. The effect of John's update has been lost due to interference between the transactions, and the bank is unhappy.

Another similar type of problem that may occur when concurrency control is not established is the **inconsistent read problem**. This problem occurs when one user reads data that have been partially updated by another user. The read will be incorrect and is sometimes referred to as a *dirty read* or an *unrepeatable read*. The lost update and inconsistent read problems arise when the DBMS does not isolate transactions, part of the ACID transaction properties.

Inconsistent read problem
An unrepeatable read, one that occurs when one user reads data that have been partially updated by another user.

Serializability

Concurrent transactions need to be processed in isolation so that they do not interfere with each other. If one transaction were entirely processed before another transaction, no interference would occur. Procedures that process transactions so that the outcome is the same as this are called *serializable*. Processing transactions using a serializable schedule will give the same results as if the transactions had been processed one after the

FIGURE 12-10 Lost update (no concurrency control in effect)

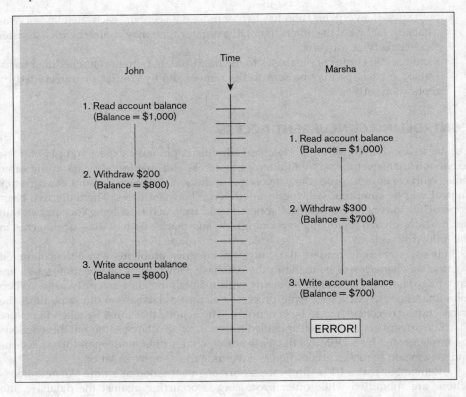

other. Schedules are designed so that transactions that will not interfere with each other can still be run in parallel. For example, transactions that request data from different tables in a database will not conflict with each other and can be run concurrently without causing data integrity problems. Serializability is achieved by different means, but locking mechanisms are the most common type of concurrency control mechanism. With **locking**, any data that are retrieved by a user for updating must be locked, or denied to other users, until the update is complete or aborted. Locking data is much like checking a book out of the library; it is unavailable to others until the borrower returns it.

Locking Mechanisms

Figure 12-11 shows the use of record locks to maintain data integrity. John initiates a withdrawal transaction from an ATM. Because John's transaction will update this record, the application program locks this record before reading it into main memory. John proceeds to withdraw $200, and the new balance ($800) is computed. Marsha has initiated a withdrawal transaction shortly after John, but her transaction cannot access the account record until John's transaction has returned the updated record to the database and unlocked the record. The locking mechanism thus enforces a sequential updating process that prevents erroneous updates.

LOCKING LEVEL An important consideration in implementing concurrency control is choosing the locking level. The **locking level** (also called **lock granularity**) is the extent of the database resource that is included with each lock. Most commercial products implement locks at one of the following levels:

- *Database* The entire database is locked and becomes unavailable to other users. This level has limited application, such as during a backup of the entire database (Rodgers, 1989).
- *Table* The entire table containing a requested record is locked. This level is appropriate mainly for bulk updates that will update the entire table, such as giving all employees a 5 percent raise.

Locking

A process in which any data that are retrieved by a user for updating must be locked, or denied to other users, until the update is completed or aborted.

Locking level (lock granularity)

The extent of a database resource that is included with each lock.

**FIGURE 12-11   Updates with
locking (concurrency control)**

* *Block or page*   The physical storage block (or page) containing a requested record is locked. This level is the most commonly implemented locking level. A page will be a fixed size (4K, 8K, etc.) and may contain records of more than one type.
* *Record*   Only the requested record (or row) is locked. All other records, even within a table, are available to other users. It does impose some overhead at run time when several records are involved in an update.
* *Field*   Only the particular field (or column) in a requested record is locked. This level may be appropriate when most updates affect only one or two fields in a record. For example, in inventory control applications, the quantity-on-hand field changes frequently, but other fields (e.g., description and bin location) are rarely updated. Field-level locks require considerable overhead and are seldom used.

TYPES OF LOCKS   So far, we have discussed only locks that prevent all access to locked items. In reality, a database administrator can generally choose between two types of locks:

1. *Shared locks*   **Shared locks** (also called **S locks, or read locks**) allow other transactions to read (but not update) a record or other resource. A transaction should place a shared lock on a record or data resource when it will only read but not update that record. Placing a shared lock on a record prevents another user from placing an exclusive lock, but not a shared lock, on that record.

Shared lock (S lock, or read lock)

A technique that allows other transactions to read but not update a record or another resource.

FIGURE 12-12 The problem
of deadlock

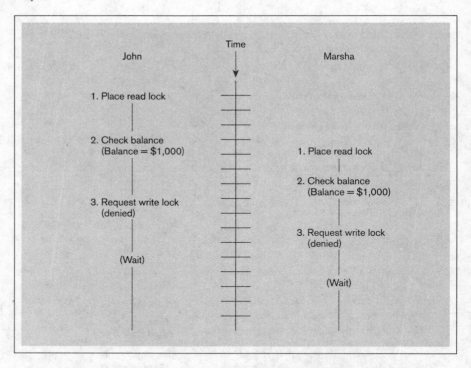

FIGURE 12-12 The problem
of deadlock

Exclusive lock (X lock, or write lock)

A technique that prevents another transaction from reading and therefore updating a record until it is unlocked.

2. *Exclusive locks* **Exclusive locks** (also called **X locks**, or **write locks**) prevent another transaction from reading (and therefore updating) a record until it is unlocked. A transaction should place an exclusive lock on a record when it is about to update that record (Descollonges, 1993). Placing an exclusive lock on a record prevents another user from placing any type of lock on that record.

Figure 12-12 shows the use of shared and exclusive locks for the checking account example. When John initiates his transaction, the program places a read lock on his account record, because he is reading the record to check the account balance. When John requests a withdrawal, the program attempts to place an exclusive lock (write lock) on the record because this is an update operation. However, as you can see in the figure, Marsha has already initiated a transaction that has placed a read lock on the same record. As a result, his request is denied; remember that if a record is a read lock, another user cannot obtain a write lock.

Deadlock

An impasse that results when two or more transactions have locked a common resource, and each waits for the other to unlock that resource.

DEADLOCK   Locking solves the problem of erroneous updates but may lead to a problem called **deadlock**—an impasse that results when two or more transactions have locked a common resource, and each must wait for the other to unlock that resource. Figure 12-12 shows a simple example of deadlock. John's transaction is waiting for Marsha's transaction to remove the read lock from the account record, and vice versa. Neither person can withdraw money from the account, even though the balance is more than adequate.

Figure 12-13 shows a slightly more complex example of deadlock. In this example, user A has locked record X, and user B has locked record Y. User A then requests record Y (intending to update), and user B requests record X (also intending to update). Both requests are denied, because the requested records are already locked. Unless the DBMS intervenes, both users will wait indefinitely.

Deadlock prevention

A method for resolving deadlocks in which user programs must lock all records they require at the beginning of a transaction (rather than one at a time).

MANAGING DEADLOCK   There are two basic ways to resolve deadlocks: deadlock prevention and deadlock resolution. When **deadlock prevention** is employed, user programs must lock all records they will require at the beginning of a transaction, rather than one at a time. In Figure 12-13, user A would have to lock both records X and Y before processing the transaction. If either record is already locked, the program must wait until it is released. Where all locking operations necessary for a transaction occur

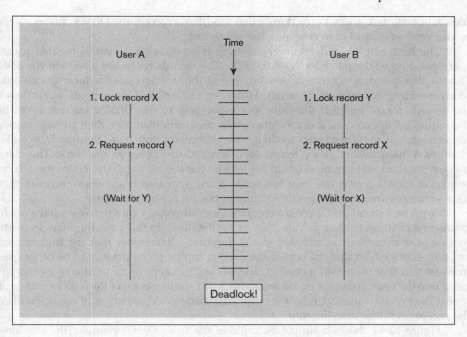

FIGURE 12-13 Another example of deadlock

before any resources are unlocked, a **two-phase locking protocol** is being used. Once any lock obtained for the transaction is released, no more locks may be obtained. Thus, the phases in the two-phase locking protocol are often referred to as a growing phase (where all necessary locks are acquired) and a shrinking phase (where all locks are released). Locks do not have to be acquired simultaneously. Frequently, some locks will be acquired, processing will occur, and then additional locks will be acquired as needed.

Locking all the required records at the beginning of a transaction (called *conservative two-phase locking*) prevents deadlock. Unfortunately, it is often difficult to predict in advance what records will be required to process a transaction. A typical program has many processing parts and may call other programs in varying sequences. As a result, deadlock prevention is not always practical.

Two-phase locking, in which each transaction must request records in the same sequence (i.e., serializing the resources), also prevents deadlock, but again this may not be practical.

The second, and more common, approach is to allow deadlocks to occur but to build mechanisms into the DBMS for detecting and breaking the deadlocks. Essentially, these **deadlock resolution** mechanisms work as follows: The DBMS maintains a matrix of resource usage, which, at a given instant, indicates what subjects (users) are using what objects (resources). By scanning this matrix, the computer can detect deadlocks as they occur. The DBMS then resolves the deadlocks by "backing out" one of the deadlocked transactions. Any changes made by that transaction up to the time of deadlock are removed, and the transaction is restarted when the required resources become available. We will describe the procedure for backing out shortly.

Versioning

Locking, as described here, is often referred to as a pessimistic concurrency control mechanism because each time a record is required, the DBMS takes the highly cautious approach of locking the record so that other programs cannot use it. In reality, in most cases other users will not request the same documents, or they may only want to read them, which is not a problem (Celko, 1992). Thus, conflicts are rare.

A newer approach to concurrency control, called **versioning**, takes the optimistic approach that most of the time other users do not want the same record, or if they do, they only want to read (but not update) the record. With versioning, there is no form of locking. Each transaction is restricted to a view of the database as of the time that

Two-phase locking protocol

A procedure for acquiring the necessary locks for a transaction in which all necessary locks are acquired before any locks are released, resulting in a growing phase when locks are acquired and a shrinking phase when they are released.

Deadlock resolution

An approach to dealing with deadlocks that allows deadlocks to occur but builds mechanisms into the DBMS for detecting and breaking the deadlocks.

Versioning

An approach to concurrency control in which each transaction is restricted to a view of the database as of the time that transaction started, and when a transaction modifies a record, the DBMS creates a new record version instead of overwriting the old record. Hence, no form of locking is required.

transaction started, and when a transaction modifies a record, the DBMS creates a new record version instead of overwriting the old record.

The best way to understand versioning is to imagine a central records room, corresponding to the database (Celko, 1992). The records room has a service window. Users (corresponding to transactions) arrive at the window and request documents (corresponding to database records). However, the original documents never leave the records room. Instead, the clerk (corresponding to the DBMS) makes copies of the requested documents and time stamps them. Users then take their private copies (or versions) of the documents to their own workplace and read them and/or make changes. When finished, they return their marked-up copies to the clerk. The clerk merges the changes from marked-up copies into the central database. When there is no conflict (e.g., when only one user has made changes to a set of database records), that user's changes are merged directly into the public (or central) database.

Suppose instead that there is a conflict; for example, say that two users have made conflicting changes to their private copy of the database. In this case, the changes made by one of the users are committed to the database. (Remember that the transactions are time-stamped, so that the earlier transaction can be given priority.) The other user must be told that there was a conflict, and his work cannot be committed (or incorporated into the central database). He must check out another copy of the data records and repeat the previous work. Under the optimistic assumption, this type of rework will be the exception rather than the rule.

Figure 12-14 shows a simple example of the use of versioning for the checking account example. John reads the record containing the account balance, successfully withdraws $200, and the new balance ($800) is posted to the account with a COMMIT statement. Meanwhile, Marsha has also read the account record and requested a withdrawal, which is posted to her local version of the account record. However, when the transaction attempts to COMMIT, it discovers the update conflict, and her transaction is aborted (perhaps with a message such as "Cannot complete transaction at this time"). Marsha can then restart the transaction, working from the correct starting balance of $800.

The main advantage of versioning over locking is performance improvement. Read-only transactions can run concurrently with updating transactions, without loss of database consistency.

FIGURE 12-14 The use of versioning

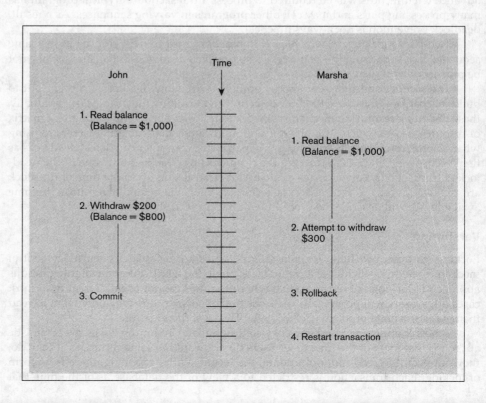

DATA DICTIONARIES AND REPOSITORIES

In Chapter 1, we defined *metadata* as data that describe the properties or characteristics of end-user data and the context of that data. To be successful, an organization must develop sound strategies to collect, manage, and utilize its metadata. These strategies should address identifying the types of metadata that need to be collected and maintained and developing methods for the orderly collection and storage of that metadata. Data administration is usually responsible for the overall direction of the metadata strategy.

Metadata must be stored and managed using DBMS technology. The collection of metadata is referred to as a *data dictionary* (an older term) or a *repository* (a modern term). We describe each of these terms in this section. Some facilities of RDBMSs to access the metadata stored with a database were described in Chapter 7.

Data Dictionary

An integral part of relational DBMSs is the **data dictionary**, which stores metadata, or information about the database, including attribute names and definitions for each table in the database. The data dictionary is usually a part of the system catalog that is generated for each database. The **system catalog** describes all database objects, including table-related data such as table names, table creators or owners, column names and data types, foreign keys and primary keys, index files, authorized users, user access privileges, and so forth. The system catalog is created and maintained automatically by the database management system, and the information is stored in systems tables, which may be queried in the same manner as any other data table, if the user has sufficient access privileges.

Data dictionaries may be either active or passive. An *active* data dictionary is managed automatically by the database management software. Active systems are always consistent with the current structure and definition of the database because they are maintained by the system itself. Most relational database management systems now contain active data dictionaries that can be derived from their system catalog. A *passive* data dictionary is managed by the user(s) of the system and is modified whenever the structure of the database is changed. Because this modification must be performed manually by the user, it is possible that the data dictionary will not be current with the current structure of the database. However, the passive data dictionary may be maintained as a separate database. This may be desirable during the design phase because it allows developers to remain independent from using a particular RDBMS for as long as possible. Also, passive data dictionaries are not limited to information that can be discerned by the database management system. Because passive data dictionaries are maintained by the user, they may be extended to contain information about organizational data that is not computerized.

Repositories

Whereas data dictionaries are simple data element documentation tools, information repositories are used by data administrators and other information specialists to manage the total information processing environment. The **information repository** is an essential component of both the development environment and the production environment. In the application development environment, people (either information specialists or end users) use data modeling and design tools, high-level languages, and other tools to develop new applications. Data modeling and design tools may tie automatically to the information repository. In the production environment, people use applications to build databases, keep the data current, and extract data from databases. To build a data warehouse and develop business intelligence applications, it is absolutely essential that an organization build and maintain a comprehensive repository.

Figure 12-15 shows the three components of a typical repository system architecture (Bernstein, 1996). First is an information model. This model is a schema of the

Data dictionary
A repository of information about a database that documents data elements of a database.

System catalog
A system-created database that describes all database objects, including data dictionary information, and also includes user access information.

Information repository
A component that stores metadata that describe an organization's data and data processing resources, manages the total information processing environment, and combines information about an organization's business information and its application portfolio.

FIGURE 12-15 Three components of repository system architecture

Source: Based on Bernstein (1996)

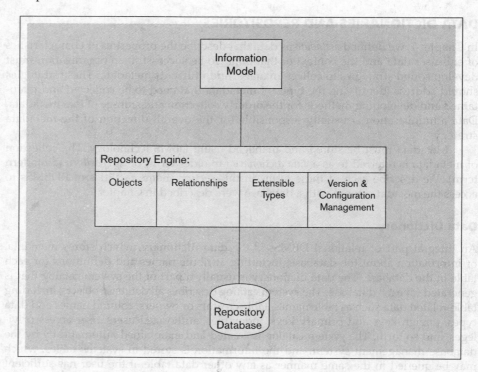

information stored in the repository, which can then be used by the tools associated with the database to interpret the contents of the repository. Next is the repository engine, which manages the repository objects. Services, such as reading and writing repository objects, browsing, and extending the information model, are included. Last is the repository database, in which the repository objects are actually stored. Notice that the repository engine supports five core functions (Bernstein, 1996):

1. *Object management*   Object-oriented repositories store information about objects. As databases become more object oriented, developers will be able to use the information stored about database objects in the information repository. The repository can be based on an object-oriented database or it can add the capability to support objects.

2. *Relationship management*   The repository engine contains information about object relationships that can be used to facilitate the use of software tools that attach to the database.

3. *Dynamic extensibility*   The repository information model defines types, which should be easy to extend, that is, to add new types or to extend the definitions of those that already exist. This capability can make it easier to integrate a new software tool into the development process.

4. *Version management*   During development, it is important to establish version control. The information repository can be used to facilitate version control for software design tools. Version control of objects is more difficult to manage than version control of files, because there are many more objects than files in an application, and each version of an object may have many relationships.

5. *Configuration management*   It is necessary to group versioned objects into configurations that represent the entire system, which are also versioned. It may help you to think of a configuration as similar to a file directory, except configurations can be versioned and they contain objects rather than files. Repositories often use checkout systems to manage objects, versions, and configurations. A developer who wishes to use an object checks it out, makes the desired changes, and then checks the object back in. At that time, a new version of the object will be created, and the object will become available to other developers.

Although information repositories are already included in the enterprise-level development tools, the increasing emphasis on data warehousing and other big data technologies are leading is an increasing need for well-managed information repositories.

OVERVIEW OF TUNING THE DATABASE FOR PERFORMANCE

Effective database support results in a reliable database where performance is not subject to interruption from hardware, software, or user problems and where optimal performance is achieved. Tuning a database is not an activity that is undertaken at the time of DBMS installation and/or at the time of implementation of a new application and then disregarded. Rather, performance analysis and tuning are ongoing parts of managing any database, as hardware and software configurations change and as user activity changes. Five areas of DBMS management that should be addressed when trying to maintain a well-tuned database are addressed here: installation of the DBMS, memory and storage space usage, input/output contention, CPU usage, and application tuning. The extent to which the database administrator can affect each of these areas will vary across DBMS products. Oracle 11g will be used as the exemplar DBMS throughout this section, but it should be noted that each product has its own set of tuning capabilities.

Tuning a database application requires familiarity with the system environment, the DBMS, the application, and the data used by the application. It is here that the skills of even an experienced database administrator are tested. Achieving a quiet environment, one that is reliable and allows users to secure desired information in a timely manner, requires skills and experience that are obtained by working with databases over time. The areas discussed next are quite general and are intended to provide an initial understanding of the scope of activities involved in tuning a database rather than providing the type of detailed understanding necessary to tune a particular database application.

Installation of the DBMS

Correct installation of the DBMS product is essential to any environment. Products often include README files, which may include detailed installation instructions, revisions of procedures, notification of increased disk space needed for installation, and so on. A quick review of any README files may save time during the installation process and result in a better installation. Failing to review general installation instructions may result in default parameter values being set during installation that are not optimal for the situation. Some possible considerations are listed here.

Before beginning installation, the database administrator should ensure that adequate disk space is available. You will need to refer to manuals for the specific DBMS to be able to translate logical database size parameters (e.g., field length, number of table rows, and estimated growth) into actual physical space requirements. It is possible that the space allocation recommendations are low, as changes made to a DBMS tend to make it larger, but the documentation may not reflect that change. To be safe, allocate at least 20 percent more space than suggested by standard calculations. After installation, review any log files generated during the installation process. Their contents will reveal installation problems that were not noticed or provide assurance that the installation proceeded as expected.

Allocation of disk space for the database should also receive consideration. For example, some UNIX backup systems have trouble with data files that exceed a gigabyte in size. Keeping data files under one gigabyte will avoid possible problems. Allocation of data files in standard sizes will make it easier to balance I/O, because data file locations can be swapped more easily should a bottleneck need to be resolved.

Memory and Storage Space Usage

Efficient usage of main memory involves understanding how the DBMS uses main memory, what buffers are being used, and what needs the programs in main memory have. For example, Oracle has many background processes that reside in memory and handle database management functions when a database is running. Some operating systems require a contiguous chunk of memory to be able to load Oracle, and a system with insufficient memory will have to free up memory space first. Oracle maintains in main memory a data dictionary cache that ideally should be large enough so that at least 90 percent of the requests to the data dictionary can be located in the cache rather than having to retrieve information from disk. Each of these is an example of typical memory management issues that should be considered when tuning a database.

Storage space management may include many activities, some of which have already been discussed in this book, such as denormalization and partitioning. One other activity is **data archiving**. Any database that stores history, such as transaction history or a time series of values for some field, will eventually include obsolete data— data that no longer has any use. Database statistics showing location access frequencies for records or pages can be a clue that data no longer have a purpose. Business rules may also indicate that data older than some value (e.g., seven years) do not need to be kept for active processing. However, there may be legal reasons or infrequently needed business intelligence queries that suggest data should simply not be discarded. Thus, database administrations should develop a program of archiving inactive data. Data may be archived to separate database tables (thus making active tables more compact and, hence, more likely to be more quickly processed) or to files stored outside the database (possibly on magnetic tape or optical storage). Archive files may also be compressed to save space. Methods also need to be developed to restore, in an acceptable time, archived data to the database if and when they are needed. (Remember, archived data are inactive, not totally obsolete.) Archiving reclaims disk space, saves disk storage costs, and may improve database performance by allowing the active data to be stored in less expansive space.

Data archiving

The process of moving inactive data to another storage location where it can be accessed when needed.

Input/Output (I/O) Contention

Database applications are very I/O intensive; a production database will usually both read and write large amounts of data to disk as it works. Although CPU clock speeds have increased dramatically, I/O speeds have not increased proportionately, and increasingly complex distributed database systems have further complicated I/O functioning.

Understanding how data are accessed by end users is critical to managing I/O contention. When hot spots (physical disk locations that are accessed repeatedly) develop, understanding the nature of the activity that is causing the hot spot affords the database administrator a much better chance of reducing the I/O contention being experienced. Oracle allows the DBA to control the placement of tablespaces, which contain data files. The DBA's in-depth understanding of user activity facilitates her or his ability to reduce I/O contention by separating data files that are being accessed together. Where possible, large database objects that will be accessed concurrently may be striped across disks to reduce I/O contention and improve performance. An overall objective of distributing I/O activity evenly across disks and controllers should guide the DBA in tuning I/O.

CPU Usage

Most database operations will require CPU work activity. Because of this, it is important to evaluate CPU usage when tuning a database. Using multiple CPUs allows query processing to be shared when the CPUs are working in parallel, and performance may be dramatically improved. DBAs need to maximize the performance of their existing CPUs while planning for the gains that may be achieved with each new generation of CPUs.

Monitoring CPU load so that typical load throughout a 24-hour period is known provides DBAs with basic information necessary to begin to rebalance CPU loading. The mixture of online and background processing may need to be adjusted for each environment. For example, establishing a rule that all jobs that can be run in off-hours must be run in off-hours will help to unload the machine during peak working hours. Establishing user accounts with limited space will help manage the CPU load also.

Application Tuning

The previous sections have concentrated on activities to tune a DBMS. Examining the applications that end users are using with the database may also increase performance. Although normalization to at least 3NF is expected in many organizations that are using relational data models, carefully planned denormalization (see Chapter 5) may improve performance, often by reducing the number of tables that must be joined when running an SQL query.

Examination and modification of the SQL code in an application may also lead to performance improvement. Queries that do full table scans should be avoided, for example, because they are not selective and may not remain in memory very long. This necessitates more retrievals from long-term storage. Multitable joins should be actively managed when possible with the DBMS being used, because the type of join can dramatically affect performance, especially if a join requires a full table join. A general rule of thumb is that any query whose ratio of CPU to I/O time exceeds 13:1 is probably poorly designed. Active monitoring of queries by the DBMS can be used to actually terminate a query of job that exhibits exceeding this ratio. Alternatively, such queries may be put into a "penalty box" to wait until the job scheduler determines that sufficient CPU time is available to continue processing the query.

Similarly, statements containing views and those containing subqueries should be actively reviewed. Tuning of such statements so that components are resolved in the most efficient manner possible may achieve significant performance gains. Chapter 5 discussed a variety of techniques a DBA could use to tune application processing speed and disk space utilization (e.g., re-indexing, overriding automatic query plans, changing data block sizes, reallocating files across storage devices, and guidelines for more efficient query design). A DBA plays an important role in advising programmers and developers which techniques will be the most effective.

The same database activity may take vastly different amounts of time, depending on the workload mix at the time the query or program is run. Some DBMSs have job schedulers that look at statistics about the history of running queries and will schedule batch jobs to achieve a desirable mix of CPU usage and I/O. A DBA can actively monitor query processing times by running so called "heartbeat" or "canary" queries. A **heartbeat query** is a very simple query (possibly SELECT * FROM table WHERE some condition) that a DBA runs many times during the day to monitor variations in processing times. When heartbeat queries are taking extraordinarily long to run, there is probably either an inappropriate mix of jobs running or some inefficient queries are consuming too many DBMS resources. A heartbeat query may also be exactly like certain regularly run user queries for which there are service-level agreements (SLAs) with users on maximum response times. In this case, the heartbeat query is run periodically to make sure that if the user were to submit this query, the SLA goals would be met.

Another aspect of application tuning is setting realistic user expectations. Users should be trained to realize that more complex queries, especially if submitted ad hoc, will take more processing and response time. Users should also be trained to submit queries first using the EXPLAIN or similar function that will not actually run the query but rather estimate the time for query processing from database statistics. This way, many poorly written queries can be avoided. To effectively set realistic user expectations, the DBA needs to realize that database statistics (e.g., number of table rows and distribution of values for certain fields often used for qualifications) must be recalculated frequently. Recalculation of statistics should occur at least after every batch load of a table, and more frequently for tables that are constantly being updated online. Statistics affect the query optimizer, so reasonable up-to-date statistics are essential for the DBMS to develop a very good query processing plan (i.e., which indexes to use and in which order to execute joins).

The preceding description of potential areas where database performance may be affected should convince you of the importance of effective database management

Heartbeat query
A query submitted by a DBA to test the current performance of a database or to predict the response time for queries that have promised response times. Also called a canary query.

and tuning. As a DBA achieves an in-depth understanding of a DBMS and the applications for which responsibility is assigned, the importance of tuning the database for performance should become apparent. We hope this brief section on database tuning will whet your appetite for learning more about one or more database products in order to develop tuning skills.

DATA AVAILABILITY

Ensuring the availability of databases to their users has always been a high-priority responsibility of database administrators. However, the growth of e-business has elevated this charge from an important goal to a business imperative. An e-business must be operational and available to its customers 24/7. Studies have shown that if an online customer does not get the service he or she expects within a few seconds, the customer will take his or her business to a competitor.

Costs of Downtime

The costs of downtime (when databases are unavailable) include several components: lost business during the outage, costs of catching up when service is restored, inventory shrinkage, legal costs, and permanent loss of customer loyalty. These costs are often difficult to estimate accurately and vary widely from one type of business to another. A recent survey of over 600 organizations by ITIC (**http://itic-corp.com/blog/2013/07/one-hour-of-downtime-costs-100k-for-95-of-enterprises/**) revealed that for 95 percent of the organizations the cost of our one hour of downtime was in excess of $100,000.

A DBA needs to balance the costs of downtime with the costs of achieving the desired availability level. Unfortunately, it is seldom (if ever) possible to provide 100 percent service levels. Failures may occur (as discussed earlier in this chapter) that may interrupt service. Also, it is necessary to perform periodic database reorganizations or other maintenance activities that may cause service interruptions. It is the responsibility of database administration to minimize the impact of these interruptions. The goal is to provide a high level of availability that balances the various costs involved. The cost of downtime escalates annually as and when the availability time decreases although the worst downtime could be as low as 1 percent. Also shown is the annual cost of downtime for an organization whose hourly cost of downtime is $100,000. Notice that the annual costs escalate rapidly as the availability declines, yet in the worst case shown in the table the downtime is only 1 percent.

Measures to Ensure Availability

A new generation of hardware, software, and management techniques has been developed (and continues to be developed) to assist database administrators in achieving the high availability levels expected in today's organizations. We have already discussed

TABLE 12-2 Cost of Downtime, by Type of Business

Industry/Type of Business	Approximate Estimated Hourly Cost
Financial services/Brokerage operations	$7 million
Financial services/Electronic transactions (card) processing	$2.5 million
Retail/Tele-sales	$115,000
Travel/Reservation Centers	$90,000
Logistics/Shipping Services	$28,000

Based on: Mullins (2002), p. 226

TABLE 12-3 Cost of Downtime, by Availability

Availability	Downtime Per Year		Cost Per Year
	Minutes	Hours	
99.999%	5	.08	$8,000
99.99%	53	.88	$88,000
99.9%	526	8.77	$877,000
99.5%	2,628	43.8	$4,380,000
99%	5,256	87.6	$8,760,000

Based on: Mullins (2002), p. 226

many of these techniques in this chapter (e.g., database recovery); in this section we provide only a brief summary of potential availability problems and measures for coping with them. A number of other techniques, such as component failure impact analysis (CFIA), fault-tree analysis (FTA), CRAMM, and so on, as well as a wealth of guidance on how to manage availability are described in the IT Infrastructure Library (ITIL) framework (**www.itil-officialsite.com**).

HARDWARE FAILURES Any hardware component, such as a database server, disk subsystem, power supply, or network switch, can become a point of failure that will disrupt service. The usual solution is to provide redundant or standby components that replace a failing system. For example, with clustered servers, the workload of a failing server can be reallocated to another server in the cluster.

LOSS OR CORRUPTION OF DATA Service can be interrupted when data are lost or become inaccurate. Mirrored (or backup) databases are almost always provided in high-availability systems. Also, it is important to use the latest backup and recovery systems (discussed earlier in this chapter).

HUMAN ERROR "Most…outages…are not caused by the technology, they're caused by people making changes" (Morrow, 2007, p. 32). The use of standard operating procedures, which are mature and repeatable, is a major deterrent to human errors. In addition, training, documentation, and insistence on following internationally recognized standard procedures (see, for example, COBIT [**www.isaca.org/cobit**] or ITIL [**www.itil-officialsite.com**]) are essential for reducing human errors.

MAINTENANCE DOWNTIME Historically, the greatest source of database downtime was attributed to planned database maintenance activities. Databases were taken offline during periods of low activity (nights, weekends) for database reorganization, backup, and other activities. This luxury is no longer available for high-availability applications. New database products are now available that automate maintenance functions. For example, some utilities (called *nondisruptive utilities*) allow routine maintenance to be performed while the systems remain operational for both read and write operations, without loss of data integrity.

NETWORK-RELATED PROBLEMS High-availability applications nearly always depend on the proper functioning of both internal and external networks. Both hardware and software failures can result in service disruption. However, the Internet has spawned new threats that can also result in interruption of service. For example, a hacker can mount a denial-of-service attack by flooding a Web site with computer-generated messages. To counter these threats, an organization should carefully monitor its traffic volumes and develop a fast-response strategy when there is a sudden spike in activity. An organization also must employ the latest firewalls, routers, and other network technologies.

Summary

The importance of managing data was emphasized in this chapter. The functions of data administration, which takes responsibility for the overall management of data resources, include developing procedures to protect and control data, resolving data ownership and use issues, conceptual data modeling, and developing and maintaining corporate-wide data definitions and standards. The functions of database administration, on the other hand, are those associated with the direct management of a database or databases, including DBMS installation and upgrading, database design issues, and technical issues such as security enforcement, database performance, data availability, and backup and recovery. The data administration and database administration roles are changing in today's business environment, with pressure being exerted to maintain data quality while building high-performing systems quickly.

Threats to data security include accidental losses, theft and fraud, loss of privacy, loss of data integrity, and loss of availability. A comprehensive data security plan will address all of these potential threats, partly through the establishment of views, authorization rules, user-defined procedures, and encryption procedures.

Databases, especially data security, play a key role in an organization's compliance with Sarbanes-Oxley (SOX). SOX audits focus on three key areas: IT change management, logical access to data, and IT operations.

Database recovery and backup procedures are another set of essential database administration activities. Basic recovery facilities that should be in place include backup facilities, journalizing facilities, checkpoint facilities, and a recovery manager. Depending on the type of problem encountered, backward recovery (rollback) or forward recovery (rollforward) may be needed.

The problems of managing concurrent access in multiuser environments must also be addressed. A DBMS must ensure that database transactions possess the ACID properties: atomic, consistent, isolated, and durable. Proper transaction boundaries must be chosen to achieve these properties at an acceptable performance level. If concurrency controls on transactions are not established, lost updates may occur, which will cause data integrity to be impaired. Locking mechanisms, including shared and exclusive locks, can be used. Deadlocks may also occur in multiuser environments and may be managed by various means, including using a two-phase locking protocol or other deadlock-resolution mechanism. Versioning is an optimistic approach to concurrency control.

Managing the data dictionary, which is part of the system catalog in most relational database management systems, and the information repository help the DBA maintain high-quality data and high-performing database systems. The establishment of the Information Resource Dictionary System (IRDS) standard has helped with the development of repository information that can be integrated from multiple sources, including the DBMS itself, data modeling and design tools, and software development tools.

Ensuring the availability of databases to users has become a high priority for the modern DBA. Use of batch windows to perform periodic maintenance (e.g., database reorganization) is no longer permissible for mission-critical applications. A new generation of hardware, software, and management techniques is being introduced to assist the DBA in managing data availability.

Effective data administration is not easy, and it encompasses all of the areas summarized here. Increasing emphasis on object-oriented development methods and rapid development are changing the data administration function, but better tools to achieve effective administration and database tuning are becoming available.

Chapter Review

Key Terms

Aborted transaction 519
After image 515
Authorization rules 508
Backup facility 514
Backward recovery
    (rollback) 518
Before image 515
Checkpoint facility 515
Concurrency control 521
Data administration 493
Data archiving 530
Data dictionary 527
Database
    administration 494

Database change log 515
Database destruction 520
Database recovery 513
Database security 500
Deadlock 524
Deadlock prevention 524
Deadlock resolution 525
Encryption 509
Exclusive lock (X lock,
    or write lock) 524
Forward recovery
    (rollforward) 519
Heartbeat query 531

Inconsistent read
    problem 521
Information
    repository 527
Journalizing facility 514
Locking 522
Locking level (lock
    granularity) 522
Open source DBMS 499
Recovery manager 515
Restore/rerun 516
Shared lock (S lock,
    or read lock) 523

Smart card 511
System catalog 527
Transaction 514
Transaction
    boundaries 517
Transaction log 514
Two-phase locking
    protocol 525
User-defined
    procedures 509
Versioning 525

Review Questions

12-1. Define each of the following terms:
  a. data administration
  b. database administration
  c. two-phase locking protocol
  d. information repository
  e. locking
  f. versioning
  g. deadlock
  h. transaction
  i. encryption
  j. data availability
  k. data archiving
  l. heartbeat query

12-2. Match the following terms to the appropriate definitions:

_____ backup facilities   a. protects data from loss or misuse

_____ biometric device   b. reversal of abnormal or aborted transactions

_____ checkpoint facility   c. describes all database objects

_____ database recovery   d. automatically produces a saved copy of an entire database

_____ database security   e. application of after images

_____ lock granularity   f. might analyze your signature

_____ recovery manager   g. restoring a database after a loss

_____ rollback   h. DBMS module that restores a database after a failure

_____ rollforward   i. extent to which a database is locked for transaction

_____ system catalog   j. records database state at moment of synchronization

12-3. Compare and contrast the following terms:
  a. data administration; database administration
  b. repository; data dictionary
  c. deadlock prevention; deadlock resolution
  d. backward recovery; forward recovery
  e. active data dictionary; passive data dictionary
  f. optimistic concurrency control; pessimistic concurrency control
  g. shared lock; exclusive lock
  h. before image; after image
  i. two-phase locking protocol; versioning
  j. authorization; authentication
  k. data backup; data archiving

12-4. What is an open source DBMS?

12-5. Indicate whether data administration or database administration is typically responsible for each of the following functions:
  a. Managing the data repository
  b. Installing and upgrading the DBMS
  c. Conceptual data modeling
  d. Managing data security and privacy
  e. Database planning
  f. Tuning database performance
  g. Database backup and recovery
  h. Running heartbeat queries

12-6. Describe the changing roles of a data administrator and database administrator in the current business environment.

12-7. List four common problems of ineffective data administration.

12-8. List four job skills necessary for data administrators. List four job skills necessary for database administrators.

12-9. Briefly describe four database administration trends that are emerging today.

12-10. What changes can be made in data administration at each stage of the traditional database development life cycle to deliver high-quality, robust systems more quickly?

12-11. List and discuss five areas where threats to data security may occur.

12-12. Explain how creating a view may increase data security. Also explain why one should not rely completely on using views to enforce data security.

12-13. List and briefly explain how integrity controls can be used for database security.

12-14. What is the difference between an authentication scheme and an authorization scheme?

12-15. What are the key areas of IT that are examined during a Sarbanes-Oxley audit?

12-16. What are the two key types of security policies and procedures that must be established to aid in Sarbanes-Oxley compliance?

12-17. What is the advantage of optimistic concurrency control compared with pessimistic concurrency control?

12-18. What is the difference between shared locks and exclusive locks?

12-19. What is the difference between deadlock prevention and deadlock resolution?

12-20. Briefly describe four DBMS facilities that are required for database backup and recovery.

12-21. What is transaction integrity? Why is it important?

12-22. List and describe four common types of database failure.

12-23. Briefly describe four threats to high data availability and at least one measure that can be taken to counter each of these threats.

12-24. Briefly describe the difference between a data dictionary and an information repository.

12-25. List and briefly explain the ACID properties of a database transaction.

12-26. Explain the two common forms of encryption.

12-27. Briefly describe four components of a disaster recovery plan.

12-28. Explain the purpose of heartbeat queries.

12-29. How can views be used as part of data security? What are the limitations of views for data security?

12-30. What is the purpose of the GRANT and REVOKE SQL commands? List some actions that can be granted to or revoked from a user.

12-31. Why is Data Quality important? What does the data governance program include as part of the broader strategy to maintain Data Quality?

12-32. What are the categories of Data transformation functions? Why is data transformation necessary?

Problems and Exercises

12-33. Fill in the two authorization tables for Pine Valley Furniture Company below, based on the following assumptions (enter Y for yes or N for no):
- Salespersons, managers, and carpenters may read inventory records but may not perform any other operations on these records.
- Persons in Accounts Receivable and Accounts Payable may read and/or update (insert, modify, delete) receivables records and customer records.
- Inventory clerks may read and/or update (modify, delete) inventory records. They may not view receivables records or payroll records. They may read but not modify customer records.

Authorizations for Inventory Clerks

	Inventory Records	Receivables Records	Payroll Records	Customer Records
Read				
Insert				
Modify				
Delete				

Authorizations for Inventory Records

	Salespersons	A/R Personnel	Inventory Clerks	Carpenters
Read				
Insert				
Modify				
Delete				

12-34. Five recovery techniques are listed below. For each situation described, decide which of the following recovery techniques is most appropriate.
- Backward recovery
- Forward recovery (from latest checkpoint)
- Forward recovery (using backup copy of database)
- Reprocessing transactions
- Switch
  a. A phone disconnection occurs while a user is entering a transaction.
  b. A disk drive fails during regular operations.
  c. A lightning storm causes a power failure.
  d. An incorrect amount is entered and posted for a student tuition payment. The error is not discovered for several weeks.
  e. Data entry clerks have entered transactions for two hours after a full database backup when the database becomes corrupted. It is discovered that the journalizing facility of the database has not been activated since the backup was made.

12-35. Whitlock Department Stores runs a multiuser DBMS on a LAN file server. Unfortunately, at the present time, the DBMS does not enforce concurrency control. One Whitlock customer had a balance due of $500.00 when the following three transactions related to this customer were processed at about the same time:
- Payment of $500.00
- Purchase on credit of $100.00
- Merchandise return (credit) of $50.00

Each of the three transactions read the customer record when the balance was $500.00 (i.e., before any of the other transactions were completed). The updated customer record was returned to the database in the order shown in the bulleted list above.
  a. What balance will be included for the customer after the last transaction was completed?
  b. What balance should be included for the customer after the three transactions have been processed?

12-36. For each of the situations described below, indicate which of the following security measures is most appropriate:
- Authorization rules
- Encryption
- Authentication schemes
  a. A national brokerage firm uses an electronic funds transfer (EFT) system to transmit sensitive financial data between locations.
  b. An organization has set up an offsite computer-based training center. The organization wishes to restrict access to the site to authorized employees. Because each employee's use of the center is occasional, the center does not wish to provide the employees with keys to access the center.
  c. A manufacturing firm uses a simple password system to protect its database but finds it needs a more comprehensive system to grant different privileges (e.g., read, versus create or update) to different users.
  d. A university has experienced considerable difficulty with unauthorized users accessing files and databases by appropriating passwords from legitimate users.

12-37. Metro Marketers, Inc., wants to build a data warehouse for storing customer information that will be used for data marketing purposes. Building the data warehouse will require much more capacity and processing power than it has previously needed, and it is considering Oracle and Red Brick as its database and data warehousing products. As part of its implementation plan, Metro has decided to organize a data administration function. At present, it has four major candidates for the data administrator position:
  a. Monica Lopez, a senior database administrator with five years of experience as an Oracle database administrator managing a financial database for a global banking firm, but no data warehousing experience.
  b. Gerald Bruester, a senior database administrator with six years of experience as an Informix database administrator managing a marketing-oriented database for a *Fortune* 1000 food products firm. Gerald has been to several data warehousing seminars over the past 12 months and is interested in being involved with a data warehouse.
  c. Jim Reedy, currently project manager for Metro Marketers. Jim is very familiar with Metro's current systems environment and is well respected by his coworkers. He has been involved with Metro's current database system but does not have any data warehousing experience.

d. Marie Weber, a data warehouse administrator with two years of experience using a Red Brick–based application that tracks accident information for an automobile insurance company.

Based on this limited information, rank the four candidates for the data administration position. Support your rankings by indicating your reasoning.

12-38. Referring to Problem and Exercise 30-7, rank the four candidates for the position of data warehouse administrator at Metro Marketing. Again, support your rankings.

12-39. Referring to Problem and Exercise 30-7, rank the four candidates for the position of database administrator at Metro Marketing. Again, support your rankings.

12-40. What concerns would you have if you accept a job as a database administrator and discover that the database users are entering one common password to log on to the database each morning when they arrive for work? You also learn that they leave their workstations connected to the database all day, even when they are away from their machines for extended periods of time.

12-41. During the Sarbanes-Oxley audit of a financial services company, you note the following issues. Categorize each of them into the area to which they belong: IT change management, logical access to data, and IT operations.

a. Five database administrators have access to the sa (system administrator) account that has complete access to the database.

b. Several changes to database structures did not have appropriate approval by management.

c. Some users continued to have access to the database even after having been terminated.

d. Databases are backed up on a regular schedule, using an automated system.

12-42. Revisit the four issues identified in Problem and Exercise 30-41. What risk, if any, do each of them pose to the firm?

12-43. An organization has a database server with three disk devices. The accounting and payroll applications share one of these disk devices and are experiencing performance problems. You have been asked to investigate the problem and tune the databases. What might you suggest to reduce I/O contention?

12-44. You take a new job as a database administrator at an organization that has a globally distributed database. You are asked to analyze the performance of the database, and as part of your analysis, you discover that all of the processing for regional monthly sales reports is being conducted at the corporate headquarters location. Operations are categorized by five regions: Eastern United States, Western United States, Canada, South America, and Mexico. Data for each region are kept on a server located at the regional headquarters. What would you try to improve the time needed to create the monthly sales reports?

12-45. An e-business operates a high-volume catalog sales center. Through the use of clustered servers and mirrored disk drives, the data center has been able to achieve data availability of 99.5 percent. Although this exceeds industry norms, the organization still receives periodic customer complaints that the Web site is unavailable (due to data outages). A vendor has proposed several software upgrades as well as expanded disk capacity to improve data availability. The cost of these proposed improvements would be about $50,000 per month. The vendor estimates that the improvements should improve availability to 99.99 percent.

a. If this company is typical for a catalog sales center, what is the current annual cost of system unavailability? (You will need to refer to Tables 12-2 and 12-3 to answer this question.)

b. If the vendor's estimates are accurate, can the organization justify the additional expenditure?

12-46. Review the tables for data availability (Tables 12-2 and 12-3). For the travel firm shown in Table 12-2, calculate the expected annual cost of downtime for the following availability levels: 99 percent and 99.5 percent. Do you think that either of these levels are acceptable for this organization?

12-47. The mail order firm described in Problem and Exercise 30-45 has about 1 million customers. The firm is planning a mass mailing of its spring sales catalog to all of its customers. The unit cost of the mailing (postage and catalog) is $6.00. The error rate in the database (duplicate records, erroneous addresses, etc.) is estimated to be 12 percent. Calculate the expected loss of this mailing due to poor-quality data.

12-48. The average annual revenue per customer for the mail order firm described in Problems and Exercises 30-45 and 30-47 is $100. The organization is planning a data quality improvement program that it hopes will increase the average revenue per customer by 5 percent per year. If this estimate proves accurate, what will be the annual increase in revenue due to improved quality?

12-49. Referring to the Fitchwood Insurance Company case study at the end of Chapter 9, what types of security issues would you expect to encounter when building a data warehouse? Would there be just one set of security concerns related to user access to the data warehouse, or would you also need to be concerned with security of data during the extracting, cleansing, and loading processes?

12-50. How would Fitchwood's security have to be different if the data mart were made available to customers via the Internet?

12-51. Examine the two applications shown in Figures 8-9a and 8-9b. Identify the various security considerations that are relevant to each environment.?

12-52. Research available data quality software. Describe in detail at least one technique employed by one of these tools (e.g., an expert system).

12-53. Visit some Web sites for open source databases, such as **www.postgresql.org** and **www.mysql.com.** What do you see as major differences in administration between open source databases, such as MySQL, and commercial database products, such as Oracle? How might these differences come into play when choosing a database platform? Summarize the DBA functions of MySQL versus PostgreSQL.

12-54. Compare the concurrency issues that must be dealt with when developing an OLTP system versus a data warehouse.

12-55. Visit the Web sites of one or more popular cloud service providers that provide cloud database services. Use the table below to map the features listed on the Web site to the major concepts covered in this chapter. If you are not sure where to start, try **aws.amazon.com** or **cloud.oracle.com.**

Concepts from Chapter	Services listed on cloud database provider site

12-56. Based on the table above as well as additional research, write a memo in support of or against the following statement: "Cloud databases will increasingly eliminate the need for data/database administrators in corporations."

Field Exercises

12-57. Visit an organization that has implemented a database approach. Evaluate each of the following:
a. The organizational placement of data administration, database administration, and data warehouse administration
b. The assignment of responsibilities for each of the functions listed in part a
c. The background and experience of the person chosen as head of data administration
d. The status and usage of an information repository (passive, active-in-design, active-in-production)

12-58. Visit an organization that has implemented a database approach and interview an MIS department employee who has been involved in disaster recovery planning. Before you go for the interview, think carefully about the relative probabilities of various disasters for the organization you are visiting. For example, is the area subject to earthquakes, tornadoes, or other natural disasters? What type of damage might the physical plant be subject to? What is the background and training of the employees who must use the system? Find out about the organization's disaster recovery plans and ask specifically about any potential problems you have identified.

12-59. Visit an organization that has implemented a database approach and interview individuals there about the security measures they take routinely. Evaluate each of the following at the organization:
a. Database security measures
b. Network security measures
c. Operating system security measures
d. Physical plant security measures
e. Personnel security measures

12-60. Identify an organization that handles large, sporadic data loads. For example, organizations that have implemented

data warehouses may have large data loads as they populate their data warehouses. Determine what measures the organization has taken to handle these large loads as part of its capacity planning.

12-61. Databases tend to grow larger over time, not smaller, as new transaction data are added. Interview at least three companies that use databases extensively and identify their criteria and procedures for purging or archiving old data. Find out how often data are purged and what type of data are purged. Identify the data each organization archives and how long those data are archived.

12-62. Visit an organization that relies heavily on Web-based applications. Interview the database administrator (or a senior person in that organization) to determine the following:
a. What is the organizational goal for system availability? (Compare with Table 12-3.)
b. Has the organization estimated the cost of system downtime ($/hour)? If not, use Table 12-2 and select a cost for a similar type of organization.
c. What is the greatest obstacle to achieving high data availability for this organization?
d. What measures has the organization taken to ensure high availability? What measures are planned for the future?

12-63. Visit an organization that uses an open source DBMS. Why did the organization choose open source software? Does it have other open source software besides a DBMS? Has it purchased any fee-based components or services? Does it have a DA or DBA staff, and, if so, how do these people evaluate the open source DBMS they are using? (This could especially provide insight if the organization also has some traditional DBMS products, such as Oracle or DB2.)

References

Anderson, D. 2005. "HIPAA Security and Compliance," available at **www.tdan.com** (July).

Bernstein, P. A. 1996. "The Repository: A Modern Vision." *Database Programming & Design* 9,12 (December): 28–35.

Celko, J. 1992. "An Introduction to Concurrency Control." *DBMS* 5,9 (September): 70–83.

Cloud Security Alliance. 2011. Security Guidance for Critical Areas of Focus in Cloud Computing, v 3.0. **https://cloudsecurityalliance.org/guidance/csaguide.v3.0.pdf**, accessed 12/18/2011.

Descollonges, M. 1993. "Concurrency for Complex Processing." *Database Programming & Design* 6,1 (January): 66–71.

Fernandez, E. B., R. C. Summers, and C. Wood. 1981. *Database Security and Integrity*. Reading, MA: Addison-Wesley.

Hall, M. 2003. "MySQL Breaks into the Data Center," available at **http://www.computerworld.com/s/article/85900/MySQL_Breaks_Into_the_Data_Center**.

Inmon, W. H. 1999. "Data Warehouse Administration." Found at **www.billinmon.com/library/other/dwaadmin.asp** (no longer available).

Inmon, W. H., C. Imhoff, and R. Sousa. 2001. *Corporate Information Factory*, 2nd ed. New York: Wiley.

Michaelson, J. 2004. "What Every Developer Should Know About Open Source Licensing." *Queue* 2,3 (May): 41–47. (Note: This whole issue of *Queue* is devoted to the open source movement and contains many interesting articles.)

Morrow, J. T. 2007. "The Three Pillars of Data." *InfoWorld* (March 12): 20–33.

Mullins, C. 2001. "Modern Database Administration, Part 1." *DM Review* 11,9 (September): 31, 55–57.

Mullins, C. 2002. *Database Administration: The Complete Guide to Practices and Procedures*. Boston: Addison-Wesley.

Rodgers, U. 1989. "Multiuser DBMS Under UNIX." *Database Programming & Design* 2,10 (October): 30–37.

Further Reading

Loney, K. 2000. "Protecting Your Database." *Oracle Magazine*. 14,3 (May/June): 101–106.

Quinlan, T. 1996. "Time to Reengineer the DBA?" *Database Programming & Design* 9,3 (March): 29–34.

Web Resources

http://cloudcomputing.sys-con.com/node/1660119/print Interesting article on some specific skills that a DBA might need as databases move to the cloud.

http://gost.isi.edu/publications/kerberos-neuman-tso.html A guide to the Kerberos method of user authentication.

http://cobitonline.isaca.org A set of best practices for IT management. See APO10 for vendor management best practices.

http://tpc.org Web site of the Transaction Processing Performance Council, a nonprofit corporation founded to define transaction processing and database benchmarks and to disseminate objective, verifiable transaction processing performance data to the industry. This is an excellent site for learning more about evaluating DBMSs and database designs through technical articles on database benchmarking.

GLOSSARY OF ACRONYMS

1:1	One-to-one	**DA**	Data administrator (or data administration)
1:M	One-to-many	**DB2**	Data Base2 (an IBM Relational DBMS)
1NF	First normal form	**DBA**	Database administrator (or database administration)
2NF	Second normal form		
3GL	Third-generation language	**DBD**	Database description
3NF	Third normal form	**DBMS**	Database management system
4NF	Fourth normal form	**DCL**	Data control language
5NF	Fifth normal form	**DDL**	Data definition language
ACID	Atomic, consistent, isolated, and durable	**DES**	Data Encryption Standard
ACM	Association for Computing Machinery	**DFD**	Data flow diagram
AITP	Association of Information Technology Professionals	**DKNF**	Domain-key normal form
		DML	Data manipulation language
ANSI	American National Standards Institute	**DNS**	Domain Name System
API	Application programming interface	**DOLAP**	Database online analytical processing
ASCII	American Standard Code for Information Interchange	**DSS**	Decision support system
		DTD	Data type definitions
ASP	Active Server Pages	**DWA**	Data warehouse administrator
ATM	Automated teller machine	**DVD**	Digital versatile disc
B2B	Business-to-business	**EAI**	Enterprise application integration
B2C	Business-to-consumer	**EDI**	Electronic data interchange
BASE	Basically available, soft state, and eventually consistent	**EDW**	Enterprise data warehouse
		EDR	Enterprise data replication
BCNF	Boyce-Codd normal form	**EER**	Extended entity-relationship
BI	Business intelligence	**EFT**	Electronic funds transfer
BI&A	Business intelligence and analytics	**EII**	Enterprise information integration
BOM	Bill of materials	**EIS**	Executive information systems
BPM	Business performance management	**E-R**	Entity-relationship
BSON	Binary JSON	**ERD**	Entity-relationship diagram
CAD/CAM	Computer-aided design/computer-aided manufacturing	**ERP**	Enterprise resource planning
		ETL	Extract–transform–load
CASE	Computer-aided software engineering	**FDA**	Food and Drug Administration
CDC	Changed data capture	**FK**	Foreign key
CDI	Customer data integration	**FTC**	Federal Trade Commission
CDO	Chief data officer	**FTP**	File Transfer Protocol
CD-ROM	Compact disc–read-only memory	**GPA**	Grade point average
CEO	Chief executive officer	**GUI**	Graphical user interface
CFO	Chief financial officer	**HDFS**	Hadoop Distributed File System
CGI	Common Gateway Interface	**HIPAA**	Health Insurance Portability and Accountability Act
CIF	Corporate information factory		
CIO	Chief information officer	**HIVEQ**	An SQL-like language
CLI	Call-level interface	**HTML**	Hypertext Markup Language
COM	Component Object Model	**HTTP**	Hypertext Transfer Protocol
COO	Chief operating officer	**IBM**	International Business Machines
CPU	Central processor unit	**I-CASE**	Integrated computer-aided software engineering
CRM	Customer relationship management		
C/S	Client/server	**ID**	Identifier
CSF	Critical success factor	**IDE**	Integrated development environment

IE	Information engineering
INCITS	International Committee for Information Technology Standards
I/O	Input/output
IP	Internet Protocol
IRM	Information resource management
IS	Information system
ISAM	Indexed sequential access method
ISO	International Standards Organization
IT	Information technology
ITAA	Information Technology Association of America
J2EE	Java 2 Enterprise Edition
JDBC	Java Database Connectivity
JDO	Java Data Objects
JSON	JavaScript Object Notation
JSP	Java Server Pages
LAN	Local area network
LDB	Logical database
LDBR	Logical database record
LDM	Logical data model
MB	Megabytes (million bytes)
MDM	Master data management
MIS	Management information system
M:N	Many-to-many
M:1	Many-to-one
MMS	Multi-messaging service
MOLAP	Multidimensional online analytical processing
MOM	Message-oriented middleware
MPP	Massively parallel processing
MRN	Medical record number
MRP	Materials requirements planning
MS	Microsoft
MVC	Model View Controller
NIST	National Institute of Standards and Technology
NoSQL	Not only SQL
ODBC	Open database connectivity
ODL	Object definition language
ODS	Operational data store
OLAP	Online analytical processing
OLTP	Online transaction processing
OO	Object-oriented
OODBMS	Object-oriented database management system
OODM	Object-oriented data model
OQL	Object Query Language
O/R	Object/relational
ORB	Object request broker
ORDBMS	Object-relational database management system
P3P	Platform for Privacy Preferences
PC	Personal computer

PDA	Personal digital assistant
PIN	Personal identification number
PK	Primary key
PL/SQL	Programming Language/SQL
PMML	Predictive Model Markup Language
PVFC	Pine Valley Furniture Company
RAD	Rapid application development
RAID	Redundant array of inexpensive disks
RAM	Random access memory
RDBMS	Relational database management system
ROI	Return on investment
ROLAP	Relational online analytical processing
RPC	Remote procedure call
SCD	Slowly changing dimension
SCM	Supply chain management
SDLC	Systems development life cycle
SGML	Standard Generalized Markup Language
SOA	Service-oriented architecture
SOAP	Simple Object Access Protocol
SOX	Sarbanes-Oxley Act
SPL	Structured Product Labeling
SQL	Structured Query Language
SQL/CLI	SQL/Call Level Interface
SQL/DS	Structured Query Language/Data System (an IBM relational DBMS)
SQL/PSM	SQL/Persistent Stored Modules
SQLJ	SQL for Java
SSD	Solid-state disk
SSL	Secure Sockets Layer
TCP/IP	Transmission Control Protocol/Internet Protocol
TDWI	The Data Warehousing Institute
TPS	Transaction processing systems
TQM	Total quality management
UDDI	Universal Description, Discovery, and Integration
UDF	User-defined function
UDT	User-defined data type
UML	Unified Modeling Language
URI	Universal resource identifier
URL	Uniform resource locator
W3C	World Wide Web Consortium
WSDL	Web Services Description Language
WWW	World Wide Web
WYSIWYG	What you see is what you get
XBRL	Extensible Business Reporting Language
XML	Extensible Markup Language
XSL	Extensible Style Language
XSLT	XML Stylesheet Language Transformation
YARN	Yet Another Resource Allocator, also called MapReduce 2.0

GLOSSARY OF TERMS

Note: Number (letter) in parentheses corresponds to the chapter (appendix) in which the term is found. A W indicates the chapter (appendix) is found on the book's Web site

Aborted transaction A transaction in progress that terminates abnormally. (12)

Abstract class A class that has no direct instances but whose descendants may have direct instances. (W14)

Abstract operation An operation whose form or protocol is defined but whose implementation is not defined. (W14)

After image A copy of a record (or page of memory) after it has been modified. (12)

Aggregation A part-of relationship between a component object and an aggregate object. (W14) The process of transforming data from a detailed level to a summary level. (10)

Agile software development An approach to database and software development that emphasizes "**individuals and interactions** over processes and tools, **working software** over comprehensive documentation, **customer collaboration** over contract negotiation, and **response to change** over following a plan." (1)

Alias An alternative name used for an attribute. (4)

Analytics Systematic analysis and interpretation of data—typically using mathematical, statistical, and computational tools—to improve our understanding of a real-world domain. (11)

Anomaly An error or inconsistency that may result when a user attempts to update a table that contains redundant data. The three types of anomalies are insertion, deletion, and modification anomalies. (4)

Application partitioning The process of assigning portions of application code to client or server partitions after it is written to achieve better performance and interoperability (ability of a component to function on different platforms). (8)

Application program interface (API) Sets of routines that an application program uses to direct the performance of procedures by the computer's operating system. (8)

Association A named relationship between or among object classes. (W14)

Association class An association that has attributes or operations of its own or that participates in relationships with other classes. (W14)

Association role The end of an association, where it connects to a class. (W14)

Associative entity An entity type that associates the instances of one or more entity types and contains attributes that are peculiar to the relationship between those entity instances. (2)

Asynchronous distributed database A form of distributed database technology in which copies of replicated data are kept at different nodes so that local servers can access data without reaching out across the network. (W13)

Attribute A property or characteristic of an entity or relationship type that is of interest to the organization. (2)

Attribute inheritance A property by which subtype entities inherit values of all attributes and instances of all relationships of their supertype. (3)

Authorization rules Controls incorporated in a data management systems that restrict access to data and also restrict the actions that people may take when they access data. (12)

Backup facility A DBMS COPY utility that produces a backup copy (or save) of an entire database or a subset of a database. (12)

Backward recovery (rollback) The backout, or undo, of unwanted changes to a database. Before images of the records that have been changed are applied to the database, and the database is returned to an earlier state. Rollback is used to reverse the changes made by transactions that have been aborted, or terminated abnormally. (12)

Base table A table in the relational data model containing the inserted raw data. Base tables correspond to the relations that are identified in the database's conceptual schema. (6)

Before image A copy of a record (or page of memory) before it has been modified. (12)

Behavior The way in which an object acts and reacts. (W14)

Big data Data that exist in very large volumes and many different varieties (data types) and that need to be processed at a very high velocity (speed). (11)

Binary relationship A relationship between the instances of two entity types. (2)

Boyce-Codd normal form (BCNF) A normal form of a relation in which every determinant is a candidate key. (WB)

Business intelligence A set of methodologies, processes, architectures, and technologies that transform raw data into meaningful and useful information. (11)

Business rule A statement that defines or constrains some aspect of the business. It is intended to assert business structure or to control or influence the behavior of the business. (2)

Candidate key An attribute, or combination of attributes, that uniquely identifies a row in a relation. (4)

Cardinality constraint A rule that specifies the number of instances of one entity that can (or must) be associated with each instance of another entity. (2)

Catalog A set of schemas that, when put together, constitute a description of a database. (6)

Changed data capture (CDC) Technique that indicates which data have changed since the last data integration activity. (10)

Checkpoint facility A facility by which a DBMS periodically refuses to accept any new transactions. The system is in a quiet state, and the database and transaction logs are synchronized. (12)

Chief data officer (CDO) An executive-level position accountable for all data-related activities in the enterprise. (10)

Class An entity type that has a well-defined role in the application domain about which the organization wishes to maintain state, behavior, and identity. (W14)

Class diagram A diagram that shows the static structure of an object-oriented model: the object classes, their internal structure, and the relationships in which they participate. (W14)

Class-scope attribute An attribute of a class that specifies a value common to an entire class rather than a specific value for an instance. (W14)

Class-scope operation An operation that applies to a class rather than to an object instance. (W14)

Client/server system A networked computing model that distributes processes between clients and servers, which supply the requested services. In a database system, the database generally resides on a server that processes the DBMS. The clients may process the application systems or request services from another server that holds the application programs. (8)

Commit protocol An algorithm to ensure that a transaction is either successfully completed or aborted. (W13)

Completeness constraint A type of constraint that addresses whether an instance of a supertype must also be a member of at least one subtype. (3)

Composite attribute An attribute that has meaningful component parts (attributes). (2)

Composite identifier An identifier that consists of a composite attribute. (2)

Composite key A primary key that consists of more than one attribute. (4)

Composition A part-of relationship in which parts belong to only one whole object and live and die with the whole object. (W14)

Conceptual schema A detailed, technology-independent specification of the overall structure of organizational data. (1)

Concrete class A class that can have direct instances. (W14)

Concurrency control The process of managing simultaneous operations against a database so that data integrity is maintained and the operations do not interfere with each other in a multiuser environment. (12)

Concurrency transparency A design goal for a distributed database, with the property that although a distributed system runs many transactions, it appears that a given transaction is the only activity in the system. Thus, when several transactions are processed concurrently, the results must be the same as if each transaction were processed in serial order. (W13)

Conformed dimension One or more dimension tables associated with two or more fact tables for which the dimension tables have the same business meaning and primary key with each fact table. (9)

Constraint A rule that cannot be violated by database users. (1)

Constructor operation An operation that creates a new instance of a class. (W14)

Correlated subquery In SQL, a subquery in which processing the inner query depends on data from the outer query. (7)

Data Stored representations of objects and events that have meaning and importance in the user's environment. (1)

Data administration A high-level function that is responsible for the overall management of data resources in an organization, including maintaining corporate-wide definitions and standards. (12)

Data archiving The process of moving inactive data to another storage location where it can be accessed when needed. (12)

Data control language (DCL) Commands used to control a database, including those for administering privileges and committing (saving) data. (6)

Data definition language (DDL) Commands used to define a database, including those for creating, altering, and dropping tables and establishing constraints. (6)

Data dictionary A repository of information about a database that documents data elements of a database. (12)

Data federation A technique for data integration that provides a virtual view of integrated data without actually creating one centralized database. (10)

Data governance High-level organizational groups and processes that oversee data stewardship across the organization. It usually guides data quality initiatives, data architecture, data integration and master data management, data warehousing and business intelligence, and other data-related matters. (10)

Data independence The separation of data descriptions from the application programs that use the data. (1)

Data lake A large integrated repository for internal and external data that does not follow a predefine schema. (11)

Data manipulation language (DML) Commands used to maintain and query a database, including those for updating, inserting, modifying, and querying data. (6)

Data mart A data warehouse that is limited in scope, whose data are obtained by selecting and summarizing data from a data warehouse or from separate extract, transform, and load processes from source data systems. (9)

Data mining Knowledge discovery using a sophisticated blend of techniques from traditional statistics, artificial intelligence, and computer graphics. (11)

Data model Graphical systems used to capture the nature and relationships among data. (1)

Data modeling and design tools Software tools that provide automated support for creating data models. (1)

Data scrubbing A process of using pattern recognition and other artificial intelligence techniques to upgrade the quality of raw data before transforming and moving the data to the data warehouse. Also called data cleansing. (10)

Data steward A person assigned the responsibility of ensuring that organizational applications properly support the organization's enterprise goals for data quality. (10)

Data transformation The component of data reconciliation that converts data from the format of the source operational systems to the format of the enterprise data warehouse. (10)

Data type A detailed coding scheme recognized by system software, such as a DBMS, for representing organizational data. (5)

Data warehouse A subject-oriented, integrated, time-variant, nonupdateable collection of data used in support of management decision-making processes. (9) An integrated decision support database whose content is derived from the various operational databases. (1)

Database An organized collection of logically related data. (1)

Database administration A technical function that is responsible for physical database design and for dealing with technical issues, such as security enforcement, database performance, and backup and recovery. (12)

Database application An application program (or set of related programs) that is used to perform a series of database activities (create, read, update, and delete) on behalf of database users. (1)

Database change log A log that contains before and after images of records that have been modified by transactions. (12)

Database destruction The database itself is lost, destroyed, or cannot be read. (12)

Database management system (DBMS) A software system that is used to create, maintain, and provide controlled access to user databases. (1)

Database recovery Mechanisms for restoring a database quickly and accurately after loss or damage. (12)

Database security Protection of database data against accidental or intentional loss, destruction, or misuse. (12)

Database server A computer that is responsible for database storage, access, and processing in a client/server environment. Some people also use this term to describe a two-tier client/server application. (8)

Deadlock An impasse that results when two or more transactions have locked a common resource, and each waits for the other to unlock that resource. (12)

Deadlock prevention A method for resolving deadlocks in which user programs must lock all records they require at the beginning of a transaction (rather than one at a time). (12)

Deadlock resolution An approach to dealing with deadlocks that allows deadlocks to occur but builds mechanisms into the DBMS for detecting and breaking the deadlocks. (12)

Decentralized database A database that is stored on computers at multiple locations; these computers are not interconnected by network and database software that make the data appear in one logical database. (W13)

Degree The number of entity types that participate in a relationship. (2)

Denormalization The process of transforming normalized relations into non-normalized physical record specifications. (5)

Dependent data mart A data mart filled exclusively from an enterprise data warehouse and its reconciled data. (9)

Derived attribute An attribute whose values can be calculated from related attribute values. (2)

Derived data Data that have been selected, formatted, and aggregated for end-user decision support applications. (9)

Descriptive analytics Describes the past status of the domain of interest using a variety of tools through techniques such as reporting, data visualization, dashboards, and scorecards. (11)

Determinant The attribute on the left side of the arrow in a functional dependency. (4)

Disjoint rule A rule that specifies that an instance of a supertype may not simultaneously be a member of two (or more) subtypes. (3)

Disjointness constraint A constraint that addresses whether an instance of a supertype may simultaneously be a member of two (or more) subtypes. (3)

Distributed database A single logical database that is spread physically across computers in multiple locations that are connected by a data communication link. (W13)

Dynamic SQL Specific SQL code generated on the fly while an application is processing. (7)

Dynamic view A virtual table that is created dynamically upon request by a user. A dynamic view is not a temporary table. Rather, its definition is stored in the system catalog, and the contents of the view are materialized as a result of an SQL query that uses the view. It differs from a materialized view, which

may be stored on a disk and refreshed at intervals or when used, depending on the RDBMS. (6)

Embedded SQL Hard-coded SQL statements included in a program written in another language, such as C or Java. (7)

Encapsulation The technique of hiding the internal implementation details of an object from its external view. (W14)

Encryption The coding or scrambling of data so that humans cannot read them. (12)

Enhanced entity-relationship (EER) model A model that has resulted from extending the original E-R model with new modeling constructs. (3)

Enterprise data modeling The first step in database development, in which the scope and general contents of organizational databases are specified. (1)

Enterprise data warehouse (EDW) A centralized, integrated data warehouse that is the control point and single source of all data made available to end users for decision support applications. (9)

Enterprise key A primary key whose value is unique across all relations. (4)

Enterprise resource planning (ERP) A business management system that integrates all functions of the enterprise, such as manufacturing, sales, finance, marketing, inventory, accounting, and human resources. ERP systems are software applications that provide the data necessary for the enterprise to examine and manage its activities. (1)

Entity A person, a place, an object, an event, or a concept in the user environment about which the organization wishes to maintain data. (1, 3)

Entity cluster A set of one or more entity types and associated relationships grouped into a single abstract entity type. (3)

Entity instance A single occurrence of an entity type. (2)

Entity integrity rule A rule that states that no primary key attribute (or component of a primary key attribute) may be null. (4)

Entity type A collection of entities that share common properties or characteristics. (2)

Entity-relationship diagram (E-R diagram, or ERD) A graphical representation of an entity-relationship model. (2)

Entity-relationship model (E-R model) A logical representation of the data for an organization or for a business area, using entities for categories of data and relationships for associations between entities. (2)

Equi-join A join in which the joining condition is based on equality between values in the common columns. Common columns appear (redundantly) in the result table. (7)

Exclusive lock (X lock, or write lock) A technique that prevents another transaction from reading and therefore updating a record until it is unlocked. (12)

Extensible Markup Language (XML) A text-based scripting language used to describe data structures hierarchically, using HTML-like tags. (8)

Extensible Stylesheet Language Transformation (XSLT) A language used to transform complex XML documents and also used to create HTML pages from XML documents. (8)

Extent A contiguous section of disk storage space. (5)

Fact An association between two or more terms. (2)

Failure transparency A design goal for a distributed database, which guarantees that either all the actions of each transaction are committed or else none of them is committed. (W13)

Fat client A client PC that is responsible for processing presentation logic, extensive application and business rules logic, and many DBMS functions. (8)

Field The smallest unit of application data recognized by system software. (5)

File organization A technique for physically arranging the records of a file on secondary storage devices. (5)

First normal form (1NF) A relation that has a primary key and in which there are no repeating groups. (4)

Foreign key An attribute in a relation that serves as the primary key of another relation in the same database. (4)

Forward recovery (rollforward) A technique that starts with an earlier copy of a database. After images (the results of good transactions) are applied to the database, and the database is quickly moved forward to a later state. (12)

Fourth normal form (4NF) A normal form of a relation in which the relation is in BCNF and contains no multivalued dependencies. (WB)

Function A stored subroutine that returns one value and has only input parameters. (7)

Functional dependency A constraint between two attributes in which the value of one attribute is determined by the value of another attribute. (4)

Generalization The process of defining a more general entity type from a set of more specialized entity types. (3)

Global transaction In a distributed database, a transaction that requires reference to data at one or more nonlocal sites to satisfy the request. (W13)

Grain The level of detail in a fact table, determined by the intersection of all the components of the primary key, including all foreign keys and any other primary key elements. (9)

Hadoop An open source implementation framework of MapReduce. (11)

Hash index table A file organization that uses hashing to map a key into a location in an index, where there is a pointer to the actual data record matching the hash key. (5)

Hashed file organization A storage system in which the address for each record is determined using a hashing algorithm. (5)

Hashing algorithm A routine that converts a primary key value into a relative record number or relative file address. (5)

HDFS HDFS or Hadoop Distributed File System is a file system designed for managing a large number of potentially very large files in a highly distributed environment. (11)

Heartbeat query A query submitted by a DBA to test the current performance of a database or to predict the response time for queries that have promised response times. Also called a canary query. (12)

Hive An Apache project that supports the management and querying of large data sets using HiveQL, an SQL-like language that provides a declarative interface for managing data stored in Hadoop. (11)

Homonym An attribute that may have more than one meaning. (4)

Horizontal partitioning Distribution of the rows of a logical relation into several separate tables. (5)

Identifier An attribute (or combination of attributes) whose value distinguishes instances of an entity type. (2)

Identifying owner The entity type on which the weak entity type depends. (2)

Identifying relationship The relationship between a weak entity type and its owner. (2)

Inconsistent read problem An unrepeatable read, one that occurs when one user reads data that have been partially updated by another user. (12)

Incremental extract A method of capturing only the changes that have occurred in the source data since the last capture. (10)

Independent data mart A data mart filled with data extracted from the operational environment, without the benefit of a data warehouse. (9)

Index A table or other data structure used to determine in a file the location of records that satisfy some condition. (5)

Indexed file organization The storage of records either sequentially or nonsequentially with an index that allows software to locate individual records. (5)

Information Data that have been processed in such a way as to increase the knowledge of the person who uses the data. (1)

Information repository A component that stores metadata that describe an organization's data and data processing resources, manages the total information processing environment, and combines information about an organization's business information and its application portfolio. (12)

Informational system A system designed to support decision making based on historical point-in-time and prediction data for complex queries or data-mining applications. (9)

Java servlet A Java program that is stored on the server and contains the business and database logic for a Java-based application. (8)

Join A relational operation that causes two tables with a common domain to be combined into a single table or view. (7)

Join index An index on columns from two or more tables that come from the same domain of values. (5)

Joining The process of combining data from various sources into a single table or view. (10)

Journalizing facility An audit trail of transactions and database changes. (12)

Local autonomy A design goal for a distributed database, which says that a site can independently administer and operate its database when connections to other nodes have failed. (W13)

Local transaction In a distributed database, a transaction that requires reference only to data that are stored at the site where the transaction originates. (W13)

Location transparency A design goal for a distributed database, which says that a user (or user program) using data need not know the location of the data. (W13)

Locking A process in which any data that are retrieved by a user for updating must be locked, or denied to other users, until the update is completed or aborted. (12)

Locking level (lock granularity) The extent of a database resource that is included with each lock. (12)

Logical data mart A data mart created by a relational view of a data warehouse. (9)

Logical schema The representation of a database for a particular data management technology. (1)

MapReduce An algorithm for massive parallel processing of various types of computing tasks. (11)

Master data management (MDM) Disciplines, technologies, and methods used to ensure the currency, meaning, and quality of reference data within and across various subject areas. (10)

Materialized view Copies or replicas of data, based on SQL queries created in the same manner as dynamic views. However, a materialized view exists as a table, and, thus, care must be taken to keep it synchronized with its associated base tables. (6)

Maximum cardinality The maximum number of instances of one entity that may be associated with each instance of another entity. (2)

Metadata Data that describe the properties or characteristics of end-user data and the context of those data. (1)

Method The implementation of an operation. (W14)

Middleware Software that allows an application to interoperate with other software without requiring the user to understand and code the low-level operations necessary to achieve interoperability. (8)

Minimum cardinality The minimum number of instances of one entity that may be associated with each instance of another entity. (2)

Multidimensional OLAP (MOLAP) OLAP tools that load data into an intermediate structure, usually a three- or higher-dimensional array. (11)

Multiple classification A situation in which an object is an instance of more than one class. (W14)

Multiplicity A specification that indicates how many objects participate in a given relationship. (W14)

Multivalued attribute An attribute that may take on more than one value for a given entity (or relationship) instance. (2)

Multivalued dependency The type of dependency that exists when there are at least three attributes (e.g., A, B, and C) in a relation, with a well-defined set of B and C values for each A value, but those B and C values are independent of each other. (WB)

Natural join A join that is the same as an equi-join except that one of the duplicate columns is eliminated in the result table. (7)

Normal form A state of a relation that requires that certain rules regarding relationships between attributes (or functional dependencies) are satisfied. (4)

Normalization The process of decomposing relations with anomalies to produce smaller, well-structured relations. (4)

NoSQL A category of recently introduced data storage and retrieval technologies that are not based on the relational model. (11)

Null A value that may be assigned to an attribute when no other value applies or when the applicable value is unknown. (4)

Object An instance of a class that encapsulates data and behavior. (W14)

Object diagram A graph of objects that are compatible with a given class diagram. (W14)

Online analytical processing (OLAP) The use of a set of graphical tools that provides users with multidimensional views of their data and allows them to analyze the data using simple windowing techniques. (11)

Open database connectivity (ODBC) An application programming interface that provides a common language for application programs to access and process SQL databases independent of the particular DBMS that is accessed. (8)

Open source DBMS Free DBMS source code software that provides the core functionality of an SQL-compliant DBMS. (12)

Operation A function or a service that is provided by all the instances of a class. (W14)

Operational data store (ODS) An integrated, subject-oriented, continuously updateable, current-valued (with recent history), enterprise-wide, detailed database designed to serve operational users as they do decision support processing. (9)

Operational system A system that is used to run a business in real-time, based on current data. Also called a system of record. (9)

Optional attribute An attribute that may not have a value for every entity (or relationship) instance with which it is associated. (2)

Outer join A join in which rows that do not have matching values in common columns are nevertheless included in the result table. (7)

Overlap rule A rule that specifies that an instance of a supertype may simultaneously be a member of two (or more) subtypes. (3)

Overriding The process of replacing a method inherited from a superclass by a more specific implementation of that method in a subclass. (W14)

Partial functional dependency A functional dependency in which one or more nonkey attributes are functionally dependent on part (but not all) of the primary key. (4)

Partial specialization rule A rule that specifies that an entity instance of a supertype is allowed not to belong to any subtype. (3)

Periodic data Data that are never physically altered or deleted once they have been added to the store. (9)

Persistent Stored Modules (SQL/PSM) Extensions defined in SQL:1999 that include the capability to create and drop modules of code stored in the database schema across user sessions. (7)

Physical file A named portion of secondary memory (such as a hard disk) allocated for the purpose of storing physical records. (5)

Physical schema Specifications for how data from a logical schema are stored in a computer's secondary memory by a database management system. (1)

Pig A tool that integrates a scripting language and an execution environment intended to simplify the use of MapReduce. (11)

Pointer A field of data indicating a target address that can be used to locate a related field or record of data. (5)

Polymorphism The ability of an operation with the same name to respond in different ways depending on the class context. (W14)

Predictive analytics Applies statistical and computational methods and models to data regarding past and current events to predict what might happen in the future. (11)

Prescriptive analytics Uses results of predictive analytics together with optimization and simulation tools to recommend actions that will lead to a desired outcome. (11)

Primary key An attribute or a combination of attributes that uniquely identifies each row in a relation. (4)

Procedure A collection of procedural and SQL statements that are assigned a unique name within the schema and stored in the database. (7)

Project A planned undertaking of related activities to reach an objective that has a beginning and an end. (1)

Prototyping An iterative process of systems development in which requirements are converted to a working system that is continually revised through close work between analysts and users. (1)

Query operation An operation that accesses the state of an object but does not alter the state. (W14)

Real-time data warehouse An enterprise data warehouse that accepts near-real-time feeds of transactional data from the systems of record, analyzes warehouse data, and in near-real-time relays business rules to the data warehouse and systems of record so that immediate action can be taken in response to business events. (9)

Reconciled data Detailed, current data intended to be the single, authoritative source for all decision support applications. (9)

Recovery manager A module of a DBMS that restores the database to a correct condition when a failure occurs and then resumes processing user questions. (12)

Recursive foreign key A foreign key in a relation that references the primary key values of the same relation. (4)

Referential integrity constraint A rule that states that either each foreign key value must match a primary key value in another relation or the foreign key value must be null. (4)

Refresh mode An approach to filling a data warehouse that involves bulk rewriting of the target data at periodic intervals. (10)

Relation A named two-dimensional table of data. (4)

Relational database A database that represents data as a collection of tables in which all data relationships are represented by common values in related tables. (1)

Relational DBMS (RDBMS) A database management system that manages data as a collection of tables in which all data relationships are represented by common values in related tables. (6)

Relational OLAP (ROLAP) OLAP tools that view the database as a traditional relational database in either a star schema or other normalized or denormalized set of tables. (11)

Relationship instance An association between (or among) entity instances where each relationship instance associates exactly one entity instance from each participating entity type. (2)

Relationship type A meaningful association between (or among) entity types. (2)

Replication transparency A design goal for a distributed database, which says that although a given data item may be replicated at several nodes in a network, a developer or user may treat the data item as if it were a single item at a single node. Also called fragmentation transparency. (W13)

Repository A centralized knowledge base of all data definitions, data relationships, screen and report formats, and other system components. (1)

Required attribute An attribute that must have a value for every entity (or relationship) instance with which it is associated. (2)

Restore/rerun A technique that involves reprocessing the day's transactions (up to the point of failure) against the backup copy of the database. (12)

Scalar aggregate A single value returned from an SQL query that includes an aggregate function. (6)

Schema A structure that contains descriptions of objects created by a user, such as base tables, views, and constraints, as part of a database. (6)

Second normal form (2NF) A relation in first normal form in which every nonkey attribute is fully functionally dependent on the primary key. (4)

Secondary key One field or a combination of fields for which more than one record may have the same combination of values. Also called a nonunique key. (5)

Selection The process of partitioning data according to predefined criteria. (10)

Semijoin A joining operation used with distributed databases in which only the joining attribute from one site is transmitted to the other site, rather than all the selected attributes from every qualified row. (W13)

Sequential file organization The storage of records in a file in sequence according to a primary key value. (5)

Service-oriented architecture (SOA) A collection of services that communicate with each other in some manner, usually by passing data or coordinating a business activity. (8)

Shared lock (S lock, or read lock) A technique that allows other transactions to read but not update a record or another resource. (12)

Simple (or atomic) attribute An attribute that cannot be broken down into smaller components that are meaningful to the organization. (2)

Simple Object Access Protocol (SOAP) An XML-based communication protocol used for sending messages between applications via the Internet. (8)

Smart card A credit card–sized plastic card with an embedded microprocessor chip that can store, process, and output electronic data in a secure manner. (12)

Snowflake schema An expanded version of a star schema in which dimension tables are normalized into several related tables. (9)

Specialization The process of defining one or more subtypes of the supertype and forming supertype/subtype relationships. (3)

Star schema A simple database design in which dimensional data are separated from fact or event data. A dimensional model is another name for a star schema. (9)

State An object's properties (attributes and relationships) and the values those properties have. (W14)

Static extract A method of capturing a snapshot of the required source data at a point in time. (10)

Strong entity type An entity that exists independently of other entity types. (2)

Subtype A subgrouping of the entities in an entity type that is meaningful to the organization and that shares common attributes or relationships distinct from other subgroupings. (3)

Subtype discriminator An attribute of a supertype whose values determine the target subtype or subtypes. (3)

Supertype A generic entity type that has a relationship with one or more subtypes. (3)

Supertype/subtype hierarchy A hierarchical arrangement of supertypes and subtypes in which each subtype has only one supertype. (3)

Surrogate primary key A serial number or other system-assigned primary key for a relation. (4)

Synchronous distributed database A form of distributed database technology in which all data across the network are continuously kept up to date so that a user at any site can access data anywhere on the network at any time and get the same answer. (W13)

Synonyms Two (or more) attributes that have different names but the same meaning. (4)

System catalog A system-created database that describes all database objects, including data dictionary information, and also includes user access information. (12)

Systems development life cycle (SDLC) The traditional methodology used to develop, maintain, and replace information systems. (1)

Tablespace A named logical storage unit in which data from one or more database tables, views, or other database objects may be stored. (5)

Term A word or phrase that has a specific meaning for the business. (2)

Ternary relationship A simultaneous relationship among the instances of three entity types. (2)

Text mining The process of discovering meaningful information algorithmically based on computational analysis of unstructured textual information. (11)

Thin client An application where the client (PC) accessing the application primarily provides the user interfaces and some application processing, usually with no or limited local data storage. (8)

Third normal form (3NF) A relation that is in second normal form and has no transitive dependencies. (4)

Three-tier architecture A client/server configuration that includes three layers: a client layer and two server layers. Although the nature of the server layers differs, a common configuration contains an application server and a database server. (8)

Time stamp A time value that is associated with a data value, often indicating when some event occurred that affected the data value. (2)

Total specialization rule A rule that specifies that each entity instance of a supertype must be a member of some subtype in the relationship. (3)

Transaction A discrete unit of work that must be completely processed or not processed at all within a computer system. Entering a customer order is an example of a transaction. (12)

Transaction boundaries The logical beginning and end of a transaction. (12)

Transaction log A record of the essential data for each transaction that is processed against the database. (12)

Transaction manager In a distributed database, a software module that maintains a log of all transactions and an appropriate concurrency control scheme. (W13)

Transient data Data in which changes to existing records are written over previous records, thus destroying the previous data content. (9)

Transitive dependency A functional dependency between the primary key and one or more nonkey attributes that are dependent on the primary key via another nonkey attribute. (4)

Trigger A named set of SQL statements that are considered (triggered) when a data modification (i.e., INSERT, UPDATE, DELETE) occurs or if certain data definitions are encountered. If a condition stated within a trigger is met, then a prescribed action is taken. (7)

Two-phase commit An algorithm for coordinating updates in a distributed database. (W13)

Two-phase locking protocol A procedure for acquiring the necessary locks for a transaction in which all necessary locks are acquired before any locks are released, resulting in a growing phase when locks are acquired and a shrinking phase when they are released. (12)

Unary relationship A relationship between instances of a single entity type. (2)

Universal data model A generic or template data model that can be reused as a starting point for a data modeling project. (3)

Universal Description, Discovery, and Integration (UDDI) A technical specification for creating a distributed registry of Web services and businesses that are open to communicating through Web services. (8)

Update mode An approach to filling a data warehouse in which only changes in the source data are written to the data warehouse. (10)

Update operation An operation that alters the state of an object. (W14)

User view A logical description of some portion of the database that is required by a user to perform some task. (1)

User-defined data type (UDT) A data type that a user can define by making it a subclass of a standard type or creating a type that behaves as an object. UDTs may also have defined functions and methods. (7)

User-defined procedures User exits (or interfaces) that allow system designers to define their own security procedures in addition to the authorization rules. (12)

Vector aggregate Multiple values returned from an SQL query that includes an aggregate function. (6)

Versioning An approach to concurrency control in which each transaction is restricted to a view of the database as of the time that transaction started, and when a transaction modifies a record, the DBMS creates a new record version instead of overwriting the old record. Hence, no form of locking is required. (12)

Vertical partitioning Distribution of the columns of a logical relation into several separate physical tables. (5)

Virtual table A table constructed automatically as needed by a DBMS. Virtual tables are not maintained as real data. (6)

Weak entity type An entity type whose existence depends on some other entity type. (2)

Web services A set of emerging standards that define protocols for automatic communication between software programs over the Web. Web services are XML based and usually run in the background to establish transparent communication among computers. (8)

Web Services Description Language (WSDL) An XML-based grammar or language used to describe a Web service and specify a public interface for that service. (8)

Well-structured relation A relation that contains minimal redundancy and allows users to insert, modify, and delete the rows in a table without errors or inconsistencies. (4)

XML Schema Definition (XSD) Language used for defining XML databases that has been recommended by the World Wide Web Consortium (W3C). (8)

XPath One of a set of XML technologies that supports XQuery development. XPath expressions are used to locate data in XML documents. (8)

XQuery An XML transformation language that allows applications to query both relational databases and XML data. (8)

INDEX